INDUSTRIAL MANAGEMENT LIBRARY

GRAPHIC METHODS
FOR
PRESENTING FACTS

BY

WILLARD C. BRINTON

McGRAW-HILL BOOK COMPANY, Inc.
NEW YORK AND LONDON

Copyright, 1914
By The Engineering Magazine Company

PRINTED IN THE UNITED STATES OF AMERICA

TO MY MOTHER

PREFACE

IN the preparation of this book there has been a constant effort to present the subject to suit the point of view of the business man, the social worker, and the legislator. Mathematics have been entirely eliminated. Technical terms are used practically not at all. Since the readers whom it is most desired to reach are those who have never had any statistical training, consistent effort has been made to keep the whole book on such a plane that it may be found readable and useful by anyone dealing with the complex facts of business or government. Though written primarily for the non-technical man, it is hoped that this book may, nevertheless, prove convenient to the engineer, the biologist, and the statistician.

A definite effort has been made to produce a work which can serve as a hand book for anyone who may have occasional charts to prepare for reports, for magazine illustration, or for advertising. Unfortunately, there are extremely few draftsmen who know how to plot a curve or prepare any kind of a chart from data presented to them in the form of tabulated figures. Most draftsmen can plot a curve if they are given the data and an example showing the general type of chart desired. The executive who desires a chart is usually too busy to stand by a draftsman and explain in detail just how the chart should be prepared as concerns those all important details of proportion, scale, width of line, etc. It is believed that the owner of this book will find it feasible to run through the various chapters and pages until he finds a chart most nearly like that which he desires to have made from his own data. A sample chart placed before any draftsman of average ability should give the draftsman practically all the instruction needed for the preparation of a similar chart from other data.

Much careful labor has been expended in so arranging the book that a busy reader may get the gist of the matter by looking at the illustrations and reading only the titles and the sub-titles. The main title under each illustration is intended to show exactly what the chart represents, just as if it were used in some publication relating to the particular subject matter of the chart. The sub-titles relate to method and give criticism of each chart as a whole. Though the text gives much more detailed information concerning method than can possibly be put into any sub-titles, the reader who examines only the illustrations and the titles, without any reference to the text, will undoubtedly get a major portion of the vital material in the book. It is believed that an average reader may go through the illustrations and the titles in about one hour.

Many of the illustrations which have been borrowed for use in this book are criticized adversely. It is the hope that all such criticisms will be accepted as an honest attempt toward an advance in the art of showing data in graphic form. In fairness to the authors of those charts which are criticized, it must be said that there has been a very rapid advance in the art of graphic presentation within the last few years and that many of these men would not present the material to-day by the methods which may have been used some years ago in the preparation of certain charts shown here. Where charts are used and criticized adversely, the charts have been included only because it is felt that they show a practice which is rather common but is nevertheless of questionable desirability.

Many of the suggestions for standard practice contained in this book should be taken as tentative only. The American Society of Mechanical Engineers has invited about fifteen of the chief American societies of national scope to co-operate by sending one member each to a Joint Committee on Standards for Graphic Presentation. Though this committee is not yet completely organized, and it will be some time before any report is available, the reader who desires further information regarding standard practice should be on the lookout for any reports which the joint committee may publish in the future.

This volume may arouse in the minds of many readers a desire for more detailed information than can possibly be given here. The following books are suggested for the person who wishes to take up the study of statistics as related to the collection and interpretation of data without special reference to the methods of graphic presentation. The present work is necessarily limited to the consideration of graphic presentation, and those who wish to go further in the general subject of statistics should by all means consult books of the type exemplified by "The Elements of Statistical Method," by Willford I. King, The Macmillan Company, New York; "An Introduction to the Theory of Statistics," by G. Udny Yule, Griffin and Company, London; "Elements of Statistics," by Arthur L. Bowley, Charles Scribner's Sons, New York; "Primer of Statistics," by W. Palin Elderton and Ethel M. Elderton, Adam and Charles Black, London; "Statistical Averages," by Franz Zizek, Henry Holt and Company, New York; "Statistical Methods with Special Reference to Biological Variation," by C. B. Davenport, John Wiley and Sons, New York. Any list of this sort is, of course, incomplete and these books are mentioned as only a few of those which may be found useful to supplement the study of the subject considered in this volume.

Part of the matter here presented was given in lectures delivered at the Graduate School of Business Administration of Harvard University, the Amos Tuck School of Administration and Finance of Dartmouth College, the Northwestern University School of Commerce, and the College of Commerce and Administration of the University of Chicago. Some of the material was presented before the American Society of Mechanical Engineers in New York. The advance presentation of matter in course of preparation for the press was made with the cordial assent and approval of the publishers of this work.

I am greatly indebted to Mr. Edward Scott Swazey, Mr. Curtis Prout, and Miss Katherine Tyng, for valuable assistance and suggestions received during the preparation of this book. Chapter XV is largely based on an article prepared at the suggestion of the author by Mr. Pierpont V. Davis of New York City and published by Mr. Davis in *Moody's Magazine*. I wish also to express my thanks to numerous friends who have given excellent suggestions and criticisms during the time the manuscript was in preparation.

If this book should receive any commendation, much of that commendation will be the result of good fortune in securing an unusually high grade of drafting skill on those charts which are original.

The author cannot be responsible for the accuracy of the data presented in many of the charts shown. The illustrations have been selected partly on account of the educational value of the facts, but chiefly because of the methods used in presentation. Though great care has been exercised to make the titles complete, the elaboration of titles beyond their wording in the original source may have resulted in some inaccuracies.

As far as the author is aware, there is no book published in any language covering the field which it has been attempted to cover here. If the presentation of the subject appears to be crude and incomplete, it is hoped that any critic will keep in mind that there is little precedent for guidance in a territory so unexplored.

It is impossible entirely to avoid errors in any book containing as much detail as results here from the numerous complex illustrations and the necessity of carefully worded language to give condensed information. Any corrections, criticisms or suggestions will be appreciated by the author.

WILLARD C. BRINTON

New York, June, 1914

CONTENTS

PAGE

CHAPTER I. COMPONENT PARTS 1
    The need for graphic methods in presenting facts. The method of presentation as important as the data. Possibility for standard methods of presentation. Tabulated figures *versus* graphic methods. A total shown with its component parts. The horizontal bar. The circle and sectors. Subdivision of components. Separate bars totalling 100 per cent. Charts giving numerous subdivisions. Organization charts. Routing charts for manufacturing plants and offices.

CHAPTER II. SIMPLE COMPARISONS 20
    Errors due to comparing by areas or by volumes instead of by one dimension only. The use of graphic methods in geography books. The data should be shown on the face of each chart if possible. Good and bad methods of including the data. "Eye-catchers" to attract the attention of the reader. Criticisms of methods commonly used. Certain bars made especially prominent. Increases and decreases. Lines connecting different bars. Examples of various good methods.

CHAPTER III. SIMPLE COMPARISONS INVOLVING TIME 36
    Impossibility of accurate interpretation when circles of different size are compared. Errors when pictures of the human figure in different size are compared. Methods which are popular and accurate as well. Examples of bad practice in arrangement and the same data correctly represented. Vertical bars giving the general effect of a simple curve. Curve plotting.

CHAPTER IV. TIME CHARTS 53
    Horizontal bars drawn to a scale of time. Complex time charts by which the relations of numerous horizontal bars may be studied. Time charts showing bars combined with a curve expressing totals. Curves to study whether time schedules are maintained. Rank charts to portray the rank of different individuals at various times. Rank charts showing actual relative rank at any time and also changes in rank at various times. Train-dispatching charts. Time-distance curves.

GRAPHIC METHODS

PAGE

CHAPTER V. CURVE PLOTTING 69
  The desirability of using only well-known methods of presentation. Curves permit a more rapid and more accurate interpretation than possible by other methods. Studies of the causes of crests and valleys of curves. Curves especially needed for complex data. The use of curves in advertising. Polar co-ordinates objectionable for presenting statistical data. Examples of good practice in curve plotting.

CHAPTER VI. CURVE PLOTTING CONTINUED 84
  Independent and dependent variables. Confusion caused if the independent variable is not used for the horizontal scale. Examples showing correct arrangement of scales. Curves to advertise newspaper circulation. Curve charts combining much complex information. The use of two sets of co-ordinate ruling for the vertical scale. Moving averages. Smoothing curves. Index numbers. Weighted averages. Curve studies of national prosperity.

CHAPTER VII. COMPARISON OF CURVES 107
  Similarity and contrast of curves plotted in the same field. The zero of the vertical scale should be shown on the chart. Advantages of plotting curves for different years one above the other for comparison. Contrast in shape of curves plotted in separate fields. Advantage from shading the space under a curve. Numerous dissimilar but related curves on the same sheet. Errors resulting if curves not having the same zero line are compared. A total curve plotted from several other curves. Inverse relations, one curve trending downward when another trends upward. Study of correlation by plotting a curve from the data of two other curves. The angle of a curve on ordinary rectangular co-ordinates tells nothing about the percentage rate of growth. Disadvantages of the arithmetical scale ruling for curve plotting. Advantages obtained by plotting curves on logarithmically ruled paper.

CHAPTER VIII. COMPONENT PARTS SHOWN BY CURVES 138
  Use of vertical bars with components totalling 100 per cent. Shaded area under a curve when the height of the total field represents 100 per cent. The use of several areas in a curve field which totals 100 per cent. in height. A contrasting method of showing all curves plotted separately but from the same zero line. Universal co-ordinate paper for convenience in curve plotting. Total curves with component areas so that any point on a curve totals 100 per cent for the height of the areas beneath.

CHAPTER IX. CUMULATIVE OR MASS CURVES. 149
  Factory production schedules and actual outputs plotted on a cumulative basis. Curves for income and expense on a cumulative basis. Various uses for cumulative curves. Cumulative curves with lines drawn to show rate

PAGE

of change. A grand total cumulative curve plotted from several other cumulative curves. Cumulative curves for the determination of storage requirements for water supplies.

CHAPTER X. FREQUENCY CURVES. CORRELATION 164

The arrangement of objects so that their position shows a crude frequency curve. Vertical bars to represent frequency. Frequency curves. The "mode." Frequency curves much easier to interpret than charts using bars or areas. Cumulative frequency curves. The use of cumulative frequency curves for business problems. Cumulative frequency curves preferably plotted on a "more than" basis instead of on a "less than" basis. Necessity for making the independent variable the horizontal scale. Wage comparisons for industrial work. Studies of the percentage of clerical work and percentage of revenue from orders of various sizes. Pin boards to record costs of doing work on orders of different size. Theoretical curves for percentage of clerical work and percentage of revenue from orders of different size. The Lorenz curve. Correlation curves. "Shotgun" diagrams. Plotting curves to represent numerous points. Shaded areas to represent numerous dots. Correlation charts for two independent variables. Isometrically ruled paper for chart work.

CHAPTER XI. MAP PRESENTATIONS 208

Map presentation of prime importance. Shading of different areas. The Ben Day method of mechanical shading. Lines of equality. Profiles. Maps with circles or dots representing quantities. Shaded areas with a key to represent quantity. Miscellaneous methods. Map charts showing traffic. Map models with built up strips to show quantities.

CHAPTER XII. MAPS AND PINS 227

Map tacks projecting above the map. Map pins pushed in till the heads touch the map. Photographing pin maps. Mounting maps for use with map pins. Wall maps for use with pins. Map cabinet systems. Pin maps for advertising work. Pins bearing identifying numbers. Spot maps to a scale with each dot representing some large quantity. Routing systems. Various types of pins and beads available. Bead maps and their great advantages.

CHAPTER XIII. CURVES FOR THE EXECUTIVE 254

Peak-top curves *versus* flat tops. Methods for combining curves with figures recording the data. Cards for plotting curves for operating records. Advantages of the card method for instantaneous comparison of different curves. Typical operating curves for a manufacturing business. Typical records for a selling organization. Arrangement of the card system for extension with increase of business. Moving average curves for operating records. Record cards for preserving all information regarding each curve.

PAGE

CHAPTER XIV. RECORDS FOR THE EXECUTIVE 288
    Need for complete records in curve form relating to all main features of a business. Curve-card filing methods. Blueprints from the curve cards allow a cross-index of all important operating curves. A complete record department for a business. Methods for keeping records as used by various large corporations. The need for education in the interpretation of curves. Curves in conference meetings by using a reflecting lantern and the curve-record cards without lantern slides. Curves on swinging-leaf display fixtures.

CHAPTER XV. CORPORATION FINANCIAL REPORTS. 307
    The annual report of corporations not usually put in form to permit intelligent comparison by the stockholders. Records of previous years not usually given. The number of stockholders constantly increasing. Best policy is to give complete and clear information. Recent examples showing bad practice. Curves for the United States Steel Corporation as a suggestion for the type of chart to be included in a corporation annual report. Charts should be a feature of the annual report of every large corporation.

CHAPTER XVI. GENERAL METHODS. 321
    Methods for collecting and tabulating data. Punched-card sorting and tabulating machines. Use of tabulating machines for manufacturing records and for analyses of selling results. The slide rule as a great convenience. The use and abuse of significant figures. Photographic copying of charts. Use of the reducing glass. Preparation of copy for the engraver. The Ben Day process. Charts for two independent variables. Card-board models. Solid models. The desirability of curves and charts in political campaigns. The projecting lantern with charts for campaign purposes. Methods for presenting election returns to large numbers of people. Charts in parades.

CHAPTER XVII. A FEW CAUTIONS 344
    The importance of clear and accurate titles. Symbols which are easily remembered. No necessity for plotting curves vertically. Errors resulting in interpretation of curves if the zero of the vertical scale is not shown on the chart. The selection of scales for curve plotting. Different impressions from curves from the same data but with various scales. Optical illusions which may affect graphic work. A checking list for final inspection of graphic presentations. Need for standard rules of grammar for the graphic language. A few suggested rules for graphic presentation. Great advantages may result if graphic methods are more widely used for portraying quantitive facts.

GRAPHIC METHODS
FOR
PRESENTING FACTS

GRAPHIC METHODS FOR PRESENTING FACTS

CHAPTER I

COMPONENT PARTS

AFTER a person has collected data and studied a proposition with great care so that his own mind is made up as to the best solution for the problem, he is apt to feel that his work is about completed. Usually, however, when his own mind is made up, his task is only half done. The larger and more difficult part of the work is to convince the minds of others that the proposed solution is the best one—that all the recommendations are really necessary. Time after time it happens that some ignorant or presumptuous member of a committee or a board of directors will upset the carefully-thought-out plan of a man who knows the facts, simply because the man with the facts cannot present his facts readily enough to overcome the opposition. It is often with impotent exasperation that a person having the knowledge sees some fallacious conclusion accepted, or some wrong policy adopted, just because known facts cannot be marshalled and presented in such manner as to be effective.

Millions of dollars yearly are spent in the collection of data, with the fond expectation that the data will automatically cause the correction of the conditions studied. Though accurate data and real facts are valuable, when it comes to getting results the manner of presentation is ordinarily more important than the facts themselves. The foundation of an edifice is of vast importance. Still, it is not the foundation but the structure built upon the foundation which gives the result for which the whole work was planned. As the cathedral is to its foundation so is an effective presentation of facts to the data.

We daily see facts presented in the hope of creating interest and action for some really worthy piece of work to benefit the people as a whole. In many of these cases the attitude of the person presenting the matter seems to be that the facts will speak for themselves and that they need little or no assistance. Ordinarily, facts do not speak for themselves. When they do speak for themselves, the wrong conclusions are often drawn from them. Unless the facts are presented in a clear and interesting manner, they are about as effective as a phonograph record with the phonograph missing.

If it were more generally realized how much depends upon the method of presenting facts, as compared with the facts themselves, there would be a great increase in the use of the graphic methods of presentation. Unlimited numbers of reports, magazines, and newspapers are now giving us reams of quantitative facts. If the facts were put in graphic form, not only would there be a great saving in the time of the readers but there would be infinite gain to society, because more facts could be absorbed and with less danger of misinterpretation. Graphic methods usually require no more space than is needed if the facts are presented in the form of words. In many cases, the graphic method requires less space than is required for words and there is, besides, the great advantage that with graphic methods facts are presented so that the reader may make deductions of his own, while when words are used the reader must usually accept the ready-made conclusions handed to him.

In many presentations it is not a question of saving time to the reader but a question of placing the arguments in such form that results may surely be obtained. For matters affecting public welfare, it is hard to estimate the benefits which may accrue if a little care be used in presenting data so that they will be convincing to the reader. If the average citizen, and especially the business man, knew how to interpret charts and curves, it would be feasible to convey to him in effective form those facts relating to broad public improvements, public-service operation, and national, State, or municipal management, which might affect the whole fabric of our civilization. Archimedes wanted only a fulcrum for his lever and he would move the world. If the world is ever moved it will probably be by facts properly presented. The method of presentation is the fulcrum without which facts, as a lever, are useless.

The preparation and interpretation of simple charts and curves should be taught in the public schools as a part of arithmetic. The work of kindergarten nature now done in the lower grades of the public schools could very readily be extended so that the pupils would be making charts and curves without realizing that the work (or play) had any relation to mathematics. Text-books for geography are already making effective use of charts. In the public schools of Newark and of Trenton, New Jersey, grammar-school pupils are preparing charts and plotting curves relating to records which show the present condition and recent development of their home city. The principles of charting and curve plotting are not at all complex, and it is surprising that many business men dodge the simplest charts as though they involved higher mathematics or contained some sort of black magic.

If an editor should print bad English he would lose his position. Many editors are using and printing bad methods of graphic presentation, but they hold their jobs just the same. The trouble at present is that there are no standards by which graphic presentations can be prepared in accordance with definite rules so that their interpretation by the reader may be both rapid and accurate. It is certain that there will evolve for methods of graphic presentation a few useful and definite rules which will correspond with the rules of grammar for the spoken and written language. The rules of grammar for the English language are numerous as well as complex, and there are about as many exceptions as there are rules. Yet we all try to follow the rules in spite of their intricacies. The principles for a grammar of graphic presentation are so simple that a remarkably small number of rules would be sufficient to give a universal language. It is interesting to note, also, that there are possibilities of the graphic presentation becoming an international language, like music, which is now written by such standard methods that sheet music may be played in any country.

With oral and written language and with tabulated figures also the reader sometimes draws conclusions regarding the relative importance of different things from the comparative length of time or amount of space used in presentation. Graphic methods overcome this difficulty by showing quantitative facts in true proportions which give instantly the correct interpretation. In tabulations like that on page 4 it is only

4   GRAPHIC METHODS

the highly skilled reader who can refrain from regarding the five different items listed as of somewhere nearly equal numerical importance, simply because the five different items are given exactly the same space and prominence when written down on the page.

PERCENTAGE OF EACH RACE IN THE POPULATION OF THE WORLD

Yellow	45
White	41
Black	11
Brown	2
Red	1

It requires mental concentration in interpreting even these simple figures to get the correct impression of the very large percentage of the two chief races and the numerical insignificance of the one last named. If these data were shown in a simple horizontal bar, somewhat like that seen in Fig. 1, the relative proportions of the different races

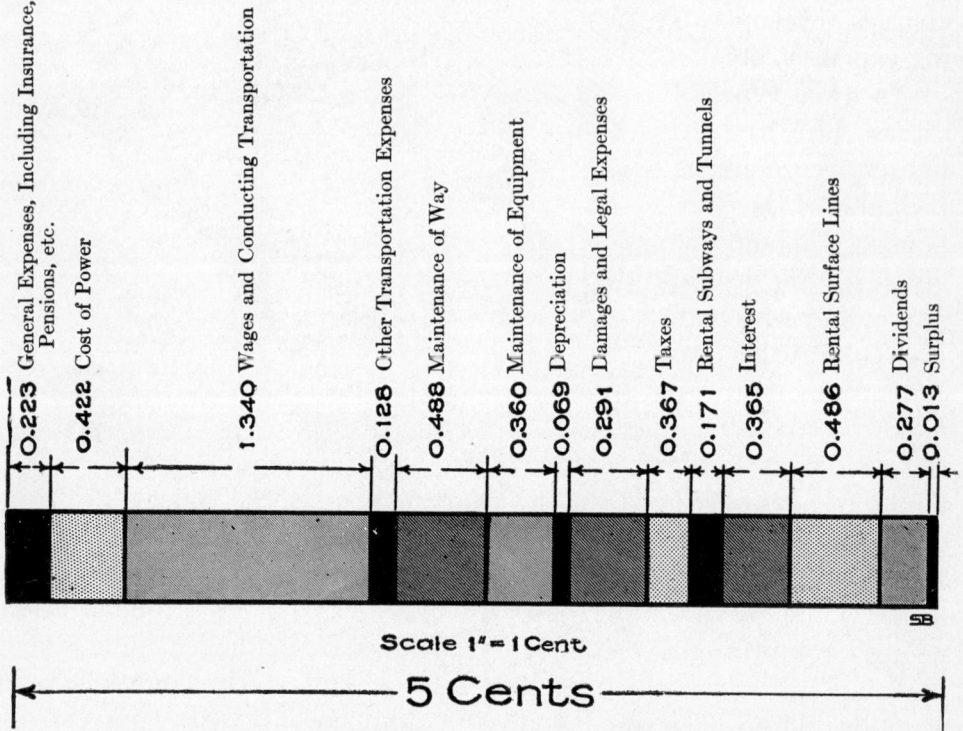

Fig. 1. Disposition of a 5-cent Fare Paid to the Boston Elevated Railroad in the Year Ending September 30, 1909

The horizontal bar gives an especially good method for showing component parts

would instantly be seen without any mental effort on the part of the reader.

Fig. 1 is a very satisfactory form of chart to bring out the component parts of any group total. The horizontal bar need be made only wide enough to show the various kinds of shading necessary to give a good contrast. Engineering dimension lines above each block in the bar are of great advantage for convenient reading. The dimension lines permit of grouping in such a manner that several of the detail blocks could be included in various sets of dimension lines to show such items as total fixed charges, total operating expenses, etc.

In this type of chart the actual figures representing the value of the components should be given for the use of any reader who may wish to draw his own conclusions or to make new combinations of figures different from those shown in the chart. As a general thing it is always desirable to have full data given on any chart. Fig. 1 gives all the data without in any way detracting from the ease of reading the chart itself.

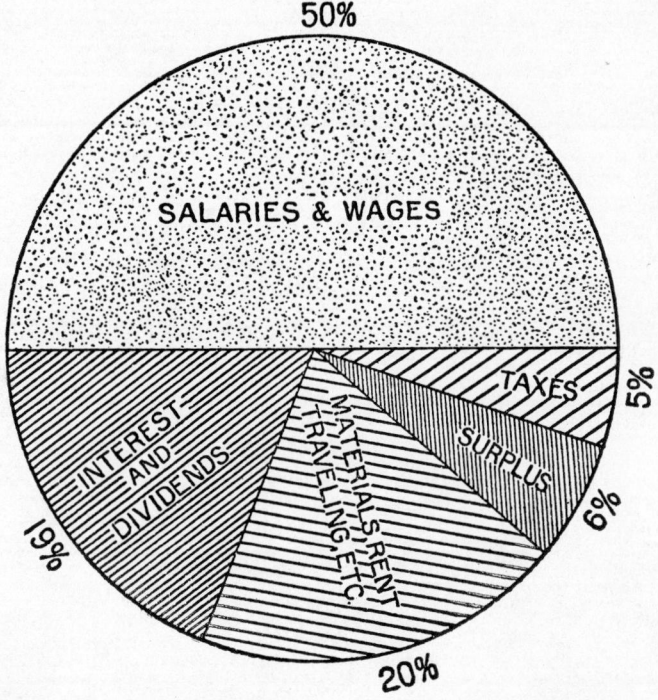

Fig. 2. Disposition of the Gross Revenue of the Bell Telephone System for the Year 1911

This chart was taken from the annual report to the stockholders of the American Telephone and Telegraph Company for the year ending December 31, 1911

The circle with sectors is not as desirable an arrangement as the horizontal bar shown in Fig. 1

It would be desirable to have a large number of the illustrations in this book printed in color. Charts which are made in color can readily bring out points which are not easily portrayed when only black ink is used. The reader should keep in mind for his own work that he should use colors in making those charts where colors are economically possible. For the purpose of this book, color printing is prohibitive on account of the cost. In printed reports, in magazine articles, and in magazine advertising, color printing is not at the present time commonly available. The illustrations of this book will accordingly show what can be done in printing complex charts with only one color of ink, under the same conditions that would be found in the preparation of material for magazine articles, printed reports, and ordinary prospectus or other advertising matter.

Fig. 2 is a form of chart used probably more widely than any other form to show component parts. The circle with sectors is not a desirable form of presentation, however, because it does not have nearly such flexibility as the method shown in Fig. 1. The sector method does not permit of convenient arrangement of names for the different components. Note that the direction of the lettering must be reversed as the eye proceeds around the circle. In this case, "Interest and Dividends" reads upward while "Materials, Rents, Traveling Expenses, etc." reads downward. Another disadvantage of the sector method is the impossibility of placing figures in such manner that they can be easily compared or added. The horizontal-bar method permits of placing figures so as to keep the decimal points in line, thus making it possible to add the whole column of figures relating to the various components.

The Survey

Fig. 3. Disposition of a Family Income of from $900 to $1000

This cut shows an attempt to put figures in popular form. The eye is likely to judge by the size of the pictures rather than by the angles of the sectors

The sector method is probably so widely known through presentation in exhibits, illustrations for popular magazines, etc., that it is more generally understood than any other method now in use. The more easy reading of the wedge or sector chart is, however, largely due to habit. If the horizontal-bar method of Fig. 1 were used as frequently as the sector method, it would be found in every way more desirable than the sector method and would, in a very short time, become so well known that it would be read much more quickly and accurately than the method involving sectors.

In Fig. 4 a double scale is used by which the same data can be interpreted from two different standpoints. On the left the scale is given in millions of tons, and on the right in millions of dollars. The reader can interpret the chart from whichever standpoint he prefers. Though this chart is arranged vertically instead of horizontally, it really makes little difference which way the bars are placed. As a general thing, the horizontal arrangement lends itself more readily to the use of type so that the reader may read type statements without having to turn the book.

In Fig. 5 the whole population of the United States is divided first into native white, foreign white, and colored, then each of these groups is subdivided according to place of birth. This is an excellent type of chart to use if subdivisions in the component parts of any unit have to be shown. If the scale to which the chart is drawn is specified, it is possible for the reader to measure, with an ordinary ruler or with an engineer's scale, the exact percentage size of each of the different components.

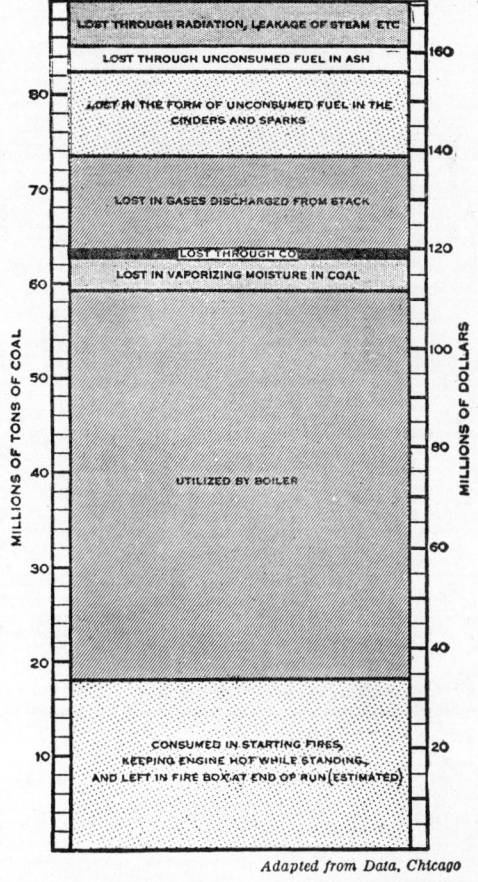

Fig. 4. Utilization and Accompanying Wastes of One Year's Coal Supply for Locomotives on Railroads of the United States

The double scale permits reading this chart in tons or in dollars

If the chart is made on co-ordinate paper with ruled squares, the reader can obtain the size of each component direct from the co-ordinate lines. The trouble, however, with using co-ordinate paper for charts of this sort is that the components are likely to begin and end at points not falling upon the co-ordinate lines, thus making it necessary to count fractions of a division at both beginning and end of the component to be measured. The best thing in charts of this kind is to use unruled paper, and specify the scale. The reader, if he wants the exact data, can take his measurements with a ruler. The engineer's scale has its subdivisions in decimals and hence is the most convenient scale for chart work. An engineer's scale should be part of the equipment of every person who has charts to make.

Another method of showing the relative size of the divisions and subdivisions of a unit or group is shown in Fig. 6. In this case we have the total population of the United States split into its component groups according to the condition in regard to marriage. The subdivision bars, given below the total bars, show the conjugal condition in each of the main groups which enter into the total population. Each of these main-group bars is cross-hatched to show the conjugal condition within the group. The combined length of the four bottom bars is equal to the length of the total-population bar shown at the top. These same data could have been presented by the method shown in Fig. 5. It will be noted, however, that in Fig. 6 all the figures have been included, and are available for reference purposes without detracting from the utility of the chart itself. The lettering was done by hand and shows the possibilities for neatness resulting from hand work when a skilled draftsman is employed. In many ways the method of Fig. 5 is preferable, but it is probably true that Fig. 6 would be more readily understood by the average untrained reader.

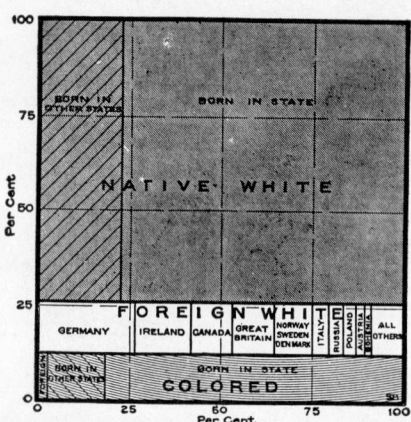

United States Statistical Atlas for the Census of 1900

Fig. 5. Elements of the Population of the United States in 1900

Here the components of the total population are shown in their relative sizes on the vertical scale. Each component is also divided into different subdivisions whose percentage size may be read from the horizontal scale. This is an admirable method of presentation if components must be subdivided

Where there are a large number of items to be compared and the components of each item are given, the method of Fig. 7 is a very convenient one. The Census Atlas for the 1900 Census contained many pages of charts of this type for its comparisons of different States. By placing bars for all the States on one page, the total for the country is shown as 100 per cent in the vertical direction. No vertical scale

COMPONENT PARTS

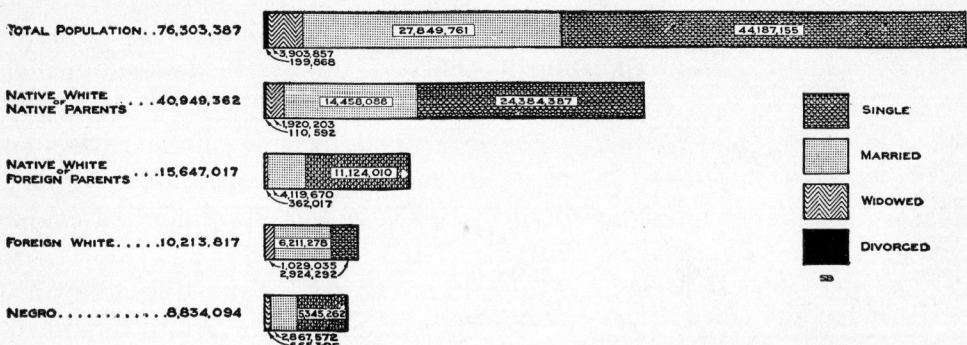

Fig. 6. Conjugal Condition of the Population of the United States in 1900

The four lower bars show components of the total population represented by the upper bar. The combined length of the four lower bars equals the length of the upper bar

is used, all the bars being made of equal width. In this particular case (Fig. 7) we have a total split into its components and again subdivided so as to show the prevalence of a second factor which is included in the first. Thus, we see the proportion of illiterates in each of the main groups of population for each State. All of the States are shown on the same basis, since all are depicted by bars of the same length representing 100 per cent. It is not easy to make a clear black-and-white drawing if one kind of cross-hatching must be placed on top of another kind. Fig. 7 shows that it is possible, however, to superimpose two kinds of cross-hatching and get a drawing that is fairly clear. The facts in this chart would have been brought out better if colors had been used for the main divisions of population. Ruled cross-hatching in black to represent the percentages of illit-

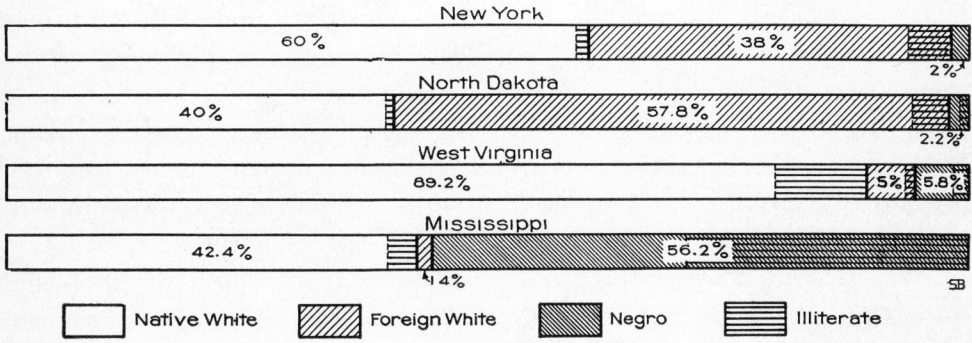

Fig. 7. Males of Voting Age in certain States, in 1900, by Color and Nativity and by Illiteracy

A method for two successive divisions into components is shown here. The proportion of illiterates in each group is brought out by the horizontal ruling

erates would show clearly through the colored ink used for the main divisions.

Though it would have been possible to portray the data given in Fig. 7 in the form of the square shown in Fig. 5, the square would take up so much room on the page that the method would be prohibitive if all the States had to be shown on one page for comparison. With the method of Fig. 7, it is possible to place on one page all the forty-eight States so that comparison between States can be made instantly and accurately.

Fig. 8 shows another method of analyzing to 100 per cent in each of two directions. The method of Fig. 5 could be used for these data, but would not be as easy to understand as the method of Fig. 8. Fig. 5 would require most careful cross-hatching to bring out the vertical subdivisions for each of the different States. By using the method of Fig. 8, each State can be shown distinctly even if it is only the width of a line, as in the case of Nevada or Wyoming. The wide space between the different bars showing the States adds tremendously to the clearness of the diagram. The vertical scale for the width of bars is made according to the number of electoral votes from each of the States. New York has more electoral votes than any other State, and is there-

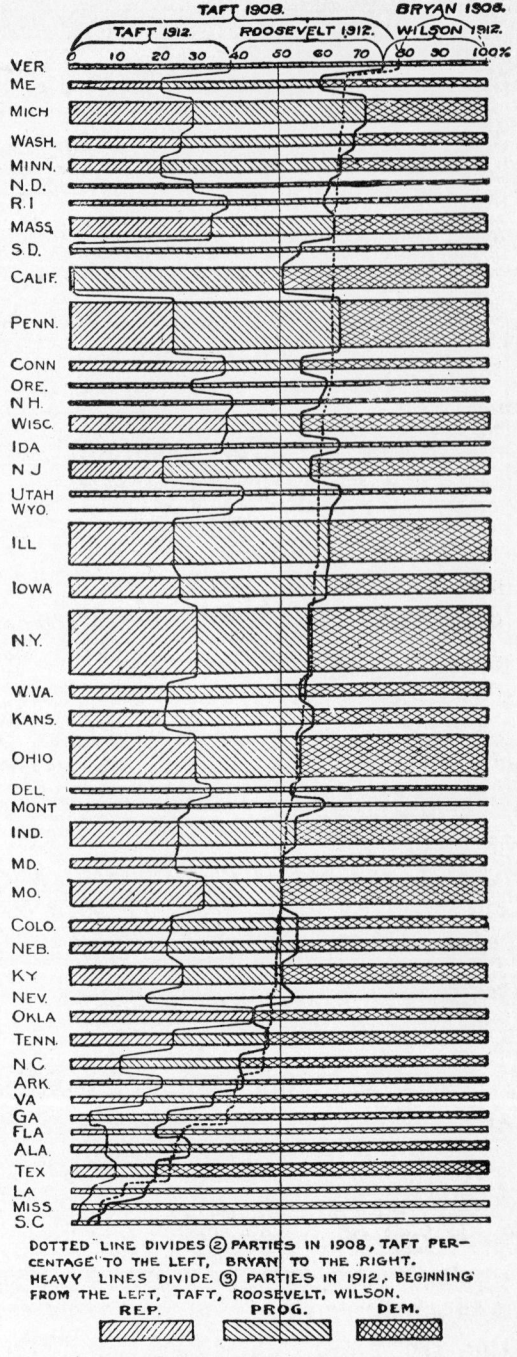

Prof. Irving Fisher in the New York Times

Fig. 8. The Vote for President in 1908 and in 1912 by States

Compare this with Fig. 5 where the vertical scale is continuous, without the gaps necessary here in order to distinguish different States.

10

fore given greater width than any other State in proportion to the greater size of its electoral vote. The horizontal division has been made according to the percentage number of votes for each of the main political parties. Two different elections are shown by using solid lines and dotted lines. The chart proves that the Democratic vote of 1913 was essentially the same as the Democratic vote in 1908, and that a Democrat was elected President in 1912 largely because there were three candidates in 1912 and only two in 1908. This is an admirable piece of presentation even though the lettering and drafting are not quite as good as they might have been if more care had been used, though probably allowance must be made for the limitations of paper and presswork in daily newspaper printing.

Relations Between Annual Cost of Motor Trucks And Characteristics of Service.

	Tires	Repairs	Battery Renewals	Lubricants	Electricity or Gasoline	Garage Expense	Sundries	Driver and Helper	Amortization or Depreciation	Interest	Insurance	Administration and Taxes
(a) Character of work:												
Size and type of truck	x	x	x	x	x	x	x	x	x	x	x	x
Nature of loads	x	x	x		x		x	x	x		x	
Number of cars	x	x	x	x	x	x	x					x
Distance per day	x	x	x	x	x				x			
Number of stops per day		x	x	x	x				x			
Days in service	x	x	x	x	x	x		x				
(b) Roads and climate:												
Road surface	x	x	x		x				x			
Grades		x	x		x				x			
Other street traffic		x	x		x						x	
Climate	x		x	x	x		x					
(c) System of operating:												
Routing	Indirectly as this item affects distance											
Loading and unloading	Indirectly as this item affects distance											
Overloading	x	x	x	x	x			x	x			
Overspeeding	x	x	x	x	x			x	x			
Garage facilities		x	x		x	x	x		x		x	x
Care of cars	x	x	x	x	x			x	x			x

Massachusetts Institute of Technology—Vehicle Research

Fig. 9. The Factors Entering into the Annual Cost of Motor Trucking Service

The scheme of this convenient form of tabulation is somewhat similar to that of Fig. 5. Here, however, the components are only named without denoting their relative size or importance

When studying a number of varied components, and the relations of each to every other one, a chart like Fig. 9 is frequently of great assistance. This chart shows that certain components are affected by features which may not affect other components. We have here the total cost of motor trucking, studied according to the components of the cost and also according to the conditions which produce those component costs. We may consider either the service conditions or the cost components. We have 100 per cent in the horizontal direction and 100 per cent also in the vertical direction. The total of the components in either direction is 100 per cent, but the actual size of each is not given because the size is not known or because it may vary from time to time.

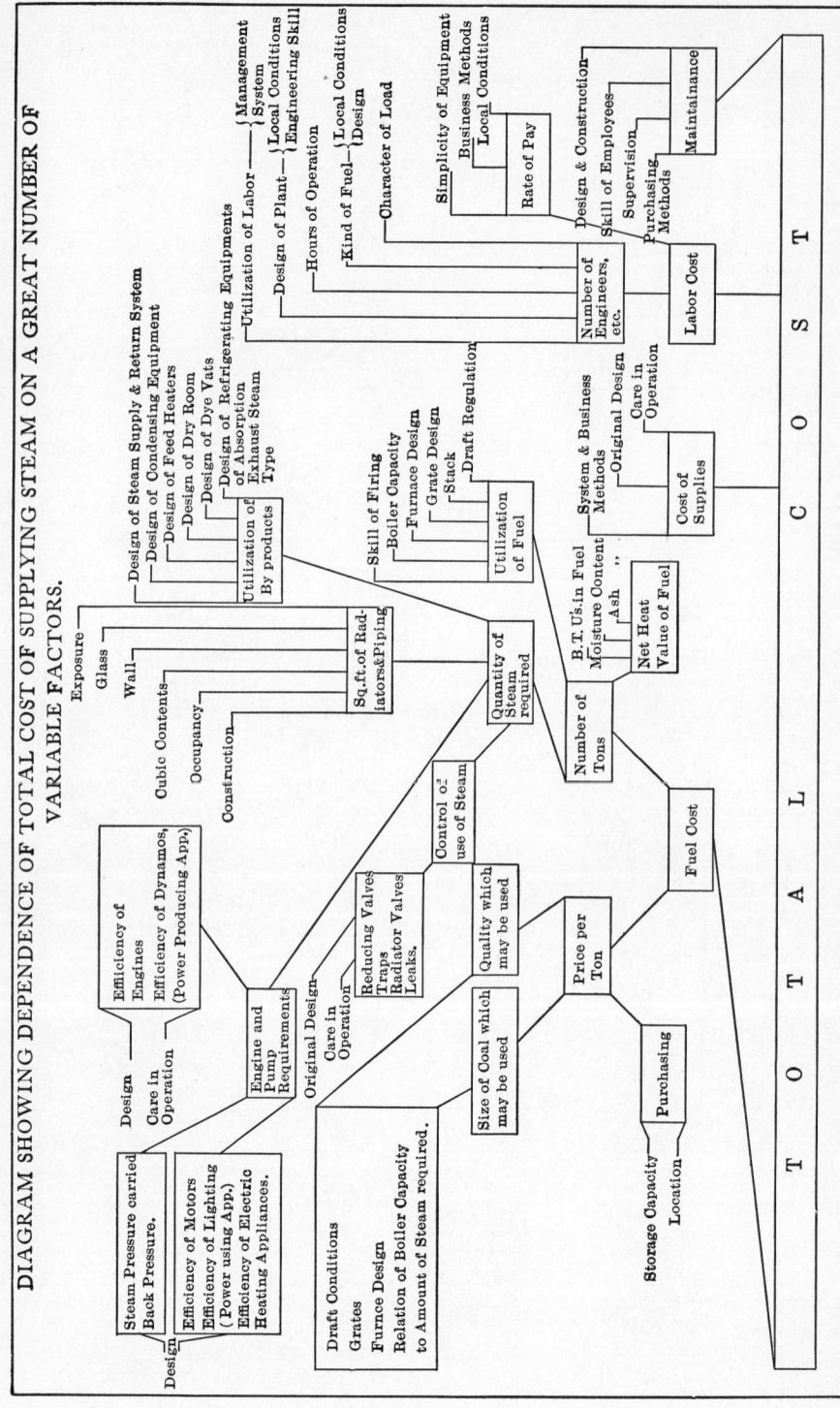

Fig. 10. Components or Factors Which May Enter into the Total Cost of Producing Steam

A chart similar to this allows making numerous subdivisions of component factors with clear expression of relations existing between different factors.

COMPONENT PARTS

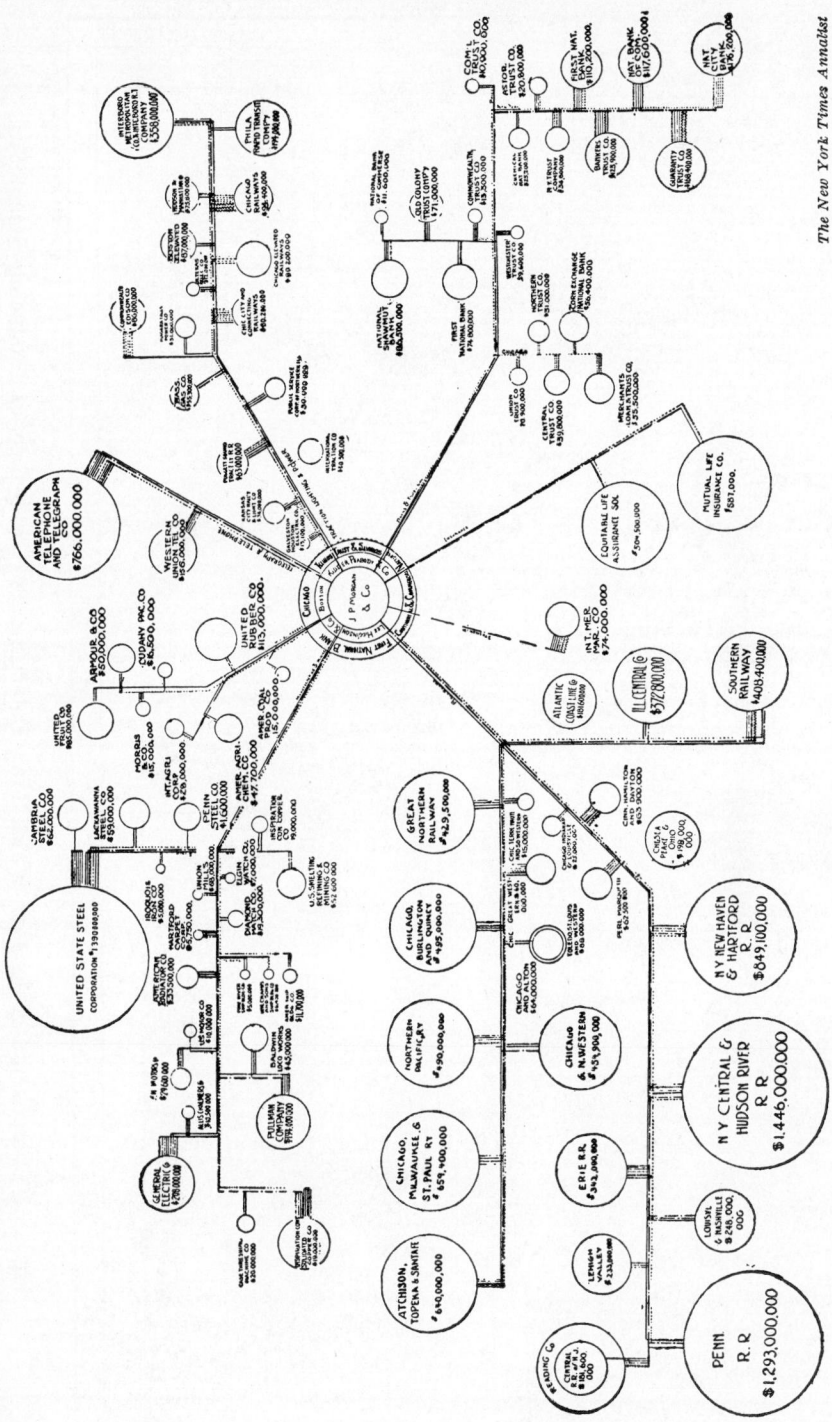

Fig. 11. **Banking Influence in Large Corporations**. The original chart had lines in three colors of ink

This illustration was adapted from a larger size chart in the Pujo Money Report.

The New York Times Annalist

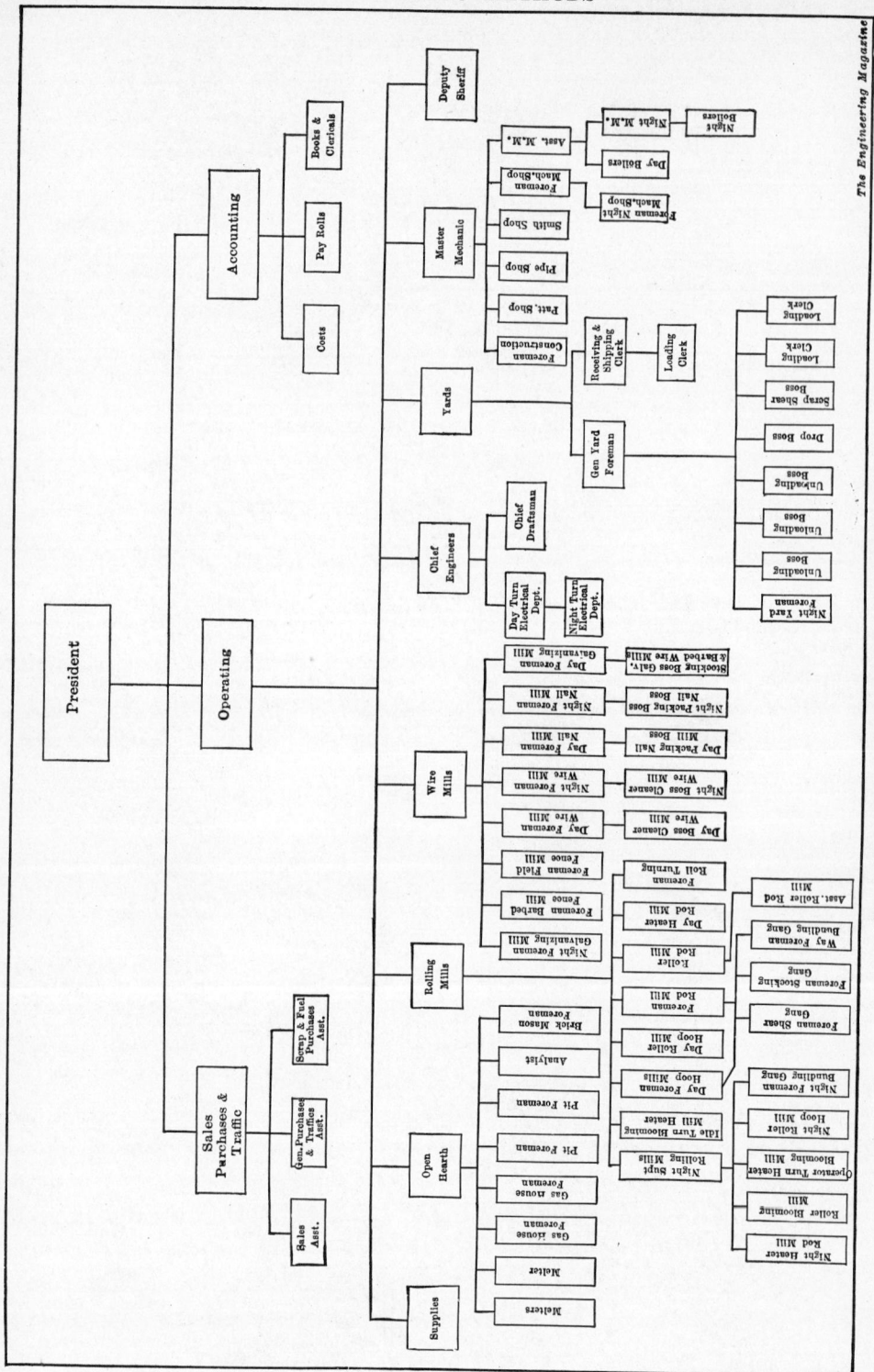

Fig. 12. Outline for an Organization Chart
It would be better to start with the stockholders as in Fig. 13

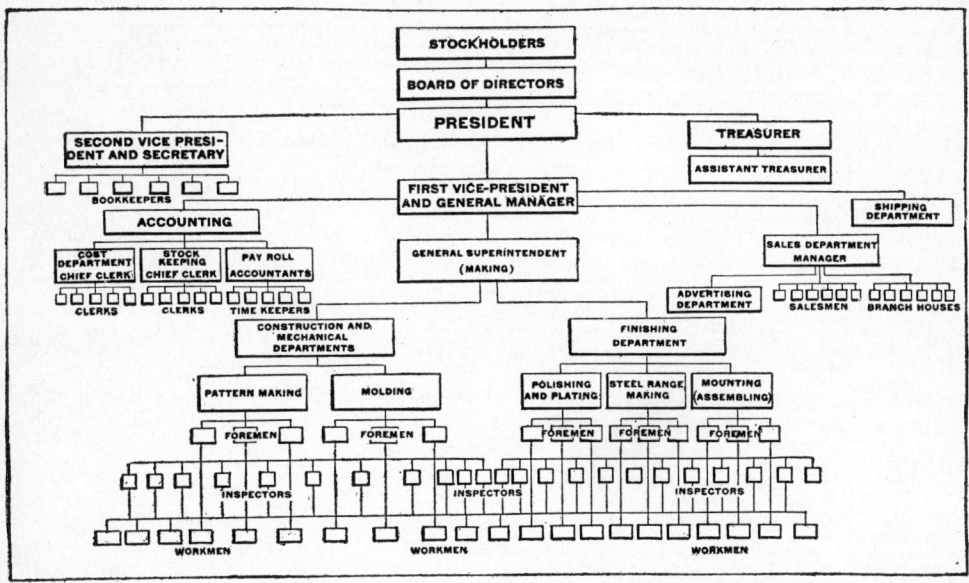

System

Fig. 13. Organization Chart of a large Company Manufacturing Stoves

A complete organization chart should always include the stockholders and the Board of Directors as shown here

A diagram like that of Fig. 10 may be of considerable assistance if a very complex relation of components has to be shown. In Fig. 9, the components have only one subdivision. In Fig. 10, however, we have fuel cost subdivided as many as five different times. Though the method of Fig. 10 could easily be used for the data of Fig. 9, that of Fig. 9 has its advantages in that it makes printing cheaper and is therefore desirable whenever it can be used. Fig. 9 can be prepared on a typewriter or can be set up by any printer, while Fig. 10 requires the making of a drawing.

In Fig. 11 the ramifications of the influence of the J. P. Morgan Company and various large banking concerns are shown. This chart, taken from the Pujo Money Report, was drawn originally in several different colors of ink. Though the windmill effect of the chart is rather disagreeable to the eye, the chart nevertheless shows the application of the graphic method to such complex situations as it is almost impossible to portray with language alone.

Organization charts are not nearly so widely used as they should be. As organization charts are an excellent example of the division of a total into its components, a number of examples are given here in the hope that the presentation of organization charts in convenient form will lead to their more widespread use.

It has been well stated that an organization chart closely resembles a genealogical tree.

Authority reaches down through the several branches of an organization like descent of blood, and, if properly planned, it will be as irregular for a factor in an organization to be in doubt as to the person in authority over him as for the child to deny the parentage of his father. Such a chart should be drawn for every organization, even more especially for those organizations which are short-handed expanding businesses in which one man holds the authority of several positions. It should be graphically shown what positions are only temporarily filled, so that when new men are engaged they will fit into the scheme with functions planned. Then there will be no irritation, no feeling on the part of some that their authority has been usurped.

If such a chart is made there will be fewer cases of conflict or of short-circuiting of orders. Every command from the general that is given directly to the private over the head of the captain weakens the authority of the captain over the private and weakens the authority of the general over the captain. A military organization is so planned that each man knows from whom to take orders, but business proceeds too much on personal authority. An organization chart will help to prevent this.

Of course, no two businesses can have identical organizations. The skeleton may be the same, however, and just as the proper study of the functions of the human body begins with the skeleton, so the study of organization should begin with those simple outlines which appear, in the main, in all completely and successfully organized businesses. Very few enterprises are organized properly. Very few have an organization that can be charted at all. That is one reason why there is such inefficiency in industry.

As a general thing it is better to have an organization chart begin with the stockholders and then show the board of directors as intermediate between the stockholders and the president. In reality, a typical organization chart represents the shape of an hour glass or a double funnel, with the large number of stockholders on one side and the large number of employees on the other. The board of directors, the president, and the officers of the company are at the narrow part, with the president as the intermediary through which all transactions take place between the large number of stockholders and the large number of employees.

The routing of work through the many processes and departments of a large plant is a subject of such great importance that charts are frequently desired for the study of such routing. Fig. 14 is a fairly good example of this class of chart. In a complete chart, the departments would of course be designated for easy reference, by names, numbers, or letters. Colored ink could be used to keep one class of work distinct from another. Colored inks would help tremendously

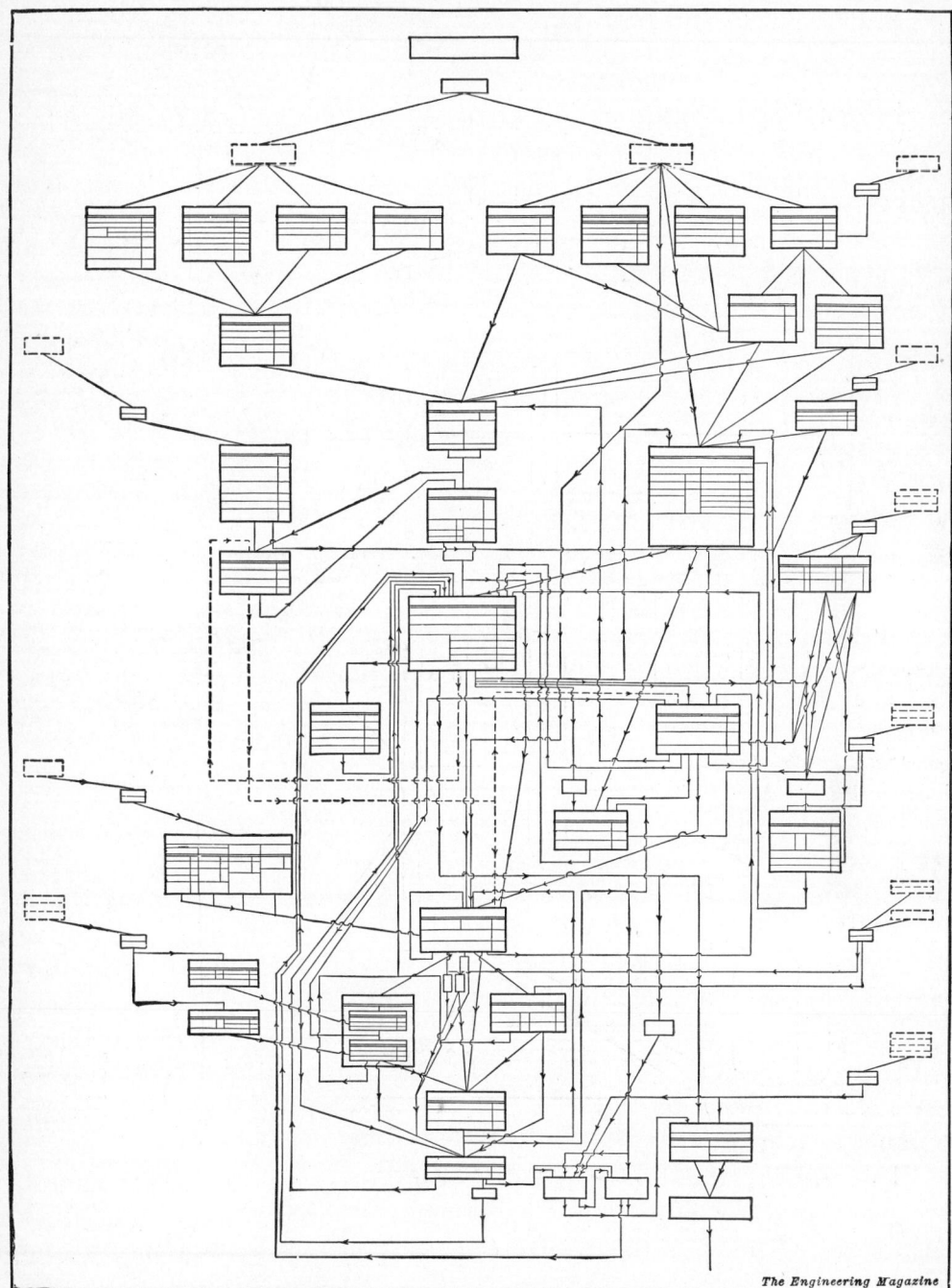

Fig. 14. Graphic Representation of Processes and Routing in a Representative Plant
Names of departments and operations are omitted by request of the proprietors of the establishment in which this chart was made

18   GRAPHIC METHODS

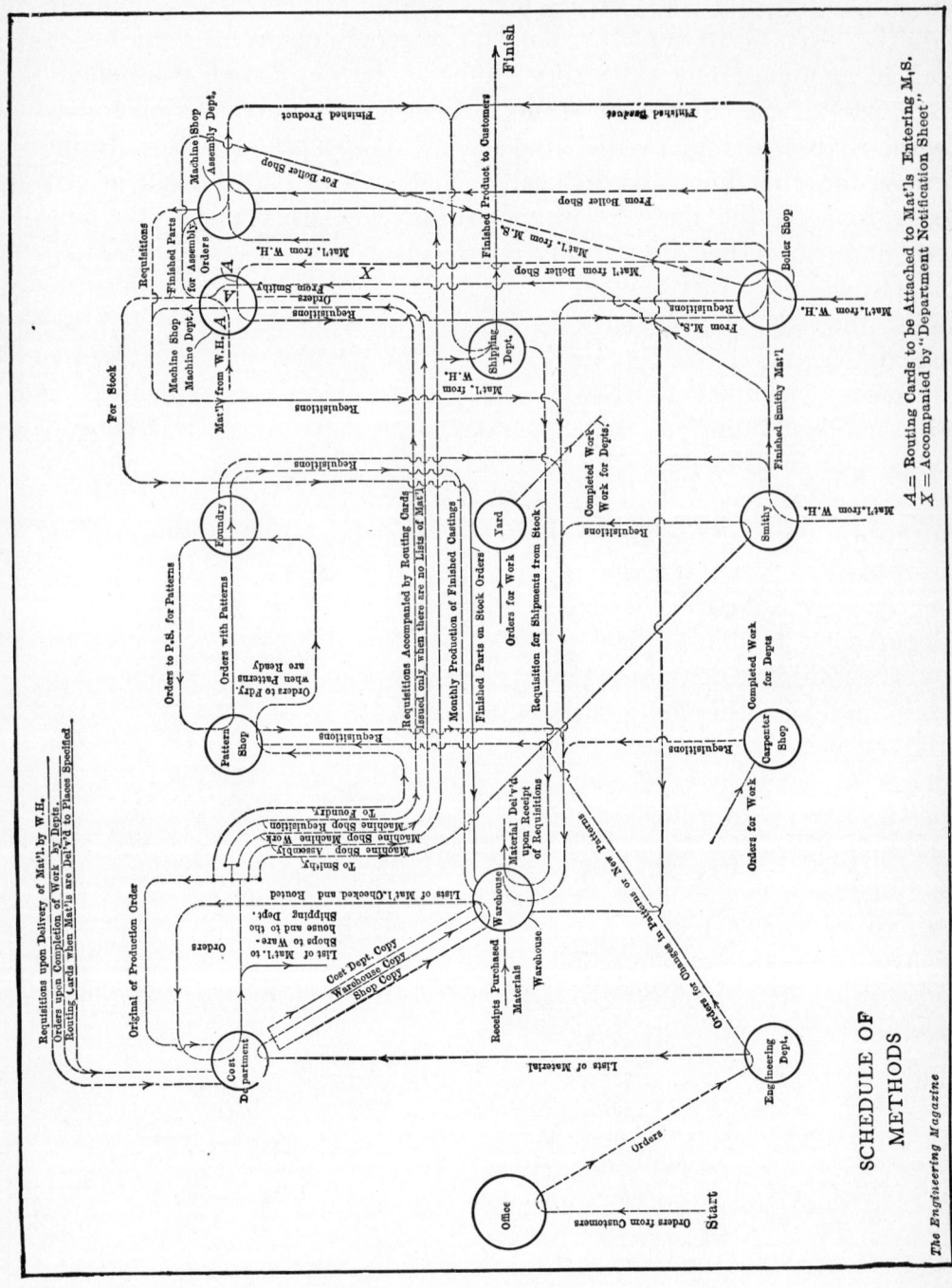

Fig. 15. Routing Diagram for Materials and for Printed Forms in a Manufacturing Plant

in simplifying Fig. 14, but are not available here because of the prohibitive expense of color printing. Colored drawing inks can be obtained at almost any stationery store. A bottle of each color should be a part of the equipment of any person who is regularly doing chart work. Note in Fig. 14 the small curves drawn where one route line crosses another line. By means of small curves like these it is very easy to keep the lines separate and to show clearly that the lines crossing each other are entirely independent.

Orders and other printed forms sent through a large organization must follow a routing entirely distinct from that actually followed by the heavy materials. The routing of printed forms in a large business is, in itself, a matter worthy of most careful study to get a true understanding of their complex movements. A clear idea of office system is almost impossible unless the data are charted. Fig. 15 may give some suggestions for a chart to show the movement of printed forms through an industrial plant. Here again printing by colored inks such as would be used on the original drawing would be of great service in making the chart easy to understand and easy to follow from department to department.

If a building contains many stories the routing diagram for materials and also the routing diagram for printed forms can be made conveniently by a rough perspective drawing showing the different floors as planes one above the other. Colored ink lines on the perspective chart will show clearly the movement of materials through the manufacturing building, and will indicate the elevator movements for material in a manner not possible if the departments are represented all in one plane on the ordinary sheet of paper. Perspective charts of floors, one above the other, are so simply made that their advantage should not be overlooked when preparing routing charts for plants having multi-story buildings.

Chapter II

SIMPLE COMPARISONS

ONE of a business man's chief assets is his ability to show things to others in their true proportions. He is continually making contrasts, and holding up for comparison different propositions which come up in his daily affairs. The graphic method lends itself admirably to use in making comparisons. It is surprising how much clearer even simple comparisons of only two or three items will appear when their numerical value is put in graphic form rather than in figures.

Fig. 16 is a cut taken from the report of the Metropolitan Sewage Commission. Most people know so little about bacteria that it would mean nothing to them to say that the Harlem River contains 15,600 bacteria per cubic centimeter of water. When, however, such a comparison is made as is shown in Fig. 16, even the most casual glance would convince anyone that the Harlem River is not the most ideal

BACTERIA PER CUBIC CENTIMETER OF WATER

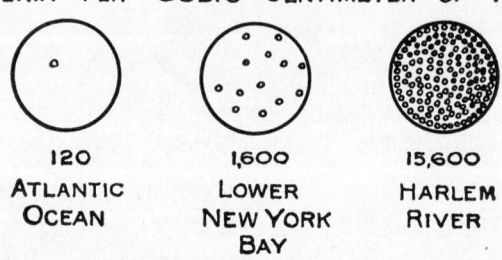

| 120 | 1,600 | 15,600 |
| ATLANTIC OCEAN | LOWER NEW YORK BAY | HARLEM RIVER |

Fig. 16. Bacteria in the Waters of New York Harbor

This illustration is taken from the report of the Metropolitan Sewage Commission. The representation as though seen through a microscope is decidedly effective

swimming place. The figures for the bacteria count are given with the chart so that all the data are available to anyone who may wish to study the facts from a scientific standpoint.

The drawing of Fig. 17 is of the cartoon type, effective for wall exhibitions or for use in the more popular magazines. This particular

SIMPLE COMPARISONS 21

diagram contains nothing by which accurate comparison may be made. No figures are given, and it is impossible to tell whether the different money bags should be compared on the basis of diameter, area, or volume. Almost the only conclusion which can be drawn from such a diagram is one regarding the relative rank of the different expenditures. The reliability of even that is likely to be questioned because of the evident lack of accuracy in this kind of chart. Nevertheless the cartoonist style should not be broadly condemned, for it has tremendous possibilities. It is possible to combine the cartoonist's wonderful power of arousing interest with methods of presenting facts which will give a numerical interpretation that cannot be misunderstood. There is a great opportunity waiting for the man who can combine cartoon methods with accuracy of numerical statement.

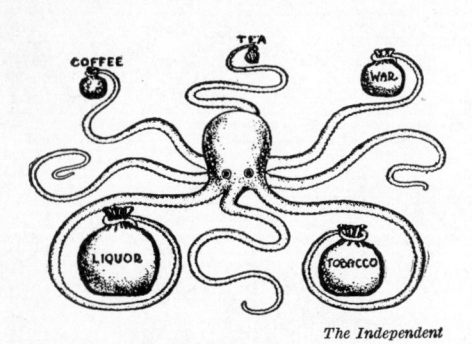

The Independent

Fig. 17. Five Forms of Our National Waste

A cartoon type of chart like this will reach a popular audience. Accuracy of statement should not, however, be sacrificed as it has been here, in that there is no way of correctly comparing the money bags

Fig. 18 gives a statement which the illustration does not support. In the first place, the dates of the two years compared are not given. In the second place, it is impossible for the reader to tell whether the diagram is drawn on the basis of one dimension, two dimensions, or three dimensions. It would be a hopeless task to fit the area of the smaller washing machine into the area of the larger washing machine. Methods like this cannot be too severely condemned.

Commercial geography, as it is now widely taught in the public schools by listing the various imports and exports of countries and the products of different cities, fails to give a clear idea of the

Good Housekeeping

Fig. 18. Illustration Intended to Show that the Sale of Washing Machines has Increased Sevenfold in the Past Three Years

In comparing the two pictures it is not likely that the reader will obtain a ratio of seven to one. There is no way for the reader to tell on what basis the drawing was prepared, whether by height, area or volume. The title of this chart is also poor in that it does not name the two years for which the comparison is made

relative importance of the materials listed. It frequently happens that the second or third item on a list may have only one-tenth the importance of the first item. Because the three names are given one after the other, the pupil is quite likely to consider the three items of equal importance, just as three persons may be of different height, yet of about the same importance. The graphic method judiciously applied to school geography and to general commercial geography would make a tremendous difference in the student's grasp of the subject.

Fig. 19. The Six Leading Cotton-producing Countries in 1910

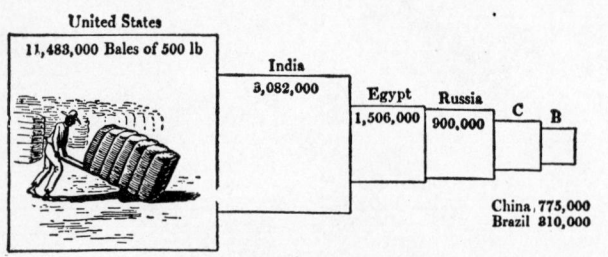

Tarr and McMurray's New Geographies

This arrangement is a bad one to place before school children. The eye cannot fit one square into another on an area basis so as to get the correct ratio

Fig. 19 is a typical example taken from a geography book in which the attempt was made to use the graphic method. The introduction of the picture of the bale of cotton in Fig. 19 is justifiable. There is, however, no justification for placing the picture inside of one of the series of squares. The picture detracts from the size of the square. Graphic comparisons, wherever possible, should be made in one dimension only. In such a case as this, one-dimension presentation is perfectly feasible by the use of bars of different lengths. The pupil would find it an almost hopeless task to fit one side of the block for Brazil into one side of the block for the United States and then square the resulting ratio in order to learn that the United States produces, roughly, thirty times as much cotton as Brazil. Bars in one dimension only would show the comparison accurately. Under any circumstances, the use of the squares of Fig. 19 with the center line through the centers of the squares gives an extremely poor arrangement.

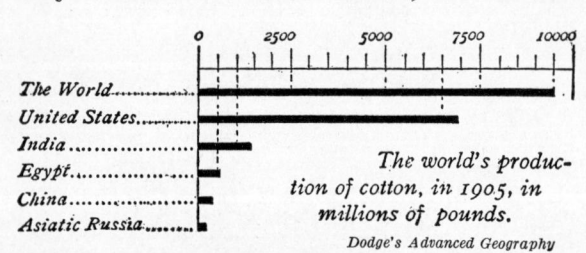

Fig. 20. The World's Production of Cotton in 1905 in Millions of Pounds

Dodge's Advanced Geography

The above illustration together with the title is shown exactly as given in a recent geography book. Charts like this greatly assist the pupil in getting the correct relative importance of the different things studied. Note the scale at the top of the chart

SIMPLE COMPARISONS 23

VALUE OF PRODUCTS FOR PRINCIPAL CITIES: 1909.

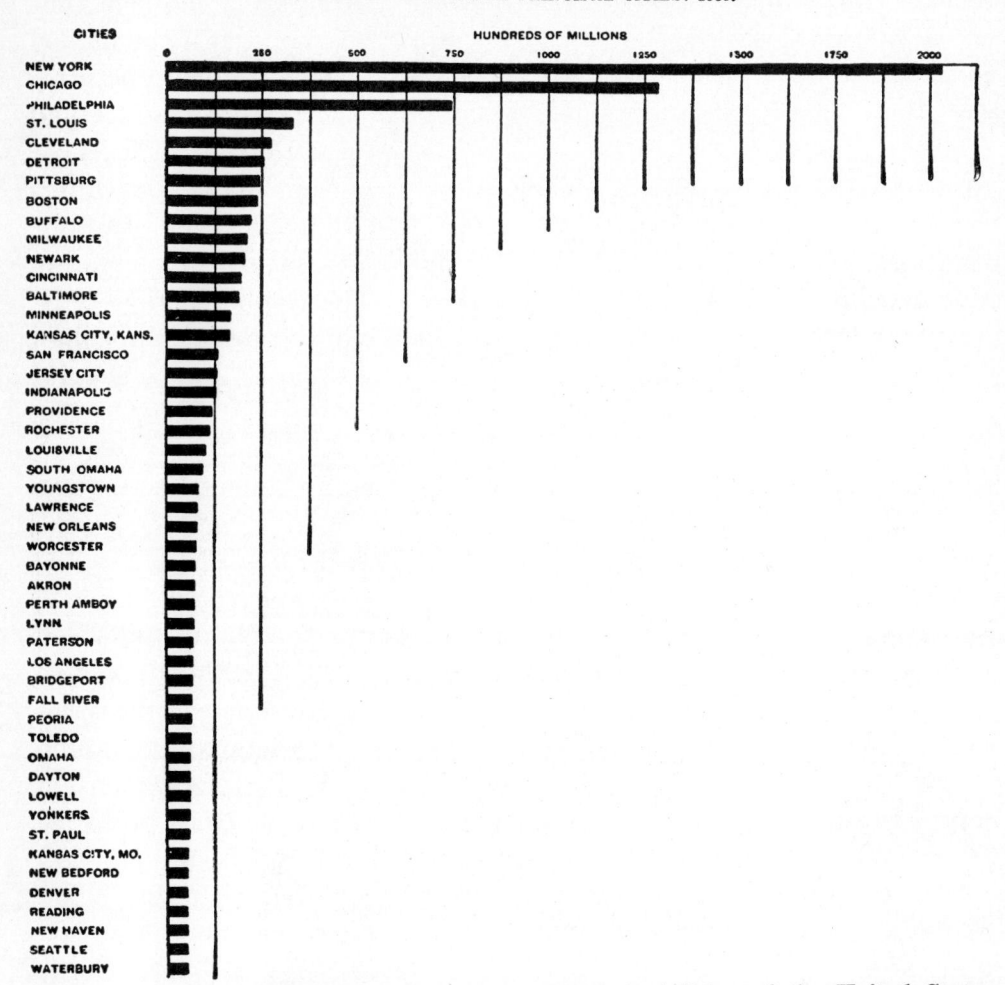

Fig. 21. Value of Manufactured Products of Principal Cities of the United States in 1909

This chart, taken from a Census office report, would have been greatly improved if the actual figures had been placed at the left of the bars in the manner shown in Fig. 27

It is stated by the author of the book in which Fig. 19 is used that tests have shown that children grasp relative quantities better when separate squares are used than when the information is shown by lines or bars. If this is the case, it is probably due to the fact that the squares appear more prominently to the eye than do the bars, and it would seem that the best kind of presentation might be made by using much wider bars so that the bars would be easily seen. Bars can be made as wide as some of the squares seen in Fig. 19 and, if it seems best, the bars could be made in outline rather than in solid black. Wide bars would give a striking visual effect and yet they would vary in one dimension only, so that relative proportions could be easily judged. Wide bars would probably have all the advantages and none of the disadvantages of the methods of either Fig. 19 or Fig. 20. Instead of showing the data of Fig. 19 by either bars or squares, another method would show pictures of bales in rows of different lengths, on the general scheme of Fig. 41. The rows would be the same as the broad horizontal bars, but their numerical interpretation would be less abstract.

Fig. 20 gives a diagram taken from another geography book. This is a much better form of presentation than used in Fig. 19. It could, however, be improved by giving the figures for each country in connection with its own bar.

Fig. 21 shows the horizontal-bar method applied to a larger number of items and proves the great utility of this method when several different items must be shown in their proper rank. In this case, however, the figures should have been given for the convenient use of any one who might wish to make ratios or to quote the actual value of products for any one of the cities. It is exasperating to run across a diagram of this kind which contains valuable information in such form that it cannot be carried away or quoted for use elsewhere.

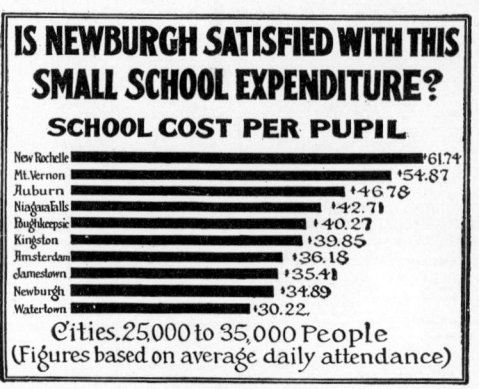

Fig. 22. Comparison of School Cost per Pupil in Cities of 25,000 to 35,000 People in New York State

This illustration was photographed down from a wall exhibit to adapt it to a printed report. The use of the figures at the right-hand end of the bars is bad practice. The eye is apt to make the comparison from the last figures rather than from the ends of the bars

In Fig. 22 an attempt has been made to show in the graphic presentation the figures from which each horizontal bar was drawn. The method of placing the figures at the right of the bar is, however, unsafe. The eye is likely to make a comparison, not from the ends of the bars themselves, but from the right-hand end of the figures. Since the figures are of about constant length, visual ratios are inaccurate when made by comparing a short bar *plus* the constant length of figures with a long bar *plus* the constant length of figures. If the shortest bar in Fig. 22 were about the same length as the space required for the figures, it would be possible to make a visual error of 100 per cent in the comparison. If the figures had been placed at the left of the bars, they would have been in a neat column and not at all likely to affect the accuracy of the visual comparison.

The chart, Fig. 22, was taken from a report devoted entirely to the city of Newburgh. On this account, it would have been much better if the word "Newburgh" had been printed in heavy-faced type so that it would stand out from the other cities in the list. Where the use of colored ink is possible, it is frequently desirable to make the item under foremost consideration stand out prominently by giving it a brilliant color such as red or green.

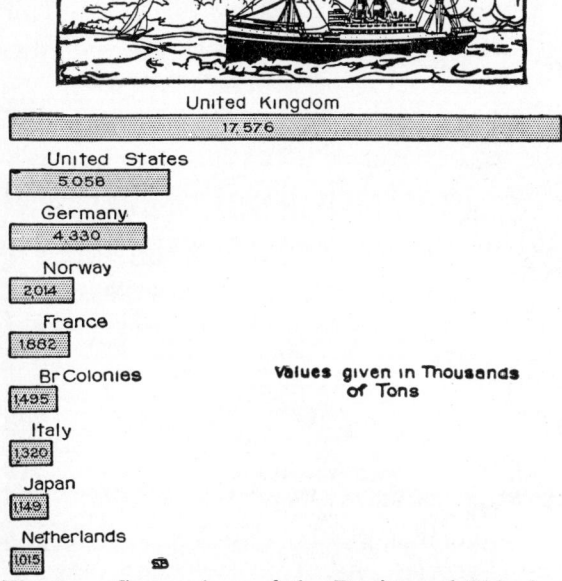

Fig. 23. Comparison of the Registered Shipping of the Principal Countries of the World

The picture at the top of the chart assists in attracting the attention of the reader. After the attention is gained, the bars set forth the comparison more accurately than it could be given by any pictures of ships of different sizes

Fig. 23 is an attempt to give a popular touch similar to that attempted in Fig. 19 by the bale of cotton. As a general thing, it is possible to attract attention by some such scheme as the steamship used in Fig. 23 and then, after the attention is attracted, to give the comparison by methods which are entirely correct and also familiar to the average observer. In Fig. 23 the figures are given for the data from which the bars are drawn. The values, however, were so large that it was necessary to leave off the last three ciphers and state that the values given are in "thousands of tons." Though the dropping of ciphers is very common, it is a practice likely to lead to serious error and should not be encouraged. Even with the ciphers omitted, the values could not possibly have been given inside the bar if more countries had been included in the list, or if the scale had been any smaller than that shown here. To place above each bar the title for that bar is not good practice. In general, it is desirable to have a title for each bar at the left, then the figures, then the bar. With such an arrangement, one title will be below another, easily perceived by the eye, and the figures will all be in one column with the decimal points in a straight line.

Figures running into millions can be easily read from long columns if sufficient white paper is left between figures in the vertical arrangement, and if each group of three figures in the horizontal arrangement is widely set off by means of a comma. For graphic work, the groups of three figures should, in general, be more widely set apart than they are ordinarily.

Fig. 24 shows the arrangement with the figures at the left of the bars. Here again, however, the ciphers have been omitted when it would probably have been just as clear if they had been included and set off by means of a comma and a wide space. The drawing for the pigs of copper shown at the left of the illustration gives an idea of what can be done by hand drawing in order to attract attention to the subject which the chart itself is intended to illuminate. In this case the lettering also has been done by hand and is a good example of what a skilled draftsman may do without any great expenditure of time. The solid black bars of Fig. 24 come out in much better contrast than the gray bars of Fig. 23.

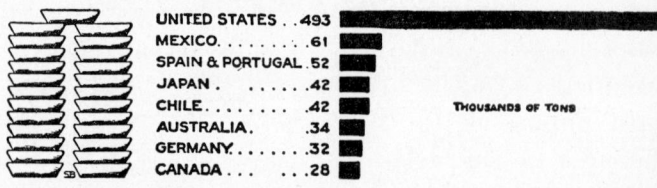

Fig. 24. Production of Copper in Different Countries for One Year

UNITED STATES ..493
MEXICO........ .61
SPAIN & PORTUGAL .52
JAPAN. 42
CHILE......... .42
AUSTRALIA. .34
GERMANY....... .32
CANADA... ...28

THOUSANDS OF TONS

This chart is a redrawing of Fig. 25. The title here should state the year, but that was not given in the book from which Fig. 25 was taken

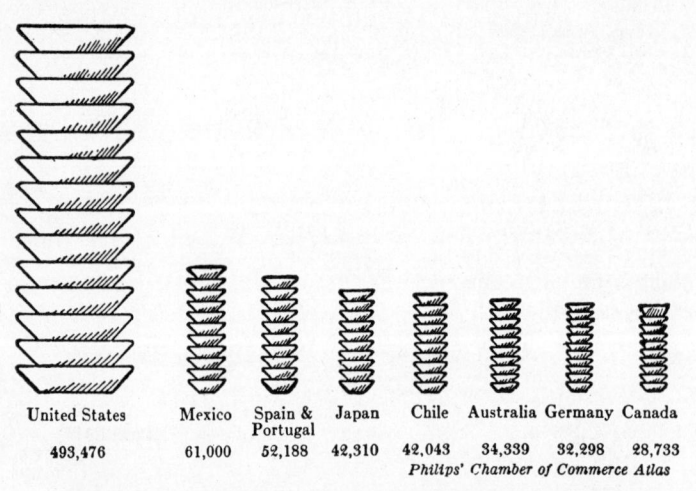

United States 493,476
Mexico 61,000
Spain & Portugal 52,188
Japan 42,310
Chile 42,043
Australia 34,339
Germany 32,298
Canada 28,733

Philips' Chamber of Commerce Atlas

Fig. 25. A Year's Production of Copper in Tons

This illustration was copied from a prominent book on international trade. Accurate interpretation of the chart is impossible. Graphic work of this sort is dangerous because it may be misleading

Fig. 25 shows a chart of the same data from which Fig. 24 was drawn. It is readily seen that it would be impossible for the average reader to tell whether this chart was drawn on the basis of height or the basis of area. The pigs of copper are not of the same size in the different piles, and it is evident that a pictured pig of copper is not intended to be the unit. If Fig. 25 is drawn on an area basis, it is almost impossible for the eye to fit the area for the right-hand pile into the area of the left-hand pile. This chart is a typical example of thousands of illustrations used by the popular magazines and even by some of the more pretentious reference books.

Fig. 26 is an even greater atrocity than Fig. 25. In Fig. 26, the observer is entirely unable to tell whether comparison is made in one, two, or three dimensions and he has an additional puzzle because of the large amount of perspective shown for the top of the pigs of tin. It would be surprising if one man in a thousand could guess anything near the ratio intended to be expressed between the largest and smallest pigs shown. In general, graphic work of this kind is much worse than the use of figures alone. There are times when an absence of knowledge is better than incorrect knowledge.

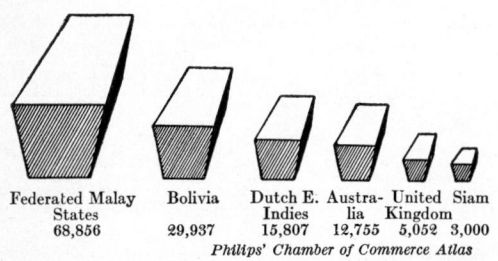

Fig. 26. A Year's Production of Tin in Tons
This illustration, taken from the same source as Fig. 25, is even more confusing. The perspective of the tops of the pigs of tin is such that there is no way of telling whether visual comparison should be made by height, area or volume

Federated Malay States	Bolivia	Dutch E. Indies	Australia	United Kingdom	Siam
68,856	29,937	15,807	12,755	5,052	3,000

Philips' Chamber of Commerce Atlas

Fig. 27 is a good example of what can be done as a standard arrangement for simple comparisons. On the left there is a symbol to attract the eye and interest the observer. Note that a dollar mark is shown on top of the picture of the bale of cotton in one case and the sheaf of wheat in the other, to indicate that the value of the crop is considered rather than the number of units. After the pictures, which may be thought of as "eye catchers," we have the figures, and then the bars plotted to scale for quick comparison by the reader. This cut could have been improved slightly if the spaces between the sep-

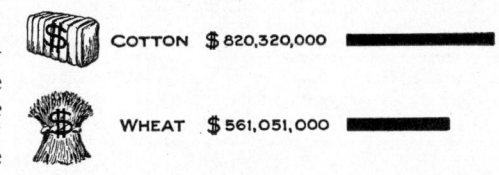

Fig. 27. Value of Cotton and of Wheat Produced in the United States in 1910
Here is a suggestion for a standard arrangement for horizontal-bar comparisons. The illustrations at the left make the presentation popular in form, yet actual figures for the data are given at the left-hand end of the bars

arate groups of three figures had been made somewhat larger and if the black bars had been made about one and one-half times as wide as shown here.

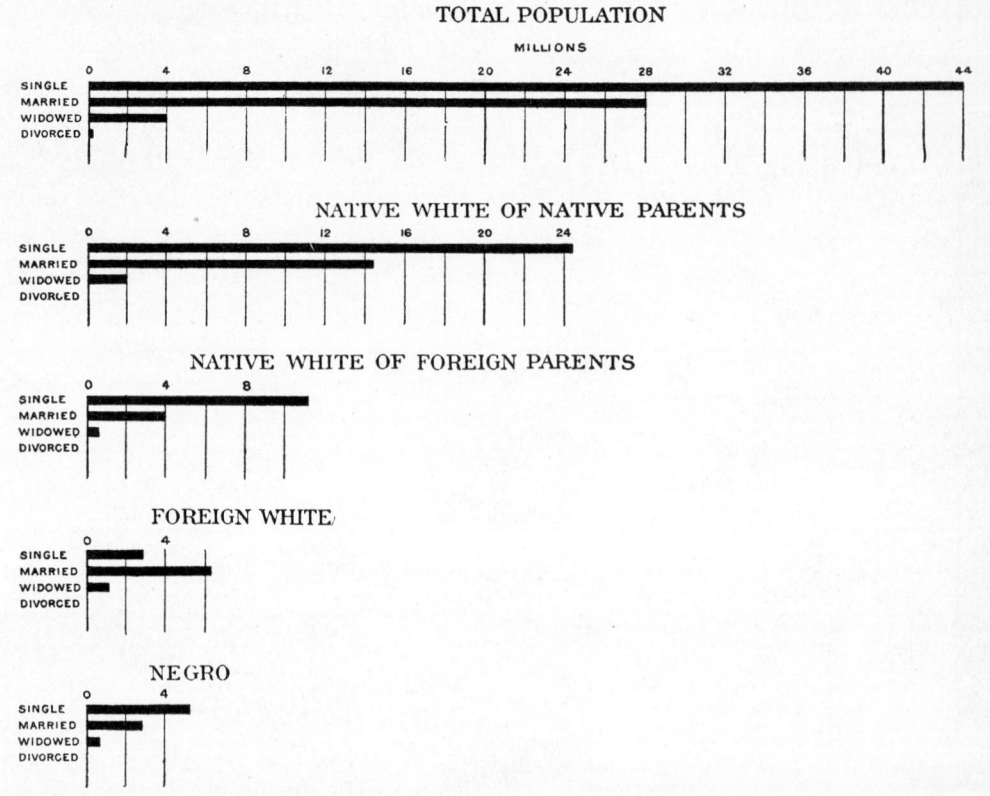

United States Statistical Atlas, 1900 Census

Fig. 28. Status of the Population of the United States in 1900, in Regard to Marriage

This chart would have been improved if the figures had been given at the left end of the bars. Note that the four lower groups of bars are a cross-index of the information given in the upper group

Another application of the bar method is seen in Fig. 28. Each of the four lower groups of population is a subdivision of the total population shown in the upper group. The same data may be seen portrayed in a different way in Fig. 6. The arrangement of Fig. 6 is more desirable, in that the size of the components is more readily grasped when all are shown in the same horizontal bar. In Fig. 28 the eye does not readily make the addition necessary to fit together the four items "Single," "Married," "Widowed," and "Divorced" as percentages of the total 100 per cent in each group.

The drawing in Fig. 29 is a portion of an illustration intended to show how far different kinds of trucks could travel for an expend-

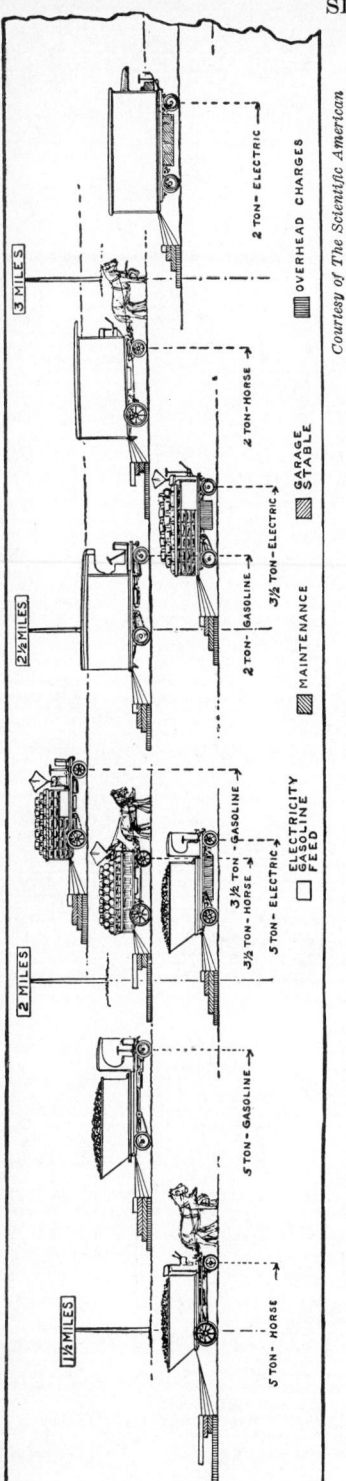

SIMPLE COMPARISONS 29

Fig. 29. The Distance Different Kinds of Trucks Can Travel for One Dollar Expenditure. The Distance They Have Covered May be Judged from the Mile Posts

The reader is likely to be misled by this illustration, because the zero point where the truck race started is not shown on the chart. Distances must not be judged from the left end of the illustration shown above

iture of one dollar. The placing of these trucks on different levels is somewhat confusing, but it was done in order that one truck would not have to be shown back of another. Note the bars behind each truck, to give the component parts of the total expenditure split into different kinds of charges. This chart is grossly misleading because the point where the race started is not shown. It appears, for instance, that for one dollar expended a five-ton gasoline truck will run about twice as far as a five-ton horse truck. This conclusion is entirely unwarranted, and would not be reached by any reader if the chart had been so drawn that the zero point or starting point for the race had been shown to scale at the left end of the chart.

The black bars used in Fig. 30 to show contagious diseases indicate an excellent method for differentiating items shown in graphic comparison. In the Boston health-report illustration from which this cut was adapted, the infectious diseases were shown in red. By making most of the bars in outline only, it was possible in Fig. 30 to use solid black to get the contrast obtained in the original report by means of red ink.

It *is* frequently necessary to show increases and decreases on the same chart so that they may

30 GRAPHIC METHODS

be in contrast. In Fig. 31 an example of the contrast of increases and decreases is given, increases being shown to the right of the zero line and decreases shown to the left of the zero line. This right-and-left arrangement of increases and decreases is fairly well known and is so convenient that it should be more widely used. The actual figures from which each of the horizontal bars is drawn can be shown on the chart even if the horizontal bars are drawn to the left of the zero line. The figures can be placed on the left-hand margin of the chart, immediately between the title for each bar and the end of the bar, in a manner similar to that shown in Fig. 27. Since the zero line must be near the center of the chart, rather than at the left-hand edge, when the right-and-left arrangement is used, it

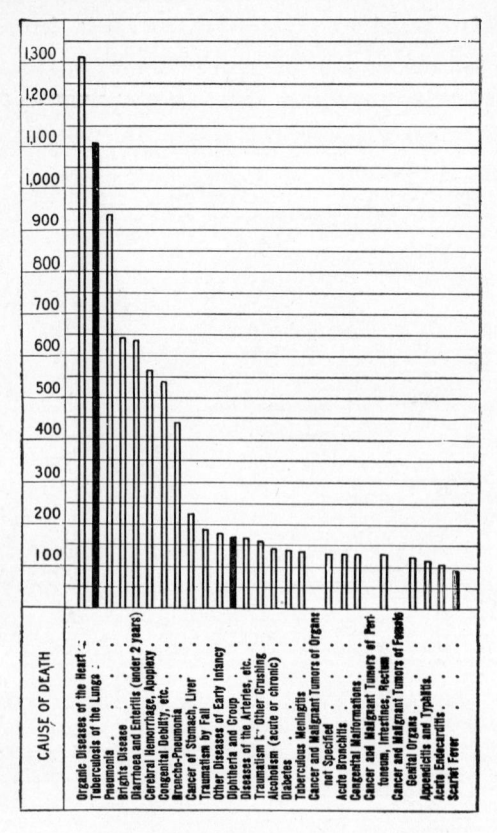

Annual Report of the Health Department, City of Boston, 1910

Fig. 30. Comparative View of Twenty-five of the Principal Causes of Death in Boston During 1910

In the Boston report, the infectious diseases were represented by red bars. Here attention is called to the infectious diseases by using solid black bars in contrast with bars shown only in outline

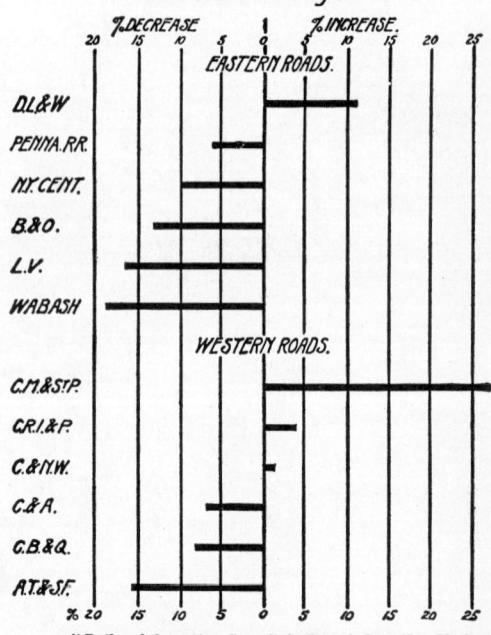

"Railroad Operating Costs," Suffern & Son, New York

Fig. 31. Increase is Here Shown to the Right of the Zero Line and Decrease to the Left of the Zero Line. A Heavier Zero Line and Arrows Pointing Right and Left from it Would Improve This Chart

would be well to have a broad line for the zero line, so that the eye may at once perceive that zero is not at the left-hand edge of the chart. It would have been better if the zero line in Fig. 31 were somewhat broader. Another help to the reader could be given by placing an arrow pointing to the right with the word "increase" and an arrow pointing to the left with the word "decrease."

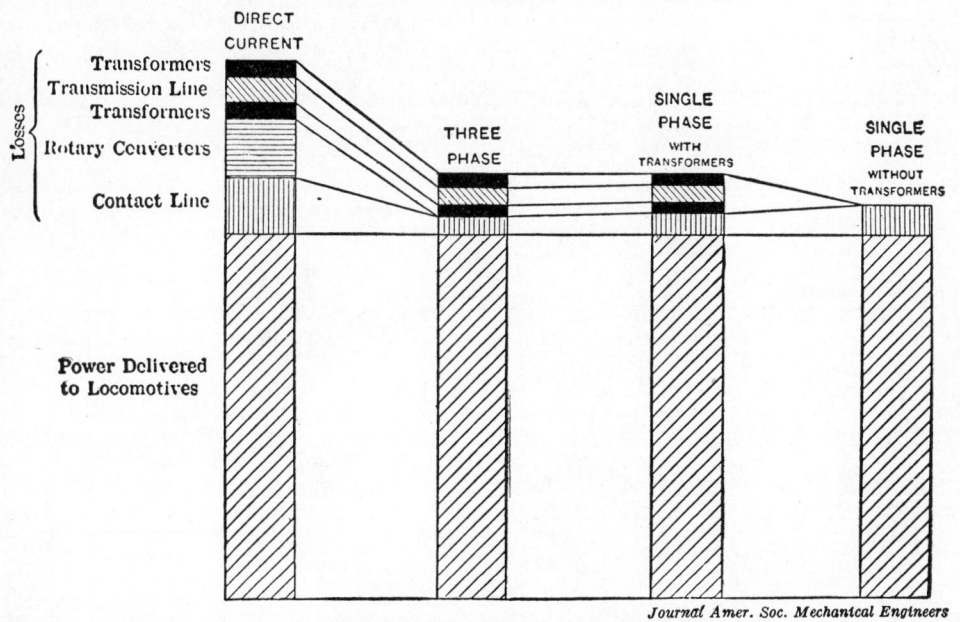

Journal Amer. Soc. Mechanical Engineers

Fig. 32. Comparative Losses Between the Power House and Locomotives with Different Systems of Electric Traction

The comparison of the losses in the different power systems is very clearly shown in this illustration, which was taken from a paper by George Westinghouse

Broad bars can be used either vertically or horizontally. The horizontal arrangement is usually the more convenient, as it lends itself more readily to the use of type and horizontal lettering for the titles, data, etc., of each bar, without forcing the reader to turn the book at right angles. In Fig. 32, however, the lettering can perhaps be more conveniently grasped by the reader with the bars placed vertically instead of horizontally.

Note the lines connecting different bars to show how the components compare in size therein. These lines assist greatly in giving a clear and rapid interpretation of the chart.

Fig. 33 is an admirable example of what the graphic method can do to boil down complex facts for quick interpretation by the reader. In this case the schools of each of the forty-eight United States were

TEN TESTS OF EFFICIENCY

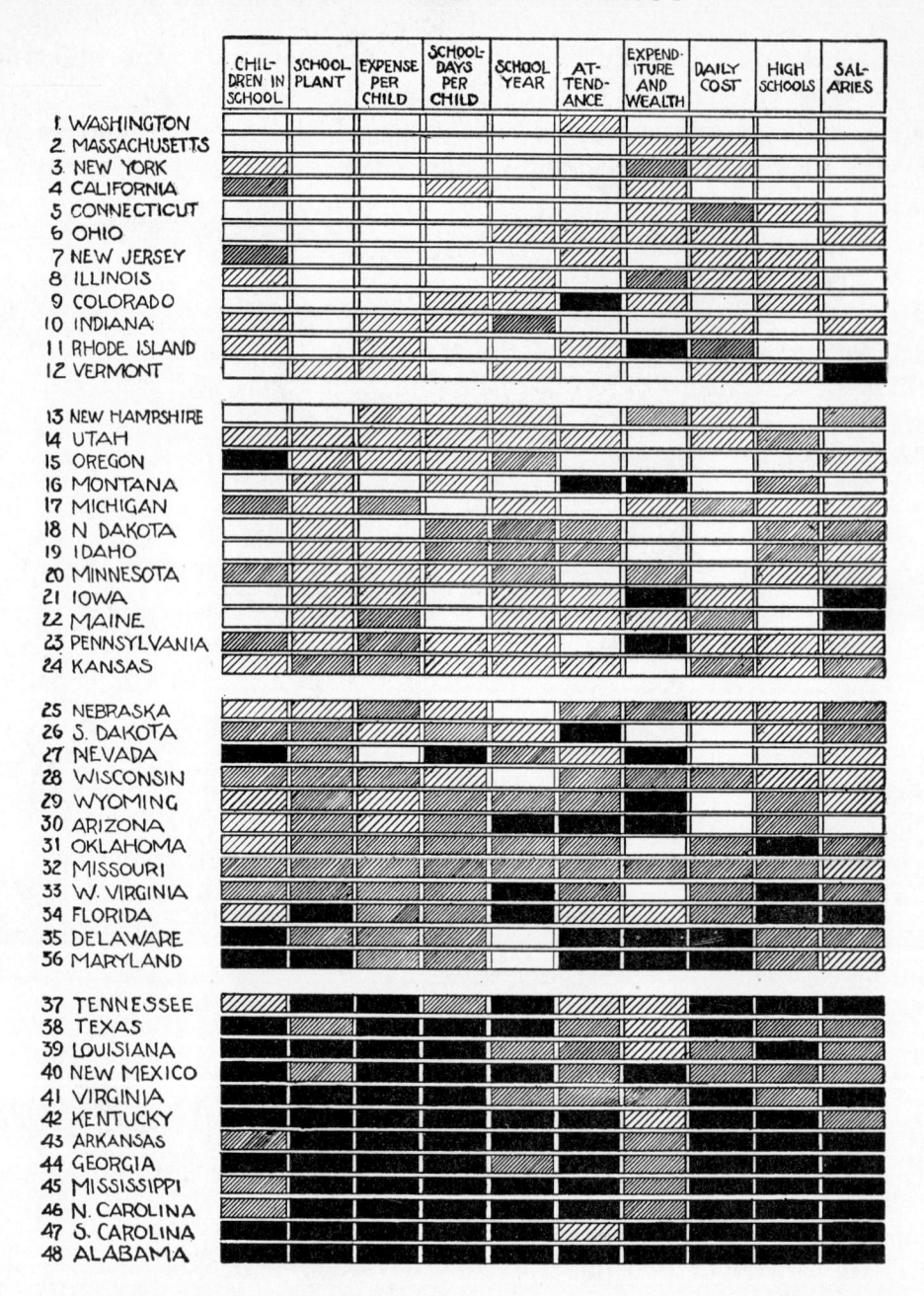

Fig. 33. Rank of States in Each of Ten Educational Features, 1910. White Indicates that the State Ranks in the Highest 12 of the 48, Light Shading that it Ranks in Second 12, Dark Shading that it Ranks in Third 12, and Black that it Ranks in Lowest 12

The above illustration is a photograph of one page of a pamphlet issued by the Division of Education of the Russell Sage Foundation, regarding the public schools of the United States. This type of chart is capable of wide application in other fields

considered from each of ten different view points. The different States were then arranged in grades one, two, three, or four, according to the efficiency of their schools from each of the ten different points of view from which they were considered. The best grade under each heading is shown by means of a white rectangle, the second grade by light cross-hatching, the third grade by dark cross-hatching, and the fourth and worst by solid black. States are shown in the complete chart in their comparative rank. The State with the best schools is shown at the top of the chart and the State with the worst schools is shown at the bottom of the chart. On the chart as a whole, one can see at a glance just how the schools of any State rank with those in the other States, and wherein the greatest defects occur.

The chart of Fig. 33 was in a thirty-page illustrated pamphlet sent broadcast over the United States by the Russell Sage Foundation to members of various legislatures, school boards, etc. This pamphlet has resulted in the appropriation of some millions of dollars for the improvement of public schools. The arrangement of the pamphlet itself is worthy of note in that each left-hand page is a chart, while each right-hand page, facing the chart, is devoted to a brief explanation of the conclusions which can be made from a study of the chart. This arrangement of alternate pages of chart matter and printed matter is tremendously effective and is well worth copying.

It is frequently necessary to contrast one grouping of components

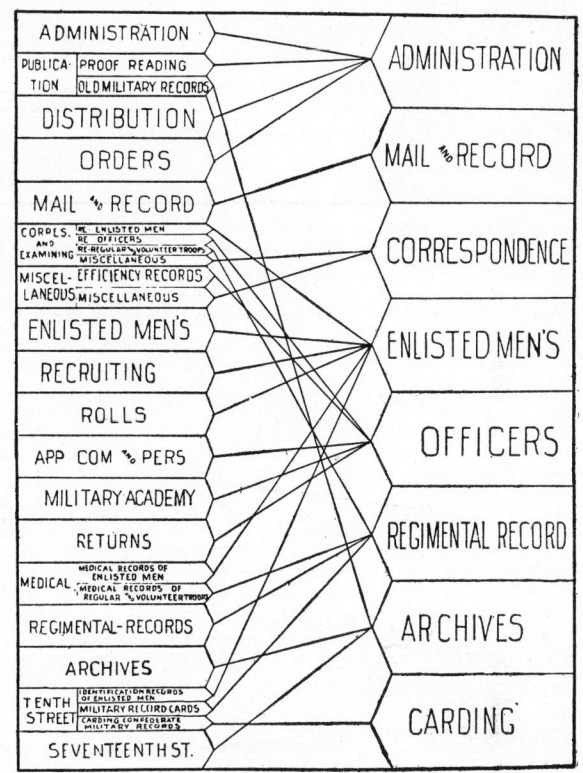

Fig. 34. Organization of the United States Adjutant General's Office Compared with Organization Proposed by President Taft's Commission on Economy and Efficiency

This method of connecting blocks with lines to show the disposition of departments can be used in many types of chart presentation with another grouping of components. In Fig. 34 we have a chart which may give a valuable suggestion to anyone who is considering the rearrangement of departments in any large organization. The present arrangement and the proposed arrangement are each clearly indicated, with connecting lines to show instantly the disposition of each of the old departments.

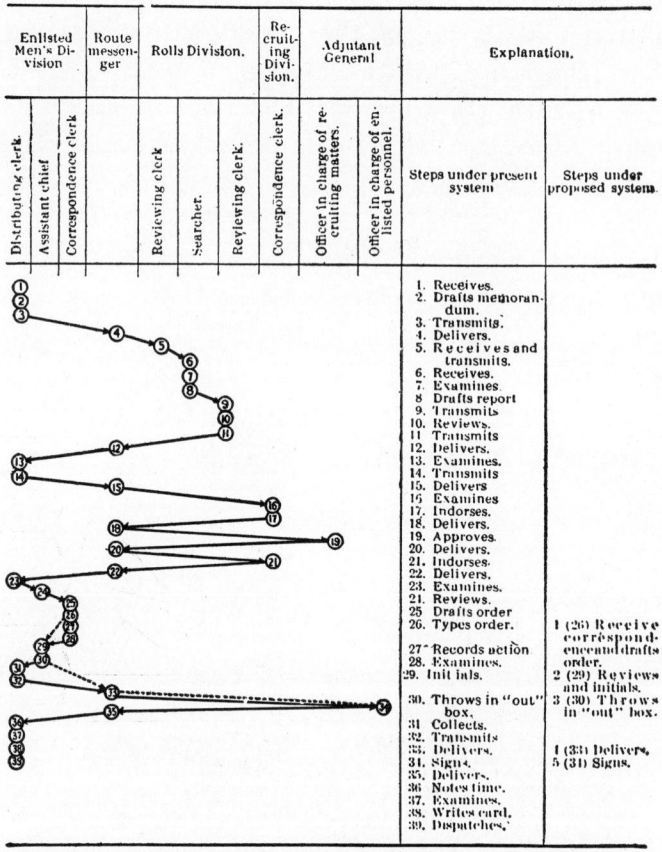

Fig. 35. Routing of a Letter Through the Adjutant General's Office Requesting the Discharge from the Army of an Enlisted Man in Recruiting Service, Contrasted with the Routing Proposed by President Taft's Commission on Economy and Efficiency

By referring to the horizontal scale and to the vertical scale the steps can be studied either by departments or by operations

In Fig. 35 is given a convenient method to show the routing of papers through a large office, together with the operations through which these papers must pass. Across the top of the chart is a scale of departments. The circles drawn immediately below the space for any department on the upper scale show that the papers receive some action in that particular department. At the right is a scale showing the nature of the work done in each of the departments. The chart is drawn on the basis of the intersection of vertical lines downward from the names of departments and horizontal lines through the names of the operations given at the right. Arrows joining the various circles then give the routing of the papers through the whole of the journey. The comparison of the existing routine with the proposed routine can be seen by considering the solid lines and the dotted lines and by comparing the two distinct columns or lists at the right. Thirty-nine operations may be counted in the present arrangement against five operations in the proposed arrangement. Though the drafting and the detail arrangement of this chart could be improved, the general scheme is nevertheless worthy of attention.

Chapter III

SIMPLE COMPARISONS INVOLVING TIME

THOUGH in making comparisons, the horizontal bar divided into blocks is superior to the circle divided into sectors, the circle and sector arrangement is not inaccurate when only the component parts of any unit are to be shown. In the case of Fig. 36, however, the comparison is between two circles, the divisions into component sectors being only an incidental feature. In this diagram, copied direct from the Statistical Atlas of the 1900 Census, it is practically impossible to tell how much larger the foreign-born population was in 1900 than it was in 1850, for it is necessary to compare the two circles on an area basis. To the average person this is an almost impossible task, because it is not feasible to fit one circle inside of the other visually as two horizontal bars may be fitted. If the circle for 1900 were estimated as twice the diameter of the circle for 1850, it would mean that the foreign-born population in 1900 was four times as great as that in 1850. If, however, the ratio were something less simple than this, interpretation of the chart would be difficult even by the processes of mental arithmetic. If the ratio between the diameters were,

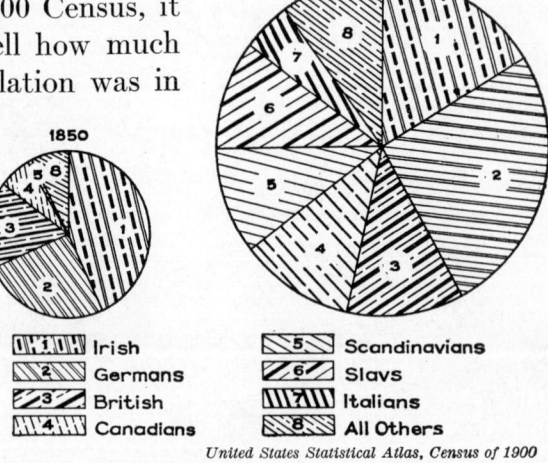

Fig. 36. Foreign-born Population of the United States in 1850 Compared with that in 1900, also the Proportion of the Different Nationalities in the Two Years Compared

The method of presentation by means of a circle with sectors is not inaccurate when only component parts are to be shown. Here, however, we have two different circles compared on the basis of total area. The reader cannot compare the areas visually so as to get the correct ratio measure of the increase in total number of foreign-born population. Horizontal bars are much preferable to circles when comparisons are to be made

for example, one and a half, the average reader would be completely nonplussed, as he would not trouble to go through the mental arithmetic of multiplying one and a half by one and a half. In general, the comparison of two circles of different size should be strictly avoided.

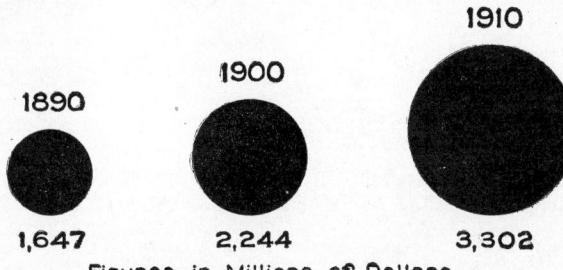

Many excellent works on statistics approve the comparison of circles of different size, and state that the circles should always be drawn to represent the facts on an area basis rather than on a diameter basis. The rule, however, is not always followed and the reader has no way of telling whether the circles compared have been drawn on a diameter basis or on an area basis, unless the actual figures for the data are given so that the dimensions may be verified.

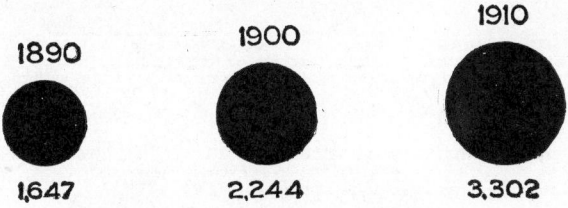

Fig. 37. Total Yearly Value for the United States of Combined Imports and Exports by Land and by Sea

In this illustration the data have been represented by circles drawn on a diameter basis. The right-hand circle appears more prominent than the data would justify. Circles compared on a diameter basis mislead the reader by causing him to over-estimate the ratios. Compare Fig. 38

In Fig. 37 the figures are given, and the circles have been drawn on a diameter basis. It will be noted that the figures for 1910 are roughly twice those for 1890. The circle, however, has roughly four times the area of the circle for 1890 and, accordingly, seems to have much more than twice the importance. In Fig. 38, the same data have been shown on an area basis as most of the authorities on statistical work recommend. If the figures were not given, the reader would be forced to fit the left-hand circle into the right-hand circle on an area basis, or else make a ratio between the diameters and then square the ratio. Either process is almost impossible to accomplish and there is

Fig. 38. Total Yearly Value for the United States of Combined Imports and Exports by Land and by Sea

Here the data of Fig. 37 have been shown by means of circles drawn on an area basis, as recommended by many authorities on statistical work. The right-hand circle, however, shows up less prominently than the figures would justify. Circles compared on an area basis mislead the reader by causing him to underestimate the ratios. Circles of different size should never be compared. Horizontal bars have all the advantages of circles with none of the disadvantages

38 GRAPHIC METHODS

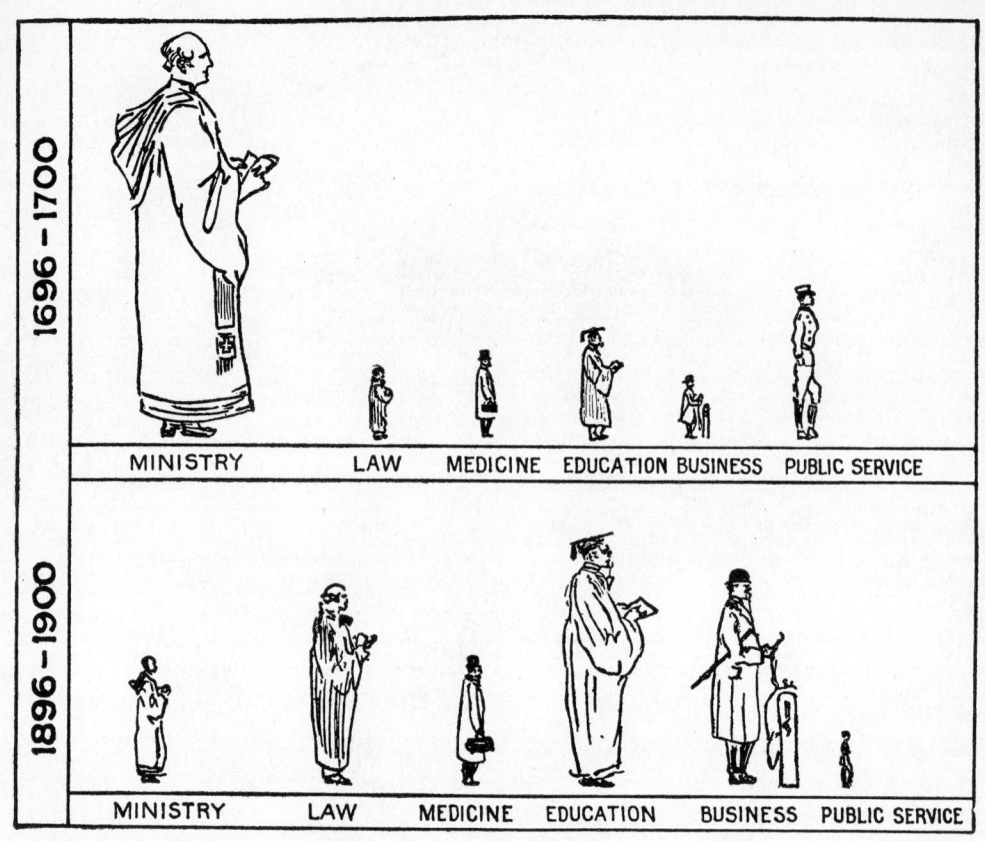

Fig. 39. Proportion of College Graduates in Different Professions in 1696-1700 and in 1896-1900

Charts of this kind with men represented in different sizes are usually so drawn that the data are represented by the height of the man. Such charts are misleading because the area of the pictured man increases more rapidly than his height. Considering the years 1696-1700, the pictured minister has about two and one-half times the height of the man representing public service. The minister looks over-important because he has an area of more than six times that of the man drawn to represent public service. This kind of graphic work has little real value

no necessity of inflicting such cruelty on a reader. Though the circles in Fig. 37, drawn on a diameter basis, exaggerate the ratios, the circles in Fig. 38, plotted on an area basis, make the reader underestimate the ratio. Comparison between circles of different size should be absolutely avoided. It is inexcusable when we have available simple methods of charting so good and so convenient from every point of view as the horizontal bar.

In Fig. 37 and in Fig. 38, it would have been better if the year had been given under each circle, with the figures for quantity placed above the circles, so as to follow the standard arrangement of having

COMPARISONS INVOLVING TIME 39

dates placed always at the base of the chart.

Another difficulty in the comparison of areas is shown in Fig. 39. No figures have been given and the helpless reader must compare by means of the pictures alone. By measurement, it will be seen that the minister in 1700 has over three times the height of the minister in 1900. Since the man in each case is shown in his natural proportions, the picture of the minister in 1700 has over nine times the area of the picture for 1900. Whether the ratio should be roughly three or roughly nine, we cannot tell.

Another example of the same kind of difficulty appears in Fig. 40, but here the figures are given and we can check up the author to see whether he has drawn the 1911 man on the basis of height or on the basis of area. The 1911 man, on account of his far greater area, looks to be rather more than two and a quarter times as important as the man of 1899. Though this type of graphic work is quite common, it should be avoided, for its visual inaccuracy is serious enough to cause distrust of the whole graphic method. In considering Fig. 40, the point

Fig. 40. Passengers Carried on the Railroads of the United States in 1899 and in 1911 Compared

This illustration has all the bad features mentioned for Fig. 39. Here the numerical data are given and we can prove for ourselves that the two pictured men are compared on the basis of height. Because of the disproportionate area, the right-hand picture gives the reader a false and exaggerated impression of growth. See Fig. 41

Fig. 41. Number of Passengers Carried on the Railroads of the United States in 1899 and in 1911 Compared

Here is a chart drawn from the same data as Fig. 40. It was not a larger passenger, but more passengers, that the railroads carried. The ratio expressing increase in business can be clearly and accurately seen from this method of portraying the facts

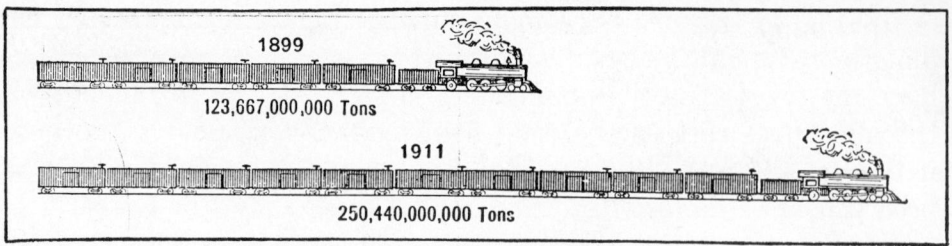

40   GRAPHIC METHODS

Fig. 42. Comparison of the Total Amount of Freight Service on the Railroads of the United States in 1899 and in 1911

It would have improved this illustration if the two locomotives had been shown one exactly above the other facing to the left. The additional cars representing the increase in 1911 would then be seen as though added to the rear of the train

to be brought out is not that the railroads carried a larger passenger in 1911, but that they carried more passengers.

If it is necessary to have a popular method, we can at least be accurate by portraying the data in the form of Fig. 41, not as in Fig. 40. Copy for an illustration of this sort is very simply made by taking proofs from a cut of one man and then pasting these proofs on a long strip of paper until a row of the correct length is obtained. The whole arrangement can then be photographed down to produce the effect shown in Fig. 41. To avoid fractional men at the end of a row, it is usually easy to express the ratio with a sufficient number of men in each row or bar to get numerical correctness. Note that in Fig. 41 the whole arrangement is similar to that of Fig. 24 or Fig. 27 in Chapter II, the actual data being given at the left of the row or bar. It would have been better if the men in Fig. 41 had been faced to the left instead of to the right. The additional men in the row for 1911 would then appear to have joined the rear of the line rather than to have come in at the front of the line.

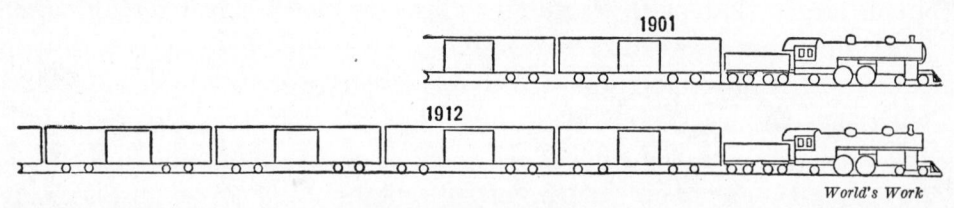

Fig. 43. Comparison in Size of Trainload on the Chicago, Burlington & Quincy Railroad in 1901 and in 1912

Here one locomotive is above the other but both face in the wrong direction. Figures for the data are not given and the reader cannot tell whether the two lengths compared should include the locomotives or only the cars. Clearness could have been assured if the cars had been shown for comparison in solid black, with the locomotives included for pictorial effect, but only in outline

COMPARISONS INVOLVING TIME 41

In Fig. 42 the idea is brought out that the railroads are now handling more freight. The drawing, however, should be reversed so as to have the two locomotives one above the other facing to the left, with the additional cars at the right-hand end. It would also be better if the dates for the two years and the figures representing tons had been placed at the extreme left in the manner shown in Fig. 41.

In Fig. 43, the two locomotives are placed neck and neck, but the whole chart reads backwards in that it reads to the left instead of to the right. Turn the page over and hold it up to the light. Through the back of the paper, the arrangement of the cars appears from left to right as it should.

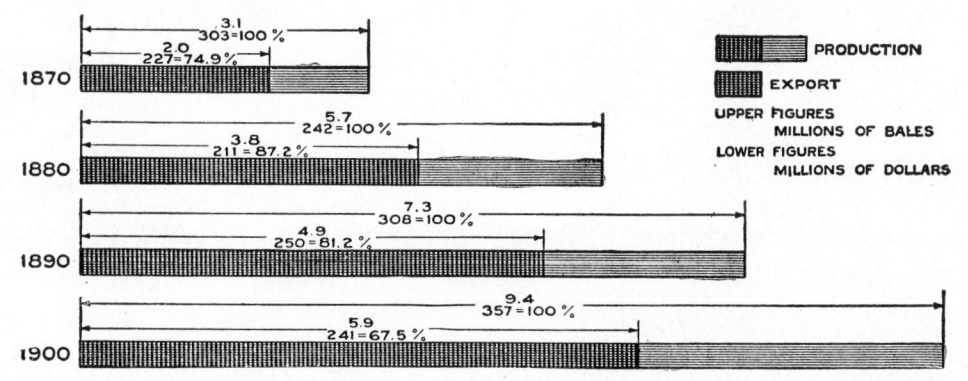

Fig. 44. Yearly Cotton Production and Export of the United States. The Figures with the Arrows Show the Number of Millions of Bales and also the Value in Millions of Dollars

If horizontal bars are used to represent years, the earliest year should be shown at the top as seen here

No data are given in Fig. 43, and it is impossible to tell whether the comparison between 1901 and 1912 should be based on the ratios of the whole length, including engines, or whether it should be based on the lengths for cars only. A ratio without the engines would be much larger than with engines. This chart is accordingly unreliable. The difficulty in regard to engines being included in the drawing could be entirely overcome if the freight cars were made in solid black, with the engines shown in outline only, so that the eye could judge the ratio between the solid black bars representing freight cars without including the outline drawings of the engines.

Often in charting information like that given in Fig. 44, vertical bars instead of horizontal bars are used. However, the figures given in Fig. 44 in conjunction with the bars make it desirable that the bars should here be horizontal in order that the figures may be read easily.

GRAPHIC METHODS

AVERAGE VALUE OF AMERICAN AUTO EXPORTS

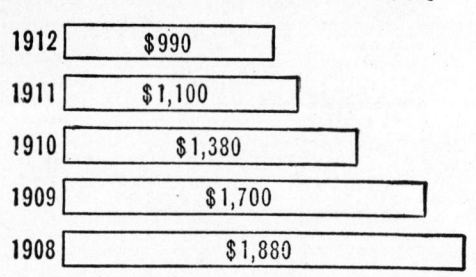

1912	$990
1911	$1,100
1910	$1,380
1909	$1,700
1908	$1,880

THE RISE OF THE LOW-PRICED CAR
SHOWING HOW THE AVERAGE VALUE OF EXPORTED AMERICAN AUTOMOBILES HAS DROPPED IN FIVE YEARS

World's Work

Fig. 45. The Illustration and the Titles are Shown Above Exactly as Originally Printed

The reader is misled if he does not notice that the earliest year has been shown at the bottom instead of at the top. The wording of the two titles, when taken in conjunction with the chart, really adds to the general confusion

The arrangement of dimension marks with an arrow-head at each end is a convenient scheme worthy of wide use. Note that the percentage figures in the illustration clearly refer to the value of the cotton rather than to the number of bales. The figures representing time, in this case years, read downward as they should do in every case in which horizontal bars are used to represent facts at different periods of time. If the horizontal bars are arranged with the earliest date at the top, any reader who wishes to do so may read the chart as a curve from the left-hand edge of the page and the dates will then appear in correct order from left to right.

In Fig. 45 the latest date has been placed at the top of the chart. This causes an impression absolutely the reverse of what it was intended to bring out by the drawing. Any one glancing at this chart is likely to suppose that the earlier year is indicated at the top and probably would not notice that the draftsman in this case, for some unjustifiable reason, has reversed the correct arrangement.

PASSENGER AND FREIGHT REVENUES
(Average for U. S.)

Date	Net Operating Revenue	PER MILE OF ROAD No. of Passengers Carried 1 Mile	No. of Tons Carried 1 Mile	Average Receipts per Passenger per Mile, Cents	Average Receipts per Ton per Mile, Cents	Average Journey per Passenger, Miles	Average Haul per Ton, Miles	Ratio of Operating Expenses to Operating Revenues, Per cent
1908*	$3 171	130 073	974 654	1.937	.754	32.86	143.83	69.75
1907	3 696	123 259	1 052 119	2.014	.759	31.72	131.71	67.53
1906	3 548	114 529	982 401	2.003	.748	31.54	132.33	66.08
1905	3 189	109 949	861 396	1.962	.766	32.21	130.60	66.78
1904	2 998	104 198	829 476	2.006	.780	30.64	133.23	67.79
1903	3 133	103 291	855 442	2.006	.763	30.10	132.80	66.16
1902	3 048	99 314	793 351	1.986	.757	30.30	131.04	64.66
1901	2 854	89 721	760 414	2.013	.750	28.58	135.03	64.86
1900	2 729	83 290	735 352	2.003	.729	27.80	130.87	64.65
1899	2 435	77 821	659 565	1.978	.724	27.89	131.04	65.24
1898	2 325	72 462	617 810	1.973	.753	26.70	132.09	65.58

Courtesy of "Data," Chicago

Fig. 46. Average Railroad Revenues from Passengers and from Freight in the United States

Here again the earliest year has been shown at the bottom instead of at the top. In tabulations of this sort there is less danger of erroneous reading if the earliest year is shown at the top. Years are usually grouped in fives, including in one group years ending from one to five inclusive, and in the next group years ending from six to ten inclusive

In Fig. 46 also, the latest year has been placed at the top of the column instead of at the bottom of the column. Though some precedent could probably be found for such an arrangement, the arrangement nevertheless seems

COMPARISONS INVOLVING TIME

an unfortunate one which should not be copied. Note that in Fig. 46 the figures have been arranged in groups of four with a blank space to assist the eye in reading across the page. In general, it is customary to have such figures not in groups of four but in groups of five, the groups including years ending in 1 to 5 inclusive and 6 to 10 inclusive.

A rapid reader seeing Fig. 47 is likely to get a much exaggerated idea of the increase in the American exports of automobiles. The arrangement of the three horizontal bars for the three years is such that the reader is justified in assuming that the years are consecutive. He is not likely to notice that the upper bar represents the year 1906 and that four years are omitted between 1906 and the consecutive years 1911 and 1912. Since there is nothing to indicate that years have been left out after 1906, the reader seeing the figure 1912 is apt to assume that the two earlier years are 1911 and 1910.

Fig. 48 is a redrawing of Fig. 47 with a change in scale to indicate to the reader that the earlier year shown for comparison must not be read as one of three consecutive years. Though the space left between the bars for 1906 and 1911 would not be sufficient for the four omitted years, if the whole chart were drawn to scale, the space is nevertheless large

VALUE, AMERICAN EXPORTS

1906	$4,409,136
1911	$21,636,661
1912	$28,300,139

VALUE, IMPORTS FROM ABROAD

1906	$4,910,208
1911	$2,446,248
1912	$2,000,000

A MARVEL OF EXPORT TRADE

SHOWING THE AMAZING INCREASE IN OUR EXPORTS OF MOTOR CARS, AND THE STEADY DECREASE IN OUR IMPORTS, IN THE LAST SEVEN YEARS

World's Work

Fig. 47. This Illustration was Originally Printed with Fig. 45 on the Same Page of a Magazine, yet in Fig. 45 the Earliest Year was Shown at the Bottom While Here the Earliest Year is Properly Shown at the Top

There is, however, danger, in this illustration, that the reader may assume that the three bars represent consecutive years without noticing the jump from 1906 to 1911. Compare Fig. 48

VALUE, AMERICAN EXPORTS

1906	$4,409,136
1911	21,636,661
1912	28,300,139

VALUE, IMPORTS FROM ABROAD

1906	$4,910,208
1911	2,446,248
1912	2,000,000

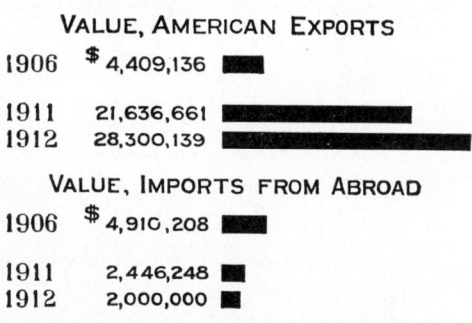

Fig. 48. The Contrast of American Exports and Imports of Automobiles

The data of Fig. 47 have here been redrawn. The values have been shown at the left of the bars, where they give the neatest and most convenient arrangement. Note that the bar for 1906 is somewhat separated from the bar for 1911, so as to indicate to the reader that the three bars do not represent consecutive years

enough to serve as a safeguard to the reader. A slight break could indicate in this manner a gap of any large number of years which it would not be feasible to denote by allowing space according to scale. In Fig. 48 the years and the figures for the chart are properly shown to the left much as they are shown in Fig. 24 and in Fig. 27.

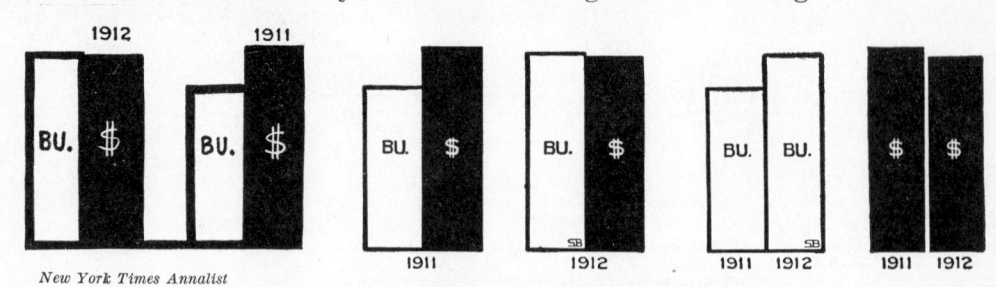

New York Times Annalist

Fig. 49. The Size and the Value of the Corn Crop of the United States in 1911 Compared with that of 1912

The object of the chart is to show that, though there were more bushels of corn in 1912, the producer received less total money than in 1911.
The left-hand illustration is incorrectly made as it shows the earlier year to the right. In the central illustration this error has been corrected and the years are named at the base instead of at the top. The arrangement still fails, however, to bring out the message clearly.
From the right-hand presentation it can be seen instantly that the number of bushels has increased while the total money received has actually decreased. The right-hand presentation is arranged in accordance with the working of the average person's mind and it gains in clearness accordingly

The left-hand group in Fig. 49 was used as an illustration in a business magazine. The purpose of the chart was to show that in 1912 the farmers of the country raised more bushels of corn than in 1911 but received less total money in return. Note that the earlier year is placed at the right instead of at the left, and that the dates are given at the top rather than at the bottom. The middle group of bars corrects the error, but the information is still not as clearly brought out as it should be. The best way to bring out this information is to show that the number of bushels has increased while the number of dollars has decreased, and this is not clear from the middle drawing. In the right-hand presentation it is clearly seen that the bushels went up though the total value came down. The right-hand drawing follows the working of the average person's mind and it gains in clearness accordingly.

As a general rule dates should always be arranged to read from left to right, and columns of figures should be arranged with the column for the earlier date at the left. A common exception is made, however, in the case of financial reports when it is desired to show the most recent year next to the various type-headings relating to earnings, expenses, etc., as in Fig. 50. In the case of financial reports it is always the latest year which is of chief interest, and for this reason the arrangement of Fig. 50 seems permissible in order that the figures and the account names may be side by side. The problem in Fig. 49 is so entirely different from that in Fig. 50, that the method of Fig. 50 cannot be held as a precedent to justify the reversed arrangement of dates shown at the left of Fig. 49. The fact that one needs an umbrella on a rainy day is not sufficient reason for carrying an umbrella at all times.

* * *

UNION BAG AND PAPER COMPANY—Reports for the year ended Jan. 31:

	1913.	1912.	1911.	1910.
Net earnings	$554,251	$1,017,835	$1,038,112	$1,055,400
Depr. and ext. fd.	122,585	122,265	120,987	149,925
Balance	431,666	895,570	917,125	905,475
Skg. fd. & bd. red.	134,925	114,095	110,745	107,605
Balance	296,741	781,475	806,380	797,870
Interest	253,748	202,480	197,135	204,611
Balance for divs..	42,993	578,995	609,245	593,259
Preferred dividend	330,000	440,000	440,000	440,000
Deficit	287,007	*138,995	*169,245	*153,259
Prev. surp.	1,921,788	2,020,471	1,851,226	1,697,968
Bond disc. & exp.	70,945	237,677	......	......
Profit and loss sur.	1,563,836	1,921,788	2,020,471	1,851,226

* * *

New York Times Annalist

Fig. 50. Brief Financial Statement Regarding the Union Bag and Paper Company

In condensed statements of this sort there seems to be good reason for placing next to the headings at the left the column of figures for the latest fiscal year, since this information is of most vital interest to the reader. Columns for other years are then printed to the right for comparative purposes. The earliest year is shown at the extreme right

Though this reversed arrangement of years seems permissible for the purpose of printed reports as here used, there is no justification for the use of the reversed arrangement in chart work. As a general rule material given by years should be shown with the earliest year at the left

Fig. 51 is an illustration photographed down from a large drawing used in a wall exhibit. It is a fair example showing what can be done to arouse interest by the judicious embellishment of charts, especially of those for wall exhibits intended to reach a miscellaneous audience having an average of rather limited education. Note the smokestacks in Fig. 51. The smoke-stack at the left is the same height as the bar for the year 1906–07, and the taller smoke-stack at the right the same height as the bar for 1912–13. As this drawing was made for a wall exhibit to show the co-operation of manufacturing companies with the college, the pictorial embellishment seems quite justifiable and useful to attract attention to this particular exhibit. A pictorial effect also relieves monotony in a large exhibition which may have hundreds or even thousands of different charts and other wall exhibits.

Fig. 52 was shown in conjunction with Fig. 51 with the idea of pointing out that the number of students in the University of Cincinnati had increased just as (according to Fig. 51) the number of firms co-operating in the engineering work of the University had increased in the same time.

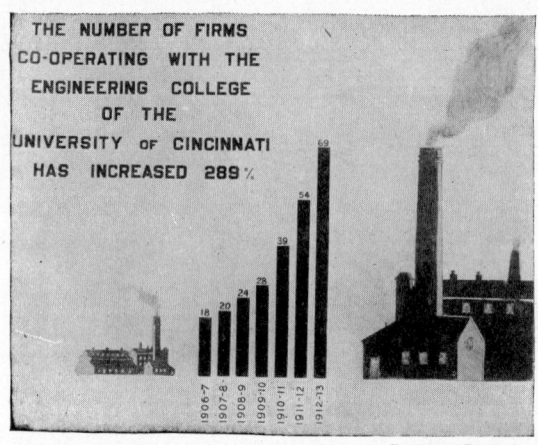

The bars in Fig. 51 and Fig. 52 are placed vertically, each bar representing a year. This vertical arrangement of bars permits reading the chart as if a curve had been made by drawing a line through the tops of all the bars. Curves are the common language of engineers and statisticians. In order that the bars may be read as curves, it is desirable to have the bars placed in a vertical position, if they represent divisions of time, rather than entirely distinct subjects such as the separate cities compared as to the value of their output of manufactured products, in the chart reproduced in Fig. 21.

American Review of Reviews

Fig. 51. The Increasing Number of Business Firms Co-operating with the Engineering College of the University of Cincinnati

When the bars represent years or other divisions of time, a vertical arrangement of the bars is usually more desirable than the horizontal arrangement seen in Fig. 44. With the vertical arrangement a line may be imagined joining the tops of the bars so as to give a "curve".

Note, in this illustration of a wall chart, the popular touch given by the pictures of manufacturing plants with smoke-stacks of the same height as the first and the last vertical bars

Lettering like that shown in Fig. 51 or Fig. 52 is conveniently made by using the gummed black-paper letters and figures which can be obtained in many good stationery stores. A thin pencil line as a guide at the bottom of the letters, and some judgment used in spacing, will assist greatly in getting a neat result from the gummed letters. Large bars like those shown in Fig. 51 and Fig. 52 can be made by cutting out strips of black paper and pasting them onto white cardboard. Such work, however, must be very carefully done or the bars will curl on the edges and give an unpleasant effect. It is generally better to use India ink in making the bars if a good result is to be assured. The liquid drawing ink sold at most stationery stores is available in many different colors. Some grades of the drawing ink are water-proof after drying. On elaborate charts the water-proof quality should always be used to make certain that a few rain drops, or handling with moist hands, will not ruin the finished work.

In the discussion of Fig. 51 and Fig. 52 it was mentioned that a line could be drawn through the tops of the vertical bars to give a curve. If the curve were actually drawn, the bars themselves would be omitted. In Fig. 53, instead of using bars, we have lines which may be considered as curves for each of the several items compared. In this case it would be impossible to use bars for each of the items shown because the bars would cover each other. The bars are entirely omitted and lines are simply drawn from the 100 per cent point in 1897 to the various points for different items in 1907. It is certain that the prices (that of pine lumber, for instance, shown by the upper curve) did not have the uniform rate of increase which the straight line from 1897 to 1907 would indicate. We are considering here, however, the changes over the period as a whole, and we can for simplicity draw a straight line and neglect all the fluctuations of intervening years. The general scheme of Fig. 53 is convenient, as the neglect of detail brings the main information out clearly. Fig. 53 has, unfortunately, been drawn in a misleading manner in that the reader is likely to interpret the curves as if zero were shown at the bottom of the chart. The general rule in charts of this kind is that zero should be shown as the bottom line, or, if not shown at the bottom, that the omission of zero should be clearly indicated. As Fig. 53 is shown on a percentage basis, the 100 per cent line should be clearly indicated by drawing a broad line on the chart for the line opposite the figure 100 in the scale. It would have been better, perhaps, to have plotted the data so that zero would replace the figure 100. On a scale so made, pine lumber would go up 83 per cent, while railroad rates would be shown

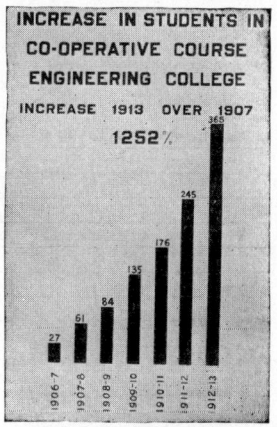

Fig. 52. The Increasing Number of Students in the Co-operative Course of the Engineering College of the University of Cincinnati

This illustration was originally used as a companion piece to the chart of Fig. 51. For a popular exhibit the use of vertical bars brings out information quite clearly. Though curves (such as are shown in later chapters) are superior to vertical bars, it is unfortunately true that most people do not know how to read even the simplest curves correctly.

Note the lettering at the upper portion of the chart. Lettering of this kind may be had by using separate gummed letters such as may be purchased ready for use

48   GRAPHIC METHODS

as decreasing 4 per cent. The scale would read upward from the zero line for increases, and downward from the zero line for decreases. By changing the scale and using a broad zero line, misinterpretation of the chart would be entirely prevented.

Fig. 54 is somewhat similar to Fig. 53 in that intervening years are neglected, and that lines drawn from left to right of the chart indicate the total movement rather than short-time fluctuations. Fig. 54 would be better if the lines around the outside of the drawing had been omitted. In general, lines of this kind around the outside of a chart are likely to be confusing. In this case, the double lines at the bottom of the chart draw too much attention to the bottom and may cause a wrong interpretation of the chart. As charts of this type are usually made so as to have the bottom at zero, the reader of Fig. 54 may get an entirely erroneous idea of the actual increase in the rates of wages. This chart of Fig. 54 should have been drawn with 7/8 inch more room at the bottom so that the scale would begin at zero rather than at $1.00. A glance at the chart as it is shown here might convey to any but a careful reader that the wages of trackmen had more than doubled, within the period of ten years covered by the records thus graphically presented, though the actual wage increase was only from about $1.12 to $1.50. Though Fig. 54 contains a good suggestion for presenting data in popular form, it is in itself misleading because it does not have its base line at zero.

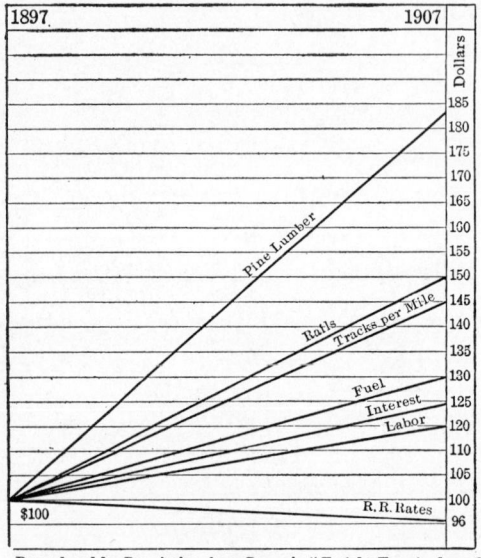

Reproduced by Permission from Droege's "Freight Terminals and Trains", copyright, 1912, by the McGraw-Hill Book Company

Fig. 53. Changes after Ten Years in Costs of Railroad Materials and in Freight Rates for a Large Railroad System

A simple chart of this kind is often advantageous, as it neglects all temporary fluctuations and shows only the important changes over a period of time considered as a whole. The line for 100 on the scale should have been made a broad line to indicate the basis of comparison. A wavy line should have been put at the bottom of the chart to show that the scale does not begin at zero

Fig. 55 is a commendable piece of work for popular presentation, as for instance in a magazine. Note the use of dimension marks in two independent horizontal rows so that the upper row indicates the material from which the ships are made while the lower row shows the method of propulsion. Dimension lines used in this way are an extremely valuable adjunct to chart work and should be used much more commonly than they are at present.

Tendencies for the future are frequently very accurately predicted by drawing a smooth curve through known points and then continuing this curve for future years in the manner shown by the broad line in Fig. 55. The trend of this curve indicates that by 1925, we are likely to have ships about 1,200 feet long. Though the method of prediction by extending a curve into the future is very valuable, care must always be used to apply the method with judgment. If in Fig. 55 a curve had been drawn from the data up to the year 1860 and extended from that point to show the probable length of vessels in succeeding years, the curve would have indicated a likelihood of 1,200-foot ships by 1870. We can see in the light of history that such a prediction would have been most erroneous. It would have assumed the continuance of side-wheel steamers and would have been based chiefly on the length of the Great Eastern alone. The Great Eastern was too far in advance of the age and was in reality an engineering failure. Hence, we see the error which would result from basing a prediction curve on too limited an amount of data.

Periodic photographs of any kind of construction work are one of the most striking forms of graphic presentation. Many large contractors and machine manufacturers now make a practice of having photographs taken of each job at least once each week. The

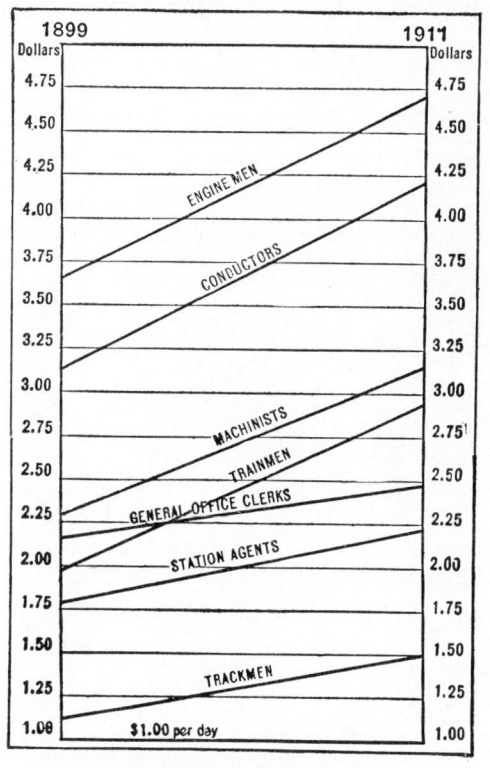

THE RISING WAGE SCALE

SHOWING THAT THE PAY OF RAILROAD EMPLOYEES HAS INCREASED FROM 30 TO 50 PER CENT. IN TWELVE YEARS. NOTE THAT THE GENERAL OFFICE CLERKS NOW RECEIVE LESS THAN THE TRAINMEN.

World's Work

Fig. 54. Wage-Scale Increase

This illustration is so drawn that wages appear to have increased much more rapidly than is proved by the actual data given in the chart itself. The chart should have been extended to show the zero line of the vertical scale so as to assist the reader in getting a correct interpretation

photographs are carefully dated and filed for reference in case there should be any dispute later regarding the progress of the work and payment therefor. If a large card giving the date of the work is placed in front of the camera so that the date is photographed directly into the picture, the date is somewhat more easily proved than it would be otherwise. Putting the date card in front of the camera with the date upon the card gives a chance for any passer-by to check the honesty of the date on the picture, much as the "amount purchased" card at the front of a cash register checks the honesty of the clerk.

Progress photographs like those described above are particularly effective for use in advertising. A series of three or four pictures placed one below another, with the dates carefully stated on each, give the best possible demonstration of the rapidity with which construction work has been completed by the advertiser. A broad use for these progress photographs is found in the preparation of reports, catalogues, magazine advertising, etc. Thus a manufacturing plant, for instance, can be pictured in a series of photographs taken some years apart showing buildings which have been added to provide for increase in the business. In the case of machinery, a series of photographs taken in different years are of value to show the increase in the size of the machines built or the successive improvements made in the design.

Moving-picture machines have opened up a whole field of possibilities in the rapid conveying of accurate information. Many companies are now using moving-picture films to show the technical operations involved in making up their manufactured product, or to show views in different parts of a factory. Moving-picture cameras have been used also in a very striking way by Mr. Frank B. Gilbreth as an adjunct to methods of time and motion study. By placing in the camera field with the worker a clock with a large dial and a sweeping second hand, an automatic and permanent record may be secured both of the worker's movements and the corresponding elapsed time. The statistics thus graphically recorded are immeasurably more accurate and more conclusive than any that could be secured in any other way. Possibilities for the use of moving-picture machines in educational work in schools are only beginning to be grasped by a few of the world leaders in thought. When the moving-picture machine becomes a feature of every school room the results will be astounding.

COMPARISONS INVOLVING TIME 51

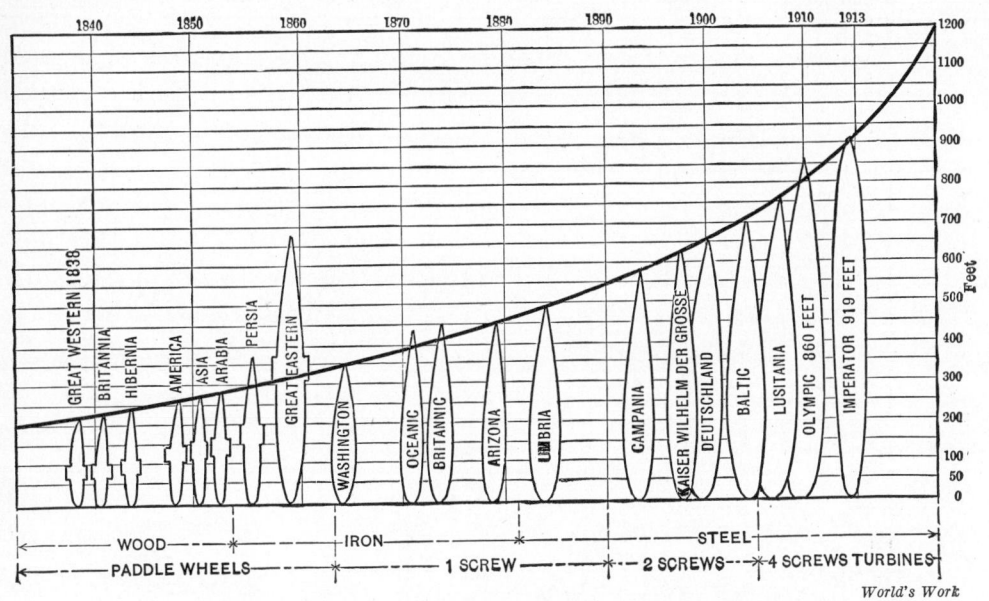

Fig. 55. The Growth in the Length of Ocean Liners

This is an excellent piece of presentation for reaching an average non-technical class of readers. A smooth curve line has been drawn through the ends of the pictured ships so as to approximate most closely the general law which seems to govern progress in ship building. The smooth curve has been extended into the future as a prediction of the length of the ships which will probably be built during the next ten years. Note the excellent use of dimension-line arrows at the base of the chart showing the materials used in ship building and the methods of driving ships at different periods in history

Bars to represent different intervals of time as in Fig. 51 and Fig. 52 may be compared to the progress photographs mentioned above. Though the bars and progress photographs are valuable, they may be said to give information only in spots. A moving-picture machine shows pictures so rapidly that the pictures blend into a continuous narrative in the eye and the brain of the observer. What the moving picture is to separate progress photographs, the curve is to detached bars representing time. In just so much as the moving picture is superior to separate pictures shown by lantern slides, in just that much is a curve superior to a series of horizontal or vertical bars for the same data. Unless a person knows thoroughly how to read and how to plot curves he cannot hope to understand the graphic presentation of facts. The use of curves will be covered in later chapters.

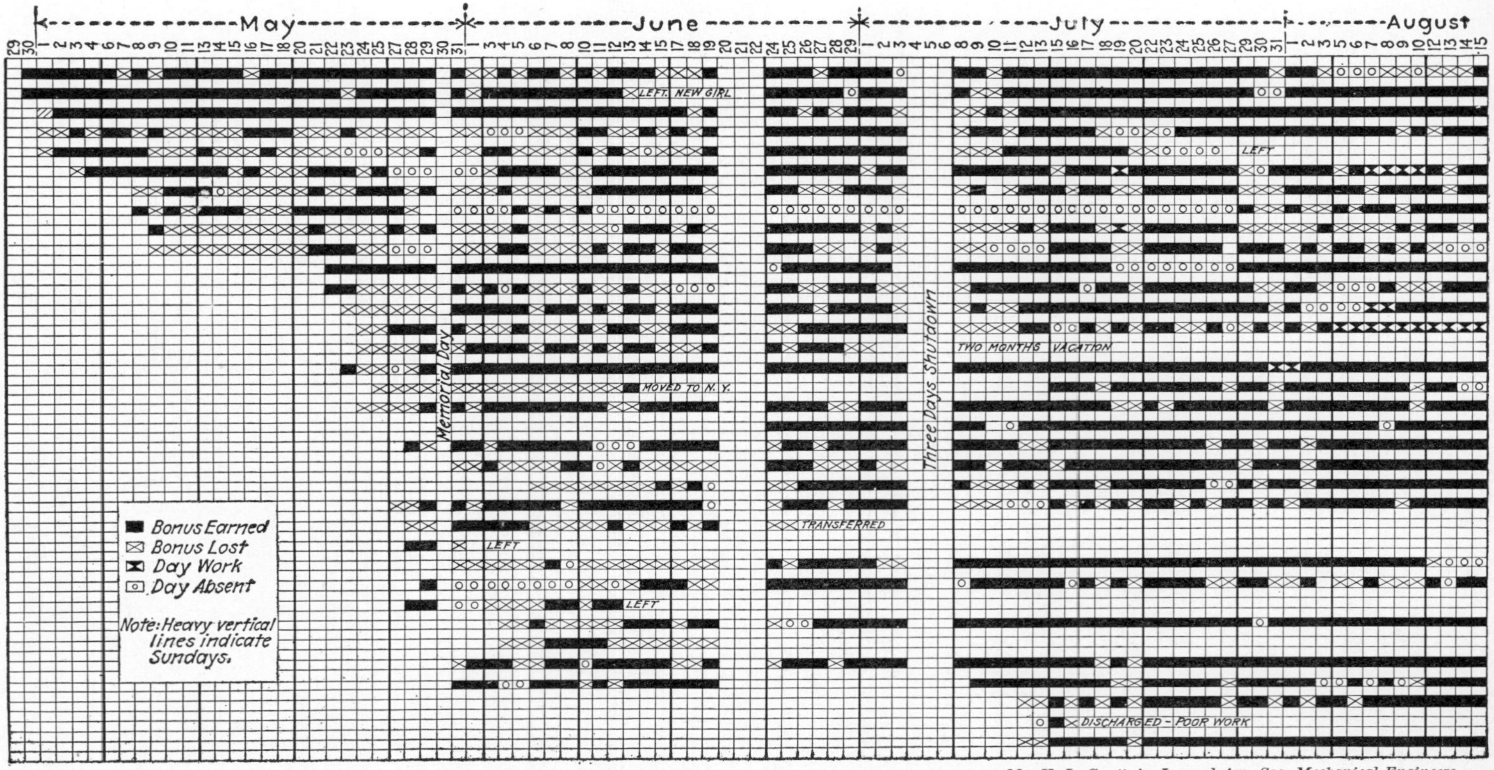

Fig. 56. Record of Work in One Room of a Worsted Mill. See page 54
Each line represents one worker and gives all the important information regarding that operative's work

Mr. H. L. Gantt, in Journal Am. Soc. Mechanical Engineers

Chapter IV

TIME CHARTS

THE horizontal-bar method used in Chapter I to show the component parts of any unit may be modified so as to represent various conditions at different hours, days, and other subdivisions of time. Fig. 57 illustrates a convenient scheme to assist the arrangement of vacations for concerns having many employees, in which it is necessary to plan the vacations so that there shall always

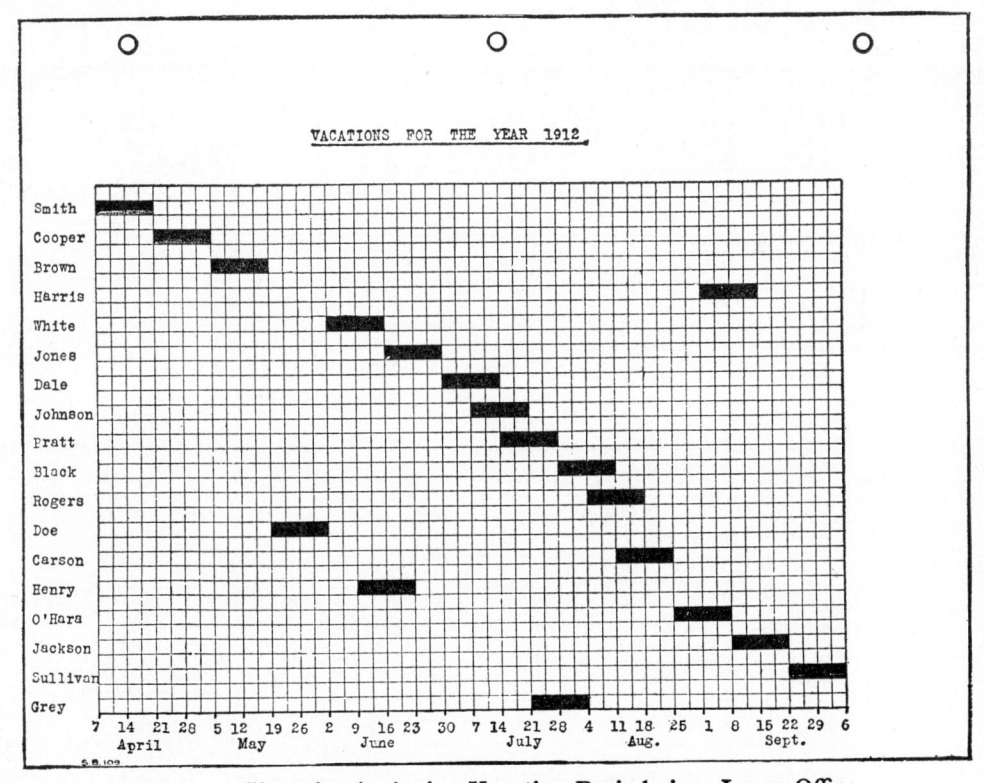

Fig. 57. Chart for Assigning Vacation Periods in a Large Office

Vacations have here been planned so that not more than two men are away at any one time

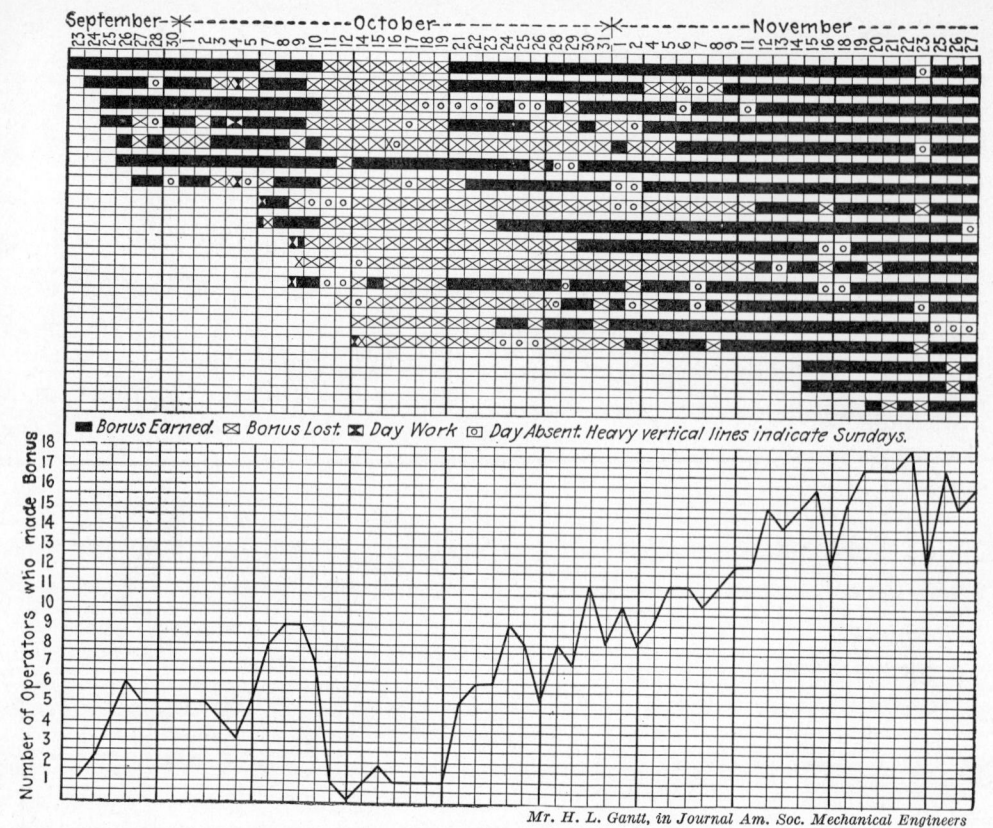

Fig. 58. Chart Illustrating Bonus Work in a Factory where Bonus Work was Introduced Too Rapidly at First

The curve at the bottom shows the total number of workers earning a bonus each day. On November 22 all the workers earned a bonus

be a good man available to take charge of responsible work. A chart of this kind can be made quickly if co-ordinate paper is used, the horizontal lines being drawn in with lead pencil. Vacations are shifted around until an arrangement is found that is satisfactory to the manager and also to the various employees. After a final schedule has been decided upon, the time given each employee can be made sufficiently conspicuous by going over the lead-pencil marks with crayon or ink. A chart of this nature posted on the bulletin board of an office would serve as a convenient means of giving information to the employees as to their respective vacation periods.

Fig. 56 (page 52) illustrates a method regularly used by Mr. H. L. Gantt to indicate conditions in a manufacturing plant. This particular chart was drawn to show progress made in training the employees of a worsted mill under scientific management. Trained employees may earn a bonus by completing a certain quantity of work each day. It will be seen at a glance that the chart becomes blacker at the right hand, thus showing that two-months training had greatly increased the output of the employees. If a chart like this is made with different colored pencils, the facts can be grasped more quickly than when only one color is used.

Fig. 58, at the right-hand end, shows that the workers were earning a bonus practically every day, and it also shows clearly that something was wrong during the middle part of October. The workers failed to earn a bonus at that time for the reason that the bonus work was introduced so rapidly that they did not get adequate instruction. The manager of a plant would realize such a situation at once if he had this kind of a chart before him.

At the bottom of Fig. 58 a curve is plotted to give the number of operators who earned a bonus every day. The horizontal scale for this curve is exactly the same as for the bar chart above, except that in the curve a day is represented by a line rather than by a space. In plotting curves, it is customary to represent time by lines rather than by spaces, and this curve is plotted in accordance with good practice. The scale at the left-hand edge of the lower part of the chart represents the number of workers who made the bonus. In order to plot the curve, one simply counts in the upper section of the chart the number of black blocks which are filled in for the particular day. Thus, for October 10, we see that there are seven black blocks. The point on the curve is then placed in the lower portion of the chart at the intersection of the horizontal line representing the number of workers earning a bonus and of the vertical line representing the day, October 10. The curve gives a convenient method of determining the total number of operators who are earning a bonus. When it is desired to know only the number of employees earning bonus each day, the curve shows the matter more clearly than do the black blocks in the upper portion of the chart. The horizontal bars give the story for each worker, the curve gives the total for all the workers.

A chart like that shown in Fig. 59 would ordinarily be made on a long sheet of co-ordinate paper so that the co-ordinate ruling could be used for the vertical lines, indicating time. Co-ordinate paper in several different rulings can be purchased in rolls so that the desired ruling can often be had in continuous lengths. Sometimes, however, the desired ruling can be obtained only in flat sheets of limited size

56 GRAPHIC METHODS

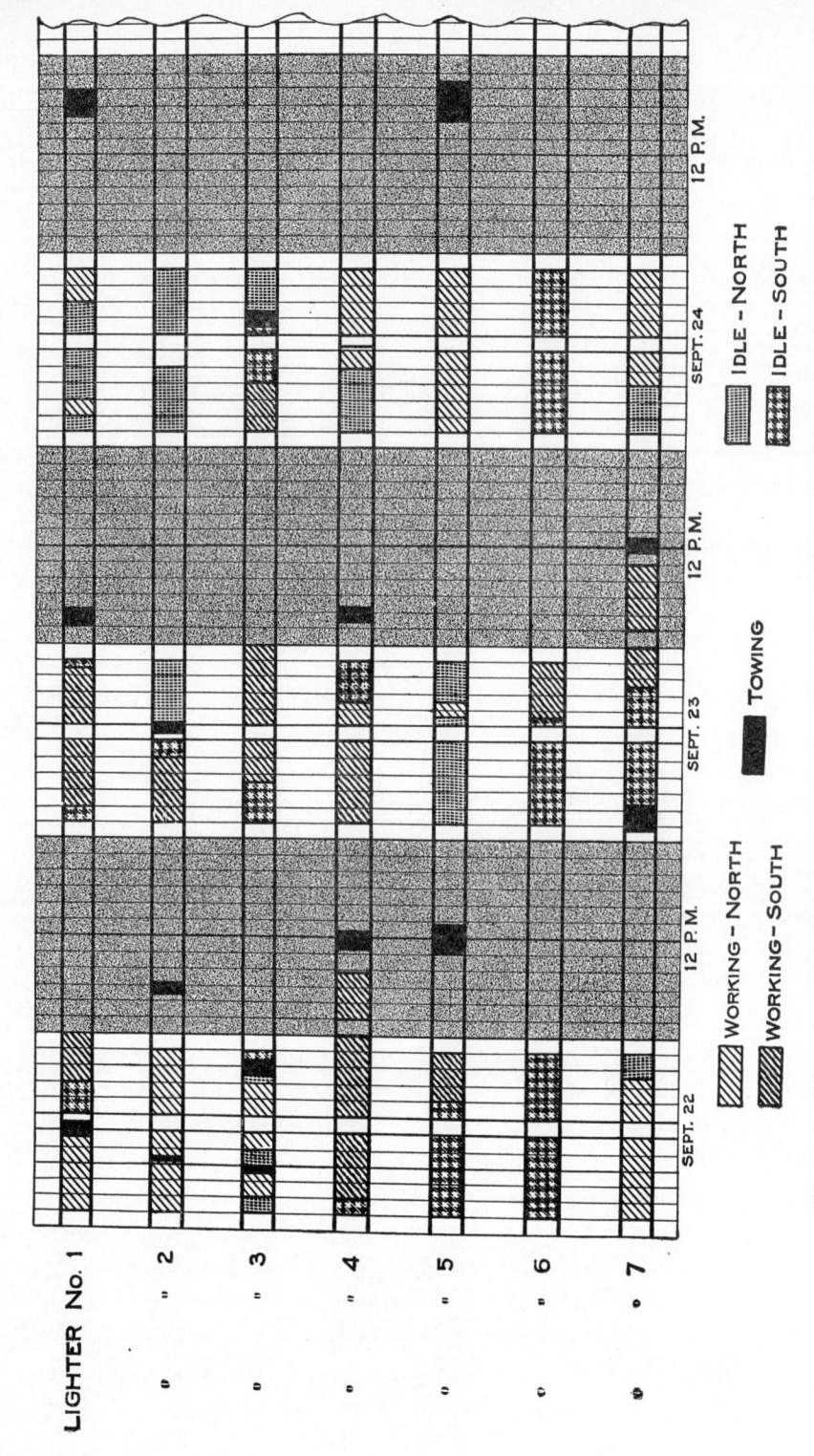

Fig. 59. Chart Showing the Operation of Some Freight Lighters in New York Harbor

Each horizontal bar represents one lighter. Night hours from six to six are shown by the gray vertical areas. Colored crayons used on the original chart made the information stand out much more plainly than possible here with black ink only

and it is then necessary to make a long sheet by pasting together several of the separate sheets. The original study from which Fig. 59 was prepared was made upon a built-up sheet seventeen inches wide and eight feet long, so that a full month of lighter operation could be shown on the one chart.

In a large working chart, such as is shown in Fig. 59, very little ruling is required except for the lines limiting the width of the horizontal bar representing each lighter. In the original chart, drawing inks of different colors were used to indicate the four different conditions—working north and working south, and idle north and idle south. Black was used to indicate towing. Solid red showed idle time in the north, and a red made up of red-ink strokes with white spaces showed idle time in the south. Thus all idle time may be indicated by red, the method of application determining whether the delay is at the north or at the south end of the trip. Working time may similarly be indicated by solid green and by green strokes with white spaces.

It is desirable in all chart work to have certain conventions by which colors would be understood to have certain definite meanings. Thus, following railroad practice, red could generally be used in chart work to indicate dangerous or unfavorable conditions, and green to indicate commended features or favorable conditions. Where neither commendation nor adverse criticism is intended, colors such as blue, yellow, brown, etc., could be used.

In Fig. 59, an ordinary atomizer filled with writing ink was used to fill in gray areas representing night hours. If a little care is used in regulating the spray, a good uniform and light shade of gray is obtained, on top of which colored crayons will show out clearly, as, for instance, in Fig. 59 where Lighter No. 7 is represented as working on the night of September 23. To prevent the ink spreading over the chart, a strip of cardboard should be laid carefully on each edge of the surface which it is desired to ink in by means of the spray.

In making up charts like that shown in Fig. 59, the data are usually recorded on the chart day by day as reports come in. This involves a large amount of handling of the chart, and the chart is likely to be much smeared by the time the last reports are entered. If colored crayons with the color embodied in paraffin are used, very brilliant colors can be obtained, yet rubbing with the hands will not smear the colored areas. Unless a non-smearing crayon is used, it is better

58 GRAPHIC METHODS

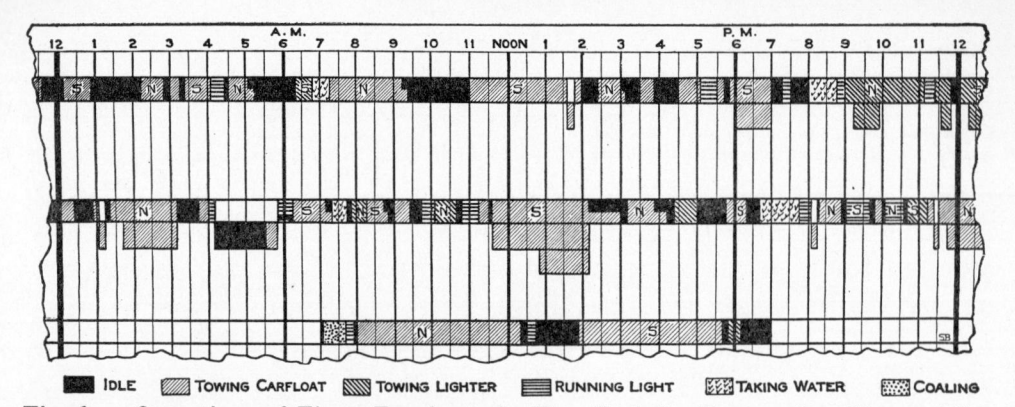

Fig. 60. Operations of Three Tug-boats in New York for Twenty-four Hours. The Boat Represented by the Lower Bar is in Service for a Twelve-Hour Shift Only

A working chart of this kind would usually be made on a long strip of co-ordinate paper. The illustration was drawn entirely by hand to show the possibilities of hand cross-hatching for bringing out information ordinarily shown in several colors

to make up colored charts by using different colors of drawing ink. The ordinary crayons smear so badly that a chart made with them is sometimes unrecognizable before it is finished.

Fig. 60 is a further elaboration of the method used in Fig. 59. The actual chart from which this illustration was made was drawn on co-ordinate paper ruled in tenths of an inch. Each of these tenth-of-an-inch spaces was made to represent ten-minutes time, so that a much larger scale was obtained than in Fig. 60. As the tug-boat captains regularly kept log-books in which their work was recorded to a five-minute interval the chart was made to the same interval by splitting the ten-minute squares to represent five-minute intervals. With a scale of this size it was feasible to use colored crayons, even though some of the divisions of time were very short.

Fig. 60 was drawn by hand and shows the possibilities in preparing an illustration of this kind when only one color of printing ink is available.

The chart from which Fig. 60 is taken was made to determine how much idle time there was in the operation of three tug-boats, and to ascertain whether the boats could be so run as to reduce the amount of idle time and give better service. The black in Fig. 60 shows the idle time vividly. By looking from bar to bar, it is possible to study all the work of the three tug-boats and to determine whether, if the work were differently assigned, there would be less waiting between jobs. Frequently the tug-boats had to tow two or more lighters or two or more car-floats, simultaneously, as will be seen from the extra bars placed below the main bar for each tug. The number of lighters and car-floats towed simultaneously is clearly shown in the chart, as well as the time at which each was picked up, and the time at which each was delivered by the tug. In the case of car-floats, a frequent break will be noticed at the end of the towing, one-half the width of the horizontal bar being marked with black. This convention was adopted to show that the idle time was occasioned by the necessity of waiting to obtain an unoccupied float bridge into which the car-float could be shifted. Though the tug-boat was standing idle it was not feasible for the dispatcher to take the tug away from the particular car-float to which it was attached, for the tug would be necessary to place the car-float in the float bridge as soon as the float bridge became free.

Charting of information frequently brings out points which would be entirely overlooked if charts were not made. The tug-boat chart from which Fig. 60 was taken at once calls attention to the time required for the tugs to obtain water. As the service of tugs was valued at about $9.00 per hour, the time spent in taking water was a serious loss. As soon as the chart showed the extent of this loss, it was comparatively simple to remedy the situation by providing different methods of getting boiler-feed water.

A time chart like Fig. 60 can often be used advantageously in conjunction with other time charts covering the same period of time. Thus, in studying tug-boats, the information on a chart for lighter operation such as is shown in Fig. 59, and on charts for the operation of car-floats or of float bridges, may be valuable. All the various kinds of equipment with which the tug-boats may be employed could be considered in the study, if it is to be determined whether or not the most effective use is being made of the tug-boats. If all the charts used in the study are drawn to the same horizontal scale, the charts can be placed immediately above each other so that the operations of all related equipment for every hour of the day and night can be instantly seen during the whole of a test period, of, say, a week or a month.

The charts thus far considered in this chapter have shown time in the horizontal direction only. In Fig. 61 we have time shown by days in the horizontal direction and by hours in the vertical direction. This type of chart is extremely valuable in determining whether or not schedules are maintained uniformly over any period of time.

By using different colors of ink a chart of this kind can be made so as to show all related operations without the drawing becoming too complex to read. Fig. 61 has purposely been made simpler than the ordinary chart of this kind to overcome the handicap of being limited to only one color of ink in the reproduction.

Charts in the form of Fig. 61 are valuable in that they show on one sheet all the operations occurring during a given period of time— in this case, twenty-four hours. Some conditions, such as the blizzard of January 7, affect all the deliveries to the different railroads. Study of the chart brings out in contrast conditions which are beyond the control of man and conditions which are the result of carelessness or poor management, which usually crop up first in connection with one railroad, then in connection with another, without being so general as to affect all of the curves, as did the blizzard of January 7.

Fig. 62 shows the possibility of simplification when so many different horizontal curves must be shown that easy reading is impossible. The simplification is made in Fig. 62 by showing only one railroad on each sheet. All the figures for one railroad are shown in curves, placed one above the other. Ordinarily curves like those in Fig. 62 will be nearly parallel, for the time interval required to complete each of the steps of work remains about the same day after day. What Fig. 62 brings out most of all is not so much the time interval between the different steps as the information as to whether each of the different steps was started promptly on schedule. Any one operation started late must delay all the following operations.

The paper on which Fig. 62 was drawn is in itself worthy of attention. This letter-sheet size of paper was carefully laid out so that a typewriter could be used for the lettering on the margins of the four sides of the sheet. The paper was purposely ruled in squares so that any of the common divisions of time might be shown. The possibilities in this direction are:

The days of the month may be used on the short edge of the paper as in Fig. 62.

Fifty-two weeks for one year can be shown by using the long edge of the paper.

Three years by months can be plotted by using the thirty-six squares on the short side of the paper.

One year by months can be shown by using every third line along the short edge of the paper.

TIME CHARTS 61

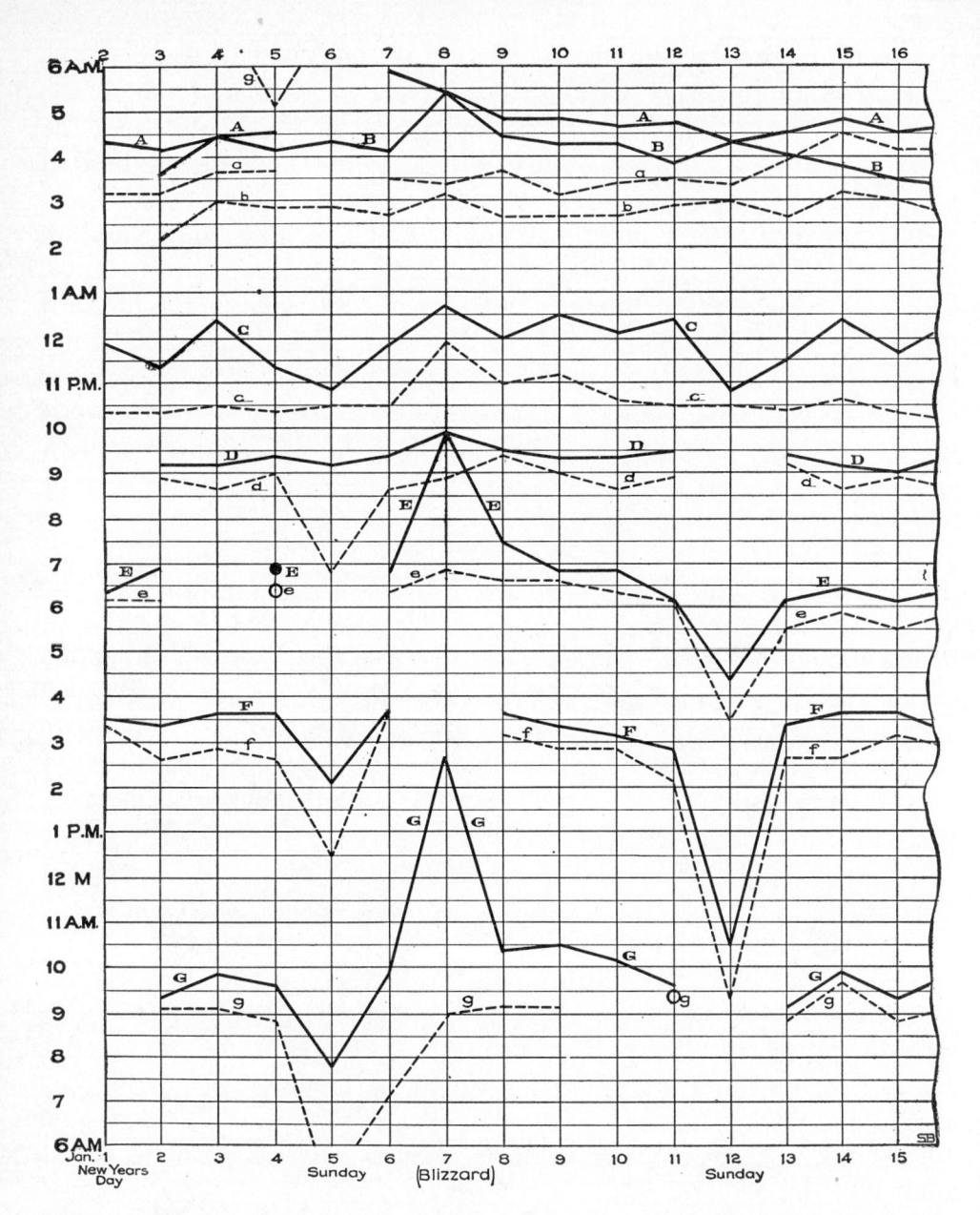

Fig. 61. Operation of Freight Car-Floats at a Railroad and Steamship Freight Terminal

Here we have time represented by days in the horizontal direction and by hours in the vertical direction. The object of the chart is to record whether car-floats are loaded and dispatched at the same hour each day.
Dotted lines show the time at which cars are pushed onto car-floats by locomotives. Solid lines show the time at which car-floats are towed away by tug-boats. Curves for any one car-float destination are in pairs bearing the same letter.
If the departure schedule is well maintained, all curve lines will be practically horizontal. Note that the blizzard of January 7 affected the locomotives less than the tug-boats

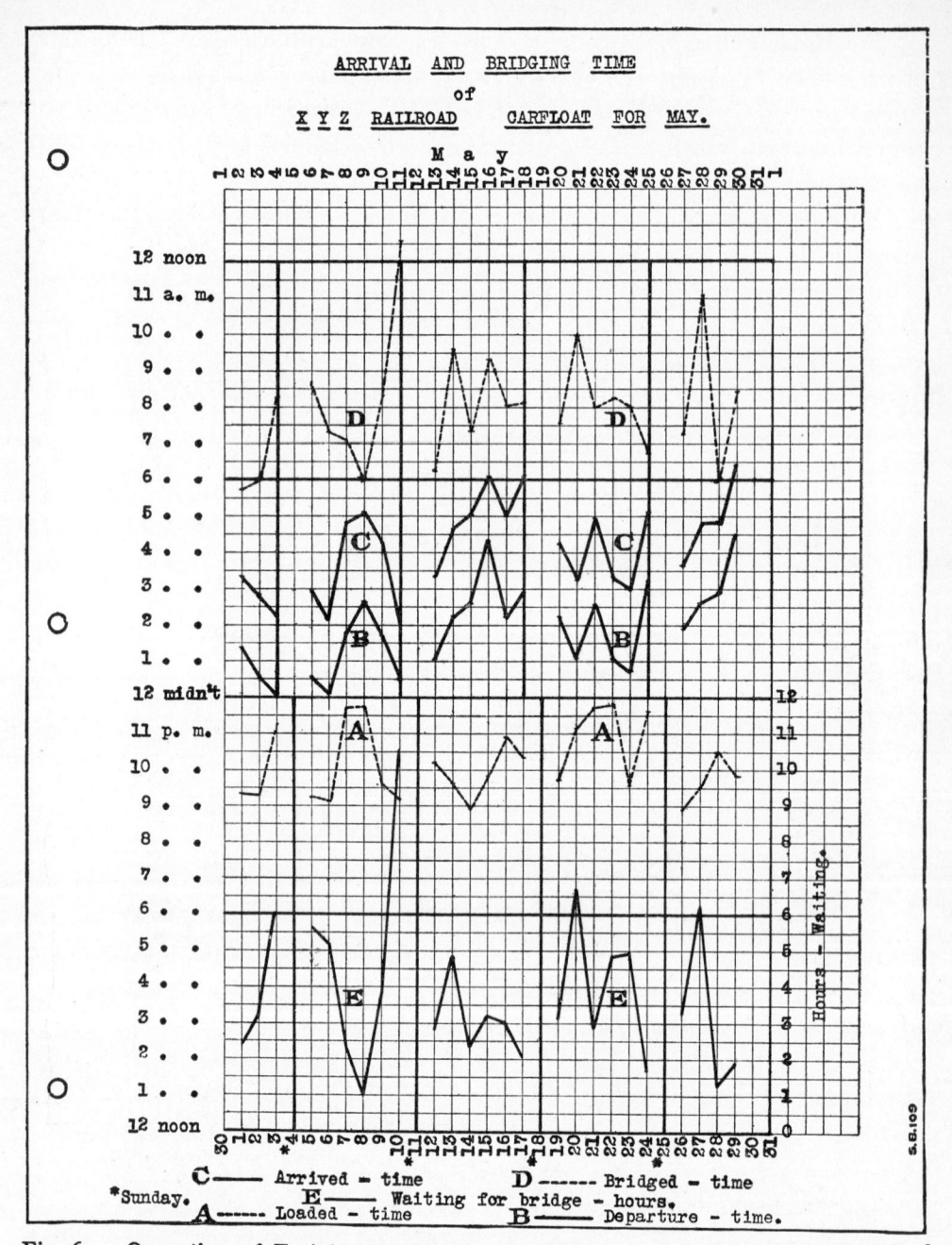

Fig. 62. Operation of Freight Car-Floats at a Railroad and Steamship Terminal

In Fig. 61 several different railroad connections were shown on one large sheet. Here, in Fig. 62, but one railroad is represented on one sheet, with the idea of using as many sheets as there are railroad connections.

This illustration is photographed down from a sheet of 8½-inch by 11-inch co-ordinate paper specially designed for use with a typewriter. The zinc cut for this illustration was made directly from the typewritten original

Percentages up to 100 per cent can be indicated by using fifty of the fifty-two squares on the long dimension of the paper. This ruling gives a co-ordinate paper which is extremely convenient for general work. Other charts drawn on this same ruling of paper may be seen in Figs. 134, 130, 103, 156.

Fig. 63 was adapted from a chart shown in the United States Statistical Atlas for the Census of 1900. The Atlas illustration was printed in color, while Fig. 63 is in black ink. The scheme of this chart is one which could be used widely, for it is an extremely convenient method of showing a frequently changing rank for a large number of units. The blocks for the various States are numbered according to the rank of each State at the first year shown at the left. The rise or fall in rank of each State at each census can be seen at once by following the lines joining the numbered blocks. The actual numerical rank at each census is seen by reading horizontally to the rank number at the right-hand margin or to the numbers in the left-hand column of blocks.

Sales managers publishing a house organ may find the method of Fig. 63 of great advantage in showing the status of each branch selling-house or the rank of each salesman. If every member of the selling organization is given a confidential number, the rank of each can be shown in the house organ sent out each month. Branch houses can be encouraged to compete with each other if their relative rank month after month is indicated on the chart. In the case of salesmen, if the numbers are kept confidential no one salesman can tell from the chart anything about any other salesman. He could, however, see very clearly that his own position in the sales force was getting better or worse, according to whether his relative-rank line pointed upward or downward. This comparison of selling units on a rank basis is in many respects fairer than any curve based on the value of sales. Good business conditions or bad business conditions affecting all alike do not show up in charts like Fig. 63. What is shown is the real progress or lack of progress made by every man or branch selling house as compared with all the others.

Printer's copy for a chart like Fig. 63 can very easily be made up if printed strips of the blocks shown in the chart are used. These, if desired, could be made from Fig. 63 itself. Simply photograph the chart, then take one vertical row of the blocks, as for the year 1900, and have a line engraving made of them, eliminating the figures for numbers which appear in the middle of each block. Print from the zinc plate a number of strips of blocks. With shears and a paste-pot, another vertical row of blocks may be added at the right-hand edge of the chart copy each month to provide "copy" for the plate to print the succeeding month's illustration. The identification could be lettered by hand inside of the vertical row of blocks for the latest month. It then takes only a short time to draw lines joining blocks having corresponding numbers. The built-up "copy" is then ready for the engraver to make a zinc plate. Zinc plates cost so little that there is almost negligible expense required for the new line cut needed each month.

In Fig. 64 the general scheme of Fig. 63 is expanded so that the chart shows not only the rank, but also the comparative size of the units under consideration. This illustration shows also some interesting combinations of shading by means of which blocks of distinctly different appearance are obtained. Fig. 64 was photographed directly from a United States Government report. Otherwise, the years would not be shown here reading from right to left instead of from left to right. Though the right-to-left arrangement is unfortunate, the general scheme of Fig. 64 is excellent, as it gives a large amount of information in a small space. The convenience due to this method of double comparisons, either horizontal or vertical, gives it a decided advantage in clearness.

Train charts like that shown in Fig. 65 are very commonly used by railroads, rapid-transit subways, etc. Fig. 65 would not look so complex if colored ink were available to show in contrast the express passenger trains, the work trains, etc. It is suggested that the reader observe the key at the top of Fig. 65 and then follow a few of the various trains from one end of the line to the other, taking into consideration the fact that this is a single-track railroad and that trains must pass at the turnouts which are available. To schedule a passenger train such as that leaving Tyrone at 12:25 p. m. is no simple proposition on such a crowded railroad as this.

In rapid-transit work in large cities a time-distance chart in the general scheme of Fig. 65 is almost essential if methods of giving high-speed service to the people are to be studied. These time-distance charts can be made on so large a scale that two horizontal lines may be used to indicate the stations, with the lines spaced a distance apart to show to scale the actual length of each station platform. Time-

TIME CHARTS

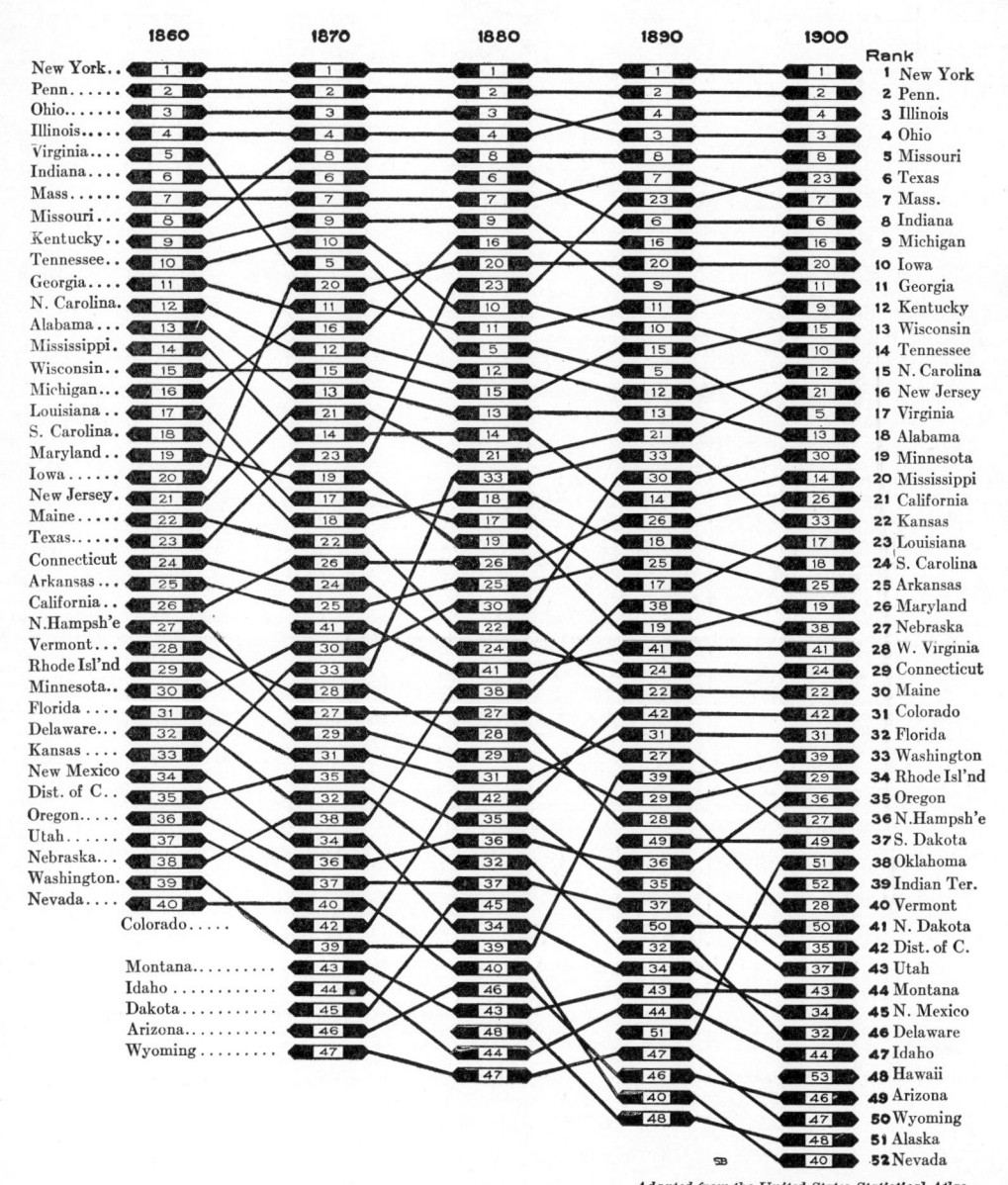

Adapted from the United States Statistical Atlas

Fig. 63. Rank of States and Territories in Population at Different Census Years from 1860 to 1900

Each State is represented by a block bearing an identifying number. The change in rank from census to census is indicated by the connecting lines. Actual rank at any census can be seen by referring horizontally to the figures at the right or to the figures at the left.

A chart of this kind can be used for showing relative rank of salesmen or comparative sales of different branch sales-houses

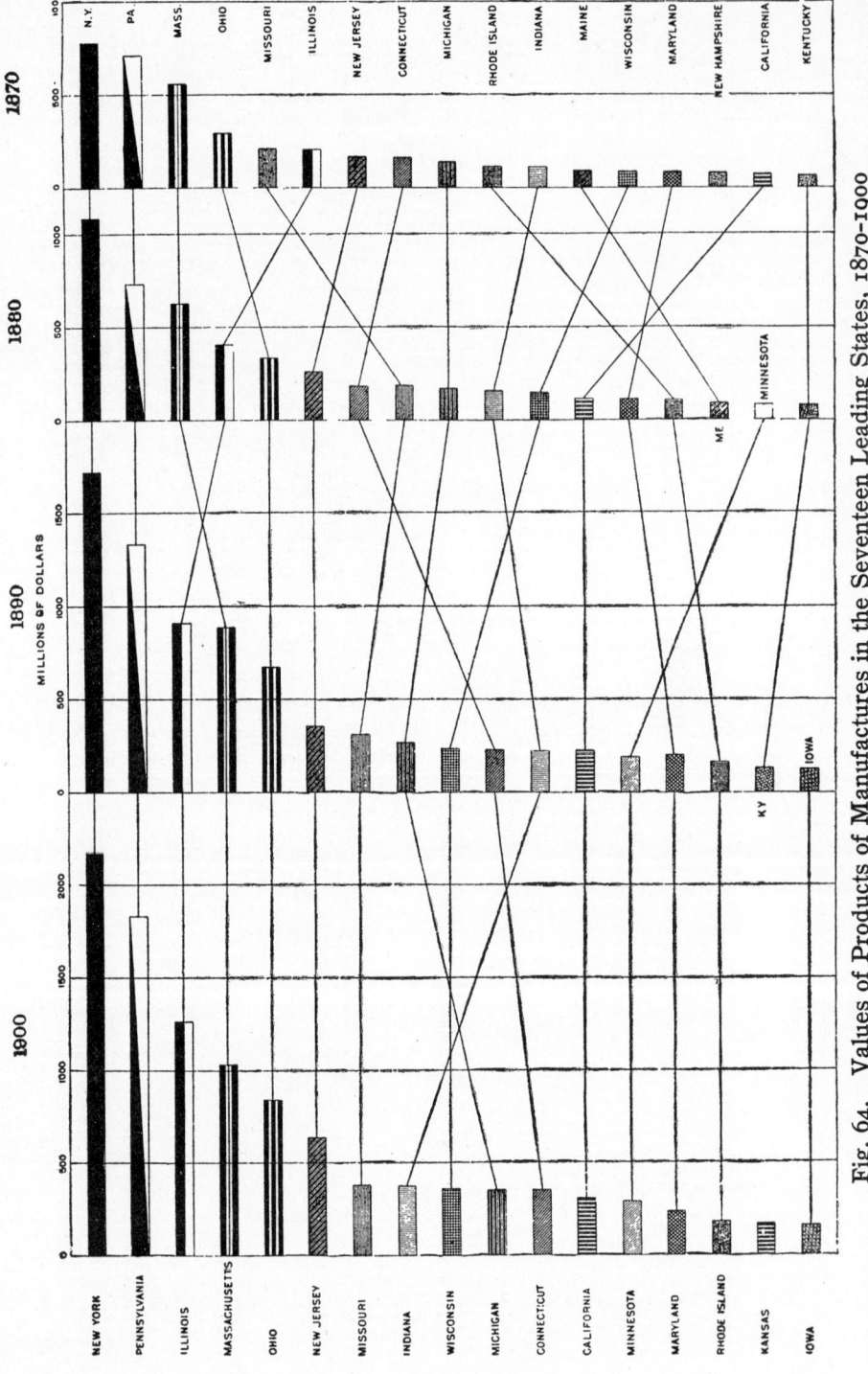

Fig. 64. **Values of Products of Manufactures in the Seventeen Leading States, 1870-1900**

In this chart are shown not only the rank, but also the comparative size of the units considered. Comparison may be made for any one State in different years or between several States in any given year. Notice that this chart, taken direct from the "Statistical Atlas of the Census for 1900", has years arranged to read backward from right to left

TIME CHARTS

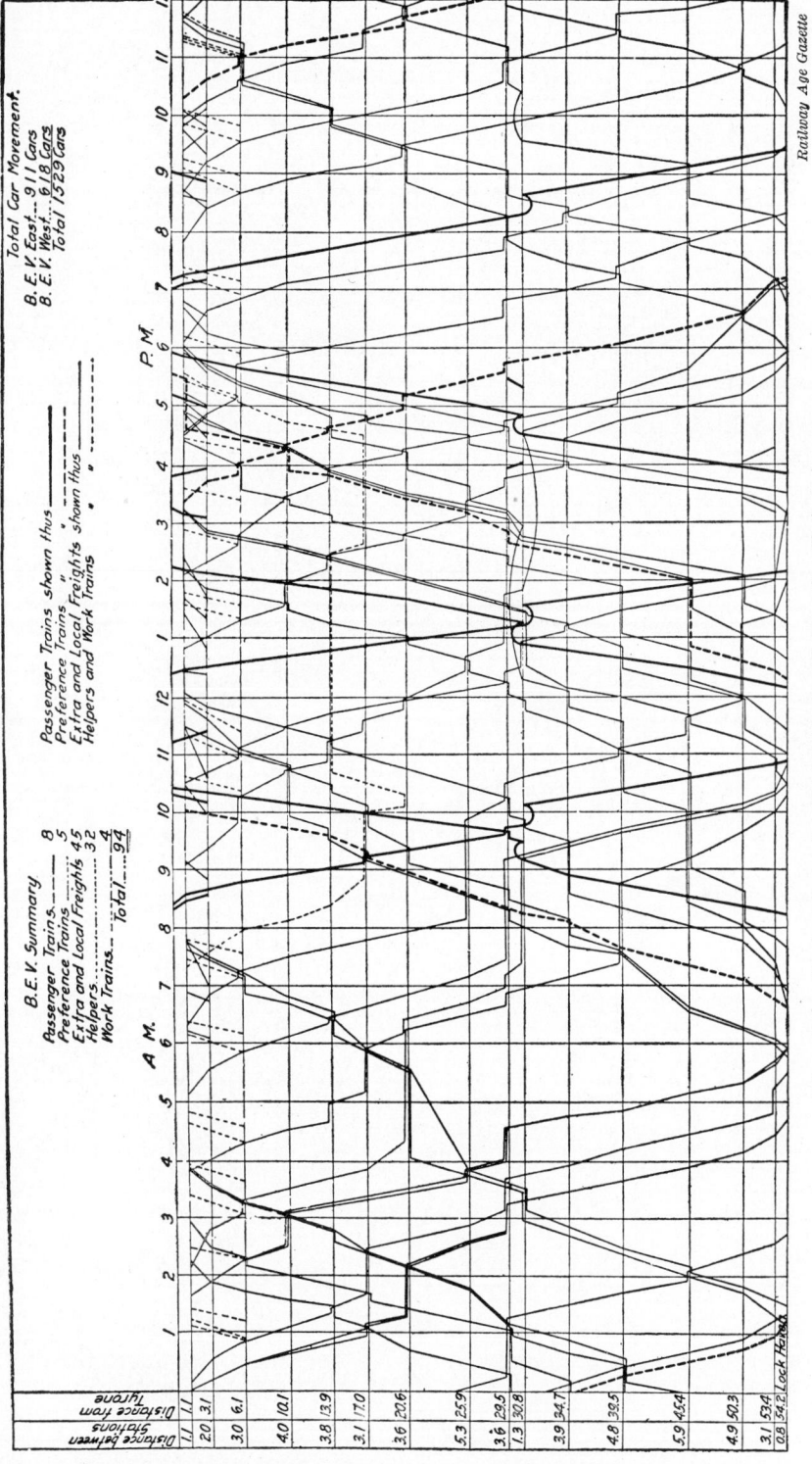

Fig. 65. Train Chart for Bald Eagle Valley for February 3, 1912

This chart shows the train movement over an extremely busy single-track railroad. Time is indicated on the horizontal scale of the drawing, and distance on the vertical scale. Trains in opposite directions must pass at points where there are turnouts, as can be seen from the chart itself

distance curves like those shown in Fig. 65 are then plotted, one for the rear end and another for the front end of each train. As the train remains constant in length throughout one whole journey it is obvious that the two curve lines must be a constant vertical distance apart throughout the length of the chart. At stations, subway trains must stop in such a way that the whole length of the train will be opposite the platform so that passengers may get in and out of every car. The trains follow each other very rapidly, and it is essential that sufficient room be left between two trains for safety. If two curves on a time-distance chart should touch each other, it would indicate a collision. The distance between different train curves on a chart gives information regarding the kind of signal and brake systems that must be used to give the desired degree of safety in operating the road.

Chapter V

CURVE PLOTTING

INFORMATION may be charted in many different ways. Under present conditions, if six men were given a set of figures and asked to chart these figures, the six resulting charts would be widely divergent in method. Though variety in method of charting is sometimes desirable in large reports where numerous illustrations must follow each other closely, or in wall exhibits where there must be a great number of charts in rapid sequence, it is better in general to use a variety of effects simply to attract attention, and to present the data themselves according to standard well-known methods.

In Fig. 66 the attempt to give a spectacular scheme of presentation seems to have overshadowed everything else in the mind of the illustrator. Though a striking architectural design has undoubtedly been obtained, the chart means nothing, for it is impossible of interpretation. No scale has been used in either the horizontal or the vertical direction, as can be seen by comparing the figures on the block for 1830 with the figures on the block for 1840. Even if some scale had been used in making up this chart, the general scheme is such that the reader would hopelessly flounder in trying to reach an accurate interpretation.

Fig. 67 puts the data given in Fig. 66 in the form of horizontal bars. Note that the values which the bars represent are given inside of the bars, for reference purposes. In order to make the shape of each bar stand out distinctly, gray dots were used which permit the figures representing the values to be read through the shading. This is an interesting attempt, but it is not satisfactory as a general scheme. Though Fig. 67 gives the data much more clearly and far more accurately than Fig. 66, the method is not satisfactory because it is difficult for the eye to follow the ends of the different bars in order to judge the increase made from decade to decade. The best method

GRAPHIC METHODS

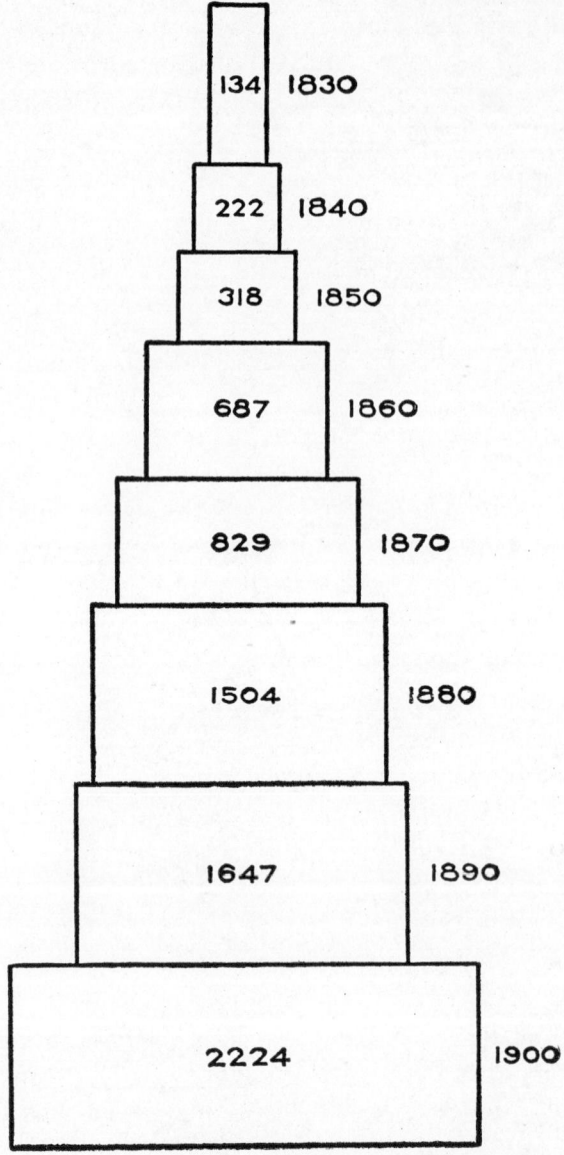

134	1830
222	1840
318	1850
687	1860
829	1870
1504	1880
1647	1890
2224	1900

The Philadelphia Commercial Museum

Fig. 66. Commerce of the United States since 1830. The Sum of Annual Exports and Imports. Values are given in Millions of Dollars

Such a chart as this is worse than none. There is no scale in either direction. The block for 1830 is drawn with a larger area than the block for 1840 which represents a larger quantity. Compare with Fig. 67 and Fig. 68

CURVE PLOTTING 71

of the three is followed in Fig. 68, where the data from Fig. 67 are plotted in the form of a curve. The curve method brings out all the information in less space and in clearer form than does the block system in Fig. 66.

An understanding of how to plot curves and of how to read them should be part of the equipment of every business man, just as it is of every engineer, physician, biologist, and statistician. The general scheme of curve plotting is so simple that instruction in it should be given as part of the work in elementary arithmetic in all public schools. Children over ten years of age can do plotting and can understand simple curves like that of Fig. 68. Curves are usually plotted on co-ordinate paper already ruled in squares, so that the person doing the plotting need not take the time necessary to rule the paper. For reports, for illustrations of magazine articles, or for advertising, it is ordinarily better to rule by hand a small area such as is shown in Fig. 68 so that the spacing of the ruling may suit exactly the data which it is desired to plot.

In Fig. 68 we have data available only by decades, from 1830 to 1900 inclusive. Lines are drawn vertically for each decade. The scale need not run above 2,300, for the largest figure to plot is 2,244 millions. A suitable scale is secured by using one line for each 200 millions.

Fig. 67. Values of Annual Exports and Imports of the United States. Figures are Given in Millions of Dollars

This chart is drawn to scale from the data given in Fig. 66, to show the use of horizontal bars for work of this nature

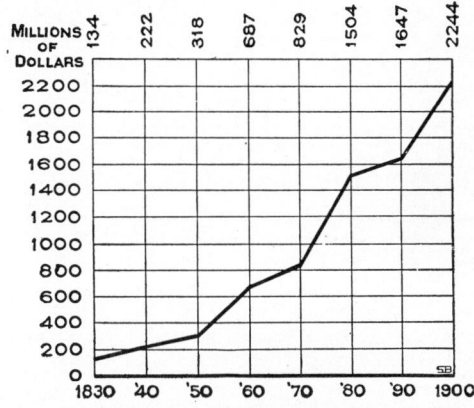

Fig. 68. Value of Annual Exports and Imports of the United States. Figures are Given in Millions of Dollars

This curve is drawn from the same data as Figures 66 and 67. The curve shows the changes from decade to decade more vividly than do the horizontal bars of Fig. 67

After the background ruling has been drawn, the figures at each census are laid off to scale, on the proper vertical lines to represent census years, and a dot is placed on each vertical line at that vertical distance which represents the data according to the scale chosen. Thus the figure 222 for the year 1840 would be indicated as a dot on the vertical line for 1840 slightly above the place where the horizontal scale line for 200 crosses the chart. After the dots for decade years have been placed on the vertical lines, the dots are joined with a heavy line and a curve appears.

The curve of Fig. 68 shows the changes from decade to decade much better than the bars of Fig. 67. It can be seen at once from the curve that the greatest gain in any decade was between 1870 and 1880 when the increase was three and a half divisions on the vertical scale. The bars in Fig. 67 have no horizontal scale to measure by and the comparison between census years is accordingly more difficult.

When plotting any curve the vertical scale should, if possible, be chosen so that the zero of the scale will appear on the chart. Otherwise, the reader may assume the bottom of the chart to be zero and so be grossly misled. Zero should always be indicated by a broad line much wider than the ordinary co-ordinate lines used for the background of the chart.

In Fig. 68, it will be noticed that figures are given at the top of the chart to represent the value for each point plotted on the curve. The use of figures at the top of the chart in this manner is very desirable. The figures are in plain sight, so that anyone desiring to know the value of any point on the curve can look above the point to get the actual figure wanted, without having to read from the scale at the left-hand edge and then estimate roughly the value for any point which happens to fall in a space between two horizontal lines of the scale. Reading from the figures at the top of the chart permits any desired figure to be obtained more rapidly and much more accurately. In addition to this, the figures are recorded in such manner that they may be quoted for use elsewhere by anyone who may wish to make use of the data in a speech or in a written article in which the chart itself cannot be used.

It would be a desirable thing if in all curve charts the figures for the horizontal scale were placed at the bottom of the chart rather than at the top. Many illustrations in this book, taken from publications of excellent standing, show dates (such as years, months, etc.) at the top of the chart. If the horizontal scale were always placed at the bottom, the standard arrangement would be a convenience to the reader and would give the additional advantage that the top of the chart would be free for a numerical statement such as is found at the top of Fig. 68.

The scales of any curve chart should be so selected that the chart will not be exaggerated in either the horizontal or the vertical direction. It is possible to cause a visual exaggeration of data by carelessly or intentionally selecting a scale which unduly stretches the chart in either the horizontal or the vertical direction. Just as the English language can be used to exaggerate to the ear, so charts can exaggerate to the eye.

A curve permits of finer interpretation than any other known method of presenting figures for analysis. Fig. 69 gives some information which many persons might not fully grasp if only a column of figures were used to indicate the average yearly earnings of Princeton graduates. The fairly uniform slope of the curve for the first six years after graduation indicates that the men were receiving

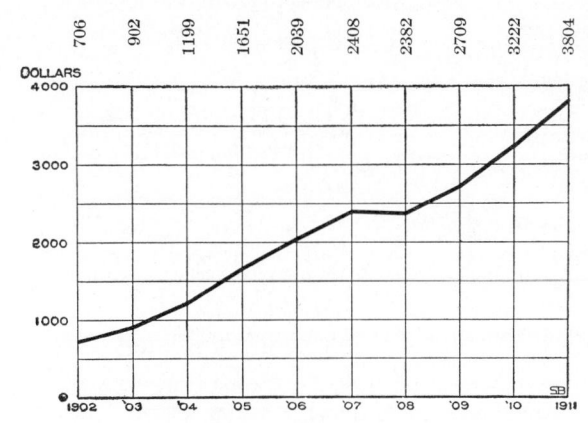

Fig. 69. Average Income of 155 Princeton Graduates of the Class of 1901 for Ten Years After Graduation

Note the effect of the 1907 panic on incomes in 1908

almost uniform raises in pay each year. It must be remembered that a straight-line curve simply indicates that the amounts of the increases year by year are uniform in numerical value. If a curve were started at the lower left-hand corner of the chart and drawn diagonally across each of the rectangles of the chart, it would be seen at once that there would be a straight line indicating an increase in salary of $500 per year. With such a straight line across the chart, the increase in salary for the first year would be $500. As compared with a zero beginning-wage there would be an increase of an infinite percentage at the end of the first year. The next year the increase would again be $500. Compared to the $500 salary, the increase would be 100 per cent. The third year the increase would be $500, and compared to a $1,000 salary the increase would be only 50 per cent. A curve of uniform slope on any chart of rectangular co-ordinate lines indicates only that there has been a uniform increase or decrease in actual numbers, not a uniform rate of change on a percentage basis. A plotted line representing a uniform rate of increase from year to year on a percentage basis may be seen in the curve given in Fig. 121.

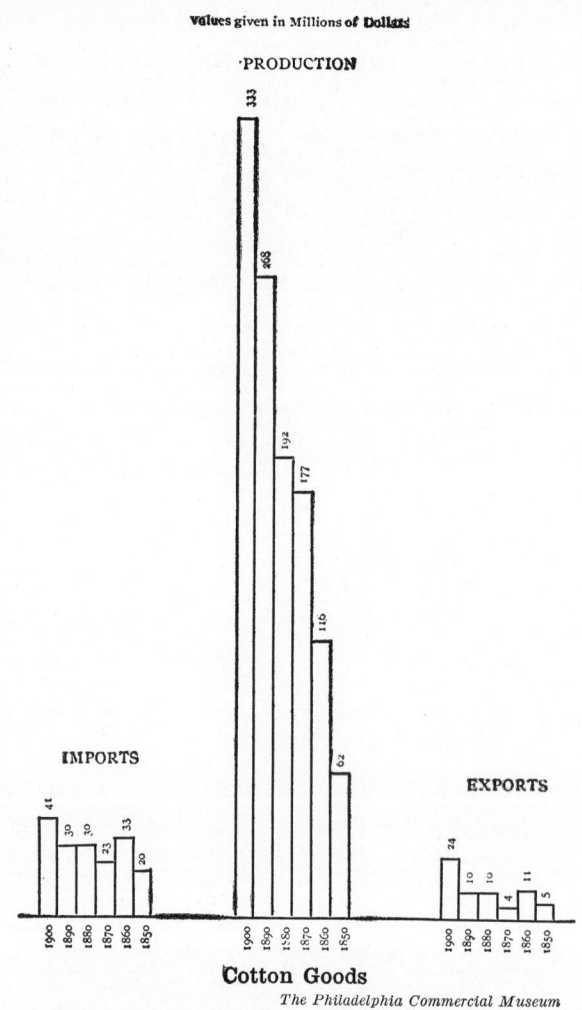

Fig. 70. Cotton Goods Production, Import and Export for the United States. Values are Given in Millions of Dollars

The order of years here reading from right to left gives the first impression that production is decreasing. Compare this illustration with Fig. 71

The untrained reader of curves will probably not be able to tell instantly what made the flat portion of the curve in Fig. 69 during the year 1907 to 1908. One of the chief advantages of the curve method of presenting information is that a curve forces one to think. A little thought here will at once bring out the fact that the flattening of the curve was caused by the 1907 panic. Though the panic started in October of the year 1907, the year 1907 was really one of the most prosperous years the country has ever known. It would be more fitting if the panic were called the 1908 panic, since the main effect of the panic came in 1908 rather than in the year 1907. It can be seen that the Princeton men had their incomes reduced during the year 1908 so that the average fell below that of 1907. By looking along the curve it will be noticed that though there was a larger yearly increase in salary after 1909, salaries at the end of 1911 had not attained the point which it would seem they would naturally have reached if no panic had occurred at a time so shortly preceding this date.

In Fig. 70 vertical bars have been placed touching each other, with the earlier years at the right. The whole arrangement of the chart is extremely poor and also misleading. In Fig. 71 the data of Fig. 70 have been replotted. The most striking thing about Fig. 71 is the falling off in the rate of increase of production in the decade between 1870 and 1880. The shape of the curve at once starts a train of thought in regard to tariff legislation and other conditions which may affect the manufacture of cotton goods.

It will be noticed in Fig. 71 that we have four curves, while only three sets of bars were given in Fig. 70. It is evident that if we add production and imports and then deduct exports, we will have a fair indication of consumption if the amounts remaining in warehouses, etc. (which are probably a negligible percentage of the whole consumption) are excepted. Note that the import and export curves follow each other in general form, though the export curve fluctuates on a percentage basis much more rapidly than does the import curve. Remember that in the fluctuations of two curves like these, the change from year to year must be judged from the zero base line rather than from the slope of the curves themselves. The drop in the export line from 1860 to 1870 was almost one-half, while the drop in the import line for the same period was much less than one-half, even though the import line does show the greater slope downward.

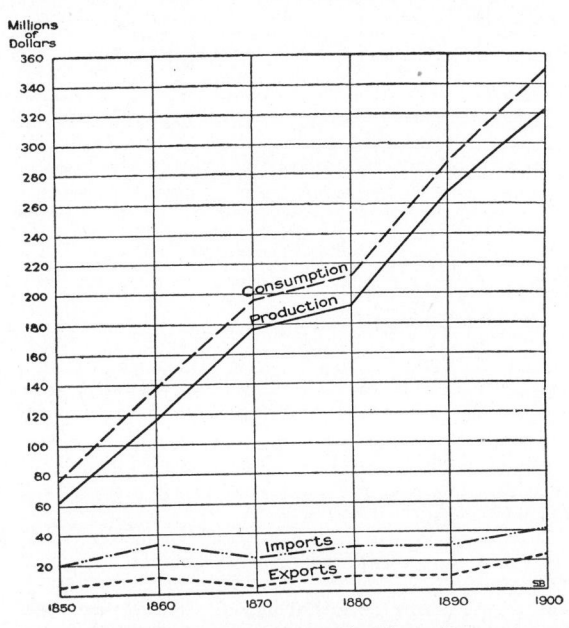

Fig. 71. Cotton Goods Production, Import and Export for the United States

These curves are plotted from the data of Fig. 70, and show the information in much clearer form

In Fig. 72 we have an example of what not to do in charting. The main effect of the circles is to give one a headache without permitting any accurate comparison between the years. The eye does not easily see each circle as an area. The tendency is to see only rings

76   GRAPHIC METHODS

between the lines of the circles, rather than the whole area included inside of each circle line.

Fig. 73 gives the data of Fig. 72 in curve form. The heavy solid line curve shows the changes from decade to decade as they could never be interpreted from either the actual figures or the circles of Fig. 72. The tremendous increase in the world's commerce between 1900 and 1910 is of very great interest, showing the effect which better means of communication have brought about as a result of the splendid increase in scientific and engineering knowledge.

If one makes comparisons between the circles of Fig. 72 on a

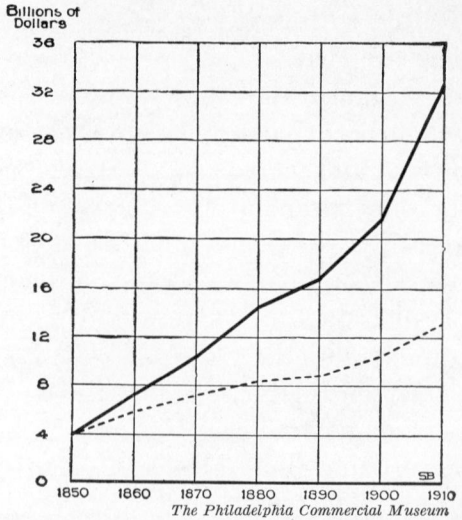

Fig. 73. Annual Commerce of the World, Imports and Exports Combined. Shown at Ten-year Periods, 1850-1910

The solid line is plotted according to the figures given in Fig. 72. The dotted line shows the erroneous impression which would be obtained by the reader if he should interpret Fig. 72 by the diameters instead of by the areas of the circles

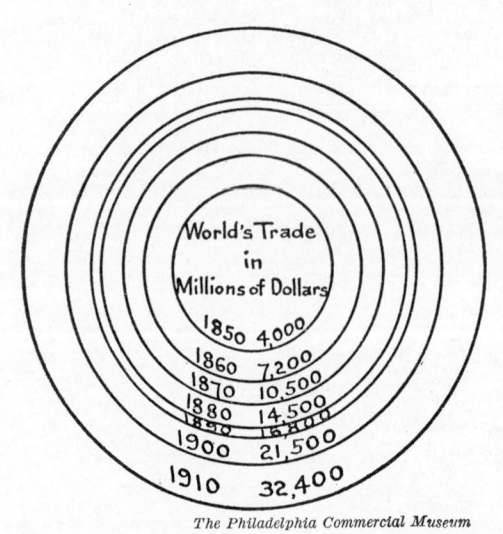

Fig. 72. Annual Commerce of the World, Imports and Exports Combined. Shown at Ten-year Periods, 1850-1910

These circles, drawn on an area basis, are even more difficult to interpret than the circles of Fig. 38. The eye is likely to see the rings rather than the whole areas of the circles. Compare Fig. 73

diameter basis rather than on the area basis to which the circles were drawn, one gets an interpretation like that indicated by the dotted line in Fig. 73. By comparing the dotted line with the solid curve the reader may see the extent of the error which arises if circles are compared on a diameter basis after being drawn on an area basis.

Fig. 74 gives a good idea of the utility of the curve method for showing concisely a large quantity of data. If the figures for the price of cement had been expressed in dollars and shown in a long numerical column, there would be very few readers who would take the

CURVE PLOTTING 77

trouble to follow the table of figures and notice the fluctuations from year to year. The curve, however, gives all the variations in price at a glance and shows in most striking manner the great reduction which occurred in the price of cement as manufacturing facilities improved and increased. A curve of this kind greatly stimulates thought, for one immediately wishes to know the cause of each of the peaks and of each of the valleys in the curve. One gets a vista of recurring periods of financial boom and of financial depression, and a glimpse of such factors as new developments in methods of manufacturing cement and the constantly increasing demand for the product.

If the reading of curves were understood by the average educated person, it would be possible to use, in almost any kind of magazine, advertising illustrations on the order of that shown in Fig. 75. Since, however, curves are not widely understood at present, this type of advertising must now be limited chiefly to the technical journals read by engineers and others who understand curve interpretation. It is really a calamity that curves are not more widely understood. Advertising men are now frequently unable to convince people of their argument simply because they have no language by means of which figures can be made interesting or even intelligible when expressed in an advertisement of limited size. The author ventures to predict that it will be only a very few years until curves are so widely understood and used that they may be presented advantageously in any high-grade advertising pages.

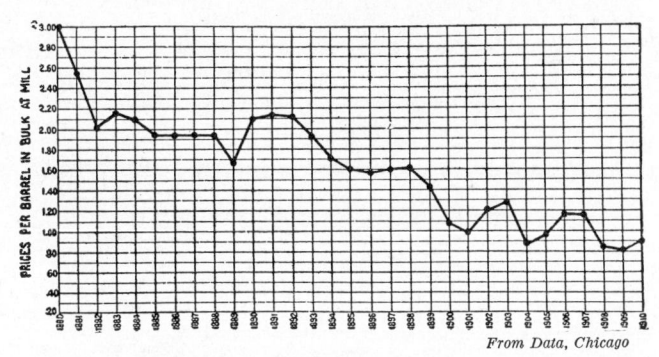

Fig. 74. Prices of Cement, per Barrel, in Bulk, at the Mill, from 1880 to 1910

Columns of printed figures or a series of vertical bars could not portray this information as vividly as it is brought out by the curve shown above

It would be almost impossible to give a clear idea of the flood indicated in Fig. 76 if only columns of figures were used. With the curve it can be seen clearly that the stream rose very rapidly and subsided rapidly, so that the stream was down almost to normal level within forty-eight hours after the beginning of the flood. This curve was probably plotted from flood-gauge readings taken once an

78 GRAPHIC METHODS

hour, or even more frequently. The curve, therefore, was plotted on much more numerous points than are indicated by the vertical lines of the horizontal scale. Frequent observations of the gauge height and the numerous points plotted on the curve in Fig. 76 explain those fluctuations in the line of the curve which occur in the spaces between the vertical lines. Ordinarily a chart is sufficiently accurate if straight lines are drawn from point to point of the plotted data for a curve, without attempting to make a smooth, flowing line.

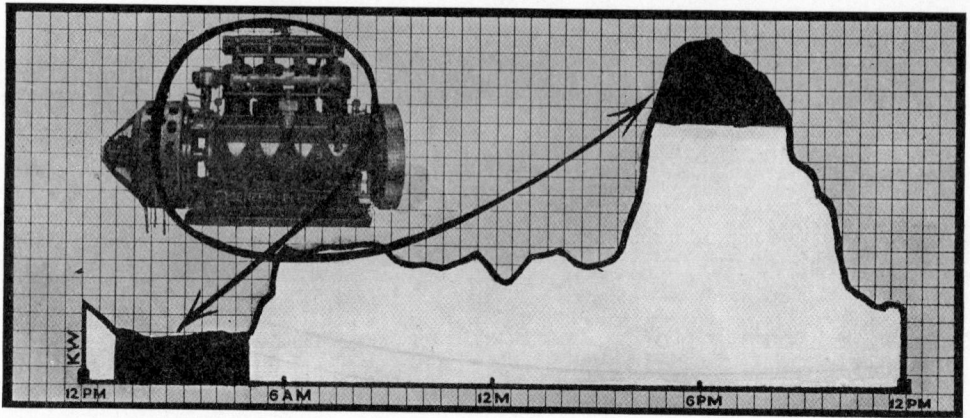

General Electric Review

Fig. 75. Advertising Illustration used in a Technical Magazine, with a Heavy-type Statement Proclaiming that "3000 Central Stations in the United States need a High Grade Gasoline-Electric Generating Set"

The black areas indicate the portion of the 24-hour power-house load for which the gasoline engine would be used

The curve looks smooth in this illustration simply because the gauge readings were taken so frequently that the nearness of the many points made the lines joining them appear curvilinear rather than angular. Such a smooth curve would not have resulted if gauge readings had been taken only every six hours and the chart made by connecting with straight lines the points plotted for the data obtained at these longer intervals.

Another flood curve is shown in Fig. 77. The speed with which the water ran off the territory drained can be judged by the shape of the curve. It is not, however, safe to compare the shapes of the curves in Fig. 76 and Fig. 77 without noticing that in Fig. 77 we have one day represented by a space approximately the same as the space used in Fig. 76 for only six hours. If the curve of Fig. 76 were plotted on the same horizontal scale as the curve of Fig. 77, the flood would appear to be much more severe and rapid than it appears from Fig. 76.

CURVE PLOTTING 79

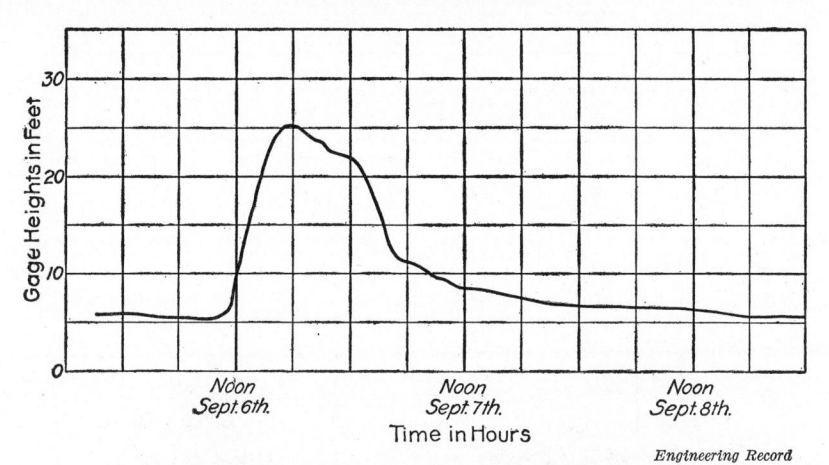

Fig. 76. Curve Showing Duration of a Flood, September 16, 1909, in the Canadian River, New Mexico

This curve was first plotted on a paper having co-ordinate lines close together. For ease of reading, the intermediate lines were omitted from the magazine illustration

In general, it is unwise to compare the shapes of two curves unless they are plotted to the same scales, both horizontal and vertical.

The curve of Fig. 77 is misleading because the scale does not begin at zero. Only the peak of the flood is shown, with no zero line from which to judge the extent by which the flood exceeded the normal flow of the river. If the co-ordinate lines were drawn so as to show the zero line, the base of the chart would be about $3/8$ inch lower than it appears in Fig. 77, and the whole curve would make a different impression. The omission of the zero line in charts of this kind is particularly irritating, yet it is a very common error made by persons drawing charts.

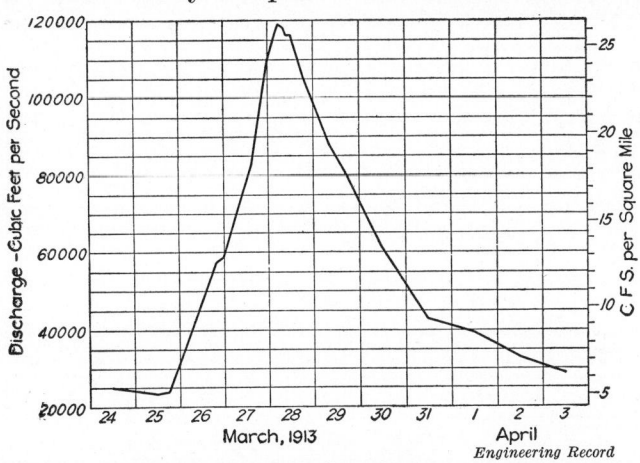

Fig. 77. Flood in the Hudson River at Mechanicsville, N. Y., March, 1913

Note the different scales at the right and the left by which the curve may be interpreted. This chart is misleading because the scales do not begin at zero

Note that in Fig. 77 the curve can be read from two distinct scales, one scale on the left side of the chart, and a different scale on the right side of the chart. If only one scale is used, it should be placed at the left-hand side of the chart. In very large charts it is sometimes desirable to repeat the scale at the right-hand side as well. Where two different units of measurement are used in the scales, the units should be carefully named so that there will be no danger of the reader's using the right-hand and the left-hand scales interchangeably as though they represented the same unit.

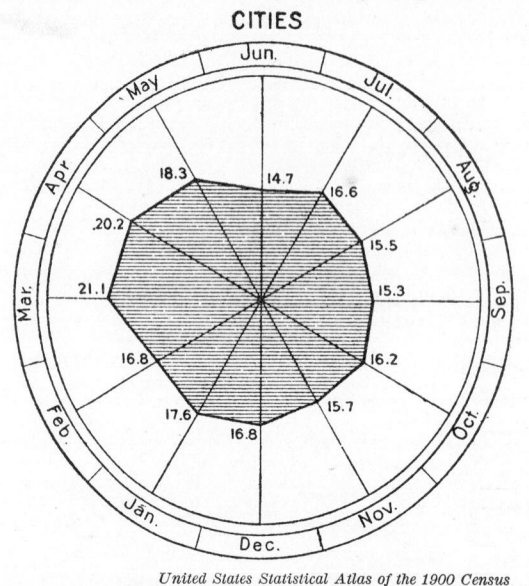

United States Statistical Atlas of the 1900 Census

Fig. 78. Death Rate from Consumption per 1000 Inhabitants for Each Month of the Year in Cities of the United States

This type of chart should be banished to the scrap heap. Charts on rectangular ruling are easier to draw and easier to understand

Charts like that shown in Fig. 78 are quite frequently used in public health reports. It is difficult to see how such an unsatisfactory type of chart ever came into general use, unless it was because there are twelve months in a year and twelve hours on the face of a clock. If the death rates for the different months of the year were plotted in a curve, using rectangular coordinates, the data would be just as easy to read and to understand as when shown by the radial scheme (polar coordinates) of Fig. 78. There would be the additional advantage that the rectangular method would be more widely understood than the circular method of Fig. 78.

Though a chart in the form of Fig. 79 might be justified in the Sunday supplement of a newspaper where an untrained audience must be reached, it is much better to use a curve in the form of Fig. 80 whenever a trained audience is assured. The most interesting thing about Fig. 79 is the slanting line which gives an unusual optical illusion if observed under artificial light, especially with a bare gas flame. The slanting line then appears blue, although it is printed black like the horizontal bars of the chart.

The dotted line in Fig. 80 corresponds to the slanting line of Fig. 79, and represents a progressive average of all the points on the curve

CURVE PLOTTING 81

above. The dotted line, of course, coincides with the solid line at the first point where there is only one point to consider in the average. Figures for the dotted line are obtained by averaging the figures for the first two years, then the first three years, then the first four years, etc., until the last point on the dotted line represents an average for all the points on the solid line.

Fig. 80 is worthy of attention as a model of good practice which may be studied carefully by anyone just beginning to plot curves.

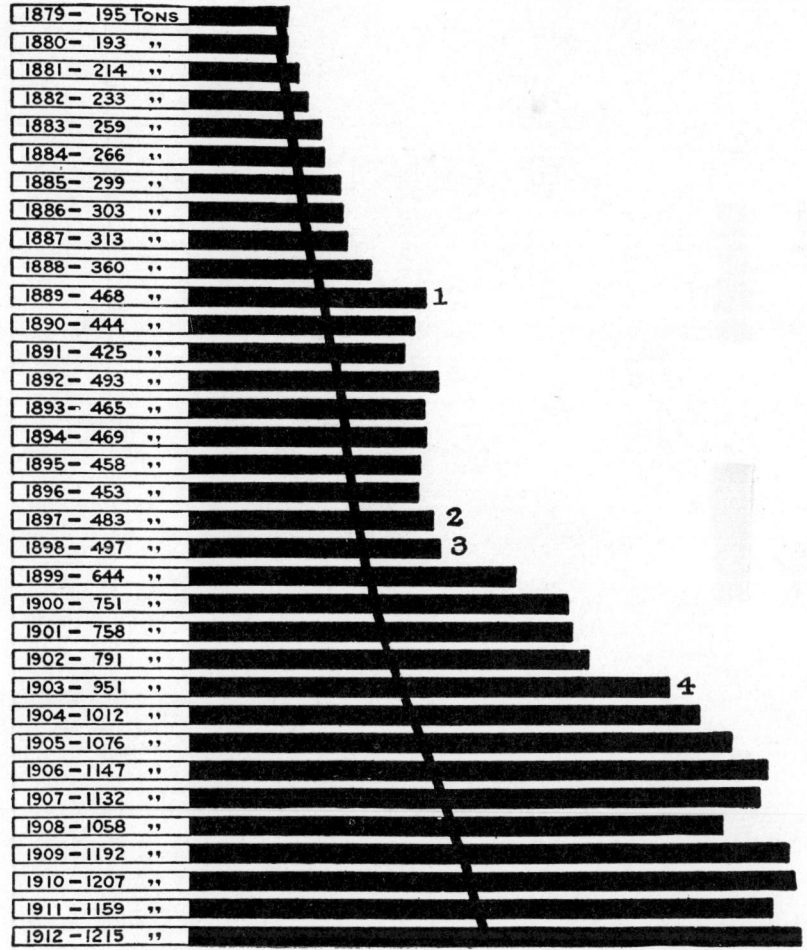

Pittsburgh and Lake Erie Railroad

Fig. 79. Yearly Average of Revenue Tons per Train Mile on the Pittsburgh and Lake Erie Railroad. The Slanting Line Shows a Progressive Average

If this illustration is observed with artificial light, an interesting optical illusion may be noticed in that the slanting line appears blue in color
The use of horizontal bars here gives a chart less easy to interpret than the curve shown in Fig. 80 for these same data

82 GRAPHIC METHODS

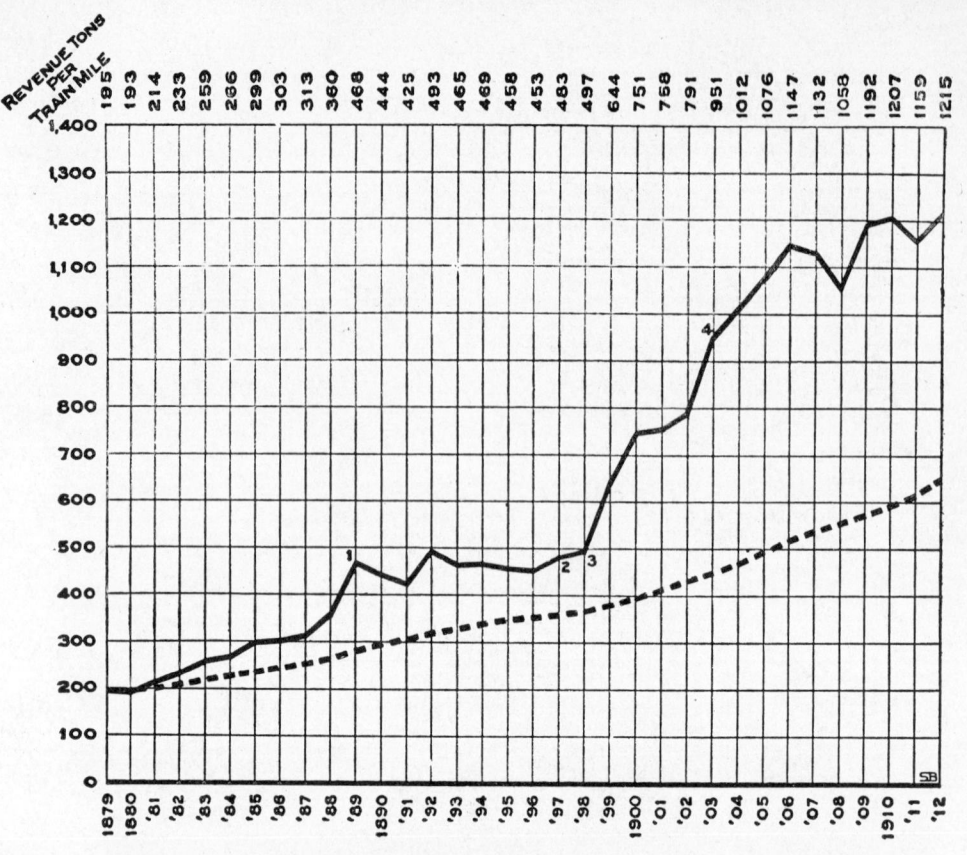

Fig. 80. Yearly Average of Revenue Tons per Train Mile on the Pittsburgh and Lake Erie Railroad. The Slanting Line Shows a Progressive Average

Here we have the data of Fig. 79 plotted in a curve which can be interpreted easily and accurately
This chart may be considered a model of good practice in curve plotting. All of the work, including the lettering, has been done by hand, thus insuring better results than can usually be obtained from printing

The following features of Fig. 80 are pointed out for the benefit of anyone who may have curves to plot:

1. The zero line is a much broader line than the co-ordinate lines.

2. Heavy lines are not used at the right- and left-hand edges, since the chart does not start or end at the beginning or end of time.

3. All lettering is so made that it can be read horizontally or from the right-hand edge of the sheet.

4. Years are given with four figures for every tenth year ending in zero. Other years are indicated with two figures so that they may be more quickly read.

5. All letters and figures on this chart were made by hand, showing the perfection which may be attained by practice in lettering.

6. The curve itself stands out clearly from the co-ordinate lines.

7. Figures at various points along the curve indicate matters which are worthy of special notice. Foot notes are not given here, however, as they are only of highly technical interest.

8. Figures for the values of points on the main curve are given at the top of the chart immediately above each corresponding point on the curve. Values may be read correctly from the upper figures rather than guessed at by estimating them roughly on the left-hand scale.

9. The statement "Revenue Tons per Train Mile" at the upper left-hand corner is purposely printed diagonally so that it may serve as a heading for each of the two columns of figures, one at the left and the other at the top of the chart. The diagonal arrangement gives a neater effect than can be obtained otherwise.

10. Though figures for the dotted curve could be shown at the top of the chart the dotted line is of only minor interest here. It is accordingly best to avoid the two columns of figures at the top in order that the figures for the main curve may stand out more prominently.

CHAPTER VI

CURVE PLOTTING CONTINUED

THERE are so many different applications of curves and such varied yet convenient methods of plotting curves, that it seems worth while to take up some of these in detail, and point out certain advantages and disadvantages of different curve-plotting schemes.

Practically all curves display relations existing between different sets of data which we may call "variables". One of the variables is used as a standard or measure by which to interpret the facts under consideration, and it may be called the "independent variable". The other variable, which is interpreted from the independent variable, is called the "dependent variable". For example, in a bacteriological examination of a pond at varying depths, distance below the surface would be the independent, and number of bacteria per cubic centimeter the dependent variable. In a seasonal gauging of a stream the dates of observation would be the independent and cubic feet per second of flow the dependent variable. Sometimes we consider more than two variables simultaneously, and we then have two or more independent variables from which to consider a dependent variable.

It is difficult to make a general rule for determining in any case which is the independent variable and which is the dependent variable. The decision depends entirely on how any set of data is approached and on the habits of mind of the investigator. When time is one of the variables it is usually, but not always, the independent variable. If we consider values or quantities at different dates, as in Fig. 80, time is very obviously the independent variable. If, however, we are interested in the length of time required to do different operations, as in Fig. 85, Fig. 86, and Fig. 87, our data are expressed in length of time and time is the dependent variable. This example is an exceptional case and it is named here only to show that, although time is ordinarily the independent variable when it enters into curve plotting, nevertheless there may be occasions when time is the dependent variable, and charts should be plotted accordingly. It is important that the person drawing a chart should in each case distinguish between the independent variable and the dependent variable, for this distinction affects the whole arrangement of the chart.

It should be a strict rule for all kinds of curve plotting that the horizontal scale must be used for the independent variable and the vertical scale for the dependent variable. When the curves are plotted by this rule the reader can instantly select a set of conditions from the horizontal scale and read the information from the vertical scale. If there were no rule relating to the arrangement of scales for the independent and dependent variables, the reader would never be able to tell whether he should approach a chart from the vertical scale and read the information from the horizontal scale, or the reverse. If charts are always plotted with the independent variable as the horizontal scale, there need be no question in the reader's mind as to how he should interpret the chart. The rule for scale arrangement is not always followed, and a few examples are shown here to indicate the difficulty of interpretation which the reader may have just because a rather simple principle of curve plotting has been neglected.

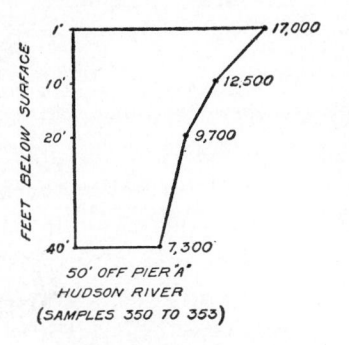

Fig. 81. Number of Bacteria per Cubic Centimeter of Hudson River Water at New York at Different Depths below the Surface

In Fig. 81 the depth of the water has been plotted downward from the top of the chart so that the reader may get the impression of measurements taken at different distances below the surface of the water. In making the tests which are represented in Fig. 81, different depths below the surfaces were selected and the bacteria determined from the water samples taken at these depths. The depth is here the independent variable, and bacteria per cubic centimeter the dependent variable. The decision as to which is the independent variable and which is the dependent variable rests entirely on how the problem is approached. Numerous samples could have been taken at different depths, and then a curve plotted to determine the depth at which certain numbers of bacteria per cubic centimeter were found. In such a case, bacteria per cubic centimeter would be the independent variable and depth would be the dependent variable. This sort of problem may be attacked from either one standpoint or the other, and it is just a question of convenience as to which method is used and which variable is made the independent variable. Though the problem can be stated in such manner that either one variable or the other can be made the independent variable, after the statement has been made the chart should be consistently drawn so that the independent variable will be used as the horizontal scale and the dependent variable as the vertical scale.

As Fig. 81 is shown it is necessary for the person interpreting the chart to select from the vertical scale some number of feet below the surface and then read the number of bacteria per cubic centimeter by the horizontal distance to the right. It is only after some little puzzling that the reader will notice that the scales for the variables have been reversed and that the chart has been practically turned on its side. How this chart would appear if the horizontal scale were used for the independent variable may be judged by turning the book and looking at Fig. 81 from the left-hand side of the page. Though it is easy to see why the person making Fig. 81 happened to arrange the chart in the manner shown with the variables reversed, the gain due to showing depth below the surface in the vertical direction does not make up for the possibility of misinterpretation which results because of the neglect to follow standard practice.

In Fig. 82 we again have depth plotted downward from the top of the chart. As we wish to determine the velocity of the stream at different depths of water, depth is the independent variable and velocity is the dependent variable. The arrangement of Fig. 82 is not as objectionable as Fig. 81, for the upper half of the illustration shows quite clearly in pictorial form that the subject under consideration is a stream having a channel shaped as shown, with widths and depths as indicated by the two scales. In the bottom portion of the diagram the scale of depths downward relates very definitely to the upper portion of the illustration so that the reader cannot easily go astray. Notice that the curves for the velocity of the water are each plotted on a separate vertical line which serves as zero line. The curves for velocity begin at various points depending upon the thickness of the ice, as will be seen from the upper portion of the chart. There is, of course, no velocity in that portion of the stream which

CURVE PLOTTING 87

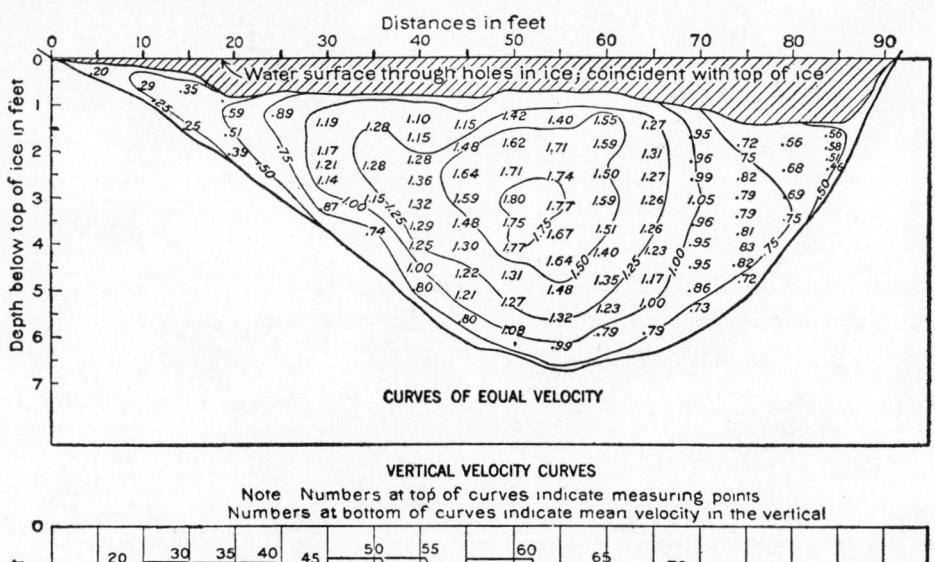

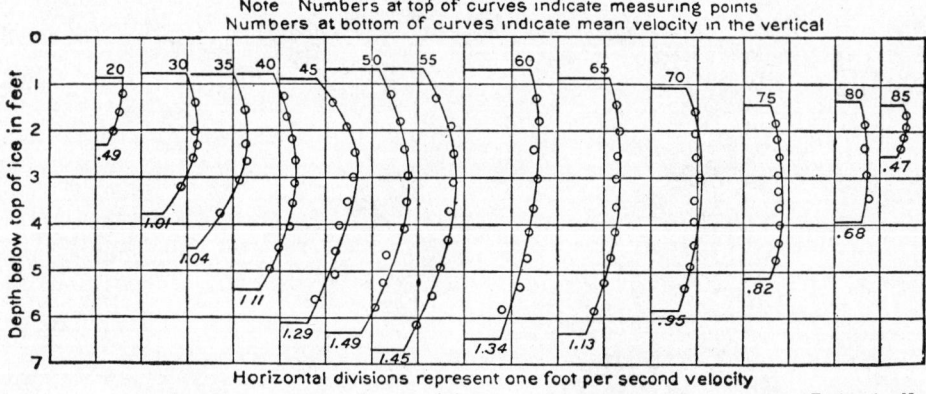

Fig. 82. The Velocity of Water in Different Portions of a Stream Flowing under Ice

The horizontal scale at the top of the illustration shows points where velocity measurements were made through holes in the ice. Velocities at different depths are indicated by the curves in the lower half of the chart, each curve being plotted to the right of a vertical zero line which corresponds with some hole in the ice. Lines are drawn in the upper portion of the chart showing different points in the stream where velocities are the same

is frozen. The velocity curves end abruptly at the bottom of the stream. It will be seen by reading velocities horizontally from the different zero lines from which the curves are plotted that the velocities are considerably greater in the center of the stream than they are near the banks or the bottom. This is natural, as the friction of the earth bottom and sides, as well as the friction of the ice at the top, causes the water to be retarded and the velocity lessened. In the upper portion of the illustration lines are drawn through all those points in the stream cross-section which have the same velocities. The lines are similar to the well-known isothermal lines on a weather map show-

88　　　　　　　　　GRAPHIC METHODS

ing where the temperatures are the same. From these lines it can be seen instantly that the highest velocity is at the center of the stream, as far away as possible from retarding influences. Velocities gradually grow less as the sides, the bottom, or the ice at the top are approached.

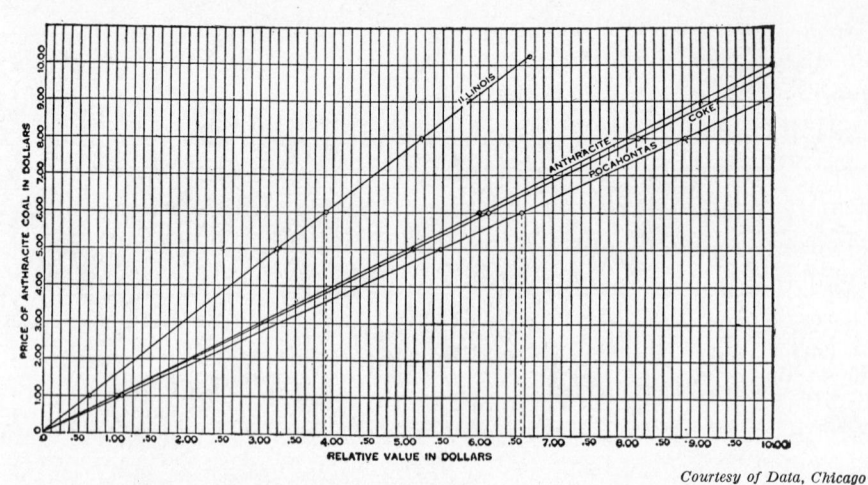

Courtesy of Data, Chicago

Fig. 83. **Relative Value of Different Coals as Compared to Anthracite Coal**
The price of anthracite coal is here the "independent variable" since it is the standard or measure by which the other variable is judged. The price of anthracite coal should have been made the horizontal scale of the chart. See Fig. 84.

Fig. 82 is an interesting piece of work and the method used in charting is justifiable, even though in this case, as in the preceding, the independent variable is plotted downward and the dependent variable is plotted horizontally.

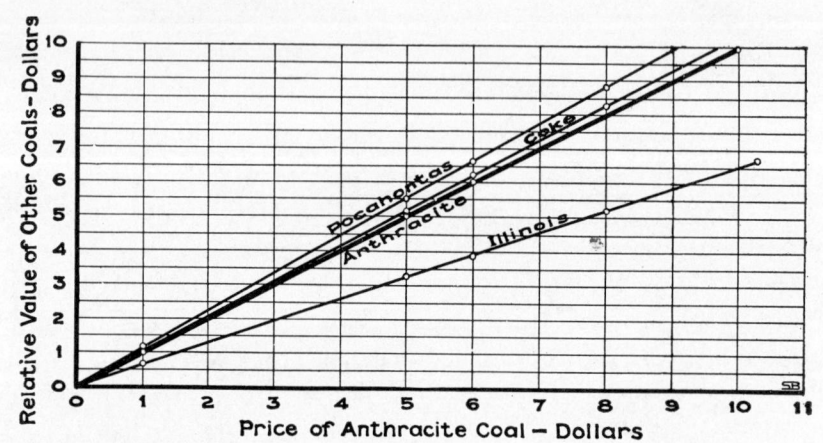

Fig. 84. **Relative Value of Different Coals as Compared to Anthracite Coal**
With the arrangement shown here the curve lines for different coals appear in their correct position. Illinois coal is at the bottom instead of at the top. The heavy line here drawn for anthracite proves at a glance which fuels are better and which poorer than anthracite

CURVE PLOTTING

Fig. 83 is intended as a comparison between different kinds of coal from the standpoint of actual heating value. At the first glance at this chart the reader sees that the line for Illinois coal is above the other lines, and he is apt to draw the conclusion that Illinois coal is better than anthracite, coke, or Pocahontas coal. It is only after some puzzling over the chart that one notices that the whole chart has been drawn in reversed order. We are considering what the relative values of other coals may be if we know the value of anthracite coal. The whole scheme of reasoning begins with the "price of anthracite coal." The "price of anthracite coal" is the independent variable and should be plotted horizontally, with the "relative value in dollars" plotted as the vertical scale. The reader may get a correct impression of the chart in Fig. 83 if he will turn over the page and read the chart by holding the page up to the light in such manner that the zeros of the two scales appear at the lower left-hand corner. When this is done, it will be seen that the relative value of Pocahontas coal exceeds each of the other fuels mentioned and that Illinois coal comes not at the top of the list, but at the bottom of the list in so far as fuel value is concerned.

Fig. 84 has been drawn with the "price of anthracite coal" as the horizontal scale, where it belongs because it is the independent variable. The lines for different fuels now appear in their correct order, and the reader sees at a glance that Pocahontas coal has more fuel value than anthracite coal. Notice that a heavy line has been used for the curve line drawn for anthracite coal. As this line is the standard by which the values are compared, it seems best to give it prominence on the chart. The position of other curve lines above or below this line shows instantly whether the fuels are better or worse than anthracite in relative value.

In Fig. 85 an effort has been made to show detail time-studies by the use of curves. There is an error here, however, in that the curve has been arranged in such manner that the independent variable is drawn vertically and the information desired as "time in seconds" must be read off from the horizontal scale. The reader wishes to know how many seconds are required for any one step or any series of steps in the whole work. The chart can be interpreted in the accustomed way if the page is turned over, and the diagram read by holding the page in such manner that the zero on the scale of "time in seconds" appears at the lower left-hand corner of the chart when the page is held up toward a light. The curve for operator No. 1 then appears below the curve for operator No. 2 and the chart shows correctly the relative merits of the two operators. Fig. 86 is a redrawing of the data shown in Fig. 85. Here the curves for the two operators appear in their correct relative position, and it is seen at once that operator No. 1 is the more rapid worker, since he uses less time. With the independent variable made the horizontal scale, a chart can be interpreted quickly. If the dependent variable is used as the horizontal scale the reader is likely to draw a conclusion the reverse of that the chart was intended to show.

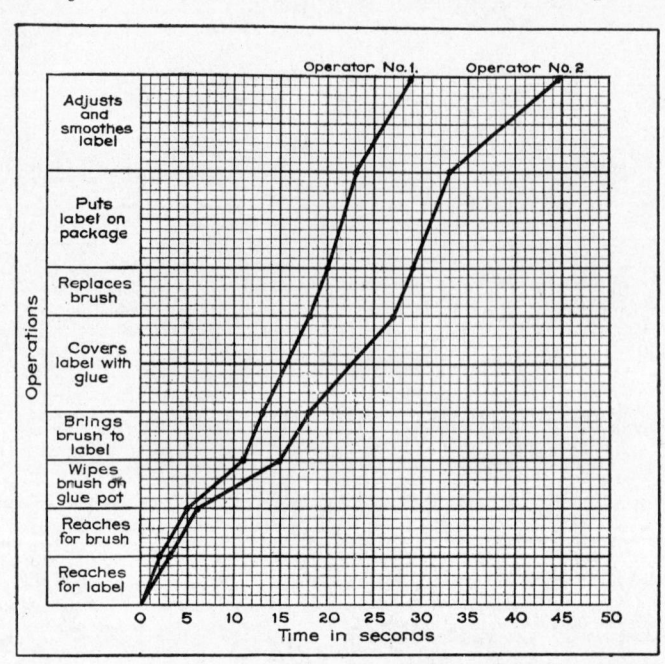

Fig. 85. Record of a Detailed Time-Study of Two Operators Labeling Packages

Adapted from System

We are here studying the time for different operations. The names of the operations constitute the independent variable while time is the dependent variable. The chart reverses the proper arrangement of scales and causes the curve for operator No. 1 to appear improperly above the curve for operator No. 2. Compare Fig. 86

Fig. 87 shows the data of Fig. 85 and Fig. 86 redrawn in the form of horizontal bars such as were seen in Chapter I and Chapter II. The relative times for the various operations are shown much more clearly by the horizontal bars than by the curves used in Fig. 85 and Fig. 86. The time in seconds required for each operation is given by detailed dimension lines above each section in the horizontal bar, and the comparative total time of the two different men can also be grasped instantly. The total time in seconds for the whole series of operations is shown by an over-all dimension line above each of the bars, and the reader, if he wishes, may make an accurate comparison between operator No. 1 and operator No. 2 by using a numerical ratio. A chart of this kind can be very quickly made for ordinary office purposes if the horizontal bars are drawn on co-ordinate paper and the different areas made to stand out in contrast by the use of colored crayons. The actual differences between the two operators would show more clearly, operation by operation, if lines were used joining the ends of the components in the two bars in a manner similar to that seen in Fig. 32. The data of Fig. 85 do not lend themselves well to presentation in curve form. In Fig. 85 and in Fig. 86 the shape of the curves means nothing, since there is no numerical scale relating to the names of operations. Fig. 87 shows a much more satisfactory method for portraying the data.

In Fig. 88 we have an application of curves to advertising in popular magazines. The curves depict the circulation of a newspaper,

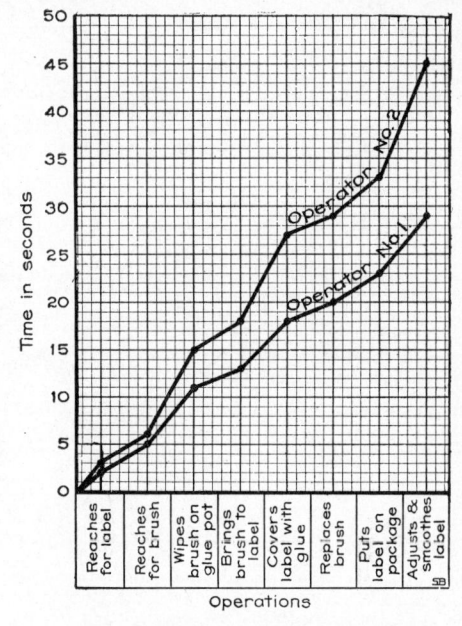

Fig. 86. Record of a Detailed Time-Study of Two Operators Labeling Packages

Here the scales have been properly arranged and the two curves appear in their correct relative position on the chart. These data, however, are not well suited for curve presentation and they are more clearly brought out by the bar method used in Fig. 87

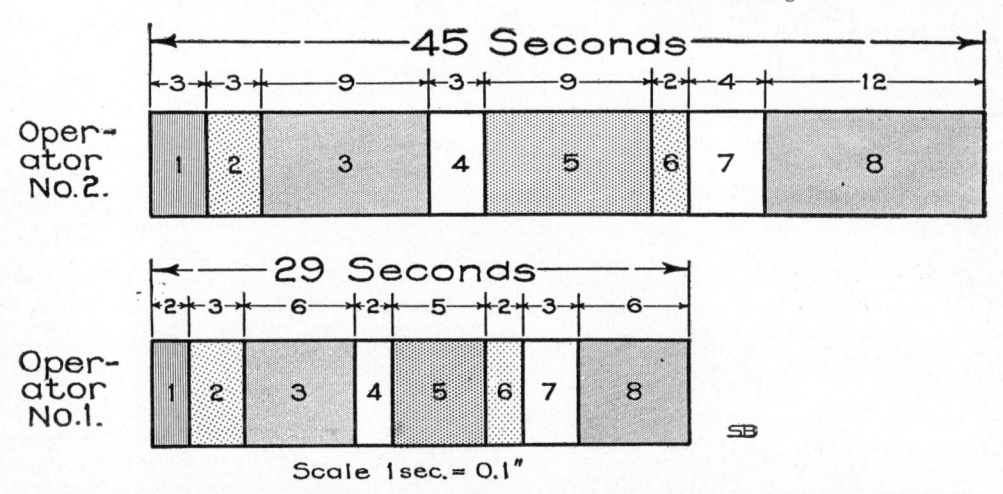

Fig. 87. Record of a Detailed Time-Study of Two Operators Labeling Packages

By this method of presentation the reader may see clearly the relative length of time for different operations as well as the comparison of total time taken by the two workers. Dimension marks and figures show conveniently the actual number of seconds required. The different operations have here been given numbers instead of names. The scale to which the chart is drawn is named

92   GRAPHIC METHODS

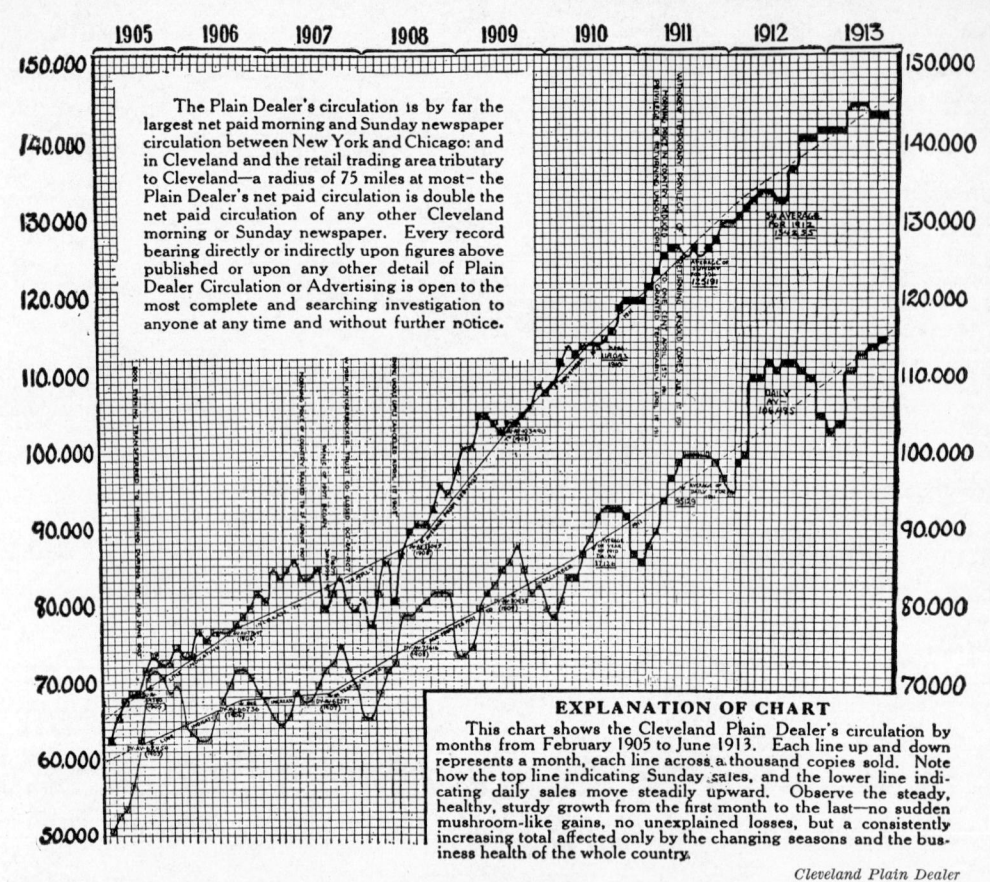

Fig. 88. The Use of Curves in an Advertisement to Show the Growth in Circulation of a Newspaper

It is unfortunate that this illustration was not made so as to show the zero line of the vertical scale. In advertising work it usually pays to avoid anything which might seem like exaggeration. Omitting the zero line makes the growth seem more rapid than it would if the zero line were included in a chart drawn to scale. Though the drafting on this chart might have been better, the application of curves to advertising deserves commendation

with the object of convincing advertising managers that this particular newspaper is a desirable one in which to place advertisements because of the rapidly and steadily increasing circulation. It is surprising that circulation managers of newspapers have not more often used charts to show circulation, instead of the wordy typed statements so frequently seen claiming great growths in circulation over a period of months or years. Though Fig. 88 shows a commendable progressiveness on the part of this particular newspaper in adapting curves to circulation statements, it seems necessary to point out the fact that the chart may cause distrust in the minds of some readers. There is a chance that the man who has advertising to place may feel

CURVE PLOTTING 93

that the chart has been drawn in too optimistic a manner because it does not show zero at the bottom of the scale. It would have given a much more conservative impression if the excellent record of circulation growth had been plotted in curves having the zero line shown at the bottom of the chart, so that the relative growth could be accurately judged visually.

In Fig. 89 a large amount of information has been condensed into a small amount of space, yet the chart is fairly clear and easy of interpretation. Several ingenious combinations have been included as, for instance, the arrows that show the prevailing direction of the wind each day. The chart gives unusually complete information in a most convenient form for any ventilating engineer or power-plant manager who wishes to keep careful track of his cost of coal in different months of the year as dependent upon weather conditions.

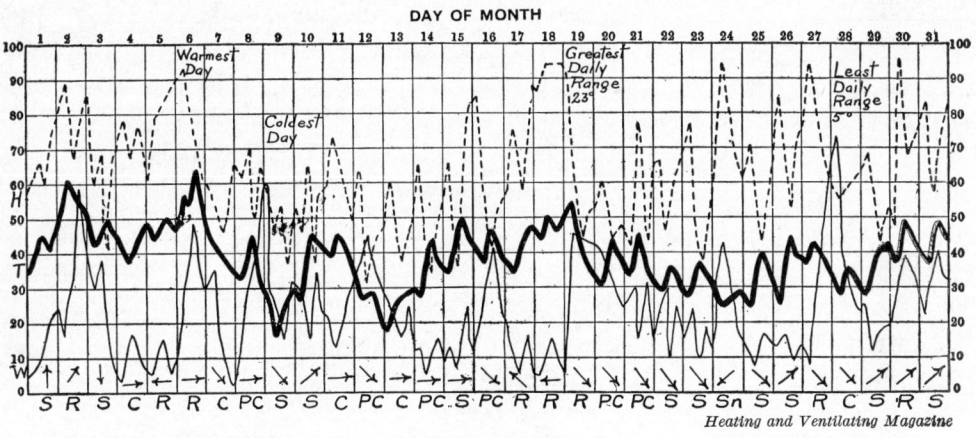

Fig. 89. Record of the Weather in New York City for December, 1912

The heavy line indicates temperature in degrees Fahrenheit
The light solid line shows wind velocity in miles per hour
The dotted line depicts relative humidity in percentage from readings taken at 8 a.m. and 8 p.m.
Arrows portray the prevailing direction of the wind
Initials at the base of the chart show weather conditions as follows: S, clear; PC, partly cloudy; C, Cloudy; R, rain; Sn, snow

Fig. 90 shows an example of double co-ordinate ruling on the same sheet of paper. The scheme of using double co-ordinates is not very well known even to engineers and it seems worthy of attention here. The solid line plotted in the general form of a curve with a flat space for each month shows the total water consumption in millions of gallons per day. The total water consumption is read from the scale of the horizontal lines as for any curve plotted by rectangular co-ordinates. The slanting lines are drawn after the total number of gallons used per day has been divided by the number of inhabitants in the district so as to obtain a figure for the average daily consumption of water *per capita*. As the population figure used depends upon census records it may be necessary to get the rate of growth in the population from records as much as ten years apart. In Fig. 90 it can be observed that the slanting lines showing the rate of growth of the city are straight lines, indicating probably that the census figures were used in the drawing of these lines because yearly figures could not be obtained. If yearly figures were obtainable the slanting lines could be extended year by year until they reached completely across the chart. The rate of growth in population determines the angle of the slanting lines, the more rapid the growth the greater the angle of the lines.

The slanting lines are located on the page so that a curve can be read from either the horizontal lines or from the slanting lines. The method of locating the slanting lines can be worked out by anyone who will experiment a little in making a chart of this type. When the population is known and the total consumption is known, it is only a matter of division to determine the consumption *per capita*. After the slanting lines are once placed upon the chart, the curve can be read either from the horizontal lines showing the total consumption or from the slanting lines showing gallons *per capita*.

Taking the peak for February, 1912, we see that the total consumption averages during the month 142,000,000 gallons per day. Reading this same month from the slanting lines we observe that the average consumption *per capita* daily was 127 gallons. Notice, that while the total consumption in gallons was much larger in February, 1912, than in January, 1909, as seen by considering the horizontal lines, the consumption *per capita* in February, 1912, read from the slanting lines, was somewhat less than in January, 1909.

If we consider the growth in the population of the city of Boston, it is permissible that the total water consumption in 1912 should be greater than in 1908. In spite of the large growth of the city from 1908 to 1912, there has been a general decrease in the total quantity of water consumed. The decrease in total consumption is chiefly due to the metering of water to individual users, eliminating a large part of the water waste which formerly occurred because of carelessness on the part of consumers. The actual percentages of the services which were metered in each one of the years considered may be seen

CURVE PLOTTING

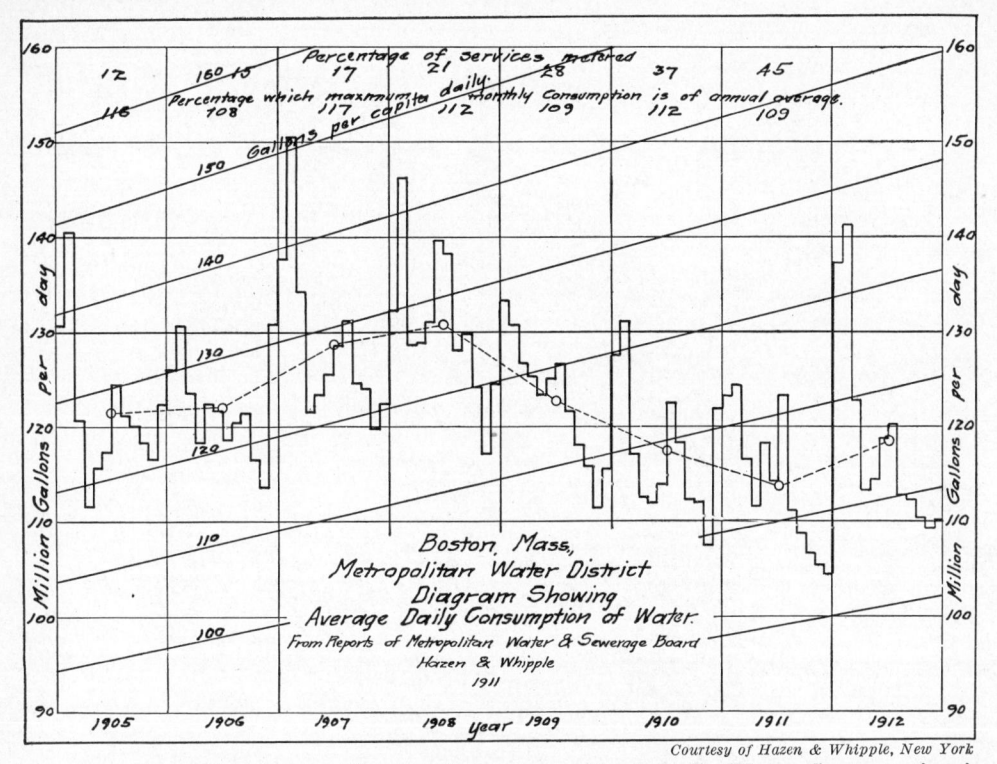

Fig. 90. Chart Showing by Months the Average Total Daily Water Consumption in Boston, and by Months the Average Daily *per Capita* Water Consumption. Also the Yearly Average of Daily Consumption Stated in Total and *per Capita*

In this illustration the curves may be read from either of two different sets of co-ordinate rulings. Using the horizontal ruled lines, we may read from the curves the average total consumption per day. By reading from the slanting lines, the same curves may be interpreted as the average consumption *per capita* per day. The scheme of using two sets of co-ordinate rulings is a valuable one. The scale for "million gallons per day" should, however, have been shown only at the left, with the slanting line scale for "gallons *per capita*" placed in the right-hand margin for the sake of clearness

by referring to the figures near the upper portion of the chart. Note that in 1908, 21 per cent of the services were metered, while in 1911, 45 per cent were metered. The proportion of the services metered in 1912 was not known at the time the chart was made and hence is not recorded.

A little study of Fig. 90 will show that there is a very striking similarity in the shape of the waves for different calendar years. Water consumption is high in the winter and again high in the summer months, with the lowest point each year usually found in November. The exact amount of resemblance of these waves to each other could be determined in an interesting manner if a separate curve were plotted for each year so that all the curves would be shown one above the other in the manner seen in Fig. 103.

Just how much the total consumption in water has been decreased, even though there was an increasing population, may be seen by referring to the dotted line on the chart. This dotted line was plotted from points which represent the average for the whole of each year. Thus, the average in 1905 was about 122 million gallons per day and in 1911 about 113 million gallons per day. There is so great a fluctuation in the main curve from month to month that it would be difficult to judge accurately whether the average consumption is going up or down if some such curve as the dotted line were not used. An average curve line run through a curve in the manner shown by the dotted line in Fig. 90 is of great assistance in drawing accurate conclusions from curves which have much fluctuation.

In Fig. 90, the dotted line, plotted through a point giving the average for each year, thoroughly eliminates all the fluctuations which would be so confusing to the reader if he had to study only the monthly curve. The dotted line shows conclusively by its slant that the total consumption from 1905 to 1908 inclusive went up just about as rapidly as the growth of the population would lead one to expect. After 1908, however, there was a tremendous drop in total consumption, even though the population kept on increasing. In 1912, the average total consumption per day went up somewhat above 1911, but yet it did not increase much more rapidly than the slanting line of the *per capita* scale might indicate as permissible. Fig. 90 could have been improved somewhat if the dotted line had been replaced by a broad black line which would bring the yearly-average curve vividly to the attention of the reader. The yearly-average curve really gives the most interesting conclusions which can be drawn from this chart and it is worthy of greater emphasis to the eye than is given to it in the chart.

It would have been better if the scale for "millions of gallons per day" had been placed only at the left-hand edge of the chart in heavy lettering so the figures would stand out clearly. The scale for the slanting co-ordinate lines could then be placed at the end of each slanting line at the right-hand side of the chart. The scale for the slanting co-ordinate lines is too difficult to find in Fig. 90.

An interesting study could be made from Fig. 90 by plotting a curve which would show each year the percentage of services which were not metered, instead of using the figures at the top of the chart which show the percentage of services which are metered. A curve for the percentages of services not metered should show some similarity in shape to the dotted line curve in Fig. 90, giving the yearly average of daily consumption.

When any curve fluctuates greatly, the general trend of the curve can be most easily determined if the method of moving averages is used. If data are plotted by months, a moving average is frequently made to include twelve months. As a succeeding month is included in the moving average, that calendar month of the preceding year is dropped out of the average so that the average always includes twelve months. The moving-average curve is a much smoother curve than a curve made from the monthly figures, and is accordingly more easily interpreted. The degree of smoothness of any moving-average curve depends chiefly on the number of points included in the moving average as compared with the number of points in one complete wave or cycle in the data curve, and the moving-average curve is most smooth if the moving average includes the same number of points as are usually found in one complete wave or cycle of the fluctuating curve.

Many curves plotted by weekly or monthly observations show a complete wave or cycle each year because of the effect of the seasons. With such a curve it is best to use for the moving average the number of points included in one year of the fluctuating curve. When, however, we study curves relating to financial conditions in any country, we find that there are complex cycles which involve several years. With such a complex curve considerable care must be used to determine the average length of one wave or cycle, so that the moving-average curve may be made as smooth as possible and most nearly represent the data being studied.

In Fig. 91 the data when plotted by years give such a complex curve that it is not easy to determine just how rapidly exports have increased. To show the effect of different numbers of points included in a moving average, curves were drawn with moving averages for three years, five years, and ten years. Since the distance between peaks on the curve making one cycle of fluctuation averages more nearly ten years than three years or five years, the ten-year curve more closely approximates a smooth curve line than either of the other two curves. As a matter of fact, the intervals between peaks change somewhat so that it is difficult to select any one number of years as the correct number for use in making up the moving average.

98   GRAPHIC METHODS

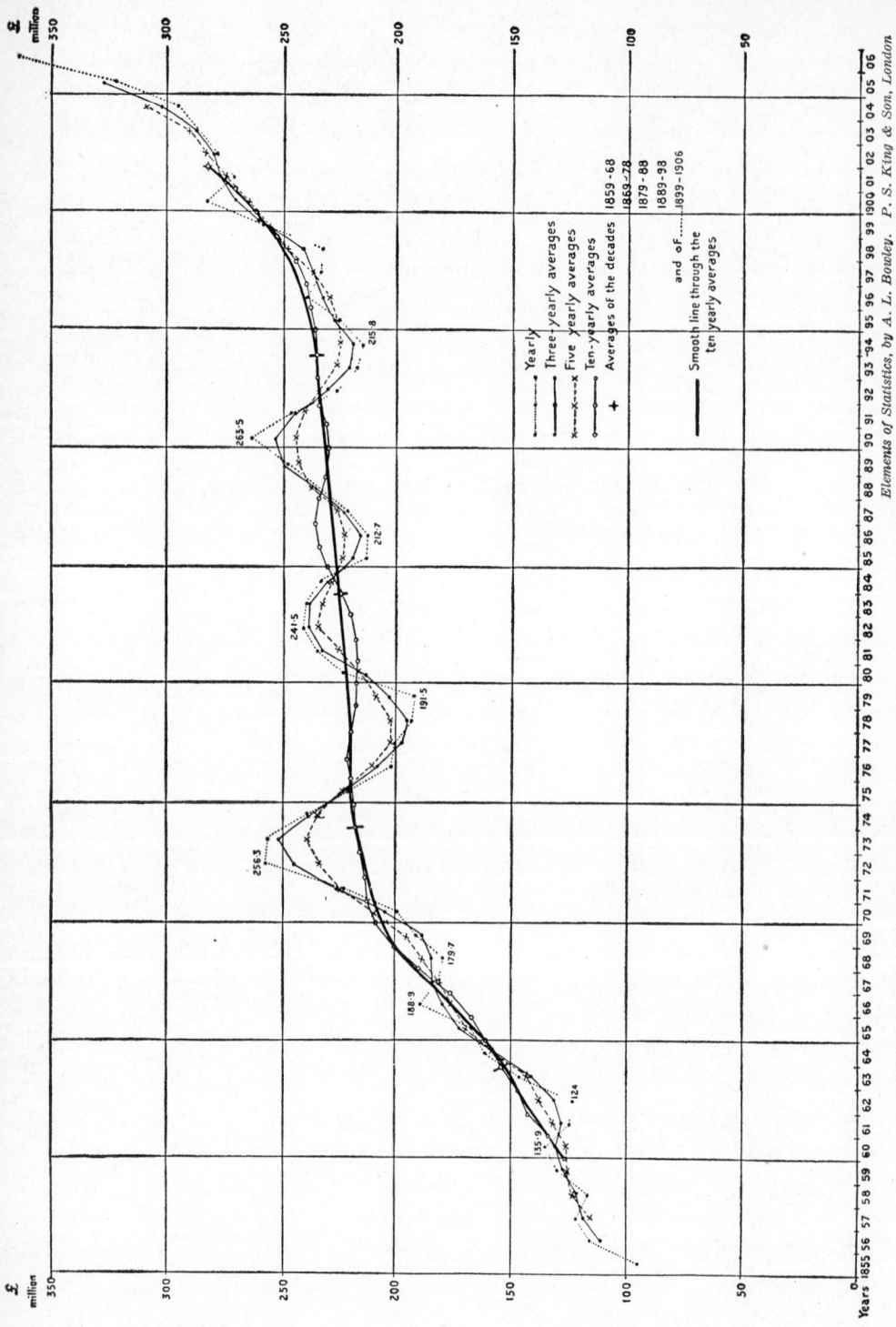

Fig. 91. Total Value of British and Irish Produce Exported from the United Kingdom, 1855-1906

Elements of Statistics, by A. L. Bowley. P. S. King & Son, London

The fine dotted line shows a curve plotted from yearly averages. This line fluctuates in such manner that it is difficult to tell the general tendency of the exports under consideration. Other curves are drawn from the same data but using moving averages of three, five, and ten years to show the effect in "smoothing" the curve. The heavy line is drawn through points which represent the average for each of the different decades, and it is smoothed arbitrarily to give the best representation of the trend of exports

The heavy smooth curve was drawn finally by using the points which represent the averages of the decades and then sketching in, free hand, a line which gives a smooth curve and removes the waves found in the ten-year moving-average curve. Notice that the heavy smooth curve is so drawn through the ten-year curve as to give approximately equal areas on either side of the smooth curve between that curve and the curve for the ten-year moving average. The curve for the ten-year moving average evidently does not give a fair interpretation of yearly data, because the ten-year average curve shows a peak in the year 1886 while the data as plotted by years show a valley for that year. The peak in the ten-year moving-average curve in 1886 was caused by the number of years included in the moving average not being a true representation of the length of one full cycle. The length of the cycle changes from time to time, so that no one selected cycle length is satisfactory for the whole curve. The heavy curve sketched in by hand is the fairest approximation to show the trend of the fluctuating curve as a whole.

In Fig. 91 the points on any smoothed curve are plotted midway horizontally in the range of years included in each moving average. It is on this account that the smoothed curves, though all plotted from the same data, do not seem to end at the same year at the right-hand side of the chart. Though it is good practice to plot smoothed curves in this manner with each point midway in the horizontal range of the points included in any moving average, there are times when it is not desirable to have the point on the moving-average curve fall behind the latest point on the data curve. For operating records in industrial work, the moving-average curve is convenient to show an average for the preceding twelve months or for any other length of time immediately preceding. With such curves it is usually best to have the last point of the moving-average curve plotted on the same vertical co-ordinate line as the last point of the data curve.

Index numbers are used very commonly in the study of facts relating to the prices of commodities over a long period of time. When making comparisons by index numbers, conditions are selected which as nearly as possible represent the normal or typical conditions for the subject under consideration. The figures for other dates are then compared with the figures representing the normal conditions, by working on a percentage basis so that the figures for the normal conditions are taken as unity or 100 per cent. Figures for the conditions to be compared with the normal are expressed in percentages, making the increases above normal in figures above 100 per cent and decreases below normal in figures below 100 per cent. Unfortunately, the reader not familiar with index numbers may not realize that a chart relating to index numbers should be read from the 100 per cent line rather than from the base of the chart. It is very common to find a chart relating to index numbers so drawn that the chart does not extend to the zero of the vertical scale. Such a chart may give a false impression of much more violent fluctuation than would be interpreted from a chart plotted on the usual co-ordinate field and showing the zero of the vertical scale.

Fig. 92 is taken from the United States Government *Crop Reporter*, a magazine widely distributed to farmers.

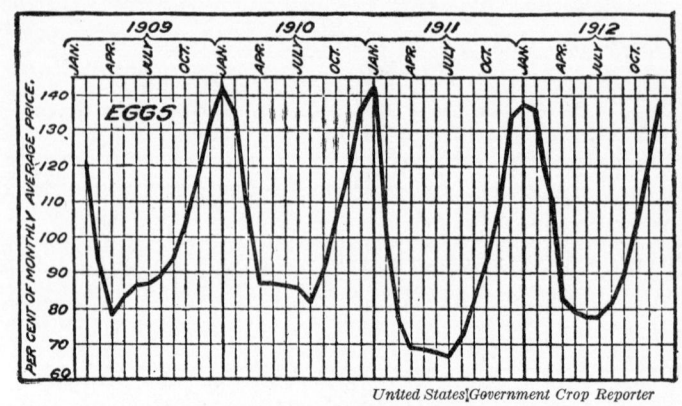

Fig. 92. Fluctuation in the Price of Eggs in the United States as Compared with the Average of the Monthly Figures for the Preceding Four Years

An untrained reader may not realize that this chart must be read from the line representing 100 per cent. Charts for index numbers, where the fluctuation is compared with 100 per cent, should have the 100 per cent line made broad, and a wavy line should be used at the bottom of the chart unless the zero of the scale is shown. An alternative arrangement is shown in Fig. 93

It has been the hope of this magazine to give producers of agricultural products an opportunity to study the price records of previous years, so that they may, in so far as possible, sell at the time of the year when prices are the highest. It is much to be doubted whether the average reader of charts like that seen in Fig. 92 would realize that the 100 per cent line must be used as a basis for interpreting the chart. The 100 per cent line has not been made any heavier than the other lines on the sheet. A man who had been at all accustomed to reading charts having zero at the base of the chart would be apt to read Fig. 92 as though the bottom line were the zero from which the curve had been drawn. On such a basis, he might think that the price of eggs in January, 1912, was more than eight times the price in July, 1911. Such a conclusion would, of course, be entirely unwarranted by the actual figures.

Where charts for index numbers are made on the 100 per cent basis, it would seem best to have a broad line for the 100 per cent line. If there is not room to extend the co-ordinate field down to the zero of the vertical scale, the co-ordinate field may be shown broken off with a wavy line at the base indicating to the reader that the bottom of the chart is not a zero line, and that the chart must be read on the 100 per cent basis.

Fig. 93 was drawn from the data of Fig. 92 as a suggestion for a type of chart which might be used where an untrained class of readers must be reached. By plotting increases above the zero line and decreases below the zero line, a chart is obtained which needs little space and which nevertheless is on a large scale, giving a great amount of detail so as to permit accurate reading of all the various points on the curve. There is very small chance for any untrained reader to misinterpret a chart made by the general method used in Fig. 93.

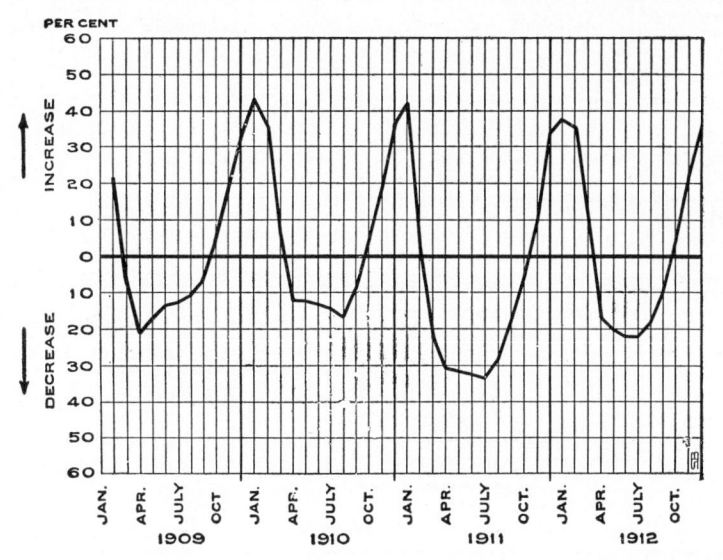

Fig. 93. Fluctuation in the Price of Eggs in the United States as Compared with the Average of the Monthly Figures for the Preceding Four Years

The Government *Crop Reporter* is intended to be of service to farmers. Any charts included should be as clear as it is possible to make them. The illustration above is submitted only as a suggestion

Fig. 94 is essentially a chart relating to index numbers. The vertical scale, instead of being shown with 100 per cent to represent unity, has zero placed opposite the line representing unity. The chart does not clearly point out that the curve drawn above the zero or unity line represents increases in revenues and not total revenues. A much greater fault with the chart, however, is found in the fact that the chart compares the operation of a railroad in different years by using the year 1908 as unity. 1908 was a panic year, with very serious business depression affecting railroads even more than some

102   GRAPHIC METHODS

of the industrial companies. All the years following 1908 are likely to show a greatly increased volume of business in practically any field of commerce or industry. Because 1908 was selected as unity in Fig. 94, the reader would be justified in feeling that the increased amount of revenue in the years following 1908 might have come solely from the improvement in general business conditions, without any assistance whatever from ability in managing the railroad. If the betterment in the general prosperity of the country were great enough, it might even be possible to show in Fig. 94 a large increase in operating revenue due only to the general improvement in business conditions and in spite of reduced efficiency in the operation of this individual railroad, considered *per se*. It is not intended here to cast any reflections upon the managing ability on the railroad in question. The only object in mentioning the matter at all is to point out the fact that the use of the year 1908 as unity puts the road unnecessarily under suspicion of attempting to mislead the public.

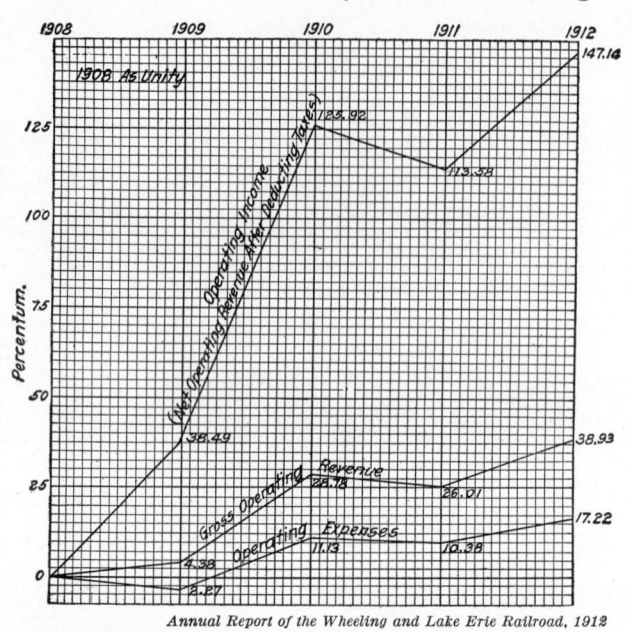

Fig. 94. Improvement in Economy of Operation of the Wheeling and Lake Erie Railroad, 1908 to 1912

It will be noticed from the upper left-hand corner of the chart that the year 1908 is taken as unity. 1908 was a year of great business depression. As business conditions naturally improved in the years following 1908, there could be a legitimate question in the reader's mind whether the better showing of the railroad is due to better management or to the increase in the general prosperity of the country

In any chart where index numbers are used the greatest care should be taken to select as unity a set of conditions thoroughly typical and representative. It is frequently best to take as unity the average of a series of years immediately preceding the years for which a study is to be made. The series of years averaged to represent unity should, if possible, be so selected that they will include one full cycle or wave of fluctuation. If one complete cycle involves too many years, then the years selected as unity should be taken in equal number on either side of a year which represents most nearly the normal condition.

Fig. 95 is an illustration reduced in size from a large chart 10 by 14 inches. The chart is of especial interest because it is one of a series of several hundred charts submitted to the board of arbitration in the concerted wage movement in the eastern territory by the Order of Railroad Conductors and Brotherhood of Railroad Trainmen in 1913. These charts cover practically all phases of railroad operation and give in condensed form a tremendous quantity of information.

RELATIVE RETAIL PRICES OF FOOD: SIMPLE AND WEIGHTED AVERAGES—UNITED STATES 1890–1912
AVERAGE PRICE FOR 1890–1899 = 100.0

Year	Simple Average	Relative Prices
1890	102.0	101.9
1891	103.6	103.4
1892	101.7	101.6
1893	104.6	104.1
1894	99.5	99.2
1895	97.2	97.1
1896	94.9	95.2
1897	96.4	96.7
1898	99.4	99.7
1899	100.6	100.8
1900	102.9	103.0
1901	109.5	108.5
1902	116.8	114.6
1903	116.9	114.7
1904	118.3	116.2
1905	118.3	116.4
1906	122.4	120.3
1907	128.0	125.9
1908	132.5	130.1
1909	140.3	137.2
1910	148.5	144.1
1911	146.6	143.0
1912	157.9	154.2

——— SIMPLE AVERAGE [1]
- - - - - RELATIVE PRICES [2]

[1] SIMPLE AVERAGE OF THE RELATIVE PRICES OF 15 PRINCIPAL ARTICLES OF FOOD. From Bureau of Labor Statistics, U.S. Department of Labor

[2] RELATIVE PRICES WEIGHTED ACCORDING TO THE AVERAGE CONSUMPTION OF THE VARIOUS ARTICLES OF FOOD IN WORKINGMEN'S FAMILIES.

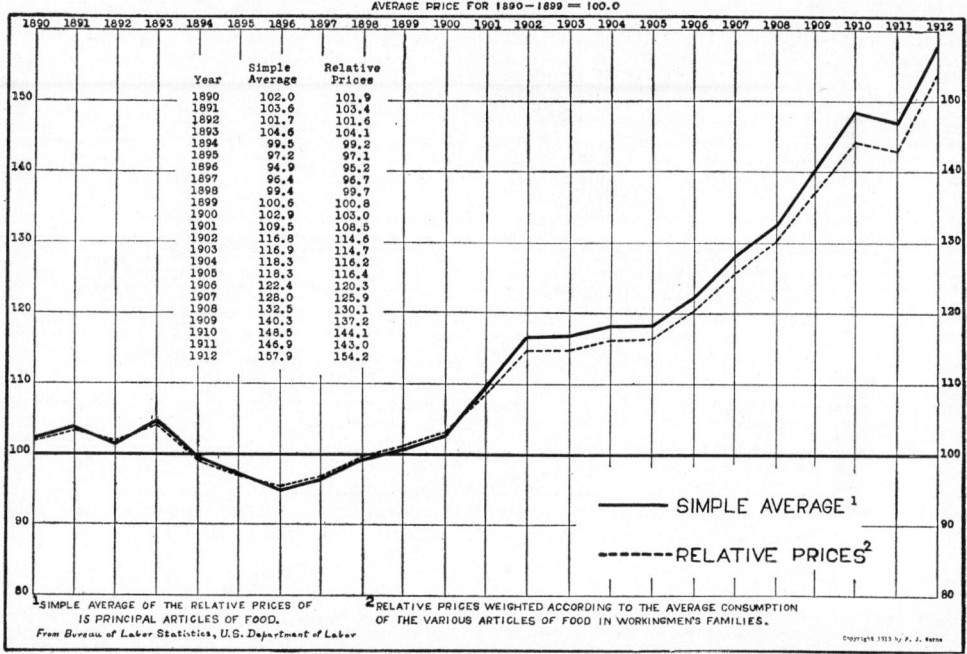

Courtesy of F. J. Warne, Washington, D. C.

Fig. 95. Relative Retail Prices of Fifteen Principal Articles of Food in the United States, 1890 to 1912, by Simple Averages and by Weighted Averages. Average Prices for the Years 1890 to 1899, Inclusive, Were Taken as 100 Per Cent

The solid line shows ordinary averages of the prices for each year considered. In order to get the data for the dotted line, estimates were carefully made of the average consumption in workingmen's families of each of the fifteen various articles of food. The food prices were then "weighted" in proportion to the quantities of each kind actually consumed and the averages shown by the dotted line were obtained. The prices of foods to the workmen did not increase as much as the simple averages shown by the solid line would indicate

There is such a great quantity of data arranged in convenient form for reference, it seems likely that a person wishing to study railroad operation could obtain more insight into present-day railroad conditions by two-hours' study of this series of charts than he could pos-

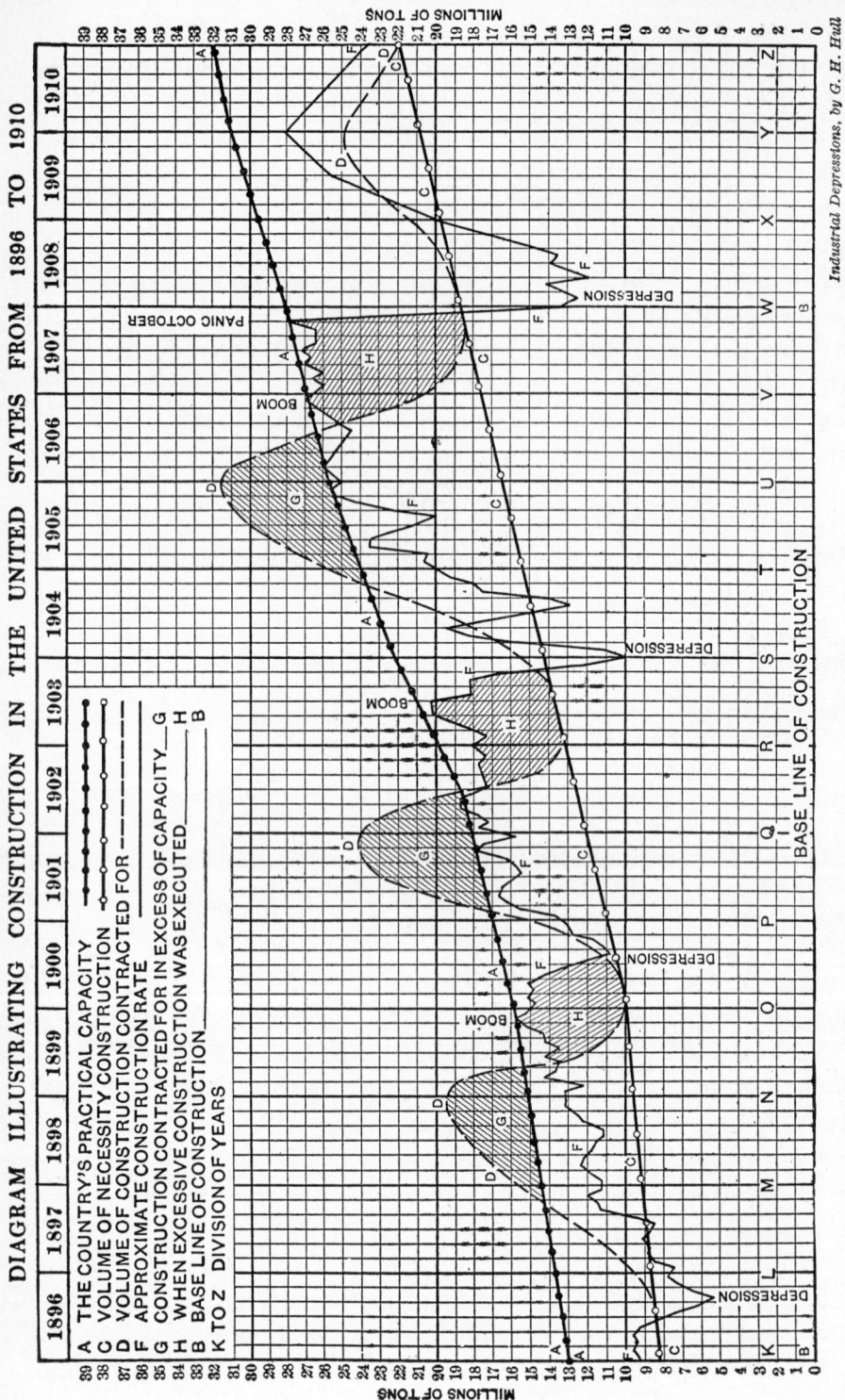

Fig. 96. A Study of Steel-Construction Work in the United States from 1896 to 1910 as Related to the Financial Condition of the Country

The key in the upper portion of the chart gives the titles for the different curves. Charts of this general type are of tremendous importance to the business man for studying financial conditions as affecting any particular industry. As no two businesses are exactly alike, it is best for each business to make up its own charts relating to the financial situation and general prosperity

sibly obtain by two months of reading the reports of transportation companies and the pages of railway journals, and of asking questions from railroad executives.

A heavy line in Fig. 95 shows the relative average prices of fifteen articles of food used in workmen's families. Since the fifteen articles of food are not consumed in equal quantities, or in equal value, it was necessary to take into account the actual quantity or value used of each kind of food. This was done by the method usually designated by the name "weighted averages". It is obviously of less importance to the workingman if the price of salt should increase 500 per cent than if the price of bread or meat should increase 50 per cent. When the fifteen articles of food are considered by simple averages, all foods are considered as though used in equal quantities and a very great increase in the value of some one food would seriously affect the simple average even though that food is consumed in only small quantity. By weighted averages the actual price of any food is multiplied by the budget percentage figure showing the percentage of that food used. The products resulting from the multiplication are added for each year, and the totals or averages are compared on a percentage basis to give a corrected comparison by weighted averages of food prices in different years. The weighted averages represent more accurately than simple averages the increases in food prices as they really affect the pocketbook of the workingman. It will be seen at the right of Fig. 95 that the heavy line for simple averages is considerably higher than the dotted line representing the weighted averages. This shows the amount of error which would have resulted in this particular study if only simple averages had been used for comparison instead of weighted averages. Weighted averages are of very great importance in most studies relating to the cost of living, and they could be used in other work much more widely than at present if their importance and utility were more generally understood. It is unfortunate that in Fig. 95 the term "relative prices" is used in the lower portion of the chart as the key for the dotted line. The simple averages show relative prices also and the term "relative prices" means practically nothing. The dotted line could more properly be referred to by the term "weighted averages" as used in the title at the top of the chart.

Fig. 96 is an example of a type of chart which can be of great assistance to the chief executive of any corporation having a business seriously affected by the ups and downs in financial conditions affecting the country as a whole. In this chart, a study has been made of supply and demand in the hope of getting some basis for prediction in regard to periods of financial depression. The various factors which might affect prosperity in steel construction work are assembled here on one chart so that the whole situation may be studied conveniently and thoroughly. In a chart of this kind some estimates and approximations must be made because it is usually impossible to obtain accurate data to the extent desired. For work of this nature it will ordinarily be found that a little "horse-sense", used in making estimates for missing data, will permit the construction of a chart giving an astonishingly large number of suggestions useful in determining the policy of a business, so that expansion and contraction may be in harmony with the basic financial conditions of the country.

Chapter VII

COMPARISON OF CURVES

THERE are many men who from long experience have become so skillful that they can glance down a column of figures and obtain quickly a good idea as to the high points and the low points shown by the figures taken as a whole. When it comes to considering two or three columns of figures simultaneously to see whether there is a similarity in the fluctuations shown by the various sets of figures, the number of men who can intelligently grasp the facts presented are rather few. It is in just such problems as these, where a number of different sets of data must be compared, that curves have tremendous advantage over presentation by columns of figures. A man must be almost a genius to grasp quickly the facts contained in several parallel columns of figures, yet anyone of average intelligence can interpret correctly a chart which has been properly made for the presentation of curves. Though there are numerous convenient methods which are useful in comparing curves, we can take up here only the few of those which are likely to be of most frequent use to the average reader.

Fig. 97 brings out the facts of its subject matter with splendid clearness. There are relatively few men who could interpret quickly the data for this chart, if the data were shown to them only as two separate columns of figures. When a chart like that shown in Fig. 97 is used, no mental effort is required to get at the gist of the matter, and the facts can be obtained much more rapidly than would ever be possible by observing columns of figures alone.

A chart like that used in Fig. 97 can be prepared from tabulated figures by any ordinary draftsman in less than one hour of work. The cost of making a line cut is probably no more than the cost of setting the type if the data are to be shown by tabulated figures. The space required for a chart like Fig. 97 is very little more than would be required for the tabulated figures, and if there is any serious limitation on space, Fig. 97 could be much reduced in size without detracting from its clearness.

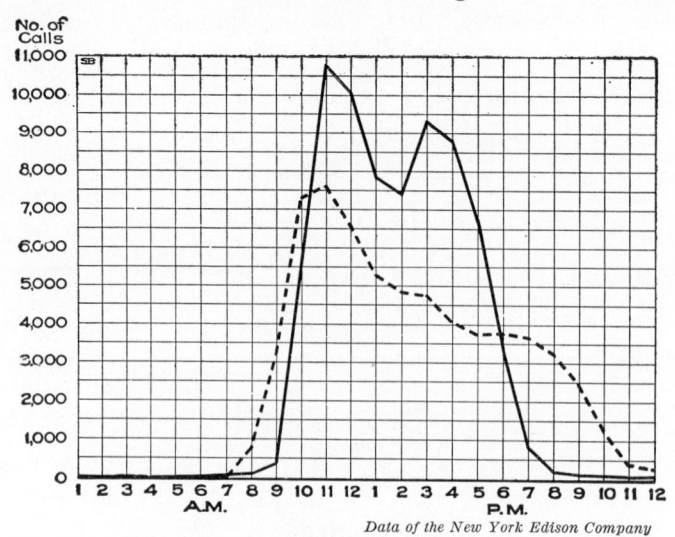

Fig. 97. Number of Telephone Messages Each Hour for One Day in a Business District in New York City as Compared with a Residence District

Solid line, the "Broad" exchange—a typical business exchange
Dotted line, the "Riverside" exchange—a typical residence exchange
Note the great number of business calls after mail has been opened in the morning and after return from lunch. In the residence district there is much morning shopping by telephone

Data of the New York Edison Company

Health-department reports are not usually of interest to the layman. Yet health-department reports, well presented, may be of as much popular interest as a well-written magazine article. Fig. 98 is taken from a commendable report by the health department of the city of Boston. In the report itself, different colors of ink were used for the various curves, with the effect of emphasizing the contrast.

Though the colored inks assisted in catching the eye of the reader, the chart with curves designated by letters is usually sufficient for all practical purposes whenever the curves do not cross over each other in such manner as to be confusing. As mentioned elsewhere, a certain slope of a curve plotted on rectangular co-ordinate paper does not in itself indicate a greater or less amount of increase or decrease than holds true for some other curve having a different slope. The slope of a curve plotted on paper with ordinary co-ordinate ruling depends largely on whether the data of the curve are in large figures, so as to bring the curve near the top of the chart, or in small figures, bringing the curve near the bottom of the chart. In Fig. 98 the fact that curve A slopes more than curve C is due to the fact that curve A is placed higher on the vertical scale of the chart than curve C. A little study will show that the reduction in mortality portrayed by curve A is much less on a percentage basis than that depicted by curve C, yet curve A has the steeper slope. The slope of these two curves can best be compared if a pencil line is drawn in such manner that the peaks above the pencil line are approximately equal to the valleys below the pencil line for each curve.

Fig. 99 contains some interesting information. Though the chart proves fairly well the close dependence of the price of cast-iron pipe upon the price of the pig iron from which it is made, the chart is nevertheless misleading in that the first glance would indicate a much greater fluctuation in the price of pig iron than actually occurred.

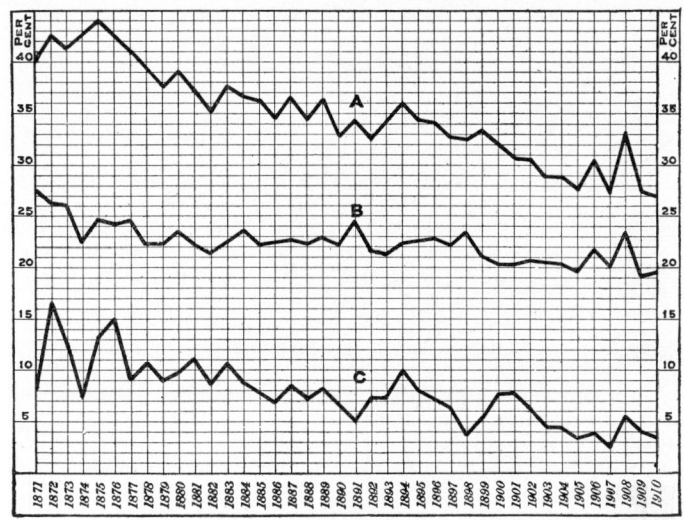

From the 1910 Annual Report of the Health Department, City of Boston

Fig. 98. Deaths in Boston of Children under Five Years of Age, under One Year, and from Five of the Principal Infectious Diseases, Expressed as a Percentage of the Total Mortality

Curve A. Deaths of children under five years of age as a percentage of the total mortality

Curve B. Deaths of children under one year as a percentage of the total mortality

Curve C. Deaths from Diphtheria, Scarlet Fever, Measles, Typhoid Fever and Smallpox as a percentage of the total mortality

Note that Curve A shows a much steeper slope than Curve C, yet Curve C drops in 1910 to less than half the figure for 1871. Curves plotted by rectangular co-ordinates should not be compared by the slope of the different curve lines

The reader is apt to overlook the fact that the vertical scale of the chart does not extend below $11 per ton. He is quite likely to think that the price of pig iron had all the rapid fluctuations which would be indicated by the changing vertical distances between the pig-iron curve and the bottom line of the chart itself. The amount of fluctuation would look much less if the chart extended to the zero line of the vertical scale.

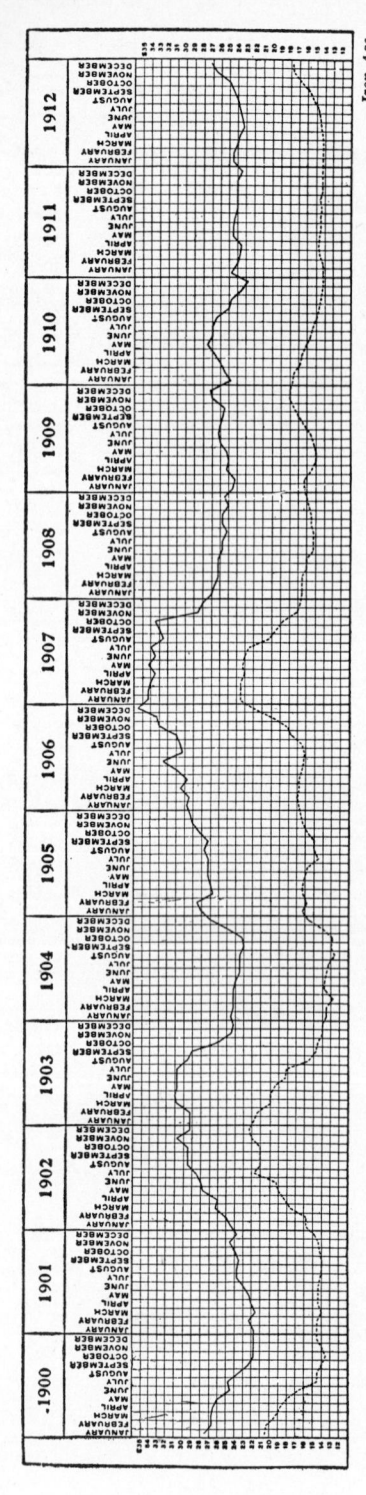

Fig. 99. Price of 6-Inch Cast-Iron Water Pipe per Net Ton in Carload Lots at New York City, Compared with Price of Gray Forge Pig Iron per Gross Ton at Philadelphia

Notice how closely the price of cast-iron pipe depends upon the price of the material used in making it. There is not great variation in the margin between cost of material and cost of product. The rapid reader is not apt to notice that the scale of prices begins at $11 per ton and not at zero. If the chart were so made as to show the zero line it would give a different impression. Dates are better shown at the base of a chart than at the top.

There is probably a fallacy in Fig. 100 because of the rise in the general standard of living between 1901 and 1906. It is not fair to the 1901 Princeton men to expect that they would earn as much immediately after graduation as men who graduated in a period of time several years later. In addition to this there is probably another serious fallacy which affects all three curves shown on the chart. The income figures from which the curves are plotted may not all be shown on the same basis. Men working on a salary have as net cash all the money they receive. Men in professions such as law, medicine, etc., where office rent and other expenses are likely to be very heavy, may report, as earnings, the total amount of money received without making corrections for the expenses of conducting their business. In other words, they may very possibly in this case report gross income instead of net income. Such procedure might tend to make the curves for average income considerably higher than they would otherwise be.

Complex charts made up of groups of bars as seen in Fig. 101 are much more common than they should be. This type of chart is very annoying to read because it is difficult for the eye to follow, through the whole series, the bars representing any one set of facts which may be of special interest. The bar method is in itself a simple one, but when the bars are combined in the manner shown in Fig. 101 the presentation becomes really more complex than if the data were shown in the form of curves.

Fig. 102 certainly brings out the information of Fig. 101 in much better form than any in which it is possible to show it by any combination of bars either vertical or horizontal. The person who is just beginning to chart data which he has used formerly in tabulated form is often surprised to find how many inconsistencies exist in the data and how many different things there are which must be allowed for by some method of estimate. In Fig. 102 the data for the United Kingdom are expressed in net tons, and for the United States in gross tons. Though some correction of the forms of the curves as they appear in this chart would of course have to be made to get a true comparison of the shipping of the two countries, for our purpose the thing of greatest interest is the general tendency of shipping in the two countries. This we can study fairly well from the general shape of the different curves, even though the curves cannot strictly be compared with each other in so far as total quantities are concerned.

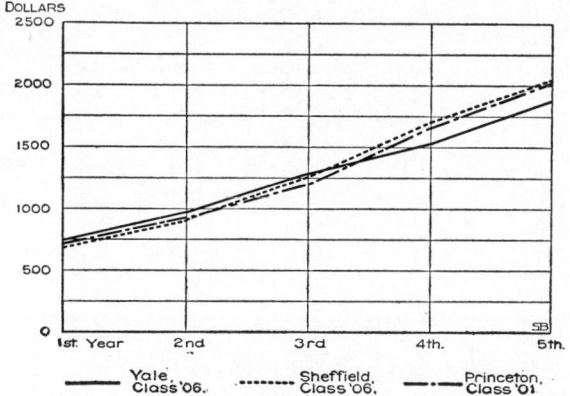

Fig. 100. Comparison of the Earnings for Five Years after Graduation of the Yale University Academic Department Class of 1906, the Yale Sheffield Scientific School Class of 1906, and the Princeton University Class of 1901

There is a fallacy in making this comparison. The standard of living undoubtedly went up between 1901 and 1906

Fig. 103 shows a convenient method for determining what fluctuations in the different months of the year are typical for any subject being studied. Instead of plotting one continuous curve by months for a long series of years to a rather small horizontal scale, a large horizontal scale is used and a separate curve is drawn for each year. The curves for different years are placed one above the other, so that any fluctuations which appear in the same months year after year

112   GRAPHIC METHODS

will be apparent from the similarity in the shape of the curves for the different years.

In order to use a fairly large vertical scale so as to make the fluctuations stand out clearly, it was necessary to avoid entirely the zero lines for the curves plotted in Fig. 103. The omission of the zero lines may cause the fluctuations from month to month to appear greater than their true size would warrant. It is sometimes possible to plot a chart on the general scheme of Fig. 103 so as to use zero lines, but many times it will be found that the zero lines cannot be used without adding confusion. Though it would be preferable to have the zero lines included, the gain due to the arrangement of the curves as shown here for comparative purposes is great enough to offset the disadvantage of not having the zero lines on the chart.

The zinc plate for Fig. 103 was prepared directly from typewritten copy, with no handwork involved except to make heavier some of the green background lines and to draw the actual curves themselves. Notice in Fig. 103 that the month at the left of the chart is December, and that the point plotted in each case for December at the left is exactly the same as the point plotted for the December shown at the right of the preceding curve. By repeating the last month of each curve in this manner, the interpretation of the curves is much simplified so that the reader can see at once what has been the tendency of the curve from December to January each year. If the December

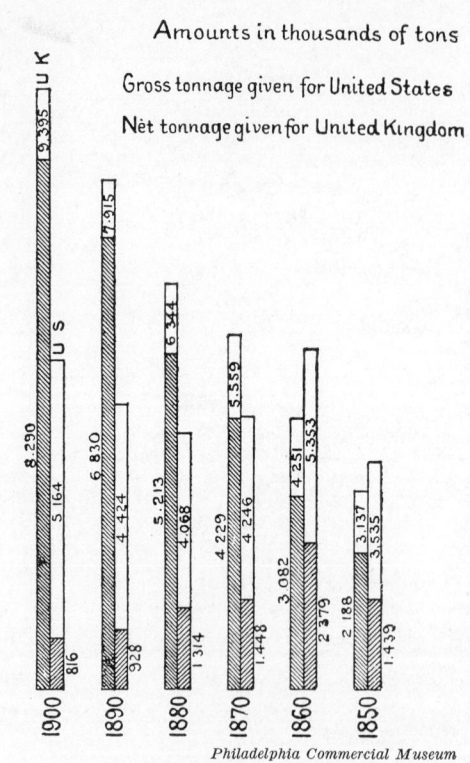

Fig. 101. Comparison since 1850 of the Merchant Tonnage of the United Kingdom with that of the United States. Gross Tonnage is Given for the United States and Net Tonnage for the United Kingdom

The chart is arranged backwards in that it reads from right to left. At first sight one thinks everything is growing smaller instead of larger. The different bars so closely grouped together are exceedingly difficult to interpret. See Fig. 102

COMPARISON OF CURVES 113

point were not represented at the left, it would be necessary for the reader to glance several times from the left-hand end of one curve to the right-hand end of the preceding curve to determine in his own mind just what changes had occurred from December to January

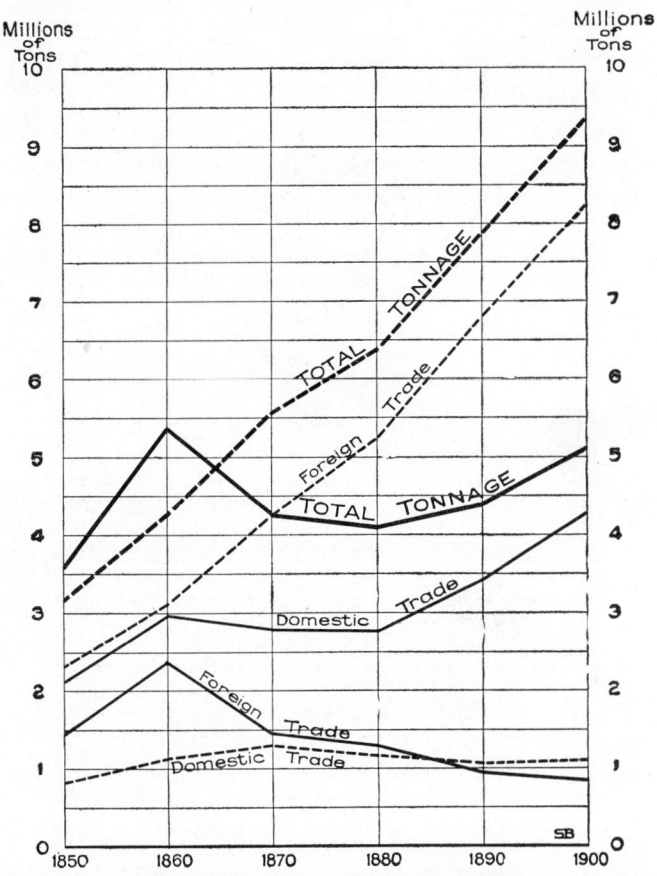

Fig. 102. Comparison since 1850 of the Merchant Tonnage of the United Kingdom with that of the United States

Gross tonnage is given for the United States and net tonnage for the United Kingdom. Solid lines United States, dotted lines United Kingdom. The "total" figures are not strictly comparable because of the difference in registration method. The general tendencies of the curves are instructive, however. Note the reduction in the foreign trade of United States since the Civil War and the steadily increasing foreign trade of the United Kingdom

at the end of each year. The repetition of the point for the last month in each year saves time to the reader and also insures against errors which might otherwise occur in the interpretation of the chart.

In Fig. 104 three distinct subjects are compared on one chart and, at the same time, the data for each subject are shown for three

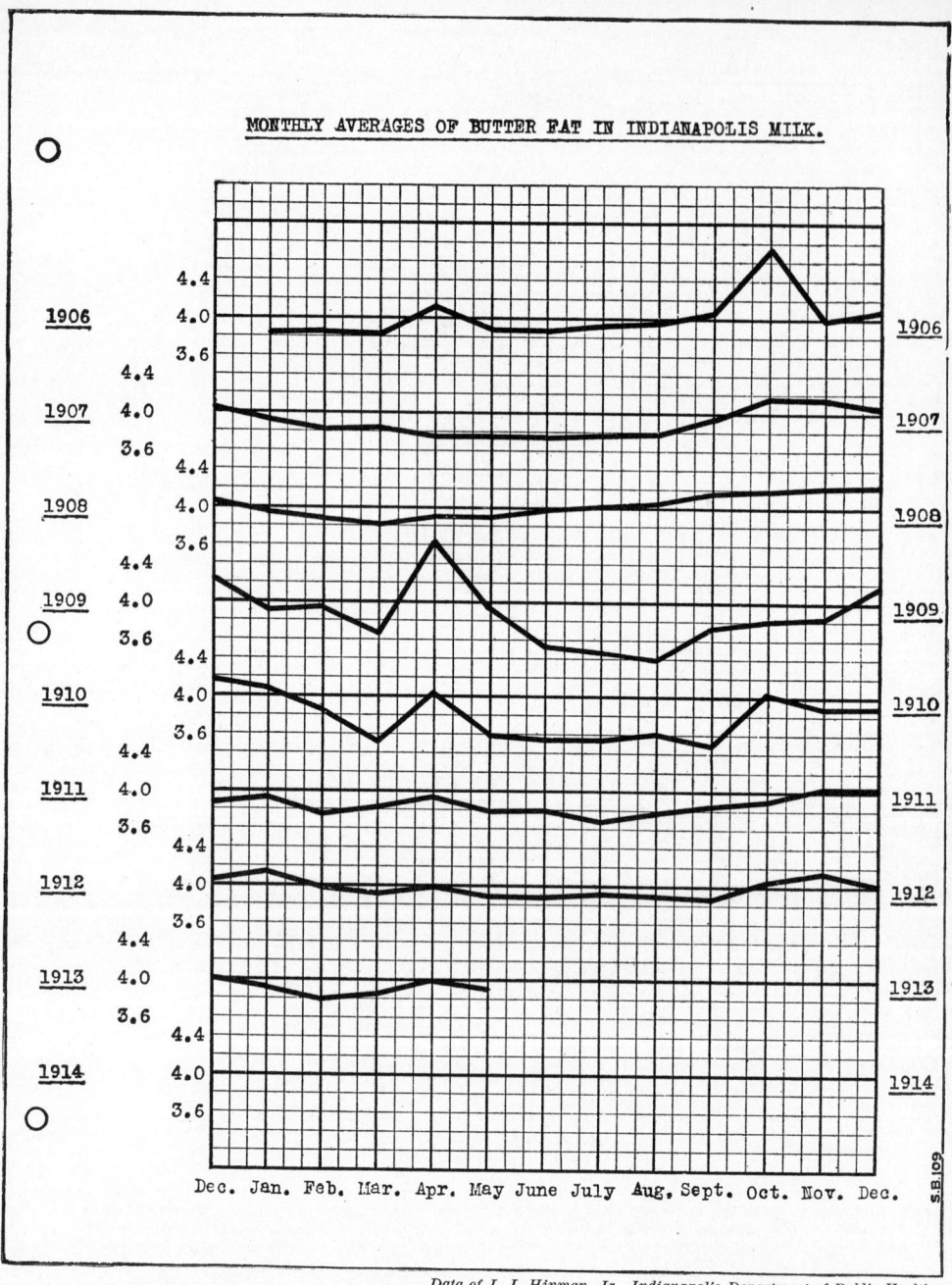

Fig. 103. Monthly Averages of Butterfat Contained in Milk on the Indianapolis Market, 1906 to 1913. The Curves Represent Averages from Several Hundred Samples each Month

In order to find what fluctuations are typical for various months of the year, it is convenient to chart the data as seen here with curves for different years one above the other. Definite peaks in April and in October or November are seen at once. This chart is drawn on the same universal co-ordinate paper shown also in Fig. 57, Fig. 130, Fig. 134 and Fig. 156

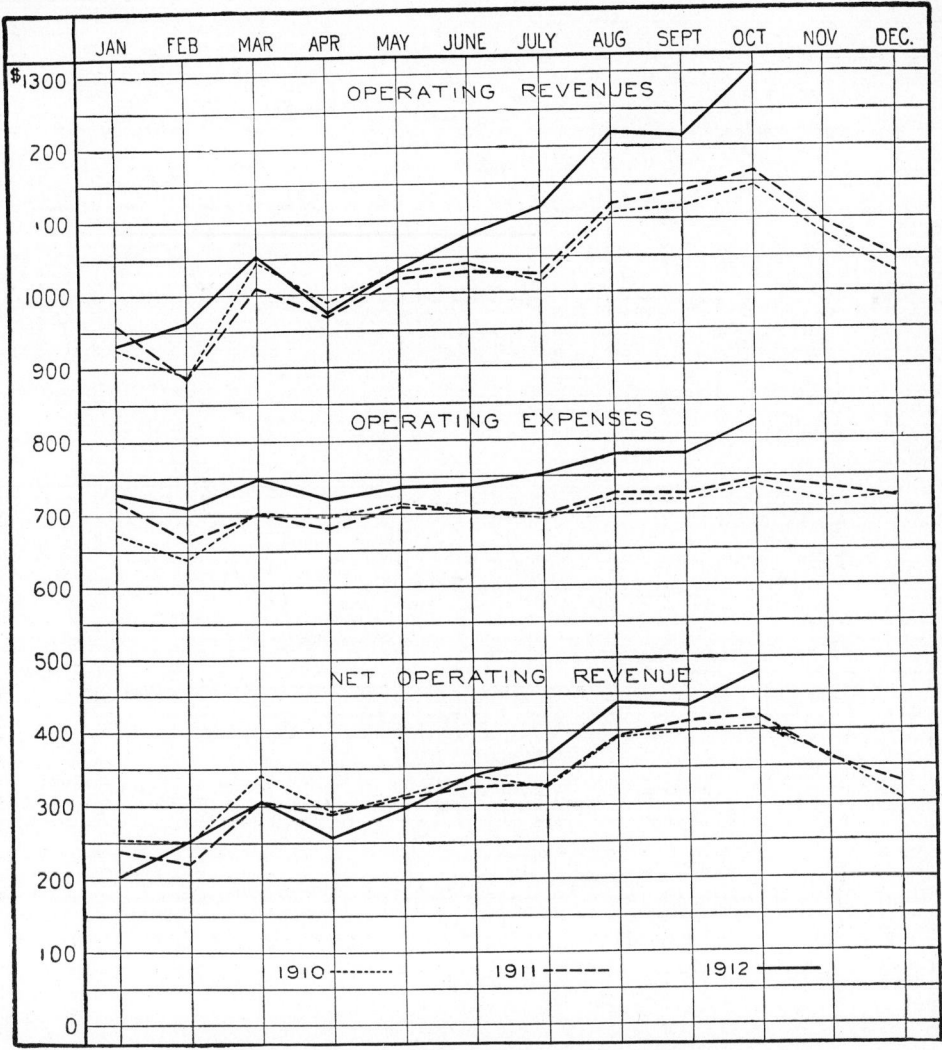

Fig. 104. Comparative Monthly Earnings and Expenses per Mile of Road of Steam Railroads in the United States Having Annual Operating Revenues of $1,000,000 or More

It is frequently convenient to superimpose curves for successive years, so that seasonal similarities and definite increases or decreases may be accurately studied. Compare this chart with Fig. 103 and also with Fig. 204. It would be better if the heavy line border around the edge of this chart were omitted. The heavy line at the bottom does not coincide with the zero line and the reader may be misled by reading the chart from the border line

different years so that comparisons between these different years are easily made. This scheme of superimposing curves for different years is a very common one that frequently gives an arrangement more convenient than could otherwise be obtained. It will be noticed

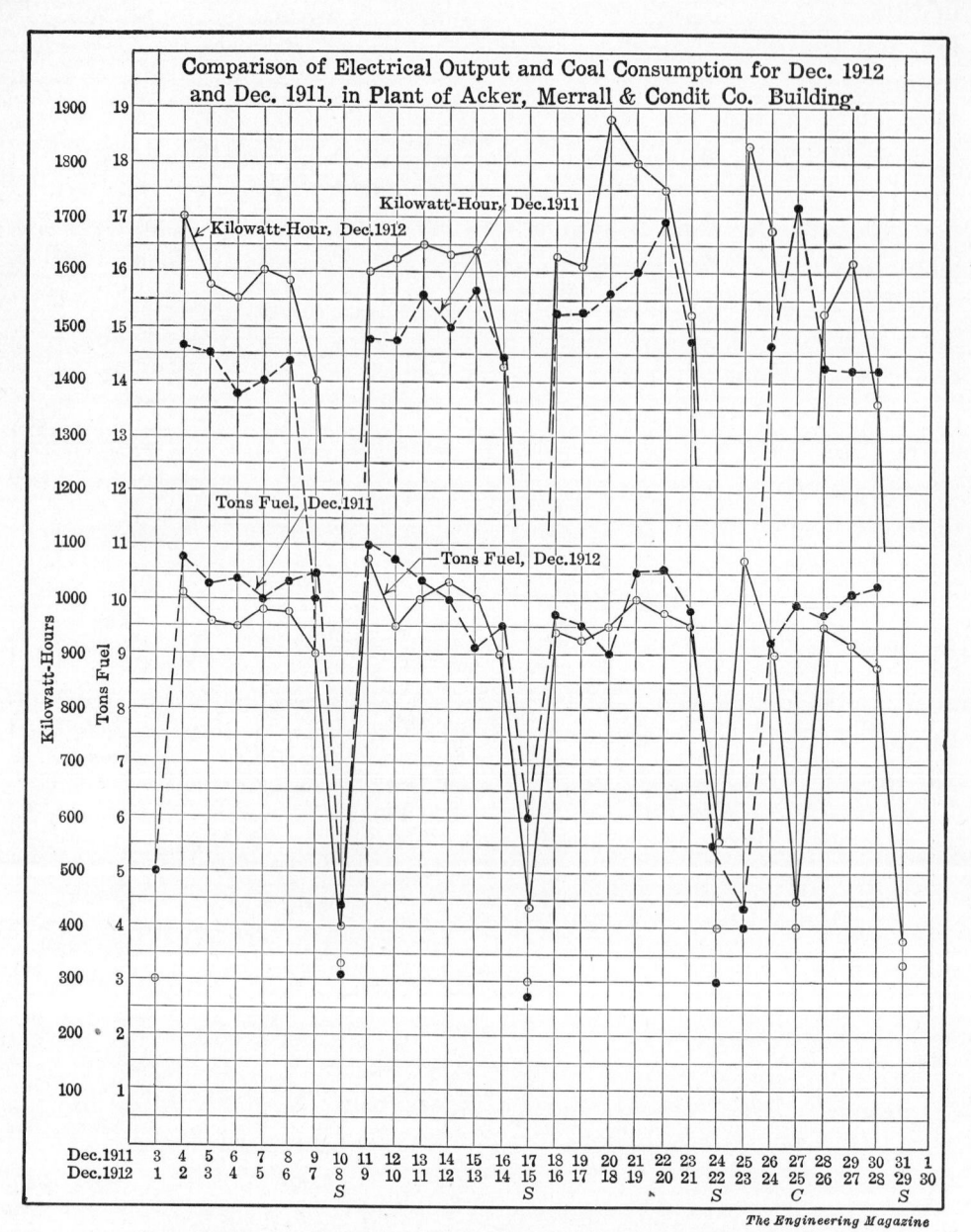

Fig. 105. Comparison of Daily Electrical Output and Daily Coal Consumption of a Power Plant for the Same Month in Two Succeeding Years

There is a relatively small quantity of power needed on Sundays. In order to make possible a comparison of the two curves for different years the horizontal scales for days were so placed that the Sundays would coincide. With curves thus arranged, the low points caused by Christmas do not fall on the same vertical line, since Christmas is fixed by the day of the month instead of by the day of the week

in this chart that the December points have not been repeated at the left and the reader is forced to glance between left and right in order to make certain in his own mind just what changes occurred from December to January each year. It can be seen that the January figures for "Operating Revenues" are all considerably lower than the December figures, but even so the reader has no clear idea of the slope of the lines which would be most typical to portray the changes from December to January in each year. This question of repeating one point for curves of different years superimposed is referred to also in Chapter XIII, Fig. 204.

Fig. 105, Fig. 106, and Fig. 107 are self-explanatory. They show some interesting applications of curves to special problems, and demonstrate the great convenience which might result if curves could be more generally used for presenting every-day facts to non-technical readers.

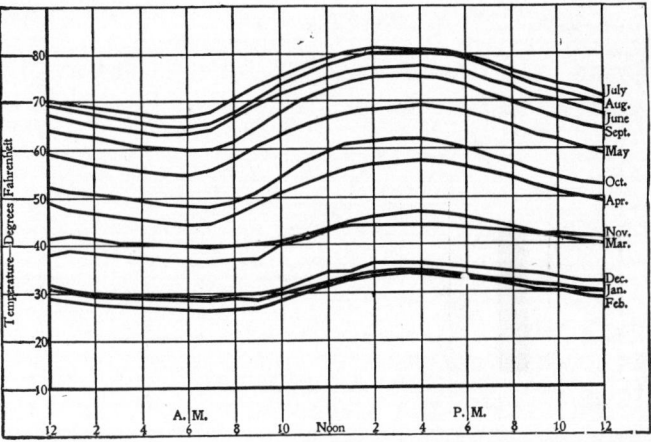

Fig. 106. Average Temperature at Pittsburgh, Pa., for Each Hour in the Day for Different Months in the Year. Plotted for Monthly Averages of Twenty-Years Observations (1891-1910) of the United States Weather Bureau

It would be impossible, using only columns of figures, to put this information in such convenient form for reference and comparison. The broad horizontal line at 10 degrees on the vertical scale of this chart and of Fig. 107 is unfortunate since that line has no special significance for persons reading the chart

In Fig. 108 we see the application of curves to the kind of data of which it would be extremely difficult to give a clear understanding if only columns of figures were available in the presentation. With these two curves we are not so much interested in the total height of the peak as in the general shape of the curve on either side of the peak, showing whether there are any laws of uniformity in the increase of the flood level and in the speed with which the flood subsided. The two curves in Fig. 108 are quite different in their shape, although they were taken for the same period of time in districts not widely separated. The size and general character of different water-sheds have

118   GRAPHIC METHODS

a great effect on the nature of the floods which may result from any definite rainfall.

In Fig. 109 also we are particularly interested in comparing the shape of the curves for the distinctly different materials under consideration. Here the curves represent reactions affected by the definite laws of physics, and we can join the plotted points resulting from different observations so as to get smooth curves. Work in engineering, physics, and chemistry depends very largely on the interpretation of smooth curves like these, and world progress would be greatly retarded if the graphic method were not available to assist in preserving and interpreting the results of elaborate experiment and voluminous research.

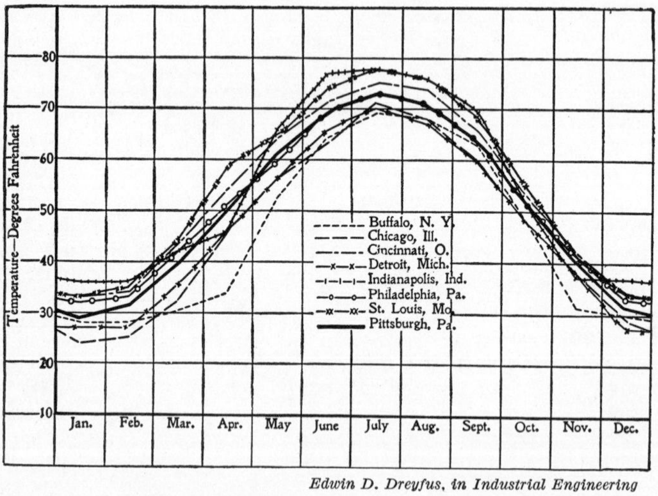

Fig. 107. Mean Temperatures for Each Month in the Year at Different Cities. Plotted from Records of the United States Signal Service and of Blodgett's Climatology of the United States

Information for eight different cities is so given that comparisons are easily made. Note the different lines used here instead of colors. Since Pittsburgh was the city under prime consideration, the Pittsburgh line was made heavy that it might be most clearly seen. This chart gives a great amount of data in smaller space than would be required to show the facts by any method other than the use of curves

In selecting a scale for Fig. 110 the draftsman is torn between a desire to show the San Francisco fire peak at its correct height, and an opposing desire to show on a large scale the data for a whole series of years so that the fluctuations from month to month may be clearly defined. It seemed best to cut off the top of the San Francisco peak so as to show the monthly data on a scale large enough to assure clearness. To get the correct slope for the two sides of the San Francisco peak, a piece of paper was laid down adjoining the chart and a point was located in the correct position for the top of the San Francisco peak. The sides of the peak were then drawn so that they would meet at that point if extended. Even though the figures for the San Francisco peak are given at the top of the chart where the peak is broken off, most readers will not imagine correctly the great height to which that peak would extend if it were shown in full. The chart could have been greatly improved if the upper portion of the peak had been drawn in full size horizontally as though hinged near the upper margin of the drawing. Since the full height of the peak is

Engineering Record

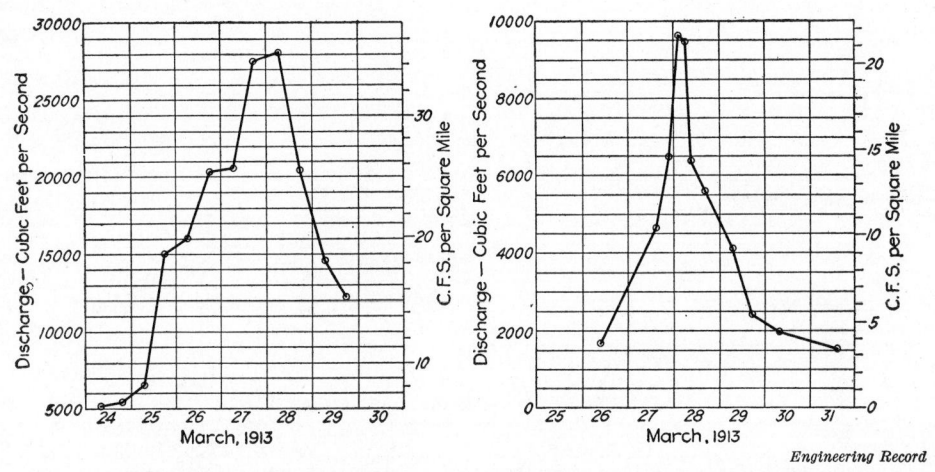

Fig. 108. Comparison of Flood Rise in Two Rivers in New York State During the Floods of March, 1913

In the preceding illustrations of this chapter there has been such similarity in the shape of the curves considered that they were superimposed for comparison. Here the curves are of different shape and they are shown in separate fields so that the contrast may be more striking. The chart at the left should have had the zero line shown. It is dangerous to base conclusions on the comparison of two curves unless the zero lines are shown in each case

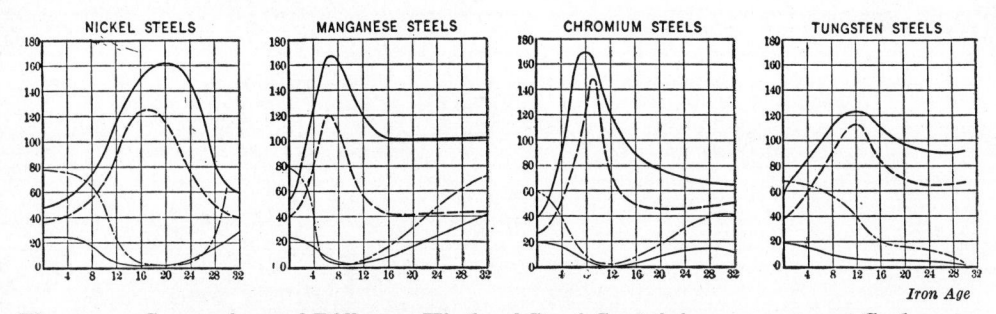

Iron Age

Fig. 109. Comparison of Different Kinds of Steel Containing 0.2 per cent Carbon, as shown by Tensile Tests on Specimens 100 mm. long and 13.8 mm. diameter. The Vertical Scale Represents Thousands of Pounds per Square Inch and also Percentage of Contraction or Elongation

The heavy line shows ultimate strength
The dash line shows elastic limit
The dash-dot line shows percentage contraction
The light line shows percentage elongation
In this chart the thing of greatest interest is the contrast seen by comparing the shapes of the curves for different steels. Though it is best to have curves of such distinct shape plotted in separate fields, it is ordinarily most convenient to have the fields themselves placed vertically instead of horizontally

120 GRAPHIC METHODS

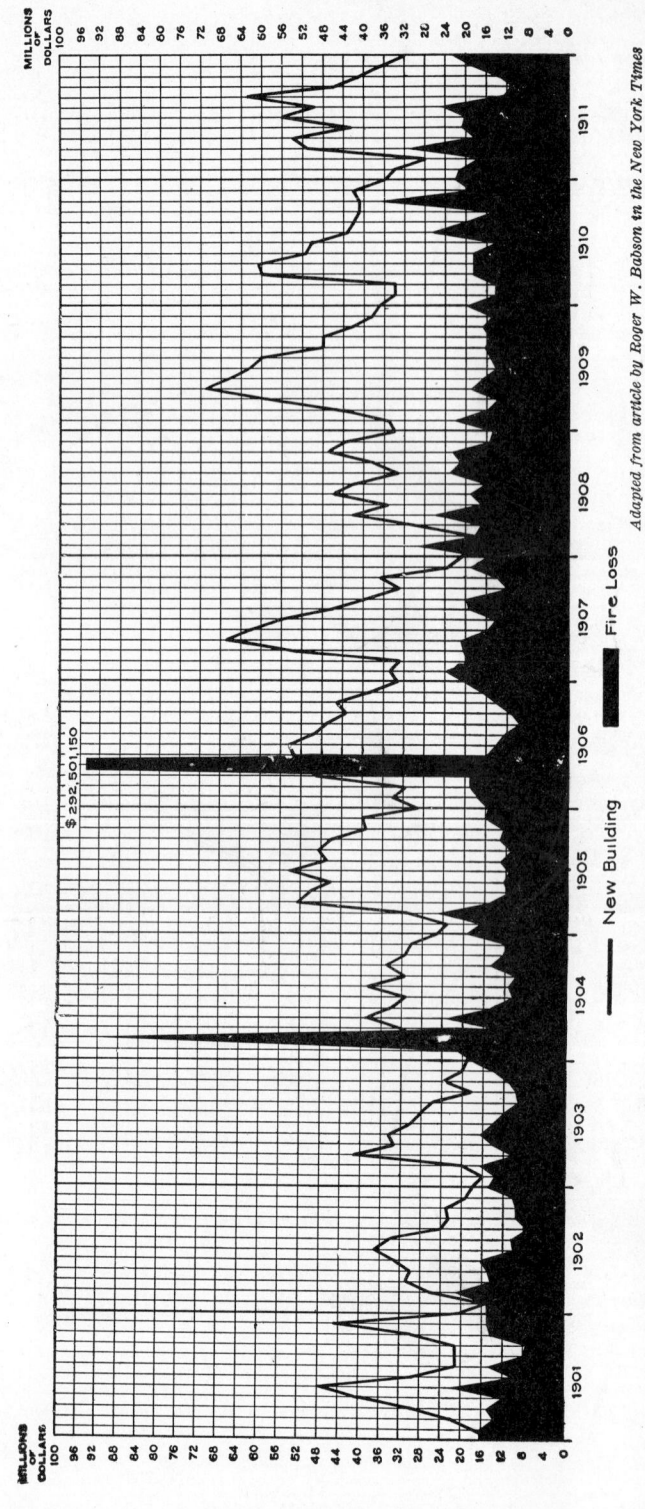

Fig. 110. Monthly Value of New Building Construction and Monthly Value of Buildings Destroyed by Fire in the United States, 1901 to 1911, Inclusive

Adapted from article by Roger W. Babson in the New York Times

The greatest volume of new building construction occurs in the spring months. Note in 1908 the effect of the 1907 panic. The peak in 1904 represents the Baltimore fire and that in 1906 the San Francisco fire. It would have been better to show the upper portion of the San Francisco peak by bending horizontally that portion which could not be shown vertically to the scale of this chart. See also Fig. 111

almost three times the height of the portion shown on this illustration, it would be necessary to make two other hinges in the horizontal extension so that the peak could be bent downward and turned backward from right to left, giving something of a spiral effect. Though this bent peak may seem rather artificial, it is quite certain that the

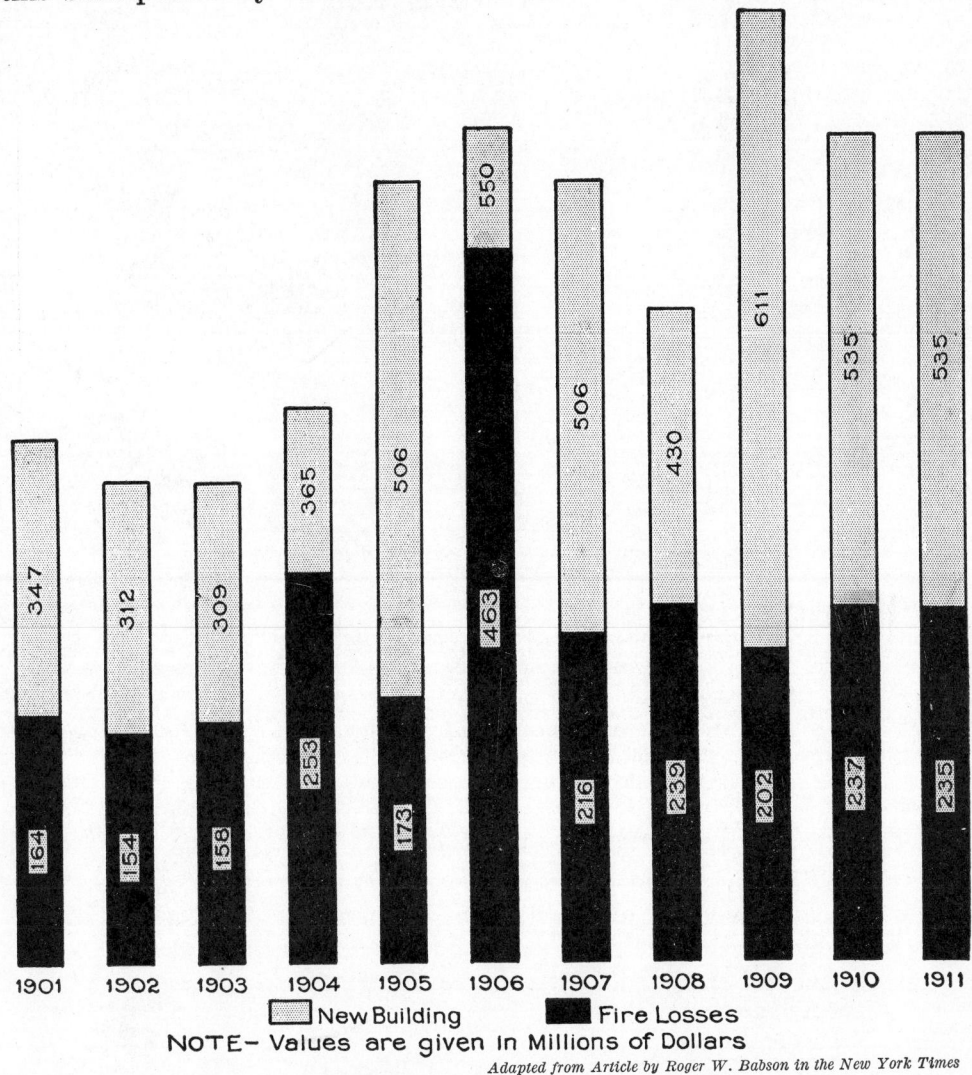

Fig. 111. **Yearly Value of New Building Construction and Yearly Value of Buildings Destroyed by Fire in the United States, 1901 to 1911, Inclusive**

With this arrangement, the percentage value destroyed by fire can be seen more readily than from the arrangement used in Fig. 110. The fluctuation from month to month cannot, however, be seen here. If both charts are used, they supplement each other very well. Remember that for these two charts the buildings destroyed are not necessarily the new buildings whose value is given. The black area represents only the value of buildings destroyed whether new or old. Note the Ben Day shading on the upper ends of the bars and the figures for the data from which the chart was made

tapering form of the horizontal extension of the peak would be understood by even the untrained reader, much more certainly than the chart as shown here with only the figures to indicate the full extent of the loss which occurred in the San Francisco fire.

While Fig. 110 gives some general idea of the proportion which American fire losses bear to the value of new building construction, the two fluctuating curves make it difficult for the reader to make an estimate of the percentage losses year by year. Fig. 111 supplements Fig. 110, and gives for each year the total values for new building construction and the total values of buildings destroyed by fire. Here the percentages of the fire loss are quite obvious when judged by the extent to which the black ink covers the shaded bar representing new building construction. Figures are given in each case for the reader who may care to work out the actual percentage ratios. It must not be assumed from the titles of Fig. 110 and Fig. 111 that the buildings destroyed by fire are the same buildings whose value is recorded in the charts as "new building construction." The rapid advance in the use of fireproof materials makes it likely that the fire losses were more largely from older buildings, built by methods which gave a structure less fireproof than the average for buildings put up in recent years.

Fig. 114 shows an error in curve plotting into which it is very easy for an inexperienced person to slip. One vertical scale is relatively

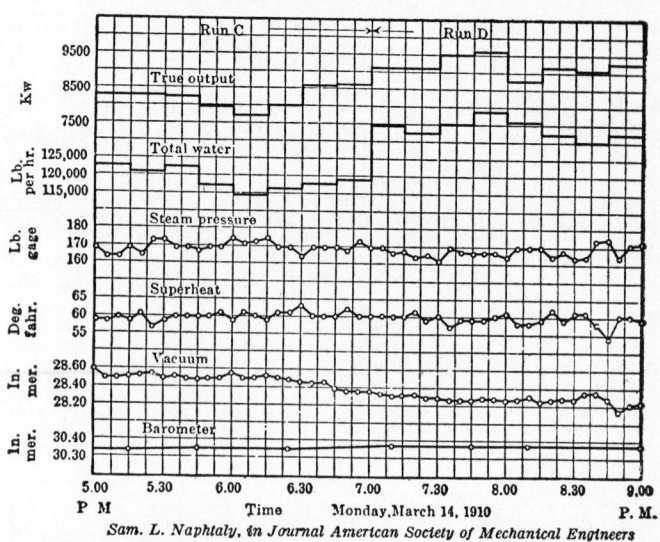

Fig. 112. Record of Test of a Steam Turbine of 10,000 Kw. Normal Rating at Plant of City Electric Company, San Francisco, California

The different curves shown in this chart supplement each other so as to give all the data on one chart in compact form. The scale for each curve given at the left is only sufficient to show the maximum and minimum value for each curve. The zero lines have been omitted entirely. Though charts of this type with numerous curves are sometimes desirable, they must be carefully made or the reader will be misled by the fluctuations of some one curve appearing more prominently than the data would justify

larger than the other, and on that account the curves have been made to coincide more closely than they would have done if both scales had the same zero line. In making comparisons of this kind care must be used to have the two scales start from the same zero line, or the person presenting the charts will be open to the unpleasant suspicion of attempting to "fake."

If the reader cares to see how these two curves would contrast if properly plotted, the left-hand scale for "corn yield" can be changed so that the different horizontal lines will be represented by the figures 0, 7, 14, 21, 28, etc. The data for "corn yield" can then be plotted to the new scale, and it will be found that the new curve does not coincide with the "rainfall" curve as closely as does the "corn-yield" curve shown in Fig. 114. Though there is some similarity in the shape of curves correctly plotted from these data, the similarity is not nearly so exact as Fig. 114 would indicate.

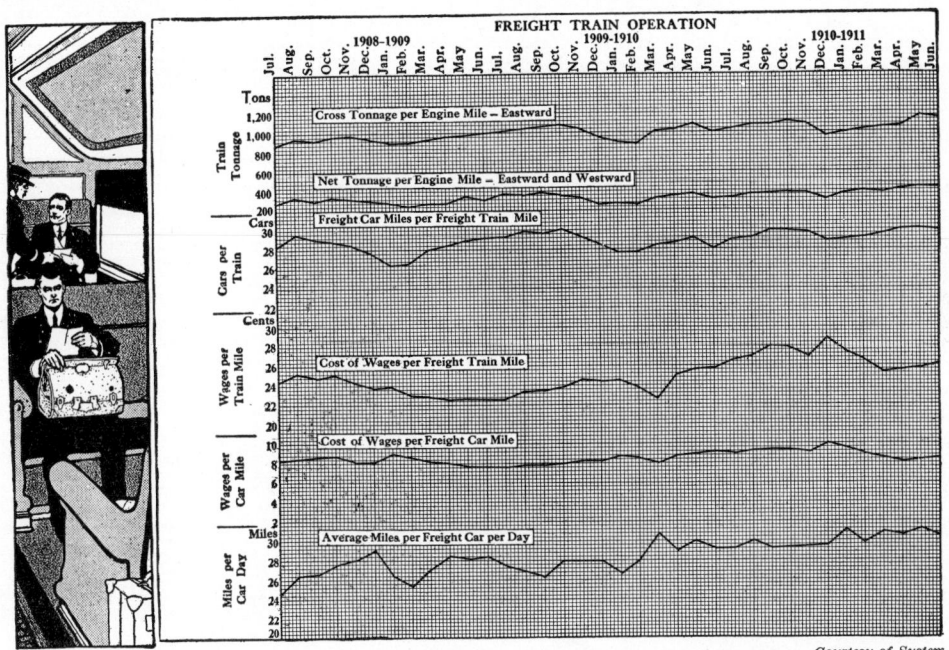

Courtesy of System

Fig. 113. Records of Freight-Train Operation on a Large Eastern Railroad

Here, as in Fig. 112, the zero lines are not given and the reader must watch the left-hand scales carefully to study percentage fluctuation. Comparison between curves cannot be made accurately by judging from the slope or from the total fluctuation of the curves on the page. Percentage increases or decreases for one curve compared with percentage increases or decreases of other curves give the best basis for comparison

Curves well made ordinarily need no embellishment. Anything used for an eyecatcher should apply definitely to the subject matter of the curves. Here the subject is freight-train operation, but the picture shows the interior of a passenger train

Fig. 115 gives a good example of a total curve made by adding the figures for different curves. Instead of using addition to get a set of figures from which a total curve may be plotted, it is easier in most cases to get the location of the total curve by the graphic method. All that is necessary is to lay off, with draftsman's dividers, successively on each vertical line, the height above zero at which each of the different curves intersects that vertical line. The totaling curve is drawn through the points thus found. When there are not too many curves, this method answers admirably. It sometimes happens that actual observations for the data of different curves are not simultaneously taken and, for this reason, it may be impossible to add the actual numerical data so as to plot a total curve. In such cases, the graphic method of stepping off the height for the total curve is practically the only one available. After each of the separate curves has been plotted from such data as may exist, it is a very simple matter by the graphic method to locate the total curve from the separate curves. A sufficient number of vertical lines are used to bring the points on the total curve close enough together to represent fairly the data of the separate curves which are totaled.

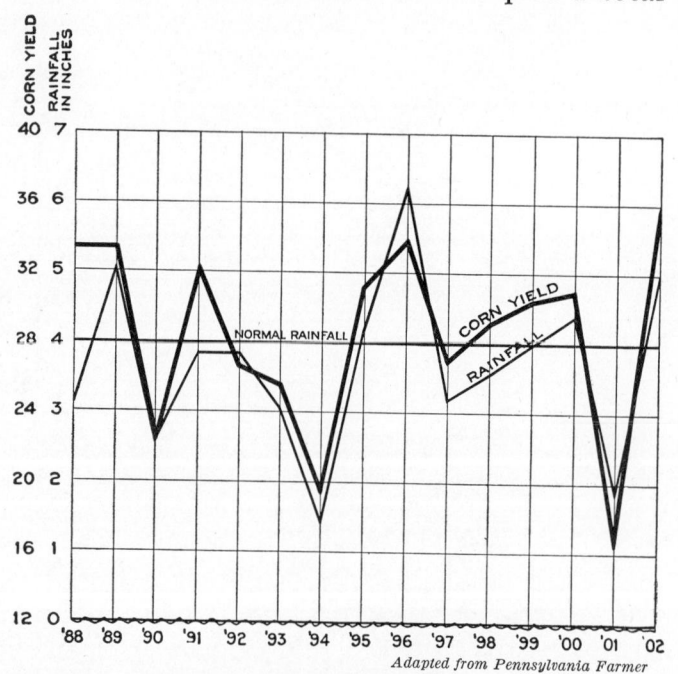

Fig. 114. Chart to Show the Dependence of Corn Yield upon the Quantity of Rainfall during the Month of July. The Yield of Corn is Given in Bushels per Acre

This chart is misleading. The close similarity of the two curves has been obtained by plotting one curve on a larger scale than that used for the other curve. The rainfall curve has been plotted with the bottom of the chart as zero. The corn-yield curve is, however, drawn with the scale starting at twelve.

In plotting curves relating to prices, it frequently happens that there is a necessity for showing in the chart both the upper and lower limits to which the prices may fluctuate in any given period of time.

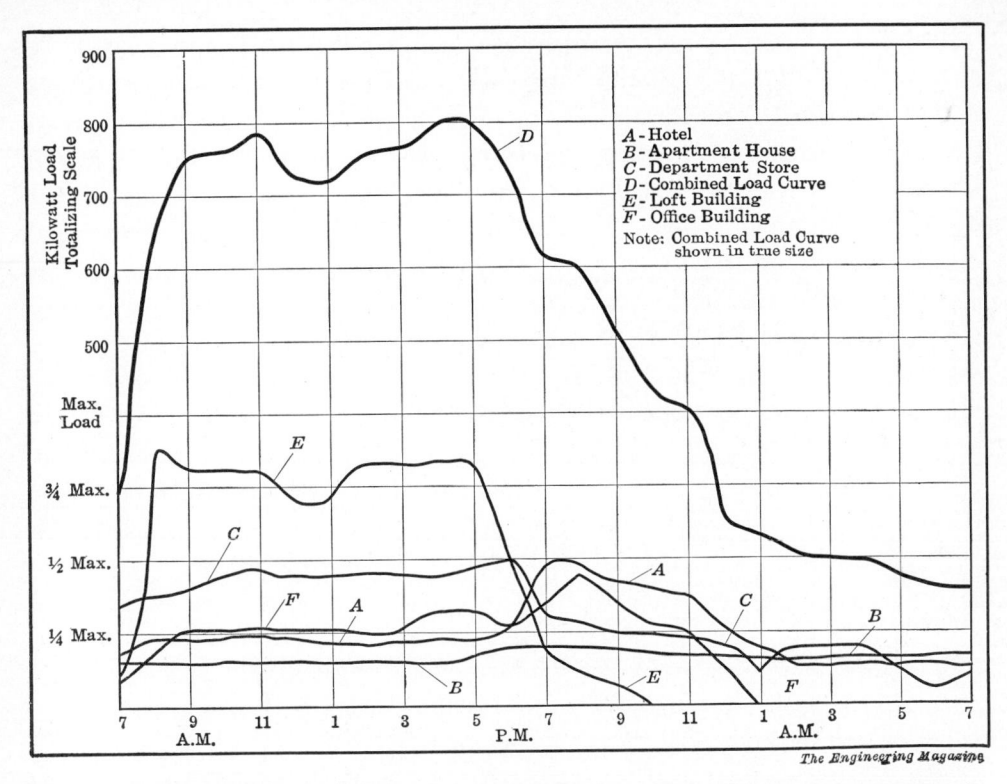

Fig. 115. **Typical Curves Showing the Twenty-Four Hour Demand for Electricity during the Summer Months in Various Types of Buildings in New York City**

Curve D shows the fluctuations in the load on a power house supplying all of the buildings represented by curves A, B, C, E and F. By combining loads of different types, the power plant can be kept more continuously busy than otherwise possible. After the other curves are all plotted, curve D can easily be located by stepping off with draftsmen's dividers on each vertical line the heights of all the different curves at that particular line

This is especially true where curves are plotted showing the fluctuations in the market prices of stocks or bonds. In such cases, it is desirable to plot two curves, one showing the minimum prices and the other showing the maximum prices. When the two curves lie quite closely together, it frequently assists in the clearness of the chart if the co-ordinate lines are erased between the two adjacent curves. The erasing of the co-ordinate lines makes the curves stand out much more distinctly than they otherwise would.

Charts on the general type of Fig. 116 are valuable to give a vivid comparison. A chart of this kind would be especially striking if used in advertising, or in a report where concentration upon only one general idea was needed, without a great amount of specific detail. Though Fig. 116 shows that telephone rates have had a constantly downward trend as the number of telephones in use has increased, there is, after all, no real proof in the chart that the rates have decreased in proportion to the increase in the number of telephones in use. Fig. 116 stimulates interest and makes one wish to plot another chart in which the number of telephones in use would be the horizontal scale and the average rate paid would be the vertical scale, somewhat on the general scheme of Fig. 119. The plotted points for different years on a chart of the kind suggested would show by the arrangement of the points whether the prices had changed exactly in accordance with the number of telephones in use.

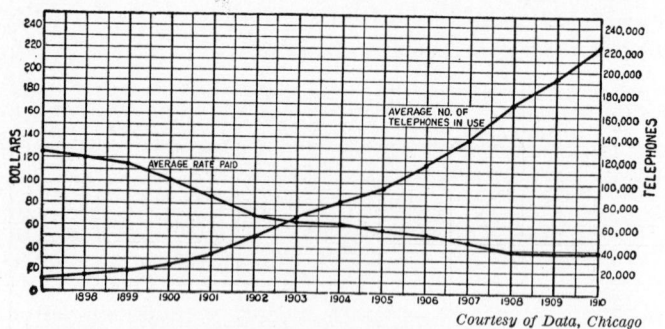

Fig. 116. Chicago Telephone Rates per Year Compared with the Number of Telephones in Use in Chicago

It is the object in this chart to show that the rates have been consistently reduced as the number of telephones has increased. The curves shown earlier in this chapter have varied directly, usually going up or down simultaneously. Here we have an inverse relation, with one curve coming down as the other goes up

Fig. 117 has been very carelessly drawn in that the two curves do not have their vertical scales start at the same zero line. The zeros for each of these scales are so close to the curves as drawn that it would have been a very simple matter to have made one zero line for both scales at the bottom line of the chart itself. The adverse criticisms of Fig. 114 may be applied to this chart also.

Though the two curves in Fig. 117 seem to show some inverse relation, since one curve frequently goes up when the other curve comes down, the chart does not permit any measurement by which the degree of correlation can be determined. The student who wishes to experiment with this interesting set of data would do well to make an entirely new chart with the two curves plotted from one zero line. After this first chart has been made, a second chart can be drawn in which the "Price" curve would be plotted exactly as in the first chart. The curve for the number of barrels of "Exports" should, however, be plotted downward from the top of the chart, after a good position has been selected for the top of the chart so that the "Exports" curve plotted downward from the top would coincide as nearly as possible with the "Price" curve plotted upward from the bottom. The scales for the curves in the second chart should be the same as those for the first chart, so that there may be no "faking" in any similarity which may show up in the shapes of the two curves. It frequently happens that the relations between two curves are such that the most striking presentation can be obtained by plotting one curve upside down so as to bring the two curves as closely into coincidence as possible, and the scheme should be kept in mind as it is frequently of assistance in making facts stand out vividly.

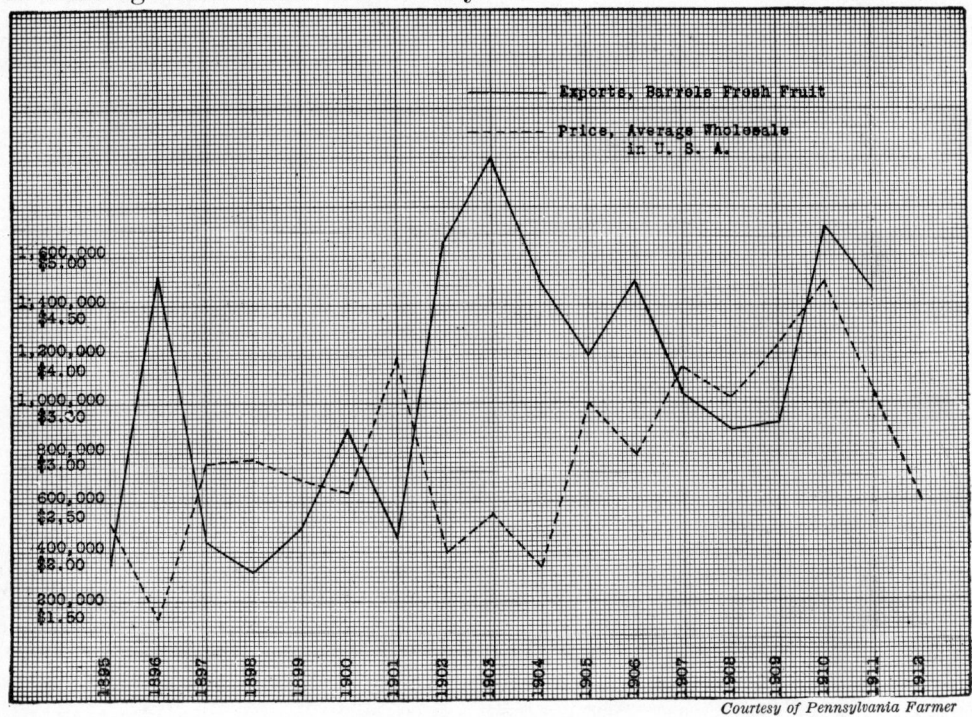

Fig. 117. Exports of Apples from the United States as Compared with the Average Wholesale Price in the United States

A little inspection shows that the export curve usually goes up when the price curve comes down. Though this fact indicates an inverse relation between the two curves under consideration it does not give satisfactory proof that exports fluctuate relatively as much as price.

This chart is likely to mislead the reader because the two vertical scales do not have the same zero line. Curves compared in this manner without having a common zero line should always be distrusted

Another interesting study can be made from Fig. 117 by drawing a chart with "Price" as the horizontal scale and quantity of "Exports" as the vertical scale. Dots for the different years placed on such a chart, after the general manner of Fig. 119, will appear so widely scattered over the whole field that the reader will find it almost hopeless to draw any general conclusion from the arrangement of the dots. Though the dots indicate by their position a general tendency for exports to decrease as prices increase, there would seem to be so many complex factors entering into the relation that no very general law of dependence can be proved.

It can be seen from inspection that the relations existing between the two curves of Fig. 118 are much closer than exist between the two curves of Fig. 117. It is unfortunate that in Fig. 118, as well as in Fig. 117, the chart was carelessly prepared so that the two curves do not have the same zero line.

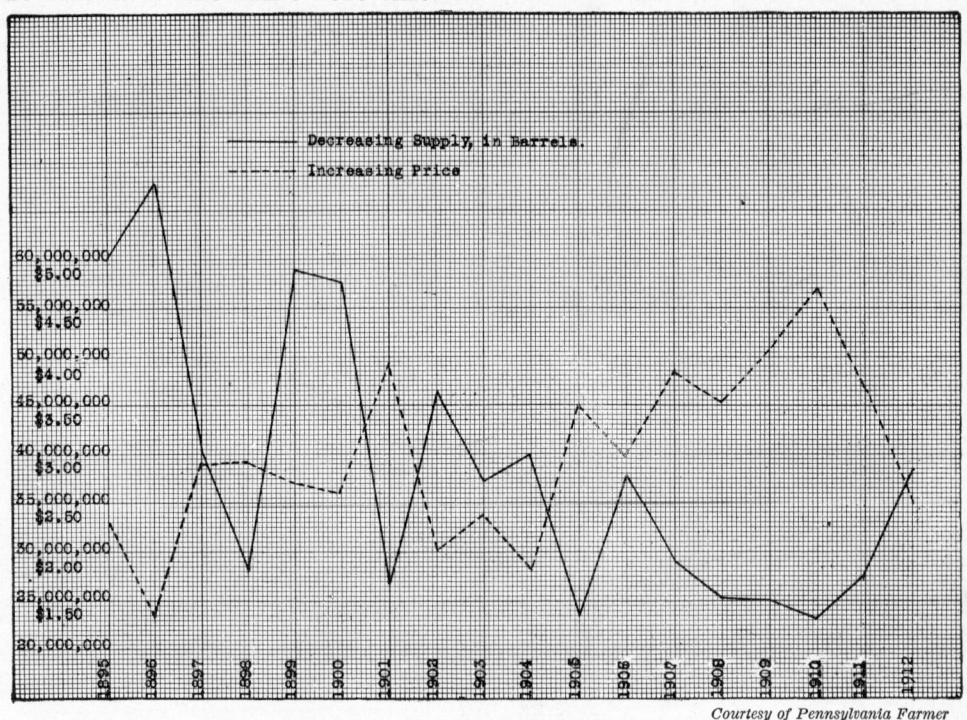

Courtesy of Pennsylvania Farmer

Fig. 118. The Average Price of Apples in the United States as Compared with the Total Supply

Here again an inverse relation is indicated, but the chart has carelessly been made with the two vertical scales starting from separate zero lines so as to cause distrust by the reader. The chart is printed showing a finely ruled co-ordinate background, though only every tenth line is desirable for the reader. The use of more lines than necessary should be avoided as it tends to cause confusion. See Fig. 119 as another method of charting the same data

In order to determine just how closely the price of apples depends upon the supply, Fig. 119 was prepared from the data of Fig. 118. Though the dots in Fig. 119 represent a rather long series of years, they nevertheless have a fairly symmetrical arrangement and the general tendency might be approximated by a smooth curve drawn as shown. It must be remembered that there are many conditions which may affect the position of these dots on the chart. For one thing, the standard of living has very greatly changed in the period of time from 1895 to 1912. Prices in recent years might be expected to be considerably higher than in the earlier years, without any regard to the size of the apple crop. Besides this, numerous diseases have affected apple trees in recent years, requiring more care than formerly to produce good fruit. This would also have some tendency to raise prices in spite of the tremendous number of apple trees which have come into bearing in the later portion of the period of time under consideration. The general method of plotting shown in Fig. 119 is of great importance and it should be kept in mind whenever two curves are found having similarities such as are seen in Fig. 118. Other examples of this method of plotting to study the correlation of two related subjects will be found in the last portion of Chapter X.

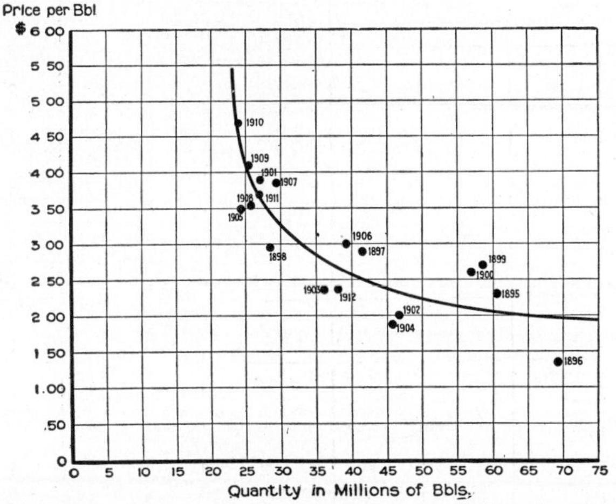

Fig. 119. The Average Price of Apples in the United States as Compared with the Total Supply

By this method, the positions of the dots on the chart show whether there is any close relation between supply and price. The dots fall in fairly regular order, proving better than Fig. 118 that the price does largely depend upon the supply. A smooth curve has been drawn to represent approximately the general relation between supply and price which the dots might seem to indicate. Note that the year is stated for each dot shown

Fig. 120 contains much information for the student of history. We are here interested particularly in the record of the United States. That curve line has accordingly been made much heavier than any of the others, so that it may be brought prominently to the eye of the reader. By visually projecting the curves for Russia and the United States beyond the limits of the chart, it appears that we should equal Russia's population within the next few decades. It must be remembered in viewing this chart that the populations of the Asiatic countries (especially the populations of China and India) are not shown here. If all the countries of the world were considered, it would be seen at once that for many years to come there is no likelihood of the United States having the greatest population in the world. It is only because Asiatic countries have been omitted that we seem to be so nearly the head of the list.

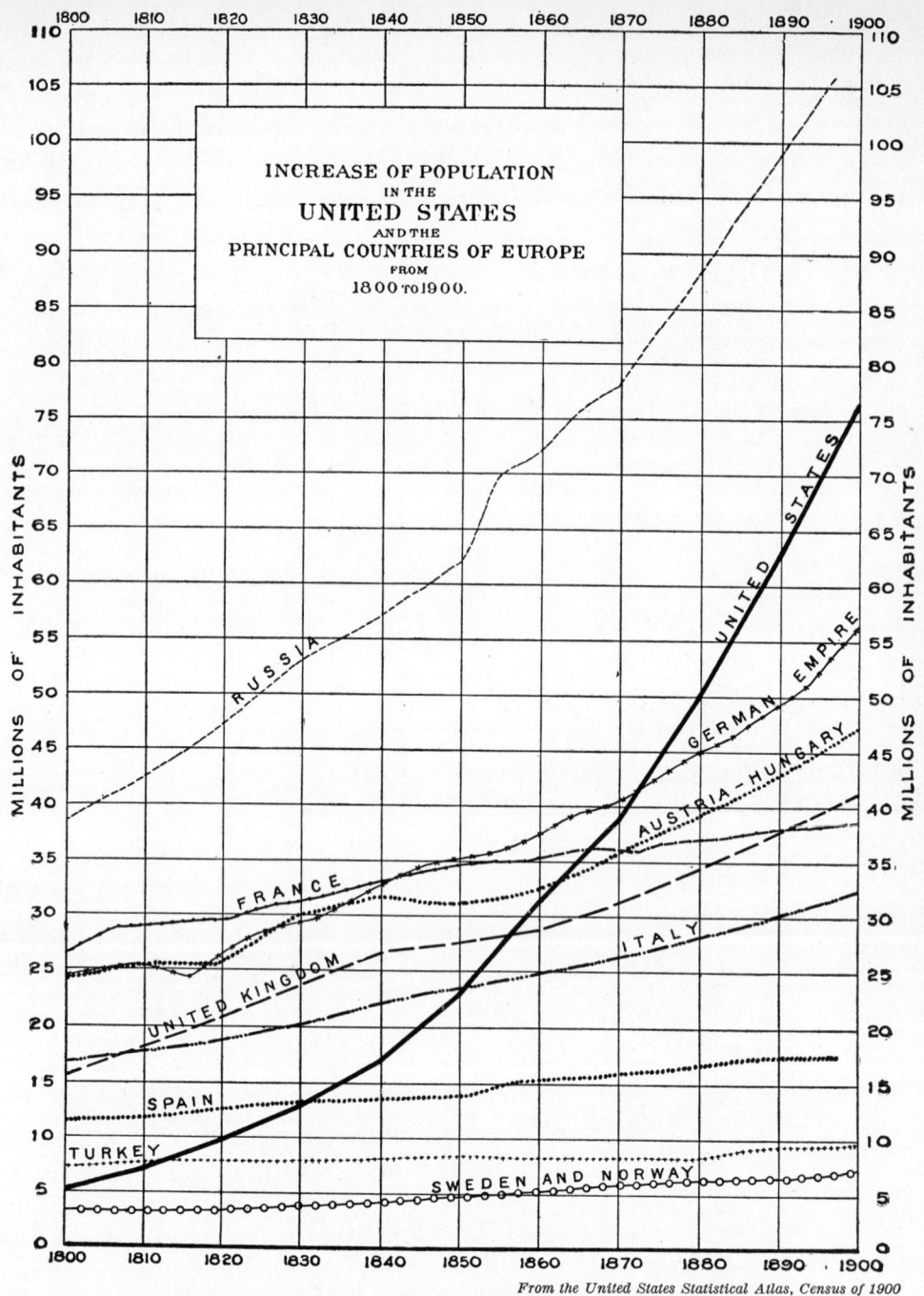

Fig. 120. **The Population of the United States Compared with the Population of the Principal Countries of Europe from 1800 to 1900, Inclusive**

Written words requiring one hour to read could not convey as much information as this chart gives. In considering the slope of the curve for the United States it must be remembered that the slope of a curve does not indicate the percentage rate of increase or decrease. The increasing slope of the United States curve does not in itself prove any increase in the percentage rate of growth. Compare Fig. 121

The reader should keep constantly in mind when viewing Fig. 120 that the slope of a curve line crossing a field ruled with ordinary rectangular co-ordinate lines on an arithmetical scale tells nothing about the percentage rate of growth from period to period. The slope of the United States curve is very much steeper in the upper portion of Fig. 120 than in the lower portion, but the greater slope does not prove that we are growing more rapidly on a percentage basis than early in the century. The slope of a curve plotted on a natural scale of rectangular co-ordinates shows only the size of the increments added from period to period and it tells nothing whatever about percentage growth.

Fig. 121 has been drawn to assist in proving the preceding statement regarding curve slope. Starting with one dollar, it was assumed that a uniform increase of 10 per cent of the accumulated amount would be made at the end of each year. This is the same as though the dollar were placed at 10 per cent compound interest. At the end of thirty-six years it can be seen that the one dollar has increased to nearly thirty-one dollars. Though the accumulated fund is shown by a smooth curve throughout the period of thirty-six years, the curve is constantly changing its slope in spite of the fact that the rate of increase remains constant at 10 per cent per year. The curve in Fig.

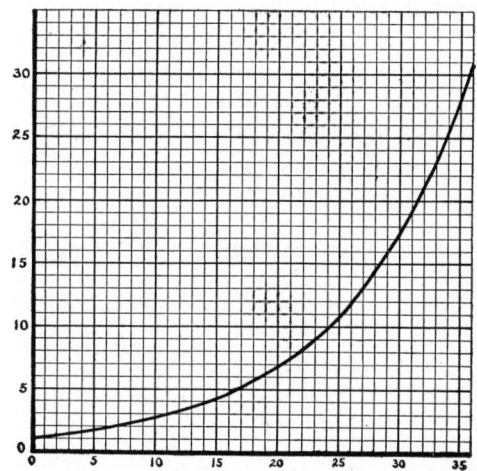

Fig. 121. Curve Showing the Growth of One Dollar at 10 per cent Compound Interest for Thirty-six Years

Here the rate of increase is uniformly 10 per cent per year, but the slope of the curve is constantly changing. The general shape of this curve is somewhat similar to the shape of the population curve for the United States seen in Fig. 120. The slope of a curve plotted on ordinary co-ordinate paper tells nothing about the percentage rate of growth. See Fig. 122 and Fig. 123

121 is very similar in shape to the curve for the United States in Fig. 120. This similarity in shape shows conclusively how much the reader would be misled if he should assume that the increasing slope of the curve in Fig. 120 proved in itself an increase in the rate of growth. The actual percentage rate of the growth for Fig. 120 can best be studied by making an entirely new chart for the purpose of observing percentage rates only.

*The ordinary form of graphic chart plotted on rectangular coordinate paper with the natural or arithmetical spacing of the lines has some serious limitations which may cause a chart to be misleading. The true function of such a chart is to portray comparative fluctuations. This desired result is secured clearly and satisfactorily when the factors or quantities compared are of nearly the same value or volume, but analysis will show that the result is not accomplished when the amounts compared differ greatly in value or volume. The extent or degree of the fluctuation as indicated on the ordinary chart depends in a measure on the proximity of the curves to the top or bottom of the chart. The chart registers the actual change in the value rather than the ratio or percentage of change. The wider the range of scale the greater the variation between the actual and the relative changes.

This same criticism applies to charts which employ two or more scales for various records or curves. If the different scales are in proper proportion the result is the same as with one scale, but when two or more scales are used which are not proportional, an indication which is absolutely false may be given with respect to comparative fluctuation. Charts made on a percentage basis are used to some extent in graphic work, and these correct the deficiency in the ordinary chart by showing the changes in the percentages of increase or decrease. In correcting one deficiency, however, another is introduced. The percentage scale gives no clue to the magnitude of the quantities represented by a curve. The true proportions of relative changes are shown, but the actual values are not indicated. The use of the percentage scale also requires considerable labor for computing the percentages of change.

As a substitute for the ordinary (or natural) scale and for the scale of percentages, as well as for compound scales, the logarithmic scale, or scale of ratios, practically meets all the requirements. The logarithmic scale permits the exhibition of both actual and relative values and actual and relative fluctuations. While some knowledge of logarithms will make plain certain features which otherwise are hard to understand, no special knowledge of higher mathematics is essential to the use of the logarithmic scale. The principles involved are the same as those embodied in the slide rule, and any treatise on the slide

---

*Portions of this discussion on charts plotted by the logarithmic scale are adapted from an article by W. J. Cunningham. in the *Railway Age Gazette*, June 25, 1909.

COMPARISON OF CURVES

rule will make them sufficiently clear. A person who can plot a chart to the ordinary scale should have no difficulty in using the logarithmic scale.

No matter what the location on the chart, if the logarithmic spacing is used on the vertical scale, for curves, the angle of the upward or downward inclination is the same for all curves affected by the same percentage of change. Curves having an increase equaling the distance from 100 to 200, 200 to 400, 300 to 600 (or the distance between any number on the scale and double that number) have an increase of 100 per cent and show the same slope. It will be noticed, for instance, from any paper ruled logarithmically, or from Fig. 123, that the distance on the logarithmic scale from 10 to 20 is the same as from 200 to 400.

In Fig. 122, we have curves plotted for comparative study in the manner most convenient when ordinary arithmetically ruled cross-section paper is used. Some of these curves represent large quantities, so that they are on the upper portion of the chart, while others represent comparatively small quantities and fall near the bottom of the chart.

Just because the curves in the upper portion of the chart represent numerically larger quantities, they have much more vertical movement up and down on the face of the chart than those curves in the lower portion of the chart which may have an even greater amount of percentage fluctuation. This wide difference in the amount of vertical movement on a page is one unfortunate source of confusion to persons who are just beginning to study curve charting.

Fig. 123 is plotted from the same data as Fig. 122, but it is on paper having logarithmic spacing for the vertical scale with the ordinary arithmetical spacing for the horizontal scale. With the logarithmic spacing on the vertical scale the fluctuations in the different curves show in true proportion. Curve F appeared insignificant in Fig. 122 because it happened to fall near the bottom of the chart where percentage fluctuations are not prominently shown. In Fig. 123, however, curve F shows up as having far the greatest percentage changes of any curve on the whole chart. For persons who understand even slightly the principles involved in reading charts plotted on logarithmic paper, Fig. 123 shows up the facts in much more convenient form than Fig. 122. To make comparison most convenient, the two figures are placed on facing pages, 134 and 135.

134   GRAPHIC METHODS

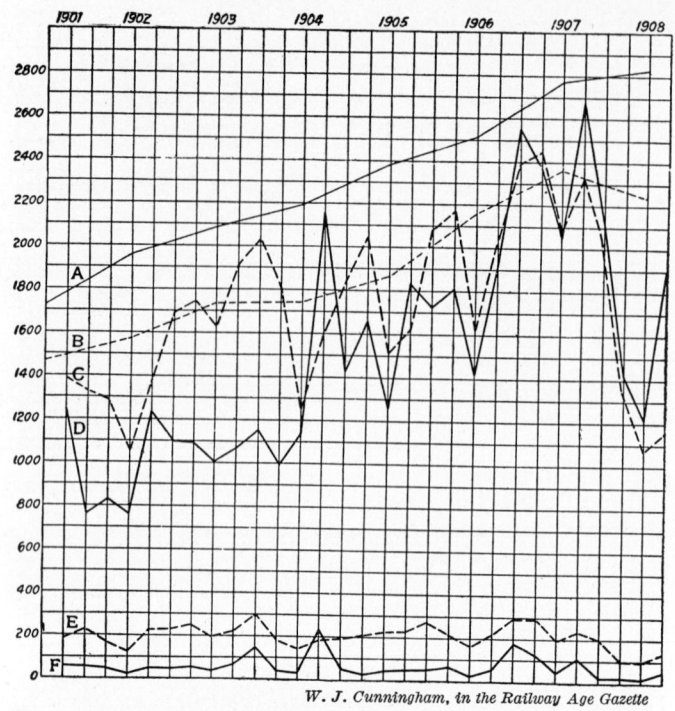

Fig. 122. Passengers and Employees Killed and Injured in Train Accidents for All Railroads in the United States. (From Quarterly Reports of the Interstate Commerce Commission)

Curve A. Passenger miles (2000 on scale equals 20 billion passenger miles)
Curve B. Ton miles (2000 on scale equals 20 billion ton miles)
Curve C. Number of employees injured
Curve D. Number of passengers injured
Curve E. Number of employees killed
Curve F. Number of passengers killed

Compare this chart with Fig. 123. The data plotted here by the ordinary natural scale of co-ordinates are replotted in Fig. 123, using logarithmic co-ordinates. Note the peak in 1904 in Curve D. The number of passengers injured was approximately doubled in a short period of time. In the same period of time the number of passengers killed increased to seven times what it had been, yet the peak on Curve F does not attract great attention. Notice these same peaks in Fig. 123 with the logarithmic scale

It is unfortunate that there is so much difficulty in obtaining paper having the logarithmic ruling in one direction and the arithmetical ruling in the other direction. The arithmetical ruling in one direction is essential for statistical work, since we must ordinarily plot as one scale data representing years or other subdivisions of time. In statistical work we cannot well use a paper having logarithmic ruling in both directions, yet that is the only kind of logarithmic paper which can be obtained from most stores selling drawing materials

COMPARISON OF CURVES

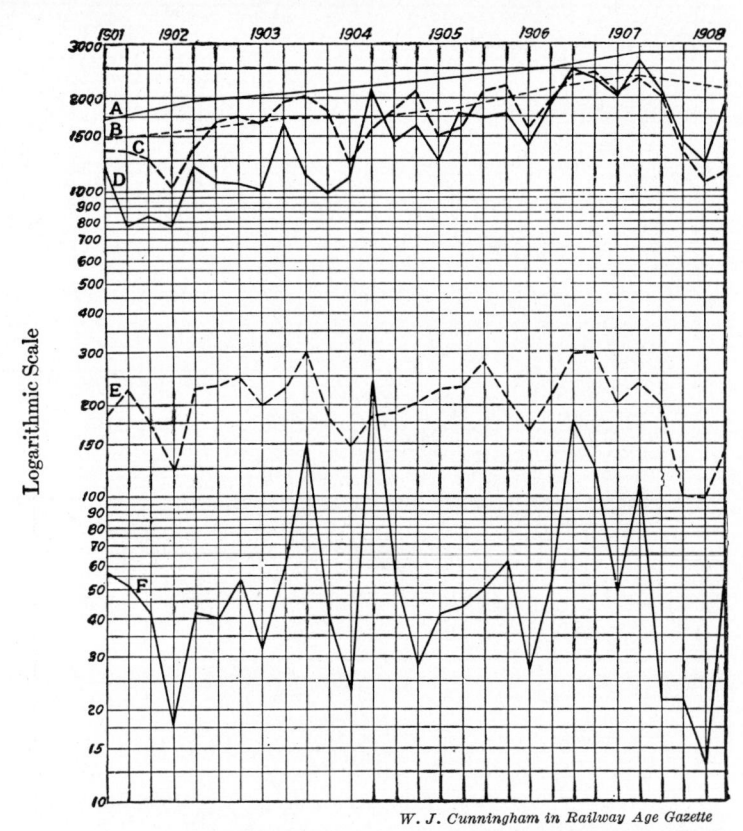

Fig. 123. Passengers and Employees Killed and Injured in Train Accidents for All Railroads in the United States. (From Quarterly Reports of the Interstate Commerce Commission)

Curve A. Passenger miles (2000 on scale equals 20 billion passenger miles)
Curve B. Ton miles (2000 on scale equals 20 billion ton miles)
Curve C. Number of employees injured
Curve D. Number of passengers injured
Curve E. Number of employees killed
Curve F. Number of passengers killed

This illustration is a replot of Fig. 122 by using the logarithmic scale in the vertical direction. In reading a chart in which a logarithmic vertical scale is used, attention may be given to the slope of the curve lines. Curves having the same slope upwards or downwards have the same percentage change. Note that curves with a logarithmic scale do not have zero for the bottom line of the chart. It is, however, desirable to have the bottom line either at ten or some power of ten on the vertical scale

and engineering supplies. A person doing statistical work for which paper with the logarithmic ruling is desirable may occasionally have to rule his own paper. This, however, is not an impossible task especially if one has a slide rule. The spacing of the lines can be copied from either scale of the slide rule, or it may be worked out easily to fit any given space by dividing into tenths and hundredths and using tables of logarithms.

It is of interest to note here that the data of Fig. 121 would show as a perfectly straight line if plotted on paper having the logarithmic ruling for the vertical scale. Since the increase from year to year is uniform, on a percentage basis, the points of the curve all fall on a straight line drawn from the first point to the last point.

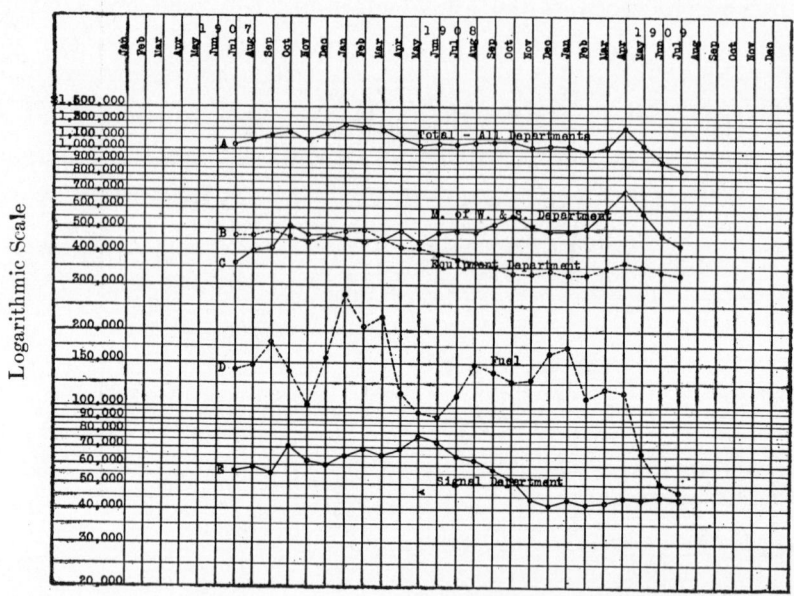

W. J. Cunningham in Proceedings of New England Railroad Club

Fig. 124. Book Value of Material on Hand for a Large Eastern Railroad

The logarithmic scale is particularly valuable for an operating chart such as this when there is a great difference in the size of the figures which must be compared. The lower curve here averages about $60,000 while the upper curve averages about $1,100,000. The logarithmic scale permits accurate comparison of various curves to determine whether any curves are out of harmony with the other curves

Fig. 124 gives an especially interesting use of curves on the logarithmic ruling. Executives who have puzzled over methods for controlling the quantity of materials or supplies on hand realize full well that it is sometimes just as important to watch the curves for materials having only a relatively small consumption as it is to watch the curves for those materials of which the greatest quantity is used. The mere fact that great amounts of capital are tied up in stocks of certain largely used materials tends in itself to cause very careful scrutiny of those accounts, while numerous small or inactive accounts may be entirely overlooked or neglected. A little study often shows that there is no necessity for carrying so much material on hand.

If charts similar to Fig. 124 are used, the executive can tell instantly whether the stocks in different departments or of different kinds of material are increasing or decreasing simultaneously and proportionately.

"To summarize—with the ordinary arithmetical scale, fluctuations in large factors are very noticeable, while relatively greater fluctuations in smaller factors are barely apparent. The logarithmic scale permits the graphic representation of changes in every quantity without respect to the magnitude of the quantity itself. At the same time, the logarithmic scale shows the actual value by reference to the numbers in the vertical scale. By indicating both absolute and relative values and changes, the logarithmic scale combines the advantages of both the natural and the percentage scale without the disadvantages of either."

Chapter VIII

COMPONENT PARTS SHOWN BY CURVES

IN Chapter I various examples were given in which the component parts or factors making up a complex whole were shown in their relative sizes. It frequently happens that it is necessary to show the changes which occur in the size of different components as time goes on. In this chapter we shall consider only examples of charts showing the fluctuating size, at different times, of components which make up a total of 100 per cent.

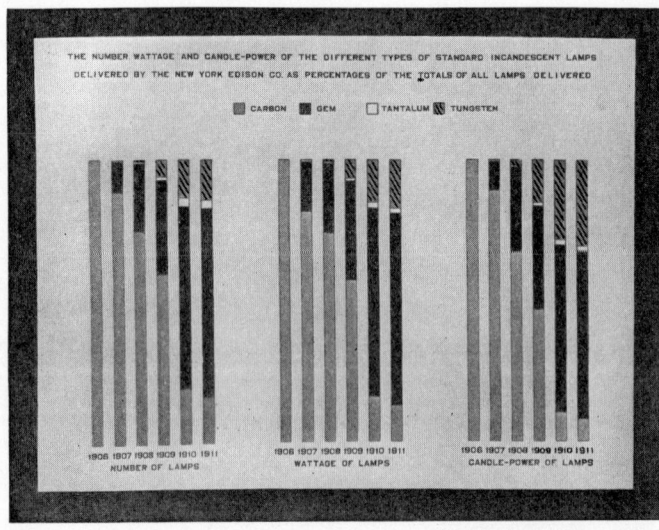

Fig. 125. The Number, Voltage, and Candle-Power of the Different Types of Standard Incandescent Lamps Delivered by the New York Edison Company in Different Years, Shown as a Percentage of the Totals of All Lamps Delivered

The chart was drawn in four contrasting colors and was framed for a wall exhibit

In Fig. 125 the proportionate number, voltage, and candle-power of various types of standard incandescent lamps delivered in different years by the New York Edison Co. are shown in a series of vertical bars which are all of the same length, representing 100 per cent. No statement is made or implied in regard to the total figures, which may have increased or decreased from year to year. All we are interested in, in this chart, is the proportion of the different components which in their aggregate make up the bar representing 100 per cent in any year.

In Fig. 126 the total height of the chart represents 100 per cent.

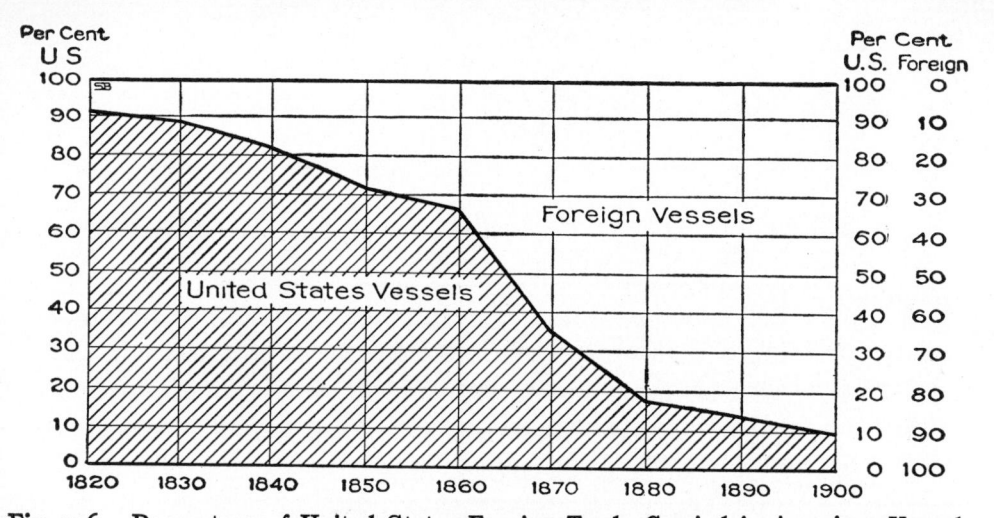

Fig. 126. Percentage of United States Foreign Trade Carried in American Vessels and in Foreign Vessels by Decades, 1820 to 1900

This type of chart requires a more highly educated reader than the type of chart shown in Fig. 125, but it gains by making the information stand out more clearly than possible with a series of bars

To show that the chart is absolutely limited to the height representing 100 per cent, we use a broad line for the zero line and another broad line at the top for the 100 per cent line. Instead of showing the percentages at different decades by the method of shaded bars used in Fig. 125, the vertical lines representing decades are first marked with points dividing the lines into component parts, then the points on the various lines are joined to give a curve. The area underneath the curve is shaded in this illustration simply to give a greater contrast between the two portions of the chart. Charts of this kind made with shaded or colored areas are understood by a surprisingly large number of people who ordinarily would not understand a chart made by using curve lines without the shaded or colored areas.

The double scale at the right of Fig. 126 is worth noting. The percentage for the United States can be read for any decade. The percentage for foreign vessels can also be read for any decade by using the reversed scale, in which zero is placed at the top and 100 per cent at the bottom. Though a double scale is scarcely necessary on a chart as simple as Fig. 126, it is frequently desirable to have a double scale.

Another very striking wall chart is shown in Fig. 127. Here as in Fig. 125 the chart was framed, but the frame shows in the photograph only as a black border. In making up this chart co-ordinate paper was used for a background. The upper half of the chart shows the 24 hours of the day divided between hours of darkness, hours of twilight and cloudiness, and hours of sunshine, totaling 100 per cent for each month in the year. The hours of darkness are definitely known from almanac figures and can be plotted as a smooth curve.

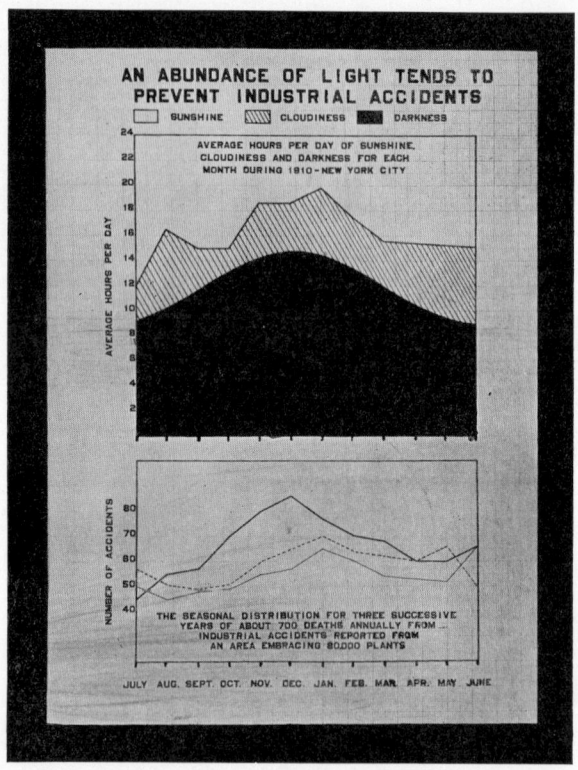

New York Edison Company

Fig. 127. Industrial Accidents in Different Months of the Year Compared with the Hours of Sunlight Each Day in Different Months According to Weather Records for New York City in 1910

Twenty-four hours in a day are shown as 100 per cent divided between darkness, semi-darkness, and sunshine. Curves showing accidents for three different years have the same general shape as the upper curve representing hours of darkness. The scale for the accident curves should have been started so as to show zero at the bottom of the curve field

The hours of cloudy weather, however, vary in different years. The area showing cloudiness and twilight was drawn from actual weather observations made in New York City during the year 1910. The percentage of sunshine in different months fluctuates considerably, as will be noticed in the chart.

The lower half of Fig. 127 contains three curves showing the monthly distribution, for three successive years, of about 700 deaths annually from industrial accidents reported from an area embracing 80,000 plants. The similarity of these curves, showing the number of fatal accidents per month, to the curves showing the percentage of darkness, is intended to convey to the person seeing the wall exhibit, the truth of the statement at the top of the chart, that "an abundance of light tends to prevent industrial accidents." Though Fig. 127 is a very commendable and effective piece of work, it should be pointed out that there is danger of exaggerating the facts in the way in which the chart is prepared. The lower left-hand scale does not begin at zero. By measuring, it can be seen that the scale begins at 20 accidents per month. The bottom line of the curve field should have been drawn near the edge of the picture frame to represent zero. This change in the bottom line would have given the reader a more accurate idea of the increase of deaths in those months having the greatest proportion of darkness. This chart really does not exaggerate the facts seriously, for the three curves for deaths and the curve for darkness would really be of approximately the same shape even if the zero line had been shown in its correct position. Yet it is a fact that the omission of the full scale in the chart may cause a person glancing hastily at the chart to distrust it simply because the zero line is not shown.

In Fig. 128 a number of different components are shown to make up a total of 100 per cent. This type of chart is especially good to give instantly a general idea of the relative size of the components or factors which enter into any total, and to show the changes in these factors as time goes on. Though it is fairly easy to see in Fig. 128 what the changes are which have occurred in, say, the item for "General" expenses, it is not at all easy to determine the changes which have occurred in the item for "Conducting Transportation." The eye cannot measure correctly the increase or decrease in width of any area as great as that representing the item for "Conducting Transportation," especially if there is no straight line to gauge by, either at the top or the bottom of the area under consideration.

Though the method of presenting the facts in Fig. 128 is excellent to give a rough general idea or to reach unskilled readers, the method of presenting the facts in Fig. 129 is likely to give the more accurate impression. In Fig. 129, each of the different expense accounts is plotted as a separate curve measured from zero as a base line. It can be seen at once in Fig. 129 that the component for "Conducting Transportation" increased rapidly until 1895, ran along fairly uniformly to 1900, then slightly decreased, then increased again. By having each curve plotted separately with the points measured from a zero base line, the eye can judge instantly and accurately the changes which have occurred over a period of years in any component which enters into the total. In an illustration like Fig. 129 it should be shown in the title, or preferably on the chart itself, that the sum of the heights of all the curves given on the chart is constantly 100 per cent as indicated by the broad line at the top of the chart. The reader will then know that if any one curve on the chart goes up, some other curve or curves must come down in order that the 100 per cent line may remain straight and horizontal.

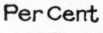

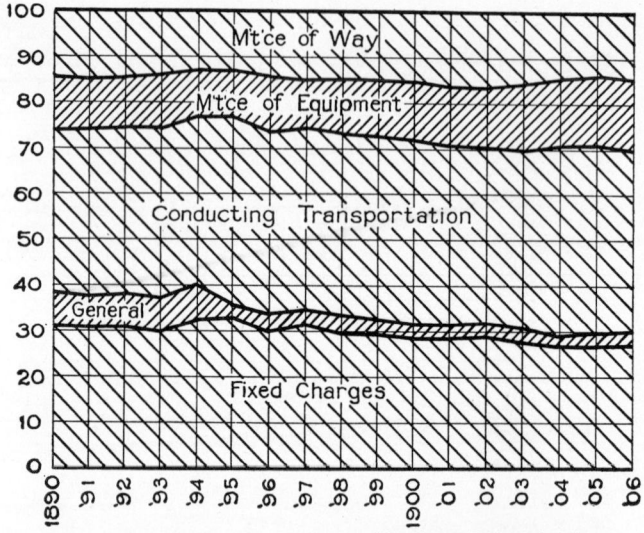

Fig. 128. Percentage Distribution of the Expenses of Operating the Railroads of the United States

Here a number of different factors enter into the total 100 per cent. Since the strips representing different expenses vary at both top and bottom, it is not easy to see from year to year how much any strip may be increasing or decreasing. Compare with Fig. 129

Fig. 130 is an interesting application of the method of using areas to show components with 100 per cent shown as a straight line at the top of the combined area. As in this case a large part of the construction work was finished, the actual number of accidents in the construction department dropped to almost nothing, and, because the shaded area for construction grew less, it was necessary that the other areas should widen out if the 100 per cent line at the top were to remain a straight line. Here the weak point in the method of charting is the same as that indicated for Fig. 128. The person observing the chart has no way of telling whether the factors included in the 100 per cent have grown less or grown greater, and whether

COMPONENT PARTS SHOWN BY CURVES 143

the quantities represented by the different areas have changed in actual size or only in relative size. Where great fluctuations occur from time to time and many factors enter into the total, it is best to draw charts in the form of Fig. 129 with a common zero line, or in the form of Fig. 131, where each factor has its own separate base line, or in the form of Fig. 132 and Fig. 133, in which the lines on the chart represent actual quantities rather than percentages of an aggregate or total sum.

Note in Fig. 130 and Fig. 131 the 8½-inch by 11-inch co-ordinate paper on which the ruling is so arranged that the paper may be used for almost any subdivisions of time, such as days, weeks, months, etc., as seen in Figs. 57, 103, 131, 134, and 156.

In Fig. 130 the paper was used for a time-scale of three years by months, the total height of the chart being put at 100 per cent, using fifty out of the fifty-two spaces on the paper. Fifty-two spaces, corresponding to the number of weeks in a year, of course are necessary when the paper is used to represent weeks on the long dimension of the sheet.

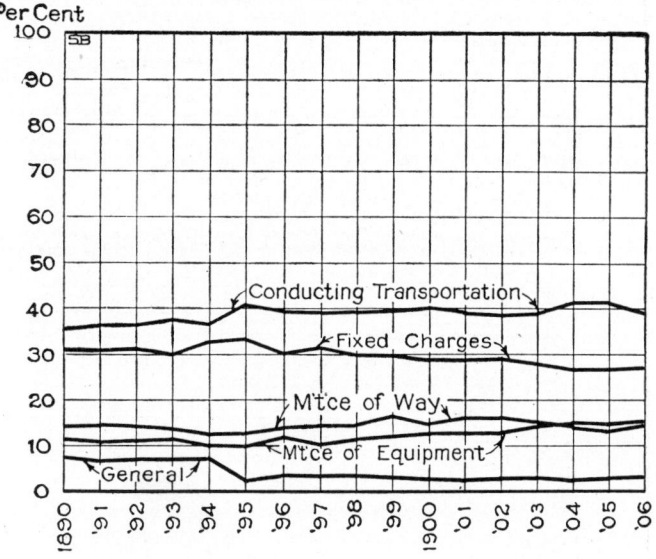

Fig. 129. Percentage Distribution of the Expenses of Operating the Railroads of the United States. The Combined Height of All the Curves Shown Equals 100 Per Cent on the Scale

This illustration represents the same data as Fig. 128. Here the percentage for each expense is read from the zero base line instead of from one to the other of the fluctuating lines on either side of an area. This method, though not so popular as the method of Fig. 128, permits more accurate reading

Fig. 131 and Fig. 130 depict exactly the same data. In Fig. 131 the facts, which in Fig. 130 were represented by areas, are shown as separate curves, each curve with its own base line. Having this series of separate curves on one sheet of paper permits an executive to compare the number of accidents in one department with the number of accidents in any other department at any one time, or to study

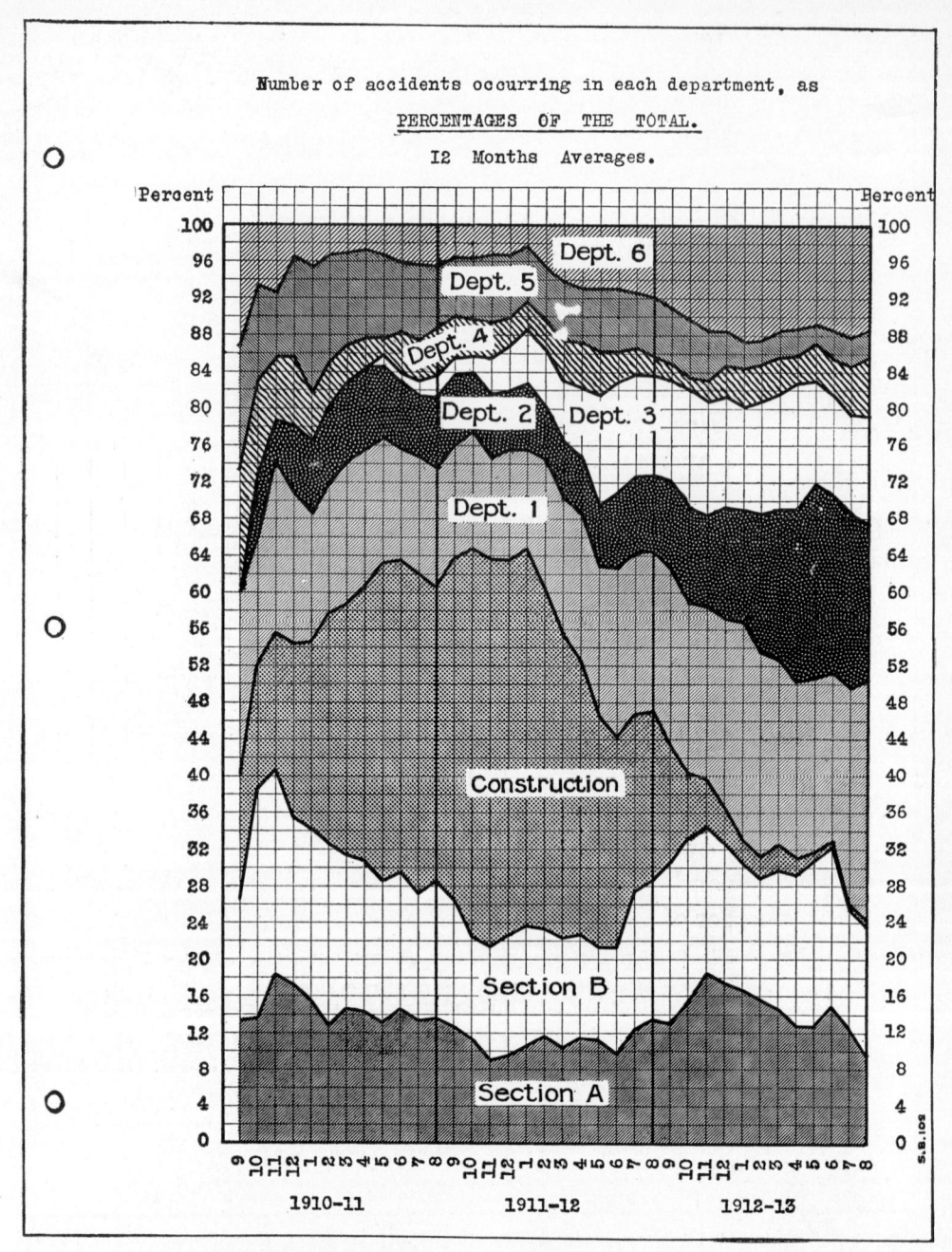

Fig. 130. Percentage of Accidents Occurring in Each Department of a Large Industrial Plant. Plotted Monthly by Twelve-month Averages

By this method, with a constant width to represent 100 per cent, any great change in any component affects all other components. Here the decrease in construction accidents causes the areas depicting other accidents to increase in width, even though there may be no increase in the actual number of accidents. Compare Fig. 131

This cut was made from specially ruled co-ordinate paper 8½ inches by 11 inches, with all lettering done by typewriter. The ruling as used here shows 100 per cent and three years by months. Note also Figs. 57, 103, 134 and 156, for which this same universal ruling has been used

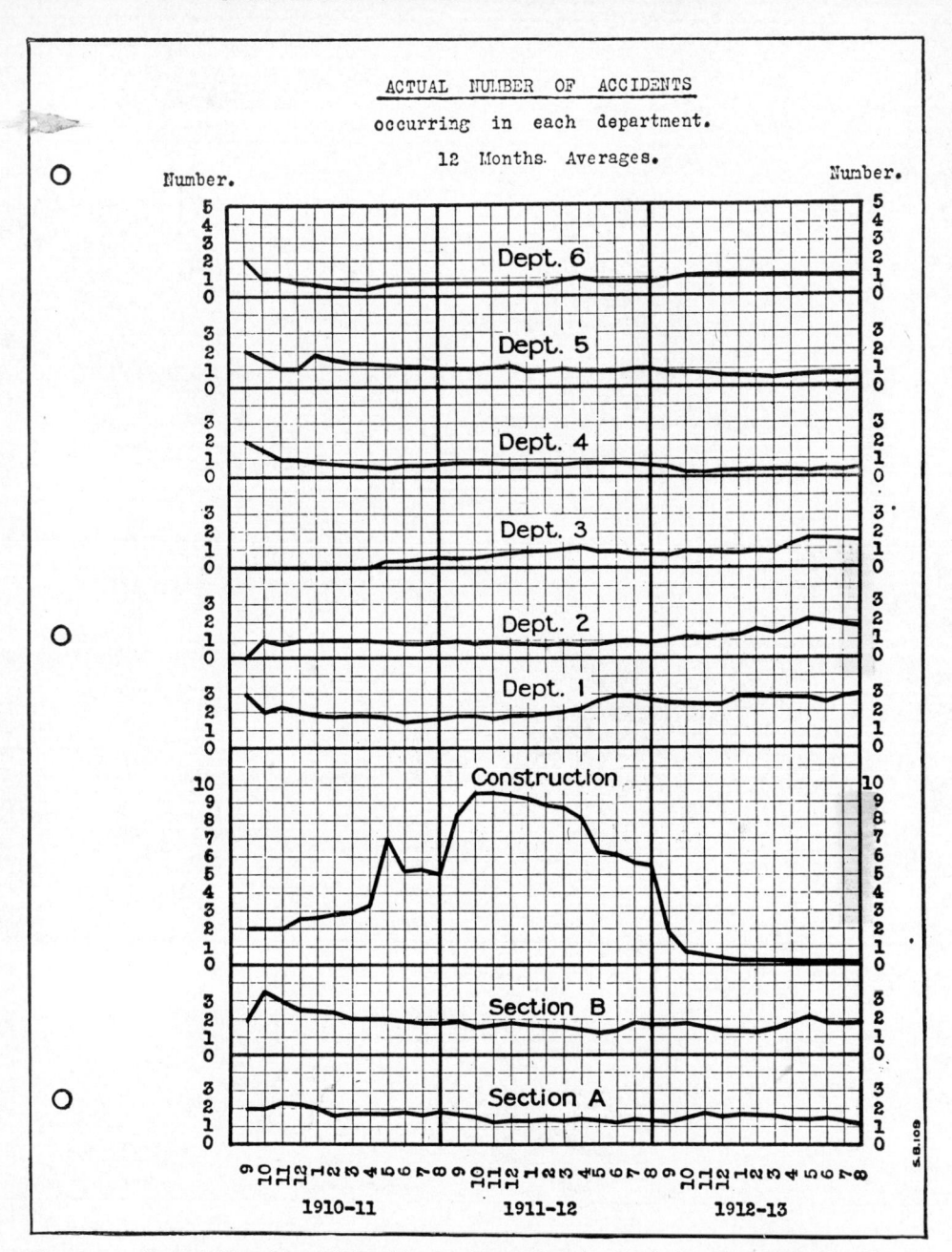

Fig. 131. Actual Number of Accidents Occurring in Each Department of a Large Industrial Plant. Plotted Monthly by Twelve-month Averages

In this chart the actual condition in each department can be seen much more clearly than by the method used in Fig. 130. Here each department is judged by its own record without danger of unjust criticism based on conditions in other departments

For a more complete discussion of Figs. 130 and 131 and of the contrast of methods followed in preparing them the reader is referred to pages 142, 143 and 146

146   GRAPHIC METHODS

the fluctuations in the accidents of any one department over a long period of time.

As accidents never occur with any regularity, curves representing the actual number of accidents are likely to fluctuate a great deal. There was such variation in the different months for the number of accidents represented in Figs. 130 and 131 that it was almost impossible to draw any definite conclusion from curves for monthly

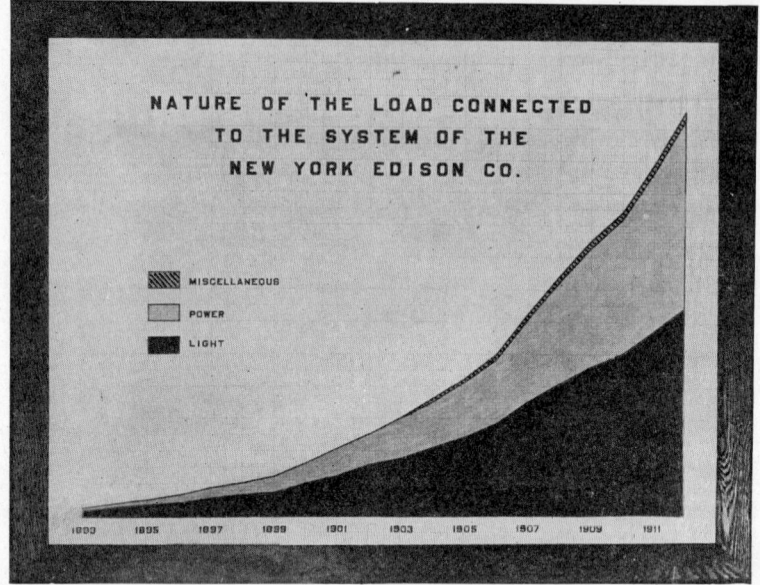

New York Edison Company

Fig. 132. Nature of the Electrical Load Connected to the System of the New York Edison Company, 1893 to 1912

In the preceding illustrations 100 per cent was indicated by a straight line at the top of the chart. Here the line representing 100 per cent is a curve. Though the actual sizes of different components can be seen by this method, percentages can only be estimated from the widths of the areas. The scale for this type of chart must read in actual quantities rather than in percentages. On this wall exhibit the scale has been omitted entirely

data. The data for Fig. 130 and for Fig. 131 were plotted on the basis of giving, monthly, the average number of accidents in each department during the last twelve months for which records were available. Actual figures in tabulated form were used to show for immediate reference the number of accidents in any month. The curves on the twelve-months average basis were consulted to determine whether there was any great increase or decrease in any department.

In Fig. 132 the vertical scale was omitted, perhaps with the idea that the chart would thus appear more simple to the average individual attending a large exhibition. If the scale were given, however, it would be plotted on the basis of actual horse-power rather than on percentage, for the top curve here represents the total quantity. Percentage scales cannot well be used in diagrams of component parts if a fluctuating curve line instead of a horizontal line representing 100 per cent is given at the top. The reader may, however, get a fair idea of the percentages if he roughly calculates the height of the areas in question on any vertical line of the co-ordinate ruling and then, using that vertical line as a measuring rod, estimates the height of the areas as a percentage of the total height of the chart.

In Fig. 133 the straight line at the top of the chart does not have any significance, as it is due only to the co-ordinate ruling which serves as a background to the chart itself. The important part of the chart ends at the top of the shaded area. We may consider the top of the whole shaded area as a curve and read the values accordingly from the scales on the right- and left-hand sides. In fact, any curve on the whole chart may be considered as a sub-total, which includes all of those components or factors shown as separate areas beneath that curve. Thus the "Total Shop Cost" includes all those components shown below the "Total Shop Cost" curve.

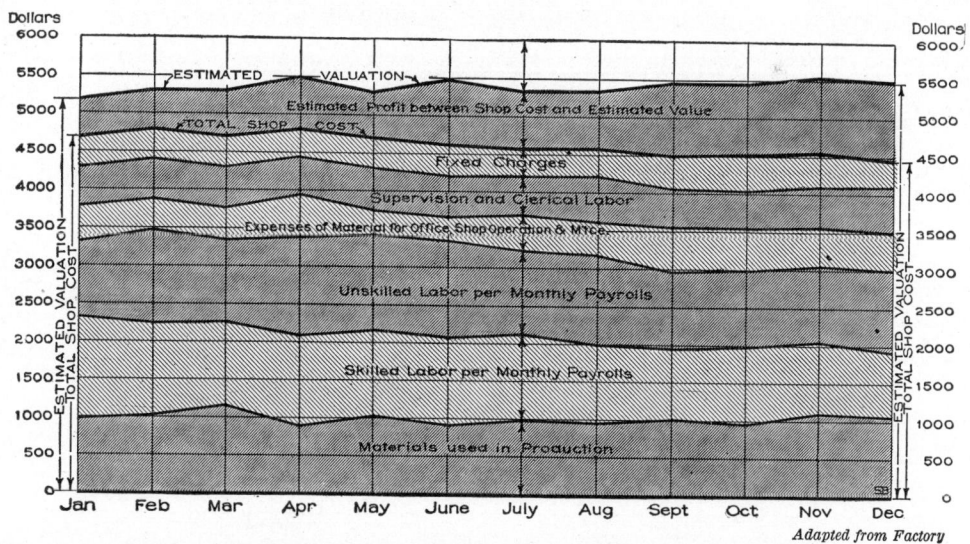

Fig. 133. Factors Entering into the Total Costs and Estimated Value of the Product of a Manufacturing Plant

The various elements entering into total shop cost are plotted, each built up on the areas below. The "Estimated Valuation" is based upon market prices for the finished goods. Vertical distances between the "Total Cost" curve and the "Estimated Valuation" curve show the estimated profit. Note the use of dimension lines in combination with the scales

The use of engineering dimension lines in Fig. 133 is of interest, for the dimension lines add considerably to the clearness of the drawing. In the center of the chart the vertical dimension lines on both sides of the names for each area show distinctly that the chart must be read on the basis of the vertical distance between the two curves on either side of any area. At the right- and left-hand edges of the chart the over-all dimension lines show the reader at once how to read the chart so as to include all the various components entering into any total which may be under consideration. The use of dimension lines should be thoroughly understood by everyone drawing charts or plotting curves, and by everyone having graphic presentations to read. Dimension lines may add much to the clearness of a chart without being in themselves unduly conspicuous.

CHAPTER IX

CUMULATIVE OR MASS CURVES

THE curves thus far shown have practically all been of a type in which the thing plotted was a value or a rate per week, per month, or per year. The tendency of such curves is to follow a horizontal direction unless affected by conditions which cause seasonal fluctuations or gradual increases or decreases. In this chapter we shall consider curves in which the data plotted concern total output, rather than the rate of output. With cumulative or mass curves, such as are considered here, each point on the curve represents a total output up to the time for which the last point is plotted. The figure for each successive period of time is added to the total already recorded, and the new total point is plotted. Because the figures relating to the last unit of time are always added to the total figures already recorded, curves of this type are called cumulative curves or mass curves. The tendency of a cumulative curve is to start at the lower left-hand corner of the co-ordinate ruling and move toward the upper right-hand corner of the sheet, according to the scale which may have been selected.

Fig. 134 is a half-tone illustration of a cumulative-curve chart representing the output of an automobile factory for one fiscal year of the business. In a conference between the sales, engineering, and manufacturing heads of this business, it was decided that the quantity of automobiles desired was fifty per week until the first of April, then sixty per week until the first of June, and seventy per week thereafter, giving a total production of three thousand two hundred automobiles for the whole season. It was thought that the rate of production on the new model automobile could be increased after the factory had been put into thoroughly good running shape, and the schedule rate of production was accordingly increased gradually in the manner shown. On account of the delay in getting drawings

150   GRAPHIC METHODS

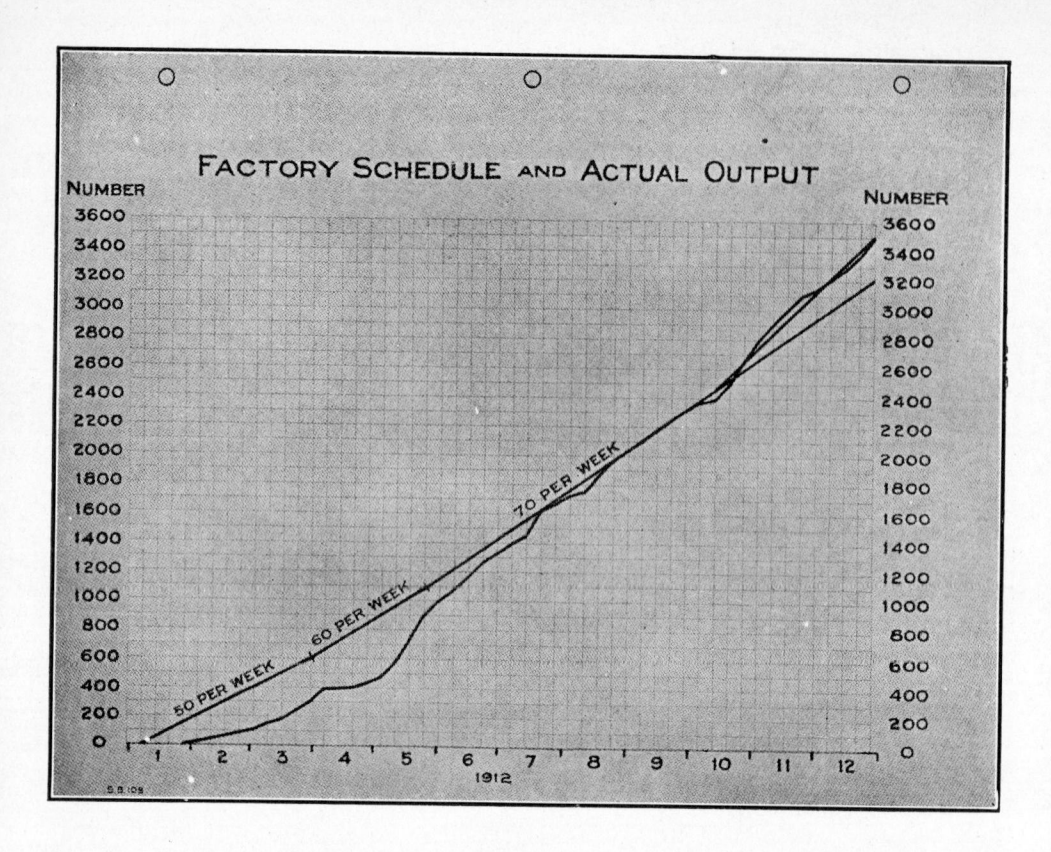

Fig. 134. Production Schedule and Actual Output of an Automobile Factory for One Year

The schedule is shown by the straight lines drawn according to the desired output per week. Actual output is indicated by the waving line showing at any date the total number of autos shipped since the beginning of the year. Note the co-ordinate paper of letter-sheet size and the scheme for marking off weeks and months so that any fiscal year may be shown on this standard ruled paper

from the engineering department, the factory was able to ship practically no cars during the month of January, though the schedule shows that one hundred and fifty cars should have been made that month. During February, the factory produced cars but fell further behind schedule constantly, as can be seen by the difference between the angle of the schedule line for February and the angle of the actual output line for February.

It must be remembered that with cumulative curves the angle between the curve and the horizontal line gives the rate of production per unit of time. The angle of the curve on the page gives much valuable information to the reader. It is for this reason that cumulative curves are sometimes much more useful than curves in which the rate of output is plotted horizontally from time to time. In the cumulative curve the total output is plotted, and changes in the rate of output, judged by the angle of the curve at different times, may be seen very easily.

During March the output curve took a rapid upward turn and we can see from its angle that, until the end of the first week in April, the output curve gradually approached the curve for schedule. During the latter part of March the factory not only got out its quota of cars each week but produced more than its quota, making up a little for the distance it fell behind during the first part of the year. Owing to a lack of material, because of a fire in a factory which supplied the crank shafts for the automobiles, not a single automobile could be shipped during the second week in April and only a few in the third week of April. The automobile factory was busy, however, accumulating a large supply of parts and assembling automobiles as completely as it was possible to do without the crank shafts which were lacking. By measuring the vertical distance between the output curve and the schedule curve, it will be seen that the factory was furthest behind its schedule during the first week in May, which is one of the best automobile-selling months of the year. If we count the squares between the output curve and the schedule curve we see that the factory was about four hundred and twenty automobiles behind schedule at the end of the first week in May. As, however, a large supply of parts and of nearly completed automobiles accumulated while the crank shafts were delayed, the factory was able to assemble and ship cars very rapidly when the crank shafts were finally received from a new source of supply. The factory turned out much more than fifty cars per week during the latter part of May and was rapidly catching up with the schedule, until the supply of accumulated parts was used up and the assembling departments were limited to the rate at which parts could be produced in the machine shop. By making every possible effort in the machine shop, the weekly rate of seventy sets of parts was exceeded, and the curve shows that during June and July the rate of shipping automobiles exceeded the schedule rate to such an extent that by the end of the third week the factory had caught up with the schedule production asked for by the sales department. There was, however, a slump in the factory output about the first of August, and it was not until the middle of August that the factory was able to furnish the desired quota of automobiles regularly.

A conference held between the sales manager and the factory manager in September resulted in a statement from the sales manager to the effect that he could sell all the automobiles that the factory could produce by the end of the year. The factory manager was told to go ahead as fast as he wished and turn out all the cars he could up to a total of three thousand five hundred cars. The schedule line was accordingly changed from the second week in October, by drawing the line so that it came out at three thousand five hundred cars at the end of the year. It will be noticed that, though the factory had a setback due to delayed material in the second week in October, it was able to exceed the new schedule during the early part of November and it made the three thousand five hundred cars by the end of the year as requested.

The foregoing account will give a fair idea of the application of cumulative curves to problems involving output and sales. In work of this sort, the cumulative curve is one of the most valuable aids to the busy executive. The last point on the curve gives him the total output since the beginning of the period for which the curve was plotted. From the angle of the curve he can see the rate of output for any period of time he may wish to consider. It must be kept in mind that a cumulative curve never trends downward. It can move only upward or horizontally. If there is no output during any period of time the curve simply moves horizontally. Like a clock recording time, it cannot go backward.

Though the cumulative curve proper cannot go backward, a modified curve may nevertheless be made to show quantities which have been added to and subtracted from, giving total net quantities. Thus the modified cumulative curve may be used to show the quantities of stock on hand, additions to stock being plotted upward and reductions to stock being plotted downward. Any point on the curve then shows the quantities on hand at that particular time. In making a curve like this it is ordinarily the practice to strike a balance of the additions and reductions for the latest period of time, and then to change the curve only by the net amount added or taken away. Such a curve gives not only a perpetual inventory in the last point plotted, but it shows the quantity on hand at different seasons of the year as a guide for future operations. A curve of this kind can be plotted for the total number of men employed in a large organization just as well as for quantities of goods in store rooms.

Fig. 134 was photographed from a sheet of co-ordinate paper specially ruled for convenience in curve plotting. The paper is eight and a half by eleven inches (a standard letter-sheet size), and has co-ordinate ruling printed in green ink with wide margins on all four edges to allow space for lettering, scales, etc. Note in Fig. 134 that the green ink of the co-ordinate lines shows much lighter in color than the black drawing ink used for the scales and the curves. Though the co-ordinate lines are distinct enough for ease in reading they are not nearly so conspicuous as they would be if a line cut had been used instead of a half-tone. In making a line cut, the green lines of the paper must, of course, be printed as black and the color value of the green lines is entirely lost. The finished line cut shows only the relative widths of lines, not relative colors. For many illustrations of curves, conspicuous co-ordinate lines are not desired. In such cases it is better to use a half-tone, as has been done in Fig. 134, than to use a line cut.

In Fig. 135 we have curves for two successive fiscal years plotted so that they may be compared easily. The double-line curves and the dotted-line curves are plotted to show the rate of shipments, while the heavy-line curves are plotted on a cumulative basis and give the total number of carloads shipped since the beginning of each fiscal year. Ordinarily it is not desirable to put on one sheet of paper curves giving both rate of output and cumulative output, as there is danger of confusing in the reader's mind two different types of curves. This illustration is included simply to show the possibility of comparing two cumulative curves for succeeding years by plotting both cumulative curves on the same sheet.

It must be remembered that cumulative curves always refer to some definite length of time and that they must always begin at the beginning of the period for which the summation is made. Cumulative curves do not extend outward indefinitely, but start over again at zero with each succeeding period of time. Thus, cumulative curves plotted by months or weeks on a long sheet of paper, for a series of years, would be seen in the shape of saw teeth, with the highest point at the end of each fiscal year and then a drop to zero again at the beginning of the next fiscal year. The saw-tooth shape makes it feasible, and sometimes desirable for easy comparison, to plot cumulative curves for several successive periods of time in the same space, as the two cumulative curves in Fig. 135 are plotted.

The progressive average shown by means of the dotted lines in Fig. 135 is obtained by averaging each month the values for all the points

154 GRAPHIC METHODS

given on each curve since the beginning of each fiscal year. For November the average includes two months, for December three months, for January four months, etc. The progressive averages in this chart mean comparatively little and can be of almost no assistance to the manager studying them. The daily averages and the progressive averages would have been much more striking if the averages for the two years had been plotted horizontally instead of as superimposed curves. A moving average could then be shown continuously so that the average would always take in twelve months without having to start over again at the beginning of the second fiscal year. The information in Fig. 135 would have been more simple in appearance and more quickly apprehended if it had been given on two separate sheets of paper, the daily average curve and the suggested moving-average curve being shown for two years horizontally on one sheet, the cumulative curves being shown on a different sheet with the two years superimposed on the same scale, as in Fig. 135.

It is frequently desirable to show two cumulative curves on the same ruled sheet of co-ordinate paper so that each curve may be studied separately and the distances between the curves noted. Thus, in Fig. 136, the upper curve shows the amount of money loaned since the beginning of the operation of a factory loan-department. The lower curve, the dotted line, indicates the amount of money repaid by the persons obtaining loans since the beginning of the department. The difference between these two curves thus represents the amount of money outstanding at the end of any month. At the bottom of the chart the actual amount of money outstanding is plotted, also in the form of a curve. On the curve showing the amount outstanding the height of each point above the zero line represents the distance between the two cumulative curves in the upper portion of the chart. It is much easier to see fluctuations if the amount outstanding is plotted in this way from the zero line than if one must gauge the amount outstanding by reading the space between two fluctuating cumulative curves. When data must be read by the length of vertical lines between two curves, the eye is likely to take as the distance between the curves the shortest distance instead of the distance measured on the vertical ruled lines.

In Fig. 136 it was very important to watch the total amount outstanding, for the fund available for loans from the beginning of the loan system until January, 1912, was limited to $200. From January,

CUMULATIVE CURVES

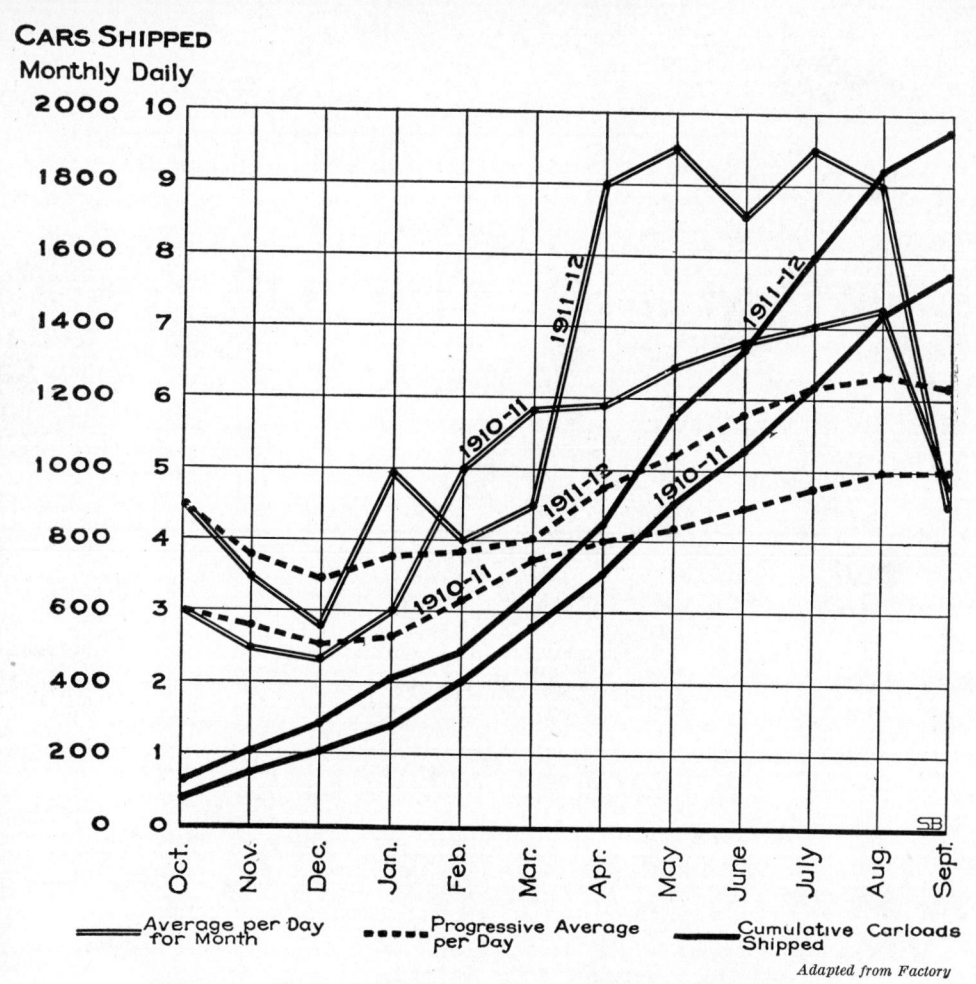

Fig. 135. Carload Shipments from a Manufacturing Plant

Two separate fiscal years are compared on the chart. The right-hand scale shows monthly averages of the number of carloads shipped per day of factory operation. The double-line curves for daily averages and the dotted-line curves for progressive averages are read from the right-hand scale. The heavy solid-line curves are read from the left-hand scale and show cumulatively the total number of carloads shipped since the beginning of each fiscal year

1912, until the end of the period under consideration the fund available for loans was $500, of which $30 (reserved for a special purpose) could not be used for the loans for which these curves were plotted. Note that in January, 1912, the amount outstanding exceeded the funds formerly available for loans, and thus required an increase in the capital of the loan fund. Though the lettering of this chart is not as clear as it should be, the chart is nevertheless an excellent presentation of facts and a good demonstration of the utility of cumulative curves.

Fig. 137 shows in detail for the same loan department the operations which are summarized in Fig. 136. In Fig. 137 the heavy line shows the actual amount of money loaned each month, while the dotted line shows the amount of money paid back each month. The data for these two curves were later added month by month on a cumulative basis and plotted into the two curves, "Loaned" and

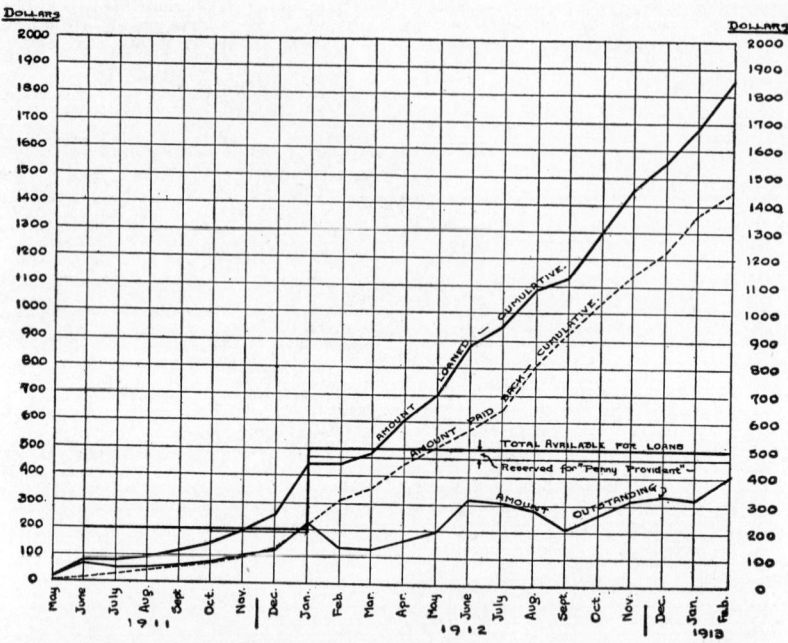

Fig. 136. Total Loans Made to Employees by a Large Industrial Corporation and Total Amount Paid Back, Shown Monthly Since the Beginning of Loans

The two upper curves are plotted on a cumulative basis. The bottom curve shows the amount outstanding and is equivalent to the vertical distance between points on the two upper curves. The capital devoted to loans is indicated, and the chart permits easy reading of the amount of capital not on loan at the end of any month

"Paid-back," in Fig. 136. Because of the great fluctuation in the amount loaned and paid back each month, the operation of the department as a whole can be seen much more easily from the cumulative curves of Fig. 136 than from the actual monthly-loan curves of Fig. 137. In general, the cumulative curve is of very great assistance in showing phenomena in which there are violent fluctuations such as are seen in the loan curve in Fig. 137.

It is interesting to note in Fig. 137 that the peaks and valleys in the curve showing the amount paid back follow ordinarily one or two months behind the peaks and valleys in the curve showing the amount loaned. This is entirely natural, for these loans were made only in cases of extreme emergency when employees were in temporary need. This relation of two curves to each other, with the peaks of one curve following at some definite distance behind the peaks of another curve, is generally referred to as "lag." Students of economics are continually finding curves which are seen to have a very great dependence upon each other when "lag" is taken into account. If "lag" is not considered, a great difference in the shape of the curves might be taken to show that there was absolutely no relation between the facts from which the curves were plotted.

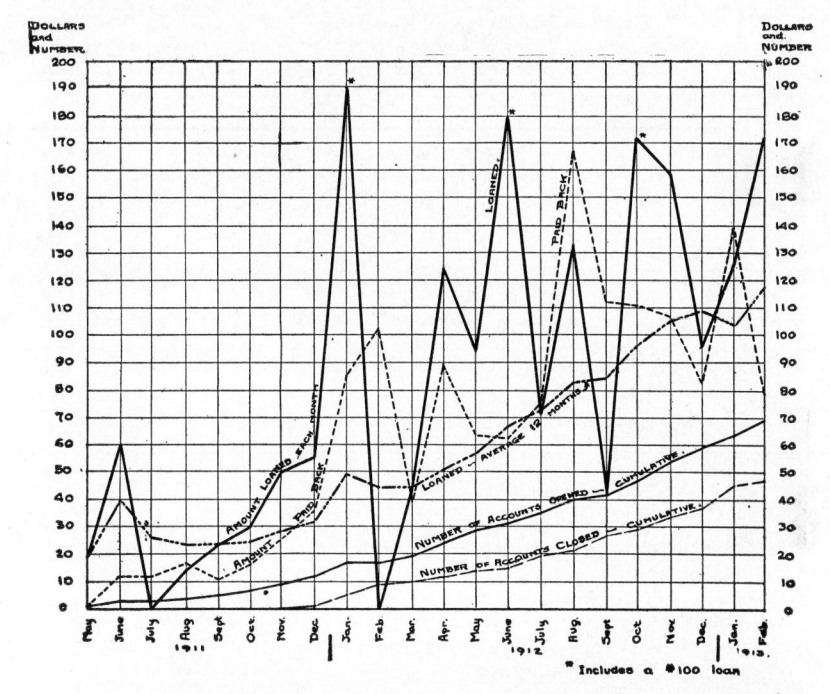

Fig. 137. Loans Each Month Made to Employees of a Large Industrial Corporation and Amounts Paid Back Each Month. Number of Accounts Opened and also Number of Accounts Closed Are Shown on a Cumulative Basis

Note how the curve for repayment lags behind the peaks and valleys of the curve for loans. The extent of the lag gives a good idea of the length of time loans are outstanding. This illustration is for the same loan department shown in Fig. 136

Great care must ordinarily be taken in determining to just how great an extent the element of "lag" enters in. The best way of determining this is to plot the two curves on separate sheets of transparent bond paper, tracing paper, or tracing cloth, plotting each curve to a separate scale, if necessary, so that the peaks and valleys in the two curves will be as nearly as possible at equal distances from the zero line. It is difficult to prove a "lag" unless the scales are selected so that the peaks and valleys in the two curves are at the same height above zero. After the two curves have been plotted separately to carefully selected scales, they may be superimposed and read through both sheets of paper held in front of a bright light. As the horizontal scales for the two curves are the same, it will be found, if the curves depend upon each other without the element of "lag," that the peaks and valleys will almost coincide. If there is "lag," it will be found necessary, in order to make the peaks and valleys coincide, to shift one sheet horizontally over the other so that the horizontal scales disagree. When the paper has been shifted back and forth until the nearest possible coincidence of the two curves has been obtained, the extent of the "lag" may be determined by seeing how far the two horizontal scales are out of agreement. "Lag" is an important feature of many different sets of curves and must be kept constantly in mind when curves are being compared.

In Fig. 137 the growth in the importance of the loan department can readily be seen by considering the twelve-months progressive moving average showing the average total monthly loans. Though there is, in January, 1912, a very high peak which overshadows all other peaks, the general tendency of the curve is still rapidly upward, because of the fact that a number of high points follow each other in close succession, each nearly as high as the peak of January, 1913, which stands out alone with low points on either side.

The number of separate loan accounts opened and the number of accounts closed is shown in Fig. 137 by means of cumulative curves. The fact that the cumulative curve for the number of accounts closed follows so nearly the angle of the cumulative curve for the number of accounts opened, shows that the number of accounts outstanding has not greatly increased. It also shows that since numerous accounts are being closed, the loans are being made to other employees rather than being repeated continually to the same employees.

Fig. 138 is a study made to determine the size of tank necessary to supply sufficient boiler-feed water for a number of locomotives and tugboats. The average amount of water used each day by all the locomotives combined is given in the lower cumulative curve. The shape of the curve shows that locomotives fill their tanks chiefly between six and nine o'clock in the morning and between five and

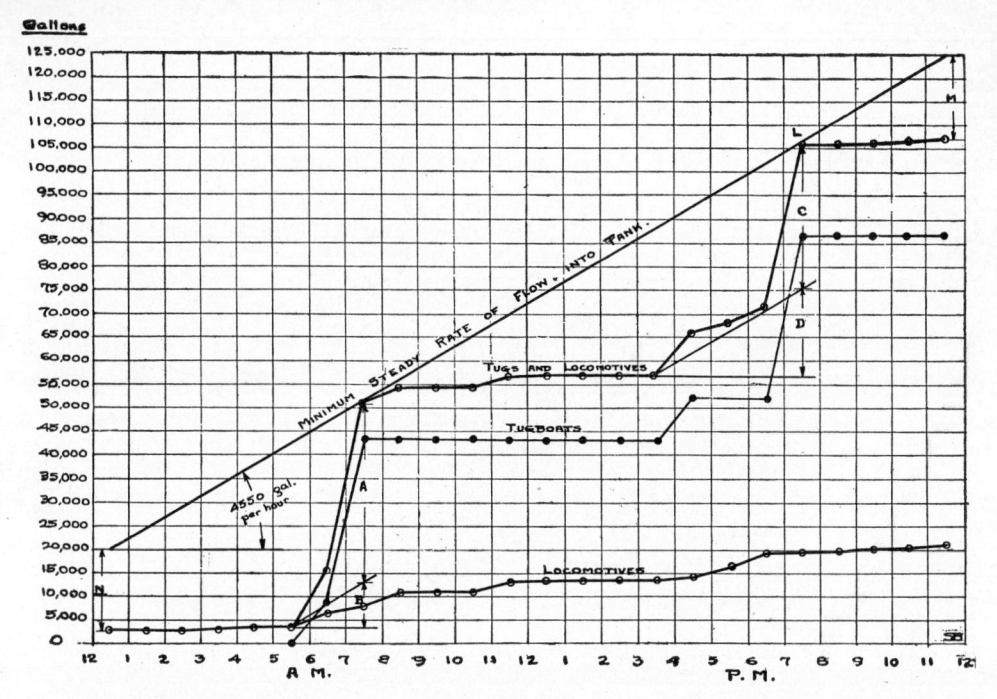

Fig. 138. Cumulative Curves Plotted to Determine the Minimum Size of Tank and the Minimum Steady Flow of Water Required for a Group of Locomotives and a Group of Tugboats Taking Boiler-Feed Water from the Same Source of Supply

Curves for locomotives and tugs are plotted separately. A third curve is then made by adding the vertical distances of points on the two curves to get the vertical distance for points on the third curve. The sloping straight line shows the minimum rate of steady flow. The greatest vertical distance between the sloping line and the combined curve shows the necessary minimum tank capacity

seven at night. The points are plotted in the middle of each space because the values are based on the average quantity of water taken between any two hours specified in the horizontal scale. The next curve above gives on a cumulative basis the average of the amount of water taken by the tugboats each day. It can be seen that the tugs take water between six and eight in the morning and between four and eight at night, the greatest quantity of water being taken between seven and eight. In order to see what would happen if the locomotives and the tugs should take water from the same tanks, the combined curve was made for both locomotives and tugboats by adding the quantities for each one-hour period. The easiest way to make a combined curve when only two curves are to be combined, is to use a pair of dividers, taking the vertical distance above zero for each point on one curve and stepping off that measured distance above each point on the other curve. The prick marks showing the

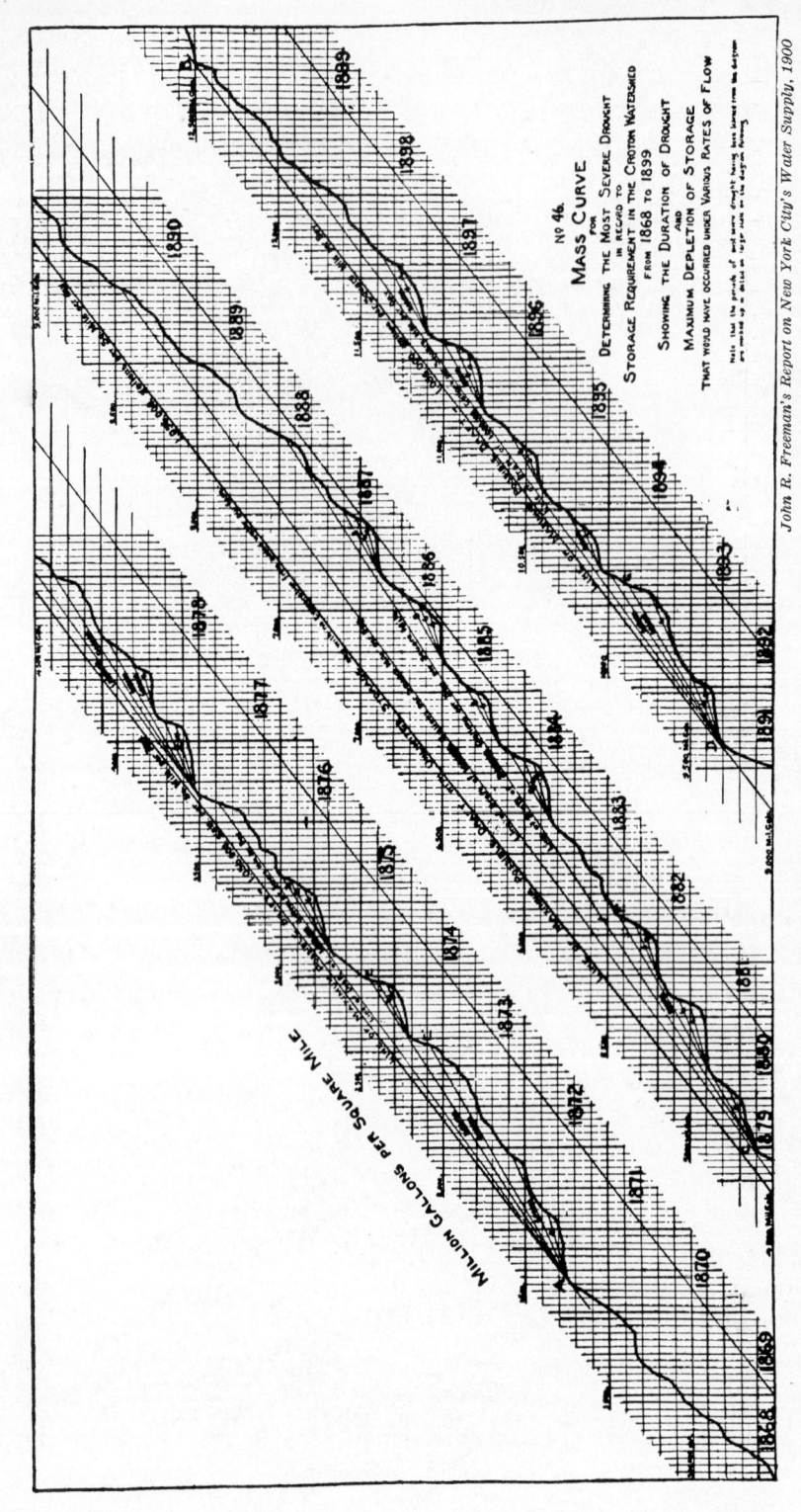

Fig. 139. Cumulative or Mass Curve, Showing the Relation of Drought to the Storage Capacity Required for Different Rates of Water Consumption from the Croton Watershed. The Rainfall in Million Gallons per Square Mile of Watershed Is Plotted from 1868 to 1899

Note the arrangement to get a long cumulative curve on a small page by showing the curve in three sections. In Fig. 138 the curve was plotted on a fluctuating consumption and the line joining humps on the curve showed the minimum rate of steady supply. Here the curve is plotted for a varying rainfall supply, and the straight lines joining different humps show the maximum possible steady rate of consumption with different sized reservoirs for storage purposes. The necessary reservoir capacity is determined by the greatest vertical distance between the rainfall curve and any sloping line drawn for rate of consumption or "draft."

distances stepped off by the dividers locate the new combined curve so that it can be quickly drawn in. The combined curve in Fig. 138 shows at a glance that the locomotives and tugs together take water in such manner that the greatest rate of flow from the tank occurs between six and eight in the morning.

One problem involved in Fig. 138 was to determine the minimum steady rate of flow into the tank and the size of the tank so that there would always be sufficient water available. By drawing a line diagonally touching the hump on the curve between seven and eight in the morning and the hump on the curve between six and seven at night, we get at once the smallest size flow which will keep the tank full throughout the whole twenty-four hours if locomotives and tugs always draw out the water as the average curves shown in Fig. 138 would indicate. The actual rate per hour at which the water should flow is obtained most easily by assuming a horizontal distance of several hours on the scale, and then reading upward to the diagonal line that vertical distance which corresponds with the horizontal distance taken. Thus, if from the point on the line for 40,000 at which the diagonal line intersects the vertical line for five a. m., we count 10 blocks horizontally to the right, we see that it takes 9.1 blocks before we again reach the diagonal line. Nine and one-tenth vertical blocks correspond on the scale to 45,500 gallons of water flowing in 10 hours, so that the minimum steady rate of flow must be 4,550 gallons per hour.

The dimension marks at "C" and "D" indicate the great amount of water used between four and eight p. m. The diagonal line drawn parallel to the minimum-flow line shows the amount of water which flows into the tank between three and eight p. m., thus reducing the quantity to be supplied from the storage space of the tank to the amount indicated on the vertical scale by the dimension mark "C". Between six and eight a. m., when the amount which can flow into the tank through the regular flow-pipe is limited to the quantity indicated by the dimension mark "B", the draught on the tank is so rapid that all of the water indicated by the dimension mark "A" must be furnished by the storage capacity of the tank itself. The water does not flow into the tank nearly so fast as it is taken out by the tugs and locomotives at that particular time of the day. If we count the squares included vertically in the dimension line "A" we find 7.6 squares. This shows that the amount of water which must be furnished by the tank during the rush hours cannot be less than

7.6 times 5,000 (the value for each square on the scale), or 38,000 gallons. The distance "A" is really the same as the vertical distance between the point representing the average for the hour from five to six a. m. and the diagonal line of minimum flow. The storage capacity necessary in any case of this sort is very simply determined by means of curves or mass diagrams on the general scheme of Fig. 138. The measurement of the greatest distance which shows between any depression in the consumption curve and the minimum-flow line which joins the peaks on either side of it gives the minimum steady rate of flow.

There is great practical value in charts like Fig. 138. In this case the minimum-flow line determines the size of the pipe, pumps, or other machinery which must be installed to provide the requisite quantity of water if the water is kept running steadily all the time. The tank capacity must be as great as the diagram demands or there will not always be sufficient water. In practice, it would, of course, be customary to put in a pump considerably larger than that needed to provide the minimum flow which the chart shows to be necessary, and the tank would also be of larger capacity than the minimum-storage determination of the curve would indicate. The extra capacity of both pump and tank are, however, only a safeguard against abnormal conditions. The graphic solution shows the exact rate of flow and the storage capacity which would be satisfactory if the conditions indicated by the data on the curves were to be constantly maintained.

Fig. 139 shows the application of the cumulative or mass curve to problems of municipal water-supply. In working up data for rainfall in different watersheds and determining the greatest possible amount of water which can be obtained from watersheds when different sizes of reservoirs are used, the cumulative curve is almost indispensable. In Fig. 139 the method is nearly identical with that used in Fig. 138, except that in Fig. 139 we are determining the greatest possible rate of uniform consumption from a fluctuating supply, instead of determining the smallest possible rate of uniform supply for a fluctuating consumption. In Fig. 139, the lines beginning at the hump in 1870 are drawn at different angles to touch the different humps and show various rates of possible consumption. These flow lines are also continued in the other sections of the curve just as if the curve had been shown continuously in one line instead of in three separate sections. The scale for Fig. 139 is selected to show "million gallons per square mile." The scale could just as well have been made to show the total gallons of rainfall in the whole watershed, but it was more convenient to put the scale on a square-mile basis, dividing the total rainfall by the number of square miles in the watershed.

Cumulative or mass curves are very frequently used for the study of quantities in earth work, especially in railroad construction. Cumulative curves showing the total quantities of earth removed from cuts and the total amount used in fills can be kept to give the whole information in the most convenient form for quick reference and accurate study.

CHAPTER X

FREQUENCY CURVES. CORRELATION

MANY business problems can be studied most rapidly and conveniently if the data are put in the form of frequency curves. Though engineers have used curves for many years to represent data relating to the laws of physics, the engineer has made practically no use of frequency curves such as are used by the biologist. This is probably due to the fact that the engineer can determine the laws of physics from mathematical computations based on a relatively small number of observations, while the biologist must deal with statistical averages based upon observations and measurements in thousands of different cases. The laws of biology are not so definitely mathematical as those of engineering and physics. The biologist must have more observations than the engineer if he is to draw accurate conclusions.

A frequency chart is based on the number of times a certain characteristic is found repeated in a large number of observations. The number of repetitions is referred to as the "frequency". A comparison

C. B. Davenport, in Popular Science Monthly

Fig. 140. Frequency Chart Based on the Number of Ribs in Scallop Shells. Shells Are Sorted into Different Piles According to the Number of Ribs, the Piles (from Left to Right) Having Respectively 15, 16, 17, 18, 19 and 20 Ribs

The heights of the different piles show the relative frequency of shells having the different numbers of ribs. Seventeen-rib shells were found much more commonly than shells with any other number of ribs. If a line were drawn through the tops of the different shell piles, we should have a frequency curve

FREQUENCY CURVES

relating to the frequency with which different characteristics or items are found repeated is commonly referred to by the biologist as "frequency distribution", and the charts showing frequency are quite often called "distribution charts" or "distribution curves".

In Fig. 140 a frequency diagram is shown at the right by photographing piles of shells arranged so that all shells in any one pile contain the same number of ribs. The pile of shells at the left, having the smallest number of ribs, contains but three shells. In the pile of shells at the extreme right, having the highest number of ribs, there is only one shell. The middle pile shows conclusively that the greatest number of the shells have seventeen ribs. There is a fairly large number of shells in the pile for sixteen ribs, and a somewhat greater number of shells in the pile for eighteen ribs. Though it is unfortunate that no horizontal scale or vertical scale is shown in the picture, the reader will nevertheless be able to see from this illustration the general scheme on which frequency curves are based.

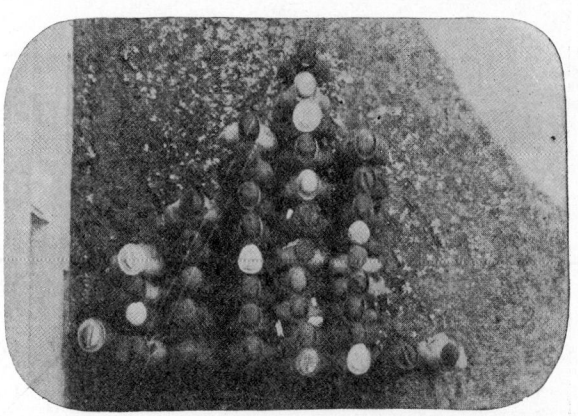

C. B. Davenport, in Popular Science Monthly

Fig. 141. Forty University Students Arranged in Rows, According to Stature by Inches, as follows: 56 to 57.9, 58 to 59.9, 60 to 61.9, 62 to 63.9, 64 to 65.9, 66 to 67.9, 68 to 69.9, 70 to 71.9

This illustration gives a good idea of the basis on which a frequency chart is constructed. A rough frequency curve could be made by drawing a line through the ends of all the different rows of men. The curve would show a definite peak for the height 64 to 65.9 inches. Such a peak is called the "mode", since it shows the type which occurs with greatest frequency

In Fig. 141 a group of men have been arranged in different rows. There is only one man in the shortest class at the left, and only one man in each of the tallest two classes at the right. Most of the men are of that height shown by the row to the right of the center of the diagram. A glance at the photograph taken looking down on this group of men shows that there are more men shorter than the most frequent height than there are men taller. If an ink line were drawn as a smooth curve to represent the outline of the whole group of men, when arranged in rows as shown here, the top of the curve at the end of the longest row would be called the "mode", as it would show the type found most frequently in all the individuals under observation.

In the following illustrations, curves of this kind will be noticed using the diagrammatic form rather than the actual photographs of a classified group like Fig. 141. In Fig. 141 it is regrettable that the illustration does not show a scale giving for each row the maximum and minimum height of men in that row. Some scheme, of course, was necessary to divide these men up into height classes, but the reader has no way of knowing the limits of height for each class except by referring to the title of the illustration.

Frequency charts are sometimes made for popular illustration by drawing vertical lines to represent the number of individuals found in each class designated by the horizontal scale. Thus, a representation could be made for the data of Fig. 141 by having a horizontal scale to represent heights, and drawing vertical lines to a scale by which the length of each vertical line or bar would represent the number of individuals of that particular height. The series of bars would then have the same general arrangement as the photograph of Fig. 141 representing the number of men actually seen. These bar diagrams to represent frequency are not of very great use, except possibly in advertising work where it may be necessary to get some kind of chart which can be understood by any untrained reader.

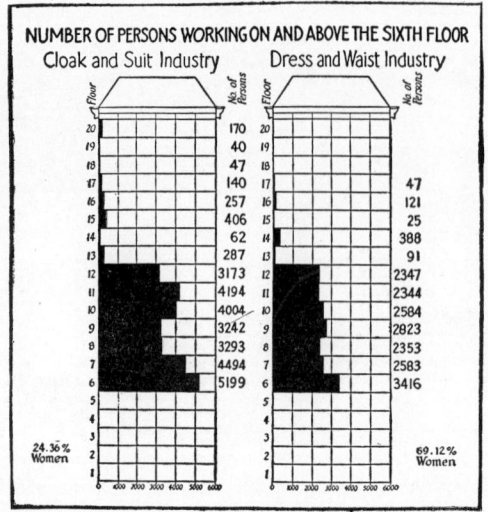

Joint Board of Sanitary Control, New York City

Fig. 142. The Number of Persons Working On and Above the Sixth Floor in the Cloak and Suit Industry and the Dress and Waist Industry in New York City

This chart was made first for a wall exhibit and was later used in a widely distributed report. The co-ordinate ruling has the shape of a New York manufacturing building. By observing this illustration from the left edge of the page the reader may get the general effect of a frequency curve

In Fig. 142 an effective use has been made of the frequency-curve scheme in a report intended for wide circulation among persons who have not been trained in reading curves. The general outline of a tall New York manufacturing building is given very clearly as a field of co-ordinate ruling, on which the actual numbers of workers for any floor level can be read from the horizontal scale with a fair degree of accuracy. The numbers working below the sixth floor are very large, and only those on and above the sixth floor are shown.

FREQUENCY CURVES

This allows the use of a large scale for the data of the upper floors. In order to see the general shape of a frequency curve when plotted with flat tops instead of peaked tops, the book may be turned so that the illustration is seen from the left-hand edge. This chart was drawn primarily as a wall exhibit, to be used later as an illustration in a printed report. The general scheme is excellent and it could scarcely be improved upon, even though the independent variable has here been made the vertical scale instead of the horizontal scale. Putting these data in the form of a curve such as is used in Fig. 143 would probably not be as effective for untrained readers as the black bars of Fig. 142, placed against a field in the general shape of a New York manufacturing building.

Fig. 143 shows a frequency diagram of the kind found most useful in ordinary work. The vertical scale here represents percentage, and the total of all the figures shown at the upper part of the chart added together is 100 per cent. Frequency curves are very often used, however, with numbers rather than percentages represented on the vertical scale, and the vertical scale then shows the actual number in each class. To assist the reader, the total number of observations made would usually be recorded, perhaps in the title of the illustration. In biological work observations are usually made in vast number, to permit making a very accurate conclusion regarding the general laws of frequency for any particular subject under consideration. For a great many problems of everyday life, however, the observations are not

Fig. 143. Age at Marriage of 439 Married Graduates of Mount Holyoke College who Graduated from 1890 to 1909

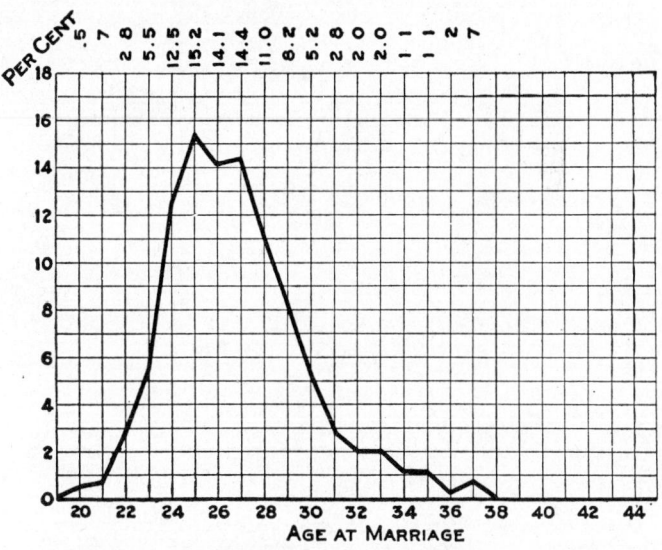

Data of Amy Hewes, in Publications Am. Statistical Assn.

The vertical scale shows the percentage of the whole 439 who married at each age given on the horizontal scale. The totals of all percentage figures at the upper margin of the chart is 100 per cent. If a greater number of persons were included in a frequency curve of this sort the curve would be less irregular and the mode would show more distinctly

of sufficient number to permit the formation of any general laws. Thus for Fig. 143 we are not justified in saying that all college women marry at the particular ages indicated by this chart. The number of women taken into consideration for the preparation of the chart was not sufficient to allow any final conclusion, certainly not to justify any general statement that college women are less likely to marry at the age of twenty-six than at either twenty-five or twenty-seven.

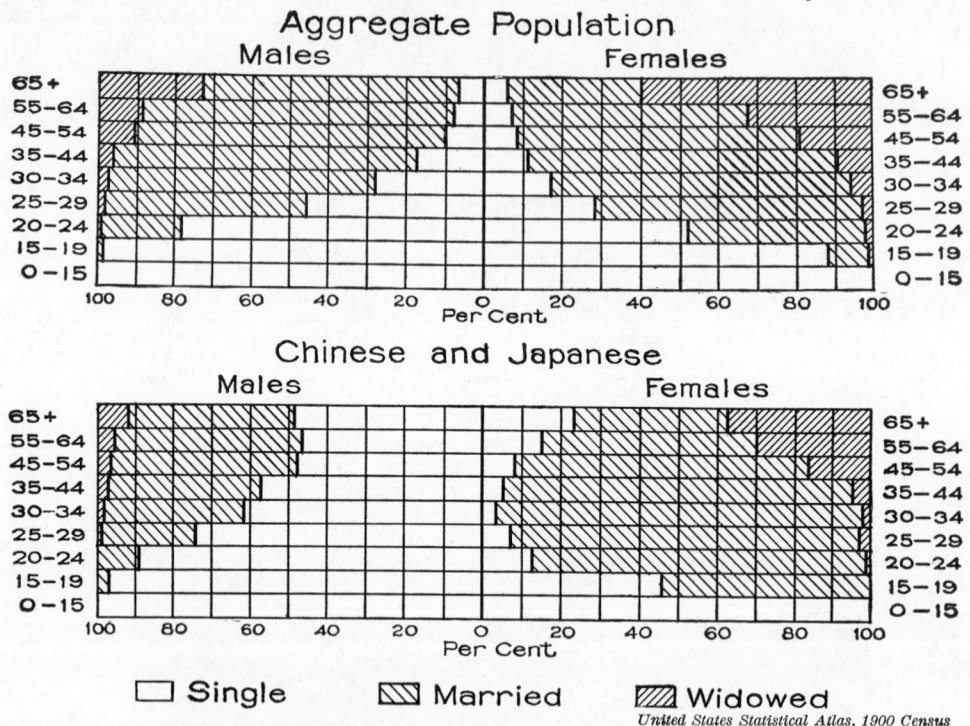

Fig. 144. Conjugal Condition of the Population of the United States in 1900 in Proportions of the Total Number of Each Age Group

This chart was printed in color in the Statistical Atlas. Here shading is used instead of color. The arrangement to the right and left of a zero line at the center makes visual comparison difficult between the data for males and females. Note the contrasts between the upper and lower charts. Compare the upper chart with Fig. 145

In biological work the number of observations taken is ordinarily sufficient to permit drawing a smooth curve to represent the general law, after a chart drawn with numerous straight lines has been made by the method used in Fig. 143. It would not be desirable to draw a smooth curve in the case of Fig. 143, as the smooth curve would be misleading because of the small number of observations made. For most business problems, and in many problems actually in the field of statistics, the laws which affect frequency are so indefinite and the number of observations so limited that it is much better to use the straight-line method of Fig. 143 than to attempt to make a smooth curve. Sometimes a smooth curve may only mislead the reader, making the chart appear very accurate when in reality the data were so crude that only the roughest approximation is possible.

Fig. 144 is copied from the Census Atlas for the 1900 Census. In the Atlas, colors were used for the different areas which must be represented here by cross-hatching. Though these illustrations hold some very valuable and interesting information, the information is contained

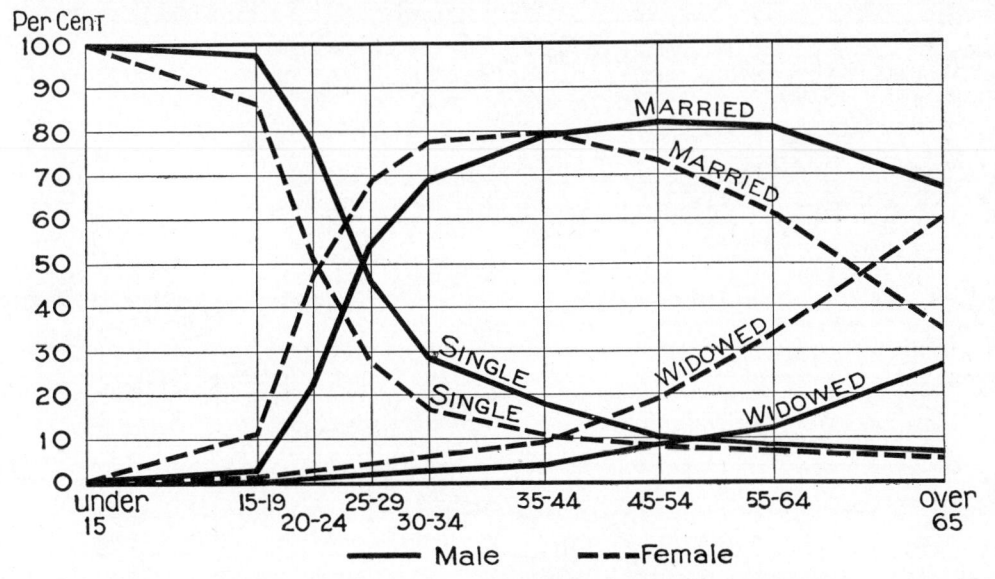

Fig. 145. Conjugal Condition of the Population of the United States in 1900 in Proportions of the Total Number of Each Age Group

Here the arrangement of Fig. 144 has been reversed so as to place age on the horizontal scale, since age is the independent variable. Having the data expressed in curves permits much clearer interpretation by the reader. Curves for male and for female may be instantly compared. The term "widowed" as applied to men was used to harmonize with the preceding illustration

in such manner that it is almost impossible for the reader to get it out. In the first place, age is the independent variable, but it has been made the vertical scale. The information sought is the percentage at different ages for each of the sexes, and this must be read from the horizontal scale, in violation of one of the most important rules for graphic work. Another bad feature of the chart is that data for male and female are shown in the right and left direction from the center line, making it almost impossible for the reader to compare the figures for male and female at any age under consideration. The data for the upper half of Fig. 144 are replotted in Fig. 145, and the reader would do well to compare the two illustrations to see just how much more clear Fig. 145 is than Fig. 144.

The bottom portion of Fig. 144 is shown here by way of contrast with the upper portion. Notice, for instance, the difference in the shape of the chart for the female Chinese and Japanese population of the United States as compared with the chart for females in the aggregate population of the United States. A very large percentage of female Japanese and Chinese are married by the age of thirty-five, but after that age there is a fairly large percentage reported as single. It would appear that many widows must be reporting themselves as single instead of as widows, or the chart would probably not be so different in shape from the chart for the aggregate population of the United States.

In Fig. 145 the scale for age has been properly placed horizontally and the scale for percentage placed vertically. The whole population is considered as single under the age of fifteen. The total of the figures for single, married, and widowed on any vertical line equals 100 per cent; thus, as the number married in succeeding years increases, the number who are single is seen to decrease. The curves prove at a glance that the women start to marry much earlier than the men. Between twenty and thirty-five the horizontal difference between the two curves shows that the women marry about four years earlier than the men, or, in other words, taking the population as a whole, the women marry men about four years their seniors. In considering these curves it must be remembered that this chart is made up on a different basis from Fig. 143. In Fig. 143 all the women who married are recorded as married, and the top of the curve (the mode) shows at once the age at which marriages are most frequent. In this chart, however, we are considering three things, and the chart shows the percentage who recorded themselves as married, rather than the actual age at which marriage occurred. The percentage of those who report themselves married is affected by the number who are single and also by the number who are widowed. If in the later age classes, deaths of husbands occur more rapidly than marriages of spinsters for any particular age, the "married" curve will trend downward even though a very large number of spinsters may be marrying at that age. It is simply a question of balancing the death rate of husbands against the marriage rate of spinsters. The curve marked "married" on this chart does not show the age at marriage, but simply shows the percentage in any age class who report themselves as married and not widowed.

The men marry later than the women. Many of the men marrying over forty marry women much younger than themselves. As the husbands are older than the wives, the expectation of life for the husband is, of course, less than for the wives, and the number of widows at any age is far in excess of the number of widowers, on this account alone. Industrial accidents, war, etc., also tend to make a high death rate among the men and cause more widows than widowers. In Fig. 145 the curve for men has been labeled "widowed" to follow the Census Office practice in Fig. 144.

With Fig. 144 some of the age classes are for an interval of only five years while other age classes have an interval of ten years, yet the different lengths of interval are shown by the same distance on the scale. For Fig. 145 the horizontal scale has purposely been made such that the ten-year age intervals are set off by twice the distance used for the five-year intervals. As there are very few marriages under fifteen, the space for "under fifteen" has been made three times the space for the five-year interval. Taking the standard life as four-score years, the space for "over sixty-five" has been made three times the distance used for the five-year intervals. This selection of horizontal distances makes the curves into much more nearly their correct shape than is possible on the Census Office chart, where five-year and ten-year class intervals are shown by equal scale distances.

Perhaps the greatest gain made in clearness in Fig. 145 is due to the placing of the curves for male and female on the same ruled field, so that they can be compared instantly and correctly without need for any right-hand and left-hand measurements such as were necessary in Fig. 144. No claim is made that Fig. 145 is suitable for untrained readers. Since, however, it is doubtful whether many unskilled readers ever refer to the Census Atlas, it would seem desirable to use the general scheme of Fig. 145 for clearness and convenience.

In Fig. 146, also taken from the Census Atlas for the 1900 Census, a right-and-left measurement must be made to compare death rates in two different years, ten years apart. The chart was drawn to bring out the data clearly and, if clearness is not attained, the data might just as well be expressed in columns of figures. Here again the variables have been reversed and the independent variable improperly made the vertical scale.

In Fig. 147 the data of Fig. 146 are redrawn into two curves by which the number of deaths occurring at different ages can be readily

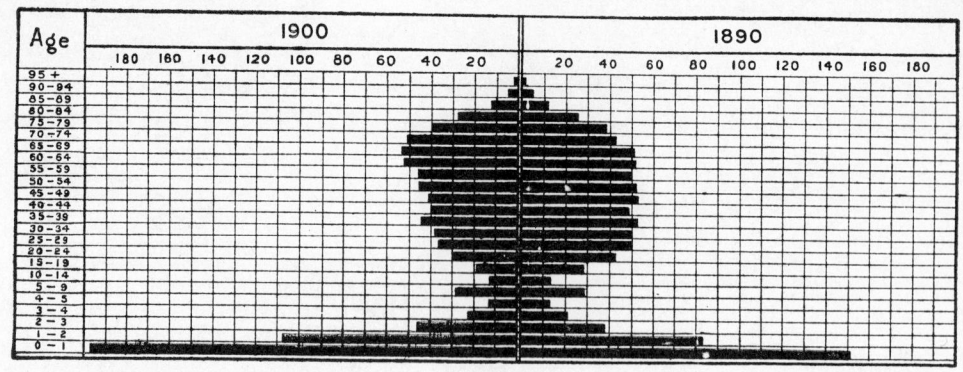

Fig. 146. Comparative Proportion of Deaths at Different Ages from Pneumonia per 1,000 Deaths from Pneumonia in the Registration Area of the United States, 1890 and 1900

The right-and-left arrangement of this chart makes comparison for the two different years almost impossible. Contrast this illustration with Fig. 147

compared for the two years under consideration. Notice that in the later year, 1900, deaths from pneumonia between the ages of ten and sixty years were much less frequent, while deaths after the age of sixty were more frequent. There was also an increase in the number of deaths at ages less than four. Certainly the facts relating to deaths from pneumonia for the two years are much more clearly brought out in Fig. 147 than in Fig. 146.

There are some peculiarities in Fig. 147 which should be pointed out. The Government figures are given by one-year intervals up to the age of five, and then on five-year intervals to ninety-five. Fig. 147 really should have been made so as to indicate a change in the horizontal scale at five years. If the chart had been made the full width of the page it would have been possible to get room enough to show the figures for single years at ages under five by using a space only one-fifth of the horizontal distance used for the five-year intervals. The large number of deaths at ages five to nine inclusive is very striking on the curve. Possibly the large death rate from five to nine may be due to the lessening of parental care at an age when exposure becomes more frequent. By ten years of age, the children have learned better how to take care of themselves and the number of deaths from pneumonia comes down to about the lowest point. Though the foregoing explanation of the large number of deaths from five to nine years may be correct, it is probable that the figures are more or less in error, due to the tendency to state ages in numbers which are multiples of five. The peaks for the period five to nine may be due largely to parents giving the age roughly as "five years".

In Fig. 148 the data in which the reader is interested are shown at the peaks of various triangles. The shaded triangles on the chart give a geometrical figure which at first glance might be considered as a curve. It is not until after a considerable amount of puzzling that one notices that the triangles have absolutely no significance and that they are only a means of showing the distance from the base line to the various points representing decrease or increase. It would have been better if plain black bars had been used for Fig. 148 instead of the triangles. Bars are so familiar to everyone that there would be no danger of error in interpretation. This illustration was used in a Sunday newspaper article where a non-technical class of readers had to be reached. For such a class of readers the solid black bars would probably be the most easily understood method of presentation.

For anything except newspaper presentation, the method of Fig. 149 would probably be more acceptable to the reader than the solid

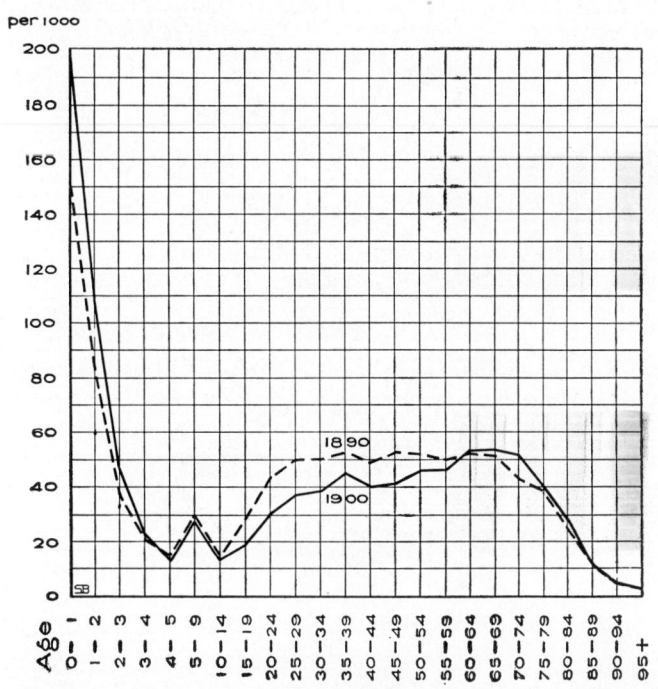

Fig. 147. Comparative Proportion of Deaths at Different Ages from Pneumonia per 1,000 Deaths from Pneumonia in the Registration Area of the United States, 1890 and 1900

Comparison of the two years can be made instantly throughout the whole range of ages. Age is the independent variable and, hence, is shown here as the horizontal scale. It would be better if a vertical wavy line or some other signal were used to show the change in the horizontal scale for ages below five years

black bars suggested in the preceding paragraph. The curve drawn in Fig. 149 shows a fairly uniform increase in death rates as ages increase up to the age of sixty. The degree of uniformity in increase is much more readily seen from the curve line than it could be shown

174 GRAPHIC METHODS

by the use of bars. Granted that the curve of Fig. 149 might not be understood by all the readers of a newspaper, it is nevertheless much more desirable, even in newspaper work, than the method shown in Fig. 148. Though Fig. 149 might not attract deep interest on the part of a newspaper reader, it would not be likely to be misinterpreted. Fig. 148 might serve to attract attention, but what is the use in attracting attention unless a correct impression is given after attention has been attracted?

Frequency curves thus far considered have permitted reading from the vertical scale only the actual number or percentage observed corresponding to any point which may be selected on the horizontal scale. Thus, in Fig. 143 (see page 167) we can read from the vertical scale only the percentage of marriages which corresponds to any selected age on the horizontal scale. In Fig. 150, however, we have the same data of Fig. 143 plotted in the form of a cumulative frequency curve. With a cumulative frequency curve the vertical scale shows not the actual number for any point of the horizontal scale, but the number cumulatively up to any point which may be selected on the horizontal scale. In Fig. 143 the percentage who married at each age is given in figures at the top of the chart. By observing the figures at the top of Fig. 143 and the figures at the top of Fig. 150, the method for plotting a cumulative frequency curve will be apparent. Beginning with the percentages for the later ages in Fig. 143, the figures for the various years are added cumulatively to give the figures seen at the top of Fig. 150. The figures and the curve of Fig. 150 thus show the per-

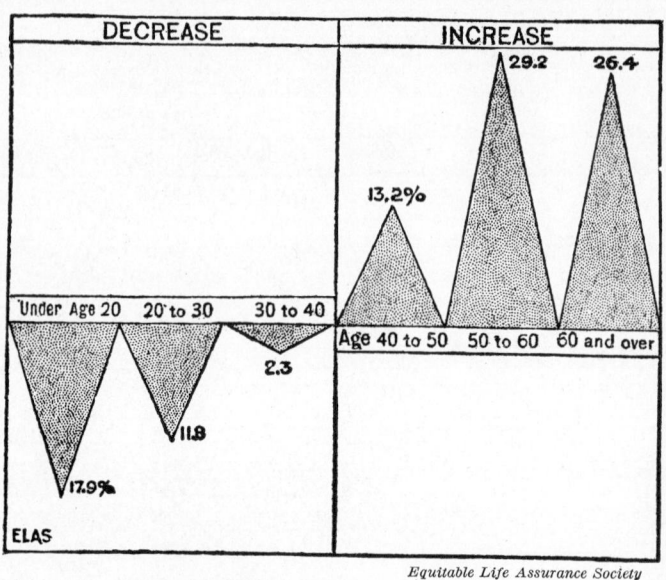

Fig. 148. Change Since 1880 in the Death Rates of Americans at Various Ages

Equitable Life Assurance Society

The use of the separate triangles here is confusing to the reader. One is apt to interpret the chart by the contour of the shaded areas rather than by the points at the tips of separate triangles. Compare this illustration with Fig. 149

FREQUENCY CURVES 175

centage who married at ages greater than any specific age selected from the horizontal scale of the chart.

Fig. 151 gives an example of a class of information which can be shown to very great advantage by the use of cumulative frequency curves. In an annual report of a railroad a tabulated statement of the number of miles of different weights of rail in use at the end of the fiscal year makes the information difficult for the stockholder to interpret. Putting the data in the form of a curve like Fig. 151 lets the stockholder see at once just what conditions are on his road, in so far as rail weight is concerned. Thus, in Fig. 151, the stockholder may see at a glance that a very small percentage of the rails on this railroad weigh in excess of 75 pounds per yard, and that only about half of the rails weigh more than 70 pounds per yard. In order to compare different years it would be well to have a chart of this kind printed in the annual report, with curves for different years plotted on the same co-ordinate ruling, so that the stockholder could see by the change in the shape of the curves just what has been done toward replacing light rails with heavy rails. If desired, rail-weight curves for different railroad systems could be shown in the same chart, so that the stockholder might see how his railroad compares with others in the matter of rail weights.

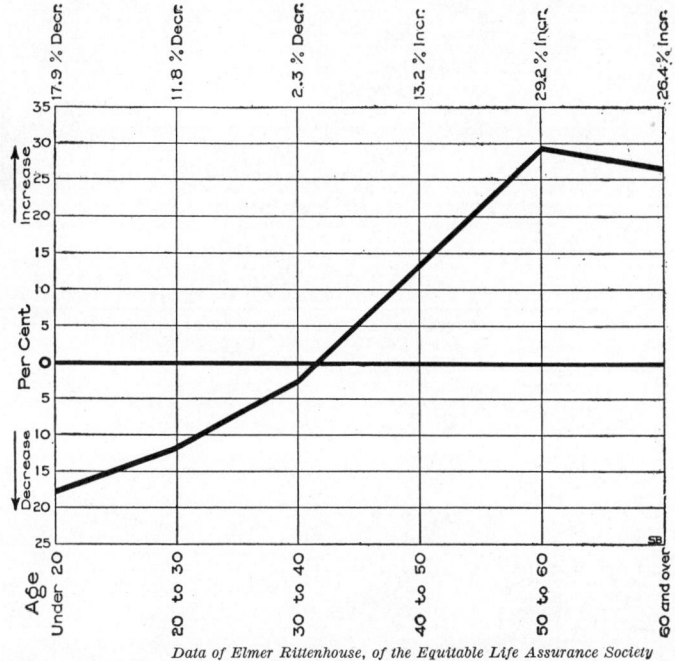

Fig. 149. Change Since 1880 in the Death Rate of Americans at Various Ages

Data of Elmer Rittenhouse, of the Equitable Life Assurance Society

The increase in death rates for ages over forty is here shown in great contrast with the decrease in death rates for ages less than forty. The heavy zero line and the arrows pointing upward and downward make misinterpretation almost impossible

It would have been better if Fig. 151 had, at the lower left-hand corner, the words "more than", with an arrow pointing horizontally to the right as can be seen in Fig. 158. In cumulative frequency curves such as this it is well to give the reader a clew that it is a cumulative frequency curve he is observing, and the arrow with the words "more than" accomplishes this result in a satisfactory manner.

There are two scales used in Fig. 151 with the expectation that the reader would ordinarily use the left-hand scale when reading the chart, using the words "more than". The right-hand scale reading downward permits the reader to get at once the complement of any figure on the left-hand scale, so that, by using the right-hand scale, the reader may interpret the curves on a "less than" basis. Thus, in considering the weight, roughly 6 per cent of all the rails on the system are more than 75 pounds per yard, and using the right-hand scale it is seen that, roughly, 94 per cent of all the rails are "less than" 75 pounds per yard. There is not ordinarily any necessity for using a double scale in this manner. It is done here only to show the difference in reading a two-scale chart.

Fig. 150. Percentage of 439 Married Graduates of Mount Holyoke College (Women) Graduating 1890 to 1909, who Married at Ages Greater than Any Specific Age Selected from the Horizontal Scale of the Chart

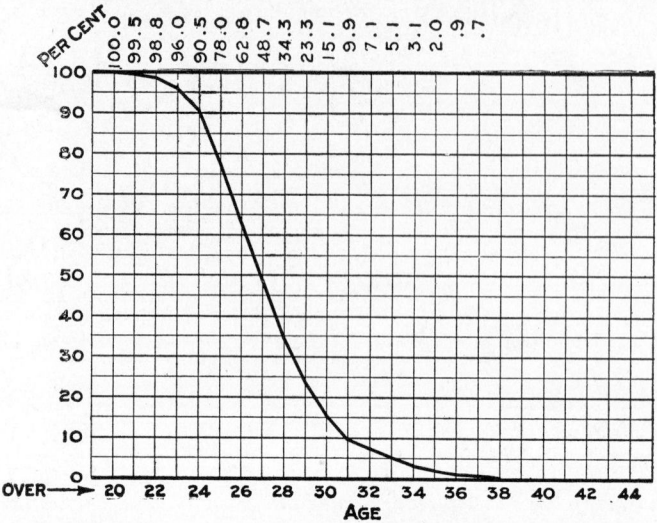

Data of Amy Hewes in Publications Am. Statistical Assn.

This is a cumulative frequency curve plotted from exactly the same data as Fig. 143. The word "over" with the arrow at the lower left-hand corner of the chart shows that the chart does not indicate the percentage who marry *at* any age but the number who marry later than any specific age read from the horizontal scale

In Fig. 152 and also in Fig. 153 the cumulative curves have been plotted on a different basis from that used in plotting Fig. 150 and Fig. 151. In Fig. 150 and Fig. 151, the curves begin at the 100 per cent line at the top of the chart and extend downward toward the right. In Fig. 152 and Fig. 153 the curves start at the zero line at the bottom and extend upwards toward the right of the chart. The differences in the shape of the curves will point out to a trained reader the manner in which he must read the curves. Fig. 152 and Fig. 153 should be read using the words "less than" instead of the words "more than". Thus,

FREQUENCY CURVES

in Fig. 152 considering the curve "A", 60 per cent of all the telephone calls of this class were answered in "less than" four seconds and 76 per cent of the calls were answered in "less than" five seconds. Of course, all those calls which were observed as having been answered in "less than" four seconds are also answered in "less than" five seconds, so that the curve is on a strictly cumulative basis. In Curve "C" it can be seen that only 30 per cent of the calls of that class were answered in less than four seconds, as against 60 per cent for curve "A". Though curve "A" is higher up on the chart than curve "C", it really represents a smaller length of time required to answer telephone calls than shown by curve "C". Since twice as large a percentage of the calls were answered in "less than" four seconds, the average time for answering calls in curve "A" is certainly smaller than the average time for curve "C", yet curve "A" appears on the upper part of the chart. It is confusing to the average reader to have curves appear on the upper part of a chart when they really represent numerically smaller quantities than other curves appearing on the lower portion of a chart. Yet this is the result when curves are plotted on a "less than" basis. In order to avoid danger of misinterpretation, it seems desirable that cumulative frequency curves should be plotted on a "more than" basis. Most of the cumulative frequency curves in this book are plotted on a "more than" basis, so that curves involving the larger quantities or percentages may appear on the chart above those cumulative frequency curves for smaller quantities or percentages.

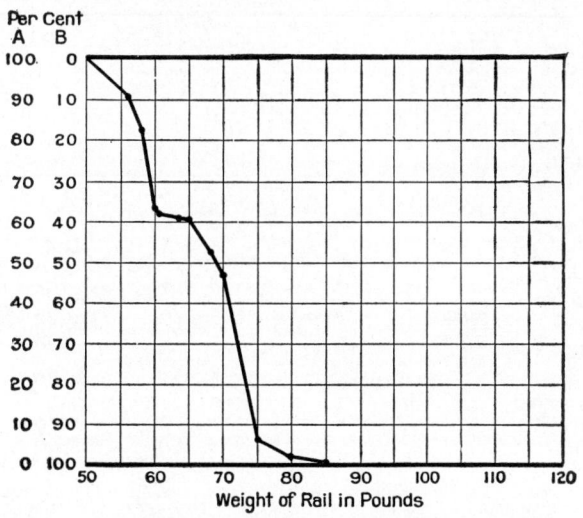

Fig. 151. Weight of Rails per Yard in the Main Line Track of the Seaboard Air Line Railway as Published in the Annual Report to Stockholders for the Fiscal Year Ending June 30, 1912

When using the left-hand scale the chart is read on a "more than" basis as if the words "more than" had been used with the horizontal scale as seen in Fig. 158. If the right-hand scale is selected the words "less than" are used

Fig. 152 and Fig. 153 show the application of the cumulative frequency curve to commercial problems. The full explanation of these two charts cannot be gone into here, but the reader can see for himself the use of the cumulative frequency curve in studying different problems in the telephone business. In Fig. 152 the curves show the time required to answer calls in different cities, while Fig. 153 shows a comparison of answering times in different classes of service. Notice that in each of these two charts it seems that two seconds is about the minimum which can be expected in answering telephone calls with the existing types of equipment. Fig. 153 certainly gives in excellent manner the comparison between the answering times for different classes of service. It would be very difficult to convey the complex information contained in Fig. 153 by using tabulated figures only. Tabulated figures would take up as much space as the chart and they would be less intelligible to any person who knows even the rudiments of reading graphic presentations.

In Fig. 154 an attempt was made to apply cumulative frequency curves to a comparison of wage rates in different sections of the United States. The chart, however, is likely to be very misleading, as it has been plotted by methods which are not in accordance with usual practice. The variables have been reversed, and the independent variable has incorrectly been made the vertical scale. Besides that, the vertical scale reads downward instead of upward. In all kinds of curve plotting it is common to have the two scales begin with zero at the lower left-hand corner of the chart. Here the two scales begin the zeros at the upper left-hand corner of the chart. Unless the reader will turn Fig. 154 on its side so as to make the two zeros at the lower left-hand corner, he may find great difficulty in interpreting the chart.

Fig. 155 shows a replot of the data of Fig. 154. Here the curves are plotted on a "more than" basis, but it would have been better if the

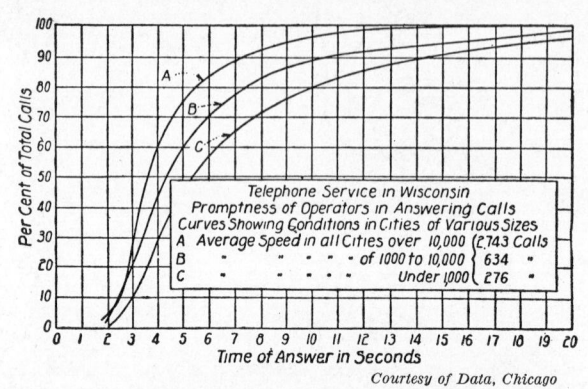

Fig. 152. Time Required for Operators to Answer Telephone Calls in Towns of Different Size in Wisconsin

These curves start at the lower left-hand portion of the field and trend upward, showing that they are plotted on a "less than" basis. Curve A shows a smaller time required to answer calls than Curves B or C, yet the actual position of Curve A on the chart is higher than either curves B or C. If cumulative frequency curves are plotted on a "more than" basis the position of several curves on a chart is relatively such that the reader is not confused so much as when curves are plotted on a "less than" basis

FREQUENCY CURVES

words "more than", with an arrow, had been placed at the lower left-hand corner of the chart. In Fig. 155 a little study will show the advantages of plotting curves on a "more than" basis. The reader can see at a glance from this illustration that the wages for the western States are very much higher than the wages in the south Atlantic States. The position of the curves one above the other would lead the reader at once to think of the upper curves as showing higher wages. Here the upper curves do indicate the higher wages, but they would not do so if they were plotted on a "less than" basis instead of on a "more than" basis. Though it may cause some confusion at first, it seems desirable as a general rule that cumulative frequency curves should be plotted on a "more than" basis rather than on a "less than" basis.

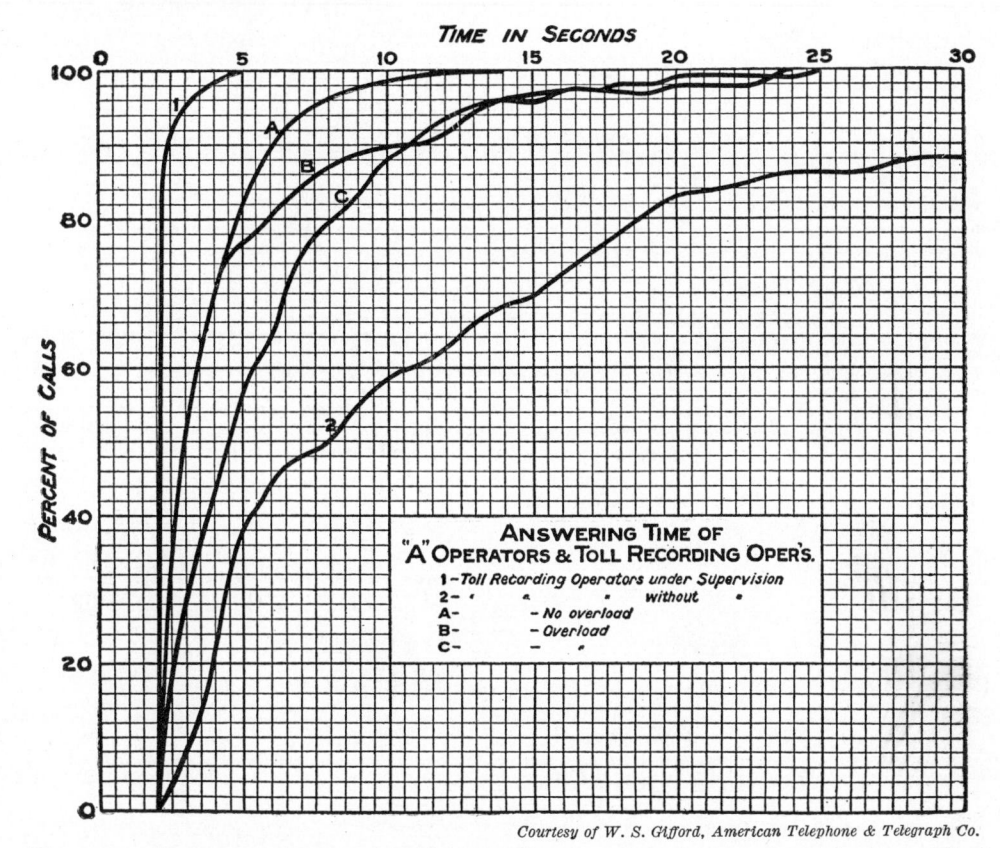

Fig. 153. Answering Time of Different Classes of Operators in Telephone Work
Cumulative curves of this sort give information in much more condensed and clear form than possible with other methods of presentation. This particular chart is read on a "less than" basis, as can be seen by the general position of the curves as related to the scales. Notice that none of the calls is answered in less than two seconds

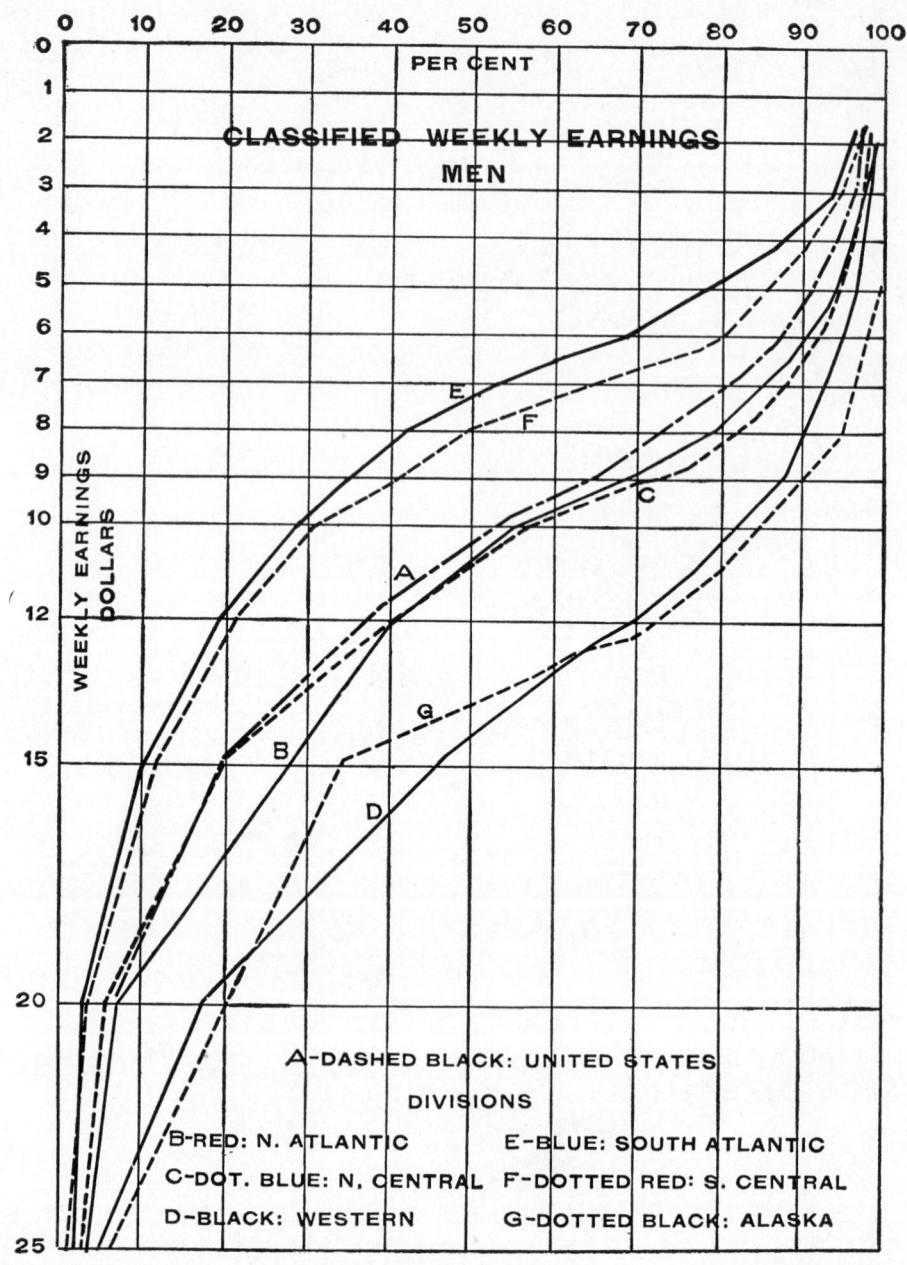

Fig. 154. Comparison of Earnings of Men Wage Earners in Different Portions of the United States in 1905

This chart is almost hopelessly confused because the scales have been so arranged that the two scale zeros appear at the upper left-hand corner of the chart instead of at the lower left-hand corner. The vertical scale reads downward when it should read upward. See Fig. 155 for these same data redrawn

FREQUENCY CURVES

In Fig. 156 we have cumulative frequency curves applied to a comparison of wages in different departments of a corporation. Here again the words "more than" and the arrow would have been desirable at the lower left-hand corner of the chart. The general position of the curves beginning at the upper left-hand corner, however, assists the reader to see that these curves are plotted on a "more than" basis. A chart of this kind is of great utility in making a study of wages. It may be noticed, for instance, in the curve for laborers, that there is a very decided change in the shape of the curve at about $9.00 per week. Only 62 per cent of these laborers make more than $9.00 per week and but 80 per cent of them get more than $5.00 per

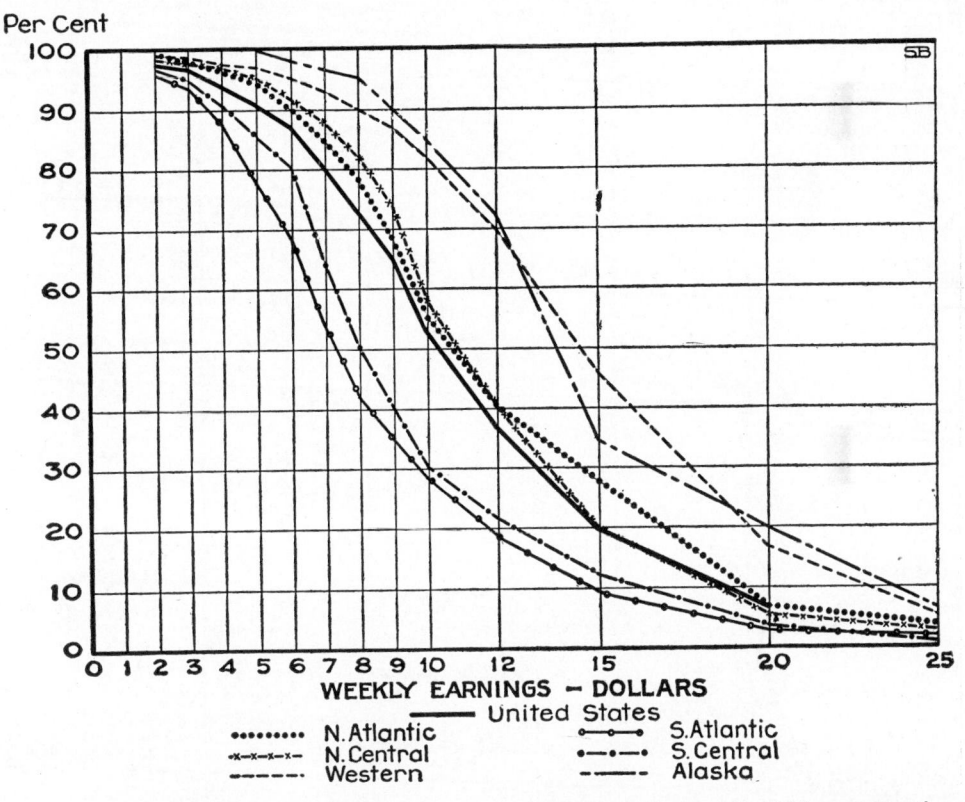

Fig. 155. Chart Showing What Percentage of the Wage Earners in Different Portions of the United States Receive More than any Specified Amount of Earnings up to Twenty-Five Dollars per Week

Here the scales are correctly arranged so that the two zeros appear at the lower left-hand corner. The plotting of these curves on a "more than" basis causes curves which show the largest earnings to appear in their proper position toward the top of the chart. Plotting of cumulative frequency curves on a "more than" basis is usually desirable, since it reduces the chances for confusion to the reader. This chart could have been improved if the words "more than" and an arrow had been placed at the lower left-hand corner on the general scheme of Fig. 158

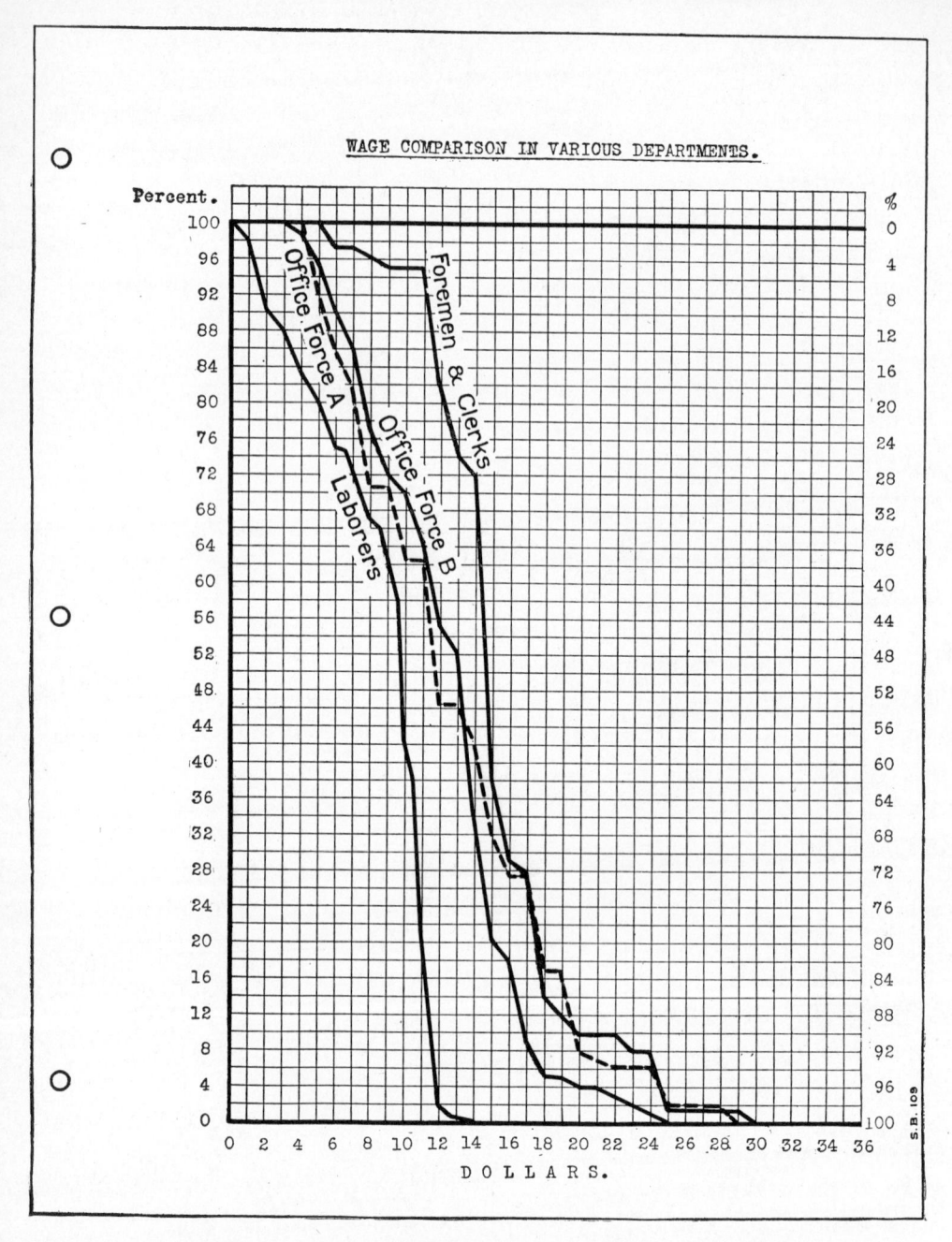

Fig. 156. Comparison of Actual Weekly Earnings in Different Departments of a Large Industrial Plant Showing Percentage of Men in Each Department Receiving More than Any Specified Amount of Earnings per Week

This illustration was made by photographing directly from the universally ruled paper shown also in Figures 57, 103, 130 and 134. The scales and the different titles were put on the paper with a typewriter. Lack of steady work caused many of the laborers to get the very small earnings shown by the upper portion of the curve marked "Laborers"

week. The fact that 20 per cent of all the laborers earn less than $5.00 per week is due to intermittent employment given laborers in this particular business. As $5.00 per week is not a living wage for any man, the shape of the cumulative curve for the laborers at once points out the desirability of some change in management by which fewer men might be employed and all the men employed more steadily than indicated by the curve for laborers in Fig. 156. Since all the laborers were paid the same rate per hour, the only possible explanation of the fact that a large number of men earn as little as $5.00 per week must be that the laborers were not employed continuously. More continuity of employment for a smaller number of laborers would, in this particular case, have resulted in more money being paid on an average to each man, so that the men would, to all essential purposes, have received an increase in pay even though the hourly wage rate were not increased.

Though that portion of the curves for the office forces seen at the upper left corner of Fig. 156 appears somewhat similar to the curve for laborers, the low earnings of a large percentage of the office force were due to the employment of office boys and other young employees who would have a fair chance to get a good training and grow up with the business. Therefore, the curves for the office forces need not attract the same attention as the curves for the laborers, who are all full-grown men having comparatively little chance for promotion.

The quick change at $11.00 per week in the shape of the curve relating to the foremen and clerks is due to the fact that some of the foremen in this business are paid by the hour and not by the week. That some of the foremen receive as low as $6.00 per week and that only 93 per cent of the foremen receive over $11.00 per week is due to the fact that some of the men were off because of sickness or on leave of absence. If the attendance of these men were more regular the curves would not have such a decided peak at $11.00 per week. Though Fig. 156 has been plotted on a "more than" basis, the reader may, if he wishes, read it on a "less than" basis by referring to the right-hand scale which has zero at the top instead of at the bottom of the page.

Fig. 156 was made directly from typewritten copy with only the curves and the marginal lines drawn in by hand. This same universally ruled paper has been referred to elsewhere as being convenient for general use. Here the paper is used to indicate 100 per cent in the vertical direction, and the horizontal scale is chosen for data unrelated to time.

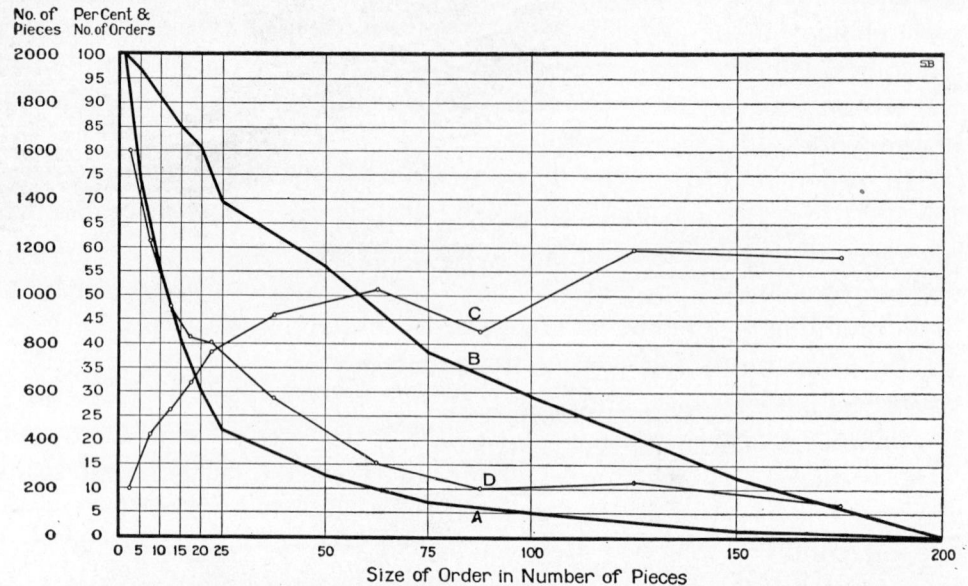

Fig. 157. Cumulative Frequency Curve Study of the Number and the Size of All Orders Handled During a Ten-days Test in a Certain Kind of Freight-handling Work

The orders are sorted into various classes or groups according to the number of pieces called for by each order. The limits for the various classes were fixed by the exercise of a little judgment and are shown by the vertical lines on the chart

Curve "D" shows by small circles the actual number of orders found in each group. The curve is read from the right-hand scale

Curve "C" shows by small circles the total number of pieces (or packages) carried by the various orders which are found in each group. Curve "C" is read from the left-hand scale

Curve "A" shows the percentage of the total orders handled which contain more than any given number of pieces considered on the horizontal scale of the chart

Curve "B" shows the percentage of the total number of pieces carried by those orders containing more than any given number of pieces considered on the horizontal scale of the chart

Curves "D" and "A" refer to the number of orders or the amount of clerical work while curves "C" and "B" relate to the number of packages handled or the actual volume of business transacted

In Fig. 157 we have an application of the cumulative frequency curve to a class of work which would be extremely difficult to understand if the graphic method were not used. In handling large quantities of freight the different orders cover many diverse kinds of material, and the jobs vary from one package up to many thousands of packages on one order. The pieces or packages referred to here may be anything from a single casting weighing 20 tons to a shipment of canned goods with 5,000 boxes or cases on a single shipping order. In the long run, however, the different classes of goods could be averaged, and it will be found that in any one locality there would be but slight change from year to year in the average size or weight of package handled. The average weight of package might happen to be 150 pounds, and, considering a whole year, there would probably be very little change in the average weight from month to month. Thus, for our purpose here, the term "piece" or "package" refers simply to the average package handled in different divisions or departments of the work under consideration.

In order to obtain the data regarding the orders referred to in Fig. 157, Fig. 158 and Fig. 159 the order slips are sorted into different piles according to some definitely thought-out plan by which there would not be too many or too few orders in any one class or size group. A little preliminary trial work in sorting would show the best places to set the class limits for sorting the orders into separate piles. After the orders have been separated into piles, it is a simple matter to count the number of orders in each pile to obtain the data from which curve "D" is plotted. It will be noticed from the shape of the curve that the upper and lower limits for each class are well selected so that there is a fairly uniform decrease in the number of orders in each group as the size of the orders increases. The order slips in the different piles sorted according to the size of the order are taken to an adding machine, and addition made to obtain the total number of packages carried by the combined orders found in any one pile or class. This gives the data from which curve "C" is plotted. Though curve "D" shows a constantly decreasing number of orders as the size of the orders becomes greater, curve "C" proves that there is an increasing number of packages handled as the orders grow larger toward the right-hand side of the chart.

Though there are not so many orders of large size as of small size, the small numbers of large orders nevertheless carry many more packages than the large numbers of small orders. The executive is, of course, interested in revenue and, for revenue purposes, as mentioned above, all packages may be considered of the same size. Revenue obviously depends upon the number of packages handled, rather than on the number of orders handled. Curve "C", then, shows at a glance that the small number of large orders are of much greater interest to the financial manager than the large number of small orders.

Fig. 157 shows that during the ten-days test period there were no orders in this particular class of work which exceeded two hundred packages. Curves "D" and "C", though interesting, do not show all the information which is desirable from the standpoint of management. In order to show up the facts more clearly, curves "A" and "B" are plotted from the same data as curves "D" and "C" respectively. Curve "A" is plotted on a cumulative basis by the same general method used for Fig. 150 and Fig. 151. The total number of orders for the whole test period is first obtained, and then the cumulative number adding up to any class-limit line on the horizontal scale of the chart is plotted as a percentage of the total number of orders. Curve "A" joins the zero line at 200, showing that none of the orders was larger than 200 packages. We can see instantly that, because of the large number of small orders, only 22 per cent of all the orders handled were larger than twenty-five pieces per order. Only 13 per cent of all the orders handled exceeded fifty pieces per order. Also, by reading from the vertical scale opposite the figure for 50 per cent, we can see at once that only half of all the orders handled carried more than twelve packages.

In a manner similar to that used in making up curve "A", the cumulative curve "B" is made up from the data relating to the number of packages shown in curve "C". It may assist the reader to follow these charts if he keeps clearly in mind that curves "D" and "A" relate to the actual number of orders of various sizes, while curves "C" and "B" relate to the number of packages, or the amount of total business carried by orders of various sizes. In other words, curves "D" and "A" relate to the amount of clerical work needed, while curves "C" and "B" show the actual amount of freight-handling labor involved and measure the amount of revenue earned. Curve "B" thus shows that, though there are not many large orders, about 69 per cent of all the revenue comes from those orders which contain more than twenty-five packages. Fifty-six per cent of the business (and the revenue) is due to orders containing more than fifty packages. Twenty-nine per cent of all of the revenue comes from orders containing more than one hundred packages, yet none of the revenue for the ten-days time considered came from orders larger than two hundred packages, since there were no such orders during the period.

It is by reading curves "A" and "B" in conjunction with each other that the manager may obtain the greatest information relating to his business. Considering first the orders which contain more than ten pieces, curve "A" shows that 55 per cent of the orders contain more than ten packages, while curve "B" shows that 91 per cent of the revenue comes from those orders which are larger than ten pieces each. In other words, the manager, because of handling so many small orders, is doing 45 per cent of the total clerical work in order to obtain 9 per cent of the revenue. Since clerical work depends chiefly on the number of separate orders, the manager would be able to reduce his clerical work on this particular class of orders somewhere near 45 per cent if he would refuse to handle orders of less than ten packages, and, by such a decision, he would lose only 9 per cent of his revenue. For most businesses, it would pay handsomely to neglect entirely 9 per cent of the revenue if 45 per cent of the clerical work could be avoided. In freight handling, the work is of course mostly under the jurisdiction of the Interstate Commerce Commission, so that even if the manager should wish to refuse orders of small size, he would not be permitted to do so.

Though the small orders must be handled to give service to the public, a chart such as Fig. 157 is nevertheless of very great assistance in pointing out the actual conditions existing. When it is seen what a large amount of clerical work is involved in handling orders which produce only a small portion of the revenue, thought could be given to the methods of handling small orders so that the small orders may not cause any more expense than absolutely necessary. Usually it is possible to handle small orders in a different manner from the large orders, and, if the true situation is thoroughly understood, small orders may possibly be handled by methods which will result in much less loss than would be incurred if small orders are handled by the same methods used for large orders.

One may see from Fig. 157 the percentages of orders and of business or revenue for any size of order which it may be desired to consider. Thus, taking orders which contain more than twenty-five packages, it can be seen that 22 per cent of all the orders contain more than twenty-five packages and that these orders carry 69 per cent of the total business and bring in 69 per cent of the total revenue. Though these orders of over twenty-five packages do not involve a large amount of clerical work, they nevertheless bring in such a large percentage of the revenue that any dividends from this particular department must probably be paid from the revenue brought in by orders in excess of twenty-five packages each.

The general methods used in plotting Fig. 157 have been considered at rather great length because it is felt that a chart of this

188   GRAPHIC METHODS

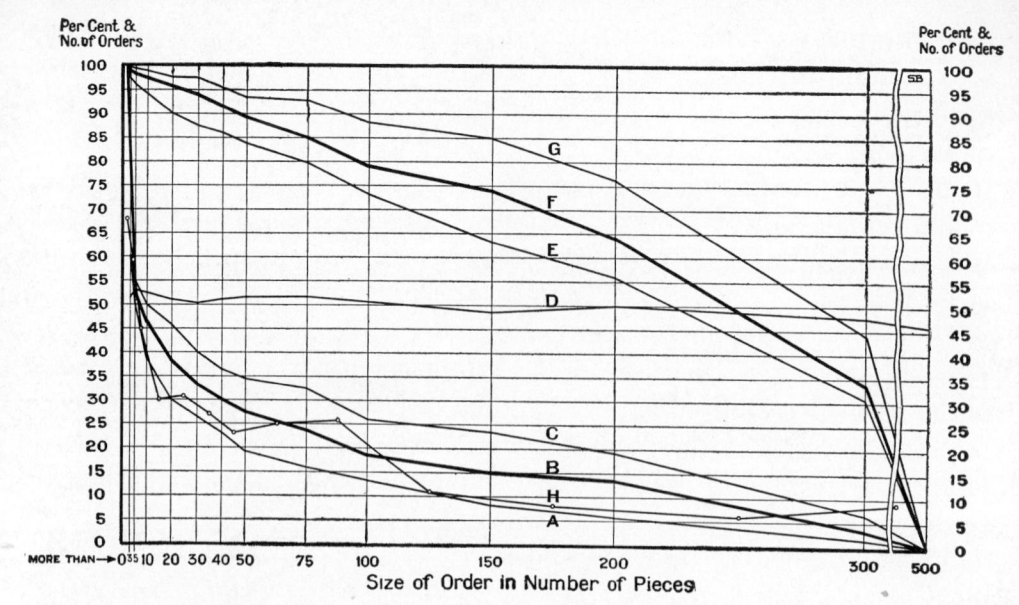

Fig. 158. Cumulative Frequency Curve Study of the Number and the Size of All Orders Handled During One Week in a Certain Kind of Freight-handling Work Carried on in Two Closely-related Departments

Curve "H" shows by small circles the actual number of orders found in each size-of-order-class. Note that at the left of the chart there are numerous orders shown in each class even though here the limits of each class have been purposely made very close together

Curve "B" shows the percentage of the total orders handled which contain more than any given number of packages considered on the horizontal scale of the chart

Curves "A" and "C" are similar to curve "B" and show subdivisions of the total number of orders according to which of two related departments handled the work

Curve "F" corresponds with curve "B" but shows the percentage of the total number of pieces carried by those orders containing more than any given number of pieces considered on the horizontal scale of the chart

Curves "G" and "E" are similar to curve "F" and show subdivisions in the total number of pieces according to which of two related departments handled the work

One sub-department of the business handled the orders portrayed by Curve "A" and Curve "E". The other sub-department handled orders portrayed by Curve "C" and curve "G". The combined work of the two departments is shown by Curve "B" and Curve "F"

The percentage of the total number of orders handled in each of the two different departments, up to any size of order read on the horizontal scale, may be seen by considering the distances on the chart above and below Curve "D"

kind can be of service in a sales analysis for almost any kind of business. A company selling fairly uniform products—shoes, for example—could use for the horizontal scale the actual number of pairs of shoes contained on various orders received for the test period of, say, a week or a month. Companies having a diversified product, as electrical machinery, could best make a chart of this kind by basing the horizontal scale on the actual value in dollars of the various orders received. Thus, the scale could be made for orders in sizes larger than $50, $500, $1,000, etc. If charts are made for different departments, very interesting comparisons could be made which would bring out information valuable to a corporation executive. Department stores might also have use for charts on the general plan of Fig. 157. Different departments could be considered by the number of orders of various sizes. As the margin of profit in different classes of goods in different quantity sold would be fairly well known, the manager could get a good idea as to how much of the time of his sales force was occupied in handling small orders, and how much in handling large orders.

Fig. 158 is drawn on the same general scheme as Fig. 157. In Fig. 158, however, we have the additional complexity that the freight under consideration must be handled by two distinct departments working in very close harmony with each other. As there is a difference in the cost of doing the work handled by the two departments, the chart was purposely so drawn as to show the number of orders and the number of packages handled by each of these two distinct departments which together do all of the work under consideration. Curves "B" and "F" show respectively the percentage of orders and the percentage of business handled as a whole. The other curves show the relative proportions of the orders and the business done by the two departments. The position of the curves on the chart gives a fairly clear idea as to whether the first department or the second department handles the larger number of orders and the larger percentage of the actual business.

In Fig. 153 it was shown that, because the curves were plotted on a "less than" basis, the curve showing the smaller length of time appears at the top of the chart, when one would naturally expect to find the smaller quantities of time recorded relatively toward the bottom of the chart. In Fig. 158 the data are plotted on a "more than" basis, and the curves are seen in their proper relation to each other. Since the reader knows that the chart is plotted on a "more than" basis (as can be seen by the words "more than" at the lower left-hand corner of the chart), he may know instantly that the curves relating to the two different departments show in their correct relation to each other. Curves "G" and "C" relate to one department, while curves "E" and "A" relate to another department. Curve "C" appears above curve "A" on the chart, and the reader may accordingly know without detail study that the department to which curve "C" relates handles larger orders than the department to which curve "A" relates. In a similar way, the upper portion of the chart shows that the department to which curve "G" relates handles a larger percentage of the total number of packages and produces a larger percentage of the revenue than the department to which curve "E" relates. If this chart had been plotted on a "less than" basis instead of on a "more than" basis, the position of these two curves giving detailed information for the main curve "F" would be exactly reversed, with curve "E" appearing above the heavy line "F" and curve "G" appearing below the heavy line.

It is perhaps well to point out an error in drafting which occurred on Fig. 158. The information most needed relates to orders containing less than three hundred packages each. It was, however, desired to show on the chart that none of the orders contained more than five hundred packages, and the right-hand portion of the chart is accordingly shown with a break, indicating that a section has been omitted. As a general rule, when making a break in a drawing in this manner, the two portions on either side of the break are made exactly as though a piece of paper had been torn out of the middle of a drawing made large enough to include the whole chart. Fig. 158 is incorrectly made in that the curve lines to the right of the figure 300 on the horizontal scale have been drawn pointing down toward the right-hand corner of the chart where they show at the left of the break. These lines would not appear this way if a piece of paper had been torn out of a large-size chart. The curve lines should have continued up to the break in the drawing more nearly on the slope seen in the left-hand portion of the chart. The lines for curves "G", "F" and "E" would, if correctly made, show much less slope also at the right of the break where they lead down to the lower corner of the chart. This error is mentioned here simply that the reader may have some guidance if he finds it necessary to make charts including a break, similar to that shown in Fig. 158.

It is customary in cost-keeping work to make costs which show only an average of the cost per unit, on an average for all orders completed during a period of time, say one month or one year. Though this method of averaging all orders together without respect to the size of the order is sufficiently accurate for many purposes, there are times when such a method may gravely mislead an executive. It is almost invariably true that small orders cost more per unit of output than orders of large size. A man who makes a selling price for his work on the average cost of small orders and large orders combined may be losing money unnecessarily, because he does not realize the true cost of work when it is done in only small quantities on different orders.

Fig. 159 proves the great variation in the cost of doing the work of handling a certain class of freight. The position of the dots on the chart shows that work done in orders of only twenty-five packages costs over twice the average for orders of four hundred or over. In keeping track of the cost of handling freight of different kinds for a large steamship terminal and warehouse company it was found impossible to get reliable cost figures by averaging, day by day, the labor cost of handling freight for preceding days. On some days all the orders for one commodity might be small orders, and on the next day a very large quantity of that same commodity might be handled all in one large order, so that a gang of men could work steadily all day on that one order. Naturally if a large gang of men work all day on one order, the cost per package handled would be very much less than if several different gangs were used in handling numerous orders of only ten or twenty-five packages each. In order to get a clear view of what was actually happening, considerable study was given to the problem and the method shown in Fig. 159 is the result.

It was decided to make a pin board about 24 by 30 inches, on the general scheme seen in Fig. 159, by which separate orders could be shown on the chart by a dot to represent each order handled. As it was desired to keep continuous records for the chief commodities, it was not feasible to make ink marks for it would then be necessary to start over again frequently with a completely new sheet of paper. To overcome this difficulty, short pins were used having spherical glass heads only $3/_{32}$ inch in diameter like those seen at the right in Fig. 186. The co-ordinate paper for the chart itself was mounted on three layers of corrugated straw-board, having the ribs of the middle layer at right angles to the ribs of the two outside layers, as described in Chapter XII. A binding of gummed cloth-tape around the edge of the board gave a neat appearance and assisted to preserve the boards during rough service and long use. These boards were very light, yet remarkably strong on account of the corrugations running in both directions.

One cost clerk could not possibly figure out the cost of all orders and all commodities handled each day. The cost method was more in the nature of an automatic inspection system or check, so that the general efficiency of the work done by numerous gangs and hundreds of men could be judged by what might be called occasional analyses

GRAPHIC METHODS

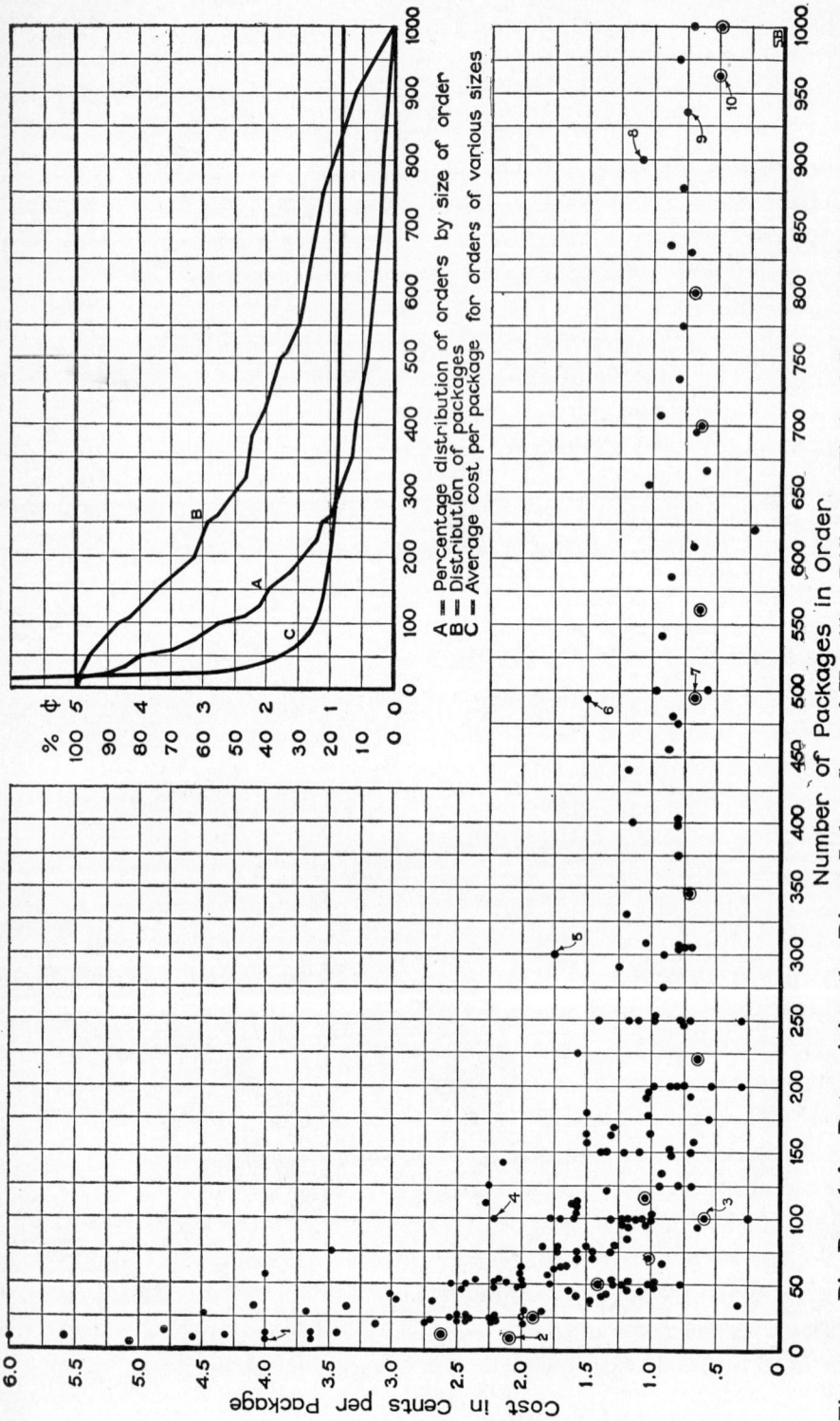

Fig. 159. Pin Board for Determining the Direct Labor Cost of Handling Different Kinds of Commodities in a Large Steamship Terminal. This Cost Method Takes into Account the Number of Packages Handled on One Order. Small Orders Naturally Have a High Cost per Package

A separate board is used for each commodity that is handled frequently enough to justify a study of the labor cost. Boards are built up of layers of corrugated straw-board with a binding of gummed cloth tape around the edges. Boards each have a sheet of co-ordinate paper about 24 by 30 inches, mounted on the surface. Short pins with spherical glass heads are pushed into the board until the heads touch the paper. With this arrangement, boards can be handled continually without danger of pins falling out and spoiling the accuracy of the record

FREQUENCY CURVES

taken at random. Because of the numerous commodities which were handled on which it was desirable to watch the cost of freight handling, the cost clerk figured the cost of any one commodity perhaps only one or two days in a month. Each morning the cost clerk would sort out all the labor tickets relating to some one particular commodity which had been handled on the preceding day. The cost per package would be figured up for each order ticket and, in the board reserved for that particular commodity, a tall pin would be placed for each order completed the preceding day, showing by the position of the pin the number of packages on the order and the cost per package of handling that particular order. In considering the pin marked 8 at the right of Fig. 159 we can see that it represents an order for 900 packages and that the cost per package was 1.1 cent. After some time in operating a pin board the position of the various pins on the board would show in the general form of a curve, and would indicate the cost of handling freight of that particular commodity in lots of different sizes. Since commodities received from ocean ships are usually packed in some standard size of bales, boxes, or bags, the pin method of charting cost is a remarkably reliable one.

The pin board can be of great assistance to the general superintendent. As the cost of handling certain orders for certain commodities for the preceding day is known about eleven o'clock each morning, the superintendent can look over the boards and note the special tall pins which show the exact cost of various orders handled. Thus, a superintendent seeing a board of the kind described would know that on the preceding day those orders had been completed which in Figure 159 are shown by numbered dots. His attention would be drawn at once to the orders represented by dots numbered 4, 5, 6 and 8. These dots show costs much above the average cost recorded for orders of those sizes. The cost clerk could furnish the order numbers of these particular orders and could also give the names of the foremen who had been in charge of the work. The superintendent could then ask for an explanation as to why these orders had cost much more than the work should have cost for lots of the size handled. Considering dot 6, notice that the average cost for 500 packages is about 0.80 cent, but the order represented by dot 6 cost 1.50 cent per package, almost twice what it should have cost. Though dot 4 shows considerably above the average dots for 100-package lots, the percentage excess is not so great as in the case of dot 6. Dot 4 shows a cost of about 2.20 cents, while the average cost for 100 packages is about 1.25 cents. What the superintendent wants to know is the percentage excess in the cost above what the chart shows should be the normal cost for any number of packages under consideration. The chart brings out this information very clearly. Since the superintendent can take the matter up with the various foremen before noon of the day after the work was completed, the foremen soon get the feeling that the superintendent knows what the cost should be, and, if anything happens to prevent work being done cheaply and quickly, the foremen are likely to report the conditions at once to see if assistance can be given them so as to keep the cost low.

After the superintendent has seen the pin boards each morning, the long pins represented by numbered dots in Fig. 159 are removed and in their places are put the short glass-head pins having shanks so short that the pins may be pushed into the straw-board until the head of the pin touches the co-ordinate paper. The pins are then quite secure, and the boards may be worked upon and handled month after month without danger of the pins becoming lost from the boards. The ordinary type of tall pins or tacks used with wooden boards would not be at all satisfactory for this class of work, as it would be impossible to work with such boards containing thousands of tacks without knocking the tacks loose, so that they would be in a continuous process of becoming lost—much to the detriment of accuracy and to the disgust of a cost clerk. The short glass-head pins pushed in until the heads touch are very convenient and they give a thoroughly accurate record.

As above mentioned, cost boards of the kind described would not be satisfactory if made with ink dots because the boards would soon have so many dots that information would be no longer easily obtainable. By using the glass-head pins it is feasible to change the color of glass heads used on any board each six months. The position of the pins of different color would then show clearly whether work was being done more cheaply than it had been done in preceding periods of time. Thus, if any particular campaign were made to reduce the cost for small orders by handling small orders on some different method from that previously used, the pins near the left-hand side of the board might appear considerably lower down on the chart than the pins of the color which had been used in the six months preceding the change in method.

When the board gets so full of pins as to make the pins crowded it is a very simple matter to remove from the board all of the pins which were inserted in the most remote period of time. Thus, it might be found feasible to keep on the chart pins relating to four different periods of six months each, so that every six months one color of pins would be removed from the board and the pins removed would be those which had been placed in the board two years previously. A board would then show at all times the record of cost in handling this particular commodity during the last two years. Boards used where pins must be put in and taken out very often may be faced with cork composition so that the pin holes may injure the surface as little as possible. Where pins are not to be changed very frequently, the straw-board covered with a layer of cloth before the co-ordinate paper is mounted will be found entirely satisfactory.

In the upper portion of Fig. 159 is shown a summary chart of the data contained on the pin board itself. Curve "C" is a smooth curve drawn through the center of gravity of all pins on any vertical line which shows the size of order. It will be noticed that the cost decreases very little when orders become larger than three hundred packages, but for this particular commodity with the methods of handling used, the cost increases rapidly as orders decrease below three hundred packages. Knowing the revenue obtained for doing the work, it is a simple matter to determine from the curve the smallest size of order of this commodity which can be handled under average conditions without incurring a loss. If the revenue for Fig. 159 were 1.5 cents per package it could be seen at once that (since the overhead expenses are not considered) there must certainly be a dead loss on orders containing less than sixty-five packages each. If the overhead expenses are taken into account as well as direct labor, there would be shown a loss on orders of larger size, probably up to one hundred or one hundred and fifty packages. Assuming that a loss occurs on all orders shown on Fig. 159 up to the size of one hundred and fifty packages per order, the number of dots to the left of the line for 150 on the horizontal scale indicates just how great the total monetary loss would be.

Curve "A" in Fig. 159 shows the percentage of orders which contain more than any specified number of packages selected on the horizontal scale of the chart. Curve "B" shows the percentage of the total packages which are found in orders containing more than any specified number of packages selected on the horizontal scale of the chart. Curve "A" indicates the amount of clerical work involved, and curve "B" shows the amount of actual labor and the amount of revenue in exactly the same manner described for Figures 157 and 158.

Curves "A", "B" and "C" are shown in Fig. 159 only by way of proving the utility of the pin-board method of keeping costs where there is a large variation in the size of the orders worked upon. The illustration shows these curves superimposed on the pin board only to save space in printing.

In Fig. 160 is shown a chart which may help to make clearer the general principles used in drawing the charts seen in Fig. 157, Fig. 158 and Fig. 159. Fig. 160 shows the appearance of the curves if there are the same number of orders in each class or group and if all classes or groups are of uniform size. It makes no difference in the shape of the curves how many orders there may be if those orders are always uniformly distributed throughout the whole length of the horizontal scale of the chart. It would perhaps have been better if Fig. 160 had been so drawn that the length of the vertical scale would be the same as the length of the horizontal scale. The actual shape of the curve line referring to the percentage of business or the percentage of the total number of pieces would then be free from any possible distortion which it may have received because of the vertical scale being of less total length here than the horizontal scale.

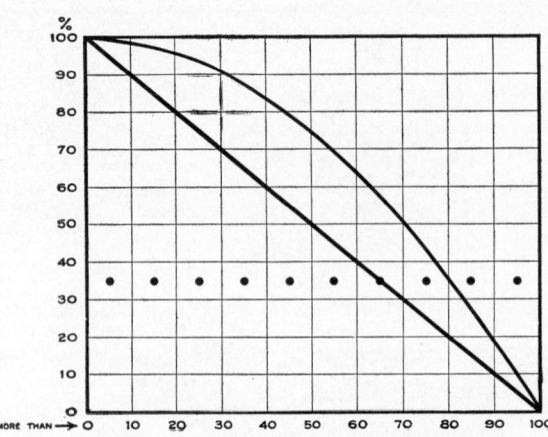

Fig. 160. Chart to Show the Theoretical Shape of Cumulative Curves for the Percentage of Total Orders and the Percentage of Total Business if There Is a Uniform Number of Orders in Each Class or Group

It makes no difference in the shape of the curves, as long as all classes contain the same number of orders, whether there is one order or one thousand orders in each class between vertical lines

The straight line shows the percentage of orders which contain more than any given number of pieces considered on the horizontal scale of the chart

The curved line shows the percentage of the total number of pieces carried by the orders which contain more than any given number of pieces considered on the horizontal scale

If there is not the same number of orders in all groups or zones the curves will take some other shape and the shape will depend on the peculiar distribution of orders as may be seen in Fig. 157, Fig. 158 and Fig. 159

It is especially interesting to compare Fig. 160 with Fig. 159. In Fig. 159 the reader may easily see for himself that there are many more small orders than there are large orders, because the pins are largely concentrated toward the left-hand side of the chart. It is this concentration at the left-hand side which has so greatly affected the shape of curve "A" and curve "B" in Fig. 159. By comparing Fig. 160, we can see that if the distribution of orders in Fig. 159 had been uniform, curve "A" would have been a straight diagonal line and curve "B" would have been a curved line bowed upward instead of bowed downward.

Though Fig. 161 somewhat resembles Fig. 160, it is nevertheless constructed on an entirely different plan. In Figs. 157, 158, 159 and 160 the independent variable related only to size of order. For charts of the type shown in Fig. 160 the independent variable is a percentage. The dependent variable is also expressed as a percentage.

Imagine the whole population placed in a long line and ranked according to income. The people in this line could be counted off into several equal groups so that each group would contain say 10 per cent of the total number. It would then be simple to compute the income of each group as a percentage of the combined income for all groups. The resulting group percentages would be plotted cumulatively as the dependent variable on a chart for which percentages of population would be the independent variable. Fig. 161 unfortunately shows the independent variable used for the vertical scale. A better arrangement may be seen by observing the illustration through the back of the paper with the two zeros appearing at the lower left-hand corner.

Fig. 161. Curves to Show the Percentages of the Total Population of Prussia in 1892 and in 1901 that Received Various Percentages of the Total Income as Considered on the Horizontal Scale

—— EQUALITY ---- PRUSSIA 1892. ••••• PRUSSIA 1901

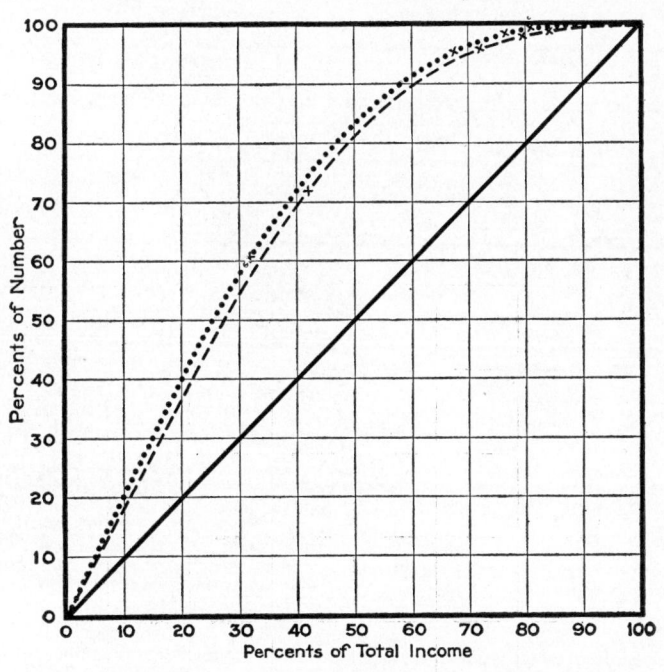

M. O. Lorenz, in the Publications, the American Statistical Assn.

If incomes were all equal the relation of population and income would be expressed by the straight diagonal line. The amount of inequality between various incomes is shown by the amount the curve diverges from the straight line. There was greater inequality of incomes in Prussia in 1901 than in 1892

198 GRAPHIC METHODS

Diagrams made on the scheme of Fig. 161 are of very great assistance in studying such matters as the distribution of wealth for any country. The subject of wealth distribution is so complex that unless data are expressed graphically there would be very serious difficulty in getting a true understanding and appreciation of the different factors involved. In Fig. 161 we have the curves for two widely separated years plotted side by side, so that we may tell from the general shape of the curves whether the distribution of wealth is approaching uniformity of tending in the direction of great concentration in the hands of a few people. The more nearly the curve approaches a straight line the more nearly wealth is distributed uniformly among all the

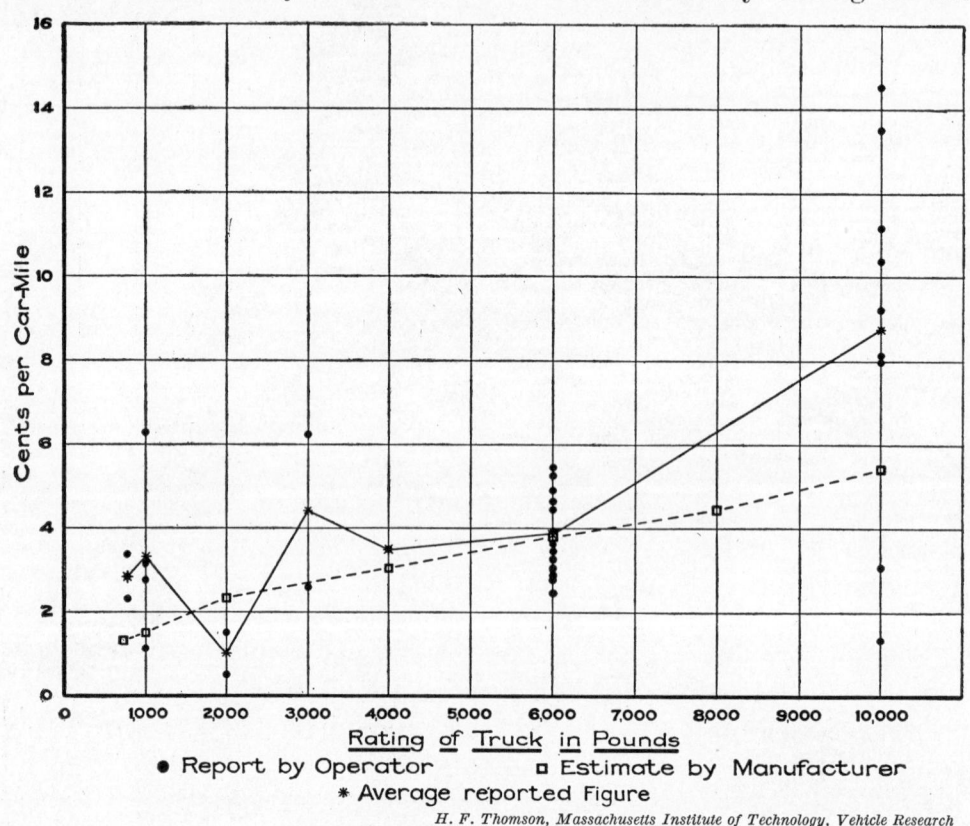

● Report by Operator   □ Estimate by Manufacturer
* Average reported Figure

H. F. Thomson, Massachusetts Institute of Technology, Vehicle Research

Fig. 162. Cost of Gasoline in Cents per Truck-Mile for Different Sizes of Motor Trucks

Since motor trucks are rated by the manufacturers in multiples of 1,000 pounds, the dots representing the records of different trucks naturally fall on the lines spaced by 1,000-pound intervals on the chart. The solid line is drawn through points at the "center of gravity" of all dots for any vertical line on the chart and represents the average condition as reported by truck operators. The dotted line is drawn through points on the chart for data furnished by the manufacturer as his estimate of good practice
A curve of this general type, proving a close relationship between two variables, may be called a correlation curve

members of the population. In Fig. 161 the line was more bowed in the later year than in the earlier year, and the conclusion may accordingly be drawn that wealth in Prussia tended toward further concentration in those years intervening between 1892 and 1901.

In Fig. 162 a study has been made to see how the gasoline consumption of motor trucks varies in trucks of different sizes. The horizontal scale shows the rated size in pounds of the trucks under consideration. On the vertical scale, the cost of gasoline is given in cents per car mile. The data of the different motor trucks were indicated by separate dots on the chart. The solid line was then drawn through a point which represents the center of gravity of all the dots on each vertical line. The total number of dots on this chart is rather small. Too much dependence cannot be placed in the resulting curve, as special conditions may have affected some of the records so as to cause the dots to be misleading. Thus, considering the two dots which are given for trucks of 2,000-pounds capacity, it will be noticed that both of these dots are far below the position on the chart which one would expect the average to occupy if one should judge by the general tendency of the curve as a whole. It may have happened that the particular trucks which these two dots represent were run with very light loads, thus making the gasoline consumption lower than would naturally be expected for trucks of that size. In Fig. 162 the object is to determine what relation, if any, exists between the cost for gasoline and the size of the truck.

"Correlation" is a term used to express the relation which exists between two series or groups of data where there is a causal connection. In order to have correlation it is not enough that the two sets of data should both increase or decrease simultaneously. For correlation it is necessary that one set of facts should have some definite causal dependence upon the other set, as seen in Fig. 162.

Correlation studies can frequently be of assistance in business problems. A manufacturer of machinery has recently revised many of his manufacturing and selling policies from the information obtained from a chart showing the relations of cost and selling price of his equipment to the actual size of the equipment. On the horizontal scale of charts used for this study the size of the apparatus was shown according to its actual working capacity. In a vertical direction a scale was selected for the cost of the apparatus and for its selling price. Dots were then placed on the chart in a manner similar to

Fig. 162, and a line was drawn on the chart through the different dots representing the factory cost of the machinery. The line was not at all straight and the chief executive spent much time in finding out why there were so many variations from uniformity. He found, among other things, that some of his machinery had not been redesigned for several years, and that the weight of material used was much greater than necessary when taking into account the greater strength of steel and iron made by modern processes. Though materials of the modern kind were being used to a large extent in his machinery, the weight of material had not been reduced and there was more weight of employed material than was actually necessary if new designs were made. Another cause for fluctuation in the curve line was found in the quantities in which the product was manufactured. Some sizes of apparatus were particularly suitable to the public, and on these sizes the quantities were much larger than on other sizes. The sizes more commonly sold were naturally better equipped with jigs and tools than other sizes, and for that reason the cost was lower than would otherwise be expected. After the cost curves had been thoroughly studied for different kinds of apparatus, the selling-price curves were drawn in on the same sheets. It was found that for selling prices, also, there were numerous inconsistencies which could be corrected with advantage to the company. Though some of the peaks and valleys of the selling-price correlation curves were to be expected, there was no justification for others and a little concentrated study brought forth methods by which the selling-price curves could be changed materially with advantage to both the producer and the consumer.

In the study of physics and of experimental engineering, there are many times when a correlation curve is of assistance in the discovery and understanding of the laws of nature. For Fig. 163, many observations were made and recorded on a sheet of co-ordinate paper. After sufficient observations had been made throughout the whole range of the horizontal scale, smooth curves were drawn which would most nearly represent the various dots plotted. In drawing curves of this kind, care should be taken to have each portion of the curve as nearly as possible at the center of gravity of the dots in any vertical section of the chart. Accuracy is not necessarily obtained by having the same number of dots on either side of the curve. If there are only three dots at some vertical line, it may be that two of these dots would be close together and their combined weight must be considered as compared with one dot which may be some distance away. As a simple rule, consider the dots in any vertical section of the chart as though arranged on a see-saw, as used by children, and then shift the point through which the curve line is to be drawn so that the see-saw will just balance evenly.

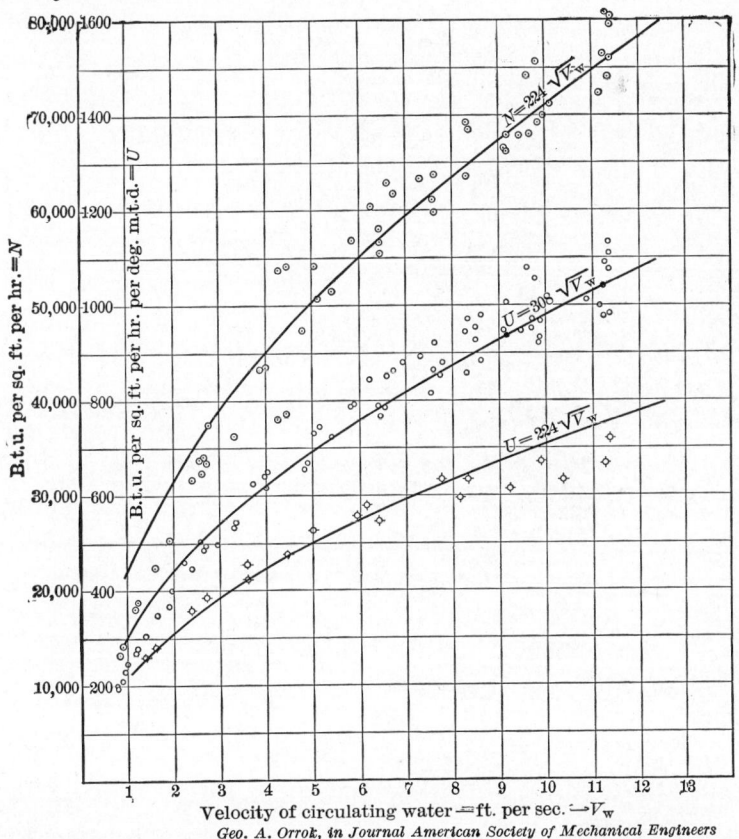

Fig. 163. Relation of the Rate of Heat Transmission to the Velocity of the Circulating Water in Surface Condensers

Correlation charts of this type have sometimes been called "shot-gun diagrams" The investigator makes a dot for each observation recorded, and then judges from the arrangement of the dots whether there is any general law expressing a relation between the two variables studied

Curves like those seen in Fig. 163 may be sketched in free-hand, or they may be much more conveniently drawn by using the irregular or so-called "French curves" which may be obtained in any store selling drafting instruments or artists' materials. As it frequently happens that an irregular curve available does not exactly fit the dots through which the curve line is to be drawn, care must be taken to shift the irregular curve along and draw only short portions of the curve line at any one stroke of the pencil or pen. Care in shifting the irregular curve will permit drawing a clean, smooth curve line, even though the irregular curve used is quite different in shape from the curve line which is drawn.

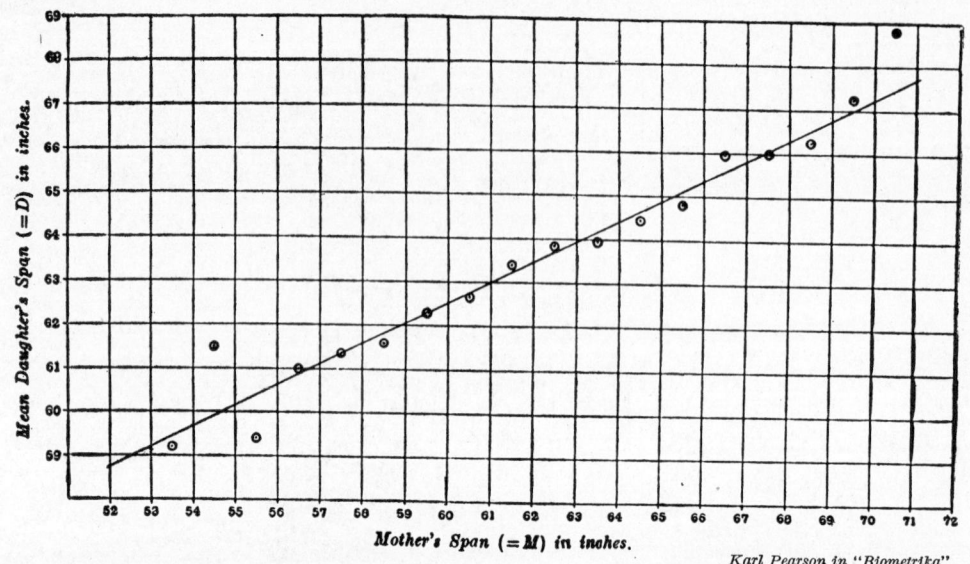

Karl Pearson in "Biometrika"

Fig. 164. Correlation Curve Showing Probable Span of a Daughter from Finger Tip to Finger Tip, for any Given Span of the Mother. 1,370 Cases were Studied in Making up this Chart

Here the dots for the 1,370 observations are not all shown. The dots seen represent the averages of all cases studied in each 1-inch range of mother's span according to the horizontal scale. The curve line is then drawn through these dots. Instead of using the curve line, the mathematical relation may be expressed by the formula $D = 34.18 + .473 M$

This chart would have been easier to interpret clearly if both the vertical and the horizontal scales began with the same figure, say 51 inches. The reader is not apt to notice that the vertical scale here begins at 58 while the horizontal scale begins at 51

Curves like those seen in Fig. 163 are properly drawn as smooth curves because they are based upon some definite laws of nature. It is only because of the crudity of the observations of mankind that the dots are so widely scattered. If human knowledge were sufficient to obtain measurements with exactness, curves for data relating to the laws of nature would fall exactly on points plotted according to the observations and there would be no difficulty in getting smooth curves. The curves in this book are nearly all plotted from statistical data for which there are ordinarily some hundreds of variables, of which many do not follow any definite laws of nature. For most statistical work it is much better to join the points showing the observations by straight lines without any attempt to draw smooth curves. Smooth curves would by their smoothness imply a degree of accuracy in the data much greater than would ordinarily be justifiable. By using the straight lines instead of the smooth curves to connect points, the reader is warned that the chart represents facts as found, rather than facts which are assumed to be in accordance with any definite laws. Where smooth curves are proper, as in Fig. 163, it is feasible to have a mathematical formula to represent the shape of the smooth curve. As the determination of mathematical formulas to suit the shape of any curve is a whole study in itself, there will be no attempt to cover that subject in this book.

Biologists have constant use for correlation curves. Fig. 164 shows a curve used in the solution of a typical problem such as biologists are constantly attacking. It was desired here to find out what laws govern the physical characteristics of the offspring when certain characteristics are found in the mother. In all, 1,370 cases were measured, both mother and daughter, to get the data from which Fig. 164 was plotted. All the cases were classed according to the span of the mother, with the class limits made 1 inch apart. A single point was plotted on the chart as an average for each class. A curve line was then drawn so as to represent most closely the data shown on the chart, and it is seen that the curve is a straight line. There were naturally fewer observations at either end of the chart, for the very small spans and for the very large spans, than for the intermediate spans. It was probably because of the small number of observations at either end of the curve that the dots there are so far away from the curve line. If more numerous observations were taken it is probable that all the averages would fall more closely on the curve line than seen in Fig. 164.

The ordinary course of procedure in making a correlation chart is to plot all the observations by the method seen in Fig. 163. Sometimes, however, the observations are so many as to make an extremely confusing chart if the observations are shown in the form of separate dots. In Fig. 164 the observations in any 1-inch class have been averaged and all the observations in one class are represented by a single dot. In Fig. 165 the dots would be very numerous, so numerous as to make it not feasible to show them on a small size chart. For Fig. 165 it was desired to show the maximum income and the minimum income, as well as the average income. Instead of showing all the dots on the chart, cross-hatching was used to represent the area in which the dots fell. The upper edge of the cross-hatching shows the maximum of the incomes, and the lower limit of the cross-hatching shows the minimum of the incomes reported for different years after graduation. The reader can thus get the whole story at a glance without being confused by the complexity which would result if all the dots were shown. Attention should be called to the fact that the curve of average income falls much closer to the bottom of the shaded area than to the top of the area. This fact shows that, though there are several graduates getting high salaries much above the average income, nevertheless, if all of the dots were shown, most of the dots would fall below the average line rather than above the average line. A few extremely large incomes near the maximum line of the chart could greatly raise the average line but still most of the dots would be found beneath the average.

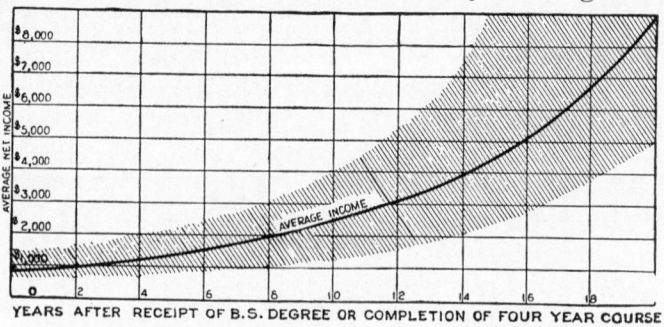

Fig. 165. Income of Graduates of Worcester Polytechnic Institute at Various Years After Graduation

Instead of showing hundreds of dots to represent the data received from different graduates, the chart was simplified by shading the area representing the range of income. The shading thus shows the maximum and the minimum incomes. This general method is a worthy one

Fig. 166 is a very interesting correlation chart. Here a single dot has been used for each observation and the dots are shown in the chart. Instead of showing each dot in its exact position, the dots have been grouped so that all the dots are arranged uniformly inside of squares formed by co-ordinate lines spaced 10 units apart in the scales for examination marks. Classification by class limits 10 units apart on the scale of marks is sufficiently accurate for all practical purposes, as is proved by the gradual change in shading on the chart as a whole. With few observations it might be desirable to show dots on the chart to actual scale rather than in classes by tens.

Ordinarily a line drawn like the heavy wavy line in Fig. 166 would be so placed that the points on the line would be at the center of gravity for the dots vertically on either side of the line. Here, however, the line is so drawn that there are an equal number of dots on either side of the line, at right angles to it at any point throughout its course.

Notice that in the upper portion of the chart the line shifts across the equality line, showing that some of the more brilliant girls obtain higher marks in arithmetic than they do in English. The lower portion of the chart shows that the larger number of girls get considerably better marks in English than in arithmetic, and that this is a general condition to be expected. In the case of those girls who do well in both English and arithmetic, there seems to be improved facility in the field of arithmetic.

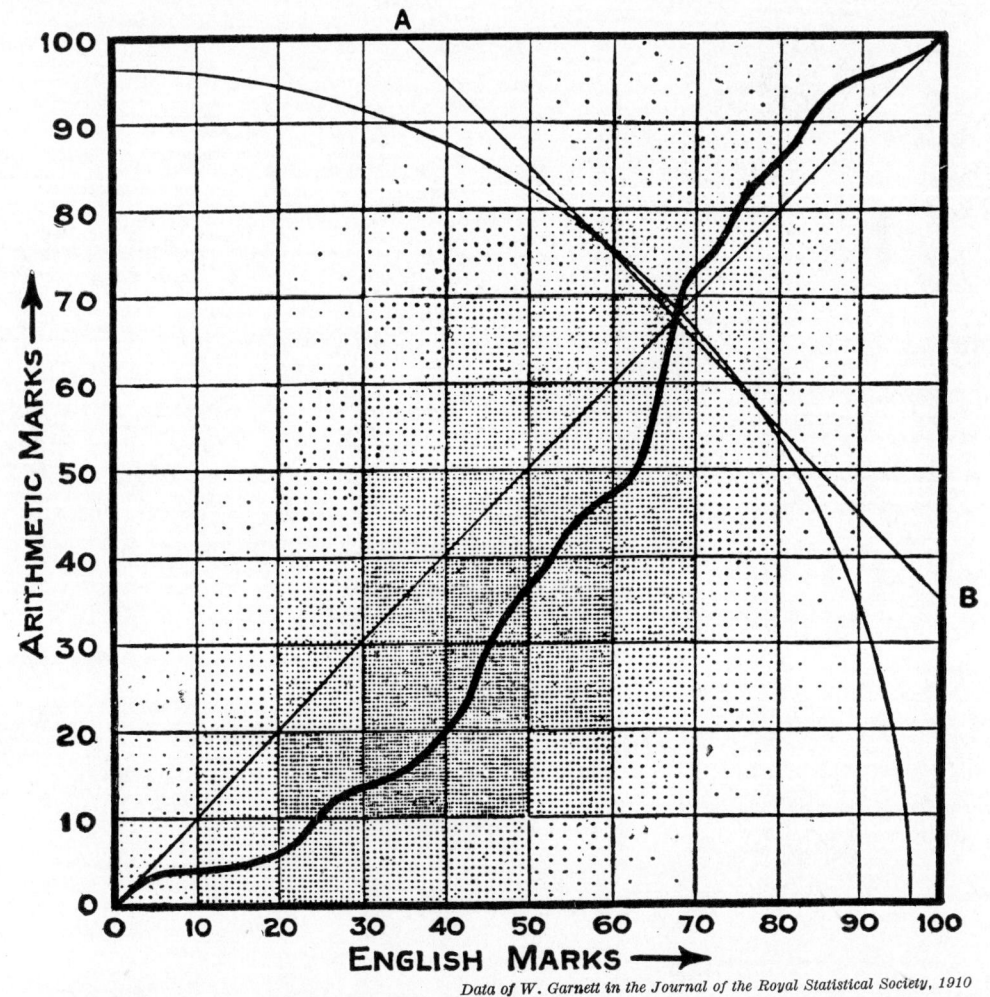

Fig. 166. Examination Marks Obtained by 9,396 School Girls in England

Each girl is represented by one dot showing to scale the grade in English and the grade in arithmetic. The dots are arranged uniformly inside of squares formed by co-ordinate lines spaced ten units apart in the scales for marks. The straight diagonal line drawn from zero shows equal ability in the two studies. The heavy wavy line is drawn through points having an equal number of girls represented on either side of the line, and its position proves that girls have much more ability in English than in arithmetic.

The data of Fig. 166 are shown by another method in Fig. 167. Though Fig. 167 appears to represent a solid model, there was in reality no solid model made in order to obtain this illustration. By using isometric paper a chart like Fig. 167 can be made with comparatively little work. Isometric paper has lines ruled on the paper right and left at an angle of 30 degrees to the horizontal. By selecting a vertical scale to portray by separate columns the number of girls represented in any square of Fig. 166, it becomes a comparatively simple matter to draw the illustration. The various necessary lines can be drawn freehand in pencil on top of the isometric co-ordinate ruling, until the chart is completed; then the various lines can be inked in to get the final effect seen in Fig. 167. The total number of girls represented in any column is shown by the figures at the top of the column.

Data of W. Garnett in the Journal of the Royal Statistical Society, 1910

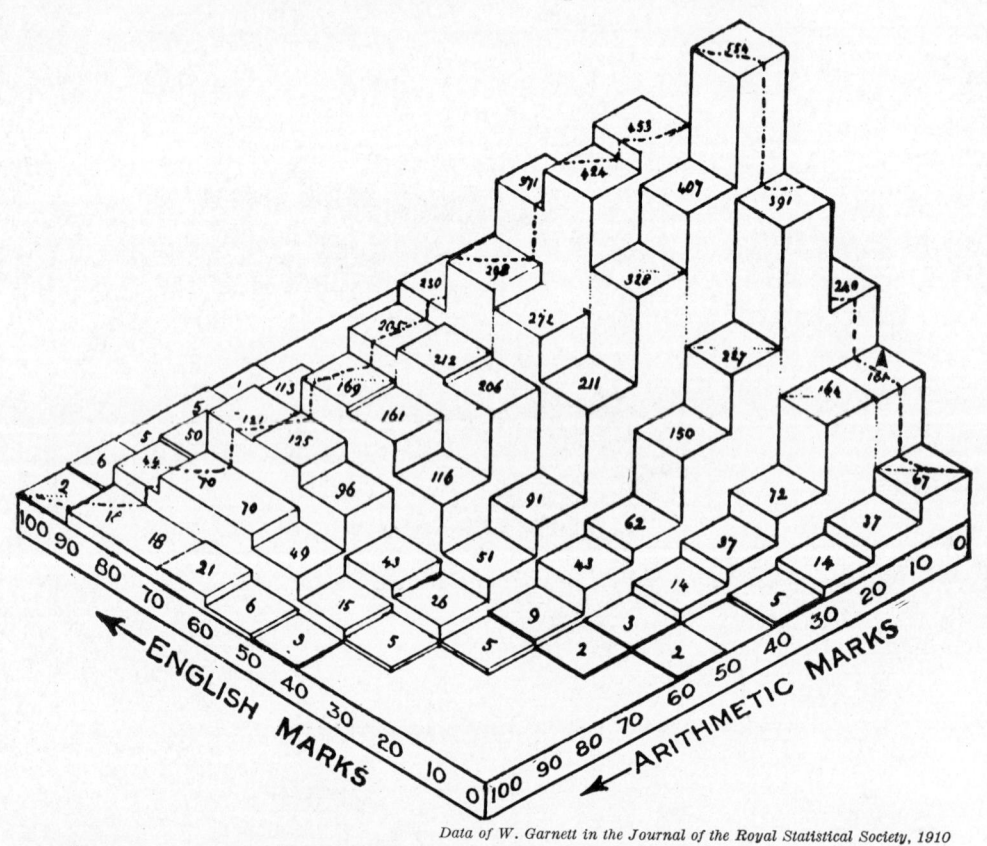

Fig. 167. Examination Marks Obtained by 9,396 School Girls in England

This illustration was made from the same data as Fig. 166. Here the number of girls in any square is shown by the height of the vertical column drawn to scale.

The arrangement of scales here is different from that in Fig. 166 as will be noticed by observing the direction of the arrows

The reader should note carefully that the scale arrangement of Fig. 167 is entirely different from that used in Fig. 166. In Fig. 166, the two zeros fall together as they ordinarily should do in chart work of this sort. In Fig. 167, however, the two scale zeros are not together and the reader is accordingly prevented from interpreting Fig. 167 directly from the location of dots seen in Fig. 166. It would seem as though a better chart could have been made if the isometric chart, instead of being as in Fig. 167, had been arranged with the two zeros together. Such an arrangement would have permitted easier interpretation, for the reader would have secured a more close similarity to Fig. 166. Another possible arrangement which would have been better than that used in Fig. 167 would put the two 100 per cent marks of the scale together, with the zero marks at the diagonally opposite corners. A chart of this nature would show as two mountain peaks, one on each side, with a valley in the center.

Where an actual model is desired more than an illustration, a very convenient, yet cheap, arrangement can be had by stringing beads on separate wires, each mounted in the center of ruled spaces, like those shown in Fig. 166. The number of beads on each wire can represent to scale the data for the particular square at the center of which the bead wire is placed. The heights of the columns of beads on the different wires would then show clearly the facts for any one section of the field in a manner similar to that of Fig. 167. The beads would probably be more generally understood by an untrained person than the isometric drawing of Fig. 167, and it is for this reason that the scheme is mentioned here. The arrangement by columns seen in Fig. 167 is satisfactory for the trained reader, but the separate beads on wires would probably give a less abstract impression, more easily grasped by the average person.

CHAPTER XI

MAP PRESENTATIONS

MAPS marked, colored, or shaded in different ways, or used in conjunction with pins or other signals, form one of the most convenient means of conveying information. Such maps may be used to advantage in a surprising variety of ways, only a few of which can be mentioned here.

Engineers who have with great labor prepared complete plans, specifications, and estimates for some proposed improvement are frequently disappointed that they cannot arouse enough enthusiasm in the proposed scheme to obtain the approval of the government or municipal officials, or members of a corporation board of directors, who must vote in favor of the plan and appropriate the money necessary to carry it into effect. It is always difficult to get non-technical persons to take an interest in proposals which are shown only by blue prints and ordinary maps. Architects realize this so well that it is common practice among them to submit carefully prepared wash-drawings to show the appearance of the building for which they are submitting plans. Most engineering work cannot be easily represented by wash-drawings, and the engineer is accordingly somewhat handicapped as compared with the architect in arousing interest in his project.

Fig. 168 shows a picture developed by H. W. Holmes, Chief of the Bureau of Highways and Bridges, of the city of Portland, Oregon, to present his plans advantageously to the common council and the taxpayers to obtain their approval for the expenditure. A photograph of the actual site of the bridge was made, and then the picture of the bridge was drawn in by hand on the photograph. Most engineers submitting plans for an improvement of this kind would send only a set of blue prints and perhaps a map marked to show the location of the proposed bridge. A picture like Fig. 168 can be used in conjunction with a map if desired. Certainly a proposition carefully worked up and submitted, as was the proposed bridge shown in Fig. 168, is more likely to receive favorable consideration than one in which only the ordinary blue prints and maps are used.

If maps must be printed in a report, a book, or a magazine, it is usually necessary, on account of the high cost of color printing, to use some arrangement of black ink for shading those areas which on a single map would ordinarily be colored by hand. Fig. 169 is a sample of what can be done without the use of color. If the drawing is made considerably larger than the finished illustration, the shading can be put on effectively by hand work. Mechanical shading by the Ben Day process, as regularly used by good engravers, gives excellent results but its use makes zinc cuts rather expensive. Many illustrations in this book are made by the Ben Day process. Anyone wishing to know more about the possibilities of this process should look up Fig. 233 or consult the engraver who is to make the line cuts.

Often the matter to be presented calls for maps of a large size, which can be obtained only at considerable

Fig. 168. Sketch of a Proposed Concrete Bridge for Portland, Oregon, Drawn on an Actual Photograph to Show the General Effect if the Bridge Is Built

Points a measured distance apart on the site of the bridge are plainly marked so that they will appear in the photograph and show both the scale of the photographic reduction and the location of the bridge. The bridge is then drawn in on the photograph by hand work

Engineering Record

expense. Sometimes only one map is available when a variety of plans must be presented. In such cases, it is not feasible to draw plans for new construction work, or alternative working schemes, on the map itself. Most draughtsmen put the map on a large drawing board and then draw the new constructions on separate sheets of tracing cloth. The tracing cloth is not very transparent, however, and it will not help greatly to get a project voted upon favorably if the plan must be presented to a board of directors on tracing-cloth drawings with the map itself only very dimly visible through the tracing cloth.

Fig. 169. Drainage Area of the Canadian River, New Mexico

Areas of different kinds may be distinguished on maps by various classes of shading when color printing is not available

A much more effective scheme is to use a sheet of almost transparent celluloid made with a rough surface that will take drawing ink fairly well. The different alternative plans may then be drawn on the celluloid in colored inks, and the different sheets of celluloid superimposed upon the map one by one as quickly as any executive committee or board considering the proposals may desire. The main difficulty with the celluloid method is that the inks will rub off if the celluloid is handled too much with moist hands. Ease of erasure has some advantages, however, for tentative schemes can be rubbed out or changed at will, simply by using a damp cloth. After the final adoption of the plan, tracing cloth can be laid over the combined map and celluloid sheet, and the important features of both may be traced for blue-printing or for general reference later. Where maps must have constant use, it is sometimes convenient to have them mounted between two sheets of clear celluloid. The celluloid-manufacturing companies are prepared to do this kind of mounting to order.

Contrasts in map areas as shown in Fig. 170, by superimposing one portion of the world on top of another portion, or by placing two portions side by side on the same scale, are of considerable value.

In geography books, and in other places where maps are most commonly seen, contrasted territories are frequently drawn to such different scales that a true idea of their proportions cannot be obtained. The relative proportion can be indicated best when care is taken to have the several areas drawn to the same scale and placed in a good position for comparison.

Fig. 171 is shown here only as an example of the almost unlimited range which the application of graphic methods may have. The average person would never think of charting a football game, yet the graphic method certainly gives the information more concisely than could words alone.

Fig. 172 will be recognized by many readers as similar in general scheme to the weather maps on which lines are drawn through all points having the same temperature or the same barometric pressure. Contour lines to show those points which are at the same height above sea level give another application of the same general method.

Profile drawings similar to Fig. 173 are commonly used by engineers, but are not as well understood as they should be by others. The main feature of the profile chart is the very great difference between the horizontal scale used to mark distance and the vertical scale showing the height of the points represented. The vertical scale of Fig. 173 should have been shown on the chart. The heights stated for different cities give a fair indication of what the vertical scale is and a reader can, if he must, measure on the drawing the height for any city and from that determine to what scale the drawing has been made. As a broad rule, the scale should be indicated in an easily seen position on every chart, if the scale can be of assistance to any one besides the maker of the chart.

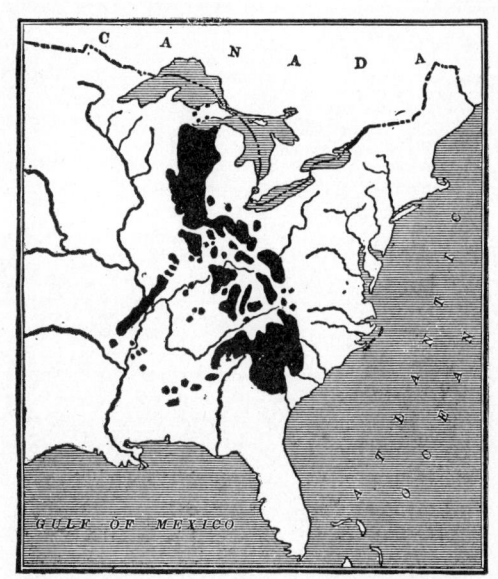

World's Work

Fig. 170. The Comparative Size of the Philippines

By drawing the islands to scale and in solid black on a map of the eastern part of the United States, the relative size is clearly brought out

Considerable time and ingenuity may be used in drawing up a

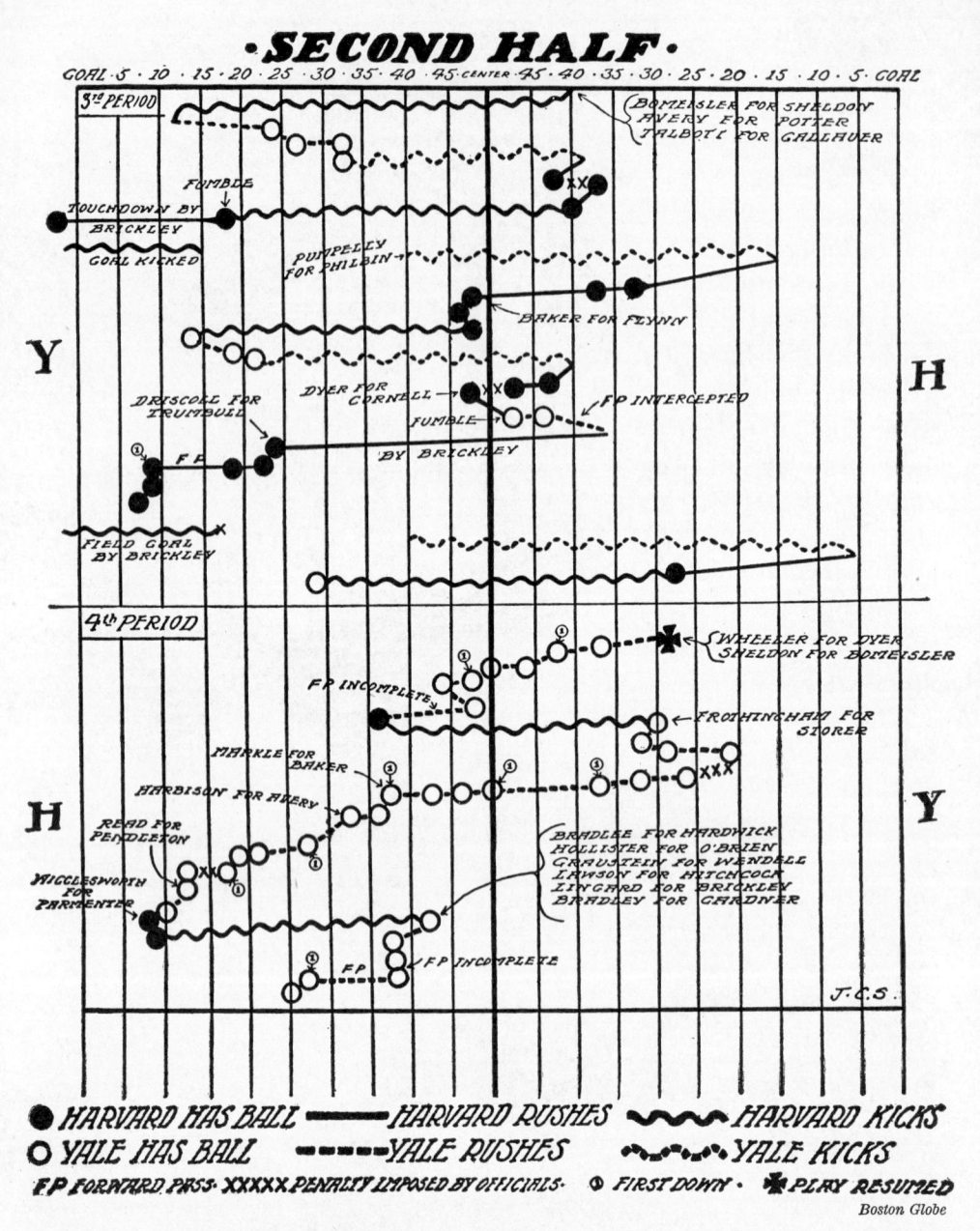

Fig. 171. Second Half of the Harvard-Yale Football Game, November 23, 1912, Final Score, Harvard 20, Yale 0

The scale of the football field has been changed so as to give sufficient width for representing the plays by lines and symbols of various kinds

chart like Fig. 174 so that the facts which it is desired to prove may be brought out clearly. Numerous methods are available for presenting such data. There is no general rule for determining which method is the best, and judgment must be used to choose the method which is best fitted to each individual case. Note that in Fig. 174 we have a scale reading to quarters of a mile, and we also have circles prominently drawn on the map at one-mile intervals to give a clear idea of the distances involved.

Country Gentleman

Fig. 172. Dates for Planting Corn, Showing How the Season Advances in Different Parts of the United States

This illustration is similar to the well-known weather maps on which lines are drawn through all points where conditions are the same

Though an illustration in the general method of Fig. 175 is attractive, and will effectively gain the attention of the reader, the method itself has all the inherent weakness of Fig. 36, Fig. 37 and Fig. 38 in Chapter III. If the reader wishes to practice some mental gymnastics, he may try to work out the ratio between the number of cattle in Idaho and the number of cattle in Texas. Though it cannot be made certain, it is probable that the chart was drawn on

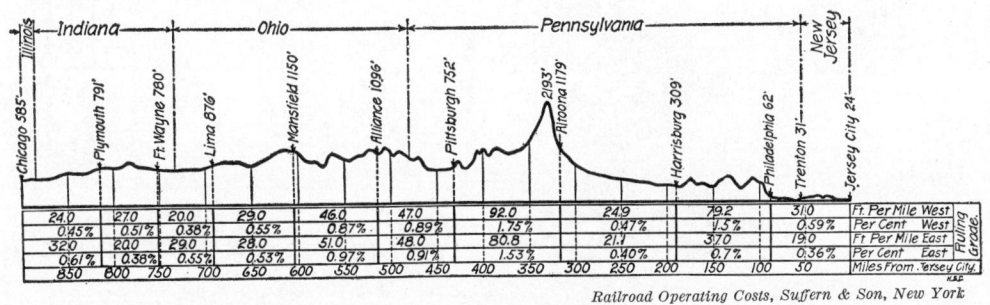

Railroad Operating Costs, Suffern & Son, New York

Fig. 173. Profile of the Pennsylvania Railroad from Jersey City to Chicago. The Tabulated Figures Below the Profile Refer to the Spaces Between the Dotted Lines

This is an example of a valuable method of presentation by which a horizontal scale much smaller than the vertical scale is used so that great distances may be represented in a small space

214　　　　　　　　GRAPHIC METHODS

an area basis. For the purpose of a visual and mental test, the area basis may be used if Idaho and Texas are compared.

The method of Fig. 176 is now quite commonly used in Government publications. This scheme for presenting data is not so striking to the eye as that of Fig. 175, but it is more accurate. The scale given with the map permits the number of cattle for any State to be read fairly accurately. The degree of accuracy depends upon the map size selected, and upon the number of dots used to represent any given quantity. The more dots used the greater the accuracy. There is,

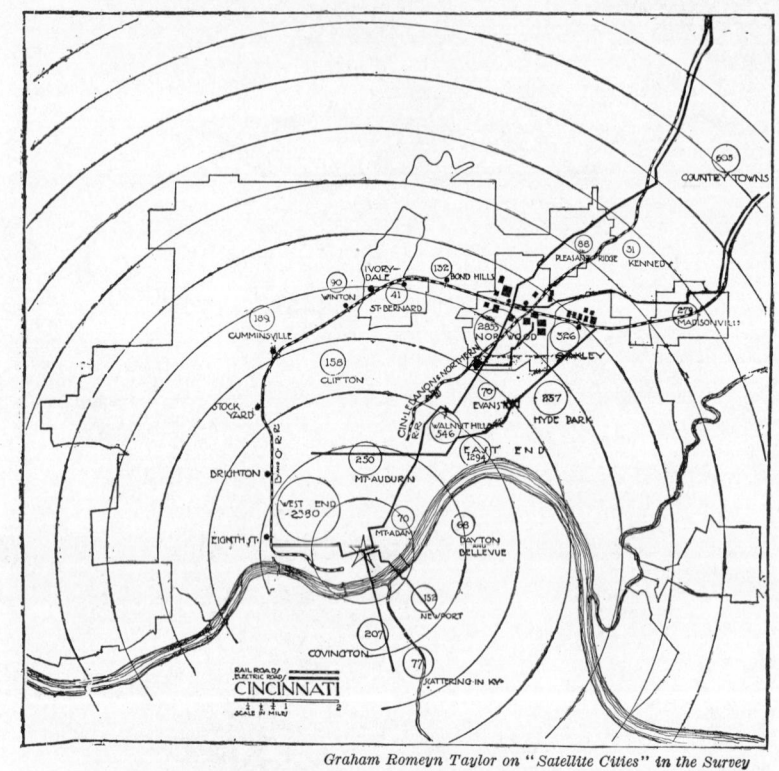

Graham Romeyn Taylor on "Satellite Cities" in the Survey

Fig. 174. Map Showing that Factory Workers of Norwood and Oakley (Cincinnati) Live Long Distances from Their Work, Many in the Heart of Cincinnati Rather than in the Suburbs Near the Factories

The use of much heavier lines on the small circles and the figures in them would have improved this chart. Pins or black-ink dots, each representing say 20 workers, would give a good result by using the method of Fig. 198

however, a limit to the number of dots which may be used, or the dots will of necessity be so small in diameter that the quarter circles will be impossible for the eye to distinguish. In Fig. 176 it would not be feasible to use a much smaller circle if the quarter-circles are used.

MAP PRESENTATIONS 215

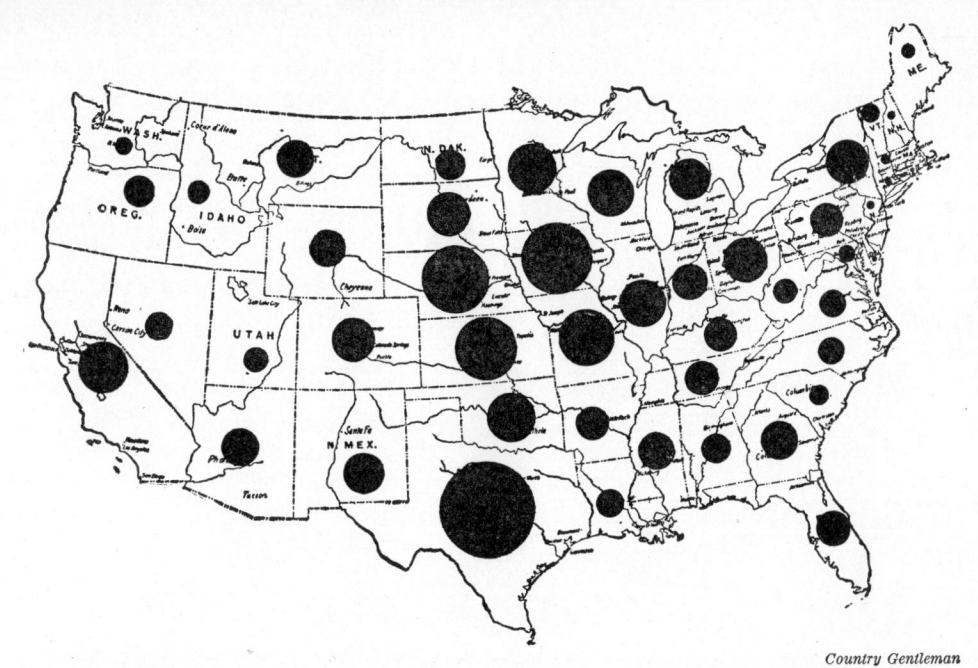

Country Gentleman

Fig. 175. Relative Distribution in the United States of Cattle Other than Dairy Cows
For popular presentation, if great accuracy is unimportant, this method of illustration would be difficult to improve upon. It is not possible to get a correct comparison between any two States because any one circle cannot be fitted visually into the area of another circle. Compare the method used in Fig. 176

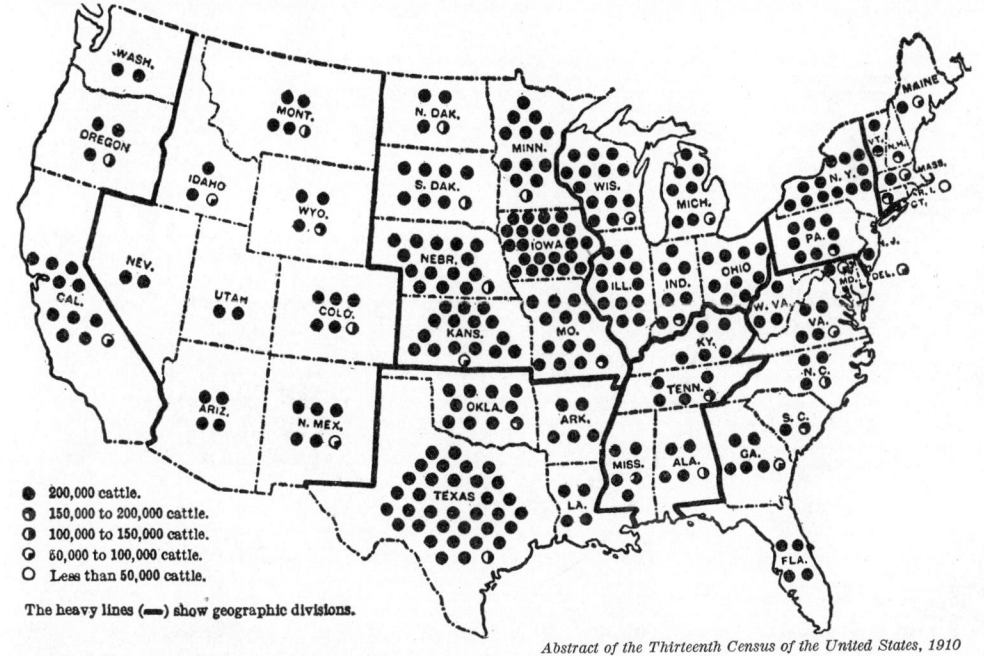

- ● 200,000 cattle.
- ◐ 150,000 to 200,000 cattle.
- ◑ 100,000 to 150,000 cattle.
- ◒ 50,000 to 100,000 cattle.
- ○ Less than 50,000 cattle.

The heavy lines (━) show geographic divisions.

Abstract of the Thirteenth Census of the United States, 1910

Fig. 176. All Cattle on Farms in the United States, by States, April 15, 1910
Here a definite scale is given which permits fairly accurate reading of the number of cattle for any State. The visual contrast between States is also quite striking. Though not so clear-cut as Fig. 175, this illustration has more accuracy

216   GRAPHIC METHODS

In making up copy for the line cut of Fig. 177 very little hand work was required. If an outline map of suitable size is available, the only hand work necessary for a cut of this kind is in drawing the small circles and placing inside them the figures serving as key numbers for the shading used. The actual shading is done by the engraver making use of the Ben Day process. For information regarding the preparation of engraver's copy for plates on which Ben Day shading is desired, see Fig. 233.

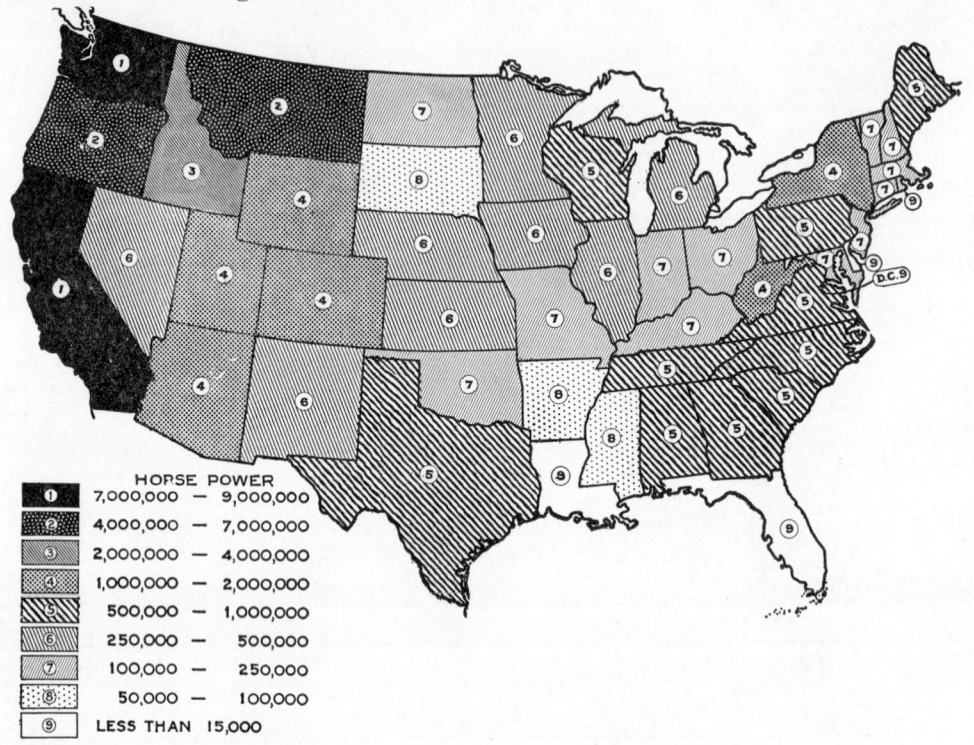

Fig. 177. Potential Water Power in the Different States of the United States
This is a splendid example of the contrasts in shading made possible by the Ben Day mechanical processes of engraving. Nine contrasting shades increasing in darkness are used here with absolute distinctness. The small number in the circle used to identify the shading is of great advantage

There is one serious error which should be avoided in the interpretation of any shaded map like Fig. 177. The key scale at the lower left-hand corner of the illustration shows that the different shades do not become darker by any uniform increase in horse power. The range included in shade number eight is 50,000—from 50,000 to 100,000. For shading number two, however, the range is 3,000,000—from 4,000,000 to 7,000,000. This numerical scale was badly selected, for the steps vary so greatly in size that the increasing degrees of shad-

MAP PRESENTATIONS 217

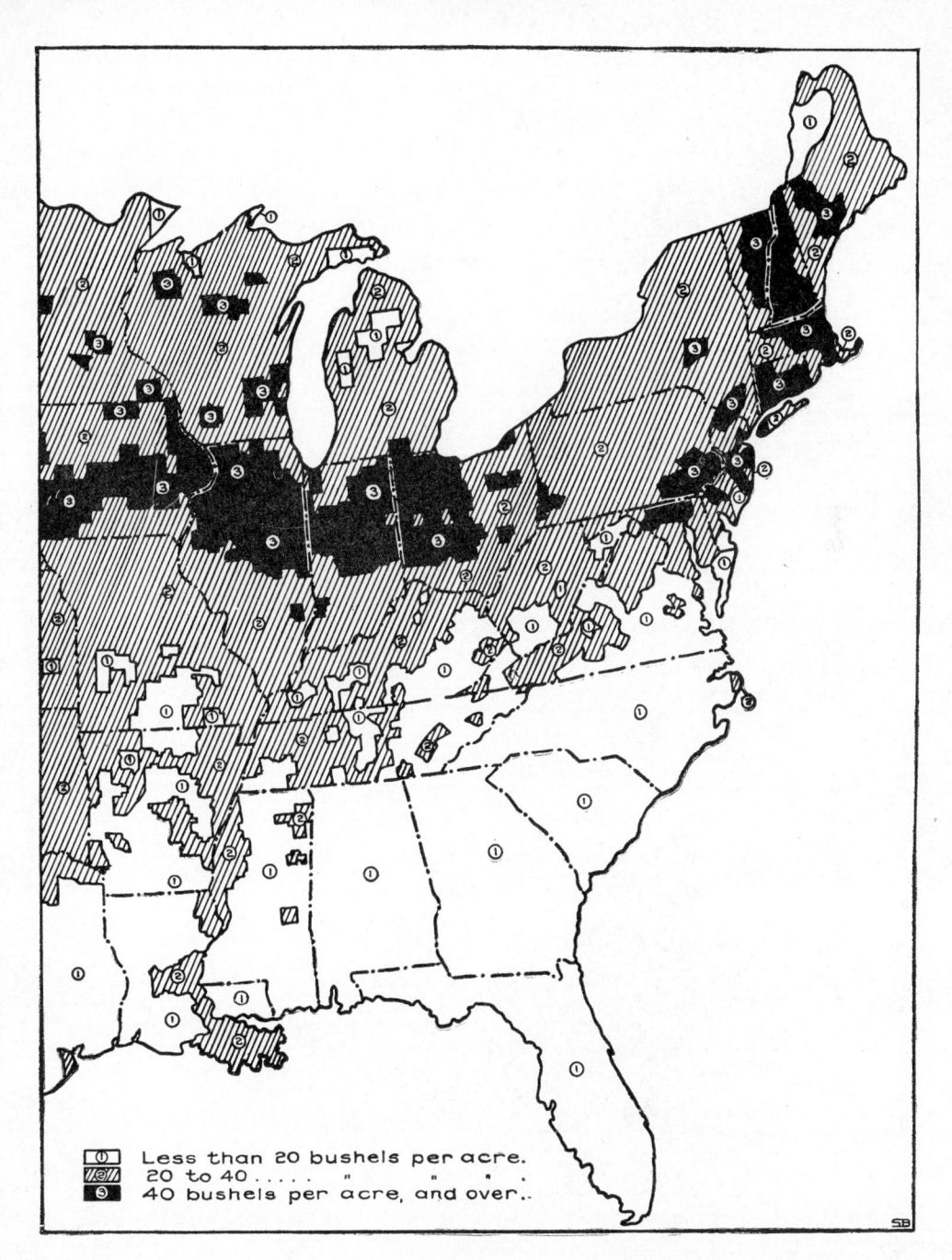

Fig. 178. Yield of Corn per Acre in the Eastern Part of the United States in 1900

Here the data have been recorded by counties rather than by States. This chart is an example of what any draftsman may do by hand shading. It would have been better to use the smaller numbers to represent the best rank, as was done in Fig. 177

218 GRAPHIC METHODS

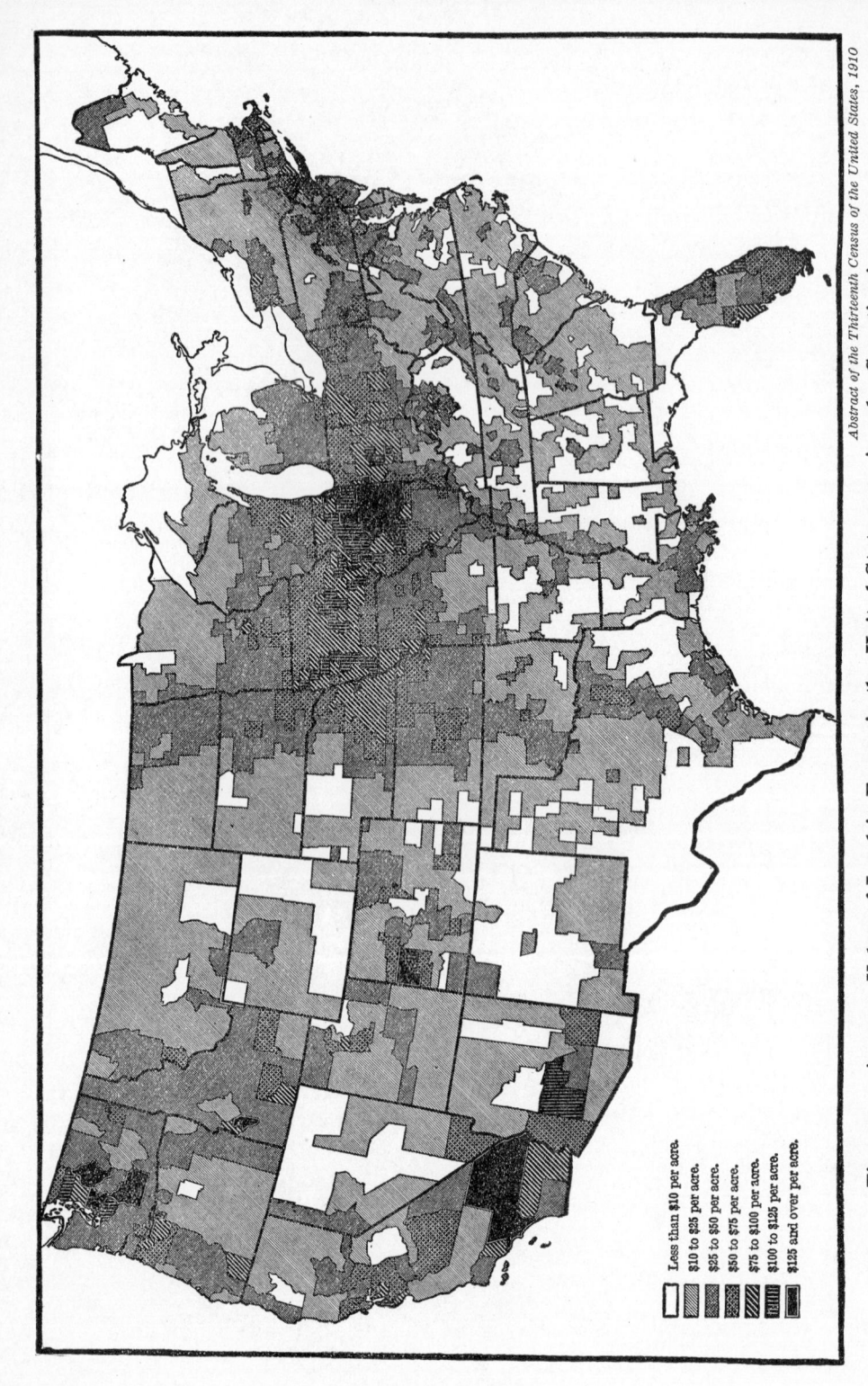

Fig. 179. Average Value of Land in Farms in the United States per Acre by Counties in 1910
Abstract of the Thirteenth Census of the United States, 1910

In Fig. 178 the shading represented unit quantities. Here it represents unit values. Maps of this nature are also of great assistance in studying the chief characteristics of cities and suburbs as regards land values, population density, etc.

ing, as they appear to the eye, mean practically nothing. States having shading number two could vary from each other in the amount of horse power by more than the whole quantity of power in States having shadings from three to nine inclusive. If the steps in the shading scale had been so made that there were nine increasing classes of shading, each representing 1,000,000 horse power, it can be seen that all the States here numbered five to nine inclusively would have the same shading. Such a map made with a scale of uniform steps would appear so entirely different from the map shown here that no one would ever recognize the maps to have been made from the same data. The selection of scale for maps of this kind is important in order that the map may tell a truthful story. Wherever feasible, the numerical scale intervals for colorings or shadings should be uniform. Frequently the data are of such kind that there is much concentration at some portion of the scale, but with important facts to show at other portions of the scale above and below the point of greatest concentration. It may then be desirable to use uniform scale-steps for the shading in the portion of the scale with greatest concentration, and to have smaller scale-steps at either end or at both ends of the scale. In Fig. 177 small scale-steps would seem desirable for the lower portion of the scale.

It will be noticed in Fig. 177 that the numbers denoting the shadings are arranged with the smallest numbers to represent the largest quantities. This arrangement was made purposely. On a map of the kind seen in Fig. 177 there may be any number of different shadings, from one to a dozen or more. In order to simplify matters for the reader it seems best to assign the smaller numbers to represent those conditions which are considered most desirable or commendable. The reader may then see instantly which areas are first, second, third, etc., in rank simply by observing the figures inside the small circles.

In Fig. 178, if it be assumed that there is a likelihood of corn crops going up to 60 bushels per acre, the scale intervals are shown as uniform. Fig. 178 is of interest chiefly because it shows what can be done by hand ruling when it is necessary to produce an illustration for a report in which an expensive cut by the Ben Day method cannot be justified.

Fig. 179 does not do justice to the possibilities of the Ben Day method of shading. The cut was made by photographing a page of the Census Abstract which was printed on rather rough paper. With an original cut made directly by the Ben Day process the distinction

220   GRAPHIC METHODS

between the different shades would be considerably clearer than it is in Fig. 179. A cut of this size and complexity is rather expensive when the Ben Day shading is used. Anyone wishing a cut made with Ben Day work would do well to get a rough cost-estimate from his engraver before actually giving the order.

It will be noticed in Fig. 179 that the numerical scale-steps for different degrees of shading are uniform except at the smaller end of the scale. It would probably not be wise to show as white area all of the land valued at from $10 to $25 an acre, since such land makes

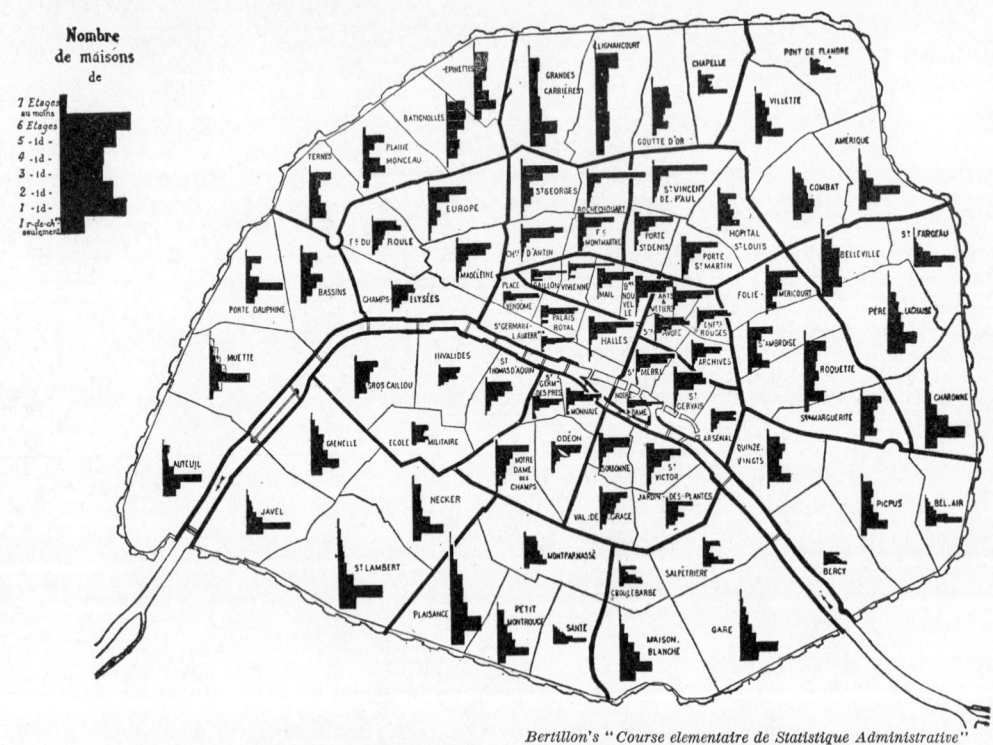

Bertillon's "Course elementaire de Statistique Administrative"

Fig. 180. Height of the Houses in the Different Districts of Paris
The scale for this illustration should have been indicated on the chart so that actual numbers of houses could be read. The vertical dimension of the group of bars for each district shows the relative total number of houses. The horizontal dimension shows the relative number of houses of each height by stories

up about half of the whole United States. A uniform scale varying by $25 per acre would give an erroneous impression regarding those important areas which contain land valued at less than $25 per acre but in which there is a large amount of farming.

Map diagrams of the type shown in Fig. 180 are sometimes useful. There is danger, however, of making a chart of this kind so popular in character that it loses in accuracy. The utility of Fig. 180 is at once

MAP PRESENTATIONS 221

POPULATION DENSITY PER ACRE.

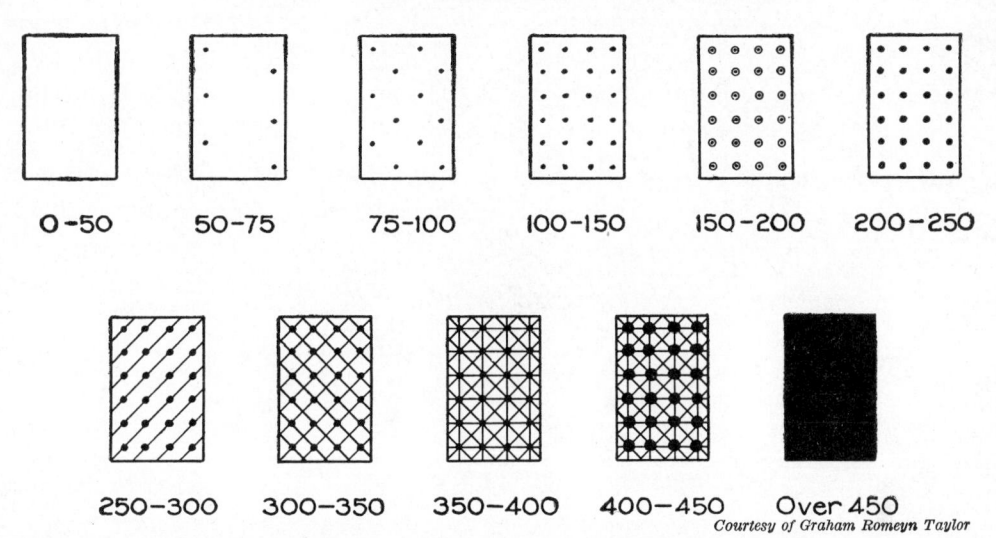

0-50   50-75   75-100   100-150   150-200   200-250

250-300   300-350   350-400   400-450   Over 450

Courtesy of Graham Romeyn Taylor

Fig. 181. Methods of Marking Maps When an Increased Density of Population May be Expected in Following Years

Each shading can be made by adding with a pen to the shading used for the next lower density. Pins of different colors placed in a map have an advantage over this scheme in that pins can be removed if population density should happen to decrease

limited by the fact that there is no key scale shown from which an exact numerical interpretation may be obtained.

The scheme for indicating population density shown in Fig. 181 is necessary only when very large and valuable maps are used. For ordinary purposes it would be better to have a new map for each Census, and then to use colored crayons on the different areas of the map, rather than to attempt the complicated scheme of Fig. 181. If, however, a photograph must be taken periodically to produce line cuts showing the map in printed form on a reduced scale, colored crayons cannot be used and the scheme of Fig. 181 may be of great assistance. The result obtained by the method of Fig. 181 may be obtained by using map pins with spherical heads and pushing the pins in until the heads touch the map. The number of pins in any city block or district would indicate the population according to some simple scale. If it is not necessary to photograph the map, pins with different colors of heads may be used to show density of population. There is one very great advantage in using pins instead of crayons or the pen-and-ink system of Fig. 181. It sometimes happens that an error is made which may spoil a very valuable map because of the impossibility of erasure. When short pins are used instead of crayon or ink, an error can be instantly

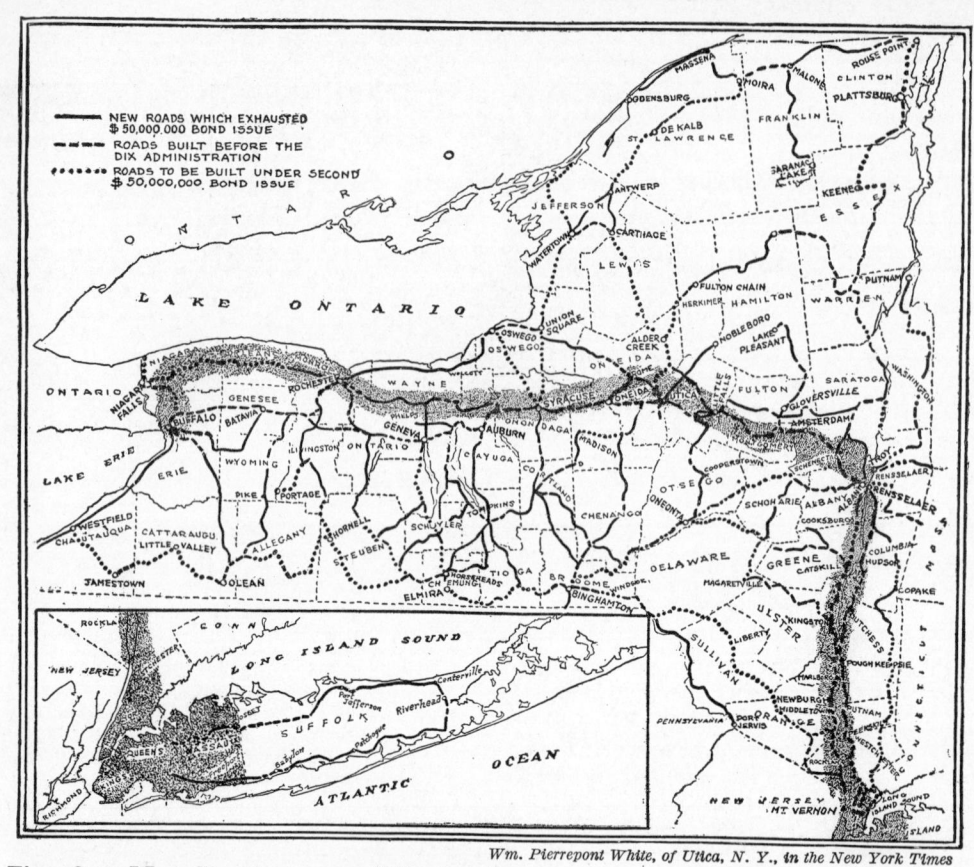

Fig. 182. Map Showing 3,500 Miles of Completed and Proposed State Roads, in New York's Proposed 12,000-Mile System. The Shaded Portion Shows a Strip Ten Miles Wide which Contains 90 Per Cent of the Taxable Valuation and 80 Per Cent of the Population

The object of the illustration is to show the necessity of a road system that will feed from the farms to the densely settled portion, permit the quick and easy transportation of farm products to the cities, lessen the cost of living, and thus justify the taxing of the State as a whole for the construction of this system

corrected by pulling out pins. Also, if there should be a reduction in the density of the population, pins can be pulled out, whereas with the pen-and-ink method of Fig. 181 it is not possible to proceed backward on the scale of marking and a decrease can never be shown without making another map or marring the old one.

In Fig. 182 is seen a good example of the graphic method applied to newspaper writing designed to convince the reader by specific argument. The presentation is very effective. The shaded portion of the map shows a strip which contains 90 per cent of the taxable valuations and 80 per cent of the population. The possibilities for the use of maps in arguments of political or economic nature are almost without limit. It is rather surprising that maps for such purposes have not been more generally employed.

Though the map record sheet shown in Fig. 183 may appeal to some business men, there would seem to be little advantage in that type of sheet over tabulated figures in a column. The column arrangement would have a desirable feature in that different entries could more easily be compared for size by judging the number of digits contained in each entry.

The method shown in Fig. 184 can be widely used in map problems relating to any kind of travel over specific routes. In this particular case the map concerns the movement of freight. Maps of this type are very commonly used to show the number of passengers carried on different city transit lines. To make an illustration on the plan of Fig. 184, the width of each broad strip is carefully drawn to some scale representing the total quantity movement. A map like this is easily drawn yet it is very effective, particularly if colors are used for the broad strips while the route itself is marked by means of a black line in the center.

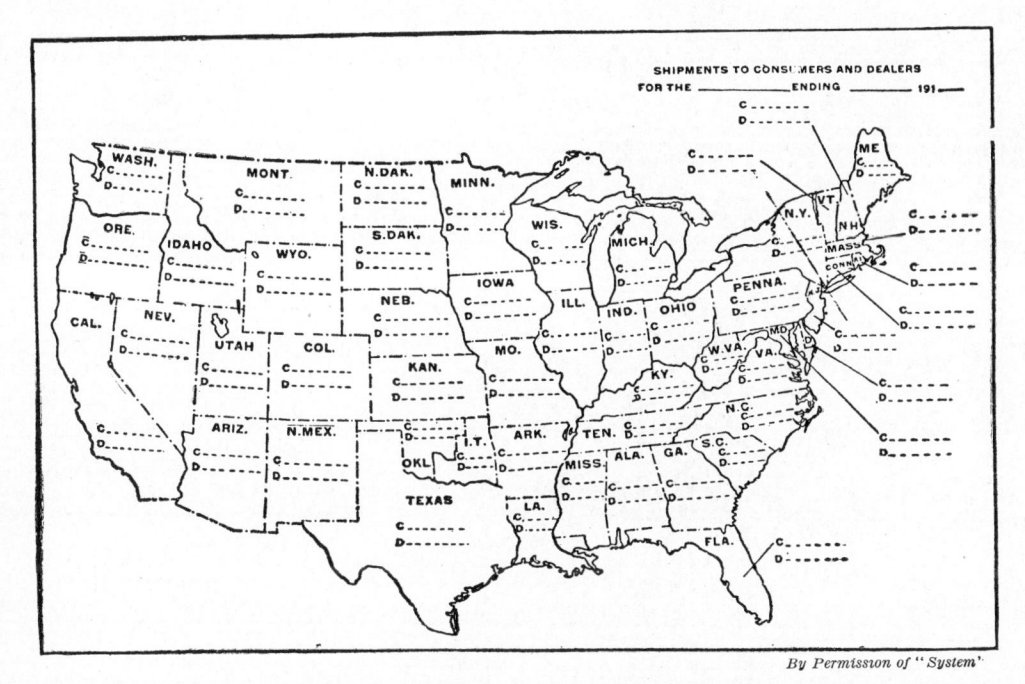

Fig. 183. Blank for Recording Sales to Consumers and to Dealers, Abbreviated by the Letters "C" and "D" for Each State

A blank like this can be filled out daily, weekly, or monthly as desired

224   GRAPHIC METHODS

Maps on the scheme of Fig. 184 are made entirely in the plane of the paper itself. In Fig. 185 we have a map presentation in which quantities are represented by building vertically above the various routes laid out on the map. For the map of Fig. 185, the vertical representation was made by strips of wood, alternately black and white, glued carefully above each one of the street-car routes. Each of the strips of wood represents 4,000 passengers carried on the street-car lines in 24 hours. The model gives the whole transit situation with surprisingly great clearness, and a better presentation than this could scarcely be imagined.

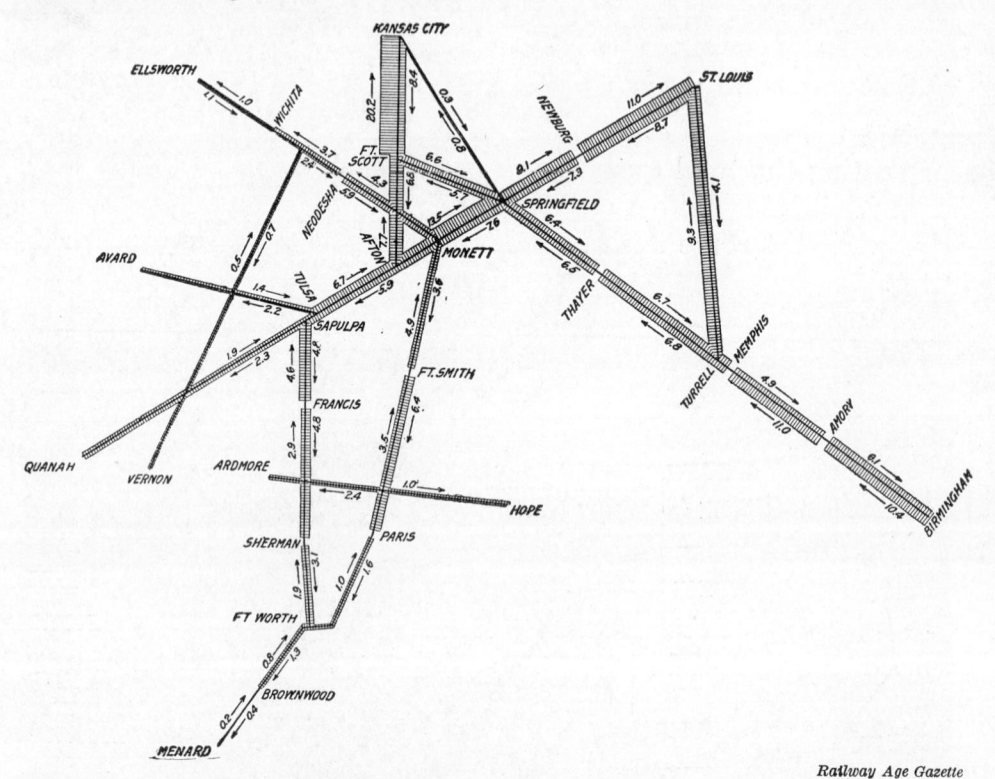

Railway Age Gazette

Fig. 184. Map Diagram Showing Freight-traffic Density and Direction on the St. Louis and San Francisco Railroad for the Fiscal Year 1912-13

The figures are in terms of 100,000 net tons hauled one mile per mile of road.
A map of this kind is easily made and is often of very great utility. The method can also be used to show the number of passengers carried on railroad, subway, or street-car lines, etc. Compare Fig. 185

The method used in the construction of the model shown in Fig. 185 gives magnificent results, but wooden strips are not practicable except on a very spacious map. The wood-strip method also involves a large amount of time on the part of a skilled workman, and workmen to

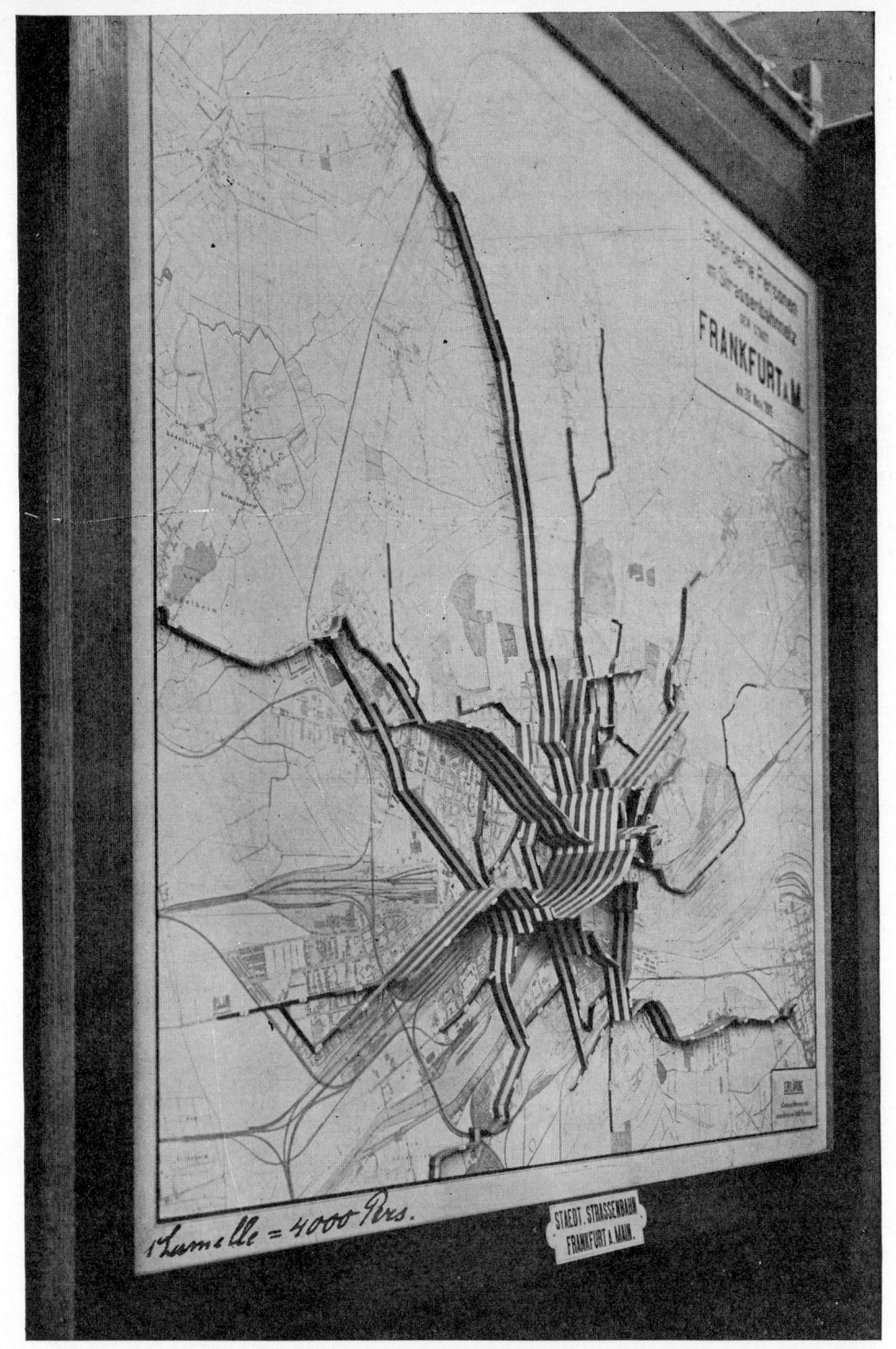

Courtesy of Dr. Ewerbeck, Internationale Baufach-Ausstellung, Leipzig, Germany, 1913

Fig. 185. Passengers Carried in Twenty-four Hours on the Street-car Lines of Frankfurt a M., Germany. Each Vertical Strip Represents 4,000 Passengers

The map is about eight feet square. Strips of wood are glued above each street having a car line. This is an excellent presentation of facts

do this class of work are not so easily found in the United States as in Germany.

An excellent map of this general type can be made by using sheet metal, as aluminum or zinc, ruled or painted with lines or colored stripes representing the vertical scale to which the information is to be shown. Where two transit lines intersect the strips of metal can be riveted or soldered together. As aluminum is not easily soldered it is best to use zinc or tinned iron if solder is to be the means of holding the vertical strips to each other. In many cases solder is unnecessary, for the strips may be held vertically by notching each strip halfway through so that the strips can be interlocked in the manner shown in Fig. 236. By using sheet metal a much cheaper construction can be obtained than by wood strips. The sheet-metal method also permits the use of a map of much smaller size and finer scale than would be feasible if wood strips were the means of obtaining the necessary vertical height.

Chapter XII

MAPS AND PINS

PIN MAPS have not been much used in the past, chiefly because a map pin which would give satisfactory service has not been available for common use. Until recently the map markers obtainable have been little more than old-fashioned carpet tacks having chisel-shaped points which cut the surface of any map into which they were pushed. Tacks with rough steel shanks cannot be pushed far into a map if the tacks are to be pulled out again. Also, rough steel is likely to rust so as to cause the whole tack to deteriorate rapidly.

Cloth heads on the map tacks make it possible to have tacks in distinct colors and plaids. The cloth tops, however, fade in the sunlight and collect dust so that in a short time the different colors of tacks on any map, exposed as a wall map must be, cannot be easily distinguished. The crudeness of the cloth-covered tack makes it unsatisfactory for many kinds of map work. Cloth-covered tacks are long, and long tacks which can be pushed only a short distance into the surface of a map are not satisfactory, for they are likely to drop out or be knocked off by any slight disturbance.

Wall maps with long projecting tacks are not practical for office use unless protected by an expensive frame with a glass cover. As it is usually necessary to open up such a glass map-case to change the position of the tacks frequently, the construction of the case becomes unduly expensive. Without a glass cover a wall map with long projecting tacks is likely to be damaged by the feather duster of the janitor.

Even when maps with long projecting tacks are safeguarded by being placed in separate drawers of a cabinet made for that purpose, there is still a probability that some of the tacks will come loose from the mounting and rattle around inside of the map drawers. This is a point not realized by most men who install map and tack systems, but it usually sooner or later sounds the death-knell of the tack system.

Generally the tacks are placed in the maps one by one as agencies are established or as data are obtained from correspondence. After the correspondence by which each tack was located has gone to the correspondence files, there is ordinarily no list showing the geographical location of the tacks. If a single tack is found loose in the bottom of a drawer of a cabinet system, or on the floor of an office where there is a wall map, it causes distrust of the whole tack installation. When there is no list showing the geographical location of different tacks, the one tack which is out of place cannot be put back without checking over correspondence and records which may extend back for years. Even

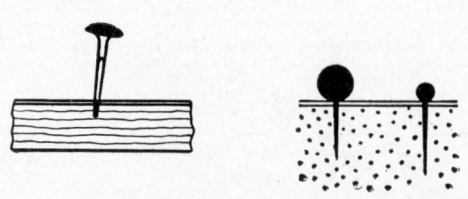

Fig. 186. A Contrast Between Long, Cloth-covered Map Tacks which are Likely to Fall Out, and Glass-head Map Pins Made with Short Needle-points so that the Pins May be Pushed in until the Heads Touch the Map

when a list of tack locations is at hand, the loose tack cannot be replaced without checking the location of all the tacks on the map one by one to determine by a process of elimination where the loose tack came from. In the ordinary course of human events it is not likely that a tack falling out of a map would be found to give warning that the map record is no longer accurate. The tack system using long projecting tacks may therefore contain unsuspected inaccuracies just because tacks may have come loose. The unpleasant suspicion that a map record may be inaccurate, because of the long tacks falling out, sometimes causes a man to abandon the tack system entirely, believing that it is not reliable enough to give data on which important decisions must be based.

Map and pin systems are of such tremendous assistance that they should not be condemned simply because the map pin itself has not been satisfactory. By using a short pin with a needle point and by having a backing for the map such that the needle point can be pushed in until the spherical head touches the map, we can secure a map system which is absolutely trustworthy. Since the pin is pushed in to its full length, a blow cannot dislodge it. The spherical head in contact with the map gives a very neat appearance, yet the spherical shape permits the fingers to remove the pin by straight pulling without any difficulty whatever. The smooth needle-point of good quality steel does not rust easily and it does not cut the surface of the map. When a pin must be removed, the hole is so small that it is scarcely noticeable.

Pins having spherical glass heads may be used on wall maps without any danger of the heads fading from sunlight. The glass surface is so smooth that dust cannot collect sufficiently to affect the color appearance of the pin head. Even if the map does get dusty, it is perfectly safe to use the feather duster on a wall map having pins which are pushed in so far that the spherical heads are in contact with the map surface. Dusting of such a map will not loosen the pins in any

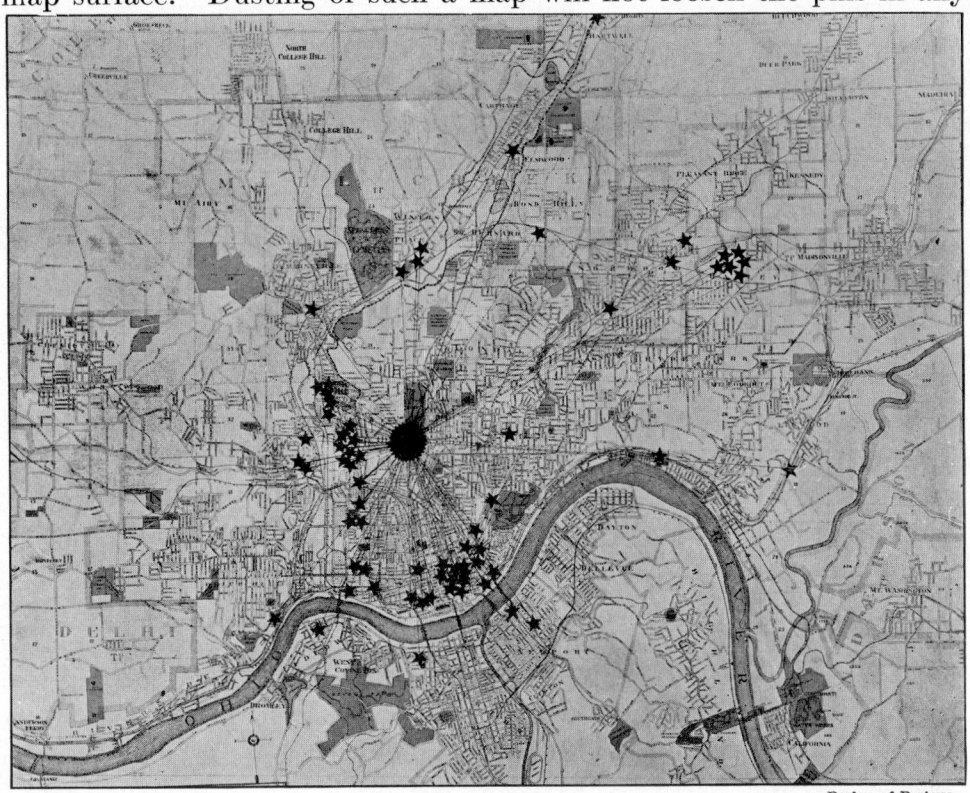

Review of Reviews

Fig. 187. Location of the Plants Affiliated with the University of Cincinnati, College of Engineering. Every Star Represents a Plant Where Co-operative Engineering Students are Employed

A wall exhibit like this is easily made by using a red legal seal and red stars such as can be purchased at many good stationery stores

way. A wall map on which pins with spherical glass heads are used can be very cheaply mounted, it needs no glass cover, and the pins can be put in or taken out instantly, thus giving a location record which is at all times in plain view, yet thoroughly accurate.

Another great advantage of the pins with spherical glass heads is that they may be obtained with small-diameter heads, which permit the use of numerous pins on maps of small size. In portraying many classes of information, it is impracticable to use the cloth-head tacks because the heads are so large that the tacks touch each other in all thickly populated regions.

Photographs taken of a map containing tall pins or tacks give an inaccurate effect, since the angle of the lens causes the head of the tack to appear at one side of the point in which the tack itself is located. Thus, in a photograph of a map of the United States the head of a long pin or tack set at Providence, R. I., might well show near Boston, Mass. There is no way of avoiding this error if projecting pins and tacks are used. The only safe plan is to use the spherical pin head which is in contact with the map surface itself. Photographic views of a sphere are the same from all directions, thus causing all pins to appear exactly the same size and shape on the photograph. Photographs taken of a large map with flat-headed tacks show the heads in the center of the picture as circles, while the heads towards the edge of the picture look of much smaller size, because they appear flattened out as ellipses. The visual effect for points toward the edge of the map is lessened when the tacks are flat headed, and an unnecessary visual error is brought into the picture.

A very cheap yet satisfactory mounting for a wall map to be used with glass-head map pins is made with three or more layers of corrugated straw-board. The straw-board used should be about $3/16$-inch thick with a facing on either side of the corrugated portion. Three thicknesses of straw-board are sufficient to give strength for any map up to one yard long. The two outside layers of straw-board should be so arranged that the corrugations will run with the length of the map, thus giving the greater strength in that direction. The middle layer should have the ribs running crosswise of the map so that the map mounting will be safeguarded from bending in either of the two different directions. Where very large wall maps are desired, six or more layers of straw-board may be used to give sufficient strength. If single sheets of straw-board cannot be found as large as the map itself, the map mounting can easily be built up of small sheets of straw-board, provided the joints in the straw-board are so placed that they will not be over each other to weaken the finished structure.

The straw-board backing for a map to be used with pins is not the best obtainable if the pins must be put in and taken out frequently. When, however, the pins are to be placed in the map and left there, the straw-board is just as satisfactory as any other backing for a map. A layer of the cheapest kind of muslin placed over the face of the straw-board will prevent the pins from tearing the surface of the map if they happen not to be pushed in exactly straight. The use of cloth over the straw-board also permits of changing the pins many more times than would be feasible with straw-board without the cloth reinforcing.

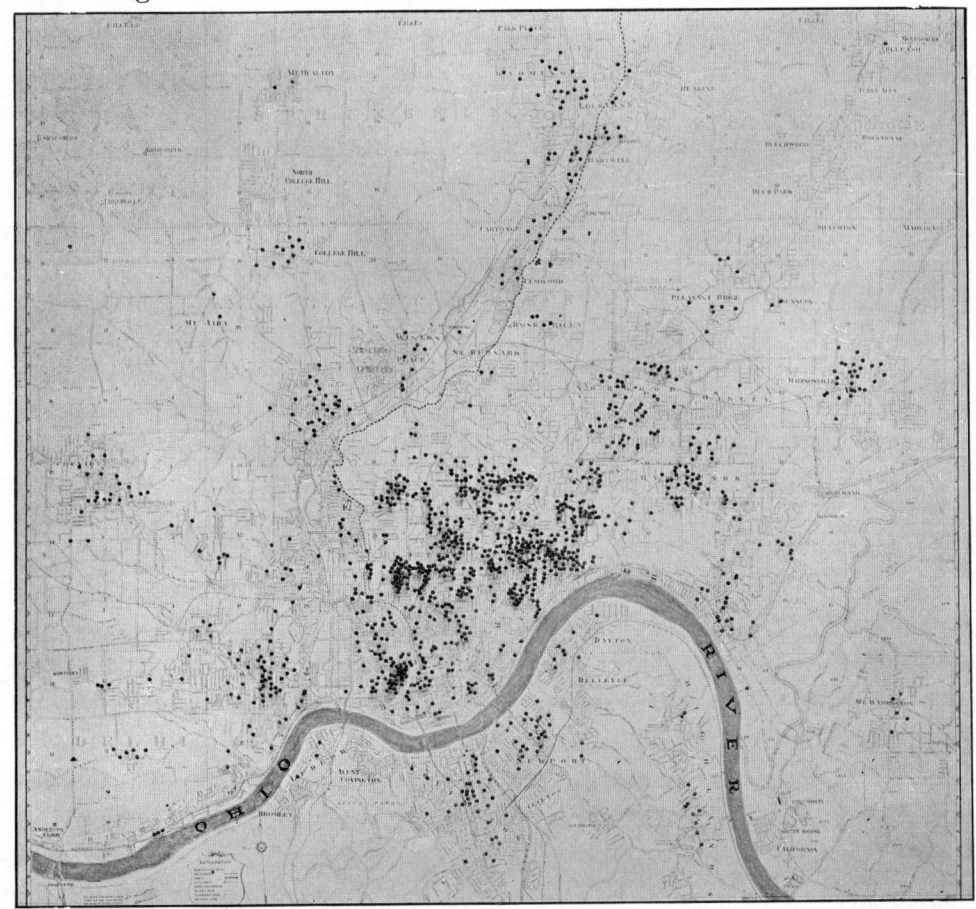

Review of Reviews

Fig. 188. Every Pin Dot on this Map Marks the Home of a Student of the University of Cincinnati

By using a map printed in colors which do not photograph as black, the pins show up distinctly on the map as a background

Before mounting a map the colors should be tested to make sure that they will not run in water. The map should then be wet all over, preferably by laying it flat for a time in a large tray. Use a flour-and-water starch paste, paper-hanger's paste, or library paste of the kind used in mounting photographic prints. Carefully remove all wrinkles and press the excess paste out from under the edge of the map. Shrinkage of the map and of the moistened straw-board surface will almost certainly cause the straw-board mounting to warp unless care is taken to prevent warping. At the same time the map is pasted on the front of the straw-board, paste a sheet of wet wrapping paper on the back of the straw-board mount. The shrinkage of the wrapping paper on the back will equalize the shrinkage of the map on the front of the mount. Place the mounted map on a flat table surface or on a smooth floor, and stack books or other heavy articles upon the mount over night or until thoroughly dry so that any tendency to warp in the drying may be overcome by the weights.

Finish the four edges of the corrugated straw-board by using gummed cloth tape or paper tape neatly folded over the edges in the manner ordinarily used with passe-partout pictures. To hang up the finished map use two combination clamps and rings such as may sometimes be obtained in stores selling window shades. These metal-clamp fixtures are of neat appearance and of strength sufficient to hold a map of any size. If two nails or hooks are used in the wall to support the map, the ring hangers allow the map to be instantly removed to a desk when additional pins must be put in.

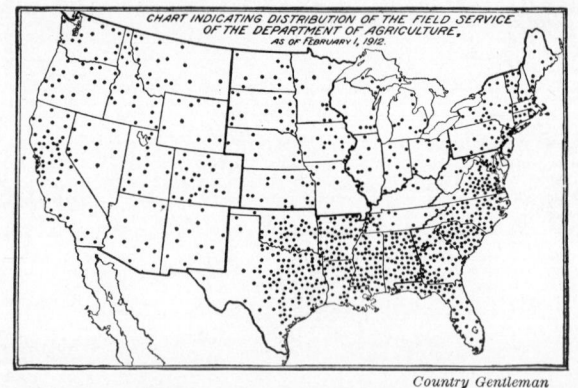

Fig. 189. Distribution of the Field Service of the Department of Agriculture, February 1, 1912
A pin map cannot be excelled for conveying information like this. Note the great activity of the Agricultural Department in the South

If pins are to be put in and taken out of a map repeatedly, it should be mounted on good quality cork composition. Exhibition-board, compo-board, wall-board, or any of the various boards generally used for wall surfaces may be used as a backing to give strength to the cork. Care should be taken to get a good quality of board which will not warp seriously. The cork composition can be glued to the wall-board and then the map pasted on the cork. A piece of wrapping paper should be pasted on the back of the wall-board at the time the map is mounted so that the shrinkage of the map may be equalized. The edge of the cork mounting may be bound

MAPS AND PINS 233

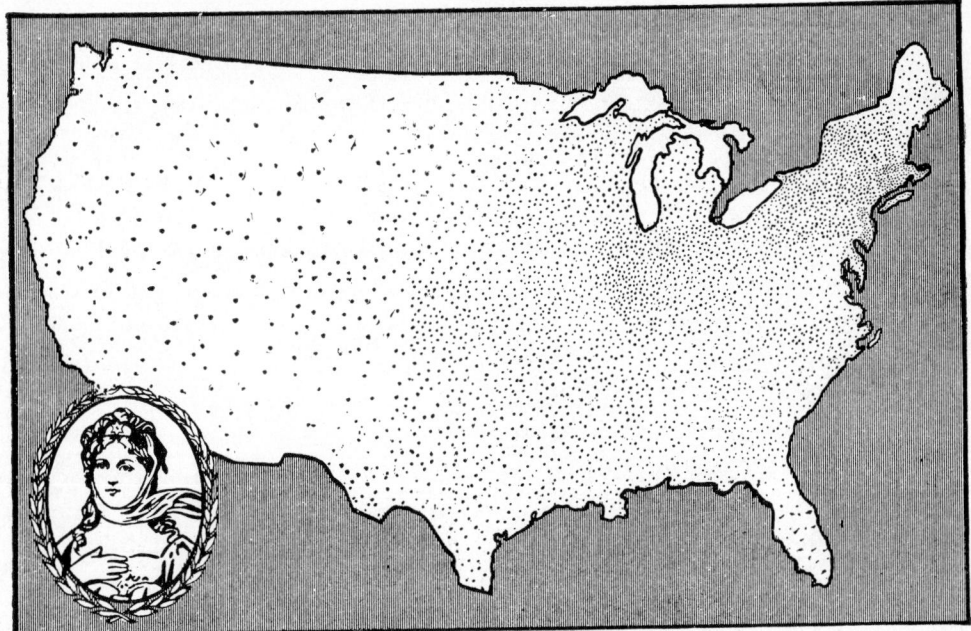

Thomas G. Plant & Co., Queen Quality Shoes

Fig. 190. The Use of Pin Maps in Advertising

A large shoe manufacturing company used this illustration in an advertisement announcing that 3,800 merchants were ready to show the latest fall and winter models of shoes

In order to make the dots stand out distinctly it would appear that agencies in any State have been shown as uniformly distributed over the State. Actual exact locations would be almost impossible to show unless a much larger map were used

with a cloth tape as suggested for straw-board mounts, or the whole built up combination may be framed with picture framing but without using any glass covering. The cork composition used should be $3/8$-inch thick. Maps backed with cork composition and used with glass-head pins having needle points will permit almost unlimited puncturing from frequently moved pins. If the map is mounted on cork composition the sharp-pointed pins are easily pushed in and removed, yet the record is always accurate because the pins cannot be knocked out.

Numerous wall maps can be very conveniently used if they are mounted on vertical swinging-leaf display fixtures similar to those shown in Fig. 219. The two surfaces of each swinging leaf should be covered with corrugated straw-board and muslin, or preferably with cork composition in order to get a good surface into which to insert the pins. As adjacent leaves are likely to strike and break the glass heads of the pins, projecting bumpers should be placed on every other leaf to allow enough clearance for opposite pins when the leaves come in contact. The rubber-covered bumpers used to prevent door knobs from striking plastered walls can be placed at the top or bottom of alternate leaf surfaces. If these rubber bumpers are not available, a narrow strip of wood at the top and bottom of each leaf will serve.

When employed with glass-head pins having needle points, the drawer cabinets for maps used to route salesman, etc., can have a layer of cork composition fastened in the bottom of each drawer. The maps are then glued to the surface of the cork composition. The drawer cabinets regularly found on the market have sufficient drawer depth to permit placing a 3/8-inch layer of cork composition in the bottom of each of the regular drawers and still allow room for the pins. Map pins may be pushed into the cork composition so securely that no pin will ever be misplaced even if a book or other heavy object should happen to drop upon the map and the map pins. Pins in cork composition are so easily inserted and removed that they can be handled more rapidly than if stuck into any kind of a board surface. When ordering maps from any map manufacturer or map store for use with glass-head pins care must be taken to specify either a cork-composition backing or a corrugated straw-board backing, else the map will probably be shipped mounted on compo-board or some other surface entirely too dense to permit of pushing the map pins in until the heads touch the surface of the map.

If numerous glass-head pins are to be put into a map at one time, the eraser in the end of a lead-pencil should be used to push the pins down until the heads touch the map. Pins can be very quickly located if only their points are pushed into the map by hand, leaving the main pressure to be applied by the lead-pencil eraser after a number of pins have been located. The pencil-eraser method saves time and it also eliminates the discomfort which may be caused if thousands of pins are pushed into a map by using the thumb and forefinger only.

Line cuts, sometimes called zinc cuts, may be made directly from pin maps if glass-head map pins of suitable color are used. At the point on the map where each pin head is located there will be a black dot on the print made from the zinc cut. As light is reflected from the surface of the glass heads of the pins, there are sometimes shown in a photograph high lights which must be retouched with a pen or a fine brush so that the whole spot shall be black, rather than black with a white center, as seen in Fig. 191. Anybody can do this retouching very quickly. It is mentioned here only as a caution that the photograph be inspected before the zinc engraving is made from it.

Photographs for line cuts must have a good contrast of white and black, or colors which photograph as black. Photographs or original drawings containing shades of gray will not produce good line cuts and frequently cannot be used at all for the zinc engraving process. When line cuts are to be made from pin maps it is best to be certain that the glass-head pins are selected in colors which will photograph as black. Red, orange, and black pins can be used without any question, since negatives made from these colors give a dead black on the photographic print. Line cuts can also be made from dark green and some of the other colors. Where it is necessary to make photographs and line cuts from a very expensive and elaborate pin map, it is wise to consult the engraver before the pin colors for the map are finally decided upon. The color blue should be carefully avoided if photographs or line cuts are to be made, since blue almost totally fails to show up on a photograph.

If half-tone engravings can be used to illustrate the pin map, many more different colors of pins may be used on the original map than when zinc cuts are the means of printing. Another advantage of half-tones is that different colors of pin heads are represented in the half-tone by different shades of gray, as can be seen in Fig. 191. On the left half of Fig. 191, fourteen different colors of glass-head map pins were used. The photograph was not retouched in any way. Fig. 191 thus represents about what can be expected of different colored pin heads for contrast in half-tone illustration. Note the high lights which give white spots on the circles of the darker pin heads. It is spots like these which should be retouched by hand on any photograph from which a line cut is to be made.

Tacks and pins have been used on maps to locate agencies, salesmen, customers, etc., more than for any other one purpose. The various possibilities in applying tacks and pins to sales-department work cannot be thoroughly covered here, but if a few general methods are known, each sales manager can work out for himself the pin scheme which best suits his own conditions.

Fig. 191 was photographed, without any retouching, direct from a section of the United States Geological Survey topographical maps. These contour maps, having a scale of about one inch to the mile, may be obtained from the Geological Survey at Washington, for most of these sections of the country which are thickly settled. The maps are very low in cost and yet are remarkably accurate. Fig. 191 was

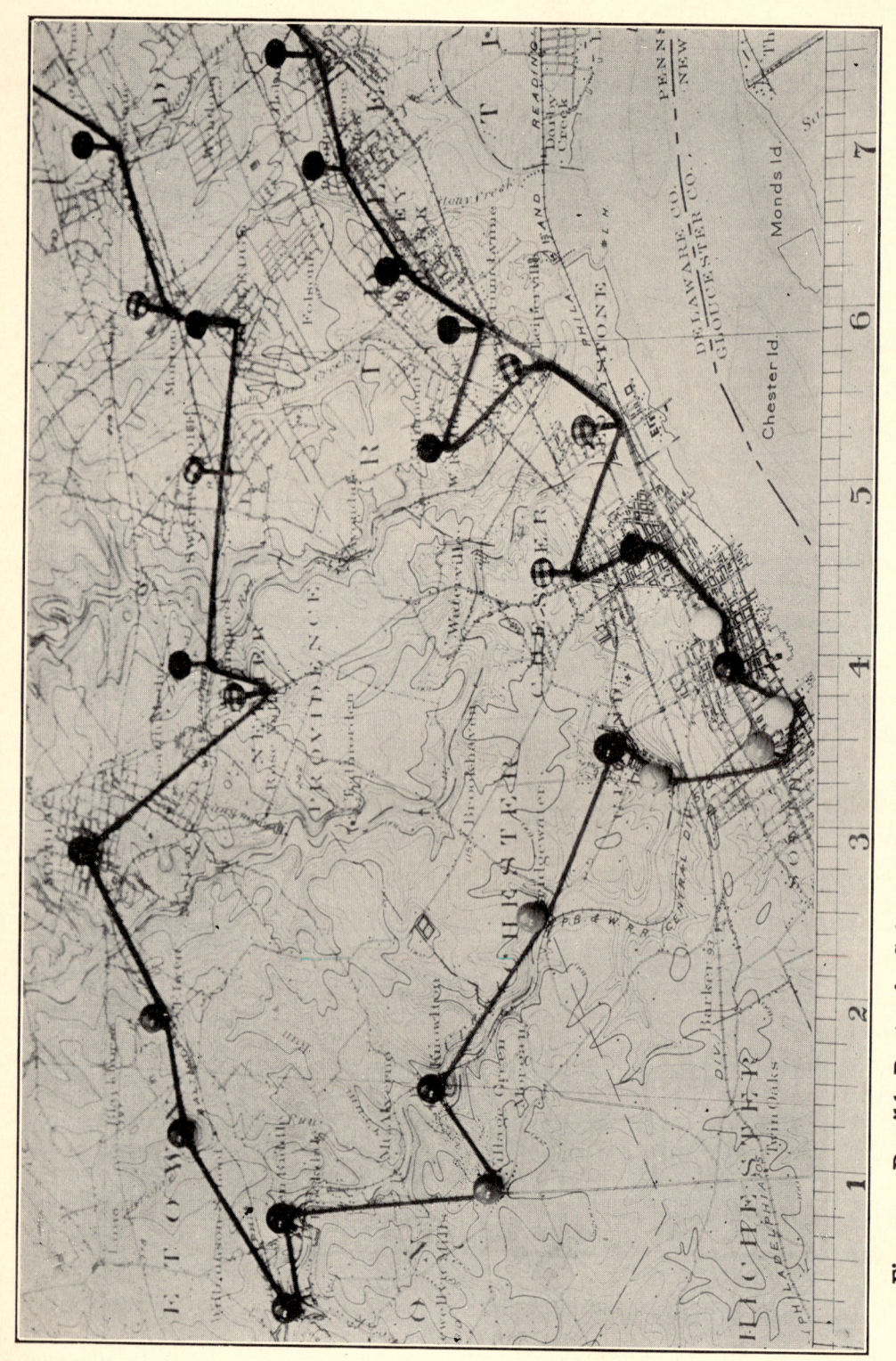

Fig. 191. Possible Route of a Salesman Traveling by Automobile to the Small Towns Southwest of Philadelphia

This illustration was photographed full size from one of the U. S. Geological Survey maps having a scale of about one inch to the mile. A ruler was included in the photograph to show inches. On the left half, glass-head map pins; on the right, cloth-covered map tacks. A red string between pins shows the route

purposely photographed at an angle of about 45 degrees. As the upper part of the illustration is out of focus because of the angle, the illustration does not do justice to the Government maps. Another reason why the map does not come out clearly is that brown ink is used to print the contour lines and these lines accordingly show only faintly in the half-tone.

When it is necessary to show the routing to various points on a map the best method is to use a fine red string or thread between map pins as seen in Fig. 191. If the routing must be changed the thread can be almost instantly moved to connect the pins in some new order. Lines could be drawn on a map in ink to show routing, but the map would be ruined if any change in routing should ever be necessary.

In the preparation of illustrations for reports, advertising, etc., whether maps with or without pins are used, great care must be taken in the selection of the map itself. Map manufacturers have a very annoying custom of purposely making maps in such manner that the maps cannot easily be duplicated by photographic processes. Maps printed in blue ink are almost hopeless for use in making zinc cuts. Maps on which large areas as States, or counties, are differentiated by the use of colors red, orange, green, etc., do not produce either good line cuts or good half-tones since the colored areas on the original maps are likely to show as solid black areas and blot out all detail on the photograph. If an illustration must be made from a map it is well to be sure that the map is printed in black, red, or orange outline so that the resulting photograph will have distinct contrast. Maps should contain as little detail as practicable, to make certain that the pin heads or other representations of specific data will show up as distinctly as possible. Fig. 192 is a good example of the kind of map to use for reproduction when pins are employed. Notice in Fig. 192 a heavy border for the country as a whole, and the outlines for each State. Towns and rivers are not shown. Each dot on the map may thus be seen with great clearness.

As maps are very carefully copyrighted by most map publishers, maps which are copyrighted should not be reproduced without consideration of the copyright. For maps which are photographed down with comparatively little change, permission should be requested from the map publisher, to make certain that unpleasant complications such as damage suits or the holding up of a publication may be avoided.

238 GRAPHIC METHODS

The 228 Principal Trading Centers

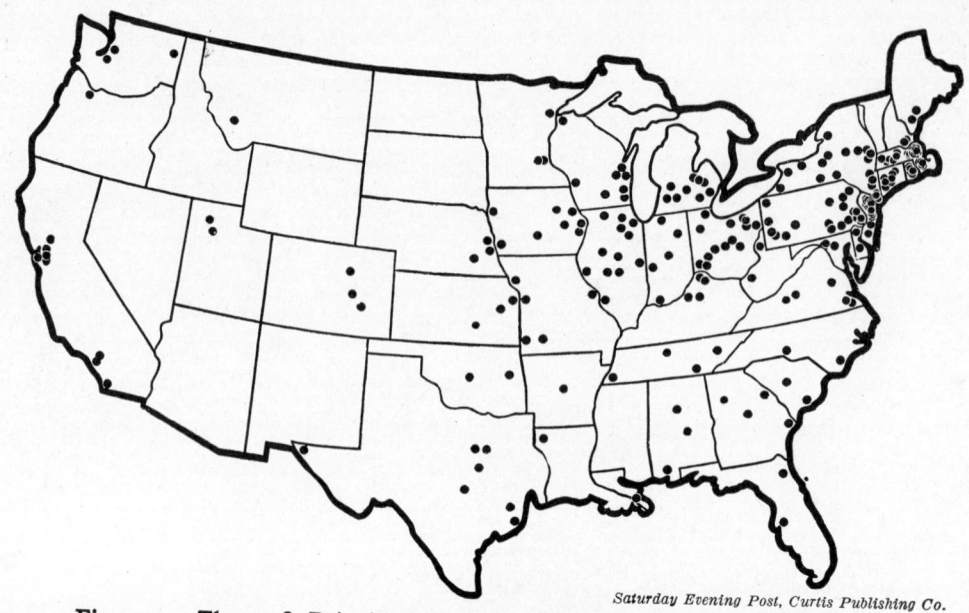

Saturday Evening Post, Curtis Publishing Co.

Fig. 192. The 228 Principal Trading Centers in the United States

This illustration was taken from an advertisement proclaiming that a certain magazine's circulation was mainly in the 228 chief trading centers of the country, and that, accordingly, the magazine must be effective as an advertising medium for merchandise

Note that in the east the dots are so numerous they are shown as crescents. The crescent scheme is a good one as it permits the use of a much larger dot than would otherwise be possible

The amount of detail which may be permitted on any map in which pins are used depends on the size of the resulting illustration and the size of the pin heads. If the pins are so numerous that the map must be very large, there is danger of reducing the map so much in size between photograph and final illustration that the pin heads will appear as indistinct dots on the complex surface of the map. In Fig. 193 a map was used in which there was more detail than really necessary or desirable for a clear illustration. In justice to the *General Electric Review* it must, however, be said that the map shown in Fig. 193 has been reduced in size and made smaller than it was in the original print. This map could not be reduced further without danger of completely losing the pin heads in the gray background resulting from so many lines on the map.

In producing an illustration like Fig. 193 considerable ingenuity must be used to make two or more classes of pins show out distinctly in zinc cuts which can be printed in only one color. The pins on the

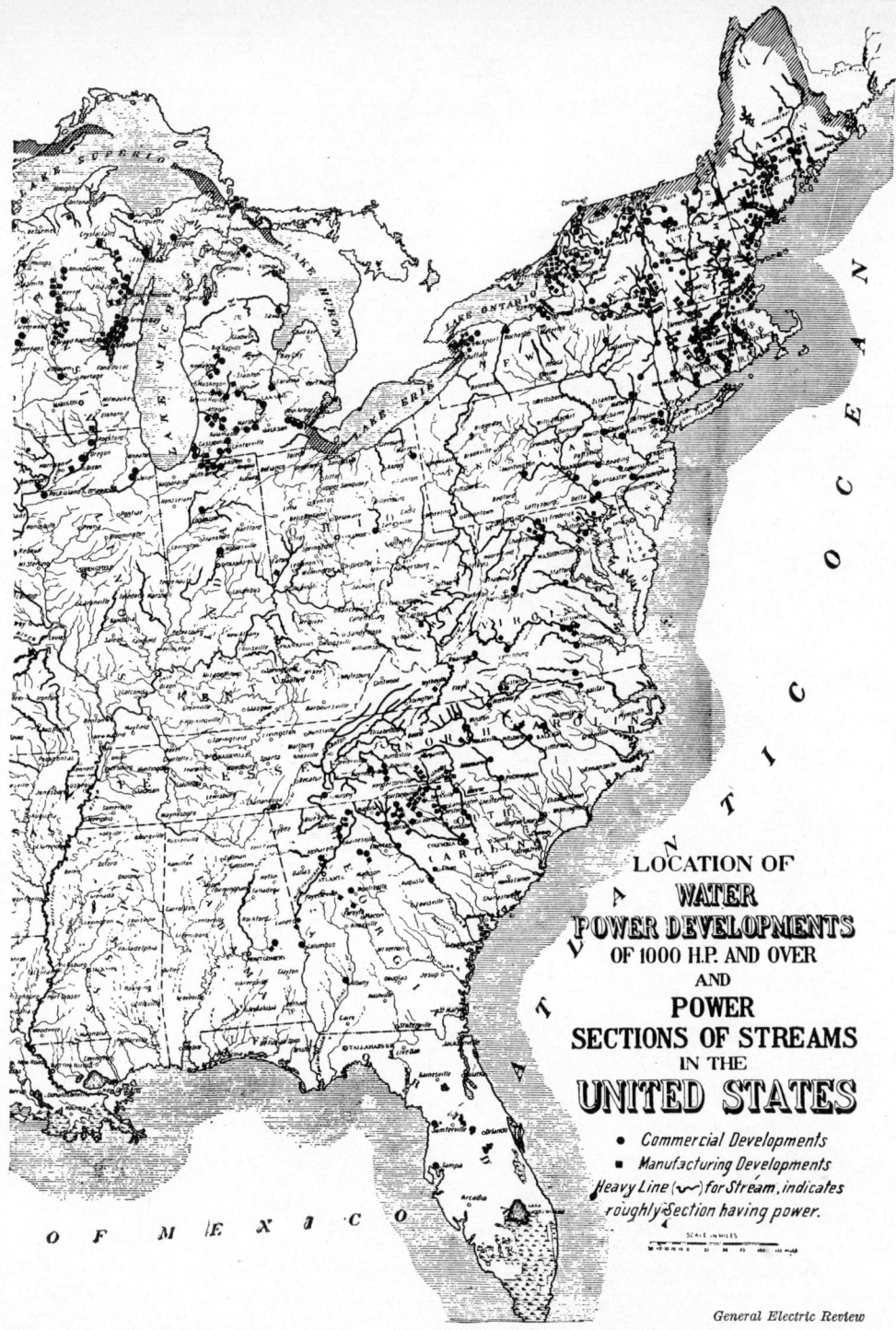

Fig. 193. Location of Water-Power Developments of 1,000 Horse Power, and Over, and Power Sections of Streams in the United States

The original of this map would have pins in two different colors. The photograph taken from the map would be retouched by the use of a pen so that squares would replace dots for one of the two colors of pins. The illustration shows a contrast of dots of two shapes rather than dots of two colors

239

240   GRAPHIC METHODS

Fig. 194. Pin Map Showing the Location of Every Telephone Exchange Point in the United States in 1912. Only One Pin is Used for Towns Having Several Telephone Exchanges

The original map is 40 inches wide and 66 inches long. It contains 19,500 pins in five different colors showing the exact competitive condition in the telephone service. This is probably the most elaborate pin map ever made

W. S. Gifford, Statistician, American Telephone & Telegraph Company

original map can be in different colors. After a photograph has been made of the pin map it is best to compare the photograph with the original, and then to make squares out of those circles which represent a certain color of pin on the original map. Squares are easily made by using a fine pen on a photograph considerably larger than the cut itself will be. When the final dots are not too small in size it is possible to make shapes with the pen such as triangles, outline circles, etc., which can be distinguished from one another.

If a great reduction in size is necessary between the original material and the finished illustration, extreme care must be used to have all the lines on any original drawing wide enough to stand the reduction in line thickness due to the decrease in size. If a drawing one foot wide is photographed down to an illustration three inches wide the lines will be only one-quarter as thick as in the original drawing. Lines on the original drawing must therefore be made very wide—in fact, much wider than is ordinarily considered desirable until experience has been gained from several disappointments in the appearance of finished illustrations. It is not easy to find maps with lines sufficiently heavy to permit of the great photographic reduction usually necessary in making illustrations from pin maps or other map representations. Quite often it is necessary for the person making a map chart to go over by hand all outlines such as borders and the divisions between States, counties, etc., to make those particular lines very much heavier than on any map which can be purchased.

A reducing glass which makes everything seen through it appear smaller is almost essential when many maps or charts must be reproduced. A convenient size of reducing glass has a single lens, about $1\frac{3}{4}$ inches in diameter, and causes objects to appear from one-half to one-quarter the size of the original. The amount of reduction can be varied by holding the glass at different distances from the original drawing. In order to tell how much reduction in size is made by the glass at any given distance, it is possible to look at the original object with one eye and through the reducing glass with the other eye so that by superimposing the two images their length may be compared. When a chart has ruled lines, as co-ordinate lines, it is a simple matter to superimpose the images from the two eyes so that one square of the original equals two, three, or four squares of the image seen through the reducing glass. When the two images are thus superimposed, study can be made of the thickness of lines or other details in the reduced size so that a decision may be had as to whether the drawing will safely stand the proposed reduction without having the lines made heavier.

Fig. 194 shows about the extreme limit of what can be done in the making of pin maps. The original map here was 40 inches wide and 66 inches long. Nevertheless, the map shows up satisfactorily in the greatly reduced size of the half-tone because care was taken to have very wide lines and little detail on the original map. Each of the 19,500 pins of five different colors had a head diameter of $3/32$ inch. It must be remembered, that most of these pins were in the characteristic blue colors commonly associated with the Bell Telephone System, and, because blue is almost impossible to photograph, the pins do not show out as strikingly as they would if other colors were used. The black splotches on the map were caused by the predominance in those areas of pins with dark blue heads. When this pin map was made there was no intention of taking a photograph of it. A much more distinct photograph would have been secured if pins in the contrasting colors of red, orange, black, green, purple, etc., had been chosen. All of these would have shown dark in the photograph, instead of white or light gray like the pale blue pins which in Fig. 194 were used in the greatest number.

Fig. 194 was photographed at an angle. The eastern half of the United States appears smaller than true scale because of the perspective in the picture. The perspective view shows that the glass-head pins had long shanks. This map, costing several hundred dollars to produce, could be injured severely by a few strokes of a janitor's feather duster. If short pins were used with spherical heads in contact with the map there would be no danger of the pins being misplaced. Another disadvantage of the long steel pins is that the steel portion exposed to the atmosphere is likely to rust, especially in cities near salt water. Pins with short needle-points pushed entirely into cork composition or corrugated straw-board have little opportunity to rust.

Fig. 195 shows a convenient map scheme by which different places on the map are numbered so that detailed information regarding each may be obtained from the annexed tabulation numbered to correspond with the pin numbers. In this scheme we have all the advantages of a pin map without the confusion of too many data on the surface of the map itself. The illustration of Fig. 195 was evidently prepared by hand. Such an illustration can, however, be made by using pins like those shown in Fig. 196, or like pin No. 20 in Fig. 199. This latter pin has black figures on a white background, and does not give as striking an effect as white figures on a black ground.

Fig. 196 gives a hint of what may be done to prepare advertising copy with almost no expense. The illustration was made direct from a map on which pins were used having black areas lettered in white. The only hand drawing necessary for this illustration was about one minute's work in darkening the high lights where there were reflections from the surface of the black pins. An illustration of this type to show the location of agencies, branches, etc., makes effective advertising because the black spots are so large in comparison with the size of the map that the whole territory of the United States appears to be well covered by agencies.

Lettered or numbered pins like those in Fig. 196 and in Fig. 199 are frequently desirable to show the daily whereabouts of salesmen, repair men, etc., in order that the nearest man may be telegraphed to in

Fig. 195. Location of the Portland Cement Plants of the Eastern Portion of the United States in 1911. Below the Map Is a Tabulation Giving the Name, Address, Capacity and Shipping Railroad for Each Plant

A pin map like this can be quickly made up by using pins such as are pictured in number 20 of Fig. 199 or pins such as are used in Fig. 196. An outline map with the pins can be photographed directly to produce an illustration like the above

case of emergency. One prominent manufacturer of locks for bank vaults uses a map which shows at all times the location of each of some fifty bank-lock experts who are routed from city to city each day by telegraph. The locations of the pins, and the railroad lines represented on the map, show instantly which man can best be sent to any bank which reports trouble regarding the door of its safe-deposit vault. Letters or numbers on the pins indicate the name of each man so that there is no danger of an error such as might occur if the pins were colored uniformly without specific letters or numbers.

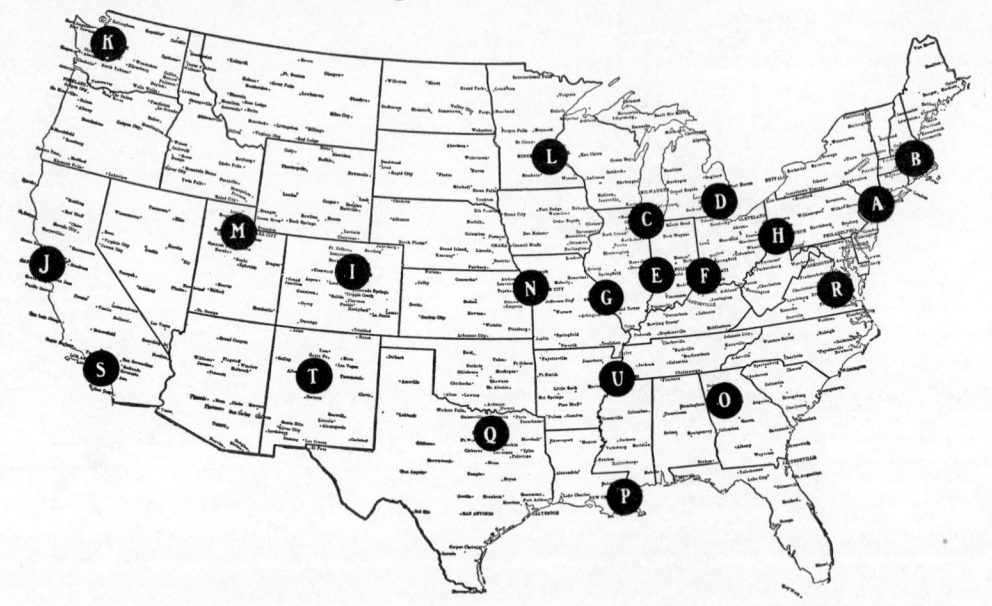

Fig. 196. Map to Show the Location of the Selling Branches of a Large Manufacturing Company

This line cut was made directly by photographing a standard map in which standard map pins had been inserted. Black pins with white letters or numbers give excellent advertising copy with absolutely no drafting work required

The argument of Fig. 197 would have been brought out better if the railroad tracks had been drawn in heavy black lines across the city map. Unless one is familiar with the city of Indianapolis, there would be no way of explaining the heavy soot deposits in that section shown on the lower portion of the map. Even the mention of railroad tracks in the title does not make up for not showing them on the chart.

In preparing Fig. 198 a scale was very carefully selected to use one dot to represent a definite number of people so as to avoid having dots crowd each other too closely on the map. A map of this kind could be made in a very large size, and then be reduced photographically to a size which could be used in a report or magazine article. The reduction must ordinarily be so great for such a map that considerable forethought and care must be used or the dots will not show up distinctly enough in the final illustration. Anyone wishing to see many maps of this type shown in very excellent manner should consult Volume II of the *Report of the Transit Commissioner*, of the City of *Philadelphia*, published in July, 1913.

In placing dots for outlying districts on maps made by the method of Fig. 198, judgment must be used to have each dot placed at ex-

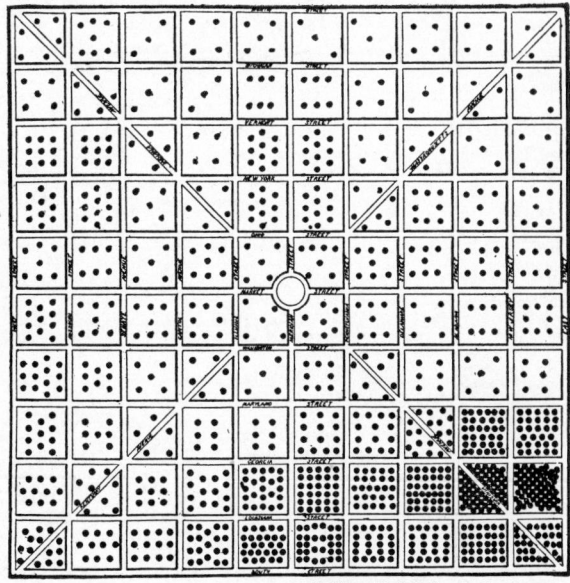

Fig. 197. Relative Soot Deposits in Indianapolis, March, 1912

The greatest soot fall is in the vicinity of railroad tracks
Carefully selected samples of snow were melted and the soot of twenty-four hours weighed after the water was evaporated. Spot maps of this kind can be quickly made by using short map pins pushed in till the pin heads touch the map

actly the right point to locate accurately the people represented. In Fig. 198 each dot represents two hundred people. A dot in the suburbs may therefore represent all the people in one square mile of territory. If a map were first made with two hundred dots for the two hundred people, the one dot actually used on the final map would have to be placed not at the geographical center of the area represented, but at the center of gravity of the two hundred dots which it replaces.

In Fig. 199 various combinations are shown of pins, beads, etc., of use in map work. Data for map presentation are frequently so complex that ingenuity is taxed to show the facts on any map of a size commercially available. A great variety of effects may be secured, however, by means of the devices shown in Fig. 199. The exhibits given in the illustration are as follows:

1. Long pin with small size glass head, available in many colors.
2. Long pin of brass wire for use with beads as shown in No. 9.
3. Long pin with glass head used in conjunction with a piece of sheet celluloid cut into the shape of a flag.

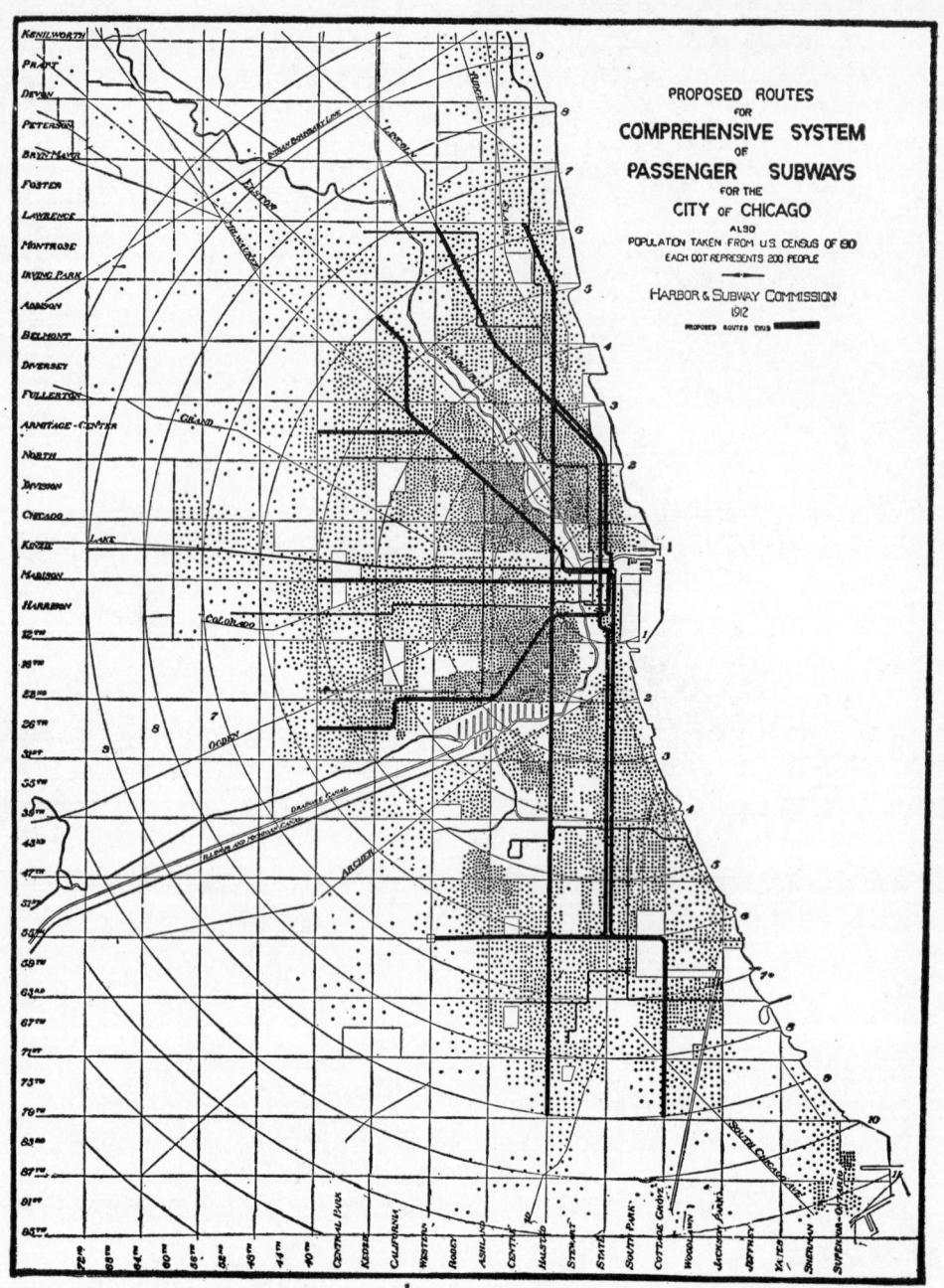

Fig. 198. Proposed Routes for a Comprehensive System of Passenger Subways for the City of Chicago

On this map each dot is carefully located to represent 200 of the population. A spot map of this kind, made to some scale whereby one dot represents several people, is essential to any reliable study of transit facilities. After the spot map is made, the transit routes can be laid out to give the best service possible. Short map pins with heads touching the paper can be used for dots on the original map

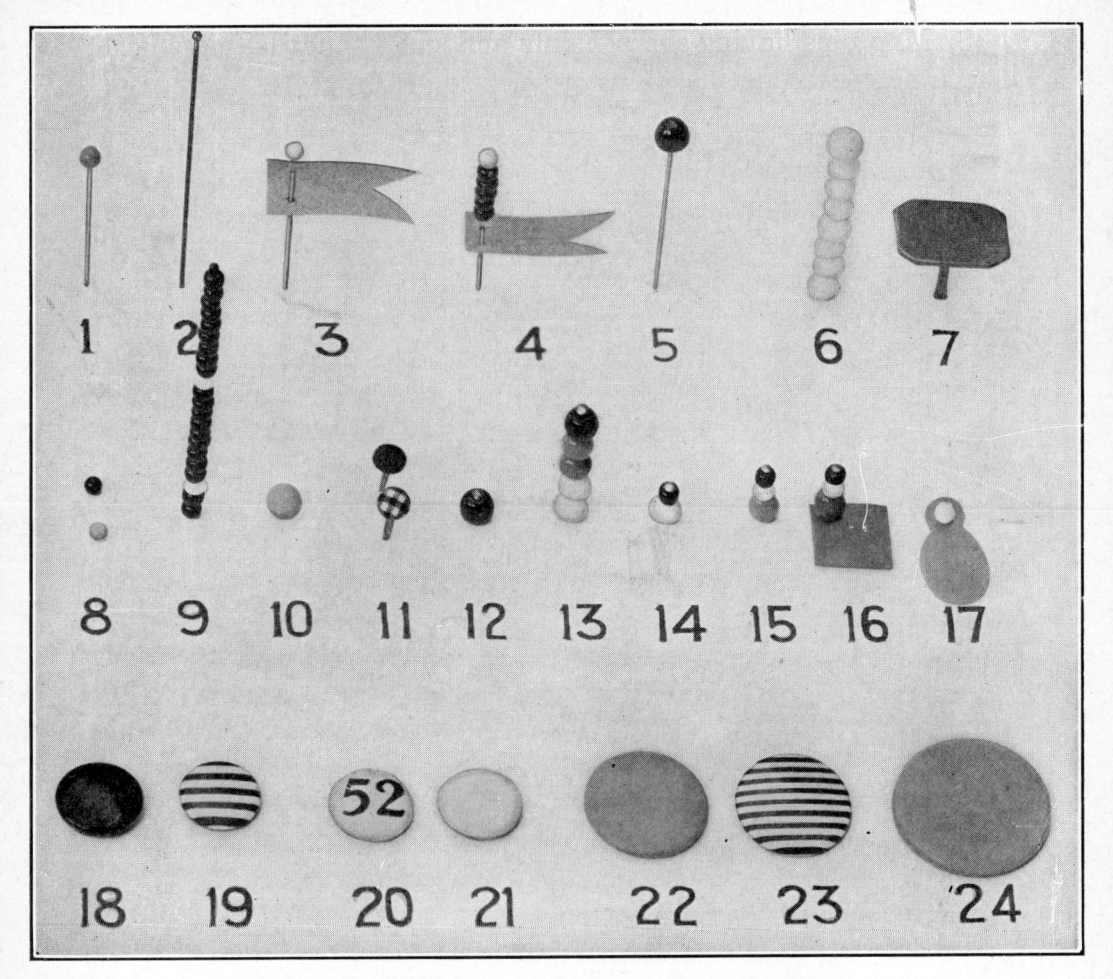

Fig. 199. **A Full-size Illustration Showing Some of the Different Arrangements of Map Pins and of Beads Which Can be Used for Map Work**

The size of the various beads and pins can be determined by measuring on the above picture with an ordinary ruler, as the articles are shown in their exact size

4. A celluloid flag, with beads above the flag to represent quantity, or beads in different colors to denote various characteristics for the data portrayed. The grip of the sheet celluloid on the pin is sufficient to hold both the beads and the flag at the upper part of the pin.

5. Long pin with large size glass head, obtainable in different colors.

6. Pin like that shown in No. 5 used with beads strung upon it.

7. A brass tack large enough to receive gummed labels which may be written upon with a pen.

8. Map pins having sharp points and small spherical glass heads in contact with the map. These pins are available in many different colors; the upper one in No. 8 is red and the lower one blue.

9. Beads in various colors of a size to correspond with the map pins in No. 8. Here the beads were red. White beads, used for every tenth position, show at a glance that there are 22 beads on the pin. Note that the color red photographs as black.

10. Map pins having sharp needle points and spherical glass heads in contact with the map. The pin is of the same general style as No. 8 but it has a head of larger diameter. This pin is obtainable in many colors.

11. Cloth-covered map tacks available in plain colors and in plaids.

12. Single bead used with an ordinary pin as a crude substitute for a regular map pin.

13. Beads in different colors corresponding in size with the map pin of No. 10.

14. Beads of two different sizes representing different things but at the same location.

15. Beads of two different sizes and three different colors. Since both sizes and colors may be varied, and almost any number of beads used on one pin, there are practically unlimited possibilities for the showing of complex data.

16. Beads on a pin which holds down on the map a sheet of colored celluloid cut to the exact shape of a small land area to which attention is directed.

17. A sheet-celluloid marker held by a map pin like that seen in No. 8.

18. Celluloid-covered tack, available in different colors.

19. Celluloid-covered tack with stripes of different colors.

20. Celluloid-covered tack with printed numbers from 1 to 99 inclusive.

21. Celluloid-covered tack having a rough surface so made that the surface may be written upon with pencil or pen, yet erased afterwards or rubbed off with a moist cloth. Lettering may be made permanent by means of a coat of varnish.

22. Large size celluloid-covered tack available in different colors.

23. Large size celluloid-covered tack with stripes of different colors.

24. Very large size celluloid-covered tack.

It will be seen from the foregoing list that the possibilities for ingenuity in map and pin presentations are almost unlimited. The celluloid-covered tacks having large flat heads, shown in Nos. 18 to 24 inclusive, are not as generally used as they might be for map work. Map pins and tacks of this sort placed upon the surface of a map can give a spot map with any desired diameter of spots, no matter what size of map is used or what the amount of photographic reduction may be. It is simply a question of selecting from the spherical heads, 8 or 10, and the flat heads 18, 22, and 24, to determine which size head is best suited to the size of the original map and to the size of dot desired in the finished illustration. Large celluloid-covered tacks 18, 22, and 24 are also valuable to show the location of main offices and different factories, or the locations of particularly important distributing points. The pins numbered 8, 10, 18, 22, or 24, are five different sizes of pins which may be used simultaneously on the same map to show different degrees of importance in the things represented.

When used for photographing to produce an illustration such as is shown in Fig. 196, lettered or numbered pins should have a black background so that the black circle outlining the tack head will show out in clear contrast against the map itself. This requires white figures on a black or red background. Pins having red letters on a black background cannot be used for photographing, as the red letters would photograph black and disappear entirely, leaving a solid black circle instead of a circle with figures. Since pins with a black background and white figures are not commonly obtainable, it may occasionally be necessary to use pins like No. 20 in Fig. 199 having black figures on a white background. Sometimes it may be feasible to draw an ink-line circle around each number which appears in the photograph so that the circles will be on the copy sent to the engraver who makes the zinc plate.

When pins must be used to locate agencies, stores, or other things which are usually concentrated in cities, the limitations are rigid because all pins should be located on the map immediately above the point representing the city. Crowded pins usually have to be spread horizontally over a wide area, and when so spread out it is impossible to tell which of several adjacent cities the various pins may represent. Fig. 200 depicts what was done in one case to get over this difficulty.

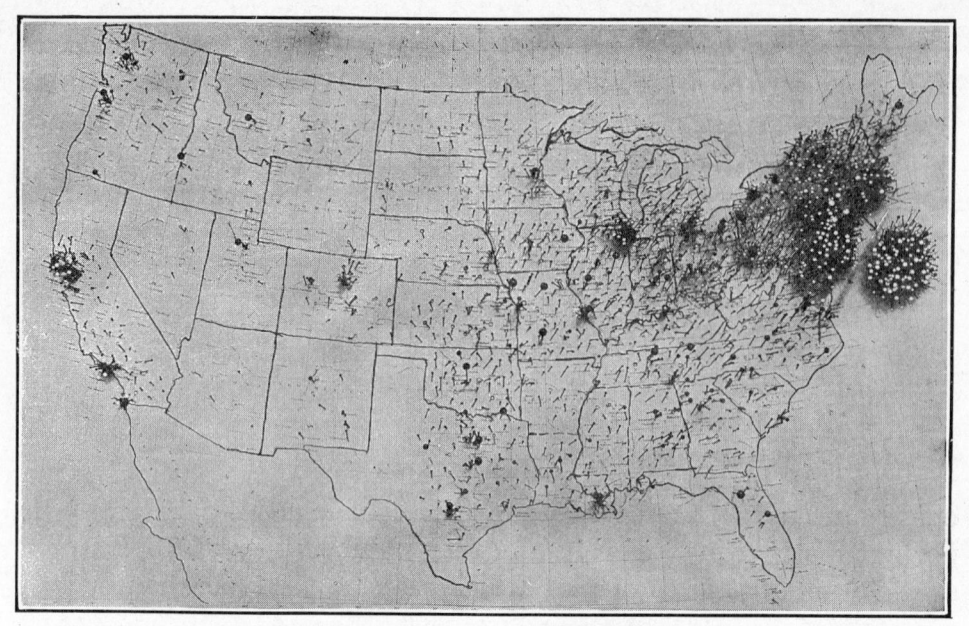

Fig. 200. Sources of the First 3,000 Letters of Appeal Sent to Mrs. E. H. Harriman. These 3,000 Letters Asked for $70,000,000

"Modern Philanthropy", W. H. Allen, Dodd, Mead & Co.

Eight different kinds of pins were used on this map to represent different kinds of appeals. Long pins like those seen here are apt to fall out of the map, and thus destroy the accuracy of the record. Note the area around New York shown on a larger scale at the right

as far as possible, by showing the more thickly crowded district as a separate area on a larger scale placed at one side of the map.

The use of beads in conjunction with pins overcomes the main difficulties encountered when pins alone are used. Beads may be placed one above each other on long pins or wires so that each pin will be exactly in the point on the map for each city, and thus portray numerical data by map location more accurately than possible with other methods. The adjoining cities can be clearly discerned by means of separate columns of beads, whereas if pins alone are used the different groups of pins frequently blend so as to be indistinguishable. If there is only one item to be represented in a town, single glass-head pins may, of course, be used in conjunction with the beads.

When there are several units in a town, the beads strung on a long pin or wire can be counted quickly if a bead of a different color is used for every tenth bead, so the whole column may be counted by tens as possible in Fig. 201. A bead map like Fig. 201 should be mounted on several layers of corrugated straw-board to allow the long pins sufficient depth in the mounting to hold fast. For this particular map six layers of straw-board were used, giving a total thickness of about 1¼ inches. Though this mounting made out of corrugated straw-board was thick, it was extremely light and very convenient to handle.

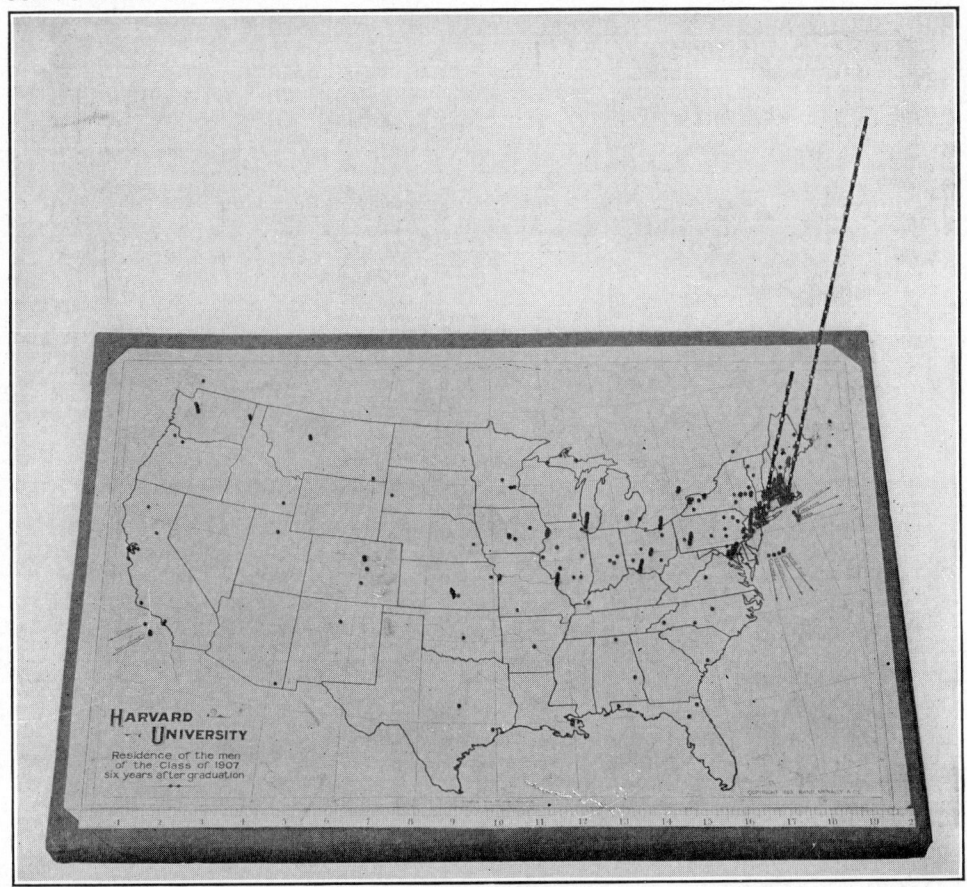

Fig. 201. Residence of the Men of the Class of 1907, Harvard University, Six Years After Graduation. The Bead Wire for Boston Includes All Men Living within Twenty-five Miles of the City Hall

Beads on long pins and wires were used here when there was more than one man in a town. A white bead was used on the wire for every tenth man. Counting from the top by tens, the exact number in any city can be seen from the illustration. 711 men are represented in this illustration less than 5 inches wide, yet the number in each city can be counted accurately

If long columns of beads must be used as in Fig. 201 for New York and Boston, the beads may be strung on piano wire such as may be secured in any good hardware store. The piano wire should be heated in a gas flame so as to remove some of the spring temper. After the wire has been heated it can be straightened and it will remain straight without continually springing back into coil form.

Brass wire should be used if the holes in the beads are large enough to take wire of a diameter sufficient to give the required amount of stiffness. Brass wire is not as stiff as steel wire. When small beads must be used having small holes, the combination of wire and beads may be given several coats of varnish, if necessary, to make a tall bead column stand up straight. The columns for Boston and New York in Fig. 201 had to be varnished as the wire was very small on account of the fact that the diameter of the beads was only about $\frac{3}{32}$ inch.

The bead map in Fig. 201 gives a great quantity of information in a small amount of space. The illustration depicts the whole United States on a page width of only $5\frac{1}{8}$ inches, yet all the facts represented by the beads are brought out clearly. The men of the group portrayed who reside in foreign countries are indicated by pins near the seacoast with arrows pointing toward the country of residence. The fact that there were large numbers of the men in Massachusetts made necessary an extremely long wire for the beads of the Boston district. Because of the small size of the finished illustration and the size of map available, large diameter beads could not be used, and the bead wire for the Boston district was necessarily very tall and slender. The Boston bead column was about as tall as could be used without the column of beads bending under its own weight, even with the bead column varnished.

Another difficulty in having very tall columns of beads is due to the fact that the bead map must be photographed at an angle of about 45 degrees in order to show a good picture of the map.

If the bead column projects more than a reasonable distance from the map it is impossible to find a camera lens which will keep in focus the whole map and the full length of the bead columns. Either the map or the top of the bead column will be out of focus and there is no way of overcoming the difficulty. When Fig. 201 was photographed the image on the ground glass of the camera showed at once that the tops of the bead columns were out of focus. The bead wires for New York and for Boston were accordingly pulled entirely out of the map and the map was photographed without these two bead wires. The two bead columns were drawn in by hand on the surface of a photograph measuring 8 inches across the base of the map. With a little care, using a fine-pointed pen, bead columns such as these can be drawn in so that the ordinary observer would never notice that they were put on after the photograph itself had been taken. The angle at which the tall bead columns should slant can be determined by observing other bead columns in the same vicinity. In the case of Fig. 201, the angle was obtained by observing the bead column for Philadelphia. The reduction in size from the photograph on which the hand drawing was done, to the half-tone (in this case, a final reduction of from 8 inches to 4¾ inches) was sufficient to eliminate most of the imperfections due to hand work.

The use of beads opens up a whole new field for map presentation of statistical data. The Board of Sanitary Control for the Cloak and Suit and the Dress and Waist Industries of New York city made up two bead maps showing the fire risks and the sanitary condition in all the twenty-five hundred factories which come under the supervision of that Board. One bead on the map represents the condition for each factory. On the fire map the height of the multi-story loft buildings in which the different factories may be found is indicated by using one bead for each floor. Thus, in some of the taller buildings, twenty stories are indicated. Different colors of beads according to the fire risk or the sanitary defect to be shown mark the stories very plainly, and the heights of the bead columns show the heights of the buildings so that the bead map itself represents in miniature the sky line so typical of Manhattan Island.

Bead maps carefully made up should be of great use in preparing illustrations for advertising purposes. The accuracy of a bead map, when data for different cities must be shown, is much greater than that of a map on which only pins are used. The bead map makes possible the giving of information in condensed form with that great clearness and accuracy necessary to good advertising. It can safely be predicted that pictures of bead maps will in the future be a common thing in the advertising pages of magazines.

Chapter XIII

CURVES FOR THE EXECUTIVE

WITH the exception of the railroads, there are relatively few businesses which make a practice of plotting curves to show operating records in convenient form for the use of executives. Railroad accounting is more highly standardized than accounting in industrial corporation work. The standardized method of accounting has made it rather easy to compare the operating records of different railroad divisions and of different railroad systems. It is probably for this reason that railroads have adopted the use of curves for operating records so much more extensively than have industrial or mercantile businesses.

The upper curve in Fig. 202 is plotted according to the method used on many railroad systems. In this form of plotting a month may be said to be represented in the middle of a space between the vertical lines. Horizontal lines are drawn in the space for each month to a scale representing the figures which it is desired to chart. Lines are then drawn vertically to coincide with the vertical lines of the co-ordinate paper, and they join the horizontal lines of different months in such a way as to give an effect like that of a stairway.

Curves for the same data plotted by the method shown at the bottom of Fig. 202 are much easier to read than those plotted by the step method shown in the upper portion of the illustration. By the method in the lower part of the illustration the plotted line more closely approaches a true curve, there is much less variation in the direction of the lines from month to month, and the general trend of the curve line is easier for the eye to grasp. Compare the two curves for the summer months of the year 1909–10. In the upper curve a series of steps, and in the lower curve an almost straight line from April to September inclusive, indicate an increase by fairly equal increments during those months. Certainly equal increments are more easily represented by the straight

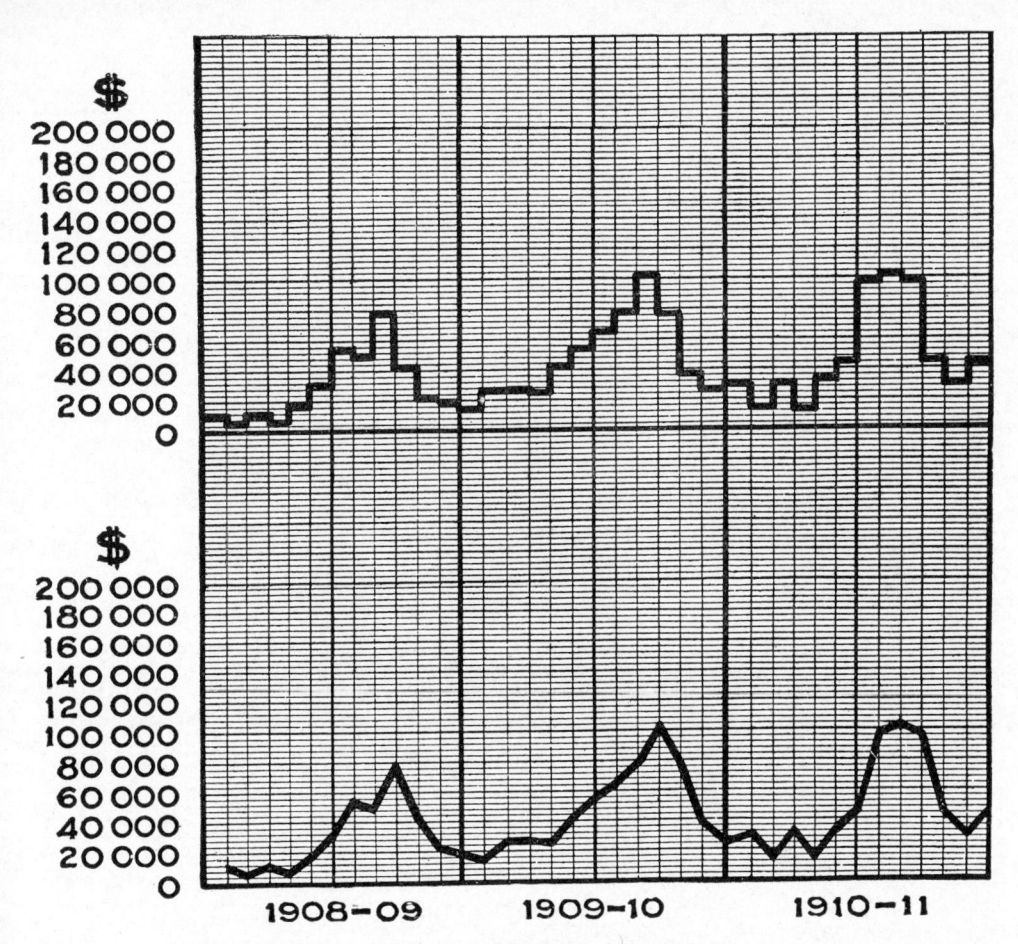

Fig. 202. Total Sales of the "Metropolis" Branch House of the "R.S.T." Automobile Company for Three Years

These two curves are plotted from exactly the same figures. The upper curve is drawn by the method still used by some railroads, but generally going out of use. The lower curve is plotted by a simpler method which should be universally used

line as in the bottom curve than by the ragged series of steps shown in the upper curve.

Another disadvantage of the method of steps with flat tops as compared with the method using slanting lines and peak tops, is seen when two or more curves are so drawn that they intersect on the same sheet of co-ordinate paper. Curves plotted with peak tops can be drawn very close together and yet be fairly distinct from each other, as will be noticed in many of the illustrations in this book. If, however, two curves with flat tops like those shown in the upper portion of Fig. 202 are plotted in such manner that they intersect each other, the re-

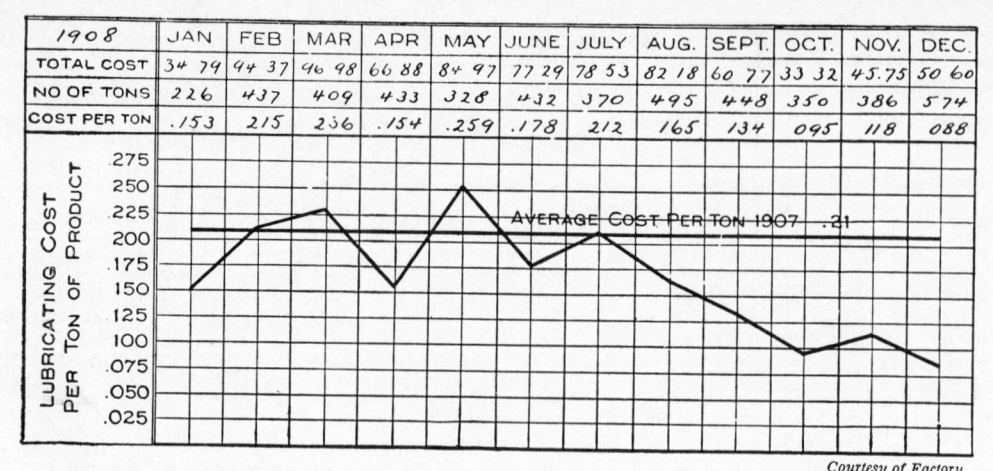

1908	JAN	FEB	MAR	APR	MAY	JUNE	JULY	AUG.	SEPT.	OCT.	NOV.	DEC.
TOTAL COST	34.79	94.37	96.98	66.88	84.97	77.29	78.53	82.18	60.77	33.32	45.75	50.60
NO OF TONS	226	437	409	433	328	432	370	495	448	350	386	574
COST PER TON	.153	.215	.236	.154	.259	.178	.212	.165	.134	.095	.118	.088

Fig. 203. Lubrication Cost per Ton of Product for a Factory in the Year 1908

The figures at the top of the co-ordinate ruling give the data from which the curve was plotted. Though data should be put on all charts, figures arranged in the direction here shown are not in convenient form for addition. See the later illustrations in this chapter for methods of placing figures above each point on a curve

sult is very confusing on account of the fact that the vertical lines connecting the flat tops may coincide. When one line falls directly on top of the other, there is no way for the reader to judge which curve is which beyond the point of intersection. Unless the curves are very carefully colored or dotted there is great danger that the reader will jump from one curve to the other in his interpretation of curves which happen to meet. This weak point in the flat-top method is particularly noticeable if blue prints must be made from original charts in which the flat-top method is used. On the original chart the curves can be fairly well distinguished by using different colored inks, but as the colors are lost in blue-printing, each blue print must be colored by hand, using the original chart as a key to show what the colors should be. If a peak-top method of plotting is used, numerous curves may be run across the same sheet and yet be distinct enough for identification even when all are reduced to uniform white lines on the blue print. It would be easy to name fifteen reasons why the method of plotting with peak tops is superior to the method of plotting with flat tops. The advantages of the peak-top method seem so obvious that it is believed the reader will agree to its desirability, without further argument being given here.

The man who plots a curve has before him the data showing the actual value for each point plotted on the curve. If any questions arise in his mind regarding the comparative figures at different points on the curve, he can refer to the data from which the curve was plotted.

The man who reads the curve, however, must ordinarily get the value of any point on the curve by referring to the scale on the left-hand margin of the chart. As most points on curves do not fall exactly on the horizontal co-ordinate lines, the only way in which the actual value at any point can be determined is by careful estimate of the fractional distance between horizontal lines, according to the scale shown on the margin. The resulting value for the point is ordinarily more or less inaccurate, depending upon the scale to which the curve is drawn. Not only is the reader's time taken in estimating the value for any point on the curve, but when he gets his result he is dissatisfied, for he cannot feel that the figure obtained is really accurate. There is a great advantage in showing on a chart the figures from which the curve was plotted. When only one curve is shown on a chart it is very easy to give the figures immediately above each point. The method used to show the figures in Fig. 203 is not, however, satisfactory, as the figures do not fall in a column. The method of indicating figures shown in the illustrations later in this chapter is much superior to the method of Fig. 203, and should be adopted as general practice by anyone preparing curves for record purposes, or for executive use.

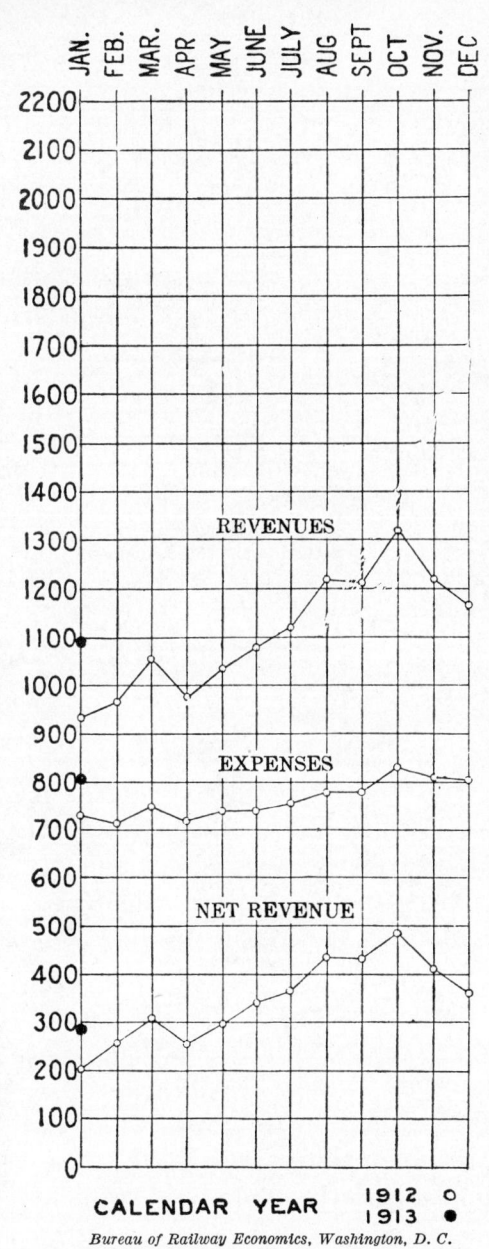

Fig. 204. Monthly Revenue, Expense, and Net Revenue per Mile of Line for Railroads in the United States Having a Yearly Revenue of One Million Dollars or More

Bureau of Railway Economics, Washington, D. C.

This illustration shows one of the difficulties encountered when curves for successive years are plotted on the same co-ordinate ruling. Here the data of January, 1913, are indicated by a dot rather than by a line. The change occurring from December to January is not easily seen. This difficulty can be easily overcome by allowing an extra space for one month as in the following illustrations

In Fig. 205 a curve is shown drawn upon a carefully designed four-by-six-inch card form. This card is designed for the plotting of data for one year by months. Thus, the fiscal year of a business can be shown on one card. Succeeding years are entered on different cards, so that by arranging the cards chronologically variations from year to year may easily be seen. In order to avoid the difficulties pointed out for Fig. 204, and Fig. 104, thirteen vertical lines are used on this four-by-six-inch card. At the beginning of each card the last month of the previous fiscal year is repeated. In Fig. 205 the fiscal year begins in August. At the beginning of the card we repeat the line for July, so that instead of showing a dot when the August figures are plotted we are able to draw a line showing the change which has occurred from July to August. In general, it is good practice to use one more vertical line than there are points to be plotted, so that the last point on one curve, sheet or card may be repeated on the next curve sheet or card.

Figures representing the value for each point on the curve are given immediately above each point, in the case of Fig. 205 to the nearest dollar. Figures for cents could, of course, be given if desired, but for executive purposes it is usually better to neglect the cents in all large numbers. The arrangement of the figures shown in Fig. 205 is such that at the end of the year the figures can be added quickly and the total given on the card. Cards for different years can easily be looked over and the yearly total figures compared instantly, to the great advantage of the executive who has these additions made for him and recorded where they are always in plain sight. Curves as they were used in the past gave the values of single points only, without any summation for a series of points. In Fig. 205 we have not only the yearly total, but also totals for every three months, so that the total for any quarter of the fiscal year can be compared with the total for any other quarter.

Fig. 206 represents a four-by-twelve-inch card used to plot data for fifty-two weeks in one fiscal year, the last point of the preceding year being repeated at the left-hand margin. Figures for the repeated week are not given above the co-ordinate ruling, as the repeated figures might then be included in the additions and cause serious error. By repeating the point, however, and not repeating the figures, the curve is made continuous without any danger of adding too many items into the total.

In the right-hand margin of Fig. 206 a short vertical line may be seen. This line may be used as the shank of an arrow to indicate, as

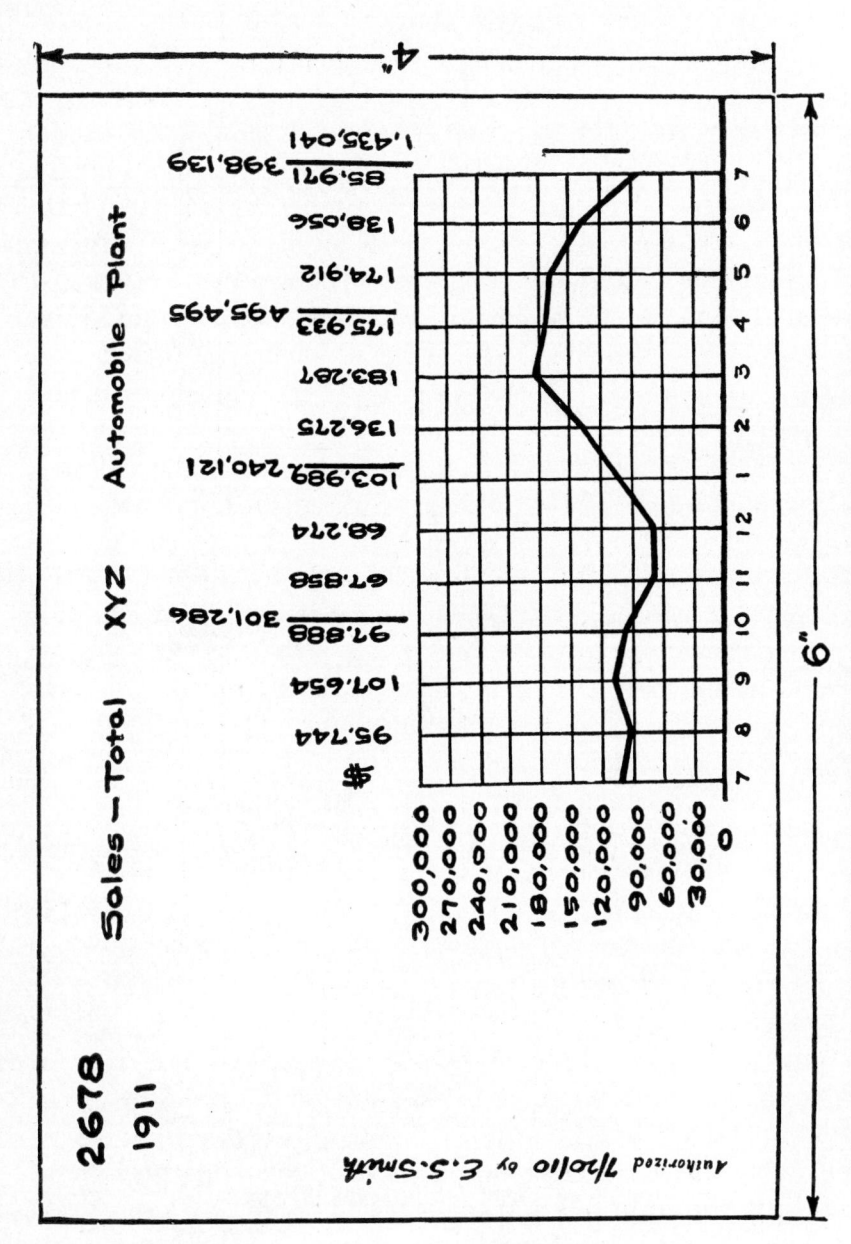

CURVES FOR THE EXECUTIVE

Fig. 205. A 4-inch by 6-inch Card Suitable for Plotting a Curve for One Year by Months

A file of these cards allows instant reference to any set of facts relating to a large business. The forms are printed on especially high grade translucent paper or card stock. Duplicates, as desired, may be made by direct contact printing on blue-print or other sensitized paper. The photostat process can of course be used if desired.

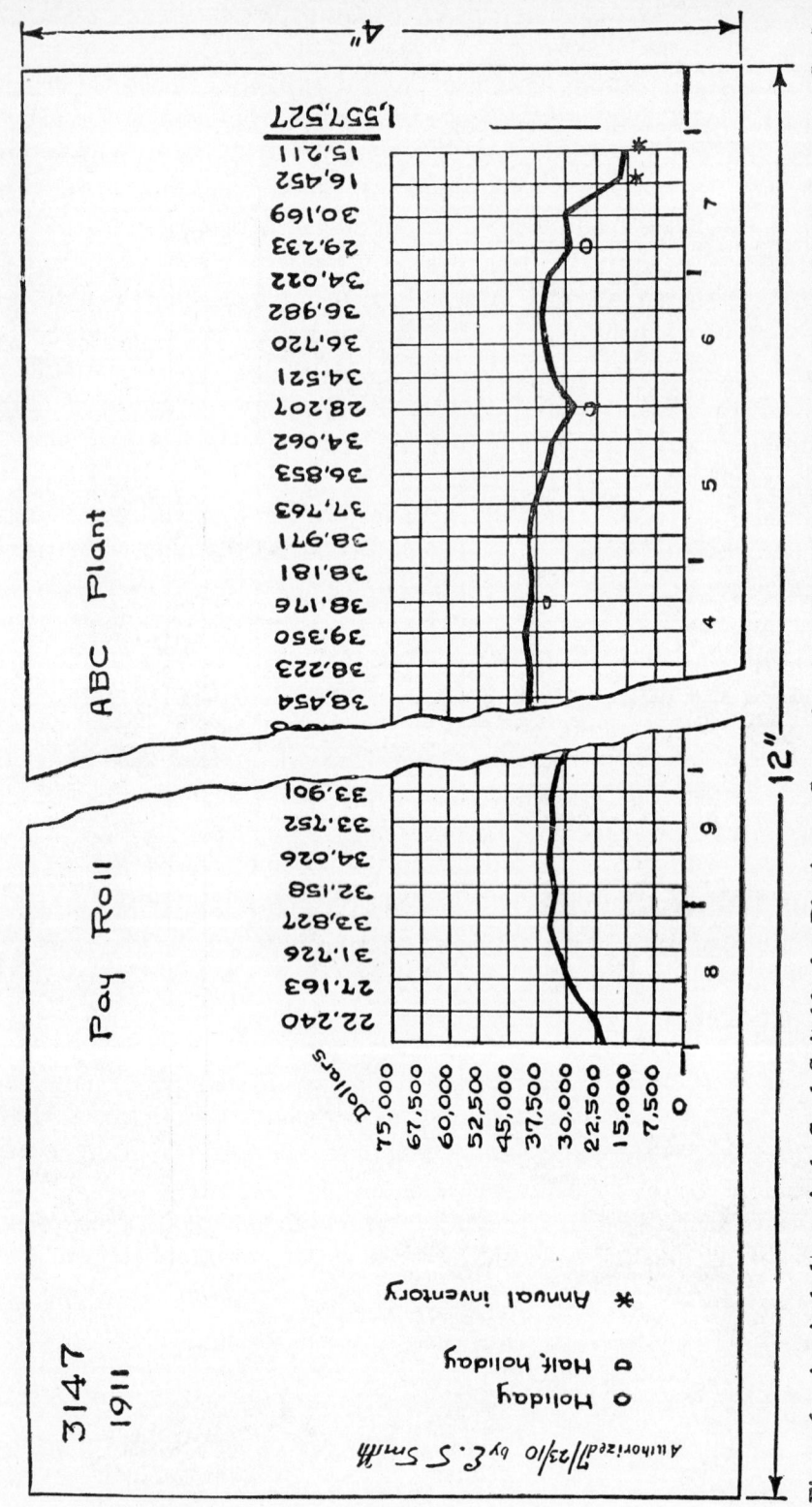

Fig. 206. A 4-inch by 12-inch Card Suitable for Plotting a Curve for One Year by Weeks, with Actual Figures on the Card Immediately Above Each Point on the Curve. The Weekly Figures Are Here Added so as to Give the Total Payroll for the Year

in Fig. 205, in which direction the executive desires that the curve should trend. In Fig. 205, which represents total sales, the head of the arrow of course points upward. If the curve is to show expenses per unit of output, the head must be placed on the vertical line so that the arrow will point downward. In Fig. 206 no head is placed on the arrow, as fluctuations in a payroll mean nothing unless we know the output of work. An increasing payroll may result either from increasing sales or from inefficient production. A decrease in payroll may result from increased efficiency of production or because sales have fallen off undesirably. Accordingly, no head is placed on the arrow and the curve must be interpreted by conditions other than those shown on the face of the card itself. In general, all curves relating to total money expenditures may trend either up or down, without meaning anything unless other conditions are considered. It is only when we express expenditures as expenditure per unit that we really get a curve for which it is safe to say that we should always desire a downward trend as long as quality is maintained.

Forms for executive records such as are shown in Fig. 205 and Fig. 206 should be printed on an especially high grade of paper. Most paper in use to-day contains sulphite pulp and chemicals which cause more or less rapid deterioration. The paper commonly used turns brown and gets brittle within five or ten years, so that records on this paper are likely to become useless in a comparatively short time. High-grade paper to be used for the record cards shown in Fig. 205 and Fig. 206 should contain only the finest selected linen stock and should be guaranteed absolutely against any deterioration for twenty years. The chief advantage of such paper, however, is that it can be used in card form, yet be transparent enough to allow of blue-printing.

The time required to blue-print cards made from such paper may best be compared with the time necessary when ordinary tracing cloth is used. Blue prints are also frequently made from bond paper. Bond paper requires an exposure of, roughly, three times as long as tracing cloth. A special card made of heavy paper would require an exposure of about six times as long as tracing cloth, or twice as long as bond paper.

When sunlight is used for blue-printing, there is no difficulty in getting a sufficiently long exposure to make good blue prints from the card forms shown in Fig. 205 and Fig. 206, if the forms are printed on selected paper. Should electric blue-print machines be used, however, it may be found that certain of the older types of continuous printing machines cannot be run slowly enough to give the required length of exposure. Some of the older machines can be changed at rather slight expense so as to have an extra belt-pulley reduction between the motor and the blue-printing machine itself. The newer types of machine can usually be run slowly enough to give the exposure necessary for this heavy paper. If a new blue-printing machine is to be ordered, however, it is well to make some preliminary tests with the cards.

The cost is not great for blue-printing a whole set of record cards once each month after the last data have been plotted. Blue-print paper of heavy weight should be carried on hand, already sensitized and cut to size, four by six inches and four by twelve inches. The original curve cards, each backed by a sensitized card of the same size, are simply fed into the blue-print machine as rapidly as the operator can put the two cards together in pairs.

There is a tremendous advantage in having all curve records made on a high-grade transparent card so that any card may be duplicated by blue-printing whenever desired. It is impossible for anyone to predict what conditions will come up in the future of a business, and the only safe plan is to install from the start such a curve-record system that any card may be duplicated by blue-printing in future years if desired. It frequently happens that an executive wishes to have a blue print made of a recent year's curve card to compare with the curve card of an earlier year, in order that the blue prints may be mailed to some higher official or to some branch-house manager to point out certain conditions which it would be difficult to describe fully if copies of the curve cards could not be sent. Unless, however, the curves for the earlier years are made on cardboard from which blue prints can be taken, it is impossible afterward to make duplicates of these cards except by hand copying or photographing. In many cases it will be found desirable to take a blue print of every record card once each month, so that blue prints may be sent each department head to show him the exact condition of his department as a guide for the next month.

The space toward the left-hand side of the cards shown in Fig. 205 is for remarks which may be necessary to explain different fluctuations in the curves. In Fig. 206 full circles along the curve show those weeks in which a full holiday reduces the amount of the payroll. In the month of April there was, for this particular plant, a half-holiday on the nineteenth. This is shown by a half circle. At the end of the fiscal year we see in Fig. 206 stars to explain why the curve showed a drop to less than one-half in the normal size of the payroll. The plant was shut down at the end of the fiscal year in order that an inventory might be taken.

The notes at the left-hand side of the card are absolutely essential to explain unusual conditions affecting the curves. In two years after an event, most managers are entirely unable to explain certain peaks or valleys in a curve, though these extreme fluctuations may be due to such events as fires, floods, or strikes. Unless the causes of unusual fluctuations are recorded, the curves would have far less than their possible utility to any new man who must take up the manager's task as his assistant or as his successor. An example of the kind of information which should be noted on the curve-card margin came up in a large public-service company, where the manager was for several minutes unable to explain a very great fluctuation which had affected the earnings of a trolley company some two years before. After careful study to explain the drop in the curve, he finally recalled that this trolley line was in a city where all cars must pass over a drawbridge between two sections of the town. At the time in question a steamer had collided with the drawbridge, making it impossible for about two weeks for any street car to cross. This accident caused the earnings of the trolley line to drop greatly during the whole of the two-weeks period. The cause of the unusual condition for the curve should have been recorded for future reference.

In Fig. 207 we have the curves for three succeeding years placed one above the other, so the eye can glance up and down the vertical lines for months and see instantly the changes which have occurred during the entire period. As automobile sales are very greatly affected by the weather conditions of different seasons of the year, these curves are important. Though weather conditions have affected the curves quite largely, we can see, by comparing the curves for 1910 and 1911, that probably conditions of management as well as weather conditions caused smaller shipments in November and December, 1911, than in those same months of 1910, when shipments were quite good. The card for 1912 is shown with the curve incomplete, just as the manager might have seen it early in the month of February, 1912, after the January reports had been received, tabulated and plotted. As Fig. 207 shows curves which are true records of the real happenings in an automobile plant, they are worthy of study for practice in curve interpretation. Notice that the changes from July to August, in 1911 and 1912, are readily seen because each curve card begins by repeating the record

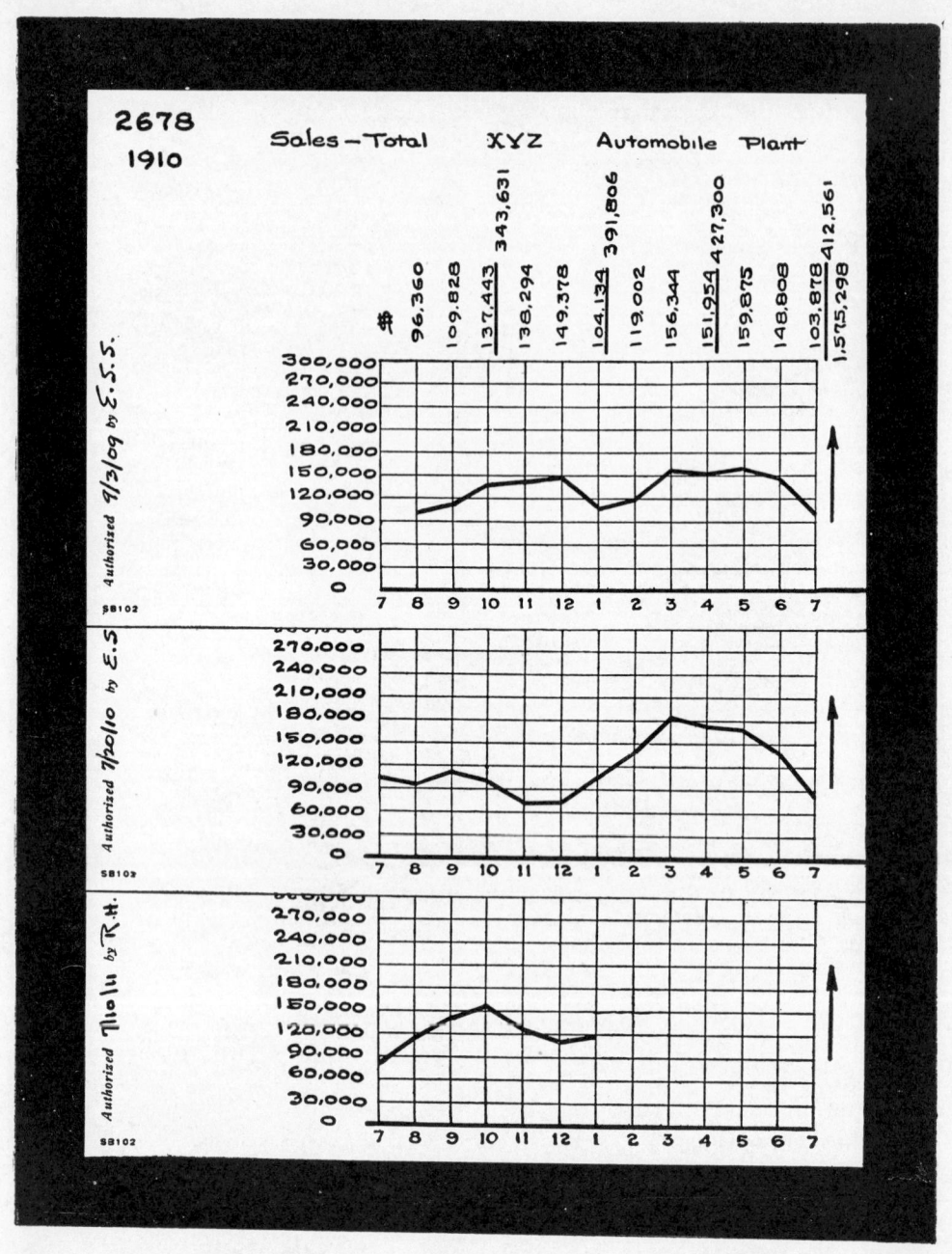

Fig. 207. Sales of the "X.Y.Z." Automobile Plant for Three Consecutive Years

The three 4-by-6-inch cards are arranged one above the other so that the curves for different years may be easily compared. Note that November and December were good months in 1910, but poor months in 1911 and 1912. The 1911 card above is the same as in Fig. 205, but here it is printed in one color only. Observe at the right the arrows showing that it is desired that the trend of the curve should be upward. Arrows like this save about two-thirds of the executive's time in looking over a large number of curves

CURVES FOR THE EXECUTIVE

for the last month of the preceding fiscal year instead of using a dot as shown in Fig. 204.

The separate cards for different years, which in Fig. 207 are arranged vertically one above the other, may be laid horizontally as in Fig. 208. Here the cards are superposed on a black background, the left-hand and middle cards each overlying the card to the right, so that the curve appears continuous. The vertical arrangement allows of a very accurate analysis of changes which have occurred from month to month of each year. With the horizontal arrangement it is not so easy to compare any month of one year with the corresponding month of another year, but it is easier to see the changes which have occurred in a curve as a whole throughout a period of years. Thus in Fig. 208 it is much easier than in Fig. 207 to see that sales dropped seriously in the first half of 1911, and that they increased far beyond any previous record during the last half of 1911. The vertical arrangement is useful for one purpose: the hori-

Fig. 208. Sales of the "X.Y.Z." Automobile Plant for Three Consecutive Years

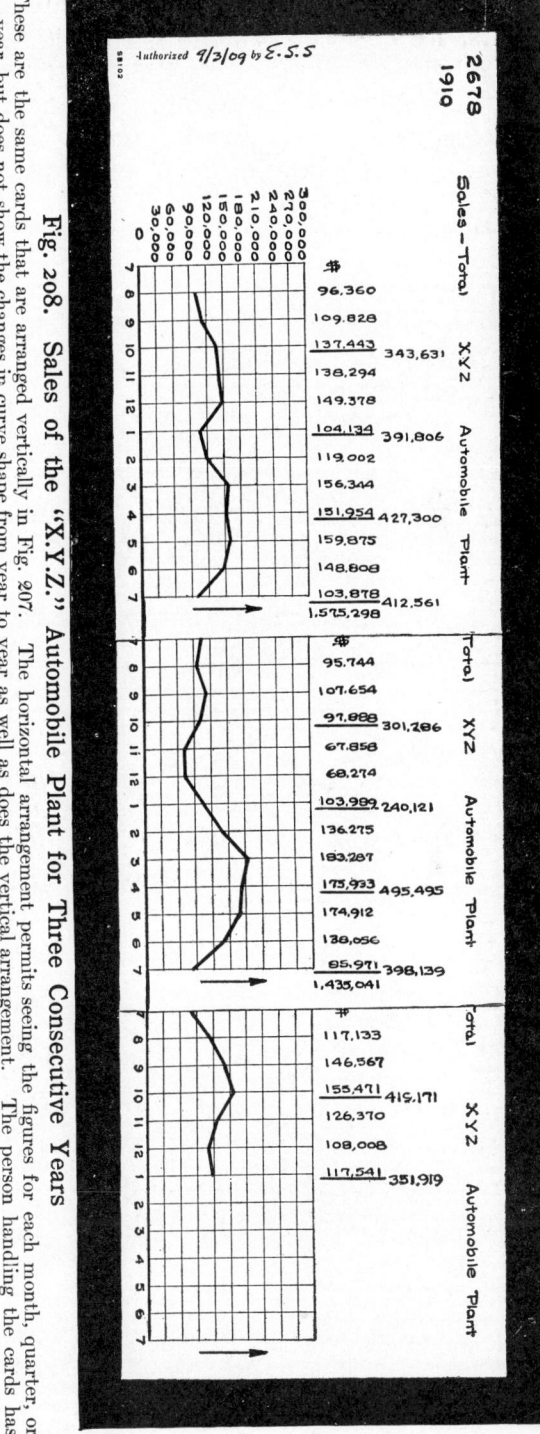

These are the same cards that are arranged vertically in Fig. 207. The horizontal arrangement permits seeing the figures for each month, quarter, or year, but does not show the changes in curve shape from year to year as well as does the vertical arrangement. The person handling the cards has his choice of the vertical or the horizontal arrangement for the cards

zontal arrangement is useful for another purpose. By having loose cards, we can arrange the cards either horizontally or vertically and get all the advantages of either position. Curves plotted in loose-leaf books, or on large sheets of paper, cannot have this flexibility of arrangement, and they accordingly handicap the executive in the analysis of data which may be vital to the success of his business.

When the cards are arranged horizontally the figures for the curve over a series of years are in plain sight, while in the vertical arrangement one card hides the figures on another card. Figures are essential to the true interpretation of curves like those seen in Fig. 208. In looking at Fig. 208 most readers are likely to feel that the business of the year 1911 was much better than the business of the year 1910. When we look at the total figures, however, we see that the sales for the year 1911 were only $1,435,041, while the sales for 1910 were $1,575,298. Not only were the total sales for 1911 much less than the sales for 1910, but there was a very great fluctuation in sales from month to month which created a very difficult problem in the operation of the manufacturing plant. In the early half of the fiscal year ending in 1911, men were not needed because of the small volume of sales, and a large portion of the working force had to be discharged. In the latter half of the fiscal year, sales increased so rapidly that men had to be hired in large numbers. Inevitably, therefore, many unskilled men were obtained who were sure to spoil a large volume of any output requiring the great accuracy needed by automobile parts. The record for the fiscal year ending 1911 was in every way bad, as compared with that for the fiscal year 1910. The company eventually ended in a receivership.

Cards only four inches by six are of sufficient height to hold the co-ordinate ruling needed for curve plotting, and yet have room above the ruled field for two separate columns of figures of seven digits each, as well as space across the top for a title which may run the whole length of the card. In Fig. 208 we have two sets of figures, one set for months and the other set for quarters. Each set of figures contains six numerals. Although the illustration in Fig. 208 is only about one half the natural size of the card, the figures themselves are clearly legible and the title at the top of the card is easily read.

One of the chief advantages in the use of loose cards lies in the fact that any set of cards may be laid out on a table and compared with any other set of cards in the manner shown in Fig. 209. It is difficult with a loose-leaf book to arrange a system for keeping hundreds of curves in such a way that quick comparisons between any of them can be made. When loose cards are used any card can be compared with any other card instantly, and, if desired, cards for any curve for a series of years may be laid out for comparison with cards for any other curve for any series of years. Anyone without experience in the analysis of curve records for large corporations may take it as a fact that no system of curve records should be installed which does not permit the instantaneous comparison of any curve with any other curve in the whole system.

Fig. 207 and Fig. 208 show the shipments from an automobile manufacturing plant as sales. Many of the automobiles recorded as sold were shipped to branch houses owned by the same company, to be stored there during the winter months when the branch-house sales are very small, for the reason that people do not wish to buy touring cars in winter. In Fig. 209 and 210 more curve records from an automobile business are given. In these cuts also, as in Fig. 207 and 208, cards are shown in groups of three, photographed against a black background. In Fig. 209 we have in the upper curve the actual sales of an automobile branch house selling direct to the automobile user. Notice that the sales in the spring months greatly exceed the sales at any other time of the year. In the first two fiscal years sales were at a maximum in May, while in the third fiscal year sales reached the maximum in April and were fairly large in both March and May.

In the lower curve we have the expenses of this same branch house. A very noticeable increase in the expenses occurred in the fall months at the beginning of the fiscal year, once in October and twice in September. This increase was due to local advertising announcing the new-model automobile for the next season. It was customary for all manufacturers of automobiles to announce their next season's models in the fall months, and the peaks in the expense curve shown here came as they did simply because of this custom of the trade.

It is quite easily seen from the upper curves that the sales for the second fiscal year were much greater than those for the first fiscal year. The total figures, however, show much more clearly the extent of the increase. Because of the excellent sales during the spring months, the curve for the third fiscal year at the right gives the impres-

268 GRAPHIC METHODS

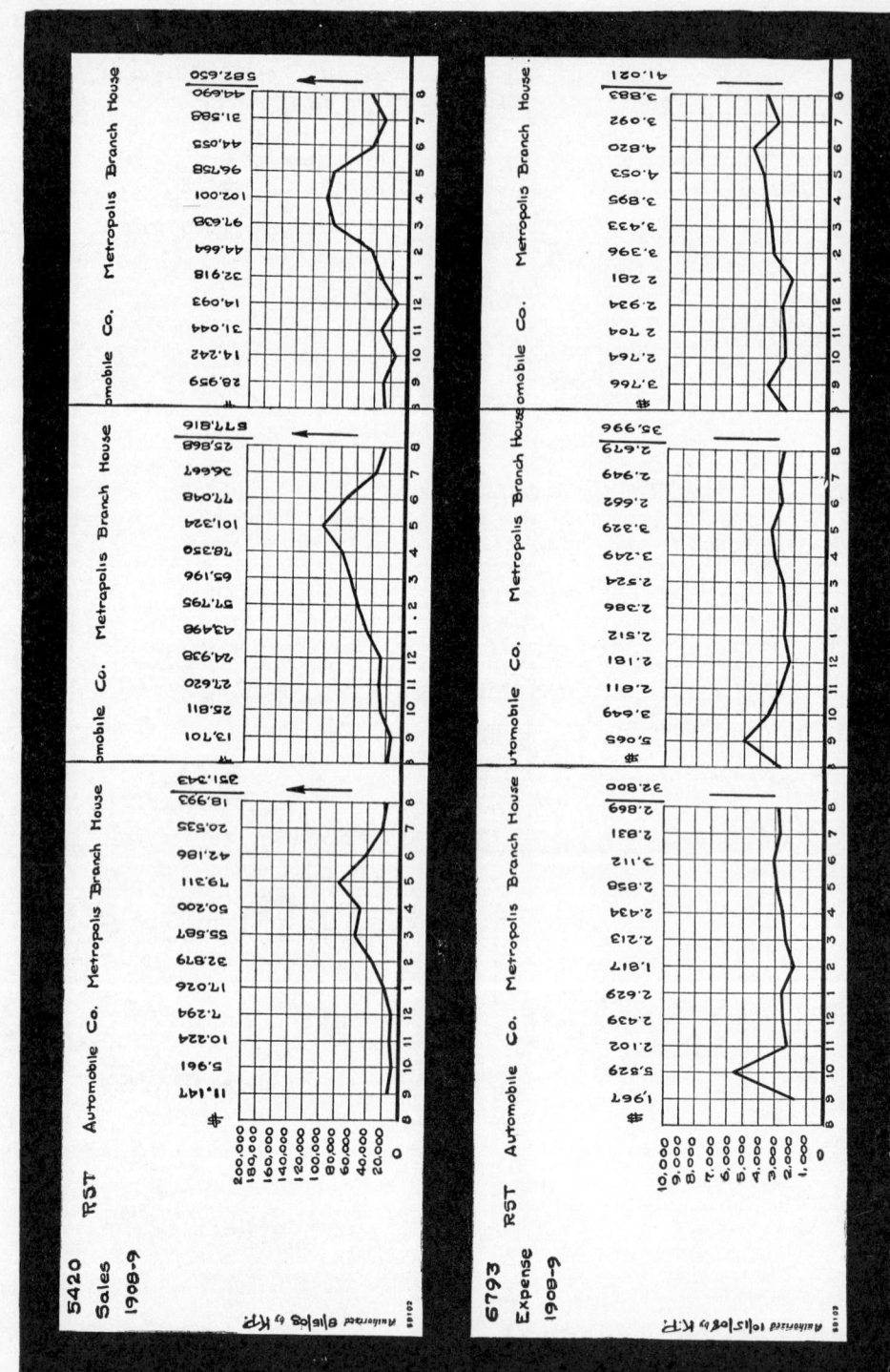

Fig. 209. Sales and Expenses of the "Metropolis" Branch House of the "R.S.T." Automobile Company for Three Consecutive Years

Compare the upper curve for sales with Fig. 202, noting the effect due to changing the horizontal and vertical scales

CURVES FOR THE EXECUTIVE 269

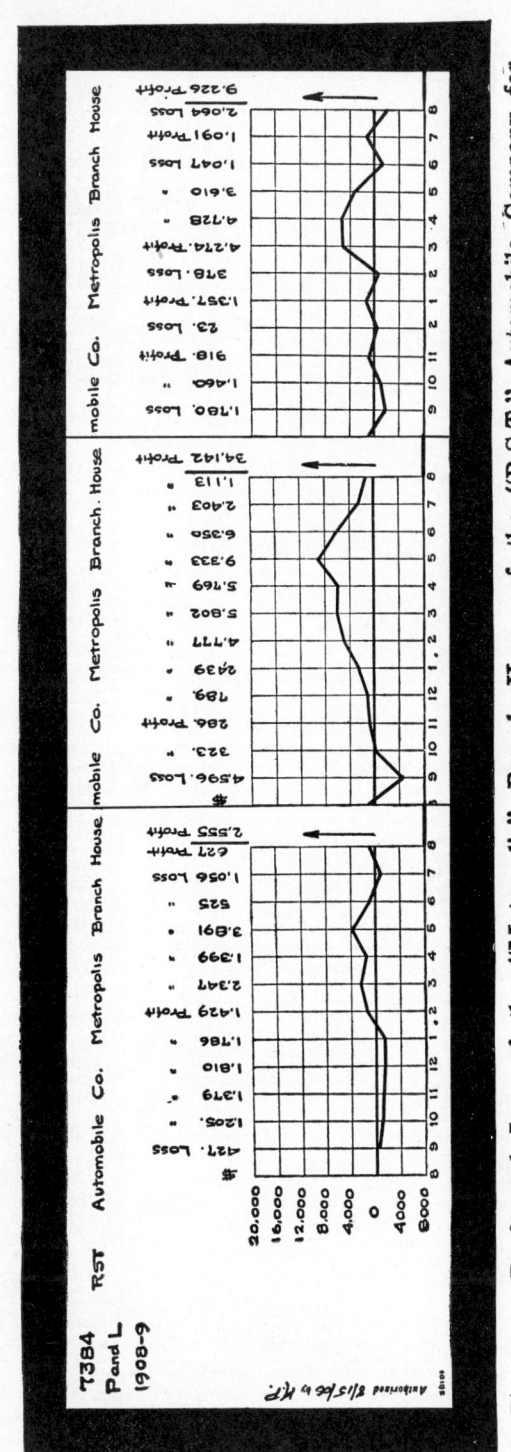

sion of a prosperous year. Reference to the figures for the total yearly sales, however, shows that the sales for the third year increased only very slightly over the preceding year. When we compare the sales of this branch house with the expenses, we get quite a different story from that read from sales curves alone. The increase in sales from the first year to the second year was very great and without a correspondingly great increase of expenses. Putting the figures for the first and second years into a ratio, sales increased 64 per cent, while expenses increased only 10 per cent. In the third year, however, the sales hardly increased at all, while the shape of the curve for expenses shows an almost constant increase. A little mental arithmetic will show further that with almost stationary sales the expenses were permitted to increase about one-seventh or, roughly, 14 per cent.

Notice that in Fig. 209 arrow-heads mark a desire that sales should go up. No arrow was used in connection with the curve for expenses.

Fig. 210. Profit and Loss of the "Metropolis" Branch House of the "R.S.T." Automobile Company for Three Consecutive Years

Read this curve in conjunction with the two curves of Fig. 209. Note the effects on profits of widely fluctuating sales and the effect of expenses which were constantly increasing more rapidly than the volume of sales

It was permissible that expenses should go up in the second fiscal year, for the volume of sales increased very rapidly. The cost per unit of sales or the ratio of expenses to total sales had decreased greatly. An arrow pointing downward would have given a wrong impression as the total expenses had increased justifiably. It is better, therefore, to avoid using arrows than to use arrows which would mean nothing.

The real story of this automobile branch house is seen in Fig. 210 which gives the profit-and-loss curve corresponding to the sales and expense curves of Fig. 209. Expenses of the branch house were fairly large throughout the whole year, because of fixed charges, while the great fluctuation in sales caused a loss during the many months in which the volume of sales was small. Note how much better the profits were in the second year than in the first year, because the business had been established long enough to have a fairly good volume of sales during the fall months. There was a profit in all the months of the second year except two, with a total profit of very considerable size, though not a tremendous one compared with the volume of sales, since the profit was only 5.9 per cent of the sales. In the third year the profits were on the ragged edge throughout the whole year except in the three spring months of March, April, and May when sales were exceptionally large. The total profits for the year, even with a slightly increased volume of sales, were less than one-third of what they had been for the preceding year.

Just to show what complex conditions enter into the comparison of business curves of this sort, it is mentioned here that the small volume of sales, the large expenses, and the negligible profits in the first half of the third fiscal year were not the fault of the manager of this branch house. The trouble went back to the factory engineering department which failed to get its next season's models designed early enough. Consequently the car could not be manufactured in sufficient quantities to give the branch manager enough cars to make a satisfactory volume of sales. The branch manager blamed the factory because the factory could not deliver a sufficient quantity of cars. The factory manager was not to blame, however, as the engineering department (reporting direct to the president instead of to the factory manager) had delayed the design for the new car, and the factory manager was, of course, unable to build a car until he had the drawings. This example will perhaps give a fair idea of the uses which can be made of curves plotted from the operating figures of a complex business.

A person who has not tried plotting curves on cards only four inches high is likely to say that the card is not of sufficient height to permit satisfactory curve plotting when there is a great fluctuation in the curve. Such a person would argue that the card is not high enough to allow the plotting of curves on a scale sufficiently large for easy reading, and that any curve for a constantly increasing business is likely to run off the top of the co-ordinate ruling within a few years. The curves as shown in this chapter certainly vary enough to allow the eye to see all the changes clearly. As the curves are in each case accompanied by the actual figures for the value of each point on the curves, it is not necessary that one should be able to measure accurately for points falling between horizontal co-ordinate lines. Instead of consulting the vertical scale to get the value at any point, reference is made to the actual figures above the various points. These figures indicate a finer fluctuation in the curve than it is possible for the eye to appreciate even in curves plotted on very large sheets of paper. Figures, then, in conjunction with curves like those shown here, make it unnecessary to plot lines of such fine width or great accuracy as would be necessary if the figures were not shown above the curve.

In Fig. 207 the bottom card shows the zero line extended to the left over the figure seven at the lower left-hand corner of the ruled field. On the middle card the zero line has been extended to the right. This right-and-left extension of the zero line is not made until a card has been completely filled out. The extension of the zero line indicates the point at which cards are to be joined when laid in the horizontal position shown in Fig. 208. It will be noticed, in Fig. 208, that the cards are overlapped in such a way that the right-hand edge of the uppermost card coincides with the left-hand edge of the ruled field of the lower card, and that the zero line is continuous. The extension line drawn at the left of any lower card shows where the extension drawn across the right margin of the upper card is to be joined. Cards may be laid together in a horizontal position almost instantly, and correctly, when these joint lines are present as a guide.

If, as in Fig. 211, a curve should rise with such rapidity as to be dangerously near the upper limit of the ruled portion of the card, the joint lines may be so drawn as to allow more vertical space on the succeeding cards. In Fig. 211 the curve for 1910 indicated that the curve for 1911 might go higher than the 1,400 line. Consequently, when the new card was made out for the year 1911, the joint lines were so

272   GRAPHIC METHODS

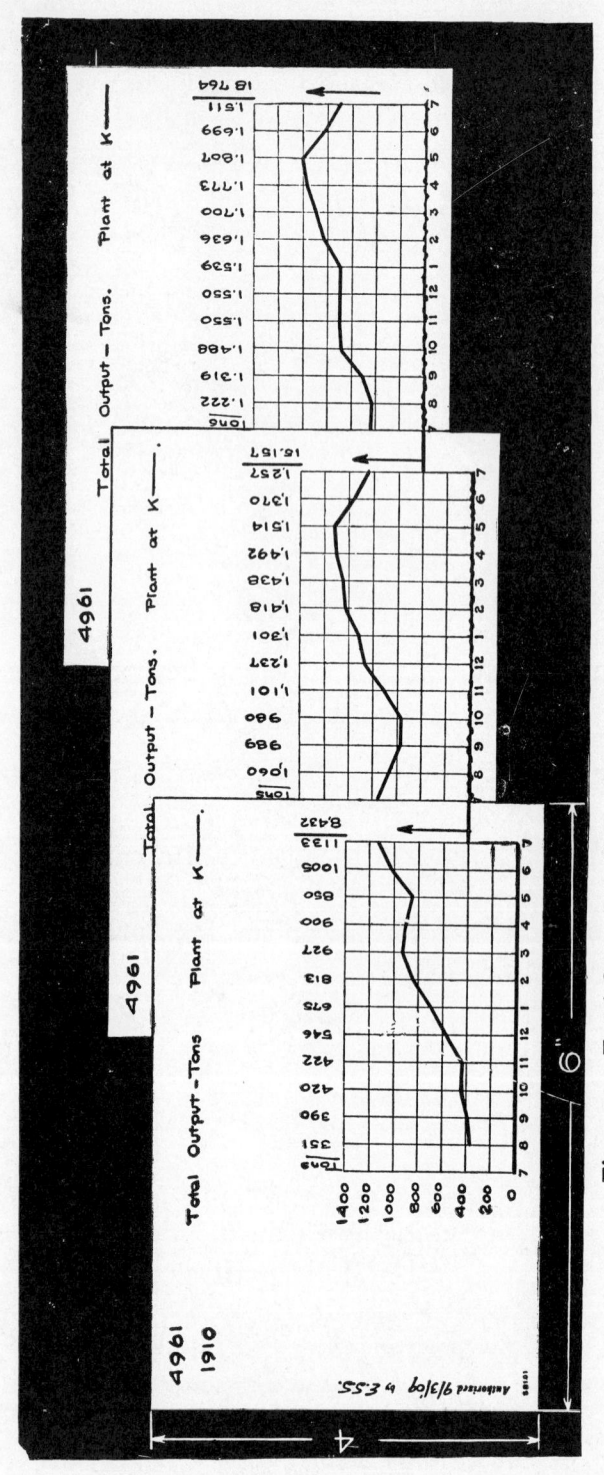

Fig. 211. Total Output in Tons of a Factory for Three Consecutive Years

When a curve shows a tendency to leave the ruled field of the card, more space can be allowed as a result of the way in which cards for succeeding years are joined

drawn that the line at the right of the 1910 card was above zero, and the joint line at the left of the 1911 card at the bottom of the ruled field. Thus, when the two cards are overlapped so that the joint lines match, it is seen that there is enough space in the ruled field at the right for the curve to rise to the scale line for 1,600. Two more spaces were again allowed in 1912 in anticipation of even further upward progress in the curve. As joint lines may be drawn in continuation of any horizontal line on either the upper or the lower card, any amount of expansion in future years may be provided for. The curve cards are small enough to be very convenient to handle and yet they may be joined together in such a way as to provide for unlimited future growth.

The card for 1910 in Fig. 211 has a broad line drawn by hand to show the zero line. On the card for 1911 the scale begins at 400, and, because the scale does not begin at zero, the bottom of the co-ordinate field is marked with a wavy line. This wavy line is made very rapidly with a pen and serves the very useful purpose of safeguarding the reader from interpreting the curve as if the lower line on the field were zero. Whenever zero is not shown at the bottom of the ruled field, this wavy line should be used. Any card can thus be read independently, with safety so far as its interpretation from the zero point is concerned. When several cards are laid out together, and the zero line is shown on the left-hand card, as in Fig. 211, it is a simple matter for the eye to imagine the zero line extended to the right below the other cards, thus permitting easy interpretation of all cards.

It sometimes happens, especially in plotting costs, that the desired direction of the curve will be downward instead of upward. In such a case, and to show small fluctuations from month to month, the scale on the curve cards may be so selected that the zero line does not appear even on the first card plotted. Should the costs be reduced so rapidly that the curve tends to run off the bottom of any card, the card for the succeeding year may have the joint line drawn in such a way as to allow an extension of the scale downward, exactly as Fig. 211 shows an extension of the scale upward. By drawing the left-hand joint line on the later cards above the bottom of the ruled space, and by putting the right-hand joint lines for the first cards at the bottom of the ruled curve field, the series of curves can be made to progress downward to any desired extent in exactly the same manner as the curves in Fig. 211 progress upward year by year. By the use of these joint lines a thoroughly universal arrangement of cards may be secured, allowing extra space for movement either up or down.

Joint lines were devised chiefly to permit of showing a large upward or downward progress in the curves for succeeding years without the necessity of laboriously replotting the curves for the earlier years. The desired result has been very satisfactorily attained. Should anyone, however, object to the presenting of a series of cards in steps as in Fig. 211, he need only replot the curve for the earlier years to some smaller scale. In general, however, it will be found that practically no replotting is necessary or desirable. By connecting the cards with joint lines and by using a wavy base line when the scale does not extend to zero, all necessary convenience and accuracy may be secured.

When plotting curves on large sheets of co-ordinate paper it frequently happens that the scale desired cannot be placed upon the kind of ruled paper available. Scales must usually be made in full size, one-half size, one-quarter size, etc., and it is usually too big a jump to change from one of these sizes to another. The ideal arrangement is to have a supply of co-ordinate paper with different rulings so that when one ruling does not suit, some other ruling may be used. On the curve cards shown in this chapter the horizontal scale is fixed, as the cards are designed for use with definite units of time, such as one year by months, one year by weeks, five years by months, etc. For the vertical scale, however, two different rulings are provided. One of these rulings has seven $\frac{1}{4}$-inch spaces as may be seen in Fig. 211. The other ruling has ten vertical spaces of $\frac{1}{6}$ inch each as seen in Fig. 209. The ratio of the two scales is seven to ten or, roughly, one scale may be said to be two-thirds of the other. This is the most desirable arrangement that it is possible to get, as these two rulings afford a great range of scales to choose from. If by using one ruling the curve comes too high on the card, simply change over to the other ruling and the peak will come lower down on the card. The two rulings, either in full size or in some fractional size, give every possible combination of scale that need be desired.

The ruling having vertical spaces of one-sixth of an inch is ten spaces high. This ruling is very convenient for curve plotting on a percentage basis when 100 per cent is shown at the top of the chart as in Fig. 126, Fig. 128 and Fig. 129 in Chapter IX. If, on the ten-space card, each space is used to represent 10 per cent with zero for the bottom line and 100 per cent for the top line of the chart, the neatest possible arrangement is secured.

In starting to plot a curve which is to be continued year after year, it is ordinarily best to allow plenty of room for future growth. In the upper curve of Fig. 209 the scale was purposely selected for the first year so that the curve would extend only about one-third of the way to the top of the ruled portion of the card. This would allow the sales to be trebled in volume before the curve would extend over the top of the ruled portion and necessitate a change in scale or a step upward so that the zero line could no longer be shown at the bottom of the card. It is well to start all curves for output or sales at about one-third of the height of the card so as to allow plenty of room for future expansion. Curves for expenses per unit, however, may be started well up on the card if there is any hope whatever of reducing the unit expenses in future years.

The man who plots curves on the cards described here keeps a supply of the printed cards in each of the two rulings of seven spaces high and ten spaces high. When starting any new curves he uses whichever of the two cards gives the scale best suited to his purpose. The cost of carrying two different kinds of ruled cards on hand is negligible compared with the great convenience resulting.

The ruling of the cards in which the vertical spaces are either $\frac{1}{4}$-inch or $\frac{1}{6}$-inch high permits the use of an engineer's scale in fortieths or sixtieths of an inch, if it should ever be desired to locate plotted points on the cards with very great accuracy. The engineers' scale in fortieths or sixtieths of an inch gives ten divisions to each space between the horizontal lines on the card and makes it possible to locate each plotted point with a very finely sharpened lead pencil or a needle. Practice, however, proves that there is no necessity for using an engineer's scale in plotting curve points on the cards here described. The man doing the plotting learns very quickly to locate the points by using only the eye and a hard lead-pencil, so that the points are practically as accurate as if spaced with an engineer's scale and a needle point. Even if the points on the curve are not located quite so accurately as they may be when a needle point and a scale are used, it makes no difference to the executive by whom the curve is read. The figures denoting the value of each plotted point are given immediately over the point in the upper margin. The executive reading the curve does not have to refer to the vertical scale. He need only glance at the figures above any point to learn the value for that point far more correctly than would ever be possible with even the most accurately plotted curve if the value of the point had to be interpolated from the vertical scale of the chart. The vertical scale of these cards on which the figures are given in the upper margin fulfills almost no purpose except that of giving a record of the scale to the man who must plot points in succeeding months, or that of giving the values of horizontal lines which are convenient in locating high points or low points on any curve.

When another point has to be added on a large number of curves for a succeeding month or week, the most convenient procedure consists in first copying upon all curve cards, immediately above the vertical line for the proper month, the figures from the typewritten reports, or

276   GRAPHIC METHODS

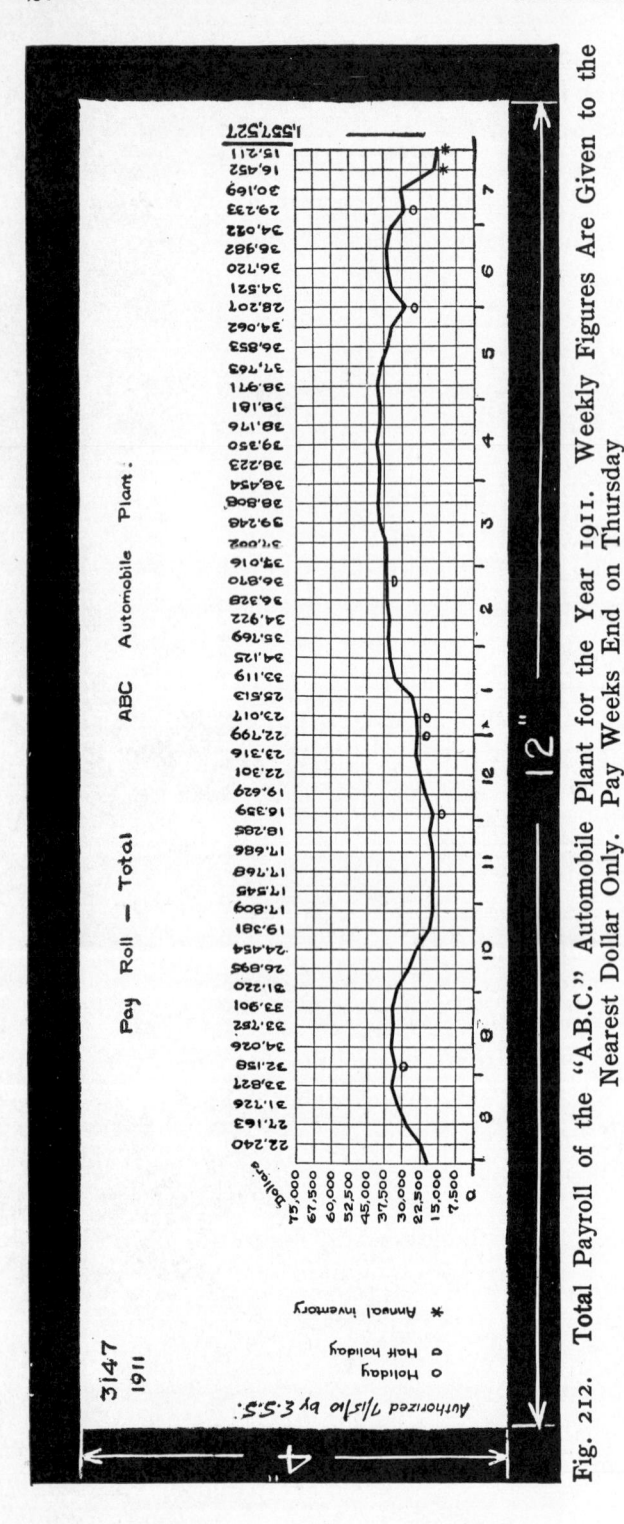

Fig. 212. Total Payroll of the "A.B.C." Automobile Plant for the Year 1911. Weekly Figures Are Given to the Nearest Dollar Only. Pay Weeks End on Thursday

other sources of information. This is straight clerical work and may be done with a pen on one card after another with great rapidity. Ordinary liquid drawing ink is the best for the figures, as the opaqueness of the drawing ink gives better blue prints than are obtainable from writing ink. This is often partly transparent and prints pale blue instead of clear white. After the figures have been entered on all the cards, the cards are taken rapidly one by one and a sharp lead-pencil is used to mark on the proper vertical line a point which, according to the vertical scale, corresponds with the newly recorded figures in the upper margin. When all the curve points have been located by lead-pencil marks on the curve cards, a drawing pen is used to draw the line on each card to show the change that has occurred since the previous point was plotted. As the new point has already been indicated in each case by the lead-pencil mark, all the ink lines can be drawn in rapidly with a draftsman's ruling pen. If the suggested procedure is used, the lines may be drawn so rapidly that there is no chance for the ink to dry on the pen and the ruling operation is almost continuous.

In Fig. 212 we find on a reduced scale the same card that was presented in Fig. 206. Fig. 206 was drawn to full scale in order to show the true size of the figures and the actual spacing. Fig. 212 gives a better idea of the proportion of this card, and though of reduced size, it nevertheless shows the appearance of a card suitable for the plotting of records for one year by weeks, and thus requiring fifty-two entries of figures in the upper part of the card.

In Fig. 212 the arrangement to show the dates along the bottom of the card, with short vertical lines dividing the horizontal scale into months, is not put on to the card until the exact year is known for which the particular card is to be used. Lines dividing the year into months so as to show exactly how many weeks are included in each month and at just which portion of the week the beginning or end of each month may occur are then put in by hand. In Fig. 212 the card has been used for a fiscal year beginning August 1. The card is marked 1911, meaning the fiscal year ending July 31, 1911. By referring to the calendar for the year 1911 one may see how the short lines for months are put in. As the pay weeks ended on Thursday, there were only four pay weeks ending in July, but there were five pay weeks ending in March. March 1 came on Wednesday. The last day of March was on Friday. The vertical co-ordinate lines for March show clearly that there were five Thursdays, and they also show the exact time relation of the Thursdays to the beginning and to the end of the month.

After the month scale for any fiscal year has been marked by hand on one card, any office boy can quickly copy the scale to other cards by superimposing the first card on the next card and copying the pen strokes from the first onto the second card. A supply of cards for any year can thus be made up at small expense, without having to have cards printed differently each year just because mankind has not yet made a calendar which always has the same relation between days of the week and days of the month. The scheme of indicating the relation of weeks and months by the short vertical pen marks permits the carrying on hand of a supply of printed cards which can be used for absolutely any fiscal year without danger of having to send the supply of cards to the scrap basket, as calendars are sent to the scrap basket

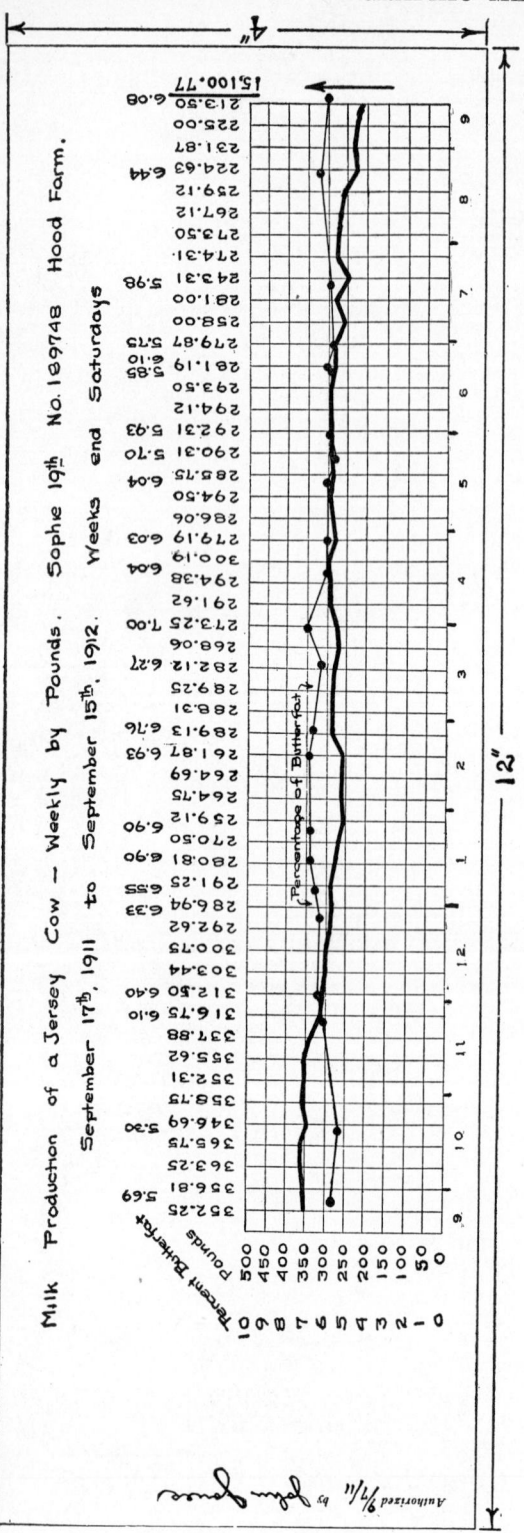

Fig. 213. Milk Production of a Jersey Cow, Weekly by Pounds

A card only 4 inches wide is ample to permit plotting two curves simultaneously. There is plenty of space to allow for two columns of figures giving data for all points on either curve and yet permit lettering a title along the top of the card. A card only four inches wide is advantageous because it can be used in a standard filing case like that seen in Fig. 217

just because last year's calendar is of no use after December 31. This assurance of a perennial form instead of one which must be renewed or replaced every year is no small advantage. Figures designating the months for any fiscal year can be printed on the weekly card if desired. In Fig. 212 the figures 8, 9, 10, etc., indicating the months, can be printed on the cards and thus leave to be inserted by hand each year only the short vertical markings indicating the relation of the weeks and the months.

Fig. 213 shows the weekly curve card used in the records of a dairy farm. The particular curve shown is for a prize Jersey cow which was being very carefully tested in the hope of breaking the world's record for milk production. The milk production each week is indicated here, in pounds, together with the butter-fat analysis taken at various intervals.

CURVES FOR THE EXECUTIVE 279

The days on which the butter-fat analysis were made are quite accurately indicated by the dots on the butter-fat curve. Figures for the milk production each week are given to hundredths of a pound in the appropriate column above, and the butter-fat analysis is given to one one-hundredth of one per cent for each date on which the analysis was made. The grand total milk production for the year of the test is given at the foot of the column. Note the diagonal arrangement of the two headings, "Pounds" and "Per cent Butter Fat". This diagonal arrangement is a convenient one as it is easy to read and refers to each of two columns of figures, one column vertical and the other horizontal.

A card for each cow as indicated above is worth while in a modern dairy. Individual records are fundamentally necessary to efficient operation. There is such a wide variation in cows that unless they are care-

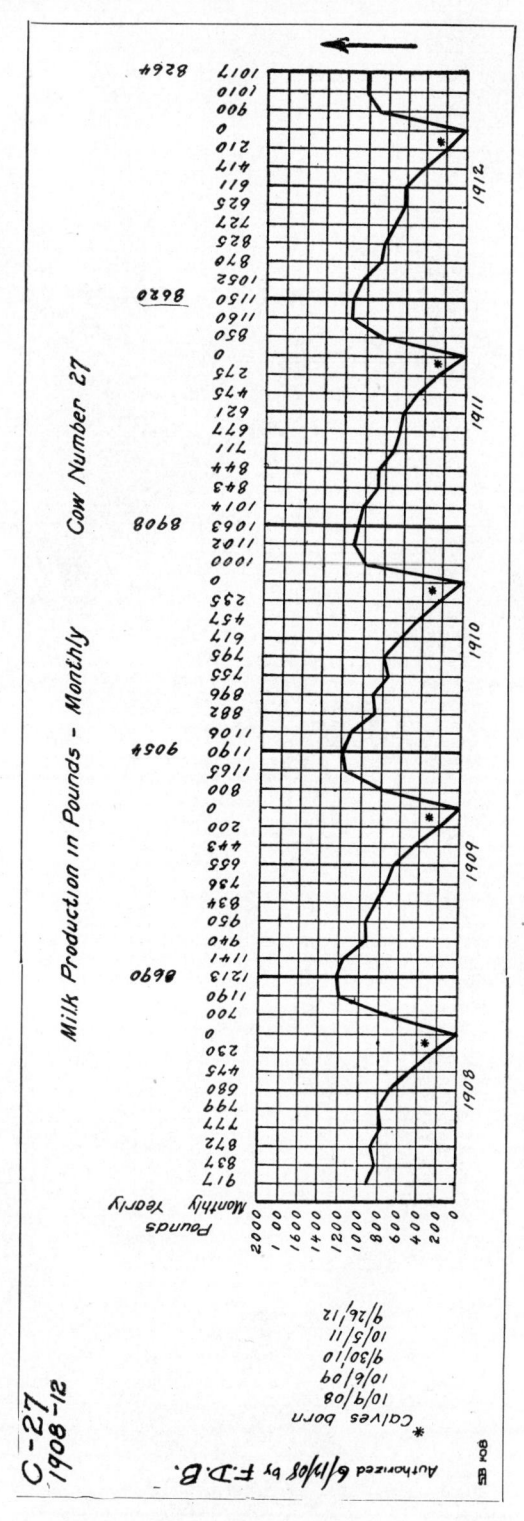

Fig. 214. Milk Production of a Cow by Months for Five Years

Since a card 12 inches long is necessary in order to show figures for fifty-two weeks in one year, we can also use a card 12 inches long for five years by months. Having five years on one card saves handling so many separate cards, but there is a disadvantage in that curve cycles for different years cannot be so easily and accurately compared as with the vertical arrangement of yearly cards seen in Fig. 207

280 GRAPHIC METHODS

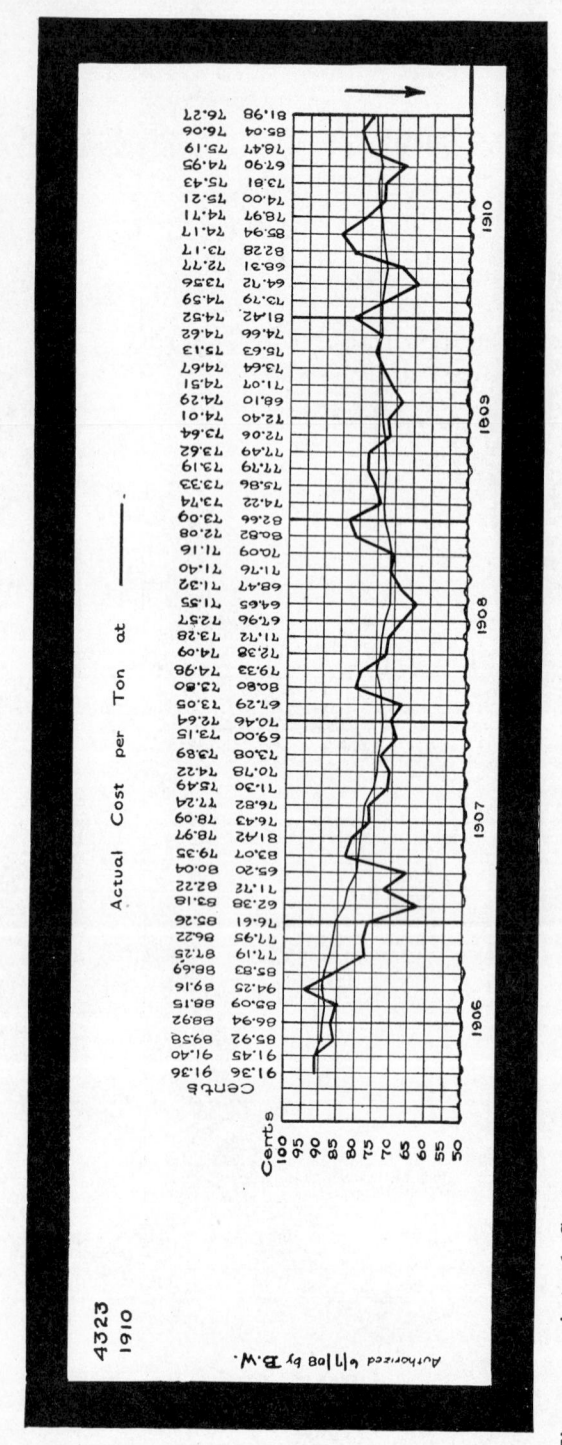

Fig. 215. Actual Cost per Ton at a Factory for Five Years by Months. The Fine Line Shows Monthly a Moving Average of the Cost for the Preceding Twelve Months

The arrow shows it is desired that the cost should go down. Since there is no hope of getting the cost below 50 cents per ton, the zero line is not shown and the bottom of the chart has a wavy line to indicate that the bottom is not at zero

fully watched there are certain to be in every herd cows whose milk production is far below the average. Individual records of each cow are now being kept regularly by up-to-date dairies, and any cow that fails to give a definite minimum of milk with a definite per cent of butter-fat is sent to the butcher. Curve cards are a convenient means of recording the output of each cow in such form that instant comparison between cows is possible.

In Fig. 214 a record for one cow for a period of five years is shown on a 4-by-12-inch card. As the card 12 inches long is necessary for weekly records, a card of the same size can be used conveniently to show five years by months instead of using five separate 4-by-6-inch cards, one for each year. In Fig. 214, the figures at the top of the card show the milk production each month and the total milk production for each calendar year. The notes in the left-hand margin show the dates on which calves were born.

In Fig. 215, also, curves are plotted on a card for five years by months. In this case there was no hope of getting the cost per ton below 50 cents, and the scale was accordingly so chosen that it began at 50 cents instead of at zero in order that fluctuations from month to month might be more carefully observed. As the zero line was not shown on the card, the wavy line was drawn at the bottom of the ruled portion, indicating clearly to the reader that he must not interpret the curve as though the bottom were at zero.

When using an arrangement showing five years by months on one card, considerable mental effort is necessary to get a clear interpretation of the fluctuations in the curve from year to year. In Fig. 215 certain peaks in the curve appear to have somewhat similar shape. Thus the peak for 1908 looks like the peak for 1907 until closer examination shows clearly that the low point for 1908 was in July, while the low point following the peak of 1907 came not in July, 1907, but in January, 1908. The waves themselves, although of somewhat similar shape, have peaks at entirely different times, the peak for 1908 being in February and the peak for 1907 in April. The foregoing examples may serve to point out the mental effort necessary in reading horizontally if the danger of misinterpretation is to be avoided. If the curves for these same years 1907 and 1908 were plotted on 4-by-6-inch cards, and one card placed above the other as in Fig. 207, there would be no possibility of error on the part of the reader. The eye would follow the vertical lines and see at once that there was no great similarity in the two waves. Having five separate cards causes the reader to take more time in handling cards in order that he may save mental effort and avoid error in interpreting the yearly waves. Having five years on one card saves handling the cards, but it takes more mental effort to be accurate in reading the curve horizontally. The choice between five cards of one fiscal year each and one card for five years must rest with the judgment or the habit of mind of each individual person.

It sometimes happens that the seasonal wave in a curve is almost completely obscured by the tendency toward a very great increase or decrease in the business. Conditions may give so large an increase in volume of business in any one year as to more than offset any decrease due to a seasonal period of slackness. The manager may think, therefore, that his business is not affected by seasons, when in reality the seasonal changes are very great. The extent of these might be very evident if, for instance, a panic year should come along and suddenly stop the upward tendencies in the curve resulting from the rapid increase in the size of the business. This is an important point for any small business to watch, for it may involve bankruptcy to assume that the particular business is not affected by slack seasons of the year such as affect most businesses. Fig. 211 gives an example of a curve in which a large amount of seasonal fluctuation might be easily seen if the rapid increase in the business did not make the upward trend from increased sales greater than the possible downward trend due to seasonal changes.

It is often necessary to compare curves for entirely different things. For instance, it is desirable to compare expenses with sales. When sales increase expenses per unit should decrease, and *vice versa*. Tremendous saving can be made in most large manufacturing plants by carefully watching the curves for the unit expenses and the output. Something is usually wrong in any department in which expenses per unit increase at the same time that the output curve goes upward. When the amount of work done is fluctuating greatly, as during periods of business depression, the executive may often get many vital hints for the operation of his plant if he will simply make periodic examinations to see whether the overhead-expense curves for each department react in the manner which would be indicated by fluctuations in the curves for direct labor or for quantity of output.

In making comparisons between separate curves there is a great advantage in having a standard arrangement of the five-year cards so that there may be no danger of comparing two curves for different years when it is intended to compare for the same year. It is desirable, as seen in Fig. 215, that all five-year cards should have the years arranged by half-decades. One arrangement includes those years ending in one to five inclusive, and the other arrangement takes those years ending in six to ten inclusive. The person reading the curves can then pick up any two cards relating to the same half-decade and compare the curves instantly and correctly, simply by placing the cards so that the edges coincide. If this half-decade arrangement were not followed there would be five different positions in making curve comparisons, and there would be grave possibility of frequent error in that different years might be compared without the reader's noticing that he was making an error. In starting a new curve on a five-year card the curve should be started in the middle of the card if the first year plotted happens to fall in the middle of a half-decade. The half-decade arrangement should be carefully followed even though it does not leave a portion of a card unfilled.

The fine-line curve running through Fig. 215 represents a twelve-months moving average of the points on the heavy curve. If the executive wishes to know the general trend of his costs, he refers at once to this fine line and sees what the cost has been for the last twelve months for which costs are known. In making up this moving average (as explained in Chapter VI), one month is dropped from the addition and another month is included in the addition, so that the twelve months added are always the most recent months for which figures are available. Note in Fig. 215 the degree of accuracy used in recording the figures for the curves. Costs are known quite accurately in this case and are recorded here to one one-hundredth of a cent. The moving-average line shown above is a much simpler line than the curve line, for the reason that the violent fluctuations in the heavy curve are largely eliminated by the method of moving averages. The general rule for smoothing a curve is that the number of points included in the moving average should be the number ordinarily found in one complete cycle or wave on the curve. This principle also was more fully discussed in Chapter VI. In Fig. 215 the length of the wave is approximately one year. It is accordingly good practice to have twelve points included here in making up the moving average, so as to give as smooth a curve as possible. If there had been a complete wave or cycle every six months instead of once a year, it would have been desirable to use six points in the moving average, rather than twelve points. The practice in many offices is to use the last twelve months in making up a moving average, though it frequently occurs that a smoother curve would be obtained if some other number of months were used.

As will be seen by reference to Fig. 91, points for a moving-average curve are usually plotted in the middle of the horizontal space covered by those points included in the moving average. In executive-control curves such as are seen here, it seems desirable to make an exception to the general rule and plot the last point on the moving-average curve so that it falls on the same vertical co-ordinate line as the last point included in the average. If the moving-average curve were made as in Fig. 91 it would be following so far behind the periodic record curve that the ordinary reader would not realize that the moving-average curve is really up-to-date. For executive work, the object of a moving-average curve is not so much to get a smooth curve as to show the average for the preceding year or other period of time considered. Under these circumstances it seems permissible to plot the moving-average curve as done in Fig. 215 instead of following the accepted method shown in Fig. 91.

In the last portion of Chapter VII some of the disadvantages of plotting curves on ordinary ruled co-ordinate paper were discussed. One of these disadvantages is due to the great difference in fluctuation with curves of small and of large numerical quantities placed near the bottom and near the top of a chart. In order to overcome this disadvantage, curves are often plotted on logarithmic paper. It seems desirable to point out that curves plotted on the curve cards described here are usually compared so that the disadvantages commonly found with curves plotted on ordinary co-ordinate paper are largely overcome. If only single curves are plotted on each curve card, and the zero line appears at the bottom of each card, then curves on different cards have approximately the same percentage scale. If two curve cards with different numerical scales are compared the comparison is much more accurate than would be the case if the two curves were plotted on a large sheet of paper to the same numerical vertical scale. The fact that the curves are all put into the same size of space on the curve cards causes them to have somewhere near the same percentage scale of height, even though the actual numerical scales may be widely different. Having all curves on the curve cards thus gives more accuracy and ease of reading than would be obtained if several curves were shown on large sheets of arithmetically ruled co-ordinate paper with one curve above the other to the same scale.

On the left-hand edge of each curve card shown in this chapter will be noticed the word "Authorized" with a space for a date and initials. When a new curve is added to the list of those curves which are regularly plotted in any organization, the man who desires to see the curve periodically must put his initials and the date of signing on the left-hand margin of the card. This is to show his approval of the general form in which the information is given, and to authorize the expense necessary in collecting data and plotting the curve week by week or month by month. A definite authorization, by which some one must sign his initials in the manner described, assists greatly in preventing unnecessary clerical work, as it eliminates any curves which are not used somewhere in the organization. The man who approves the curve can be told just about what it costs to plot each curve. For instance, if three thousand dollars a year is expended for the labor, materials, etc., necessary in plotting all the curves in an organization, and there are three thousand curves kept regularly, it can be seen that the expense per curve per year will be about one dollar. Therefore, if the man should wish one hundred curves plotted for different data relating to his department, he would be approving an expenditure of about one hundred dollars per year.

At odd times before the end of any year the person who does the curve plotting should begin to get titles and scales in place upon the new cards, which will be necessary at the end of the year when the current curves have reached the right-hand edge of the cards. As most curves continue on the same basis as before, the man who has charge of the plotting would take the new cards to those different men who had approved the curves in the preceding year. If, during that year, any change in departmental organization had occurred which would affect the manner of plotting a curve or the facts which should be shown in any curve, the change would automatically be brought to light by the man who must authorize the continuance of the curve. In large corporations, department heads and officials change so rapidly that continual vigilance is necessary to weed out those records and clerical procedures which are no longer of any use. The authorization plan here outlined, if any man leaves a corporation, would automatically give his successor an opportunity to consider how much of the curve plotting should be continued on the basis formerly used. There is always a great personal difference in the manner in which executives desire reports prepared. The authorizing of curves periodically gives each executive an opportunity to think the matter over and to have data prepared in the manner which is most effective for his individual use. In most organizations the president or the general manager would be likely to have certain standard ways of assembling data and plotting curves, since the chief executive officer must usually refer at some time to each of the records of the different departments. The standards of the chief executive would thus tend to prevent any freak methods being introduced into the general curve-plotting scheme by any department head further down the line.

Each curve plotted regularly is assigned a serial number for convenient identification. This serial number remains the same year after year, even though changes are made in the manner of assembling data or in any other minor details affecting the curve. The serial number is placed at the upper left-hand corner of the card, where it can easily be seen when the cards are filed in card-index filing cabinets. The cards are identified by the number and year, as may be seen in Fig. 211 where the three cards are $\frac{4961}{1910}$ $\frac{4961}{1911}$ $\frac{4961}{1912}$. When two curves appear on the same card, as in Fig. 215, they may be identified by the letters "A", "B", "C", etc., placed on the chart near each curve, and any reference to the several curves may be made as4323A-1910, 4323B–1910, etc. When five years are placed on one card the last year given is marked in the upper left-hand corner of the card, as in Fig. 215, to identify the card and show that it represents all the data for the half-decade ending in that year.

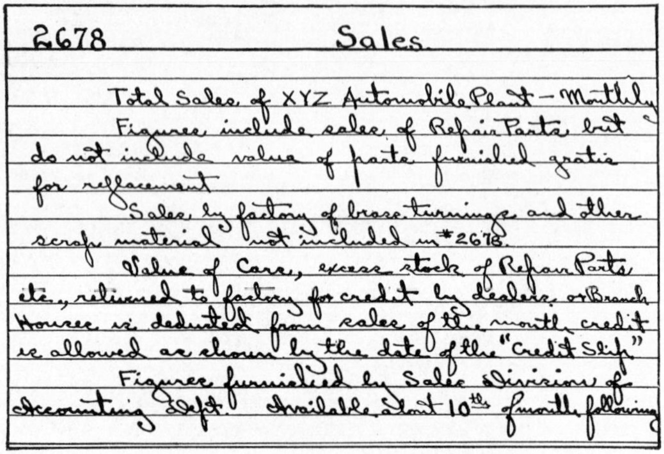
2678 Sales

Total Sales of XYZ Automobile Plant – Monthly

Figures include sales of Repair Parts but do not include value of parts furnished gratis for replacement

Sales by factory of brass turnings and other scrap material not included in *2678.

Value of Cars, excess stock of Repair Parts etc., returned to factory for credit by dealers or Branch Houses is deducted from sales of the month credit is allowed as shown by the date of the "Credit Slip"

Figures furnished by Sales Division of Accounting Dept. Available Start 10th of month following

Fig. 216. Each Curve Card Plotted Periodically Has a Serial Number. A 4-inch by 6-inch Record Card is Filed by the Curve Serial Number to Give the Complete Information Necessary so that Anyone May Know How to Collect the Data and Plot the Curve. The Card, Shown Above, Refers to Curve 2678 Shown for Three Years in Fig. 207 and in Fig. 208

It is not feasible or desirable to place on each curve card a title so complete that it gives all the information concerning the source of the data used in plotting the curve. It is better to use a fairly short title, and then have all supplementary information given on a separate card to which reference, if necessary, can easily be made. Fig. 216 shows a 4-by-6-inch card such as is used in conjunction with each curve card regularly plotted. The number on this card corresponds with the serial number on the curve card as will be seen by referring to Fig. 205 and Fig. 207. If two or more curves appear on the curve card, a card like that in Fig. 216 would have subheadings such as 2678A, 2678B, etc., all shown on the same card No. 2678. It will be seen that the information given on the card in Fig. 216 is much too lengthy to be included as a portion of the title of any curve card. The information on the record card is so specific that a new man in an organization should be able to follow the card instructions and assemble all the data necessary to plot each curve in the whole set.

Information cards such as are shown in Fig. 216 can sometimes be simplified by expressing the information as a formula. Curve numbers used in a formula may greatly simplify the method of expressing the fact that several sets of data must be added and one total divided into another total to obtain a desired ratio. Though information cards like that depicted in Fig. 216 are used principally by the man who plots the curves, they are filed in such convenient location that they may be referred to by any executive who wishes to know the source of the data plotted on any curve card, or who wishes to see just what figures are included and what are excluded in making up any grand totals. The use of the serial numbered information card gives full information in condensed and easily accessible form.

Chapter XIV

RECORDS FOR THE EXECUTIVE

A GOOD executive has been described as a man who decides quickly and who is sometimes right. Probably ninety per cent of the answers "Yes" or "No" given by a business man are based on opinion rather than on fact. The trouble is that the average executive cannot obtain and analyze facts quickly enough to base his decision on them. He is forced to decide quickly and his one hope is that he will guess "right".

The problems confronting the executives have grown, in the last few years, to such an extent in volume and in complexity that it is increasingly difficult to find men with endurance and capacity great enough to match the jobs. The executives of our corporations, the men who are mayors of our cities, and the men in active charge of the government of our country are, without exception, the hardest worked men in the world. The stoker heaving coal into the furnaces of an express steamer has a better chance for long life than the man who accepts the presidency of even our best managed railroads and industrial corporations. The stoker can at least sleep soundly at the end of his day's work. The railroad president is likely to be kept awake wondering whether his guess was a good one, whether his decision was "right".

The men now steering the courses of our big corporations are men who have come up the line, step by step, through each department. They know accurately the relation of every department to every other department in their own company. They have available, also, a tremendous fund of information as to what has been accomplished by their competitors. The present executives of corporations are fortunate, in that they have seen, in their own business experience, each of the steps toward the greater division of labor and the consolidation of executive control which have done so much to make economic production possible by large-scale production.

The present executives are extremely fortunate in that they had an opportunity to develop themselves at the same time that their jobs grew bigger. What are we going to do ten years hence, when executives who have had such thorough training have all retired or have been killed off by the strain of the job? Where shall we find men with broad enough knowledge and experience to decide, instantly and correctly, each problem placed before them?

The answer is that the executive of the future will be forced to depend on the analysis of facts which have been collected and arranged for his instantaneous and continuous use. The executive of the future will decide quickly, and he will be more than "sometimes" right, because he will base his decisions on the analysis of actual facts. His value as an executive will depend chiefly upon his powers of accurate analysis.

Corporation directors are changing rapidly these days. Suppose a new director were to come into your corporation, what could you show him of the history and present standing of your business that would permit him to give an intelligent director's vote within a year of his election to the board?

It is perfectly feasible to focus a whole business into records so simple that a trained man could see, in half a day, all the important tendencies well enough to give an intelligent director's vote. This, too, without a spoken word of explanation from anyone. The records themselves could tell the complete story in every detail if placed in proper graphic form. It is the purpose of this chapter to show how such a thing may be done.

Fig. 217 shows a standard 4-by-6-inch filing case used to file curve cards and information cards. The right-hand drawer shows the 4-by-6-inch cards filed with appropriate guide cards. In this particular case, the guides give the names of branch houses by cities. The left-hand drawer shows the 4-by-12-inch cards filed according to the location of factories. As factory payrolls must be watched closely, weekly records of the payrolls were kept for this corporation, though monthly curves were found to be sufficient for the sales. There is no difficulty in filing the 4-by-12-inch cards in a standard 4-by-6-inch filing cabinet. The follow-up block in the drawer is placed 12 inches from the end of the drawer, then the cards are filed lengthwise with a sufficient quantity of blank cards at the back to keep all the cards in an upright position. Of course a special filing cabinet 12 inches wide can be made if desired, but it is not really necessary. In a cabinet like that shown in Fig. 217, the original curve cards would ordinarily be filed behind the guide cards showing the factory or selling-house locations, or behind guide cards showing the names of departments in any large business. All the cards for succeeding years would be filed behind the proper guide cards, with the curve card for the earlier year at the front. Having the card for the earlier year at the front instead of at the back permits comparison of curves for different years with a very slight lifting of the cards, and without any danger of the cards being put back in the drawer in mixed order.

Information cards like those shown in Fig. 216 would be filed in the same filing cabinet. These 4-by-6-inch information cards are filed by curve serial numbers, with appropriate numbered guide cards so that any information card may be quickly located by its serial number. As the numbered information cards are needed only for occasional reference, they can be put in the back portion of a file drawer, leaving the front portion of the drawer available for the curve cards more frequently needed.

In checking up the condition of his business, the executive usually considers it department by department. For this reason the original curve cards should be filed by departments so that the complete history of any department may be had from the cards behind the guide card for that department. A large portion of the executive's work, however, involves the study of his general business not by departments but by functions. For instance, the executive may wish to know how many employees he has in his whole business, and how many employees there are in each department, if he is considering the departmental increases or decreases which affect the total payroll. It is therefore desirable that the executive should have available for instant reference a cross-index of information which will show his whole business by function instead of by department. Such a cross-index can easily be provided, when curve cards are used, by taking a blue print of each curve card and then filing the blue print by function, instead of by department. In such an arrangement, there would be a complete set of guide cards giving different headings, such as "Number of Employees", "Total Sales", "Total Expenses", etc., with guide cards having suitable sub-headings placed behind each one of the main guide cards. A blue print of the curve showing the total number of employees in the corporation would be filed at the front of the division for employees. Back of this total card would be filed blue prints showing the employees in each department of the whole plant. Thus, if a total card at the front showed that the employees were increasing, the manager could refer to each one of the department cards filed immediately back of the total card to see in just which departments there had been an increase during the last month, and in which department there had been a decrease.

Fig. 217. A Standard 4-inch by 6-inch Filing Case Is Used for the Curve Cards. Cards Twelve Inches Long Can Be Filed Lengthwise in a Drawer without Inconvenience

Guide cards separate the curve cards by departments. If desired, blue prints can be made from each curve card and the blue prints filed by expense-account numbers, as a cross-index of the data on the white cards which are filed by departments

In a similar manner, the blue print showing total expenses would have filed back of it cards showing the detailed expenses by departments or by account numbers. If expenses had increased the manager could refer to the departmental or account-number cards and see just which departments or accounts were responsible for an increase or decrease in the curve giving the total. The cards in a large business would be filed by expense-account numbers, with the total card referring to any expense account for the whole business filed at the front of each group of cards giving the figures for that expense account by departments. Thus, in a manufacturing plant, the card showing the loss from spoiled work as a percentage of the total payroll could have filed back of it cards showing the percentage loss in each department. If the spoiled-work curve for the whole business should go up in any month, the manager could see instantly in which departments the percentage of loss had increased and in which the percentage had decreased. Letters could be sent to the foremen of the departments having bad records, calling their attention to the bad showing made.

The cross-index of curves, obtained by filing the cards according to function or by expense-account number instead of by department, is of tremendous importance to the busy executive. This feature alone may save a large amount of his time by making necessary information more accessible, and by affording information which may show leaks in his business that he would otherwise never know to exist. In a business of any size the cost of making one blue print each month from each original curve card is almost insignificant. The guide cards showing functions or account numbers remain useful year after year, and it is necessary only to discard a blue print for each card each month and to substitute the latest blue print made from the original curve card after a new point has been added. Having the original cards filed by departments and the blue prints filed by function or account number, the manager may instantly consider his business from whichever point of view he desires. He may study the whole operation of a given department, or he may study one function or expense account in its effect upon his business as a whole.

Practically every company which does an annual business of $1,000,000 or more would find it a paying proposition to have a room reserved in the office as a general record or information department regarding all the facts of the business. Though such a room might be combined with a technical library for books relating to the particular art or industry in which the company finds its field of operation, it is advisable to have the amount of furnishings in the room limited so that there may be no likelihood of valuable confidential papers being lost or misplaced. Such a room really needs to have no more furniture than filing cases like those shown in Fig. 217, a large table, and a drawing table or a flat desk for the man who plots curves.

It would be the function of a man having an office like that described to collect for the business all the data and facts which would be of any assistance to the executive, the officers, or the department heads. Most of his work would relate, of course, to getting data and plotting curves for all the operating reports of different departments of the business. The operating reports regularly furnished by the accounting departments of the business would be gone through carefully, and figures transcribed from these reports to the curve cards mentioned previously. There could also be in the record room a series of maps, large wall charts in the form of curves, and perhaps loose-leaf books or large vertical card files for cumulative curves such as are shown in Fig. 134. Since the information contained in this room is practically a history of every phase of the business, it would be desirable to have the room enclosed with fire-proof walls and fire-proof doors and equipped with fire-proof file cases and furniture so that the destruction of the records by fire would be absolutely impossible. As good light is essential in such a room, large windows are necessary. The windows can ordinarily be sufficiently protected against fire by using polished plate glass reinforced with wire to prevent breaking of the glass from fire in adjoining buildings.

The title given the man who does the work described is really not important. Ordinarily, in a large corporation, he would be ranked as assistant to the president, as he should report only to the chief executive officer in the particular office in which he is located. He could, if desired, be given the title of chief of the record department, or, in a larger business where much specialized information is sought from outside sources, the title of "statistician" might be justified. In the work of most corporations it would soon be found desirable to have a man of the type described collect and record, for convenient use, data from sources entirely outside of the business itself. Most companies have to buy large quantities of raw material which fluctuates greatly in price. To assist in making decisions relating to purchases, it would usually be found desirable to have curves plotted for the chief materials entering into the finished product, such as pig iron, copper, tin, zinc, cotton, lumber, coal, etc. Very desirable information could also be obtained concerning the business conditions of the country as a whole. Since practically every business is affected by the general waves of financial prosperity and depression, a good man in this position could be of great assistance to the chief executive, by carefully studying some series of curves (which might, after long experience, prove to be the best barometer available) to indicate changes for better or worse in the general financial conditions affecting the particular business in question.

In a business of ordinary size, the yearly outlay for an office like that described and a man to run it would be comparatively small. It would probably be best to get a young man graduated within a few years from one of the technical schools, or from one of the schools of business administration now established as separate departments in several of the large universities. If a man of the right type were told that he would report directly to the chief executive, and that he would have a confidential position with complete access to the records of every department of the whole business including both manufacturing and selling, he would be quite willing to start the work at a reasonable salary, knowing full well that the opportunities given would soon permit him to demonstrate his ability. A recent college graduate could be obtained for $20 or $25 per week, as he would see for himself that there would be chances for him to make himself worth much more inside of the first year or so.

A man starting a record department of the type described would at first find his chief work in getting records for a series of years so that comparisons would be possible. In most corporations it is extremely difficult to get any kind of good records further than two years back, because of constant changes in personnel and changes in accounting systems without any reliable notes to tell just what these changes were and when they were made. In large manufacturing companies, subdivisions and changes in the expense accounts are likely to occur as new departments are added or as new men of different training in accounting come into control of the accounting procedure of the company. After the back records have been fairly well tabulated and plotted in the form of curves, the work of keeping the curves up to date would be comparatively simple. One man can add one more point monthly to several thousand different curves, and do also a certain amount of the clerical work involved in making up ratios, grand totals, etc. If a record file of curves like that shown in Fig. 217 is once made thoroughly up to date, for any business, it is easy to keep it up to date with only routine work such as any man of even ordinary mental caliber can do. Information cards 4-by-6-inch, such as are shown in Fig. 216, explain every step of the work required in plotting any curve, and even a new man just out of college would be able to follow the instructions well enough to take charge of a record system which some one else started. Thus, if it is desired after a year or two to promote a man who has built up a record system of this kind, it would be quite easy to have him break in a successor so that there would be no change in the methods of collecting data and plotting curves. This possibility of taking on a new college graduate every few years permits having an excellent record department, even for a small-size business in which it would be thought undesirable to spend more than $3,000 or $4,000 a year to cover the total yearly departmental cost.

It should be a strict rule for a record department of the type described that no original papers shall be taken from the room. The record department should be in a quiet place to which the president or any other official may retreat to get completely away from the distractions which are common in his own office because of the telephone and constant visitors. In the record room the executive would be free to concentrate his whole attention on the records of what his business has been doing in the last weeks or months, so that he may be able to formulate plans for the future. Though the arrangement of the files in the record room would be well known to the executive, so that he could lay his fingers instantly on any desired curve or other record, the chief of the record department would be at hand most of the time so the executive could send word ahead to have certain curves or other records laid out for instant reference when he arrived. To save time the executive should not be required to put back into the card files the curve cards which he has taken from any file drawer. By using a large table the executive could simply push to the other side of the table any cards which he may have laid out for careful comparison. The man who has charge of the room can later put the cards back in the files. There is an advantage in having one man put all the cards back in the files, as in this way there is less chance of the cards being misplaced in the file than if several different executive officers were to use the cards and themselves put the cards back. It should be stated here that in the ordinary use of curve files such as are shown in Fig. 217 an executive would not need to remove the cards from the drawer. He would simply turn the cards over one at a time, raising any card of special interest about three inches to look at it, but not removing it sufficiently to cause any danger of restoring the card in a wrong position. It is only when cards for a series of years are taken out and laid down for comparison with some other series of cards that there is any necessity for removing the cards from the drawer.

The Westinghouse Electric and Manufacturing Company of Pittsburgh regularly plot about four thousand curves which record the activities of all departments of the business. The majority of the curves have one more point added each month, but some of the curves are on a weekly basis. Day and Zimmermann, of Philadelphia, are plotting a total of about eight thousand curves, most of the curves on a cumulative basis somewhat as shown in Fig. 134. In order to allow space enough for a cumulative curve (which naturally takes up more room than a curve plotted on a non-cumulative basis), the curves are plotted on cards $8\frac{1}{2}$ inches by 11 inches, and these cards are filed vertically in a tray desk so that a man sitting at the desk can instantly lay his hand on the proper card for any one of the eight thousand curves. Guide cards are of course used to make card location easier. To prevent cards being replaced at some wrong position in the file, Day and Zimmermann have worked out the clever scheme of notching in a similar manner the tops of all cards which are filed in any one division of the file. When cards are filed one after another the notches of individual cards form a groove in the group of cards. If any card should be filed out of place it would break the continuity of the groove and would instantly be noticed. In using the notched-card scheme two notches may, if desired, be placed in the top of each card, thus permitting many more group combinations than would be possible if only one notch were used. The notches may be cut with a special instrument of rather simple construction so as to insure their uniform spacing right or left from the upper corners of the card. A notch in the form of a segment of a circle is the most satisfactory.

In order to keep the general rule that original curve cards shall not be taken out of the record room, it is well to provide means by which blue prints can be made quickly from any curve card. In a business of reasonable size, blue prints may easily be made with a small-size printing frame and sunlight printing, if the record room is located on the southern side of the building where there is sunlight most of the time. In large businesses electric blue-printing machines are a part of the regular equipment of the drafting office. If the drafting office is not near the record room, however, it may be well to equip the record room with an electric blue-printing machine and a small washing tank, so that blue prints of each card may be made without the necessity of taking confidential record cards out of the room. Photographic processes for copying records have recently been much improved. A machine called the photostat makes black and white copies quickly without the expense of glass negatives. With a blue-print machine or a photostat in the record room, it would be a very simple matter to copy periodically the complete current set of curves so that the cross-index of cards by function or account may be provided for the executive, as described in the preceding paragraphs.

The plan suggested for a record department sounds much more complex than it really is. In considering the space and expense necessary for such a department it must be borne in mind that the time of the chief executive of a modern corporation is of a great value—almost beyond computation. The value of the president's time in a large corporation cannot be figured out on the basis of his salary, for it is certainly true that the executives of large corporations receive salaries much less than the value of their services to their corporation. A single "yes" or "no" decision of the corporation executive usually involves a gain or loss in the earnings of the corporation greater than the executive's salary for a whole year. Anything that can be done to give the president and the other executives better and more quickly available information on which to base decisions is justifiable and should be installed practically without regard to cost.

In a large office it will be found desirable to give a number of department heads access to the record room. As no one would ever be admitted to this room except the chief executive, and department heads who were given written permission by the chief executive, there would be no danger of confidential information coming into the hands of outside parties. As it may not be desirable to have department heads in a business know anything about the finances of the company as a whole, or anything regarding the records of departments other than their own, it may be best to have the curve cards filed in several drawers with a separate drawer for the cards relating to the work of each department head. If the drawers are equipped with spring locks, each department head could have a key to his own drawer, yet it would be impossible for him to go through the records of departments other than his own. The chief executive would, of course, have a master key to all the drawers, so that he could compare the records of one department with the records of any other department whenever he desired. The presence of the man in charge of the record department would in itself tend to keep minor officials from going through the cards relating to bank deposits, earnings, etc., for the corporation as a whole. There would necessarily be times when the head of the information department would not be in the room while minor officials were there, and the expedient of locking up the summarized control curves for the whole corporation is therefore mentioned here as a possible safeguard.

Directors and executives change quite frequently in large corporations. When a new man comes into a corporation as an executive or a director, the value of his service to the corporation is at first practically nothing, and he may even for a while be considered a handicap to the corporation in that it is necessary for men who have been associated longer with the corporation to spend a great deal of their time in explaining to the new member the facts relating to the various departments and to the present scope of the business. This information is generally passed on from man to man by word of mouth. Usually there is no written statement giving in condensed form a bird's-eye view of the whole history and present field of the corporation. Broadly, it is now almost impossible for any new director in a corporation to give an intelligent director's vote on any proposition brought up within a year after he has joined the directorate.

It will not be long before every man holding the position of a corporation director or a corporation executive will be able to read, quickly and intelligently, simple curves and figures like those combined on the curve cards here. With a card-index file of curves and a record department like that described in this chapter, it should be possible for any trained man coming into a corporation as a new director or new official to give a fairly intelligent vote after only half a day's study of the curves, and this too without having spoken a single word to anyone. If the record department and the curves are properly kept, the whole situation would be shown on the face of the cards with far more clearness than it would ordinarily be possible to give by words alone, even if the whole history and present status of the corporation were told.

Consider the value of a record department like that suggested, if such a department were part of the equipment of the mayor's office of any city. The department could be maintained continuously by civil-service employees who could keep the records in standardized form year after year, no matter what shake-ups there might be in political parties and in spite of the numerous changes in personnel usual when one set of city officers follow another with great rapidity. In municipal work there would be no necessity for keeping any except the original curve cards under lock and key, as all the information would be public property and, of course, available to properly authorized persons. It would certainly make a great difference to any new mayor if he could go to a record room and study a set of curves showing, for instance, the total number of men in the employ of the city year after year under different administrations. He would be able to see over a period of years the number of men in each city department such as fire, police, street-cleaning, etc., together with the average rate of pay. He would also have complete information over a long series of years regarding taxable property in the city, tax rates, total population, death rates, etc. All this information would be available instantly, not only to the mayor but to each member of the council, who might apply to the record department very much as he would apply to any good reference library when in search of information. The only rule necessary would be that no curve cards should leave the room. To safeguard information files to which numerous councilmen have access, it would be wise to use only blue prints in the open files, keeping the original cards in separate locked files, available only to the man who plots the data on each card, point by point, as information is received. Councilmen, civic organizations, newspapers, etc., wanting copies of any record card should be able to get blue prints or photographs at a nominal charge of say ten cents per card copy. The New York Public Library is successfully working a plan by which photographs of any page of any book in the library can be provided to readers in a few hours at a cost of only twenty-five cents per page. A similar plan could be used for the suggested copies of official curve records.

Progress in the government of the world, and especially in the government of cities and of industrial corporations, has been greatly retarded by the fact that the only information available to executive officers has been provided to the executive in the form which is most convenient for the use of the accountant. It is, of course, necessary that records should be kept accurately from the standpoint of good accounting, and the author has no complaint to make of accounting methods in so far as accuracy is concerned. It is not, however, right that executive officers who must determine policies and who must make instant decisions should be forced to base all their decisions on information provided to them only in the form of the accountant's standard arrangement of balance sheet and operating statement.

The accountant must necessarily take a bird's-eye view of the whole business from time to time, so that he may see how all the component parts add together, to make certain that he gets a balance. The result is that the accounting officer usually makes up a periodic report, in which he gives at the end of any month or at the end of any year a complete bird's-eye statement of the status of the business at that particular time. Because of the nature of his problems, the executive's mind must necessarily work in a manner absolutely different from that of the mind of the accountant. The executive does not often want a bird's-eye view of his whole business at any one period of time. What the executive must have is a cross-index of the accountant's information, so that he may see over a long period of time the whole history of any portion of his business. Most managers are forced to work from the accountants' monthly statement, and their procedure is accordingly to go through the separate operating statements for several months and take off on scratch pads the figures for the items in which they may be particularly interested at the moment. These figures may have to be added together in order to compare a certain number of months this year with the same months of last year. This work not only takes the time of the highest paid man in the organization, but the hasty scratch-pad figures are likely to contain errors. It is absurd that executive officers should be forced to make their own cross-indexes of the accountant's statement, and not only make these cross-indexes but make them while holding the long-distance telephone or at other rush times when seconds are important.

The information as it comes from the accountant's office should be passed to the man in the executive department whose function it is to provide information for the executive by cross-indexing all information from the accountant's reports and putting this information in the form of curves. The accountant's report would, of course, be filed carefully for future reference purposes if reference is ever necessary, but for the purposes of the executive the curve cards with the figures they contain are sufficient. Not only is the information for any subject shown on the cards as a curve over a long period of time, but the actual figures of the accountant's report are visible in such manner that they may be found instantly and quoted directly from the curve cards without having to refer back month by month to the original figures in the accountant's report.

The manager or chief executive of any business using curves in order to keep in close touch with all departments will find that he needs a liberal education in logic to enable him to draw the correct conclusions quickly from the large number of facts available. There are certain general principles which are gradually being recognized, and which within the next few years will doubtless be well enough known to classify and make available for the executive's use. At present, however, each executive must work out for himself his own means of recording data and of determining policies in operating his business. An example showing some of the difficulties involved in correct interpretation is one concerning overhead-expense ratios. Some managers consider the ratio of indirect expenses to the direct labor in any department of a manufacturing business as an infallible barometer by which each department of the business can be run. They little realize the absurdity of paying too much attention to overhead-expense ratios and the danger to the business of using overhead-expense ratios as a yard-stick by which to measure accomplishment. In this particular case, that of a large manufacturing plant, a new department manager changed the manufacturing methods so radically that he was able to produce an increased output with less than half the former payroll for direct labor. The expenses for the foremen, clerks, supplies, etc., in the department remained about the same as before. Because of the reduced amount of direct labor the overhead-expense ratio was of course doubled, much to the astonishment of the chief executive, who accordingly considered this department as the worst managed in his whole works. This executive had been running his plant for so many years on the expense-ratio basis that the new department head found it almost impossible to convince the chief executive that the department was making money more rapidly than ever before, even though the overhead-expense ratio had doubled. The overhead expense itself had not increased, and the ratio was doubled simply because the amount of direct labor had been decreased.

It is perhaps worth while to point out here that there is danger in giving too much information and too many facts to executives of small brain capacity who do not know how to use their authority intelligently. Curves such as those described in this and the preceding chapter, placed for the first time in the hands of the executive who does not know the technology or the general underlying principles of the business which he controls, are likely to prompt such a narrow-minded director to send out a regular deluge of letters unjustly criticising the actions of his subordinates. There is a possibility that a small-caliber man in the manager's chair may send out too much destructive criticism and not enough constructive criticism. If such a misfortune should occur it would cause every department head in the organization to withhold information and consider the whole curve-record system as a new form of diabolical torture. Curves are not intended to give any chief executive an excuse to "jump on" any department manager or foreman. The curve records are intended only to point out those danger points at which construction work is needed. An executive of the right type will soon realize as he uses the curves that he must do the constructive work himself, and that the curves will really have more effect in changing the procedure in his own office than in changing the detailed routine in the departments of his various subordinates.

One of the first tasks confronting any modern executive is that of training, on the one hand, his board of directors and executive committee, and on the other hand, his various department heads and their subordinates, to read curves accurately so that the facts presented may be intelligently grasped and applied to the benefit of the business as a whole. It is unfortunate that so many men serving to-day on boards of directors and in executive positions of large businesses are not able to read even the simplest curve with any real grasp of the facts portrayed. Engineers and other trained men who have real facts available are tremendously handicapped in presenting the facts if it is not feasible to use the graphic method of presentation. A man prepared to show his data in the form of curves, for example like Fig. 157 or Fig. 159, feels that he would have an almost hopeless task to convey the vital facts if only spoken words might be used. The writer ventures to predict that within ten years practically all corporation directors and executives will be able to interpret curves with satisfaction to themselves and with great benefit to their business. The executive who cannot read curves will in the near future be the exception rather than the rule.

If any general manager will take the trouble to train his department heads to read curves and will then supply to them curves showing the facts of his business, he will be tremendously repaid in the interest, enthusiasm, and real progress toward improvement which will be aroused in his men.

It is possible to use a reflecting lantern like that pictured in Fig. 218 to show on a screen the curves from the curve cards described in Chapter XIII. Lantern slides are not practicable when frequent meetings of department heads must be held. The expense of making lantern slides each time a new point is plotted on each curve would be too great for even the largest corporations. Another disadvantage of using lantern slides is the impossibility of getting slides made quickly enough to represent always the latest points plotted on the curves. By using the original curve cards directly in the reflecting lantern there is always a certainty that the picture shown on the screen represents the very latest data which are available in curve form. When these curve cards are used in a reflecting lantern a simple slide carriage is made

Fig. 218. Reflectoscope as Made by A. T. Thompson & Co., Boston, Mass.

Lantern slides may be used as shown at the top of the picture. The stand holding the book may be replaced by a simple carriage arranged to take the 4-by-6-inch and the 4-by-12-inch curve cards. The very latest data from the file shown in Fig. 217 may then be instantly reflected onto a screen for use in a meeting of the department heads of a business.

to replace the stand holding the book in Fig. 218. As the card is laid down flat in its natural position and in plain view of the operator, there is no likelihood of cards being put into the machine incorrectly. If a carriage about two feet long is used, the carriage may be moved alternately from right to left, and while one side contains the cards which are being reflected on the screen, the other side may be loaded with the cards next desired. On account of its length the carriage will hold curve cards for several succeeding years. By pushing the carriage slowly across the lantern the fluctuation in any curve may be shown for as long a series of years as may be desired. Simple spring clips on the carriage may be used to hold the overlapping cards in their exact position. Not only are the curves themselves shown on the screen, but the whole face of the card is seen so that the figures for any points on the curve which are of special interest may be read directly from the screen.

If the information or record room is large enough to serve for holding conferences the lantern and the screen may be installed permanently as part of its equipment. Ordinarily, however, it will be found best to have the record room more private than any room used for general conferences can be made, and the lantern would be part of the equipment of the conference room rather than of the record room. With this arrangement it will be necessary to take the curve cards from the record room to the place where the lantern is installed. The file for the curve cards (see Fig. 217) had better be equipped with spring locks so that there will be no danger, when the file is carried, of drawers slipping out and spilling the cards. A rod arrangement is never desirable with such cards as these, for the rod would spoil the bottom portion of the card and would also make it impossible to lift cards out for quick reference or comparison. Brass handles on the sides of the file case would make it easy to carry the case to the conference room. There, on a table beside the lantern, the cards in the file case would be available for use almost exactly as lantern slides are used with the ordinary lantern. In fact, the arrangement of the cards is even more convenient than the usual arrangement of lantern slides in that the cards have a guide index so that any desired card may be instantly located.

An executive who wishes to have a meeting of his department heads need not make any very definite plan before the meeting begins as to what cards he is to show on the screen. He can start talking to his men, and, at pleasure, ask the lantern operator (ordinarily the statistician) for any set of curve cards which may be of interest to him at the moment, or which may be referred to at any time during the discussion. The use of curves on a lantern screen in the manner suggested would entirely revolutionize the meetings of the department heads of a business, or the meetings of branch-house sales managers. In sales work especially, the use of the various cards would make it possible to show the whole assembly the recent records made by selling houses in the different parts of the country. The cards for those houses which made particularly good records could be shown, the records could be commended, and conclusions could be drawn as to how the success had been attained. Records for the less successful houses could also

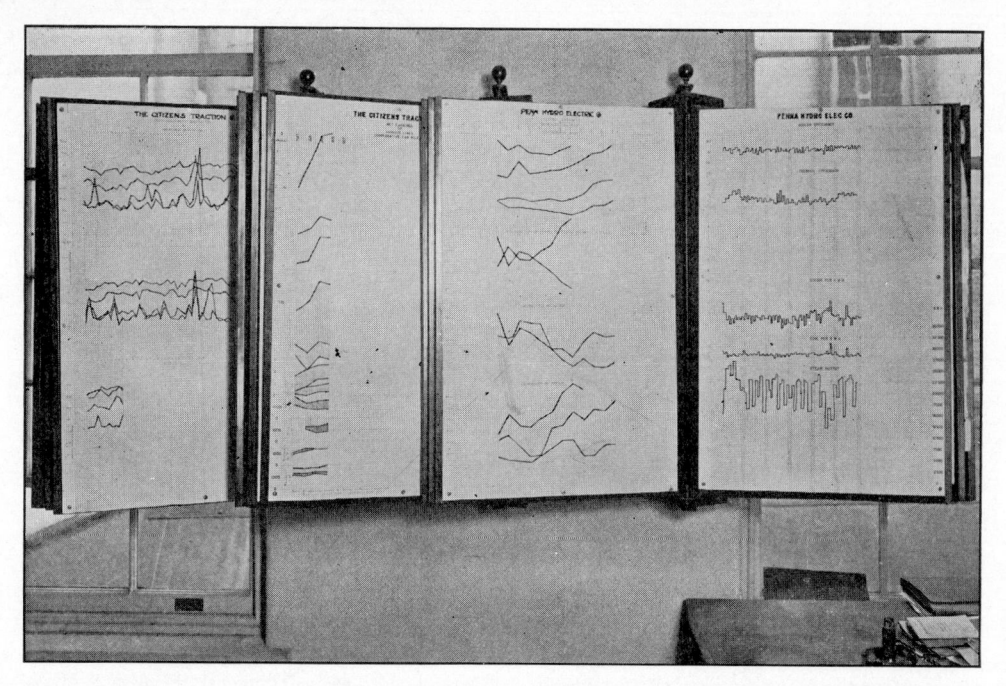

Fig. 219. Curves on Swinging-leaf Display Fixtures Used for Ready Reference in the Office of Day and Zimmermann, Philadelphia. Each Leaf May Be Easily Carried to a Desk when Additional Points Are to Be Plotted on the Curves

This same type of display fixture is often convenient for showing pin maps of different territories

be shown, with comments by the sales manager giving his own suggestions and asking for suggestions from the other branch-house managers present.

Reflecting lanterns can be used at directors' meetings as soon as corporation directors know how to read curves. By using the lantern, the president could show facts relating to the business much more rapidly, much more clearly, and with greater accuracy than would be possible with any spoken words. The showing of curves would give the directors a chance to check the president's statements so that there would be less danger than at present of a corporation president so choosing his words that, though the words might be strictly truthful in themselves, they would be over-optimistic because they did not tell all the truth. The presence of the whole file of curve cards immediately beside the lantern would enable any director to call for facts relating to any phase of the business on which he might desire information. The use of these curve cards, and a lantern, would permit a properly educated set of directors really to direct the business for which they are responsible to the stockholders.

It is sometimes desirable to have the chief facts relating to a business plotted on wall charts which are instantly visible in a conference room. Fig. 219 was photographed in the record room which adjoins the directors' room of Day and Zimmermann, of Philadelphia. On the swinging-leaf fixtures a series of curves are plotted giving all the salient facts relating to a group of public-service corporations. Though this type of wall chart is in many cases desirable, there are limitations to the use of wall charts because the number of charts cannot be sufficiently increased to give all the detailed information which is usually necessary. Wall charts are suitable chiefly to furnish summarized information to directors or other men whose time is limited or who come to an office only at rare intervals.

Wall exhibits of curves can sometimes be used with satisfactory results if special care is taken to draw the curves on a very large scale and arrange them on all four walls of a room. A prominent financier of New York City is said to have a large room, on the top floor of his residence, where the walls are completely covered with curve charts on which points are plotted as rapidly as data can be obtained. This man is so limited for time that he keeps in touch with general financial conditions by referring to the charts in this room for only a brief time each evening. He disappears to his reference room to meet his private secretary immediately after dinner. In the center of the room is a revolving desk chair with an ash tray fastened to one arm. For the length of one cigar the financier sits in his chair slowly revolving the chair until he has covered the information given on all of the wall charts, perhaps, if necessary, asking a few brief questions of his secretary. Though very little of the financier's time is taken, he is able by concentrated thought on the facts shown by his wall charts to keep in full touch with world finance and to map out his own plans for future operation.

Chapter XV

CORPORATION FINANCIAL REPORTS

THE annual report of a corporation is usually mailed to each stockholder. The report, as commonly gotten up, contains practically nothing except a brief statement by the president in regard to the last year's business, together with the balance sheet and operating statement furnished by the accounting officers of the company, and perhaps an audit by some firm of certified public accountants. The report sent to a stockholder is essentially in that form necessary for the auditor to check the financial figures and to certify to their being in balance and correct.

Though the balance sheet and operating statement, with the letter of approval by the certified public accountant, are necessary and desirable, they do not contain, in themselves, the information most desirable and most intelligible to the average stockholder. What the stockholder needs most is a report from which he can make comparison with preceding years. The bankers and large investors who can preserve in their files annual reports of a corporation over a long period of years probably number less than one per cent of the total number of stockholders to whom the annual reports are sent. It is only in very large, well managed offices that a file of corporation reports is made so that a complete set of reports for a long period of years is available for comparison with any new report which may be received. The average stockholder cannot preserve his annual reports from year to year in such manner that he can lay his hands on the earlier reports, and thus compare the last report with the record of preceding years. Even if every stockholder should have some yet uninvented type of filing system by which everything is preserved and everything can be found instantly when needed, that would not solve the problem. Stockholders are changing so rapidly that, of the total number of stockholders to whom reports are sent in any one year, a comparatively small percentage have been stockholders for more than two or three years. Because they have not been stockholders for any length of time, they cannot have available the annual reports of earlier years to compare with any annual report just received. The only way a new stockholder can possibly determine whether he wishes to buy some more stock or sell what stock he already has, is to hunt up some other stockholder or some banker who may happen to have a file of the annual reports over a period of years. Assuming that a complete file of annual reports can be found, most stockholders, if left to their own resources, would be hopelessly confused in trying to reach any correct basis for analyzing the figures. Each stockholder would have to take a sheet of paper and copy off, into different columns for various important items of the operating statement and balance sheet, figures for a number of years so that the figures for different years could all be seen at one time and compared. This means that each stockholder would have to make practically a cross-index of the most important data contained in a series of annual reports in order to study the different phases of operation independently. Even if the stockholder should know how to make such a cross-index properly, there are very few stockholders who would be willing to give the time and the mental effort requisite to make a tabulated comparison of the kind necessary.

The absorption of good securities by the public has increased in the last ten years at a tremendous rate. *The Wall Street Journal* has compiled statistics of the stockholders of the larger railway and industrial corporations showing that the numbers have grown as follows:

1901	227,000
1906	431,000
1911	865,000
1913	1,250,000

Mr. Samuel Rea, the president of the Pennsylvania Railroad, recently stated that there are nearly 100,000 stockholders in the Pennsylvania Railroad and its affiliated companies, and that the number of its bondholders probably exceeded 200,000. Therefore, if there are 1,250,000 stockholders of the railways and industrial corporations, there are doubtless considerably more than 2,000,000 bondholders. Though there are many duplications in these figures, the fact remains that the prosperity of probably 3,000,000 investors is largely dependent upon the success of these corporations.

While the number of stockholders has been increasing, the average holdings of each stockholder have been steadily decreasing, and now average ninety-eight shares. The stocks of the United States Steel Corporation are great favorites among small investors. Taking the stockholders' list, it was found that among one hundred people, chosen at random, only nine own one hundred shares, or over, of both preferred and common stock, while forty-seven have less than ten shares each.

It is highly desirable that corporations should not only keep their old stockholders, but should attract new ones. The surest way to accomplish this end is to treat stockholders with the utmost frankness. Although considerable publicity is already given to the affairs of the larger corporations, further publicity is desirable. The average stockholder does not as a rule understand a balance sheet, and has only the vaguest idea of his company's affairs. So long as dividend payments are maintained, he is content. To be sure, a stockholder can always get an impartial and valuable opinion from an investment banker concerning the past records and future prospects of any company, but it would be well if the annual reports of boards of directors to stockholders contained material from which the investor could judge for himself to a greater extent. The material included should show the records of the company over a period of years, for the company's achievement in any one year may be unnecessarily discouraging, or fictitiously encouraging. These records are most easily understood when put in graphic form. With such graphic presentations any stockholder can learn instantly how the fiscal year under review compares with the several years preceding.

The American Telephone and Telegraph Company have for several years shown on the back cover of their annual report a chart like Fig. 249 portraying the growth in their business. Fig. 2 also appeared in an annual report of the same corporation to give a clear conception of what becomes of the company's revenue.

Though Fig. 1 has not been used in any annual report, it shows a type of chart which could very readily be included in a financial report to give complete facts to stockholders regarding complex conditions on which the average stockholder would gather very little information from the kind of corporation financial report ordinarily sent to him.

The railroads have used charts in their annual reports to a greater extent than the industrial corporations. Some of the railroad charts, however, are not put up in such form as to be easily understood and, with many of the charts, there is danger of misinterpretation. For instance, it is not at all easy to analyze Fig. 220 so that its four different subjects may be compared.

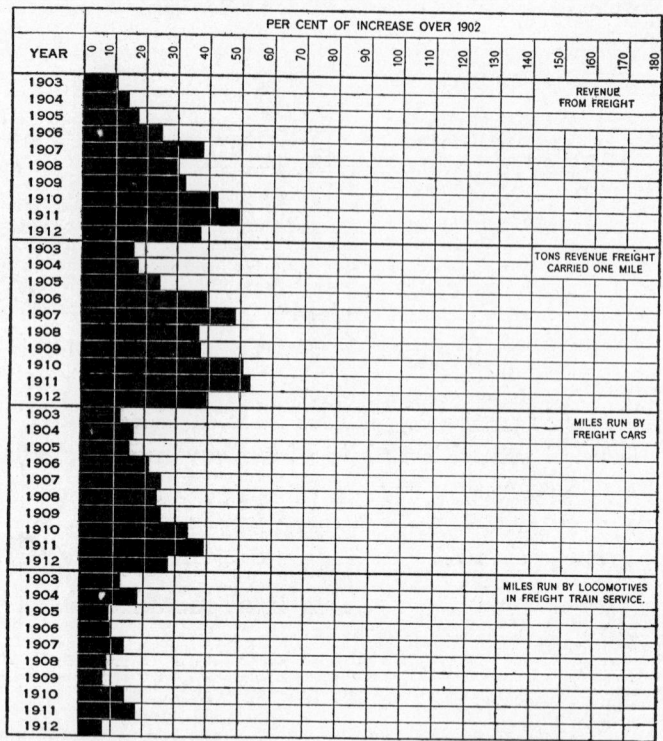

Fig. 220. Percentage Increase in Freight Service on the Illinois Central Railroad Since 1902. This Illustration Was Taken from the 1912 Annual Report of the Company

Four distinct subjects are treated in this chart, but the horizontal bars are arranged in such manner that the reader is likely to think there is only one subject. Probably most readers would prefer to turn the chart so that it may be read from the left-hand edge as four separate curves. To a trained reader this information would be much more clear if put in the form of curves like those seen in Figs. 224, 225, 226, 227

Fig. 221 also shows several different subjects which should be compared, but for which comparison is not very feasible on the chart as given. In Fig. 220 the four different subjects were so widely separated that comparisons were almost impossible, while in Fig. 221 the four different subjects have the bars so arranged that it is difficult for the eye to follow any one subject through the maze of bars.

In Fig. 222 the method of presentation is somewhat similar to that used in Fig. 221. As seen in Fig. 222, however, the bars are

CORPORATION FINANCIAL REPORTS 311

arranged horizontally with the earlier year at the bottom, while in Fig. 221 the bars are arranged vertically with the earlier year at the right. In both of these charts the arrangement for successive years is incorrect, for the charts give the impression that all quantities portrayed are becoming less instead of greater as years go on. The indiscriminate mixture of so many different kinds of bars in one chart makes a complex diagram to interpret, and it is probable that the chart would at least be no more difficult to apprehend if made entirely in the form of curves i n s t e a d of bars. Though it is true that curves are not understood by some people who can readily grasp the bar method of presentation, there is no use in keeping to the bar method if the bar presentation is made as complex as a chart involving curves.

Fig. 223 was not printed in a corporation annual report, but it is included here because it may show some possibility for the inclusion of curves in financial reports to give the stockholder more complete information than he would otherwise receive. The data of Fig. 223 are of interest when considered along with the charts seen in Fig. 224, Fig. 225, Fig. 226, and Fig. 227. Fig. 223 is, however, misleading because the vertical scale does not extend to zero and the chart gives the impression of a much larger percentage difference between net earnings and dividends than really

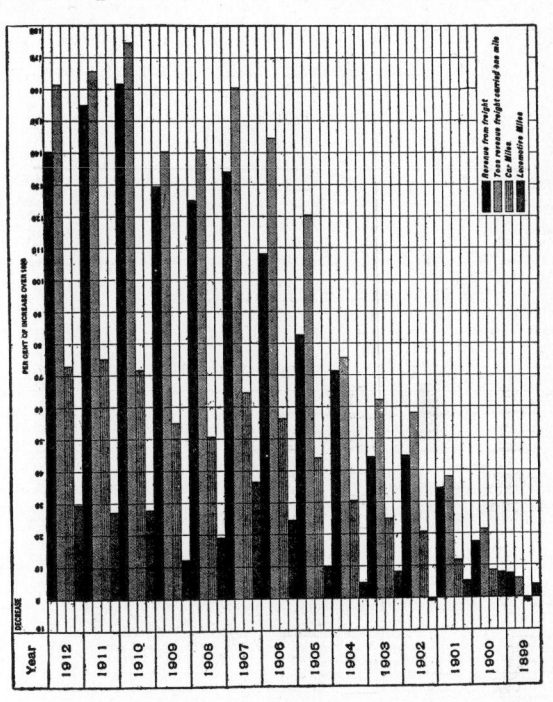

Fig. 221. Freight Service and Traffic on the Union Pacific Railroad and Auxiliary Companies

This chart shows by years the per cent of increase over the year ended June 30, 1898, in the gross revenue from the transportation of commercial freight, the number of tons of commercial freight carried one mile, and the number of miles run by cars and locomotives in freight-train service. Locomotive miles include revenue freight-train miles, all mixed-train miles, and helping-train miles

The illustration is reduced from the 1912 annual report to stockholders. The backward arrangement of years from right to left causes the first impression that all quantities are growing less instead of greater. Four subjects shown combined in one chart in this manner are confusing. Either four distinct groups of bars or four curves would be superior to the method used here

existed. Omitting the bottom of the chart makes the dividends appear a smaller percentage of net earnings than they really were. Fig. 223 could have been considerably improved, also, if the line showing net earnings were made much heavier than it is seen in the illustration.

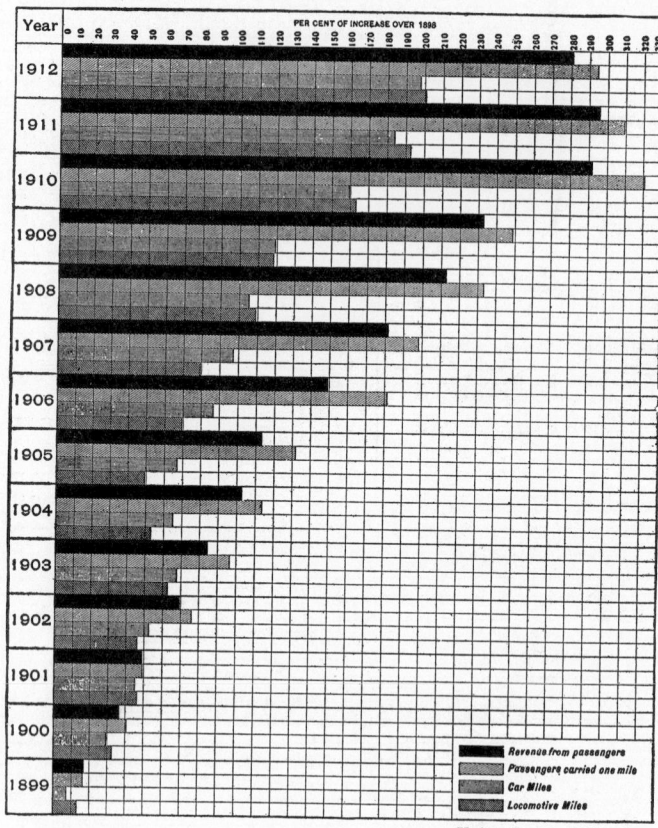

Fig. 222. Passenger Service and Traffic on the Union Pacific Railroad and Auxiliary Companies

This chart shows by years the per cent of increase over the year ended June 30, 1898, in the gross revenue from the transportation of passengers, the number of passengers carried one mile, and the number of miles run by cars and locomotives in passenger-train service. Locomotive miles include revenue passenger-train miles, all mixed-train miles and helping passenger-train miles, but do not include miles run by motor cars

Here the reversed arrangement with the latest year at the top gives the erroneous impression that passenger business is decreasing. A chart like this does not assist greatly in conveying information to the stockholder

What figures for an annual report should always be shown in chart form to make comparisons most clear is hard to determine, but it will doubtless be agreed that, if possible, the charts should

CORPORATION FINANCIAL REPORTS 313

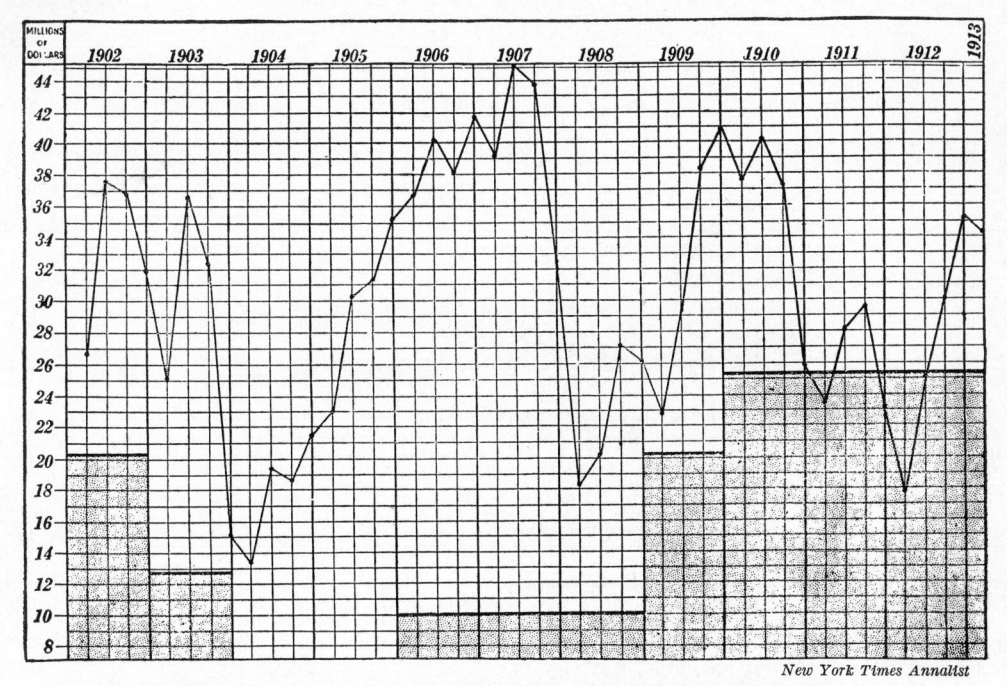

Fig. 223. Net Earnings and Dividends of the United States Steel Corporation

The figures for net earnings are plotted by quarters. Dividend figures are plotted to show the total dividends each year. The line at the top of the shaded area shows the dividend paid. Dividends exceed net earnings in portions of the years 1911 and 1912, but the total earnings of those years were nevertheless great enough to justify maintaining the dividend rate

Though this illustration contains some interesting information, the chart is misleading because the scale does not extend to zero. At first glance, the dividend of 1909 would seem to be more than four times the dividend of 1908 when in reality it is only about twice as large

attempt an answer to these questions that naturally arise in the stockholder's mind:

1. Has the earning power of the company been maintained?
2. Is the property being kept in proper physical condition?
3. Is the financial condition sound?

For the purpose of illustrating the advantages of the graphic method for annual reports, the United States Steel Corporation has been selected. The chart shown in Fig. 224 is designed to answer the first question: "Has the earning power of the company been maintained?" In order to bring out more clearly the very important relation between the surplus for dividends and the dividends paid, curves Nos. 3 and 4 are redrawn on a considerably enlarged scale as seen in Fig. 225. Curves No. 3 and No. 5 are therefore identical, as are also curves No. 4 and No. 6.

Fig. 224 and Fig. 225 show that the Steel Corporation, like a large number of railways and industrial companies, reached the zenith

314   GRAPHIC METHODS

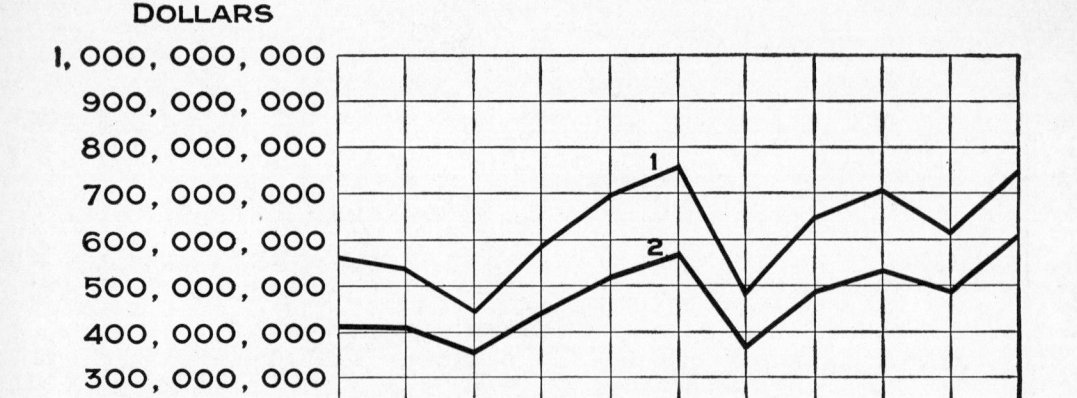

Fig. 224. The Earning Power of the United States Steel Corporation

Curve 1. Gross earnings
Curve 2. Operating expenses
Curve 3. Surplus earned available for dividends
Curve 4. Preferred and common dividends paid

This chart and the following charts relating to the United States Steel Corporation are submitted as a suggestion to show how the annual report of a corporation could easily give comparisons over several years. The space required for the charts is insignificant, yet the stockholders would receive the vital facts in such form as to permit a full understanding of the condition of their company as compared with previous years

of its earning power in the year 1907. In that year more than 15 per cent was earned on the common stock, while only 2 per cent was paid. Curve No. 1 shows that the gross earnings in 1907 were $757,-000,000. Then follows, in 1908, the terrific slump in business due to the financial panic, with a gradual but uncertain recovery. By 1912, the corporation succeeded in bringing its gross business up to $745,-000,000, still somewhat under the 1907 high-water mark.

The movement of operating expenses is depicted by curve No. 2. A glance at the chart shows that, during 1905–6–7, gross earnings tended to increase faster than operating expenses, which is again true in 1909 and 1910. In 1908 and 1911, it proved impossible to reduce operating expenses to conform to the reduction in gross earnings, with the result that profits were sharply reduced in both these years. In 1912, a unique situation occurs. Curves 1 and 2 run practically parallel, showing that although the gross earnings were largely increased, operating expenses kept pace. The largest factor in operating expenses is naturally labor, and the reports of the corporation

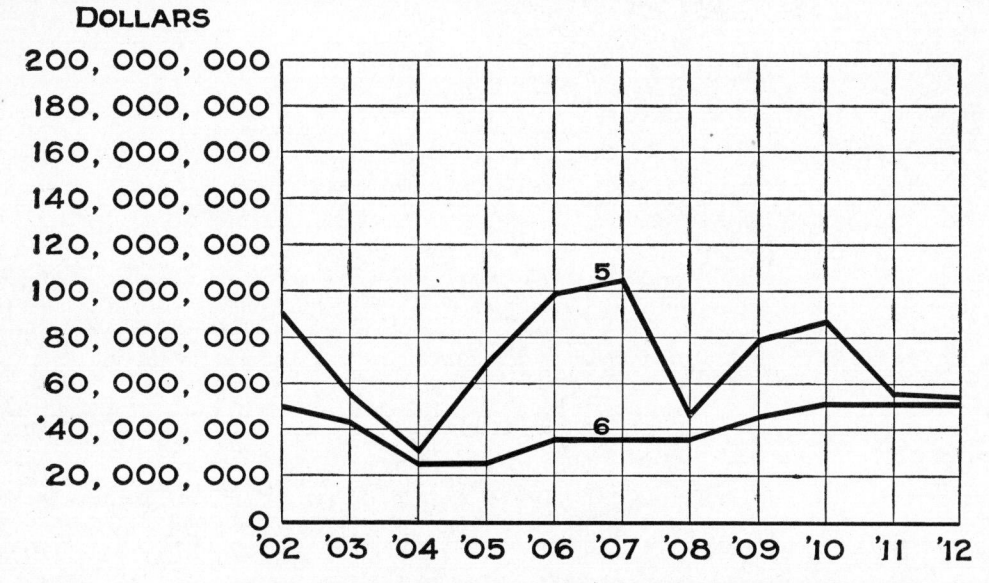

Fig. 225. The Surplus Earned and the Dividends Paid by the United States Steel Corporation

Curve 5. Surplus earned available for dividends
Curve 6. Preferred and common dividends paid
These curves are the same as Curve 3 and Curve 4, respectively. The data are depicted here on a large scale so that the relation of dividends to surplus earned may be seen clearly

throw the necessary light on this item. The average wages per man in 1907 were $765 per annum, and in 1912, $857. It has been shown that gross earnings in 1912 were less by $12,000,000 than in 1907, yet operating expenses in 1912 were $45,000,000 more than in 1907, being, as the curve shows, over $600,000,000 for the first time in the Corporation's history.

Curves 3 and 5, representing the surplus for dividends, are of most interest to the stockholder. It will be recalled that when the Steel Corporation was organized in 1901, the common stock was immediately placed on a 4 per cent basis. In 1903 the disbursements to the common stock ceased altogether and even the 7 per cent upon preferred was seriously questioned. During 1906, 1907, and 1908, 2 per cent was paid on the common, and then in 1909, the rate was first raised to 3 per cent, later to 4 per cent, and finally to 5 per cent. Conservative people have always criticised the 5 per cent dividend, believing that a 4 per cent rate would be more likely to be permanent. However, a consideration of the relation of curve No. 5 with No. 6 will show that the Corporation has avoided the payment of unearned dividends throughout its career. The margin was very slim in 1903 and 1904 and again in 1911 and 1912. As the balance of earnings for the common stock in 1911 was only 5.9 per cent and in 1912 only 5.7 per cent, a continuance for another year of such narrow margin would probably have meant the reduction of the 5 per cent rate, especially in view of the reduced appropriations for new construction and betterments, as disclosed in Fig. 226. Fortunately, however, for the stockholders, conditions in 1913 improved enormously and 11.17 per cent was earned for the common stock. Considering only the figures charted here, it is evident that the earning power of the Corporation during 1912 was not maintained.

To answer the question "Is the property being kept in proper physical condition?" the chart shown by Fig. 226 has been constructed.

As seen from curve 7, depreciation and repairs have shown a fairly constant increase, the amount in both 1910 and 1912 exceeding that of 1907, although the gross earnings were larger in 1907 than in either 1910 or 1912. This is a satisfactory sign.

Curve 8 portrays the total amount of money invested in the construction of new plants, mills, etc. This curve reaches its height in 1907 (running up to $67,000,000) and represents in large part the creation of the great plant at Gary. Curve 8 shows that even the panic of 1907 failed to curtail new construction to any great extent. But the poor profits in 1912, coupled with the higher rate of dividend on the common stock, did produce a sharp contraction—from $50,-000,000 in 1911 to less than $15,000,000 in 1912—the latter figure being the smallest since 1902. This, however, is not to be criticised too severely, since it is clear that a continuous expansion in productive capacity might easily outrun the normal consumptive demand.

Curve 9 represents the extent to which surplus earnings have been "ploughed back" into the property. This tells how the water has been squeezed out of the common stock. The report of the Bureau of Corporations in 1912 shows that, whereas there was a capitalization over indicated investment amounting to $625,353,559 in 1902, such excess was only $281,051,222 in 1910. Furthermore the report expressly states that this excess is not necessarily, nor entirely, "water". Up to 1908, curve 9 follows curve 8 very closely, indicating that the new construction was largely paid out of earnings, and not capitalized. Since 1907, there has been a tendency to finance such additions by the sale of bonds. This tendency, if not carried too far, is not open to criticism. One may, therefore, answer the second question in the

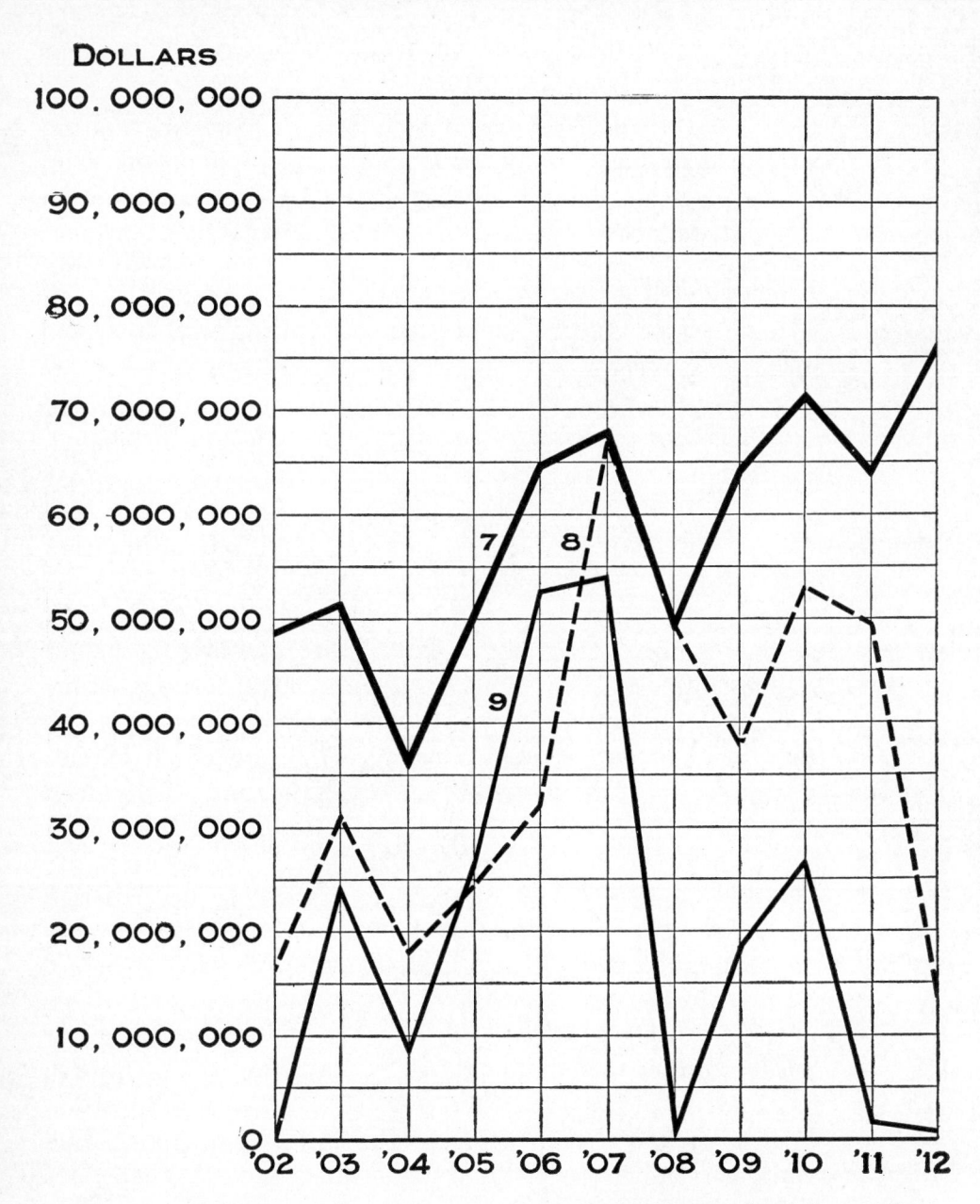

Fig. 226. The Maintenance of Property by the United States Steel Corporation

Curve 7. Depreciation, repairs, etc.
Curve 8. Expenditure for new construction
Curve 9. Appropriation from surplus earnings for construction and betterments
No more lines or figures are placed on this chart than are really necessary. The intention was to make the chart just as simple and clear as possible. Note the large quantities expressed by the numbers in the vertical scale, yet the wide spacing of the groups of three figures makes interpretation very easy

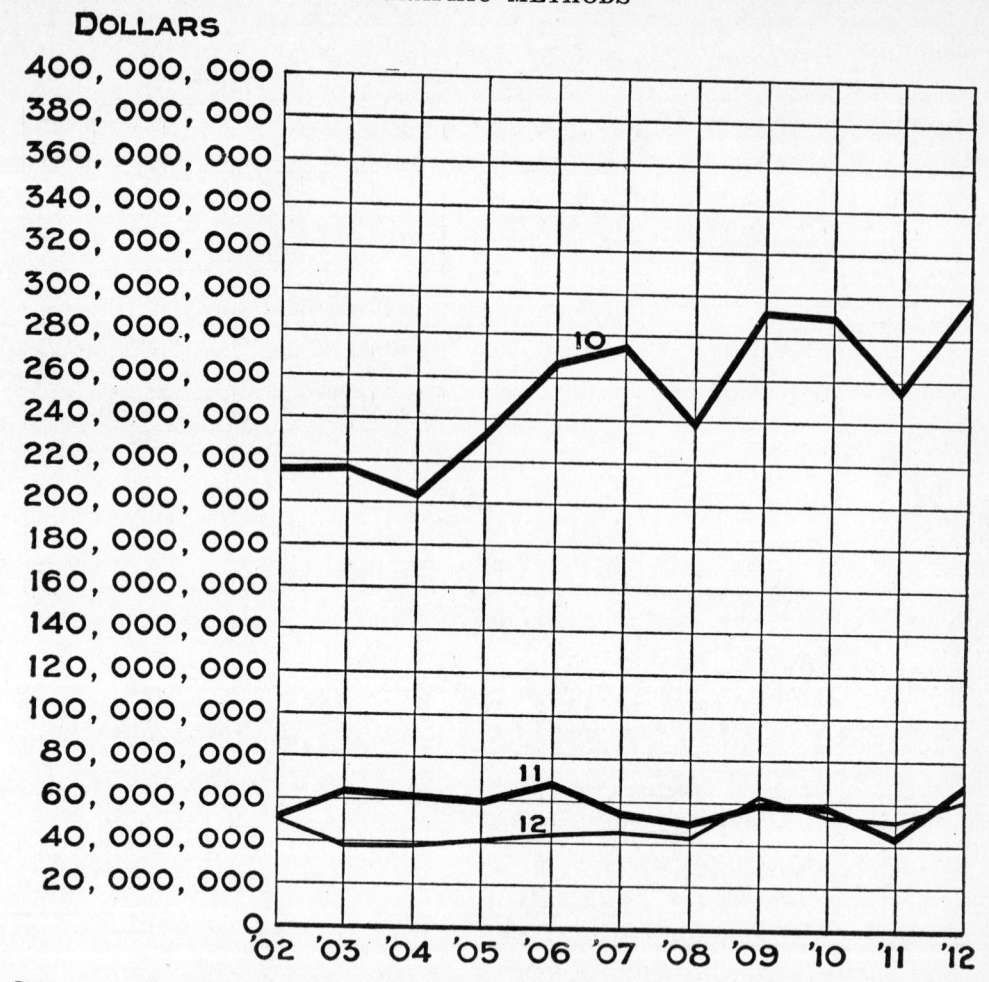

Fig. 227. Financial Condition of the United States Steel Corporation in Different Years as Shown by the Balance Sheet

Curve 10. Current assets
Curve 11. Cash holdings
Curve 12. Current liabilities

Here the numbers in the vertical scale represent larger quantities than in Fig. 226 and the spacing is closer in the vertical direction. Nevertheless, the numbers are easily read. To avoid any chance of error in interpretation it seems well to write out in full even the large numbers necessary here

affirmative, for from the evidence given, the property has been adequately maintained.

Fig. 227 illustrates the financial condition of the company as disclosed by the balance sheet. This chart is very conclusive, for it shows a very large excess of current assets over current liabilities, while cash holdings have tended to equal or exceed the total current liabilities. The balance sheet, therefore, indicates continuous and increasing financial strength. Current assets in 1912 reach nearly

$300,000,000, compared with $275,000,000 in 1907. Current liabilities were $60,000,000 in 1912 and $45,000,000 in 1907, but cash increased from $54,000,000 to $67,000,000. The Steel stockholder has, therefore, good evidence that his company is being managed with great sagacity in all departments.

An exhaustive study of the United States Steel Corporation would require a great many charts similar to the foregoing, but those given probably bring out clearly the main results in each annual report. The use of graphics to drive home statistics is yet in its infancy, and the next few years will doubtless witness a rapidly growing employment. There seems no good reason why any management, desiring to tell the whole truth to its stockholders, should not adopt graphic methods to supplement, as well as to illuminate, the statistical tables.

The famous economist, Stanley Jevons, wrote in 1875:

> There is much to be learnt about money before entering upon those abstruse questions, which barely admit of decided answers. In studying a language, we begin with the grammar before we try to read or write. In mathematics, we practice ourselves in simple arithmetic before we proceed to the subtleties of algebra and the differential calculus. But it is the grave misfortune of the moral and political sciences, as well shown by Mr. Herbert Spencer in his "Study of Sociology," that they are continually discussed by those who have never labored at the elementary grammar or simple arithmetic of the subject.

To-day, everyone still believes himself competent to discuss corporation finance, which is a branch of political science, in the same cheerful ignorance of the fundamentals of the subject. Everything, therefore, which will help to throw light on the dark corners of finance and make ignorance less excusable should be welcome. Never have corporation managers been more sensitive to public opinion, and if charts in annual reports make the truth more easily grasped (which they do) they will soon command an established place in corporation records.

This chapter is largely based on an article prepared at the suggestion of the author by Mr. Pierpont V. Davis, of New York City, and published by Mr. Davis in *Moody's Magazine*.

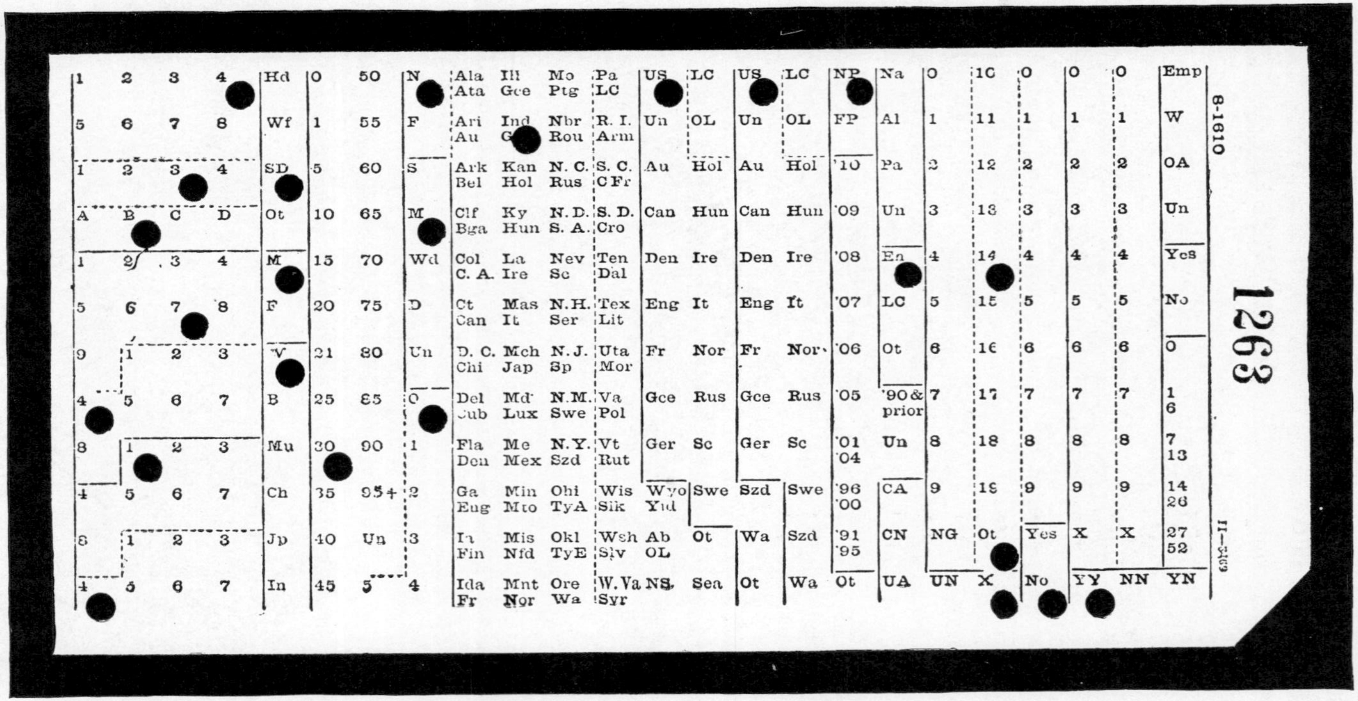

Fig. 228. Punched Card Such as Was Used by the United States Government for Tabulating the 1910 Census by Electric Card-Sorting and Tabulating Machines

There was a card similar to this for each inhabitant of the country. Holes punched at different positions in various columns represent the answers to all questions asked by the census enumerator regarding race, place of birth, age, etc. Punched-card systems can often be used advantageously for the cost and statistical work of corporations

CHAPTER XVI

GENERAL METHODS

THERE are a number of comparatively little known short cuts and convenient methods available in the collection and recording of statistical facts. If obsolete or unsuitable methods are used it may make a difference between success and failure in the work of keeping records of any complex business. When the methods of tabulation are too laborious, not only are the records so extensive as to be in disfavor, but they may occasionally include errors, in spite of the greatest care that can be taken by even the highest grade of employees. Anything which will reduce the amount of mental concentration necessary on the part of persons collecting and tabulating facts, will ordinarily assist in the production of more accurate final results. In large statistical studies, such as are made by the United States Census Office, it would be practically impossible to get all the information now obtained if tabulating machinery were not brought to the aid of the human brain and hand.

The punched-card system now widely used in statistical work has made possible an almost unlimited amount of subdivision of analysis with very little extra expense. Fig. 228 shows the card used by the United States Census Office for the 1910 census. One of these cards was punched for each inhabitant in the United States in accordance with the data obtained by the Census enumerators. It will be noticed that the card contains different columns of names or numbers and that there are twelve classifications possible in each vertical column in which a punched hole may be made. Ordinarily the different columns are used for different subjects, and the position of the punched hole in each column records the classification of the data relating to that particular subject.

The punched cards are stacked so that all are right-side up. It will be noticed from Fig. 228 that the lower right-hand corner of the card is clipped off. If any card in the stack is arranged improperly, it will show because the card will project beyond the other cards at the clipped corner of the pile. The stacks of cards are run through a sorting machine such as is seen in Fig. 229. Needles connected to electric wires make a contact through the holes in the card, and operate the sorting mechanism automatically in such manner that the cards are dropped into compartments in accordance with the position of the punched hole on the card. Cards are sorted for one particular characteristic at a time, so that all cards having that characteristic are obtained for tabulating purposes. After the data on one set of cards have been tabulated, the cards can then be run through the sorting machine again and sorted for other characteristics. This permits using the punched cards over and over again until all of the different data which may be of interest have been taken from the cards by the tabulating machines.

Fig. 230 shows the tabulating machine as used in the general commercial work of corporations, and for State or municipal departments. The cards are placed in the machine at the left and are fed

Courtesy of the Tabulating Machine Company

Fig. 229. Hollerith Card-Sorting Machine Suitable for Use by Corporations for Statistical Work Relating to Sales, Costs, Etc.

This machine will sort about 12,000 cards per hour, and place in the right compartment all cards having the hole punched in the same position in the particular column for which the sorting is done

through automatically, one by one, so that electric contacts are made wherever there are holes punched in the card. The electric contacts cause the counting dials to revolve by just the right amount to record properly the data for each punched hole.

After any group of cards has been run through the machine the totals can be read off from the counting dials and written down by the operator. Then the machine is ready for some other set of cards. Machines are built with different numbers of counting heads to suit the complexity of the data in any kind of business. By having several counting heads on the same machine, different sets of information may be taken from the cards simultaneously, thus frequently permitting one run of the cards through a tabulating machine to give all the data which may be required.

The punched-card machines are proving to be of very great usefulness in commercial work. Fig. 231 gives a view of a completely equipped office for the use of the punched-card system by an electric lighting company. The data are transferred from the original records to the cards by very simple punching machines with keys somewhat similar to typewriter keys. The punching is usually done by girls. A little training and practice gives high speed. Once punched, the cards are always available and may be filed for record purposes. It is frequently a great convenience to be able to run through the machines cards for several years back so that comparative statistics may be made. The preservation of the cards makes it unnecessary to dig out the original records. The uniform size of the cards makes it possible to preserve large quantities of them with comparatively little labor.

In punching the cards there are certain holes relating to departments, dates, etc., which are repeated time after time for large numbers

Courtesy of the Tabulating Machine Company

Fig. 230. Hollerith Tabulating Machine for Totalling the Data Contained on Punched Cards

The machine illustrated has four counters, permitting the simultaneous taking off of the data contained under four different headings on the punched card. The sorted cards are placed at the left of the tabulating machine and run through at the rate of about 3,000 per hour. Totals are read from the dials shown at the right

of cards. Instead of the operators punching these repeated holes one by one in each card, the cards are punched by a gang punch, which at a single stroke punches several holes in many different cards. The gang punch can be seen in Fig. 231 on a table near the right-hand side of the illustration.

Manufacturing companies now use the tabulating machines for keeping track of the cost of different orders and of different classes of work in the factory. The data from the original time slips of the workmen are transferred by the punching machines to the cards day by day as the time slips are turned in. The punched cards can then be sorted by order number and department, so that when each order is completed the total cost of all work on that order is obtained. The distribution of the value of work done by different departments can be had also if desired.

In keeping the records of a sales department, the facts relating to the various sales orders are transferred to the punched cards and the cards sorted and tabulated in any manner desired. A very large manufacturing business having many kinds of machinery as a product, uses the punched-card system for each order as it is received in the plant. At the end of each month the records show the total sales of each branch house, the total sales of each salesman, the total sales of each main class of product, and many other kinds of information. In this particular plant tabulating machines are of very great assistance, because they can be used to make a sales analysis for any one class of product. The punched card for each order shows the catalogue number of the product called for by that order. Whenever desired, cards for a definite length of time can be run through the machines so as to sort out all the cards for any catalogue number of product on which a study is to be made. The resorting of these cards by sales districts shows the distribution of the total sales of this particular product by distinct districts, or States, and, if desired, by different salesmen. The sales for the various months or seasons of the year may be had if wanted. Though the data relating to the many kinds of product need not be regularly tabulated, the facts are nevertheless preserved so that tabulation for any particular class of goods or any territory can be made whenever a study seems desirable.

The multitudinous uses to which these card-sorting and tabulating machines can be put are far beyond any possibility of naming here. The very great flexibility, speed, and accuracy of the machines make

Courtesy of the Tabulating Machine Company

Fig. 231. **A Completely Equipped Office for Collecting and Tabulating the Operating and Sales Statistics of an Electric-Lighting Company**

The girls at the left are operating the key punches for punching the cards. A gang punch is shown on the table at the extreme right. In the corner is the card-sorting machine, and the tabulating machine is in the center. Files for punched cards are seen along the wall

them almost indispensable in any work where there is large quantity of complex data to be analyzed. It has been found feasible and profitable to use machines of this type in businesses of only moderate size.

The adding machine is now so commonly used that it seems scarcely worth while to mention it here. There are, however, frequently times when special investigations must be made, but adding machines do not happen to be available, and the investigator feels seriously handicapped because he must take from the original records only those items which may be of especial interest to him. In work of this kind, it is sometimes convenient to use one of the small-size pocket adding machines of which there are several different makes now on the market. Though these machines are not at all in the same class as the large key-operated machines, they are of assistance in taking off occasional items because they overcome the necessity for putting down the items on a piece of paper for addition later by mental effort. With the portable adding machine the data are taken from the original work directly and added automatically as the work proceeds.

Engineers do the greater portion of all of their computing work by means of the slide rule. By others than engineers, however, the slide rule is very little used. In the preparation of data for curves and charts for corporation work, or for any investigations where numerous percentages are necessary, the slide rule is almost indispensable. A 10-inch slide rule as shown in Fig. 232 is sufficiently accurate for most work, and, as it costs only a few dollars, it should be a part of the equipment of everyone who is doing even the simplest form of statistical work, or who is periodically plotting curves involving ratios or percentages. By using a slide rule the percentage ratios of numbers can be determined almost instantly and with no mental effort. It can be confidently predicted that anyone who has much multiplication or division to do in relation to curve-plotting and chart-making will find the slide rule of such a great assistance that the rule would not be parted with under any circumstances if a new one could not be obtained.

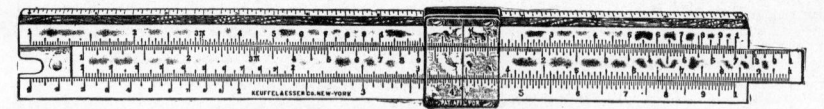

Fig. 232. A 10-inch Slide Rule

The slide rule is of great convenience in doing work involving multiplication or division. It is especially valuable for obtaining ratios or percentages in statistics for industrial work

Judgment must be used in the showing of figures in any chart or numerical presentation, so that the figures may not give an appearance of greater accuracy than their method of collection would warrant. Too many otherwise excellent reports contain figures which give the impression of great accuracy when in reality the figures may be only the crudest approximations. Except in financial statements, it is a safe rule to use ciphers whenever possible at the right of all numbers of great size. The use of the ciphers greatly simplifies the grasping of the figures by the reader, and, at the same time, it helps to avoid the impression of an accuracy which is not warranted by the methods of collecting the data.

A recent government report[*] contained this statement: "The cotton crop of last year (1911) aggregated 16,250,276 500-pound

[*] "The Packing and Marketing of Cotton," by John M. Carson.

bales, the total value of which is $1,000,000,000 and, including the seed, $1,200,000,000." The figure for the number of bales implies that every single bale of cotton raised in the United States was accounted for and that these figures are absolutely accurate down to one bale of cotton. This denotes an accuracy of 1 part in 16,000,000 parts, or an accuracy within 0.000006 per cent. It is very doubtful indeed whether the figures for the cotton crop are accurate within 1,000 or even 10,000 bales. Suppose a possible error of 10,000 bales were assumed, and the cotton crop put down as 16,250,000 bales, the accuracy would still be 1 in 1,625, or within 0.06 per cent. For most purposes it would be much preferable to use the round number 16,250,000 instead of the detailed figures which were given in the Government report. The particular report from which the figures are taken is not a tabulation, but a written report in regard to the methods used for packing cotton. Since the report was intended to be read by merchants and planters, rather than by statisticians, it is all the more important that the figures should be presented in round numbers so that they may be easily grasped. The mere fact that values for the cotton in the latter part of the quotation given above are in very rough estimates of such round numbers as "$1,000,000,000", calls special attention to the use of detailed figures for the "16,250,276 bales".

Misleading figures implying a greater accuracy than justifiable are very often found as a result of the addition of different quantities some of which are large and some small. The small quantities may have a great degree of accuracy, but this does not give accuracy to the sum of all the quantities, for the total cannot be any more accurate than the most inaccurate item included in the total. If a very large item is not accurate within ten thousand, then it is useless to include in the grand total the three right-hand digits which may be obtained as the result of addition. When some of the items included are so small that they are in tens or hundreds, the addition should be made to include all the digits. After the sum is known then all those digits whose accuracy is doubtful in the total should be replaced by ciphers.

Fictitious accuracy is quite often implied in the results of computations where a slide rule has been used. The ordinary 10-inch slide rule can give an accuracy of only three significant figures, and, on the right-hand portion of the scale, the third figure is often somewhat in doubt unless very great care is used in manipulating the rule. This means that with the 10-inch slide rule the accuracy is ordinarily no greater than 1 in 1,000, or one-tenth of one per cent. Though two quantities each running into five figures may be multiplied on the slide rule, the product would not be accurate beyond three significant figures, and ciphers must be put down to express the remainder of the number for the product.

If very large quantities obtained by slide-rule computation are added together with a number of small quantities, the total cannot, of course, be accurate beyond the third or fourth digit toward the right of the largest quantity included in the total. The fourth digit may be fairly accurate in the total, because in the process of addition the various figures added would tend to give a close approximation of the fourth digit and that digit might accordingly be put down in the total because it has at least a fair possibility of accuracy.

It must not be assumed from the preceding paragraph that the slide rule gives figures too crude for ordinary use. There are comparatively few sets of data relating to costs, output, or other records of industrial work which have an accuracy greater than one-tenth of one per cent. For the great majority of ordinary problems, the data are so crude that the 10-inch rule has more than sufficient accuracy. The use of the slide rule on many classes of work has a desirable psychological effect, in that it calls attention to the accuracy of the data and assists in preventing unnecessary detail work which it is very easy to drift into if any assumptions of great accuracy are permitted to creep in.

The question of significant figures in statistical work and even in ordinary commercial reports is an important one which should have greater attention than it ordinarily receives. Unfortunately the subject can be only briefly touched upon here and the reader would do well to look the matter up in some of the books on statistical theory.*

It sometimes happens that a few blue prints are required from some complex chart made on heavy paper or cardboard. Instead of making a tracing from the drawing by means of tracing cloth and with great expenditure of labor and time, it is sometimes feasible to treat the original drawing with a transparentizing solution so that blue prints can be obtained directly. The transparentizing solution is put on the paper with a brush or sponge and then blue prints are made in the ordinary manner. There are several different makes of the trans-

---

* A chapter on "Approximation and Accuracy" will be found in "The Elements of Statistical Method," by Willford I. King, published by the Macmillan Company, New York City.

parentizing solution on the market and a supply can be obtained from most shops selling drafting materials.

During the last few years very convenient photographic machines have been put on the market which photograph directly on sensitized paper without the use of any negative. With this type of machine, copies of drawings can be made very cheaply and clearly. One of the convenient features in doing work by this machine is that drawings can be enlarged or reduced within a wide range of sizes. The machine most commonly used for this work is called the photostat. In most large cities there are companies equipped with the photostat apparatus who will at reasonable cost make copies of drawings sent to them, much as the blue-printing companies make copies from tracings. Some of the best equipped libraries have now installed photostat machines as a convenience to their patrons. In a library so equipped it is possible to have a copy made from any page in any book or periodical in the library. In the New York Public Library, the reader need only fill out an order form giving the exact page and the name of the publication from which the copy is to be made, and state the size desired in the reproduction. Usually the copy is available within a few hours, but, if desired, it may be mailed, thus avoiding any necessity for waiting on the part of the person ordering the copy. In case of rare books or manuscripts, copies may be made page by page so that a complete copy of the book is obtained without prohibitive expenditure.

Charts from which plates must be made for printing are nearly always drawn considerably larger in size than the completed illustration. Most of the charts in this book were drawn two or three times as large as seen here. A photographic reduction in the size of the chart tends to eliminate minor irregularities and gives a much better result than can possibly be obtained from drawings in the exact finished size. In making the original large-size drawings it is almost essential that a reducing glass should be used to make certain that the finished drawing will have the desired appearance. With complex drawings it is often difficult to tell whether the lettering and figures are of large enough size to be read easily after they are reduced to the size to be used for printing. By looking through a reducing glass it can be determined at once whether the drawing is in correct proportions. A reducing glass is similar in appearance to the ordinary magnifying glass, but the lens is ground concave instead of convex so that everything seen through the glass appears of smaller size. The ordinary reducing glass can be used for a reduction through quite a range of different sizes by holding the glass at different distances from the drawing which is being considered.

One of the commonest errors made by the beginner in preparing charts from which printing plates are to be made is that he does not allow for the reduction in widths of the various lines. If the printing plate is to be made one-third the lineal dimension of the original drawing, it is essential that the lines on the original drawing should be made three times as wide as they are to appear when printed. The novice will find that even though he uses a reducing glass with great care, his heavy lines will at first nearly always appear less wide and black than he had expected and hoped that they would be.

Quite often it is desired to change the proportions of some chart so that the ratio between height and width may be different from that of the original drawing. Though the photographic process used in the photostat machine or by the engraver (in making plates for printing) permits a change in size, the same proportions remain between width and height. There would seem to be enough demand to justify an engraver making a combination of lenses by which one dimension of a drawing may be changed more than the other dimension. By using two lenses having cylindrical surfaces and having the axes at right angles, there might be a possibility of changing the proportions of drawings which are copied without any great amount of expense after the apparatus has once been designed.

Very often persons owning cameras do not know that the camera manufacturers are in many cases able to supply auxiliary lenses by which pictures and copies of drawings may be made practically full-size with ordinary cameras. Though the arrangement is not as convenient to use as a regular copying camera, it may be of great service to supplement the work of a camera already owned.

It is not generally known that line plates may be made from charts drawn on co-ordinate paper ruled with green ink. Such charts sent to many zinc engravers are returned with the statement that it is impossible to make a line cut from green-ink copy. The statement is made in most cases by the engraver without even attempting to make the cut. There is no difficulty in making excellent zinc cuts from copy using the ordinary green ink, and many of the cuts in this book have been so made, as, for instance, Fig. 156, Fig. 207, and Fig. 215.

Of course, when line cuts are made from charts having a green-ink background, the printed illustration shows both the black and green-ink lines as black, and there is no distinction between the different lines. On this account, it is necessary for the person ordering the charts made from paper having green-ink lines to make certain that the main features of the chart stand out with prominent broad lines, so that there may certainly be a contrast in the width of the lines when printed, to make up for the contrast obtained in the original drawing by the difference in color of the two inks used.

Color printing is not yet ordinarily available unless a very large number of copies are to be made. In order to make areas stand out in contrast, different kinds of cross-hatching put on by hand ruling have been used very commonly. One trouble with the hand ruling is that it lacks uniformity unless done with very great care and to a scale considerably larger than the finished illustration, so that there may be enough photographic reduction to eliminate many of the defects which would otherwise appear. It is not widely known that there is a method available in the form of Ben Day mechanical shading, which is far superior to cross-hatching for line-plate work. Most good engravers can do Ben Day work, and it is just a matter of specifying what kind of shading is desired on the different portions of the drawing. With the Ben Day shading, more degrees of shading from light to dark are feasible than with hand work, and, in addition, there are many varieties of lines and patterns which may be used.

Since Ben Day work must be applied on each area separately by means of a transfer process, it is necessary for the engraver to make certain that the Ben Day shading shall not appear on some portion of the zinc plate where it is not desired. This requires that the engraver must protect the different portions of the zinc plate by a paint-like covering, and this must be done for each of the different kinds of shading used. It is almost impossible to make any square-inch price rate for Ben Day work because each new plate is a problem in itself. The work is ordinarily charged for on a time basis, the usual rates being from $1.00 to $1.50 per hour.

When copy to receive Ben Day work is sent to the engraver it is marked somewhat as shown in Fig. 233, so that the instructions to the engraver may be explicit. Crayon marks specify by number the kind of Ben Day shading desired, and arrows point to the different areas to be shaded. This marking of instruction is done with a blue pencil because blue does not photograph easily and has such a small effect on a photographic plate that it does not spoil the copy for making a good zinc plate. In order to make the zinc plate from which Fig. 233 was actually printed, a red pencil was used for the bottom portion of the illustration referring to Ben Day work. Red photographs as black, and a zinc plate was obtained which shows the marking such as would be used with a blue pencil when Ben Day work is ordered from an engraver. Ben Day work has been used on a great many illustrations in this book, and it is believed that the reader will have no difficulty in distinguishing the cuts with Ben Day work from those cuts for which hand shading was used.

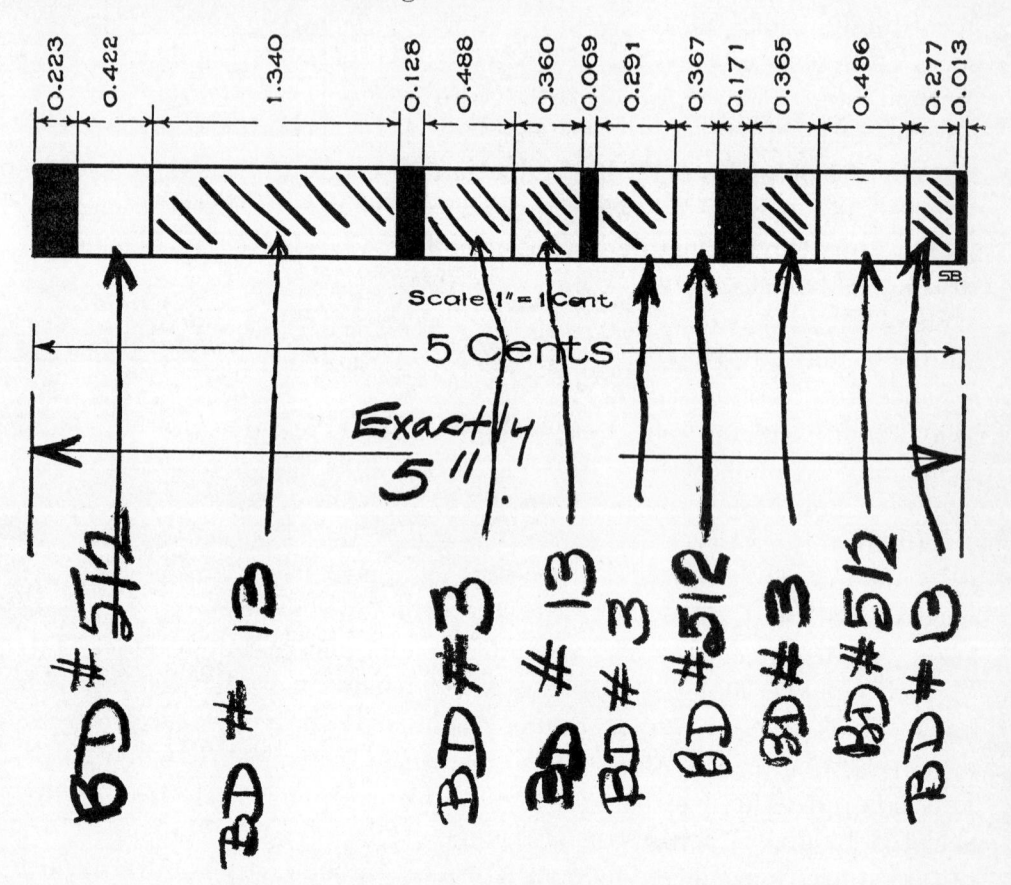

Fig. 233. Copy from Which a Zinc Plate Is to Be Made with Ben Day Mechanical Shading

This is the copy from which the plate for Fig. 1 was made. The areas to receive the Ben Day work are designated by arrows and numbers naming the particular kind of shading desired. Sample books give a wide choice of shadings. The markings on the face of the copy regarding the Ben Day work are made with blue pencil, since blue does not photograph dark enough to affect the line engraving

GENERAL METHODS 333

There are a great many problems in graphic work which puzzle the person getting up a chart if there are three different variables to deal with. The problem, as ordinarily found, involves two different independent variables, and a dependent variable depending upon each of the two independent variables. Isometric drawings like Fig. 235, or solid models such as are seen in Fig. 236 and Fig. 237, can be used, but they require a great deal of labor and care to make and are accordingly not often seen. There is another method not perhaps so obvious as a solid model but nevertheless of great value. When the data follow any definite natural laws a chart on the style of Fig. 234 is often simple to make and easy to interpret. By such charts many computations may be made with accuracy and ease.

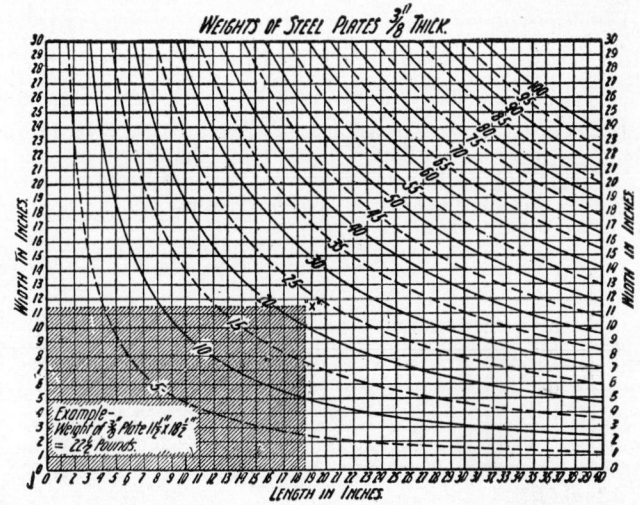

Fig. 234. Chart for Obtaining the Weight of Steel Plates $3/8$-inch Thick and of Various Widths and Lengths

A chart of this general type permits using three variables. The two independent variables here are length and width. Weight is the dependent variable. This kind of chart is much simpler to construct than an isometric drawing like Fig. 167, or a model like Fig. 236 or Fig. 237

In obtaining curves like those shown in Fig. 234 one of the variables is made some constant quantity, and the other two variables are then used to work out the data from which the curve is drawn. It can be seen, for instance, that if a definite weight and length of steel plate $3/8$ inch thick is assumed, the width is absolutely fixed. To obtain a curve like that seen for 5 pounds in Fig. 234, it is necessary only to assume a weight of 5 pounds, then choose separate lengths one by one, and compute the widths which would correspond with the lengths selected to give a weight of 5 pounds. The various figures of width obtained are then plotted as points for the 5-pound curve, and a smooth curve is drawn through all of the points, giving the result seen in the illustration. After one curve has been plotted another weight is assumed in a similar manner, and new computations are made for various lengths on the horizontal scale. Though this method of charting requires some little labor in making the various computations, it is a very excellent one where the chart must be used for frequent reference. The information from such a chart as seen in Fig. 234 may be read from any portion of the chart, even though the intersection of the length and width lines for the size of the plate under consideration does not fall on one of the curve lines drawn. It can be seen for the example stated in the lower left-hand corner of the chart that the intersection of the vertical and horizontal lines of the independent variables falls halfway between the curve for 20 pounds and the curve for 25 pounds. The weight is accordingly taken as 22½ pounds.

Though the subject cannot be fully gone into here, it may be suggested for those who care to consider further the general type of charts represented by Fig. 234, that much work may be saved by making such charts on logarithmic paper. This subject has been discussed at greater length in a preceding chapter. There are many classes of data which, when plotted on ordinary squared co-ordinate paper, involve plotting many points to produce curves like those seen in Fig. 234, but for which the same data shown on paper with logarithmic ruling would give straight lines. When the curve lines are straight lines, it is necessary to plot only two points for each curve and then draw a line connecting those two points. This permits a very rapid construction of the chart. A little practice in the making of charts is necessary before one can determine clearly the best method to use so as to produce

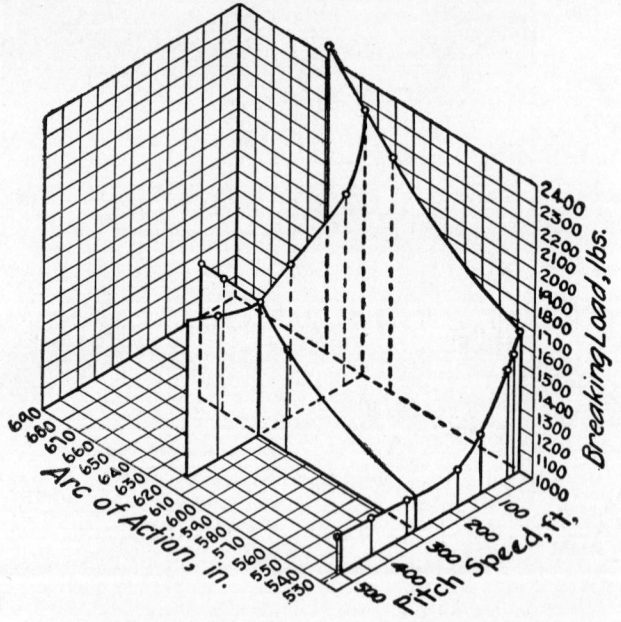

Data of Guido H. Marx.   Courtesy of the Standard Corporation, Philadelphia

Fig. 235. Relations Between Arc of Action in Inches, Pitch Speed in Feet per Minute, and Breaking Load in Pounds, for Cut Cast-iron Gears of Ten Diametral Pitch

This illustration is drawn on isometric ruling, with the ruling itself seen only as a background so as to give the appearance of a solid model in three dimensions

a simple chart. Paper having logarithmic ruling in both directions is the kind most frequently used for mathematical charts. Such paper can be purchased from almost any good store selling engineering supplies. Readers wishing to go further into the preparation of charts of this rather highly specialized character are referred to the excellent work of Mr. John B. Peddle, entitled "The Construction of Graphical Charts", published by the McGraw-Hill Book Company of New York City.

The use of isometric paper for drawing charts representing three dimensions was mentioned for Fig. 167. In Fig. 235 we have another application of this same isometric ruling. Instead of showing the whole sheet of isometrically ruled paper as a background, Fig. 235 shows only enough of the isometric ruling to give the impression of three planes meeting like one corner of a box. The chart illustrating the data is drawn on the isometric ruling so that it appears as though placed in a corner made by the three planes. Parallel ruled lines then permit reading the chart from any one of the three different scales. The dependent variable is made the vertical scale here, just as in most charts where there is only one independent variable instead of two. The use of the isometric ruling is not as common as it would be if it were more widely realized how easily charts may be prepared to give the effect of solid models without the great labor which a solid model necessarily involves.

Fig. 236 shows another method which may be used instead of the more laborious and costly solid model. Different curves are plotted by assuming at frequent intervals constant values for one of the vari-

Data of E. S. Farwell.   Courtesy of the American Machinist

Fig. 236. Tests of a Direct-connected Fan and Engine. The Model Shows the Effect on the Efficiency of the Fan of Different Outlet Openings and of Different Speeds of Operation

Curves are plotted on cardboard by assuming constant values for one of the three variables, and then plotting the relations for the other two variables. Each of the curves is cut from the cardboard and slit halfway up or down the line for intersection with the cards at right angles to it. Cards are fitted together to give the effect seen above

ables of the data, and then plotting curves for the other two variables. These curves are made to the same scale on sheets of cardboard, and then the outline of the curve is cut out with shears so as to give a series of different cardboard curve sheets. The several sheets are carefully marked for their intersecting points, and are then cut halfway through in the upward and downward direction on the intersection lines so that the curve sheets may be fitted together to give an effect like that seen in Fig. 236. A cardboard exhibit on the scheme of Fig. 236 is, in many cases, just as satisfactory as a solid model and it has the advantage of being quite easy to prepare without any special apparatus or materials being required.

Fig. 237 shows a solid model of the type which may be considered the acme of graphic work when there are two independent variables. A model of this kind is ordinarily made of plaster of Paris, as that is a material easily handled and capable of being made into any shape desired. In making such a model the usual procedure would be to rule a flat board with lines at properly spaced intervals for each of the two horizontal scales. Computations made by methods similar to those described for Fig. 236 would give the value, on the vertical scale, for each set of conditions corresponding to the intersection of each two lines ruled for the base and showing the horizontal scales. In Fig. 237 the cost computations can be considered to give points on curves drawn on the surface of the solid model. These curves correspond exactly with the curves drawn on cardboard in Fig. 236. In order to locate the curve points which determine the surface of a solid model like Fig. 237, wires are driven into the bottom board at the intersection of the ruled lines of the two horizontal scales, and these wires are made just the proper length to represent the figures computed for the dependent variable. When all the wires are in position on the board, a box is made the right size for the base of the finished solid model, and with sides as high as the solid model is to be made. This box serves as a mold into which the wet plaster of Paris is poured. Care must be taken to have the bottom edges of the box fit well on the board so that the liquid plaster of Paris may not leak out.

The powdered plaster of Paris may be obtained from any store selling building supplies, or from a drug store. Water is added and the mixture carefully stirred until it is free from lumps and of about the consistency of very thick cream. The fluid is poured into the box up to the desired height and allowed to stand for several hours

GENERAL METHODS 337

or over night until it becomes thoroughly hard. The box is then removed. In order to get the shape of the model as seen in Fig. 237, the plaster of Paris is very carefully scraped away with a piece of tin or some other simple tool until the ends of the vertical wires just show through. Before the plaster of Paris is poured in, care should be taken to mark the different sides of the board so that it will be

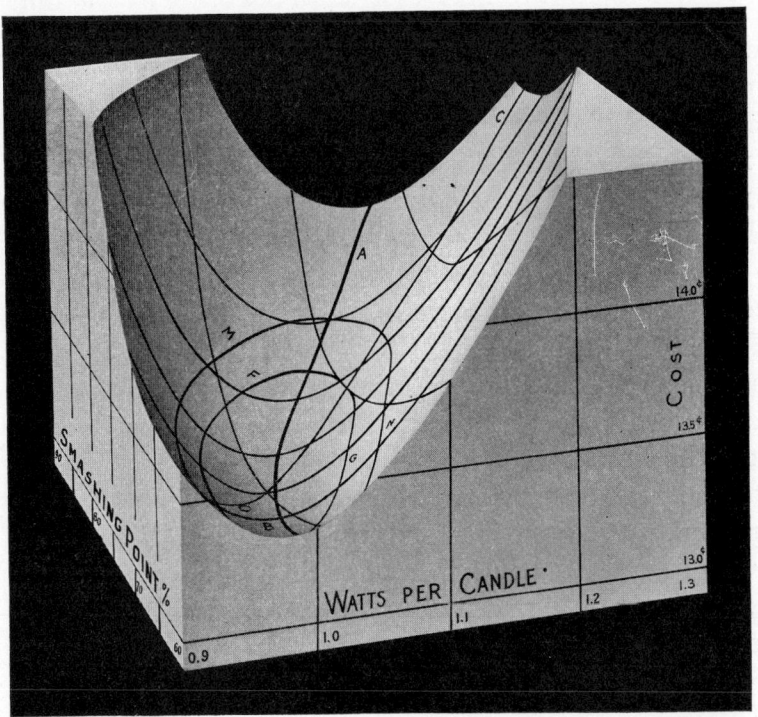

R. E. Scott, in Harvard Engineering Journal

Fig. 237. Three-dimensional Model Showing Cost of Light in Cents per 1,000 Candle-hours with 40-watt "Mazda" Lamps for Any Practicable Combination of Efficiency and Smashing Point. Price of the Lamp is 50 Cents and Cost of Electric Current is Assumed at 10 Cents per Kilowatt Hour

Three variables are considered here. The two independent variables are represented at the base of the model and the dependent variable, "cost", is read from the vertical scale. A model of this kind can be made from plaster of Paris by following the methods described in detail in this chapter

known in which portions of the plaster of Paris block the greatest amount must be removed before the wires come in sight. Knowledge of the position of the wires in the block of plaster of Paris permits removing the plaster rapidly without danger of taking off too much. After the wires do come into sight, the model must be carefully scraped so that the surfaces will have uniform curves without any humps or hollows. If all the surfaces are concave, as they are seen to be in Fig. 237, the scraping is rather a simple matter since the surfaces between the two wires are lower than the wires themselves. If a solid model were made for data such as that of Fig. 236, much care would be necessary, for in that case some of the surfaces are convex and it would be essential that enough material should be left between the different wires to permit giving the nicely rounded smooth surfaces which would correctly represent the data. When the surfaces have been scraped as nearly as possible to the proper shape they may be smoothed by rubbing with fine sandpaper. The external flat faces of the model may also be sandpapered advantageously to remove any marks which may remain from the surface of the box used as a mold. Lines such as are seen in Fig. 237 can be ruled on the surface and the different scales can be lettered by hand. A few coats of boiled linseed oil will harden the surface and give an attractive finish.

In Fig. 237 the lines giving oval figures represent certain operating conditions which, from experiment and from study of the model itself, have been found to be most desirable in practice. The oval lines show the limiting conditions best for actual practical operation, and give the real conclusions which the model itself greatly assists in portraying. Solid models and three-dimension charts like those shown are of supreme value in studies of complex data. It is to be regretted that these methods of presentation involve so much labor that they cannot be used as frequently as might be desired.

In political campaigns frequent use is made of statistical information. Campaign orators use figures which sound impressive when combined with a certain amount of eloquence. Too many of the statements, however, tell only a portion of the whole truth, and that portion is, of course, assumed to be the portion which the speaker most desires to have put forward. It is not ordinarily feasible in a speech to give all the facts over a series of years so that the hearer may draw any conclusions for himself. The whole system is weak in that the audience are forced to depend too largely on the statements made by the orator, rather than to draw conclusions of their own from data which are warranted to be authentic. When we have a larger number of people who know how to read curves, it will be a simple matter to present the arguments of a political campaign by means of a projecting lantern with properly prepared charts thrown on a screen. Even now the charts could probably be so made as to be understood and correctly interpreted by the average person attending a political meeting, with resultant increase in the effectiveness of the arguments they support.

In municipal campaigns, especially, the lantern talk could be of very great interest to the voters if the slides were carefully prepared and arranged in a logical sequence. By using simple methods of charting, almost any kind of facts could be portrayed so that they would surely be correctly understood. Concise statements in conjunction with the charts should, of course, be used, somewhat as the main titles are placed under the illustrations of this book. Slides showing snappy questions could be thrown on the screen rapidly, and the succeeding slides could then answer the questions. Recent public improvements, bridges, etc., could be illustrated by maps and actual photographs. Pictures of fire apparatus and views showing the efficiency of the street-cleaning methods, etc., could be used to add interest and to bring out certain points in regard to the operation of specific departments. There is no doubt that properly prepared lantern slides would have great weight with the voters, for lantern slides might seem to present a less biased point of view than would the average partisan campaign orator.

In using lantern slides for campaign purposes it is not necessary to have a large hall for each showing of the lantern slides. Automobiles could readily be equipped so that two cars could work together. One auto would carry a screen, which could be very quickly put up, somewhat in the manner of a sail, when that part of the town had been reached where the lantern talk was to be given to a crowd in the street or on some vacant lot. The other automobile could carry the lantern on a stand between the front and rear seats. The power for the lantern would be obtained in the ordinary manner from tanks of oxygen and hydrogen carried in the car. A car containing the lantern equipment would be entirely self-contained and no electric wires or other attachments would be necessary. The lantern car would be stopped the proper distance away from the lantern screen on the other car, and the slides could be shown on the screen within three minutes after arrival in any desired section of the city. In thickly populated districts it would probably not be necessary to announce a political meeting of this kind, as word would be passed very rapidly that a lantern talk was in progress and the desired crowd would collect spontaneously.

One very great advantage of the lantern presentation in political work comes from the fact that after one good set of slides has been prepared, these slides may be duplicated at very small expense. Twenty or even fifty sets of slides might be shown in different parts of a city simultaneously on the last few nights just before election. The main candidates are never able to make speeches at all of the desired points during the last few days, and they probably always feel that the last days or hours before an election are the most valuable of the whole campaign. When many sets of lantern slides are made from the same original charts there is very little additional expense, and the number of people who may get the benefit of the carefully prepared slides is tremendously increased. In every city there are many young lawyers or business men who would be willing to make a speech to accompany the slides if they could depend upon the slides for their main material. The number of people who may be reached during the last few hours of a campaign is thus almost unlimited if the lantern-slide method of presentation is used.

From the educational point of view, it would probably be very desirable to have lantern slides used in campaign work, because there would be a very great amount of valuable information conveyed by the slides shown. With lantern slides showing well prepared charts, probably ten times as much information could be absorbed by an audience as could be obtained by listening to the most expert campaign speaker. In addition, there would be the great advantage that the facts presented by lantern slides would be understood and remembered months after the oratory of a campaign speaker had lost its beguiling effect and his statements been forgotten.

It need not be thought that lantern talks such as are suggested need be devoid of all those spectacular climaxes which are so common with a campaign orator. Whenever it is desired to raise some enthusiasm, a photograph of a candidate could be thrown on the screen and a cheer would be sure to follow. There is an almost unlimited field for the exercise of ingenuity in the preparing of campaign charts. The sets of slides would have tremendous educational value, as well as great power in presenting political arguments in such manner as would most positively affect the vote.

Methods used by newspaper offices and political clubs for giving out election returns to great crowds in the streets on the night of election day are not all that they might be made if a little thought were given to the subject. Though the projecting lantern is now used almost universally in presenting election returns in large cities, thus far the lantern slides give only very brief scrawled statements that certain cities or certain districts have gone for some particular candidate with some estimated plurality. A person coming out into the street after an evening at the theater has no way of knowing the import of the various telegraphic statements which may have been thrown on the screen earlier in the evening. It is only by watching the bulletin-board screen for half an hour or more that a newcomer is able to get any definite idea of how things are going.

When arrangements have already been made for using a lantern to show the returns on a screen, it would cost comparatively little more to give election returns which would be of much interest to the whole gathering, as well as of great effectiveness in showing the situation clearly to any newcomer who might join the crowd. For a national election, slides could be prepared to the number of twenty-five or more, giving an outline map of the United States and showing only the State lines. As the returns come in, some man well acquainted with the political situation could summarize the telegrams received up to the last moment and give his opinion as to which candidates are leading each State. A person accustomed to coloring lantern slides could then immediately color in one of the map slides according to some key, so the colors red, green, yellow, etc., on different areas would show that certain candidates were ahead in those States or districts. For municipal elections, the wards and different divisions of the city could be colored in exactly the same manner as suggested for the States. The appearance of the suggested map as thrown on a screen may be judged somewhat from the map seen in Fig. 177. It would add much to the enthusiasm of the crowd if it were announced before election day that some well-known person would make the summary estimates from which the colored slides would be prepared. It would probably take less than fifteen minutes to color a lantern slide after the summary had been made up by the person watching the telegrams, and it would be feasible to show on the slide itself the hour at which the slide "went to press", as 9.30 p.m., 9.45 p.m., etc. As a new slide could be prepared about every fifteen minutes, a map summary shown on the screen need be only about fifteen minutes behind the latest telegraphic reports.

In addition to the actual colored map, each slide should contain colored bars which would show by their length the estimated summary of all the States or districts, so that the totals of different candidates might be easily compared. Thus, in a presidential election, the counting of the number of States for each candidate does not by any means give the whole story. The important thing is the number of electoral votes, and these would be best represented by the bar summary which would take into account the number of electoral votes of each State estimated as won by any candidate. With the combination slide showing, in the form of bars, both a map and estimated totals, any person coming out of the theater to join the election-night crowd could see instantly how the situation stood up to the moment the last slide was colored.

With the election-return method outlined, the concise telegrams in handwriting would still be shown on the screen one by one as the news came in over the wire. A popular appeal to a large crowd can always be made by snappy statements such as "Jones concedes Chicago to Smith", or "California goes for Brown". Instead of holding statements of this kind on the screen until other news could arrive, however, any statement in written words would be taken off as soon as it had been grasped by the crowd and one of the colored maps would be thrown on the screen. Slides with colored maps and colored bars would be used as fillers, to be kept on the screen continuously whenever there were no telegraphic reports to be projected on the screen in written words. It would probably be found desirable, in many cases, to show telegraphic reports in such manner that a map would be thrown on the screen between each two telegraphic reports, and also held on the screen whenever telegraphic reports should not come in fast enough.

Election returns are sometimes told to a whole city by search lights thrown from the top of some high building. National, State, or municipal election returns can be kept distinct by the search-light method if certain directions, north, east, south, or west are announced for the lantern beams referring to the different kinds of election returns. Until complete reports have been received the lantern beams can be moved gradually up and down. After complete reports are in the beam can be held steady, so that the watchers even miles away may know from the angle of the light and its position that a conclusion has been reached, and who wins.

Educational material shown in parades gives an effective way for reaching vast numbers of people. Fig. 238 illustrates some of the floats used in presenting statistical information in the municipal parade by

Photo by the International News Service

Fig. 238. Statistical Exhibits in the Municipal Parade by the Employees of the City of New York, May 17, 1913

Many very large charts, curves and other statistical displays were mounted on wagons in such manner that interpretation was possible from either side of the street. The Health Department, in particular, made excellent use of graphic methods, showing in most convincing manner how the death rate is being reduced by modern methods of sanitation and nursing

the employees of the City of New York, May 17, 1913. The progress made in recent years by practically every city department was shown by comparative models, charts, or large printed statements which could be read with ease from either side of the street. Even though the day of the parade was rainy, great crowds lined the sidewalks. There can be no doubt that many of the thousands who saw the parade came away with the feeling that much is being accomplished to improve the conditions of municipal management. A great amount of work was necessary to prepare the exhibits, but the results gave ample reward.

Chapter XVII

A FEW CAUTIONS

THE title for any chart presenting data in the graphic form should be so clear and so complete that the chart and its title could be removed from the context and yet give all the information necessary for a complete interpretation of the data. Charts which present new or especially interesting facts are very frequently copied by many magazines. A chart with its title should be considered a unit, so that anyone wishing to make an abstract of the article in which the chart appears could safely transfer the chart and its title for use elsewhere. In the preparation of this book it has been found that a number of the charts used have been copied from one magazine to another, and that the titles under the charts have suffered much in the copying. This is due chiefly to the fact that the titles are not considered as an integral part of a chart, and that many magazine editors feel at liberty to use for a chart whatever title they happen to see fit. If each chart as first presented has a complete and clear title it will greatly assist in establishing a practice that anyone making a copy of a chart should copy the title as well as the chart itself.

It is unfortunate that so many authors send in illustrations or charts for magazine articles without the titles to be used with the illustrations when printed. This often forces the editor to make the titles, and if he does not have complete information before him he cannot be blamed if he makes a mistake by using a title which does not correctly represent the data of the chart. To avoid the possibility of error, the editor may use only the most brief title under the illustration, and then trust to the chart being fully described in the context which goes with it. In such a case, the reader who may happen to be especially interested in the chart is forced to plow through a great quantity of context to find the particular paragraph which may happen to explain the chart. Though it is true that great care is necessary to give in a few words a title for a complex chart, the result is well worth the effort and a chart should not be considered complete until such a title has been made.

When large numbers of curves and charts are used by a corporation, it will be found advantageous to have certain standard abbreviations and symbols on the face of the chart so that information may be given in condensed form as a signal to anyone reading the charts. Fig. 240 is shown here as an excellent example of what may be done in making symbols which would be instantly understood by anyone seeing them. Though these particular symbols are not fitted for use in chart drawing, they may give a suggestion of the possibilities which exist for abbreviating into symbol form certain remarks or instructions, which it may be frequently convenient to place on the face of a chart as a guide to prevent misinterpretation by the reader. If the symbols for chart work are not too numerous, they would very soon be understood by each of the persons who regularly go over the operating charts of a company.

Fig. 239. A Clear and Accurate Title is of Great Importance

The clipping above, taken from the front page of a very prominent newspaper, shows an absurd title. If a thing is reduced 100 per cent, it is all gone. How can drinking be reduced 2,000 per cent?

It may be well to point out here that very large charts are sometimes a disadvantage rather than an advantage. In preparing reports, especially those reports which are used in typewritten form for limited distribution, there is a tendency to accompany the typewritten report with charts on very large sheets of paper, bulky and inconvenient to handle. Sometimes the scales of these accompanying charts are so large that the reader is puzzled to get clearly in his mind what the whole chart is driving at. There is a possibility of making a simple chart on such a large scale that the mere size of the chart adds to its complexity by causing the reader to glance from one side of the chart to the other

346   GRAPHIC METHODS

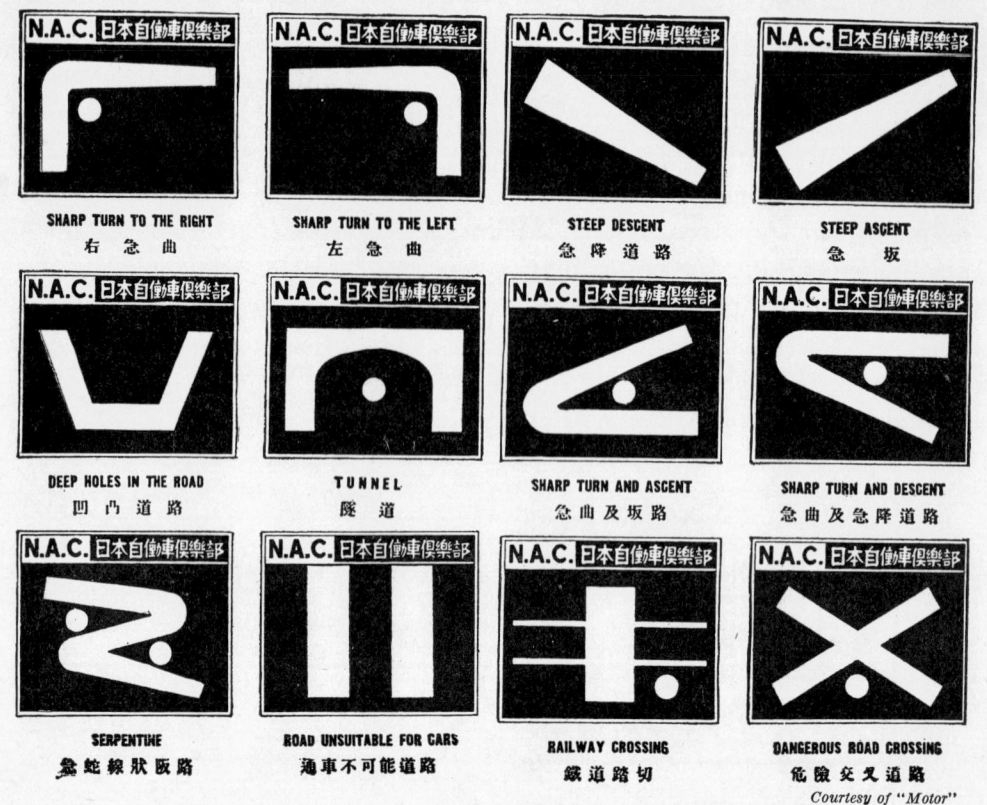

Fig. 240. International Road Signs that Are Being Erected on the Highways of Japan by the Nippon Automobile Club

Any conventional symbols or signals adopted for use in graphic work should be as clear and suggestive as it is possible to make them. The above illustration is shown here as an admirable example of good practice in the making of graphic symbols

in trying to get a condensed visualization of the chart. There are relatively few curve charts which cannot be presented for report purposes on paper 8½ by 11 inches, the commonest size used for a typewriter. Though the placing of a chart on paper of typewriter size requires more care than is necessary if a very large sheet of paper is used, the resulting chart is frequently more easy to interpret than it would be if made to a larger scale.

A warning seems justifiable that the background of a chart should not be made any more prominent than actually necessary. Many charts have such heavy co-ordinate ruling and such relatively narrow lines for curves or other data that the real facts the chart is intended to portray do not stand out clearly from the background. No more co-ordinate lines should be used than are absolutely necessary to guide the eye of the reader and to permit an easy reading of the curves. Too

A FEW CAUTIONS

many magazine articles and transactions of scientific societies contain charts which are reproduced direct from finely ruled co-ordinate paper and show all of the lines of the co-ordinate paper in the finished illustration. Co-ordinate ruling does not appear prominently on most original charts because the ruling is usually printed in some color of ink distinct from the curve itself. When, however, a chart is reproduced in a line engraving the co-ordinate lines come out the same color as the curve or other important data, and there may be too little contrast to assist the reader.

Curves are sometimes shown plotted vertically when a horizontal arrangement could be used without any difficulty. There seems to be no

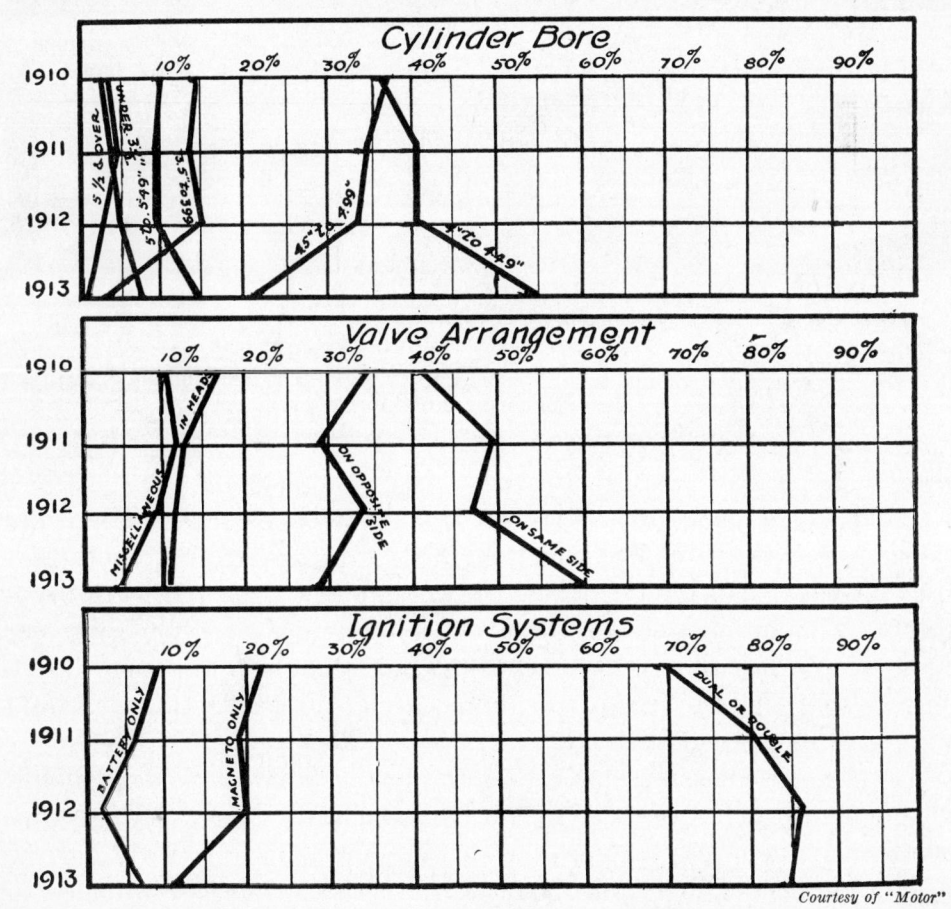

Courtesy of "Motor"

Fig. 241. Comparison of American Automobiles for Four Years, in Cylinder Bore, Valve Arrangement, and Ignition System

There is no necessity for plotting curves in the vertical position shown here for it is only confusing to the reader. These curves cannot be read conveniently even by turning the book to read from the left because some of the type would then be upside down. See Fig. 242

348 GRAPHIC METHODS

real reason why Fig. 241 should have the curves arranged in the vertical direction. The vertical arrangement confuses the reader until he ascertains how the curves may be read by turning the book so that the curves may be read from the left in their proper position.

Fig. 242 shows the data of Fig. 241 plotted in standard manner Fig. 242 is also of interest because it shows curves plotted from only a few points for each curve. Though one may be tempted to use some other method than curve presentation when only few points

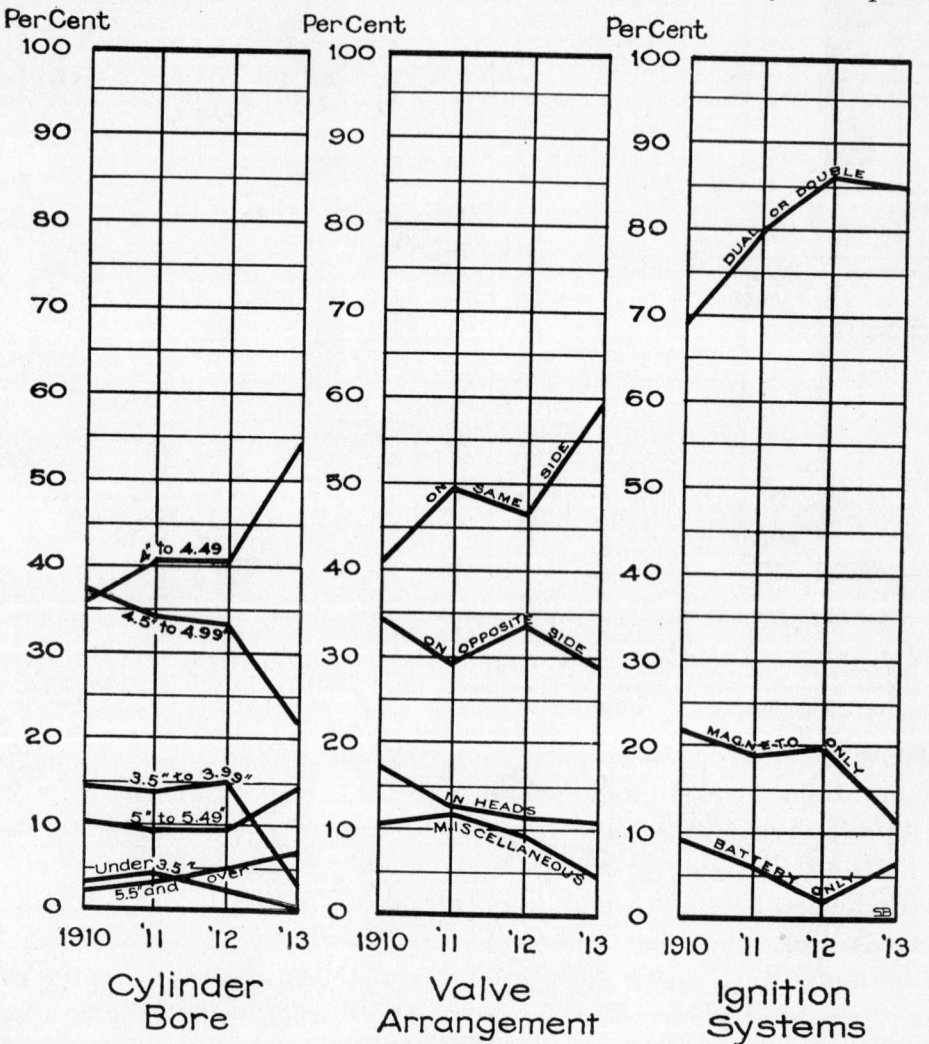

Fig. 242. Comparison of American Automobiles for Four Years, in Cylinder Bore, Valve Arrangement, and Ignition System

The standard arrangement of the curves on this chart permits easy reading. Notice that curves are perfectly feasible as a method of presentation even though there are only a few points available for each curve

A FEW CAUTIONS 349

for a curve are available, it can be seen that even if there were only three points instead of four in Fig. 242, the curve would still be valuable to convey the desired information. In Fig. 53 and Fig. 54 methods are shown by which charts which are essentially curve charts may be drawn even though there are available only two points for each curve.

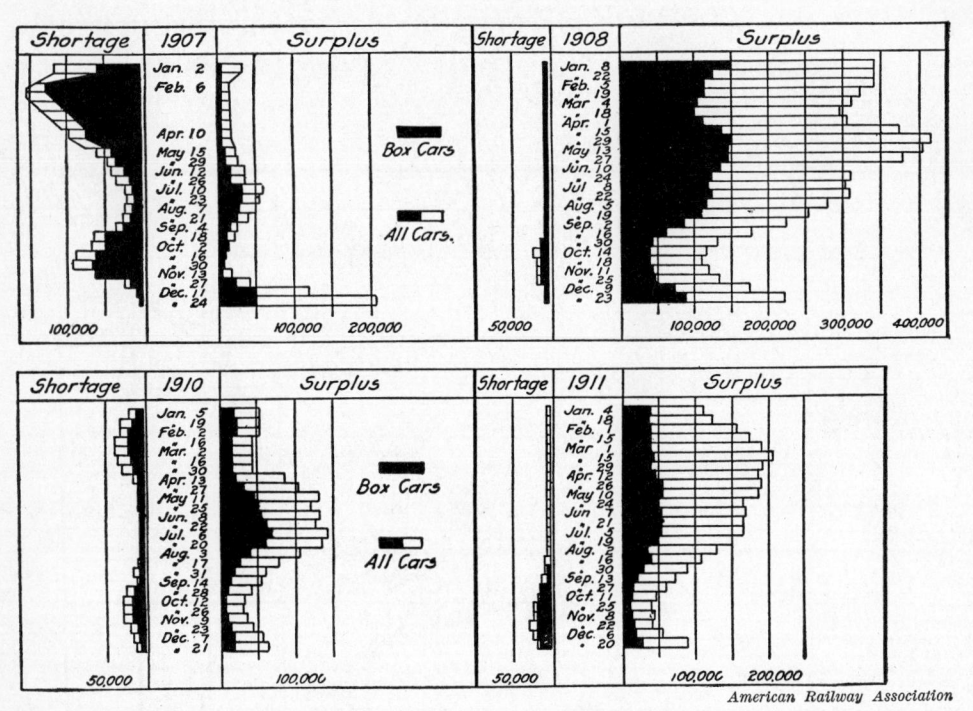

Fig. 243. Freight-Car Shortage and Surplus in the United States for Four Years, 1907 to 1911, Inclusive

The horizontal bars here are so numerous and are placed so close together that the charts have practically the general form of curves drawn vertically instead of horizontally. It would seem just as well to represent the data by real curves drawn with the standard horizontal arrangement

When curves become as widely understood as the bar method of presentation, it will be found that curves can be used advantageously in almost every case where it is now common to use either vertical or horizontal bars.

In Fig. 243 the horizontal-bar method has been elaborated so that the resulting chart has practically the general effect which would be obtained by a curve chart. The reader who wishes to read Fig. 243 in the form of curves is, however, forced to turn the book so that he may see the chart from the left with the curves running in a generally horizontal direction. The data would likely be just as well understood by railroad men if shown by real curves drawn in the standard manner.

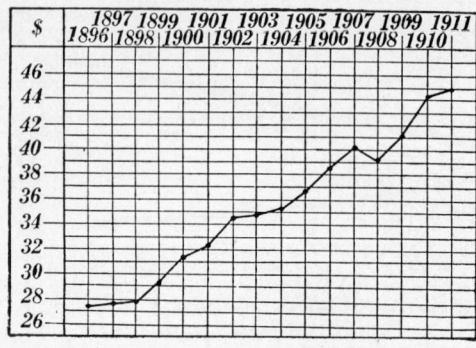

Fig. 244. Average per Capita in the United States of Total Savings-bank Deposits

At first glance the impression is that Americans are growing rich very rapidly. Yet total deposits per capita have not doubled in the sixteen years shown. If the bottom line of the chart were at the zero of the vertical scale, an entirely different impression would be given. See Fig. 245

At numerous places throughout this book criticisms have been made of curves and charts in which no zero line for the vertical scale was shown on the chart. Though this subject has been mentioned elsewhere it seems best to show here a few examples on the same general argument. In Fig. 244 the first glance impression that savings-banks deposits have increased with great rapidity is not entirely confirmed when it is noticed that the left-hand scale does not begin anywhere near zero. It is nearly always possible to make a chart so that the zero of the vertical scale will show. Usually, of course, the zero line is at the bottom of the chart unless there are negative quantities so that the curve crosses over the zero line and extends below it. In all cases the zero line can be made a heavy line. If the curve should extend below the zero line the width of the zero line should be so great that the reader will be certain to interpret the chart from the zero line rather than from the bottom line of the chart itself.

It sometimes happens that the data for a chart involve high numerical figures so that a large amount of space must be used if the zero line of the vertical scale is to be shown in the final illustration. In such a case, the bottom of the chart may have a wavy line as seen in Fig. 245 which portrays the same data as Fig. 244. Fig. 244 could have been extended so that the bottom line would be the zero line if a

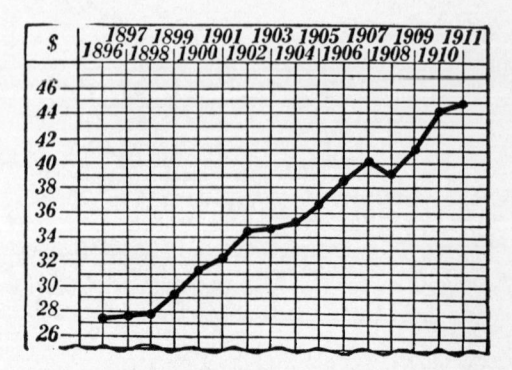

Fig. 245. Average per Capita of Total Savings-bank Deposits in the United States

Whenever possible a chart containing curves should be so drawn that the zero of the vertical scale appears in the chart. If the zero line is not shown on the chart, that fact should be indicated by a wavy line at the bottom warning the reader that interpretation must be made from the vertical scale and not by visual measurement from the bottom line of the chart

A FEW CAUTIONS 351

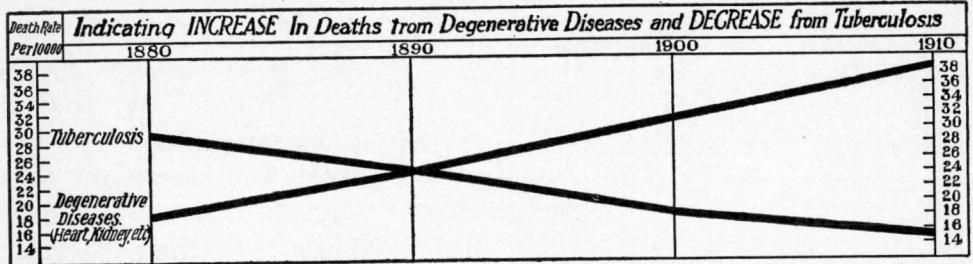

Fig. 246. Comparison of Death Rates in the United States, Showing Reduction in Death Rate for Tuberculosis and Increase in Death Rate for Degenerative Diseases

The chart gives the impression of very rapid decreases and increases, chiefly because the bottom line is not at the zero of the vertical scale. The figures used for the vertical scale are rather small in size and the rapid reader is not likely to notice that the scale does not begin at zero. Compare Fig. 247 and Fig. 248

somewhat greater amount of photographic reduction had been used in making the line engraving or if the proportions between the horizontal- and vertical-scale distances had been changed somewhat. There is really no necessity for using the wavy line for the bottom of Fig. 245 since the chart would have been better made with the zero line showing the bottom. Fig. 245 will serve, however, as an example to illustrate how the wavy line can be drawn to any chart where it is really inconvenient to extend the chart itself so that the zero line may show.

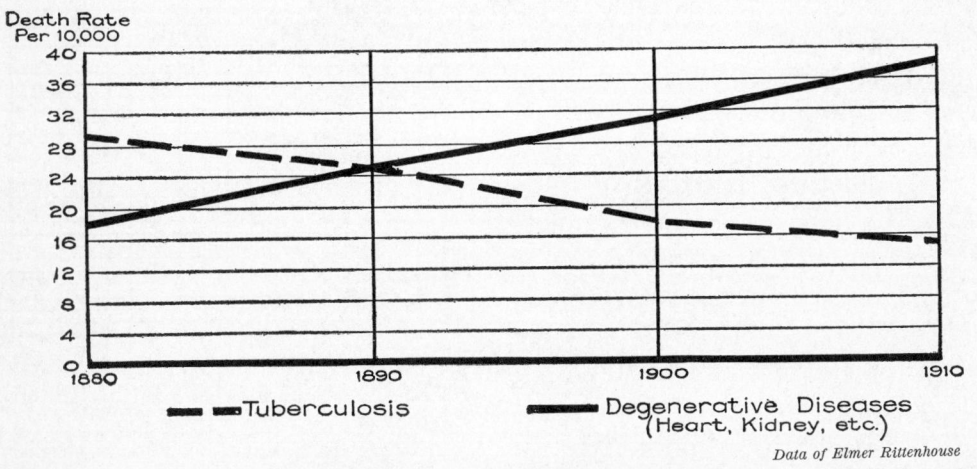

Fig. 247. Comparison of Death Rates in the United States, Showing Reduction in Death Rate for Tuberculosis and Increase in Death Rate for Degenerative Diseases

This chart is made from the same data as Fig. 246. Here the zero line is shown and the changes in death rate appear much less rapid than they do in Fig. 246. See also Fig. 248

352   GRAPHIC METHODS

Fig. 246 gives another example where neglecting to show the zero line may cause an entirely erroneous impression regarding the facts which the chart is intended to bring out. The failure to show the zero line at the bottom of a chart is so common a fault, found in nearly all publications, that some typical examples are shown here in the hope that a bad practice may be somewhat reduced.

Fig. 247 gives the data of Fig. 246 redrawn so that the zero line is shown at the bottom of the chart. It is believed that this illustration will prove conclusively how great an error may be made if charts are read hastily on the assumption that the bottom line of the chart is the zero line. Since some persons are almost sure to read a chart from the bottom line, it seems desirable that all charts should be so made that the reader may interpret from the bottom line as a zero line, or else receive positive warning that he should not do so.

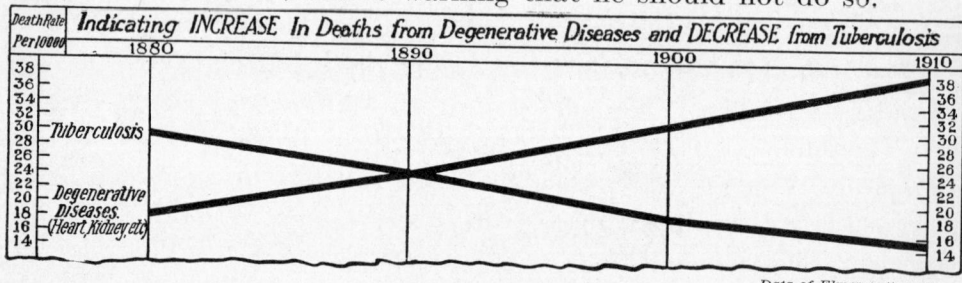

Fig. 248. Comparison of Death Rates in the United States, Showing Reduction in Death Rate for Tuberculosis and Increase in Death Rate for Degenerative Diseases

This illustration is identical with Fig. 246 except that here a wavy line is used at the base showing that the bottom of the chart is not at the zero of the vertical scale. It is always desirable to have the bottom line at zero. If that is not possible the wavy line should be used as a warning to the reader

Though there is no necessity for showing Fig. 246 without having a zero line at the bottom of the chart, Fig. 248 is presented here to prove how easy it is to make a wavy line at the bottom of a chart if there should be any real reason why the chart cannot be made so as to include the zero line of the vertical scale. Fig. 248 is exactly the same as Fig. 246 except that the wavy line is used instead of the straight line at the bottom.

The beginner in curve plotting and in curve reading is apt to be somewhat puzzled by the different effects which may be obtained by changing the ratio between the vertical scale and the horizontal scale. It is difficult to give any general rules which would assist in overcoming the beginner's confusion. Ordinarily the best way to get facility in making the proper choice of vertical and horizontal scales for plotting curves is to take one set of data and plot those data in several different ways, noticing the changes which the different scales selected give in the proportions of the chart. Just as the written or spoken English language may be used to make gross exaggerations, so charts and especially curves may convey exaggerations unless the person preparing the charts uses as much care as he would ordinarily use to avoid exaggeration if presenting his material by written or spoken words. Most authors would greatly resent it if they were told that their writings contained great exaggerations, yet many of these same authors permit their work to be illustrated with charts which are so arranged as to cause an erroneous interpretation. If authors and editors will inspect their charts as carefully as they revise their written matter, we shall have, in a very short time, a standard of reliability in charts and illustrations just as high as now found in the average printed page.

Fig. 249 shows an interesting application of the use of charts to corporation reports. The back page of the annual report of the American Telephone and Telegraph Company has the proportions seen in Fig. 249. As a report to stockholders is intended to be as optimistic as possible within the limits of truthfulness, there can scarcely be any criticism that the chart was so made that the growth in business was shown on the long direction of the page instead of on the short dimension of the page. The chart in Fig. 249 is simple to understand, and probably very few stockholders would have any difficulty in making a fairly accurate interpretation. For the annual report of a corporation, it is likely that the vertical-bar method of Fig. 249 is preferable, from an advertising standpoint, to a smooth curve like that shown in Fig. 250.

One special point relating to Fig. 249 is worthy of mention. At the bottom of the chart will be noticed the statement that the figures recorded are those of "January 1st of each year". This statement may lead to an erroneous conclusion on the part of the reader, for he may feel that the difference in height between the bar marked 1911 and that for 1912 shows the number of telephones installed during 1912, when, in reality, it shows the number of telephones installed during 1911, since the bars represent the number of 'phones installed to the first of January of each year. If the statement at the bottom of the chart had been made "December 31st of each year" there would be no danger of misinterpretation. If the statement were made for December 31 it would, of course, be necessary to change the numbers at the bottom

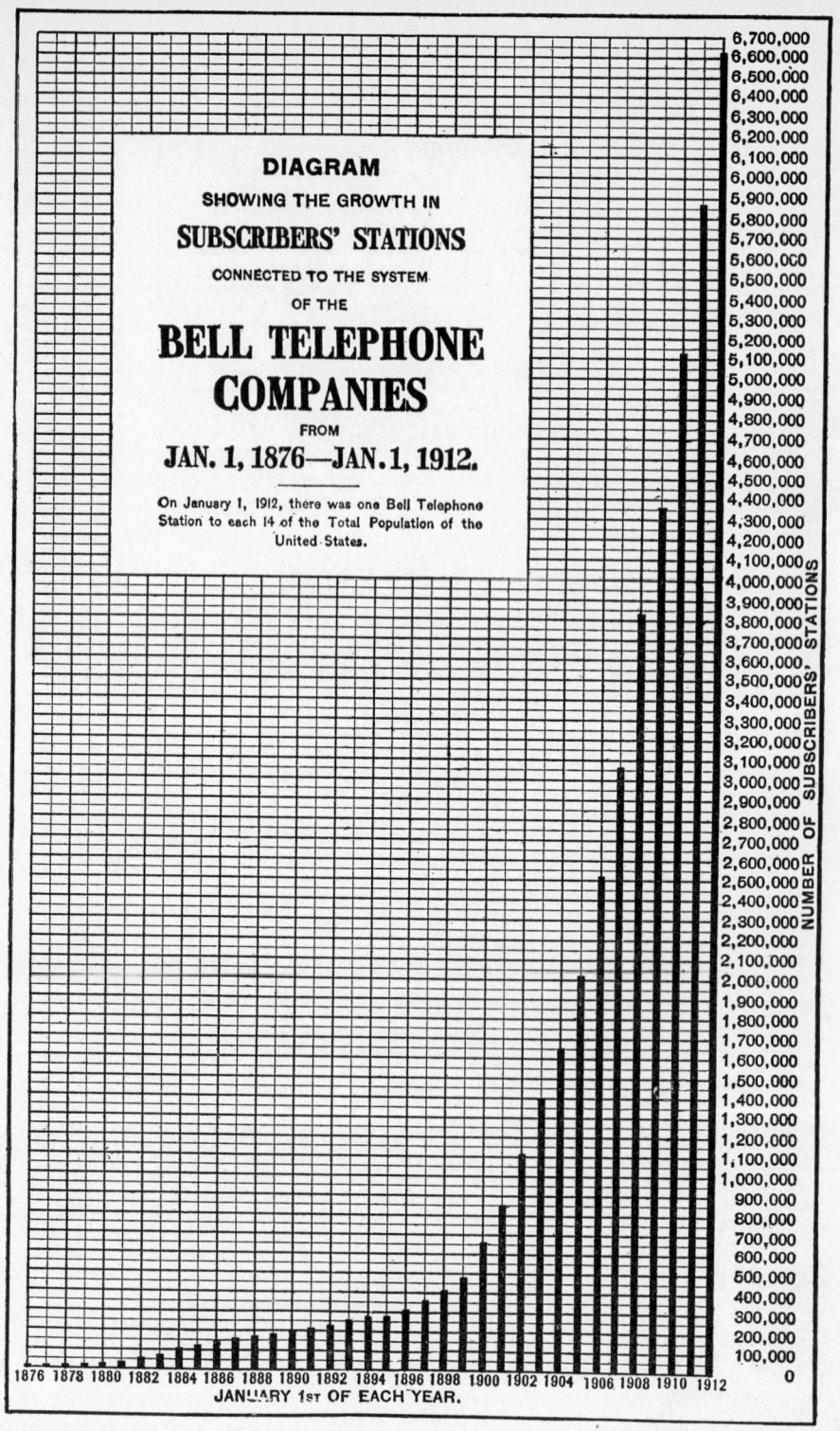

Fig. 249. The Number of Subscribers' Stations Connected to the System of the Bell Telephone Companies

This illustration was shown on the back cover of the 1911 annual report to stockholders of the American Telephone & Telegraph Company. For the average stockholder the vertical bars would probably be understood more readily than the curve shown in Fig. 250. Compare with Fig. 250 and Fig. 251.

DIAGRAM SHOWING THE GROWTH IN SUBSCRIBERS' STATIONS CONNECTED TO THE SYSTEM OF THE BELL TELEPHONE COMPANIES FROM JAN. 1, 1876—JAN. 1, 1912.

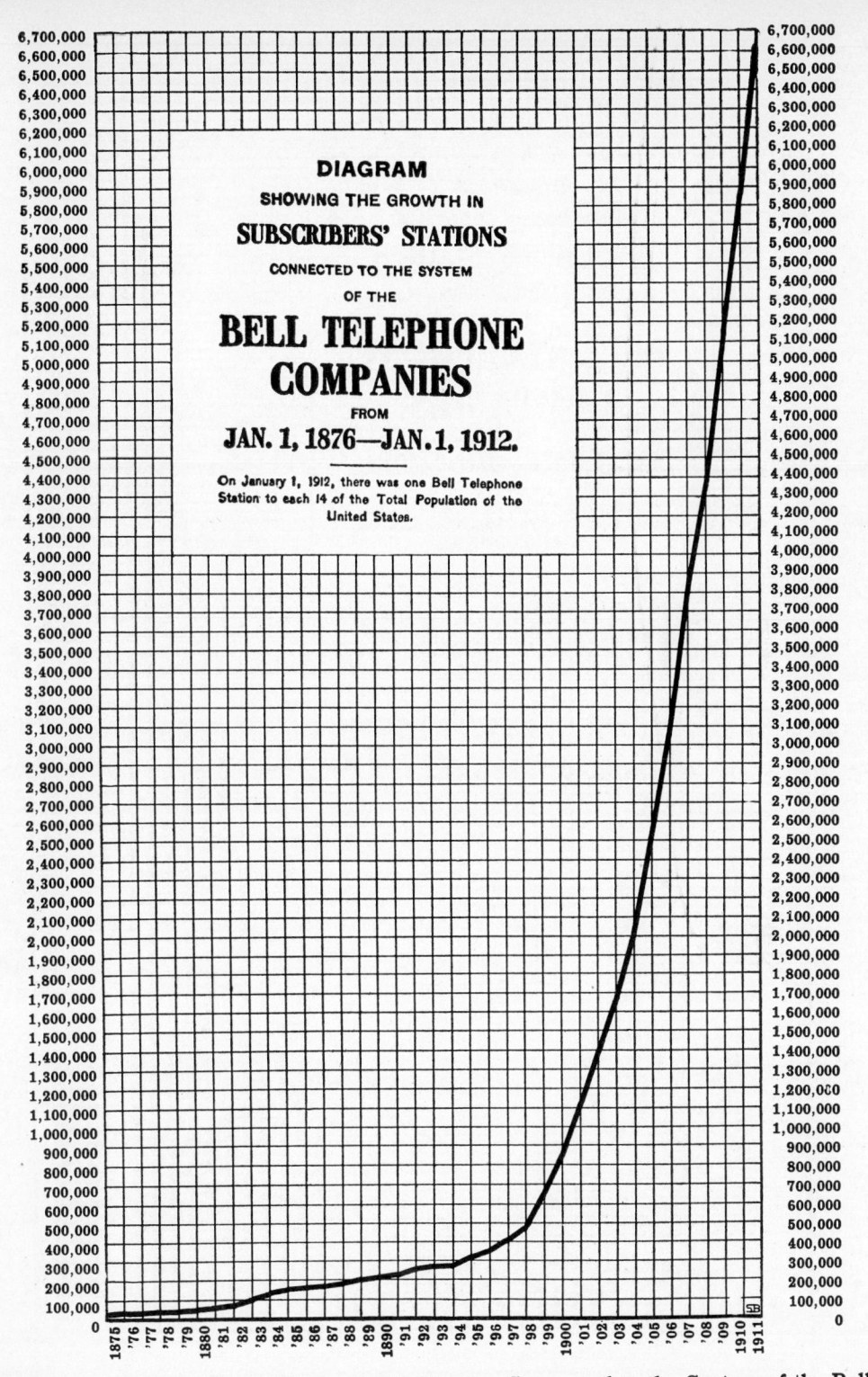

On January 1, 1912, there was one Bell Telephone Station to each 14 of the Total Population of the United States.

Fig. 250. The Number of Subscribers' Stations Connected to the System of the Bell Telephone Companies, December 31st of Each Year

The curve permits quicker and more accurate interpretation than the vertical bars but unfortunately curves are not readily understood by as many people. Note that the date on which the telephones are recorded is here specified as December 31st instead of as January 1st. Compare Fig. 251

356 GRAPHIC METHODS

Fig. 251. The Number of Subscribers' Stations Connected to the System of the Bell Telephone Companies, December 31st of Each Year

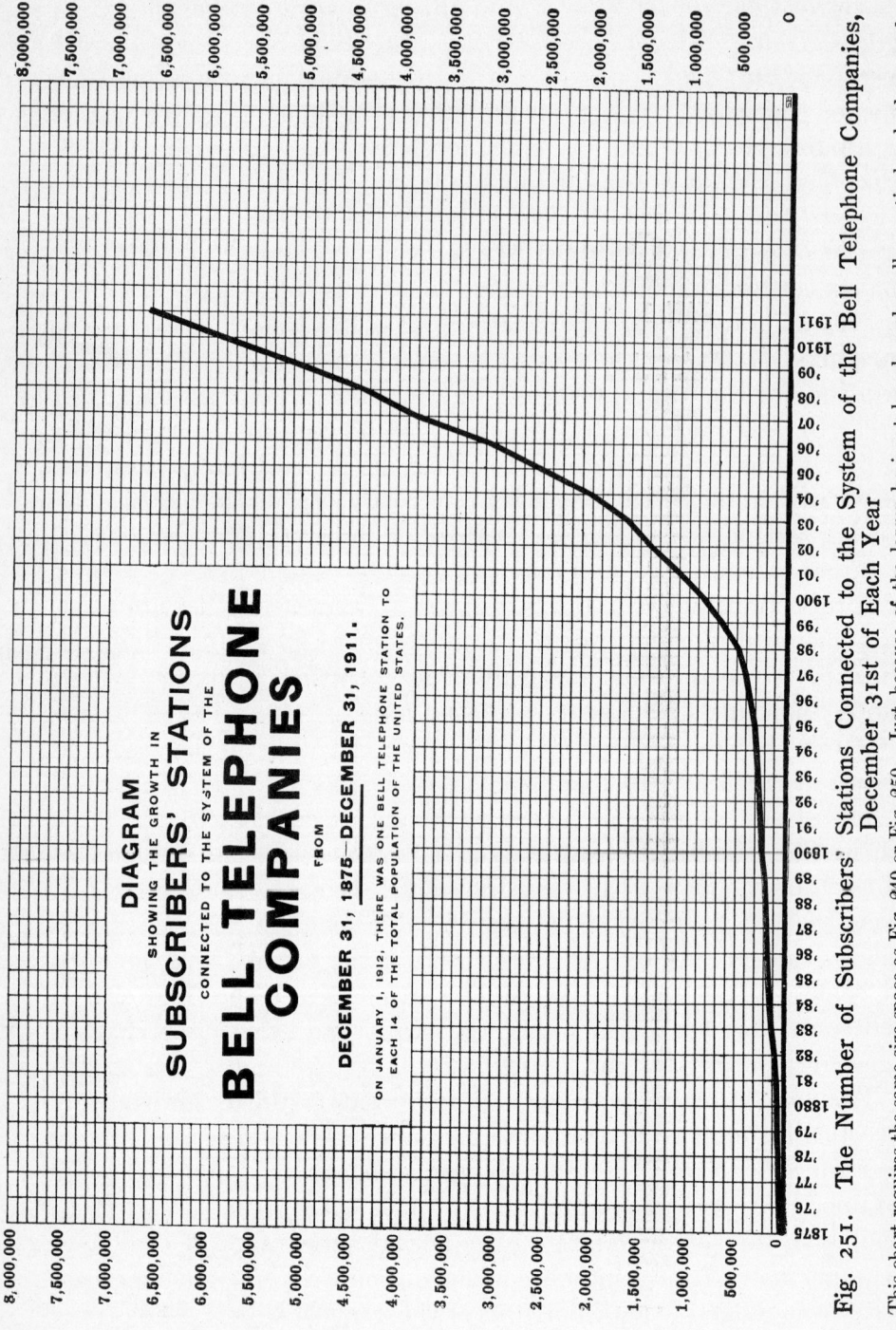

This chart requires the same size space as Fig. 249 or Fig. 250. Just because of the larger horizontal scale and smaller vertical scale the growth of the telephone industry appears much less rapid than would be thought from observing Fig. 250. Both charts are correct. The different visual impressions are caused only by the arrangement of scales. The proper selection and interpretation of scales plays an important part in graphic work

DIAGRAM
SHOWING THE GROWTH IN
SUBSCRIBERS' STATIONS
CONNECTED TO THE SYSTEM OF THE
BELL TELEPHONE COMPANIES
FROM
DECEMBER 31, 1875—DECEMBER 31, 1911.

ON JANUARY 1, 1912, THERE WAS ONE BELL TELEPHONE STATION TO EACH 14 OF THE TOTAL POPULATION OF THE UNITED STATES.

of each vertical bar so that they would appear in each case one less than the figures given. With Fig. 249 as it is, the 1908 bar shows a great increase over 1907 and the reader is quite justified in wondering how it happened that a greatly increased number of telephones were installed during a panic year. From the chart as shown the reader is not likely to realize that 1908 is getting credit for the telephones installed during 1907, which happened to be a very prosperous business year. Having the data recorded as of December 31 each year overcomes the difficulty and makes certain that no false impression can be obtained.

Fig. 250 shows the data of Fig. 249 plotted as a smooth curve. For a trained class of readers the curve presentation is preferable to the bar presentation, for it permits seeing the fluctuations which have occurred from year to year more easily than they can be seen by glancing from bar to bar in Fig. 249. Within a few years it is probable that curves will be so well understood that a report to stockholders could best be made using the method of Fig. 250 instead of the method of Fig. 249.

In order to show the different impressions which may be had if various proportions between the horizontal and vertical scales are used, Fig. 251 has been plotted from the same data as Fig. 249 and Fig. 250. For Fig. 251 an assumption was made that the chart would be printed on exactly the same size page as was used for Fig. 249. The scales for Fig. 250 were, however, arranged in the other direction on the page and the co-ordinate ruling was made so that some space would be allowed for extension of the curve in future years. As seen from Fig. 251 the growth in the telephone business does not appear nearly so rapid as would be thought from observing Fig. 250. Each of these charts is, however, plotted to exact scale and the difference in the impression obtained is caused only by the proportions of the vertical and the horizontal scales. The appearance of less rapid growth in Fig. 250 is assisted somewhat by the fact that the large-type title of the chart is arranged horizontally instead of in the form of a square as seen in Fig. 250. The heavy black type with much greater spread horizontally than vertically tends to overshadow the curve itself and causes for the curve a more distinctly horizontal impression than would otherwise be obtained. A person reading charts must take great care that he does not give too much weight to the actual appearance of the curve on the page, instead of basing his conclusions on the percentage increase or decrease as judged from the figures of the vertical scale. The proper choice of scales for curve plotting is largely a matter of judgment, and

358   GRAPHIC METHODS

the judgment can be trained very greatly if it is kept in mind to examine every curve chart which comes to one's attention to see whether the vertical and horizontal scales have been so selected that the chart gives a fair representation of the facts.

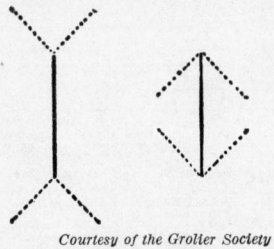

The English language has so many words with double meaning and so many words for which the shades of meaning are rather indistinct that there are really many more chances of false impression from the written or spoken language than there are from the data expressed in graphic form. Nevertheless, a few examples of optical illusions are shown here so that the reader may have some idea of those peculiar things which may enter in to cause strange impressions if charts do not receive some degree of preliminary care and final inspection. Though many of the effects seen in Fig. 252, Fig. 253, Fig. 254, Fig. 255, and Fig. 256 are not likely to appear in ordinary chart work, they may notwithstanding cause difficulty in some kinds of very large wall exhibits. Fig. 254, in particular, shows an effect which is to be avoided where large quantities of black ink are used. In a recent series of charts comparisons were made between different white squares, surrounded in each case by a black border practically as wide as the square at the center. It is not likely that a reader seeing a series of black squares with white centers of different size would be able to judge correctly the relative size of the white squares at the center.

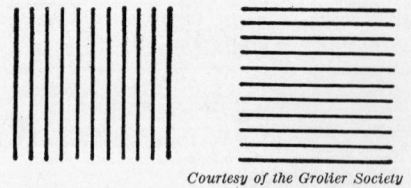

Courtesy of the Grolier Society
Fig. 252. An Optical Illusion
The black line at the left appears longer than the one at the right. The two lines are, however, of the same length

Courtesy of the Grolier Society
Fig. 253. An Optical Illusion
The left-hand arrangement looks wider than it is high while the right-hand arrangement looks higher than it is wide. On each side the height is the same as the width

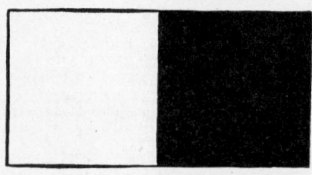

Courtesy of the Grolier Society
Fig. 254. An Optical Illusion
The white square appears larger than the black one, yet the two are of the same size

Fig. 256 shows some of the difficulties which may be encountered if an attempt is made to present data by comparing the relative heights of pictures of the human form. There are few people who will believe until they make measurements that the figure of the girl in Fig. 256 is really of greater length than that of the policeman. The illusion

A FEW CAUTIONS

is caused chiefly by the perspective lines of the drawing which force one to estimate relative height to a certain extent by the number of perspective lines intersected instead of by the actual size of the black pictures.

Before charts are sent to an engraver to have plates made for printing it is wise to have each chart run the gauntlet of a series of questions, so that the time of the person doing the checking may be saved and also that the points more frequently overlooked may be thoroughly considered in each case. Below are given a series of questions which may be found convenient to anyone having charts to prepare. This list is not by any means complete, and the questions are given here as general suggestions only. The person checking a chart simply reads the questions one by one from the book, and then carefully observes the chart to see whether it comes up to the standard. Whenever possible it is well to have the chart checked by some person other than the one who drew it. In every editorial office the fact is recognized that one proof-reader will find important errors that were overlooked by another reader equally expert. Further, a mind much occupied with an idea may often fail to see important gaps in its statement, verbal or graphic, until perhaps they are noted by someone less familiar with the subject. Two points of view are always better than one.

Courtesy of the Grolier Society and of Popular Mechanics.

Fig. 256. An Optical Illusion
The policeman appears much taller than the girl. In reality the figure of the girl is $\frac{1}{16}$ inch taller than the figure of the policeman

Courtesy of the Grolier Society

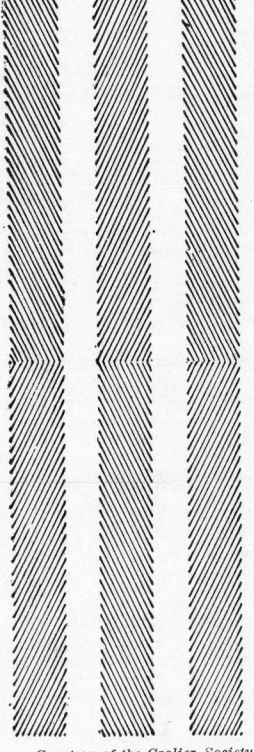

Fig. 255. An Optical Illusion
The columns appear bent. The left-hand pair seem closest at the ends, while the right-hand pair seem closest at the center. The sides of the columns are really straight and parallel

CHECKING LIST FOR GRAPHIC PRESENTATIONS

1. Are the data of the chart correct?
2. Has the best method been used for showing the data?
3. Are the proportions of the chart the best possible to show the data?
4. When the chart is reduced in size will the proportions be those best suited to the space in which it must be printed?
5. Are the proportions such that there will be sufficient space for the title of the chart when the chart has been reduced to final printing size?
6. Are all scales in place?
7. Have the scales been selected and placed in the best possible manner?
8. Are the points accurately plotted?
9. Are the numerical figures for the data shown as a portion of the chart?
10. Have the figures for the data been copied correctly?
11. Can the figures for the data be added and the total shown?
12. Are all dates accurately shown?
13. Is the zero of the vertical scale shown on the chart?
14. Are all zero lines and the 100 per cent lines made broad enough?
15. Are all lines on the chart broad enough to stand the reduction to the size used in printing?
16. Does lettering appear large enough and black enough when seen under a reducing glass in the size which will be used for printing?
17. Is all the lettering placed on the chart in the proper directions for reading?
18. Is cross-hatching well made with lines evenly spaced?
19. Can Ben Day work be used advantageously instead of cross-hatching?
20. Do the Ben Day shadings selected have sufficient contrast?
21. Are all instructions for Ben Day work given so that it will be impossible for the engraver to make a mistake?
22. Are dimension lines used wherever advantageous?
23. Is a key or legend necessary?
24. Does the key or legend correspond with the drawing?
25. Is there a complete title, clear and concise?
26. Is the drafting work of good quality?

27. Have all pencil lines which might show in the engraving been erased?

28. Is there any portion of the illustration which should be cropped off to save space?

29. Are the instructions for the final size of the plate so given that the engraver cannot make a mistake?

30. Is the chart in every way ready to mark "O.K"?

The English language has a grammar with hundreds of detailed rules concerning almost every possible construction. Though graphic presentations are used to a very large extent to-day there are at present no standard rules by which the person preparing a chart may know that he is following good practice. This is unfortunate because it permits every one making a chart to follow his own sweet will. Many charts are being put out to-day from which it would seem that the person making them had tried deliberately to get up some method as different as possible from any which had ever been used previously. Anyone of us would be thought of as a freak instead of as a genius, if he tried to invent his own constructions for the English language and to place words in some order never before seen, yet many persons are doing something akin to this when they attempt to present data by some new and outlandish method of charting. Below are given a few rules which may be of assistance toward getting graphic presentations more on a standard basis so that they may be instantly read. These rules are included here simply as suggestions, and they should be considered as only tentative until such time as definite rules have been agreed upon and sanctioned by authoritative bodies.

RULES FOR GRAPHIC PRESENTATION

1. Avoid using areas or volumes when representing quantities. Presentations read from only one dimension are the least likely to be misinterpreted.

2. The general arrangement of a chart should proceed from left to right.

3. Figures for the horizontal scale should always be placed at the bottom of a chart. If needed, a scale may be placed at the top also.

4. Figures for the vertical scale should always be placed at the left of a chart. If needed, a scale may be placed at the right also.

5. Whenever possible, include in the chart the numerical data from which the chart was made.

6. If numerical data cannot be included in the chart, it is well to show the numerical data in tabular form accompanying the chart.

7. All lettering and all figures on a chart should be placed so as to be read from the base or from the right-hand edge of the chart.

8. A column of figures relating to dates should be arranged with the earliest date at the top.

9. Separate columns of figures, with each column relating to a different date, should be arranged to show the column for the earliest date at the left.

10. When charts are colored, the color green should be used to indicate features which are desirable or which are commended, and red for features which are undesirable or criticized adversely.

11. For most charts, and for all curves, the independent variable should be shown in the horizontal direction.

12. As a general rule, the horizontal scale for curves should read from left to right and the vertical scale from bottom to top.

13. For curves drawn on arithmetically ruled paper, the vertical scale, whenever possible, should be so selected that the zero line will show on the chart.

14. The zero line of the vertical scale for a curve should be a much broader line than the average co-ordinate lines.

15. If the zero line of the vertical scale cannot be shown at the bottom of a curve chart, the bottom line should be a slightly wavy line indicating that the field has been broken off and does not reach to zero.

16. When curves are drawn on logarithmically ruled paper, the bottom line and the top line of the chart should each be at some power of ten on the vertical scale.

17. When the scale of a curve chart refers to percentages, the line at 100 per cent should be a broad line of the same width as a zero line.

18. If the horizontal scale for a curve begins at zero, the vertical line at zero (usually the left-hand edge of the field) should be a broad line.

19. When the horizontal scale expresses time, the lines at the left- and right-hand edges of a curve chart should not be made heavy, since a chart cannot be made to include the beginning or the end of time.

20. When curves are to be printed, do not show any more co-ordinate lines than necessary for the data and to guide the eye. Lines ¼-inch apart are sufficient to guide the eye.

21. Make curves with much broader lines than the co-ordinate ruling so that the curves may be clearly distinguished from the background.

22. Whenever possible have a vertical line of the co-ordinate ruling for each point plotted on a curve so that the vertical lines may show the frequency of the data observations.

23. If there are not too many curves drawn in one field it is desirable to show at the top of the chart the figures representing the value of each point plotted in a curve.

24. When figures are given at the top of a chart for each point in a curve, have the figures added if possible to show yearly totals or other totals which may be useful in reading.

25. Make the title of a chart so complete and so clear that misinterpretation will be impossible.

The American Society of Mechanical Engineers has invited about fifteen of the societies of national scope in America to co-operate in a Joint Committee on Standards for Graphic Presentation. The societies included are largely societies whose members have extensive use for graphic presentation in their daily work. One member from each society will be on this committee. It is hoped that the committee will be able to recommend a small number of brief and simple rules which may be used as a sort of grammar by persons who have graphic presentations to prepare and to interpret. Reports from this joint committee should be watched for so that any rules which may be agreed upon may be put into effect as soon as possible.

Improvements in the means of transportation by water, rail, automobile, wire, and wireless in recent years have caused a tremendous increase in the amount of printed matter and the amount of statistical material read by the average person. Newspapers and magazines are daily presenting more and more statistical information. If we study the subject even a little, it will be seen that each of us deals daily with a vast number of facts of a quantitative nature which could preferably be presented in graphic form. When graphic methods are more widely used for portraying quantitative facts, there will be a tremendous gain to accuracy of thought as well as a great saving of that most valuable thing in the world—time.

THE END

INDEX

Abbreviations for chart work, 345, 346
Accidents, as affected by daylight, 140
   in industrial plants, 144, 145
   on railroads of United States, 134, 135
Accountants, viewpoint of, 300
Accuracy and significant figures, 326
Acker, Merrall & Condit Co., 116
Adding machines, pocket, 325
Advertising, bead maps for, 253
   maps for, 238, 239
   use of curves for, 77, 78
Allen, William H., 250
American Jersey Cattle Club, 278
American Machinist, 335
American Railway Association, 349
American Review of Reviews, 46, 47, 229, 231
American Society of Mechanical Engineers, ii, 31, 52, 54, 122, 363
American Statistical Association, 167, 176, 197
American Telephone & Telegraph Co., 5, 179, 240, 309, 353, 354, 355, 356
Analysis of sales, 188
Angle of a cumulative curve, 150
   of a curve, 131
Annalist, the, see *New York Times Annalist*
Annual reports, corporation, 307
Apples, price curves of, 127, 128, 129
Arithmetically ruled co-ordinate paper, 132
Atlas of the U. S. Census, see Statistical Atlas
Atomizer for spraying ink, 57
Authorization for curve records, 284
Automobile exports of United States, 41, 43
   factory records, 263
   factory schedule curves, 150
   sales records, 255, 264
Automobiles, comparison of, 347, 348
Averages, moving, 97, 283
   progressive, 153
   weighted, 103

Babson, Roger W., 120, 121
Bacteria in river water, 20
   in river water at varying depths, 85

Bald Eagle Valley Railroad, 67
Bar diagrams *versus* curves, 310
Bars combined with a curve, 54
   certain made prominent, 29, 30
   for use in comparison, 22
   horizontal, 4
   horizontal, representing time, 53
   vertical, 46, 47
   vertical, for components, 138
Bead maps, 251
Beads for map use, 247, 248
   for statistical charts, 207
Bell Telephone system, 353, 354, 355, 356
Ben Day shading, 216, 220, 331, 332
   shading on maps, 209
   work, 331, 332
Bertillon, 220
Biologists, use of curves by, 203
Biometrika, 202
Blue-printing, 328
   cards, 259, 261
   curve cards, 291, 296
   machines, 261, 296
Boards for pin records of costs, 191, 192
Bonus earned chart, 52, 54
Boston Elevated Railroad, 4
Boston *Globe*, 212
Boston Health Department Report, 30, 109
Bowley, Arthur L., ii, 98
Breaks in drawings, 190
Bridges, drawing, upon photographs, 209
Brotherhood of Railroad Trainmen, 103
Building construction in United States, 120, 121
Buildings, maps for showing height of, 220
Bureau of Railway Economics, 257
Butter-fat curves, 279

Camera lenses, 330
Cameras, motion picture, for time study, 50
Campaigns, political, 338
Car-floats, dispatching, 61, 62
Cars, shortage and surplus, 349
Cardboard for blue-printing, 259, 261
   models, 336

Card-sorting machines, 322
Cards for blue-printing, 259, 261
 for curve-plotting, 256
 for curves, 275
 for tabulating machines, 320
Cards, information, 287
Carson, John M., 326
Cartoon drawings, 20, 21
Cattle distribution in United States, 215
Cautions, a few, 344
Celluloid-covered tacks for maps, 247, 248
Celluloid, erasing drawings from, 210
 flags for maps, 247
 for drawings with maps, 210
 for mounting maps, 210
 tacks for writing, 247, 248
Cement plants in United States, 243
 price of for thirty years, 77
Census Abstract, 218
Census Atlas of United States. See Statistical Atlas
Census-Office methods, 320, 321
Census tabulating card, 320
Charts, best size for, 345
 in political campaigns, 338
 on walls, 306
Checking list for graphic work, 359, 360
Chicago Burlington & Quincy Railroad, 40
Chicago pin map for population, 246
Chicago telephone rates, 126
Choice of scales, 352
Cincinnati, homes of factory workers, 214
Circle and sectors, 5
Circles compared, 36, 37
Clamps for hanging maps, 232
Cleveland *Plain Dealer*, 92
Cloak and suit industry in New York, 166
Coals, comparative value of, 88
Coloring maps, 209
Color-printing, 5, 331
Colors for chart work, 57
Columns of figures, order for, 45
Combined curves, 125
Commerce of the United States, 70, 71
 of the world, 76
Commercial geography, 21
Commercial Museum of Philadelphia, 70, 74, 76, 112
Commission on Economy and Efficiency, 33, 34
Comparisons, 20
 involving time, 36
Comparison of curves, 107
Compo-board, 232

Component parts, 1
 parts grouped, 33
 parts shown by curves, 138
Compound-interest curve, 131
Conjugal condition of population, 9
 of population of United States, 168, 169
Construction of graphical charts, 335
Co-ordinate lines, spacing of, 362
 paper, 55
 paper for weekly records, 150
 paper, universal, 60
 ruling, 284
Copper production, 26
Copying drawings, 329
Copyrights on maps, 237
Cork composition for map mounting, 232
Corn crop in United States, 44
 planting dates in United States, 213
 yield and rainfall, 124
 yield per acre in United States, 217
Corporation directors, 289, 298
 executives, 289
 financial reports, 307
 record department, 292
Correlation, 129, 199
 definition of, 199
Corrugated straw-board for map pins, 191
Cost analysis by pin boards, 191, 192
 of handling freight, 184, 188, 192
Cotton goods, production and export, 74, 75
Cotton production, 22
 production and export of United States, 41
Country Gentleman, 213, 215, 232
Cows, individual record curves for, 278, 279
Crayons for coloring maps, 57, 221
Crayons, paraffin, 57
Crests and valleys of curves, 79
 of curves, 79
Crop Reporter, 100
Cross-hatching, 9
Cross-index of curves, 291
Croton water-supply curves, 160
Cumulative curves, 149
 frequency curves, 174, 176, 177, 182, 184
Cunningham, Wm. J., 132, 134, 135, 136
Curtis Publishing Co., 238
Curve comparison, 107
Curve plotting, 47, 69, 84
Curves and vertical bars, 47
 for the executive, 254, 288
 interpretation of, 357
 inversely related, 126
 plotted on cards, 259, 275

INDEX

Curves and vertical bars, reading of, 302
   serial numbers for, 287
   shown by reflectoscope, 303
   versus bar diagrams, 310
Cycles of curves, 97, 283
   in curves, 97, 283
Cylindrical lenses, 330

Data, 7, 42, 88, 126, 178, 204, 243, 333
Data for curves, on face of chart, 80, 258
   for curves, shown on chart, 80, 258
   included in a chart, 24, 25, 26
Dates, position of, in curve charts, 72
Davenport, C. B., ii, 164, 165
Davis, Pierpont V., ii
Day & Zimmermann, 296, 305, 306
Death rates in United States, 174, 351
Decreases shown graphically, 30
Degenerative diseases, 351
Department of Agriculture Field Service, 232
Dependent variable, definition, 84
Depressions, financial, 104
Dimension lines, 5, 148
Directors of corporations, 289, 298
Dispatching charts for trains, 61, 62, 67
Display fixtures for curves and maps, 305
   fixtures for maps, 233
Distribution charts, 165
   curves, 165
   of wealth, 197
Dividends and earnings of Steel Corporation, 313, 314
Dixon, Frank Haigh, 115
Dodd, Mead & Co., 250
Dodge's Advanced Geography, 22
Double co-ordinates for curves, 95
   scales for curves, 95
Draft curves for water consumption, 160
Drawing ink, 46, 47, 276
Dreyfus, Edwin D., 117, 118
Drinking, reduction in, 345
Droege, John A., Freight Terminals and Trains, 48

Earnings and dividends of Steel Corporation, 313, 314
   of college graduates, 111
   of wage earners in U. S., 180, 181
Earthwork curves, 163
Edison Company, New York, 108, 138, 140, 146
Eggs, price of, 100
Elderton, W. P. & E. M., ii
Election returns, methods of giving, 341

Engineering Magazine, 12, 14, 17, 18, 116, 125, 246
Engineering News, 87
Engineering Record, 79, 119, 209, 210
Equitable Life Assurance Co., 174, 175
Errors in comparison, 20
Ewerbeck, Dr., 225
Exaggeration due to scales used, 353
Examination marks, charting, 205, 206
Executive control curves, 254, 288
Executives of corporations, 289
Exhibition board, 232
Exports and imports of United States, 37
Exports from the United Kingdom, 98
Eye-catchers, 25, 26, 27, 123

Factory, 147, 155, 180, 256
Fan tests, 335
Farm-land values in United States, 218
Farwell, E. S., 335
Figures included in a chart, 27
   misleading, 326
   significant, 326
Files for curve cards, 289, 291
Financial charts, 104
   prosperity curves, 293
   reports, corporation, 307
Fire losses in United States, 120, 121
Fisher, Irving, 10
Fixtures for displaying curves and maps, 305
Flags, celluloid, for maps, 247
Flat-top curve-plotting, 256
Flood curves, 77, 79, 119
Food prices in United States, 103
Football games, charting, 212
Foreign trade of United States, 139
Forms, routing printed, 18
Formulas for curves, 202
Frankfurt a.M., Map of, 225
Freeman, John R., 160
Freight-car shortage and surplus, 349
   handling, curves for analysis of, 184, 188, 192
   service on Illinois Central, 310
   service on Union Pacific, 311
   traffic density map, 224
   train operation, 123
French curves, 201
Frequency curves, 164

Gang punch for cards, 324
Gantt, H. L., 52, 54
Garnett, W., 205, 206
Gasoline costs for motor trucks, 198

Gasoline-electric generator advertisement, 78
Gear teeth, strength of, 334
General Electric Review, 78, 239
General methods, 321
Geography books, 22
Gifford, Walter S., 179, 240
Gilbreth, Frank B., 50
Good Housekeeping, 21
Grammar for graphic work, 361
Graphic presentation, rules for, 362
Graphical charts, construction of, 335
Green ink, making line cuts from, 330, 331
Grolier Society, 358, 359
Grouping of component parts, 33
Grooves in cards for filing, 296
Gummed letters, 46
  tape for map mounting, 231

Half-tones from pin maps, 235
Handling freight, cost of, 184, 188, 192
Harriman, Mrs. E. H., 250
Harvard Engineering Journal, 337
Harvard University, 212
Harvard University graduates, 251
Hazen and Whipple, 95
Health-department reports, 108
Heating and Ventilating Magazine, 93
Height of university students, 165
Hewes, Amy, 167, 176
Himman, J. J., 114
Hollerith tabulating machines, 229, 230, 231
Holmes, H. W., 208
Horizontal bars, 4
  for comparison, 24
  representing time, 53
Hull, G. H., 104
Human figure in comparisons, 39

Illinois Central Railroad, 310
Illusions, optical, 358, 359
Imports and exports of United States, 37
Incandescent-lamp tests, 337
Income curves, 197
Income of technical graduates, 204
Increases shown graphically, 30
Independent, the, 21, 38
Independent variable, definition, 84
Index numbers, 100
Indianapolis Department of Health, 114
Indianapolis smoke deposits, 245
Industrial depressions, 104
Industrial Engineering, 117, 118
Infectious diseases shown in contrast, 30
Information cards, 286, 290

Ink, drawing, 46, 47, 276
Internationale Baufach-Ausstellung, 225
Inversely related curves, 126
Inverted curves, 96
Iron Age, the, 110, 119
Irregular curves, use of, 201
Isometric drawings, 333
  ruling, 167, 334, 335

Japanese road signs, 346
Jersey Cattle Club, American, 278
Jevons, Stanley, 319
Joint Board of Sanitary Control, 166, 253
Joint Committee on Standards for Graphic Presentation, ii, 363

Keuffel and Esser Company, 326
Key for charts, 360
King, Willford I., ii, 328

Labeling packages, 90, 91
Lamps, types in use, 138
  tests of incandescent, 337
Land value in United States, 218
Lantern slides for election returns, 341
  slides in political campaigns, 339
  talks in political campaigns, 340
Legend for charts, 360
Lenses, camera, 330
  cylindrical, 330
"Less than" basis for frequency curves, 179
Lettering on charts, 26, 82
Letters of appeal for money, 250
  gummed, 46
Lighter operation, chart for, 56
Line cuts from pin maps, 234
  made from green ink, 330, 331
Line thickness in reduced drawings, 242
Lines connecting different bars, 31
Loans to industrial employees, 156
Locomotive feed-water curves, 159
Logarithmic co-ordinates, 132
  paper, 334, 362
  ruling, 334
  scale for curves, 132
Lorenz curve, 197
Lorenz, M. O., 197
Lubrication cost at a factory, 256

Manufactured products of cities, 23
Map and pin systems, 226
Map copyrights, 237
  models, 225
  pins, 225
  pins used for cost analysis, 192

Map pins with numbers, 243, 247
  presentations, 208
  tacks, 225
Maps, coloring, 209
  for corporation records, 293
  for election returns, 341
  for wall use, 225, 229
  mounting of, 231
  shading, 209
Marx, Guido H., 334
Mass curves, 149
Massachusetts Institute of Technology, 11, 198
Mazda lamps, 337
McAbee, William D., 245
McGraw-Hill Book Co., 335
Mechanical shading, 331, 332
Merchant tonnage of United States, 112, 113
Methods, general, 321
Metropolitan Sewage Commission, 20, 85
Milk-analysis curves, 114
Milk-production curves, 278, 279
Misleading figures, 326
Mode, 165, 170
Models, card-board, 336
  solid, 336
"More than", basis for frequency curves, 179
Morgan, J. P. & Co., 15
Motion picture cameras for time study, 50
Motor, 346, 347
Motor trucks, cost for gasoline, 198
  cost of operating, 11
Mount Holyoke College, 167, 176
Mounting maps, 231
Moving-average curves, 97, 283
Municipal parades, 343
  record departments, 298
Muslin facing for pin boards, 231

Naphtaly, Sam. L., 122
Natural scale for curves, 132
Need for graphic methods, 5
Newark, N. J., public schools, 2
Newburgh, N. Y., report on schools, 24
New York Edison Company, 108, 138, 140, 146
New York municipal parade, 343
New York Public Library, 299, 329
New York Times Annalist, 15, 45, 313, 350
New York Times, 120, 121, 222, 351
Newspaper circulation curves, 92
Nippon Automobile Club, 346
Numbered map pins, 243, 247

Optical illusions, 80, 81, 358, 359
Order of Railroad Conductors, 103
Orders, routing, 19
Organization charts, 14, 15
Orrok, George A., 201

Panics, financial, 104
Parades, charts shown in, 342, 343
  municipal, 343
Paraffin crayons, 57
Paris, height of buildings in, 220
Paris, plaster of, 336
Passengers carried on railways, 39
Passenger service on Union Pacific, 312
Payroll curves, 260
  record curves, 276
Peaked-top curves plotting, 256
Peaks of curves, 99
Pearson, Karl, 202
Peddle, John B., 335
Pencil lines, erasing, 361
Pennsylvania Farmer, 124, 127, 128
Pennsylvania Railroad, 308
  profile of, 213
Percentage scales for curves, 132
Perspective routing charts, 19
Philadelphia Commercial Museum, 70, 74, 76, 112
Philadelphia Transit Commissioner, 245
Philip's Chamber of Commerce Atlas, 26, 27
Philippines, comparative size of, 211
Photographing bead maps, 252
  pin maps, 230, 234
Photographs, drawing upon, 209
  progress, 49, 50
  used with maps, 209
Photostat, the, 296, 330
  use of, 329
Pin boards for cost analysis, 191, 192
Pin maps to scale, 246
Pins for map use, 225
  for population density on maps, 221
Pipe, cast-iron, 110
Pittsburgh & Lake Erie Railroad, 81, 82
Plant, Thomas G. & Co., advertisement, 233
Plaster of Paris, 336
Plates, weight of steel, 333
Pneumonia, deaths from, at different ages, 172, 173
Polar co-ordinates for curves, 80
Political campaigns, charts in, 338
Popular Science Monthly, 164, 165
Population curves, 130
  density maps, 221

Portland, Oregon, 208
Power development in United States, 239
Presidential election analysis, 10
Princeton graduates, class of 1901, 73
Princeton University, 111
Production schedule curves, 150
Profile drawings, 211
Progress photographs, 50, 51
Progressive averages, 153
Prominent bar for contrast, 30
Prout, Curtis, ii
Proportions of charts, 355, 356
Prosperity charts, 104
Prussia, distribution of wealth in, 197
Pujo Money Report, 13
Punched-card tabulating machines, 320, 321, 322, 323, 324
Purchasing-department curves, 293

Queen Quality shoes, advertisement, 233

Races in population of the world, 4
Railway Age-Gazette, 115, 142, 224
Railroad annual reports, 309
  earnings in United States, 115
  operating costs, 142, 143
Rank charts, 32, 63, 65, 66
Rea, Samuel, 308
Record departments for cities, 299
  room for corporations, 292
Records for the executive, 288
  needless, 285
Rectangular co-ordinates, 132
Reduction of earnings, 329, 330
Reducing glass, use of, 241, 329
Reduction in size of drawings, 241
Reflecting lantern for curves, 303
Reflectoscope for curves, 304
Reports of corporations, 307
Returns, election, 341
Revenues of railroads of United States, 257
Review of Reviews, 46, 47, 229, 231
Rittenhouse, Elmer, 175, 351, 352
Road signs, Japanese, 346
Roads in New York State, map, 222
Routing charts, 17
Routing of papers in an office, 34
  salesmen, 236
Royal Statistical Society, 205, 206
Rule, slide, 326, 328
Rules for graphic presentation, 361
Russell Sage Foundation, 24, 32, 33

St. Louis & San Francisco Railroad, 224
Sales analysis curves, 188, 269

Sales records by tabulating machines, 324
  record map, 223
Salesmen, chart for ranking, 63
  routing of, by pins, 226
San Francisco fire, 120, 121
"Satellite Cities", 214
Saturday Evening Post, 238
Savings-banks deposits in United States, 350
Scale arrangement for charts, 362
Scales, choice for horizontal and vertical, 352
  double, for curves, 79
  for charts, 8
  on charts, rule for, 211
Scallop shells, 164
Schedule curves for factory output, 150
Schools of the United States, 32
Scientific American, the, 29
Scott, Roscoe, E., 337
Seaboard Air Line Railway, 177
Sections omitted from drawings, 190
Serial numbers for curves, 286
Shading, Ben Day, 331, 332
  mechanical, 331, 332
Sheffield Scientific School, 111
Shipping of various countries, 24
Ships, length of, 49, 51
Shot-gun diagrams, 201
Significant figures, 326
Simple comparisons, 20
  involving time, 36
Slide rule, use of, 326, 328
Slope of curves, 130, 131
Smoke deposits, measuring, 245
Smooth curves, 118, 119, 201, 357
Smoothing curves, 98
Solid models, 336
Soot deposits, measuring, 245
Sophie 19th, milk record, 278
Spot maps, 246
Standard corporation, 334
Standards for graphic presentations, 363
Statistical Atlas, 8, 28, 36, 65, 80, 130, 168, 172, 215
Statisticians for corporations, 293
Steam, cost of producing, 12
Steam turbine, tests of, 122
Steel, curves for strength of, 119
Steel plates, weight of, 333
Stockholders of corporations, number of, 308
Storage capacity curves, 159
Straw-board for mounting maps for pins, 230
  for use with map pins, 191

INDEX

Street-car service map, 225
String for routing salesmen, 237
Stream velocity, 87
Swazey, Edward Scott, ii
Subdivision of components, 8
Suffern & Son, 30, 213
Survey, the, 6, 245
Swinging display fixtures for maps, 233
Symbols for charts, 345, 346
System, 15, 90, 123, 223.

Tabulating Machine Company, 322, 323, 324, 325
Tabulating machines, 320, 321, 322, 323, 324
   machines for cards, 323
Tacks, celluloid-covered, for maps, 247, 248
   map, 225, 247, 248
Tarr and McMurray's new geographies, 22
Taylor, Graham Romeyn, 214, 221
Telephone load curves, 108
   rates, 126
   service curves, 179
   service in Wisconsin, 178
Telephones in United States, pin map, 240
   number used in United States, 354
Temperature curves, 117, 118
Thompson, A. T. & Co., reflectoscope, 303
Thomson, H. F., 198
Three-dimensional charts, 205, 206
Time charts, 53
Time-distance charts, 64, 67
   curves, 64, 67
Titles for charts, 344, 345
Topographical maps, 235
Totalizing curves, 125
Tracing cloth used with maps, 210
Trading centers in United States, 238
Train-dispatching charts, 61, 62, 67
Train-operation curves, 123
Transparentizing solution, 328
Trenton, N. J., public schools, 2
Trucks, costs for gasoline, 198
   cost of operating, 29
Tuberculosis death rates, 351
Tug-boat operation, 58
Turbine, steam, tests of, 122
Two independent variables, charts for, 205, 206

Union Bag & Paper Co., 45
Union Pacific Railroad, 311, 312
United States Census Office methods, 320, 321
United States Steel Corporation, 313, 314
University of Cincinnati, 46, 47, 229, 231

Vacation chart, 53
Variables for curves, 84
Variables, two independent, 333
Velocity of water in streams, 87
Vertical arrangement of curves, 347, 349
   bar charts, 354
   bars, 46, 47
   for components, 138

Wage charts, 180, 181, 182
   comparison on railroads, 49
Wall board, 232
   charts, 306
   exhibits, 358
   maps, 225, 229
Wall Street Journal, 308
Warne, Frank J., 103
Water power in United States, 216
Water storage-capacity curves, 159
Wave lengths on curves, 283
Waves in curves, 97
Wavy line for bottom of chart, 350, 352, 362
Weather charts, 93
Wealth, curves showing distribution, 197
Weight of steel plates chart, 333
Weighted averages, 103
Westinghouse Electric & Manufacturing Co., 295
Westinghouse, George, 31
Wheat, production of, 1910, 27
Wheeling & Lake Erie Railroad 102
Whipple, George C., 95
White, William Pierrepont, 222
Worcester Polytechnic Institute, 204
World's Work, the, 39, 40, 43, 49, 51, 211
Worsted mill operation, 52, 54

Yale University, 111, 212
Years, methods for naming on curves, 82
Yule, G. Udny, ii

Zero lines for curves, 82, 140, 350, 351, 352
Zero lines on curve cards, 271
Zizek, Franz, ii